The Palgrave Handbook of African Traditional Religion

Ibigbolade S. Aderibigbe • Toyin Falola
Editors

The Palgrave Handbook of African Traditional Religion

palgrave
macmillan

Editors
Ibigbolade S. Aderibigbe
Department of Religion
University of Georgia
Athens, GA, USA

Toyin Falola
Department of History
University of Texas at Austin
Austin, TX, USA

ISBN 978-3-030-89499-3   ISBN 978-3-030-89500-6 (eBook)
https://doi.org/10.1007/978-3-030-89500-6

© The Editor(s) (if applicable) and The Author(s), under exclusive licence to Springer Nature Switzerland AG 2022

This work is subject to copyright. All rights are solely and exclusively licensed by the Publisher, whether the whole or part of the material is concerned, specifically the rights of translation, reprinting, reuse of illustrations, recitation, broadcasting, reproduction on microfilms or in any other physical way, and transmission or information storage and retrieval, electronic adaptation, computer software, or by similar or dissimilar methodology now known or hereafter developed.

The use of general descriptive names, registered names, trademarks, service marks, etc. in this publication does not imply, even in the absence of a specific statement, that such names are exempt from the relevant protective laws and regulations and therefore free for general use.

The publisher, the authors and the editors are safe to assume that the advice and information in this book are believed to be true and accurate at the date of publication. Neither the publisher nor the authors or the editors give a warranty, expressed or implied, with respect to the material contained herein or for any errors or omissions that may have been made. The publisher remains neutral with regard to jurisdictional claims in published maps and institutional affiliations.

Cover illustration: Twins SEVEN SEVEN 1944, Tortoise and Squirrel, Ink on board, Grant of Prince Yemisi Shyllon, 2018, © Yemisi Shyllon Museum of Art, Pan-Atlantic University

This Palgrave Macmillan imprint is published by the registered company Springer Nature Switzerland AG.
The registered company address is: Gewerbestrasse 11, 6330 Cham, Switzerland

Acknowledgments

The completion of this book could not have been achieved without the contributions of several key participants. Therefore, we would like to thank many colleagues and friends who guided and provided various forms of assistance associated with compiling and reviewing the contributed chapters. In specific terms, we would like to thank Dr. (Mrs.) Olutola Akindipe for coordinating the communications with contributors regarding the invitation, submission, and compilation of chapters and associated materials. Also, we are grateful to Dr. David Olali, Bukunmi Ogunsola, Olumida Ajayi, and Samaria Divine for assisting in converting and standardizing the referencing formats. In addition, Alexis Mulkey deserves special mention for the final review of the chapters.

Our contributors also deserve immense gratitude for their patience in bearing with us throughout producing the book, particularly with our several requests for corrections and submissions of associated materials. We would like you to know that without your contributed chapters, this book would not have materialized. We believe that this project's success would serve as enough compensation for the inconveniences and the amount of hard work you invested.

Finally, Palgrave Macmillan's publication team deserves our special gratitude for being patient and bearing with sometimes unusual logistical difficulties and delays in meeting deadlines. We appreciate the amount of hard work of the team in the successful production of this book.

Contents

1. Introduction to Handbook of African Traditional Religion ... 1
   Ibigbolade S. Aderibigbe and Toyin Falola

Part I Basic/Essential Features of African Traditional Religion ... 27

2. Origin, Nature, and Structure of Beliefs System ... 29
   Ibigbolade S. Aderibigbe

3. African Traditional Religion and the Sociocultural Environment ... 49
   Olutola Akindipe

4. Metaphysical and Ontological Concepts ... 61
   Alloy S. Ihuah and Zaato M. Nor

5. The Concept and Worship of the Supreme Being ... 87
   Dorothy Nguemo Afaor

6. Beliefs and Veneration of Divinities ... 97
   Lydia Bosede Akande and Olatunde Oyewole Ogunbiyi

7. Beliefs and Veneration of Ancestors ... 107
   Benson Ohihon Igboin

8. Beliefs and Practices of Magic and Medicine ... 119
   Kelvin Onongha

9	Cosmological and Ontological Beliefs Ibigbolade S. Aderibigbe	131
10	Liturgy, Rituals, Traditions, Sacrifice, and Festivals Mensah A. Osei	143
11	African Circle of Life Segun Ogungbemi	155
12	Death, Burial Rites, and After-life Segun Ogungbemi	163
13	Reincarnation and Eschatology Beliefs Ibigbolade S. Aderibigbe	173
14	Religious Leaders: Priests/Priestesses, Medicine Professionals, and Kings Danoye Oguntola-Laguda	185
15	Illnesses and Cures Kelvin Onongha	197
16	Secret Societies: Fraternities, Witches, Wizards, and Sorcerers Andrew Philips Adega	207
17	The Role of Women in African Traditional Religion Atinuke Olubukola Okunade	219
18	Arts, Music, and Aesthetics AdeOluwa Okunade	231
19	Oral and Non-Oral Sources of Knowledge in ATR: Orality and Secrecy Ethos in the Yoruba Traditional Religion within the Latin American Diaspora Félix Ayoh'Omidire	241

Part II	Contemporary Interconnections: Contents and Discontents	255
20	African Traditional Religion and Religious Ethics David Olali	257

21	Traditional Religion, and Morality in Society Dauda Umaru Adamu and Amidu Elabo	271
22	African Traditional Religion and African Philosophy Alloy S. Ihuah and Zaato M. Nor	289
23	African Traditional Religion, Gender Equality, and Feminism Adepeju Johnson-Bashua	303
24	African Traditional Religion, Sexual Orientation, Transgender, and Homosexuality David Olali	317
25	African Traditional Religion, Conflict Resolution, and Peaceful Societal Co-existence Noah Yusuf and Raji Shittu	329
26	African Traditional Religion and Democratic Governance Kwaku Nti	347
27	African Traditional Religions and Economic Development Kwaku Nti	357
28	African Traditional Religion, Social Justice, and Human Rights Samson O. Ijaola	365
29	African Traditional Religion and Contemporary Functionalism: Divination Eric Adewuyi Mason	383
30	African Traditional Religion and Contemporary Functionalism: Medicine Sarwuan Daniel Shishima	391
31	African Traditional Religion and Contemporary Functionalism: Festivals Tenson Muyambo	403
32	African Traditional Religion and Diaspora Transplantations: Nature and Formats Martina Iyabo Oguntoyinbo-Atere	413

33	African Traditional Religion and Sustainable Cultural, Social and Economic Dynamics Mensah A. Osei	427
34	African Traditional Religion and Sustainability: The New Indigenous Religious Movements Danoye Oguntola-Laguda	441
35	African Traditional Religion and Christianity in Contemporary Global Religious Space Rotimi Williams Omotoye	457
36	African Religion and Islam in Contemporary Religious Space Yushau Sodiq	473

Part III	On Pedagogy, Research, and Foundation Scholars	485
37	'Outsider' and 'Insider' Study of African Traditional Religion Raymond Ogunade and Grillo Oluwaseun	487
38	Codification, Documentation, and Transmission of Knowledge in African Traditional Religion Toyin Falola	497
39	African Traditional Religion and Indigenous Knowledge System Toyin Falola	515
40	Gnostic and Epistemological Themes in African Traditional Religion Marcus L. Harvey	535
41	African Traditional Religion in African and African Diaspora Scholarship Raymond Ogunade and Olorunfemi Dada	547
42	African Traditional Religion in Global Scholarship Toyin Falola	559

43	African Traditional Religion in the Context of World Religions: Challenges to Scholars and Students Robert Yaw Owusu	577
44	African Traditional Religion Scholarship: E. Bolaji Idowu and John S. Mbiti Rotimi Williams Omotoye	589
45	African Traditional Religion and Humanities' Scholarship: The Contributions of Edward Geoffrey Parrinder and Kofi Asare Opoku Olatunde Oyewole Ogunbiyi and Lydia Bosede Akande	599
46	Scholarship in African Traditional Religion: The Works of Joseph Omosade Awolalu and Peter Ade Dopamu Danoye Oguntola-Laguda and Joseph Moyinoluwa Talabi	613

Index 631

Notes on Contributors

Dauda Umaru Adamu is a lecturer at Gombe State University, Nigeria, and a Ph.D. student at Rice University, Texas, USA. His research curiosities are in African religions, histories and religion of ethnic groups, religion and development, religion and trauma, especially how trauma connects with spirituality and ritual, economy, migration, politics during colonial and post-colonial periods, childhood development, and environmental issues such as climate change and cultural norms, environmental laws and justice, environmental films, waste recycling, and conservation of animal species.

Andrew Philips Adega holds a Bachelor of Arts (B.A. Hons.) Degree in Religion and Philosophy from Benue State University, Makurdi, from 1997 to 2001. He equally obtained a Master of Arts (M.A.) Degree in Religious Studies from Benue State University, Makurdi, between 2002 and 2005 and further proceeded to the University of Jos, Jos, between 2008 and 2015 and received a Doctor of Philosophy (Ph.D.) Degree in African Traditional Religion with research interests in African religion and culture, ritual practices in Tiv religion, history of religions and phenomenology, and social anthropology of religion. Adega is a senior lecturer in the Department of Religion and Cultural Studies at Benue State University, Makurdi, and a member of the Editorial Board, *The Tiv Encyclopedia*. Adega is a member of numerous professional bodies and associations including Nigerian Association for the Study of Religions (NASR), Nigerian Association for the Study of Religions and Education (NASRED), Association of Scholars of African Traditional Religion and Culture (ASARC), International Research and Development Institute (IRDI), and the Nigerian University Scholars in Religions (NUSREL). Adega is a fellow of Tiv Professionals in Development Ftpd.

Ibigbolade S. Aderibigbe is Professor of Religion and African Studies at the University of Georgia, USA. He is the Associate Director of African Studies Institute. He teaches African religion and the religions of Africa in the Diaspora. Previously Aderibigbe taught at the Lagos State University, Ojo, Lagos,

Nigeria, where he also served as head of the Department of Religions. His areas of interest and research are the philosophy of religion, African indigenous religion, and the religions of Africa in Diaspora. Aderibigbe has written and co-edited numerous books. His articles have appeared in refereed journals and his works have been included in edited volumes. For many years, he served as the editor of *Religions Educator*, the *Journal of Nigerian Association for the Study of Religions and Education*. His latest single authorship and co-edited books are *Contextualizing Eschatology in African Cultural and Religious Beliefs* (2019), *Gender and Development in Africa and Its Diaspora* (2019), *Contextualizing Africans and Globalization: Expressions in Sociopolitical and Religious Contents and Discontents* (An imprint of The Rowman and Littlefield Publishing Group, 2016), *Contemporary Perspectives on Religions in Africa and African Diaspora* (Palgrave Macmillan, 2015), and *Contextualizing Indigenous Knowledge in Africa and Its Diaspora* (2015).

Dorothy Nguemo Afaor is a lecturer in the Department of Religion and Cultural Studies at Benue State University, Makurdi, Nigeria. She holds her First Degree in Religious Studies from Benue State University, Makurdi. She has also bagged a Master's Degree (M.A.) in African Traditional Religion from the same university. She further obtained a Ph.D. in African Traditional Religion from the prestigious University of Nigeria, Nsukka, Enugu State. She has written many scholarly works both locally and internationally on various subjects.

Lydia Bosede Akande is a senior lecturer in the Department of Religions at University of Ilorin, Nigeria. She obtained her B.Ed., M.A., and Ph.D. Degrees in Christian Studies from Ahmadu Bello University, Zaria, and University of Ilorin, Nigeria, respectively. Her areas of interest are church history and inter-faith relations, with a mission to investigate church history as instrument for smoothening national inter-faith connection through dialogues. She has good number of local, national, and international publications. She has attended conferences both at national and at international levels.As a visiting scholar to the Department of Religion and African Studies Institute, University of Georgia, Athens, USA, between January and May 2015, she exposed the international community of scholars to the cultural values of African songs at war times, naming and marriage ceremonies, and their spiritual significances. She was appointed a member of the committee for the review of academic programs in the Department of Religions and Peace Studies at Lagos State University, Ojoo, Nigeria, where she recently completed a one-year sabbatical leave.

Olutola Akindipe holds a Bachelor's Degree in Psychology as well as Master's and Doctoral Degrees in Educational Psychology from the University of Georgia, USA. She is a seasoned educator with over ten years of college teaching experience of which several were in different administrative capacities. Some of her areas of research interest include students' motivation, achievement, parental involvement, home-school collaboration, and gender issues.

She is also very passionate about education and enjoys working with students of all educational levels. She has facilitated and presented in several local and international conferences and volunteers for educational non-profit organizations within her local community. She is a member of several professional bodies such as the American Psychological Association, American Educational Research Association, and the Graduate Student committee of the Kappa Delta Pi, an international Honor Society in Education. Akindipe is Visiting Assistant Professor of Psychological Science at Salem College, North Carolina, where she teaches introduction to psychology and developmental psychology.

Félix Ayoh'Omidire teaches Luso-Brazilian literary, ethnic, and cultural studies at the Obafemi Awolowo University, Ile-Ife, Nigeria. He received his B.A. and M.A. degrees from the same university and holds a Post-Graduate Specialization Degree in the Teaching of Portuguese as a Foreign Language from the University of Porto, Portugal. For his doctorate degree he undertook a research in Afro-Brazilian and Latin-American literary, cultural, ethnic, and diasporal studies at the Federal University of Bahia (UFBA), Salvador-BA, Brazil, where he developed and propagated a theory of Afro-Brazilian identity construction dubbed *YoruBaianidade*. During the same period (2002–2006), he was an exchange professor and coordinator of the academic program on Yoruba language, culture, and civilization at the Centre for Afro-Oriental studies (CEAO/UFBA). He is currently a major link and resource person between Brazilian and Nigerian governmental and academic institutions. He is also the accredited examiner in Nigeria for the *Certificado de proficiência em língua portuguesa para estrangeiros* (CELPE-BRAS), organized and held twice yearly by the Brazilian Ministry of Education (MEC) for foreigners willing to study in Brazil.Ayoh'Omidire has authored various books and has to his credit numerous academic publications in reputable journals in different countries of the world.

Olorunfemi Dada is a Ph.D. candidate in the Department of Religions (Comparative Religious Studies) at University of Ilorin, Nigeria. He won the University of Ilorin undergraduate scholarship from 2008 to 2012 in the Department of Religions, and graduated as the best student of the department in 2012. He is an assistant lecturer in the Department of Religious Studies at McPherson University, Seriki-Sotayo, Ogun State.

Amidu Elabo is a Ph.D. candidate at Princeton Theological Seminary, USA, currently working on his dissertation in the religion and society program. His research interests include religion, space, and place; critical spatial theories; African indigenous religions; material religion; ArcGIS software for cartography and spatial analysis; remote sensing, mobility; African religions in the Diaspora; indigeneity, land, ethnicity; urbanism, post-coloniality; interaction of religions in sub-Saharan Africa; spatiality of African ethics; and world religions.

Toyin Falola is Professor of History, University Distinguished Teaching Professor, and the Jacob and Frances Sanger Mossiker Chair in the Humanities at the University of Texas at Austin, USA. He is an Honorary Professor at the University of Cape Town, and Extraordinary Professor of Human Rights at the University of the Free State. He had served as the General Secretary of the Historical Society of Nigeria, the President of the African Studies Association, Vice-President of UNESCO Slave Route Project, and the Kluge Chair in the Countries of the South, Library of Congress. He is a member of the Scholars' Council, Kluge Center, the Library of Congress. He has received over 30 lifetime career awards and 14 honorary doctorates. He has written extensively on Nigeria, including *A History of Nigeria*, *Nigerian Political Modernity and Postcolonial Predicaments*, *Violence in Nigeria*, and *Colonialism and Violence in Nigeria*.

Marcus L. Harvey is Associate Professor of Religious Studies at the University of North Carolina Asheville, USA. His research expertise encompasses African indigenous and Atlantic religions, the corpus of Zora Neale Hurston, religion and literature, epistemology, and the phenomenology of religion, with a central focus on exploring the interpretive relationship between African epistemology and black religious experience. Having written nationally and internationally on topics related to the study of African thought and black cultural experience, Harvey is currently developing a related book manuscript that builds upon fieldwork conducted in southern Ghana and Nigeria.

Benson Ohihon Igboin is a professor and head of the Department of Religion and African Culture at Adekunle Ajasin University, Nigeria. He has interest in African religion and culture, religion and politics. He has attended many conferences within and outside Nigeria. He edited *Corruption: A New Thinking in the Reverse Order* (2018) and co-edited *The Changing Faces of African Pentecostalism* (2018), and *African Pentecostalism: Probity and Accountability* (2019). He is co-editing *African Pentecostalism and Christian Social Responsibility* and *African Pentecostalism and the Challenges of COVID-19*. He is also an academic associate of the Research Institute for Theology and Religion, University of South Africa. He has over 100 publications in reputable national and international journals and books.

Alloy S. Ihuah is Professor of Philosophy at Benue State University, Makurdi, Nigeria. He was the winner of the 2014 Asante Award for Outstanding Research of the University of Georgia, USA. He served as the Director of Centre for Research Management at Benue State University, Makurdi, from 2016 to 2020. He has previously served as the National Secretary of the Nigeria Philosophical Association (NPA) from 2012 to 2016. He, in addition, served as the President of the Nigeria Philosophical Association (NPA) from 2018 to 2020. He is the President of Association of Philosophy Professionals of Nigeria (APPON). Ihuah researches and publishes in *Inter-Cultural Philosophy*, *Philosophy of Science*, *Epistemology* and *Existentialism*. He has authored 9 books and over 50 peer-reviewed articles in edited books and journal contributions locally and internationally. Ihuah is a member of many distinguished professional bodies and learned societies, locally and internationally.

Samson O. Ijaola teaches in the Department of Philosophy and Religious Studies at Samuel Adegboyega University, Ogwa, Edo State, Nigeria. His scholarly works have appeared in national and international edited volumes and peer-reviewed journals. His research areas include Christian studies, philosophy of religion, science and religion, gender studies, peace and conflict studies, and African studies. He is also the editor of *SAU Journal of Humanities*.

Adepeju Johnson-Bashua is Associate Professor of Comparative Study of Religions. She received her B.A. and M.A. in Religious Studies from the University of Ibadan, Ibadan, Nigeria, and Ph.D. from Lagos State University, Ojo, Lagos. She teaches comparative study of religions and African religion in the Department of Religions and Peace Studies at the Lagos State University, Ojo, Lagos, Nigeria. She is the Ag. HOD of the Department. Her areas of interest and research are comparative religion, African indigenous religion, and the religions of Africa in Diaspora. She has written a number of books, and her articles have appeared in refereed journals and edited volumes. Her latest works are (1) *Interrogating Problematic Issues in the Humanities and Education*, A Gedenkschrift for Prof Abdul Lateef Mobolaji Adetona (Co-Edited) (2019) Free Enterprise. (2) "Gender Equality: A Comparative Narrative in African Religious, Christian and Islamic Traditions" in Akinloye Ojo et al. (ed) *Gender and Development in Africa and Its Diaspora*. (2019) New York. (3) "Modern Religious Movements as Panacea/Painkiller for African Women" in *Kwara Journal of Religious Studies*. Vol. 2, No. 1. (2018) Kwara State University, Malete. (4) "Religious Rituals in the Context of Identity Empowerment: The Experience of Trans-Atlantic Slave Trade African Slave and Descendants in the Americas" in Falola and Alexius (ed) *The Democratization of Africa: Dynamics and Trends*. (2017) New York. (5) "Libation, Homage and the Power of Words" in Falola and Akintunde (ed) *Culture and Customs of the Yorùbá* (2017) USA.

Danoye Oguntola-Laguda is Scholar of Religion with specialization in philosophy of religion. He is Professor of Philosophy of Religion. He has been working in the Department of Religions and Peace Studies at Lagos State University (www.lasu.edu.ng), Ojo, Lagos, Nigeria, where he lectures and researches into the social values of religions, especially those dominant in Nigeria religious space. He was a senior research fellow in the Department of Philosophy and Religious Studies at the Simon Muzenda School of Arts, Culture and Heritage Studies, Great Zimbabwe University, Mashava, Masvingo (2019). His areas of interest include, but not limited to, religion and conflicts, religion and culture, teaching and study of religion, and religion and social institutions. He is a member of America Academy of Religion (AAR) and Africa Association for the Study of Religion (AASR) and African Consortium for Law and Religion Studies (ACLARS). His work has been published in several journals of international repute including *Journal of Religion in Africa* and *Journal of Africa and Oriental Studies* (JOAS).

Eric Adewuyi Mason is a Ph.D. student at the University of Georgia, USA, studying the religions of West Africa. His work charts the impacts of Western education on the education and training of priesthoods within African and African-derived religions. Prior to pursuing an academic career, Mason served as president of a multi-million-dollar government consulting firm, trained executives in the art of leadership and management, and aided small businesses in executing their growth strategies. He also holds a B.A. and an M.B.A. from the University of New Orleans. Additionally, he has been an Ifa priest within Yoruba Traditional Religion for over 18 years.

Tenson Muyambo is Professor of Gender and Religion at Great Zimbabwe University, Zimbabwe. His research interests lie in the areas of African religions, HIV and AIDS, religion and environment, African indigenous knowledge systems, education and emergencies such as COVID-19, just to mention a few. He has written articles and book chapters in the said areas.

Zaato Matthew Nor holds a Doctor of Philosophy Degree (Ph.D.) in Metaphysics/Phenomenology from Nnamdi Azikiwe University, Awka, Nigeria. He is Associate Professor of Philosophy in the Department of Philosophy at Benue State University, Makurdi, Nigeria. He also holds a Postgraduate Diploma in Education. Apart from his specialization in metaphysics/phenomenology, his areas of research and competence include African socio-cultural philosophy and hermeneutics, social philosophy, philosophy of education, Marxism, and philosophy of social change. His work is widely published with 35 articles in journals and book chapters both locally and internationally. He is a member of many professional and socio-cultural associations.

Kwaku Nti is Associate Professor of History at the Georgia Southern University, Armstrong Campus, Savannah, GA, USA. His research interests include everyday life in coastal Southern Ghana and the historic African Diaspora experiences in Ghana. In addition to having done peer reviews for some publishers and institutions, Nti has written several book chapters, peer-reviewed articles, and book reviews in journals. He is currently working on the manuscript "Society, Maritime Culture, and Everyday Life: Coastal Southern Ghana in the Nineteenth and Twentieth Centuries." Nti was educated at the University of Ghana, Central Michigan University, and Michigan State University.

Raymond Ogunade is a Fulbright and Study of the United States Institute on Religious Pluralism and Public Presence Fellow in the Department of Religious Studies, University of California, Santa Barbara (UCSB), USA (2011), and the Association of Commonwealth Universities Fellow at College of Human and Health Sciences, Swansea University, Wales, UK, 2010–2011. He is a Prize Award Winner of the prestigious Science and Religion Course Program, Center for Theology and the Natural Sciences, Berkeley, California, USA, 2001. His research interests include sociology of religion, African religion, inter-faith dialogue, and the interface between religion and science. He has written widely in academic journals and edited books. He also has two books to his credit. He teaches comparative religion in the Department of Religions at University of Ilorin, Nigeria.

Olatunde Oyewole Ogunbiyi is a senior lecturer in the Department of Religions at University of Ilorin, Ilorin, Nigeria. He is Scholar of Comparative Religions with emphasis in African Traditional Religion. An area of interest for him is the relationship between different religions of African religion, Christianity, and Islam in Nigeria. This is with an aim to forge harmonious relationship thereby avoiding inter-religious crisis. He is researching on the synergy between segments of the media and African religion in a rapidly globalized environment. He has several papers to his credit. He has delivered papers both in local and in international conferences.

Segun Ogungbemi is Professor of Philosophy and recipient of 2014 The University of Texas at Austin Distinguished Award for the Advancement of Pan-African Dialogue. He is also a recipient of 2014 Adekunle Ajasin University, Akungba-Akoko, Ondo State, Nigeria, Distinguished Merit Award for Excellent Services. He received his Ph.D. in Philosophy and Humanities from the University of Texas at Dallas Richardson Texas in 1984. He has taught in several universities. His university teaching career began at Bishop College Dallas, Texas, USA, before he went back to Africa and continued his teaching career at Ogun State University now Olabisi Onabanjo University, Ago-Iwoye, Nigeria; Moi University Eldoret, Kenya; Lagos State University, Lagos, Nigeria; and currently at Adekunle Ajasin University, Akungba, Ondo State, Nigeria. He has attended and presented papers at several local and international conferences. He was the editor of *JAPHIL: Journal of Applied Philosophy*, Department of Philosophy, Adekunle Ajasin University Akungba, Akungba-Akoko, Ondo State, Nigeria. He had been Head of Department of Philosophy at Ogun State University, Ago-Iwoye, Ogun State, now Olabisi Onabanjo University, Ago-Iwoye, Ogun State, Nigeria, and served on several committees of Senate. He also served as the founding Head of Department of Philosophy at Moi University Eldoret, Kenya, and was Acting Dean of School of Social Cultural and Development Studies in the same university. He was Head of Department of Philosophy at Lagos State University, Ojo, Lagos State, Nigeria. He was formerly Head of Department of Philosophy and Religious Studies at Adekunle Ajasin University, Akungba, Ondo State, Nigeria, and former Head of Department of Philosophy in the same university. He was the Chairman of the Ceremonies Committee and member of several committees of Senate. His research areas are African philosophy, ethics, environmental ethics, social and political philosophy, epistemology, philosophy of religion, philosophical theology, African traditional religion, metaphysics, existentialism, philosophy and conflict resolution, African aesthetics, and gender studies. He currently lives in Texas, USA.

Martina Iyabo Oguntoyinbo-Atere is Professor of Religious Studies at Adeleke University, Ede, Nigeria. She graduated with B.A. (Hons.) in Christian Studies with a second-class Upper Division from University of Ilorin in 1987. She enrolled for her M.A. in New Testament Studies in the Department of Religious Studies at the University of Ibadan in 1992 and graduated in 1994. She proceeded directly to the Ph.D. program in March 1995 and was appointed as an assistant lecturer in her department in April 1995. She was granted a scholarship by the World Council of Churches, Geneva, for a Doctor of Ministry Program of the San Francisco Theological Seminary (SFTS) with an International Feminist Emphasis. She lectures in the Religious Studies Department and is also serving as the Dean of Students Care Services in Adeleke University Ede, Nigeria.

AdeOluwa Okunade is Professor of Ethnomusicology in the Department of Music at the University of Port Harcourt, Rivers State, Nigeria. His current area of research includes African music in the Diaspora. He was once the President of Pan African Society for Musical Arts Education (PASMAE), 2010–2014. His scholarship activities earned him the Asante Award for Outstanding Research of the University of Georgia, Athens, USA, in 2012, among other laurels. He is an active member of Association of Nigerian Musicologists and Society of Music Educators in Nigeria.

Atinuke Olubukola Okunade holds a PhD in Philosophy of Religion, from the Lagos State University, Ojo, Lagos, Nigeria. She started her career from Adeniran Ogunsanya College of Education, now Lagos State University of Education, Ijanikin, Lagos, Nigeria. She has held several administrative positions in the college and has contributed articles to both local and international publications. She is a member of several professional bodies and has attended and read papers at many conferences, both local and international. As a Senior Academic in the University, her research interest covers use of herbal medicine among African immigrants in the Diaspora.

David Olali is the comparativist scholar and founding director/curator at Comparative Heritage Project (CHP), a transdisciplinary, scholarly research unit with broad-based thematic foci which creatively and analytically explores the complex and often-complicated ways by which meaning is produced and consumed within what is deemed to be social, political, and cultural settings for *homo sapiens* as psycho-relations-based beings. Olali's work and interest with CHP converges around heritage formations issues with their ramifications for identity politics whether through inflections of ethnicity, race, gender, or religion. Prior to CHP, Olali was the pioneer Research Fellow in Global Leadership at Interdenominational Theological Center, directing the T'Ofori-Atta Institute for the Study of the Religious Heritage of the African World (TRHAW) in Atlanta, GA. Olali received a Ph.D. in Religion from Claremont Graduate

University, CA. With expertise in critical comparative scriptures, his ongoing research centers around formations, de-formations, and reformations of heritage as instruments of power negotiation in human relations, social and political blocs, relations, and/or communities that negotiate power, hierarchies, and privileges.

Grillo Oluwaseun is a Ph.D. candidate in the Department of Religions (Comparative Religious Studies) at the University of Ilorin, Nigeria. He lectures at University of Ibadan Centre for Degree Programs at Federal College of Education, Osiele, Abeokuta, Ogun State. He is the author of *The Seven Wonderful Sentences of Jesus on the Cross.*

Rotimi Williams Omotoye is a professor in the Department of Religions at the University of Ilorin, Ilorin, Nigeria. He is the author of "The Study of African Traditional Religion and Its Challenges in Contemporary Times" in the *Ilorin Journal of Religious Studies* (2011); and "The Use of African Traditional Medicine, Orthodox Medicine, and Christian Faith Healing in Yorubaland, South Western Nigeria" in the *Ilorin Journal of Linguistics* (2103). He is an editor for *Science and Religion* in the Service of Humanity.

Kelvin Onongha is an ordained Minister of the Seventh-day Adventist Church. He holds a Ph.D. in Religion in Mission and Ministry from the Seventh-day Adventist Theological Seminary at Andrews University, Michigan, USA, in addition to a Doctor of Ministry Degree in Global Mission Leadership from the same institution. He has held leadership positions in the church and academia, having served as an Executive Secretary of the South East Conference in Nigeria, and as Associate Vice-President for Student Development at Babcock University, Nigeria. Onongha has also taught as an adjunct professor at Andrews University and on a few Adventist university campuses around the world. He is an author and has written a number of articles in professional journals. He is Associate Professor of Missions and the Director of Doctor of Ministry and M.A. Missiology Programs at the Adventist University of Africa, Kenya.

Mensah A. Osei is Interrelated Special Education educator with Clarke County School District, Athens, GA, USA. He received his Doctoral Degree in Religious Studies from the University of South Africa, Pretoria. He also is Oracle Certified Database Administrator and Associate of Chartered Institute of Marketing, England. He has taught in elementary, middle, high schools, and tertiary institutions in Ghana, Nigeria, and South Africa. Osei taught religious studies and social studies education at the University of Transkei (now Walter Sisulu University) in Umtata, South Africa. He is the co-author of *Digging Up Our Foremothers: Stories of African Women, African Traditional and Oral Literature as Pedagogical Tools in Content Area Classrooms, Contemporary Study in Religions of Africa and African Diaspora,* and *African Traditional Oral Literature and Visual Cultures as Pedagogical Tools in Diverse Classroom Contexts.* Osei's areas of research interest are African religion in Africa and African Diaspora, new religious movements, and gender studies.

Robert Yaw Owusu is a part-time professor at Morehouse College and Clark Atlanta University both in Atlanta, Georgia, USA. He teaches introduction to religion, biblical heritage, and religions of Africa. He has taught world religions for eleven years at Southern Polytechnic State University (now part of Kennesaw State University) also as adjunct faculty. Owusu received his Ph.D. in Church-State Studies from Baylor University in 2003 after receiving his two Master's Degrees in Religion and Theology from Boston University and Emory University, respectively. Owusu is an ordained Minister of the Ghana Baptist Convention, senior pastor of Amazing Grace Baptist Church of Atlanta, USA, and former president of the Ghanaian Ministers Association of Georgia. He is the author of *Kwame Nkrumah's Liberation Thought: A Paradigm for Religious Advocate in Contemporary Ghana* (2006), co-author of *Exploration of World Religions* 1st ed. (January 2015), author of *Introduction to Religion* (2016), and has written some articles, book reviews, and contributing author in *Contemporary Perspectives on Religions in Africa and the African Diaspora* (Oct 2015).

Sarwuan Daniel Shishima is Professor of African Traditional Religion (ATR) with interests in African traditional religion and culture, African traditional medicine, and African ethics and philosophy. Shishima has spent his entire career in teaching which he began in 1983 at the Mbagba Community Secondary School. After serving the nation under the National Youth Service Corps (NYSC) scheme, he continued his career in teaching, working in several schools between 1988 and 1992. When in 1992 he joined the Department of Religion and Philosophy (now Religion and Cultural Studies) at Benue State University, he committed himself to doing his job, a trait that earned him several promotions until he became Professor of Religious Studies in 2007. During his 28-year service at the Benue State University, he has held many administrative positions including dean, Faculty of Arts, head of department, and coordinator of different programs. He spent his sabbatical leave at National Institute of Policy and Strategic Studies (NIPSS) between 2011 and 2012 and has held several visiting positions in the country including Gombe State University, Kogi State University, and Taraba State University. He has been external examiner to University of Jos; Lagos State University, Ojo; Kogi State University, Anyigba; Nasarawa State University, Keffi; Federal College of Education, Obudu; and Reformed Theological Seminary (RTS) Mkar, Gboko. Shishima has over 60 publications to his credit in both local and international journals including books and book chapter contributions. Shishima is a Christian and the Grand Patron of Lordship of Christ Family Ministry, Makurdi.

Raji Shittu is a senior lecturer at the Centre for Peace and Strategic Studies (CPSS), University of Ilorin, Nigeria. He is the Chairman of the Society for Peace Studies and Practice (SPSP), Kwara State, Nigeria, and member of the Institute of Chartered Mediators and Conciliators of Nigeria. Shittu is an Alumnus of the University of Notre Dame, USA, and the co-winner of the Council for the Development of Social Science Research in Africa (CODESRIA)

2014 Research Grant. His research interests include international relations, governance and conflict management, and peace and strategic studies.

Yushau Sodiq is Professor of Religion and Islamic Studies at Texas Christian University, Fort Worth, USA, since 1992. He specializes in Islamic studies, Islamic law, African religions, and Islam in America. He taught at Virginia Commonwealth University, Richmond, from 1990 to 1992 and was a lecturer in the Faculty of Law at University of Sokoto, Nigeria, 1980–1983. He has also lectured in the Muslim Teacher's College, Farmville, VA. Born in Sagamu, Nigeria, he holds a B.A. (1976) in Islamic Studies and an M.A. (1979) in Islamic Law from the Islamic University of Medina, Medina, Saudi Arabia, and an M.A. and Ph.D. (1991) in Religious Studies from Temple University, Philadelphia, PA. Sodiq has presented papers and participated in panels at numerous scholarly meetings and has provided Islamic legal and professional advice to Muslim communities in Philadelphia, Richmond, Fort Worth, and Dallas.

Joseph Moyinoluwa Talabi received his B.A. in Theology from Crowther Theological Seminary, and then proceeded to obtain his Master's Degree in Philosophy of Religion from Ajayi Crowther University, Oyo, Nigeria. He is a prolific writer and had contributed to learned journals and books in the course of his academic and professional career. He is a Ph.D. student with Department of Religions and Peace Studies at Lagos State University.

Noah Yusuf is Professor of Sociology at the University of Ilorin, Nigeria. His research interests include industrial sociology, industrial relations, and peace and security studies. He is a fellow at Society for Peace Studies and Practice (SPSP) and a member of the Chartered Institute of Mediation and Conciliation (CIMC). He is the Vice-Chancellor of Al-Hikmah University, Ilorin.

CHAPTER 1

Introduction to Handbook of African Traditional Religion

Ibigbolade S. Aderibigbe and Toyin Falola

There is hardly any doubt that the practice and study of African Traditional Religion have generated significant interest globally. Such interest is clearly traceable to the importance of religion as the "barometer" of the African spiritual and cultural hegemonies that have shaped the fundamental identities of African ethnic groups and societies both on the continent and in the Diaspora. Unfortunately, the high levels of interest have not been matched with the same levels of recognition, acceptance, or even respect for the religion as a competing partner in the global religious space—both as an "authentic" practicing religion and as a theologically grounded faith worthy of adherence and serious intellectual or academic engagements.

This situation has been further compounded by the advents of Christianity and Islam on the African continent. The two religions have successfully decimated African Traditional Religion at its "home base" by securing the loyalty of the vast majority of the African population between the two over the centuries. Also, the Christian and Islamic hostilities toward and dismissiveness of the religious/spiritual worthiness of African Traditional Religion are legendary. Indeed, such attitudes constitute the center of their salvific propagations. For

---

I. S. Aderibigbe (✉)
Department of Religion, University of Georgia, Athens, GA, USA
e-mail: iaderibi@uga.edu

T. Falola
Department of History, University of Texas at Austin, Austin, TX, USA
e-mail: toyinfalola@austin.utexas.edu

© The Author(s), under exclusive license to Springer Nature
Switzerland AG 2022
I. S. Aderibigbe, T. Falola (eds.), *The Palgrave Handbook of African Traditional Religion*, https://doi.org/10.1007/978-3-030-89500-6_1

example, Christianity regards African Traditional Religion as paganism, while Islam consigned it to al-Jahilliyya, the time of barbarism.

However, it is important to acknowledge that some attention has been given to the concerns raised above, no matter the arguable inadequacies. The efforts at addressing the concerns have emerged in different forms and strategies. They consisted of pro-active engagements in formal and informal organizational paradigms of conferences, symposia, workshops, among others, to create and advance better understanding and, by extension, greater appreciation of both the practice and study of African Traditional Religion. Indeed, there have been countless numbers of such activities both in and outside of the African continent. The second addresses the nature, content, and focus of literature available in African Traditional Religion. As scholarly engagements, the efforts have documented the findings and views of various scholars on different aspects of the beliefs, practices, and study of African Traditional Religion. Worthy of mention here is the foundational yet, pivotal works of E. Bolaji Idowu, Joseph Omosade Awolalu, Edward Geoffrey Parrinder, John S. Mbiti, Kofi Asare Opoku, and Peter Adelumo Dopamu, among others. Their works, no doubt, have created a platform that has been instrumental to the growth of scholarship in African Traditional Religion, particularly the fundamental philosophical and religious beliefs and practices. Such works have highlighted African religion's essence in its holistic worldview of blending the divine and mundane spaces.

However, such works should be appropriately credited with laying only the foundation on which there should always be the need to build upon significantly. Consequently, these efforts should necessarily entail a deliberate re-situating and re-examining of the religion's beliefs and practices to account for their relevance in contemporary dynamics of global competitive religious space, in beliefs, in practices, and in study. It is also important that such efforts are not limited to just the nature and structure of the religion's beliefs and practices. They must transcend these fundamentals to explore the contents and discontents, exhibiting currency and the transformations that have taken place with regard to the religion. There should always be probing further and further, not only to delve into the basic components of beliefs and practices of the religion, but also more importantly to demonstrate its interconnectedness with other religious traditions globally in shaping cultural, historical, social, and political issues as they emerge at every turn of human and societal developments.

It is precisely within this context that this *Handbook of African Traditional Religion* becomes relevant and unique as a comprehensive volume. Such relevance and uniqueness entail two-dimensional strategies. The first is to avoid observed "limitations" of available works on African Religion. The second is to provide a more robust and comprehensive objective, focus, content, scope, organization, and contributions combining both the basic components with the desired contemporary orientations. Thus, the volume can be seen, not just as an apologetic three in defense of the religion but more significantly as a holistic or comprehensive manual.

In achieving these twofold objectives, the Handbook begins with an Introductory Chap. 1. The subsequent chapters are then divided into three parts. The first part consists of Chaps. 2 to 19. These chapters focus essentially on the nature, structure, and significance of African Traditional Religion's beliefs and practices. However, at the same time, they attempt to provide narratives and explore their interpretative and influence dynamics. In addition, these chapters seek to address the evolving sustainability strategies of the beliefs and practices of the religion as an authentic spiritual-religious tradition. Part II, consisting of Chaps. 20 to 36, shifts the focus to contemporary interconnectivity of issues in African Traditional Religion. Contributors through these chapters explore the contents and discontents of the interconnectivity of African Traditional Religion with various social, political, economic, and ethical issues dominating contemporary discourses. They also situate African Religion in its contacts and interface with the two dominant religions on the continent—Christianity and Islam. Also, the transition and transformation of African Traditional Religion in the Diaspora are discussed. Chapters 37 to 46 are in Part III. Issues discussed in this section are associated with academic and scholarship in African Religion. Essentially, these chapters seek to approach this task in two formats. The first explores the challenges of and furthering African Religion's teaching in institutions both on the African continent and globally. The second is uniquely designed to review some selected key or prominent foundation scholars/writers in African Traditional Religion.

Consequently, covered in 46 chapters, this volume, the *Handbook of African Traditional Religion*, interrogates and presents robust and comprehensive contributions from interdisciplinary experts and scholars. This is to achieve the ultimate objective of proffering balanced opinions of the authors of these chapters through the prism of understanding the past about African indigenous religion and, more importantly, capturing its dynamics in the present and projecting its sustainability and relevance for the future. There is also no doubt that the contents and discontents discourses articulated by a diverse pool of authors will undoubtedly promote informed sources of knowledge and understanding of African Traditional Religion in the global space of religious traditions. Therefore, in specific terms and to harness and synthesize these contributions, these chapters are summarized as follows:

The Introductory Chap. 1 constitutes the general introduction to the Handbook focusing on aims, objective, and focus of the book. It also presents a synthesis of each of the chapters of the book. It concludes with the significance, uniqueness, and target audiences of the book.

Part I: Basic or Essential Features of African Traditional Religion

Ibigbolade S. Aderibigbe's Chap. 2 starts off presenting essential features of African Traditional Religion with a detailed discussion on the religion's fundamental beliefs and practices. This is done through a discourse that illuminates awareness and understanding of the religion's nature and structure. This discussion also emphasizes the comprehensiveness of the religion as an inseparable part of the African people's total life experience in that it understandably permeates every sphere of the people's lives. It encompasses their culture, the social, the political, and ethical, as well as the individual and societal expectations—serving as the cornerstone of every aspect of African "ways of life." The chapter further attempts to succinctly but thoroughly dispel Western misrepresentations and misinterpretations of African Traditional Religion by highlighting its features as a viable and unique religious tradition in its own right. Finally, Aderibigbe explores both the internal and external challenges facing religion in today's contemporary world's sacred space. He argues that despite these challenges, the religion has a bright prospect of future existence and relevance in global religious space, particularly in its Diaspora complexities—known as African Derived Religion.

In Chap. 3, Olutola Akindipe advances discussion on the fundamentals of African Traditional Religion, dwelling on its tremendous influence on Africans' perspective not only on the continent but also among the African Diaspora despite stiff competition from other foreign religions such as Christianity and Islam. The author, however, concentrates her discussion on the sociological paradigm. In doing this, she employs some concepts from Vygotsky's sociocultural theory. The theory is used to understand African Tradition Religion worshippers' functional prisms of beliefs in the existence of a Supreme Being, spirits, ancestors, and the practice of magic and medicine. She argues that the survival of the religion, despite many challenges, is consequent upon the formidable socio-cultural dynamics provided by such functional beliefs and practices. Akindipe then submits that there is a lot to understand in applying this theory to African Traditional Religion. However, she argues that the theory should provide an understanding of the underlying perspective of African religious worshippers in their socio-cultural environment. This understanding ultimately suggests the continued existence and sustenance of African Traditional Religion now and in the future.

In turning away from the general discussion on the fundamental nature and structure of African Traditional Religion, Alloy S. Ihuah and Zaato M. Nor, in Chap. 4, open the discourse on specific concepts, beliefs, and religions' practices. Here, the authors focus on the metaphysical and ontological concepts. The chapter begins with basic definitions, explanations, and characteristics of metaphysics and ontology as universal concepts. It then details the two concepts' functionalities in understanding both the physical and transcendent realms in which human beings exist and participate in paradoxical relationships combining the two as reality paradigms. After this general description of the concepts' characteristics and significance, the authors proceed to give a detailed expository account of the different metaphysical and ontological concepts in the African Traditional Religion. This is effected through a predominantly expository and deconstructive examination of the Africans' existential worldview that encompasses and shapes African people's totality as spiritual entities.

In Chap. 5, Dorothy Nguemo Afoar continues discussing specific beliefs and practices of African Traditional Religion. She focuses on the concept and worship of the Supreme Being in the religion. The author begins the chapter with the argument of the universality of the belief in a spiritual being who is the creator and sustainer of the universe, and human beings occupying it. She then submits that this belief is also prevalent among African people as expressed through their religious worldview. According to the author, this worldview provides fundamental understandings of African peoples' devotion to this creator through their various worship rituals. However, she endeavors to explain the reality of the diversity of application of such worship rituals. This leads the author to argue that despite a general belief in a Supreme Being, there are differences in applications in specific terms. Therefore, while a strictly monotheistic approach is adopted among some ethnic groups, in others, it is not so clear, and this has led to the perspective that the religion is polytheistic among such ethnic groups. The author concludes that these differences, notwithstanding the concept and worship of a Supreme Being, are fundamental to the practice of African Traditional Religion.

For Lydia Bosede Akande and Olatunde Oyewole Ogunbiyi in Chap. 6, their concentration is on the dynamics of beliefs and veneration of divinities in African Traditional Religion. The chapter starts by illuminating and stressing the significant position occupied by divinities in the religion. It then discusses the relevance of such a belief and how and why it does not contradict the belief in one Supreme Being in African religious consciousness. Having clarified this, the authors focus on detailing the divinities' categories beginning from the relatively unknown divinities to the very prominent ones. They also attempt to examine the transition and sustenance of belief and veneration practices of the African continent's divinities in the African Diaspora. The authors also posit that the divinities occupy an intermediary position between the Supreme Being and the world. According to the authors, this functional role of divinities and the efficacy attributed to it have ensured unassailable recognition and veneration among practitioners of the religion both on the African continent and on its Diaspora. Finally, the authors believe that given the current revitalization and rejuvenation of African Traditional Religion, there is every indication that it will exist for a long time.

In a discussion on beliefs and veneration of Ancestors in African Traditional Religion, Benson Ohihon Igboin, in Chap. 7, explores how and why these have assumed a pivotal place and influence for religion practitioners. According to the author, this perspective is singularly linked to their conviction of the nearness of the ancestors to the living in terms of commonality and spirituality and because they are believed to reincarnate in new babies. The chapter then focuses on both the reality of the existence of the "spiritual domain" of the ancestors and also the required qualifications for the revered position. Such qualifications are tied to the ancestors' pristine standing in various life stations in the community's moral, economic, political, and religious accretions while they were alive. Also, the author situates the beliefs and veneration of ancestors in the contemporary African and global religious spaces. This is achieved by the author interrogating the characteristics and conditions that admitted people into their ancestors' communion. He then argues that such conditions need to be interpreted in light of contemporary reality. He concludes that if this is done, there would be a re-conceptualization of ancestor veneration that would be at once ancient and modern. Essentially, this will promote a reflective dynamism of African Traditional Religion as a living faith, not just for today but also for the future.

In Chap. 8, Kelvin Onongha takes up examining the beliefs and practices of Magic and Medicine. The author opens the discussion by submitting that the beliefs in the existence and efficacy of magic and medicine are very strong in African Traditional Religion. He then compares and contrasts the two concepts based on definitions and explanations while noting that in some cultures and languages, the terms used for both are similar and are often practiced by the same person as a profession. However, along the same vein, the author alludes to the distinctions that may characterize the two. Thus, he describes magic as a form of cosmic power that may be used for good or evil, often through manipulating spiritual entities.

On the other hand, medicine is seen as the engagement of cosmic powers of spiritual agencies to prevent and heal illnesses. The chapter then focuses on exploring the significance that magic and medicine beliefs have in African Traditional Religion, both in the past and until the present. In conclusion, the author examines the functional impacts of magic and medicine's beliefs and practices in the lives of Africans in the traditional setting and now in contemporary realities. He then highlights developing revolutionary factors contributing to their continued practices even in a modern technological age.

Ibigbolade S. Aderibigbe returns in Chap. 9. This time focusing on cosmological and ontological beliefs in African Traditional Religion. The chapter opens with the author, indicating that the beliefs as narratives are usually embedded as themes of various African ethnic groups' oral traditions. They are also very important in drawing attention to the true or authentic exposition and understanding of the religion, without which such an understanding will not be complete. This is because they constitute the essential starting points in any meaningful discourse of Africans' traditional religious worldview regarding the relationships between humans and the Supreme Being in particular and between the mundane and the spiritual spaces in general. In alluding to this position in specific terms, the author submits that the dynamics are prisms of the African "theology." That "theology" or doctrine explains not just the origins of human beings (individually and collectively) and the universe itself, but also their envisaged ends ultimately. For a meaningful understanding of this "theology," the chapter focuses on its three thematic components—the creation and nature of the world, the creation and nature of human beings, and the relationship between humans and the Supreme Being. The author discusses the themes by addressing the overall significance as paradigms of the beginning and end stations of humans and the universe. Particularly in that, they reflect the "outcomes" of cosmic destinies, instituted, sustained, and executed as divine pre-determined "journeys" for humans and the universe. The agencies employed by the author are mythical narratives from some African ethnic groups in their similarities and differences located in oral sources of the people.

Discussions on liturgy, rituals, traditions, sacrifices, and festivals in African Traditional Religion constitute the focus of Chap. 10. The author, Mensah A. Osei, refers to these religious components as forms of customary public worship. According to him, they are means of communication with the Supreme Being and ancestors within the context of worship. The adherents of African Traditional Religion, for example, utilize the media of traditional festivals to mark important religious, social, and cultural events in the lives of the people or their community. Usually, activities during such festivals culminate in a series of performances, entertainments, rites and rituals, liturgies, and sacrifices as forms of worship to communicate with the divine. The author also submits that individual and communal values for the community's well-being are promoted during the festivals. Viewed from this perspective, the liturgical rituals and sacrifices embedded in the celebrations provide epitomes of traditional cultural-educational paradigms. Based on all these characteristics, the author highlights and discusses the importance of festivals with illustrations from some ethnic groups in West Africa. In conclusion, he avers that promoting rejuvenized and contemporary compliant traditional festivals will give currency to the meaning and relevance of the festivals in the social, political, and religious life of the participants celebrating them. Also, such dynamics are needed if the festivals are to survive and remain significant for future generations of Africans.

In Chap. 11, "African Circle of Life," Segun Ogungbemi gives a general explanation of this concept in African Traditional Religion as a doctrine of the religion predicated on the ontological and cosmological nature of human existence. While the ontological component speaks of human beings deriving their existence from the Supreme Being, the cosmological equally alludes to the creation of the universe by the same Supreme Being. A combination of the two's dynamics and processes as a doctrine addresses the Africans' belief that human beings enjoy a continuous existence that is paradoxically shared between the mundane and spiritual domains. Such navigation of existence between the two domains constitutes the dynamics of the concept of "circle of life." Enjoying this form of eternal existence is further predicated on the Africans' belief in ancestorship. This belief denotes that souls of ancestors who had lived morally upright lives while in the mundane domain can be reincarnated in their immediate family or clan. The author subjects the African doctrine of the circle of life to a rigorous interrogation employing rational arguments to unravel the religious interpretations of its narratives of myths, paradoxes, and contradictions. The author concludes that African forebears have left behind the concept of the circle of life as a practical demonstration that death is not the end of life. However, the present generation and future generations should employ the scientific and robotic engineering available to them to navigate such a belief and accord it the necessary contemporary functional interpretation. The author, therefore, suggests that this portends the only format in which life could be said to be a continuum as intended in the African doctrine of the "circle of life."

In Chap. 12, Segun Ogungbemi continues with African themes of life, death, and the hereafter. He begins with the question of why is it that, of all the living things in the universe, it is only human beings who concern themselves with the phenomenon of death and the afterlife. In addressing this all-important question, the author highlights the narratives associated with the phenomenon in African Traditional Religion, particularly before foreign religions' thoughts began to influence such narratives. The chapter then goes on to navigate the traditional epistemological expressions addressing the phenomenon. It further addresses the spiritual, cultural, and intellectual dispositions available in the traditional African religious settings about the phenomenon and how these may now be challenged by those with modern civilization perspectives. After interrogating the African traditional doctrines on death, burial rites, and the afterlife, the author submits a paradigm shift in epistemological applications. However, he further argues that such a shift should not be seen as a total rejection of the traditional paradigm but its rational revisitation. He concludes that such an exercise is likely to show that while these were the best epistemological explanations available to African forefathers at the time, such explanations may not necessarily be adequate or relevant for the present descendants and future generations.

Continuing with the themes of life, death, and the hereafter in Chap. 13, Ibigbolade S. Aderibigbe examines the interconnectivity of the beliefs in reincarnation and eschatology in African Traditional Religion. The author states that this connectivity, though more glaringly evident in African Traditional Religion, can also be found in other religious traditions such as Hinduism, Buddhism, Jainism, and the Native American religion. Also, he submits that belief in reincarnation is fundamental to African Traditional Religions' doctrine of the "circle of life," which has significant implications for Africans' belief in eschatology. He then refers to this connectivity as a paradigm of relationships between the mundane and spiritual domains that demonstrates that reincarnation is the reality of an end status for the individual and the cosmos. The chapter then focuses on integrating this connectivity and its implications as a "theology" of the paradoxical relationship of human existence in the physical world and "end" destination in the spiritual domain. To give a concrete demonstration of this, the author focuses on two ethnic groups as case studies: Yoruba and Illa.

Interestingly, the two ethnic groups represent the two types of reincarnation in African Traditional Religion—partial reincarnation and universal reincarnation. The characteristics and application of the two typologies are highlighted and explained in detail. The chapter finally discusses the implications of the linkage between reincarnating and eschatology. The submission here is that from the perspective of African Traditional Religion, this linkage, through the implications involved, presents the crucial explanations for the circle of life of the individual human being and the end envisaged for not just them but also for the universe they live in.

In Chap. 14, Danoye Oguntola-Laguda shifts the discussion from basic beliefs and practices to their custodians, called religious leaders, with their different roles. Here, the focus is on Priests/Priestesses, Medicine Professionals, and Kings. The author opens with the all-important statement on the importance of leadership in any religious institution and the challenges or problems that may develop if the style and quality of such leadership are questioned. The consequences of poor, ineffective, or even morally bankrupt leadership usually lead to an inability for development and growth in such religious organizations. Coming specifically to African Traditional Religion concerning the priests/priestesses, medical professionals, and kings, Laguda extensively discusses how the quality of their leadership roles has impacted religion's development and growth. His opinion is that these leaders have not measured up to the standard based on several vices he identifies and discusses. Using the Yoruba ethnic group as a case study, Laguda seeks to identify and critically examine these religious leaders' anticipated roles, focusing on the religious, economic, social, political, and cultural lives of the adherents of the religion in particular and the relevant society in general. He concludes the chapter with suggestions on how these leaders can meet the required expectations and thereby enhance the practice and relevance of the religion presently and in the future.

In Chap. 15, titled "Illnesses and Cures," Kelvin Onongha writes on how the occurrences of illnesses and their cures have been addressed in traditional African society. Because illnesses and their cures are not regarded as just physiological but also spiritual in nature, they have always constituted a very important aspect of African Traditional Religion. Indeed, the belief in medicine, under which they are addressed, is usually seen as a significant belief in the religion. Thus, as traditional medical practitioners, traditional healers have always occupied an essential and indispensable place in African society. The author highlights and discusses the role these traditional healers have always played from one generation to the other in various African communities. He alludes to the fact they have always enjoyed clientele. He also states that the diagnostic and treatment methods they employed have been transmitted from generation to generation orally and through apprenticeship. Such methods of diagnosis often entail observation, inquiry, and in some cases, consultation with divinities to discern the cause of the disease condition and the necessary treatment procedure. The author also raises and discusses the advent of modern medical science in Africa today. However, while he accepts that this has produced new reliable methods for diagnosing illnesses and treating infirmities, he believes that reliance on traditional healers' services is far from over. Thus, there is still a need to explore the beliefs underlying the origins and causes of illness in African Traditional Religion and the remedies for treating and curing these maladies. He concludes by submitting that it is only by engaging in such an exploration that one can fully understand why traditional healing methods, although affected by the advent of modern medicine, will continue to thrive and persist.

The theme of roles in African Traditional Religion continues in Chap. 16. Here, Andrew Philips Adega discusses secret societies' roles such as fraternities, witches, wizards, and sorcerers. The author indicates that these agents in secret societies by classification fall under the canopy of mystical powers or spiritual forces. He then takes up what he calls the "raging debate" about the reality or fiction of these spiritual forces or mystical powers, particularly in contemporary African communities. Based on the author's research, it leads him to submit that fraternities, witches, wizards, and sorcerers are realities in African societies. They also possess some form of mystical power or spiritual forces that seem to defy immediate scientific explanations. The author then describes their characteristic spiritual powers and how they are employed, mostly for negative purposes. Examples of these dynamics are given in some African ethnic groups. According to the author, because witches, wizards, sorcerers, and fraternities are associated with evil deeds, they usually conduct their activities in the darkness of the night. Indeed, their evil deeds have produced death, illnesses, ill-luck, bewitchment, calamity, and loss in the communities they live in. As a result of this, these personalities are mostly hated and feared by people in their communities. In conclusion, the author highlights and discusses the emergence of specialized medicine men and women who fight the menace of these spiritual forces. He then suggests that there should be a de-emphasis on these spiritual forces' acquisition and employment for evil purposes. Rather, they should be directed for the positive engagements of enhancing the overall development of different African societies where such spiritual forces exist.

Atinuke Olubukola Okunade continues with the theme of roles in Chap. 17. For her, the focus is on the role of women in African Traditional Religion. She begins the chapter by asserting that women play essential roles as mothers and caregivers. According to the author, this is why they are mythologically revered as "mother of mankind, from whom all people originated." She cites an Ibibio myth claiming that human beings originated from the divinity Obumo, the son of the mother divinity Eka-Abbasi. The main idea here is to link human life directly with God through a woman. Also, Africans credit women with the role of giving birth to humans and caring or nursing them thereafter. Apart from the role of motherhood and demonstrating their roles as caring agents, women are usually seen as teachers and enforcers of moral values in society. Atinuke Okunade also discusses another area where women play significant roles in African Traditional Religion. This is in the area of religious activities such as the offering of prayers for their families in particular and their community in general. This is why, according to the author, there are women as priestesses, diviners, and traditional medical practitioners in many African communities. Also, the experience of spirit possession is almost exclusively the preserve of women in African Traditional Religion, and are, in most cases, women. Based on all the above, the chapter concludes that women's role is all-encompassing in African Traditional Religion as this role covers every communal activity for the overall welfare of the women themselves, their family, and the society at large.

Shifting the focus from personalities to objects in Chap. 18, AdeOluwa Okunade writes on the roles of Arts, Music, and Aesthetics in African Traditional Religion. The chapter begins with the author stressing the significant value of arts in African religious belief systems. This, according to him, obtains, despite the attempts by the perpetrators of the Atlantic Slave Trade to both erode and denigrate African cultural heritage in its totality. Thus, the author submits that art, either in visual or performative style, gives full values and life to the meaningful worships in African Traditional Religion. He then discusses how and why the arts should not be seen just as fantasies or decorative elements to determine their aesthetic value for religious purposes. Rather, they are to be taken to encompass the post-worship lifestyle of the religious adherents as they navigate the experiences of the norms, values, and ethos derived from the religious aesthetics. The chapter then discusses how arts and music transmit these values through both tangible and intangible forces. In conclusion, the author submits that arts and music are imperative purposeful aesthetics of African Traditional Religion determinants.

In Chap. 19, which concludes Part I, Félix Ayoh'Omidire writes on Oral and Non-Oral Sources of Knowledge in African Traditional Religion. Here, the author seeks to accomplish this by exploring the ethos of secrecy, orality, and power in knowledge transmission within the Yoruba Traditional Religion. He does this with particular reference to their dynamics in Afro-Latin-American and Caribbean societies such as Brazil, Cuba, and Trinidad. This chapter discusses the epistemological fundaments of the Yoruba's understanding of human essence and power relations, which he believes cuts across physical and metaphysical spheres and strata of existence. According to him, this can be found in Òtúrúpòn méjì, more popularly referred to by knowledgeable Ifá priests and practitioners of Yoruba traditional Ifá-Orisa religion as Olọgbọ́n méjì. This is the twelfth Odù in the vast compendium of Ifá oracular and literary corpus, which totals 256 great volumes. Olọgbọ́n méjì, that is, the two wise men, points out that knowledge and knowledge transmission represent a major quest and, indeed, a mark of respect and leadership in Yoruba traditional religion that can be said to represent African Traditional Religion as a whole. His conclusion is that a good grasp and utilization of these paradigms are veritable sources of deep understanding and transmission of knowledge in all its ramifications about Yoruba Traditional Religion in particular and African Traditional Religion in general.

Part II: Contemporary Interactions: Contents and Discontents

In Chap. 20, David Olali opens the discourse in this section by writing on the interactions between religious ethics as a general religious concept and in the particular case of African Traditional Religion. The chapter begins with a description of religious ethics as a concept and its link to the Africans' religious worldview. According to the author, religious ethics summarize the logic and mythologies of existence among African peoples. This dynamic is significant in that existence or living a human life requires knowing what is right and the performance of what is both right and true. For the Yoruba, a summation of these requirements' credible performance designates a person as "Omoluabi"—a person with all-around good moral character. Having provided this background, Olali then argues that, as fundamental aspects that foreground both the humanity and beingness of Africans, religious ethics embody interpretive tropes that form important sites through nearly every fiber and fabric of the social and political sphere. Thus, for Africans, there is no demarcation between the secular and the religious. All secular human functions are seen as originating and embedded in religious connections and vice versa. He further posits that, although religion and ethics point to truths that cut across complex strata of existence as socially locatable realities, they are equally subject to manipulations through human agents' whims and caprices. Based on such possibilities, the author concludes the chapter by submitting that there is a need for new critical readings in the dominant taxonomies about religion as a category when discussing power and its utilization at the community level.

Dauda Umaru Adamu and Amidu Elabo continue the conversation in Chap. 21, with the title "Traditional Religion, and Morality in Society." They begin by submitting that African Traditional Religion and moral values have a relationship that is arguably inseparable. According to them, Africans believe that moral values are essentially derived from religious beliefs and cultural values. Thus, though one can develop moral ideals and sensitivity without religion, this position is not shared by Africans since they hold that morality is intrinsically connected to traditional religious beliefs to the extent that they are considered one and the same. Based on this background explanation, the authors explore and discuss this connectivity in African societies within the context of some African religious beliefs. These include beliefs in the Supreme Being, humanity and its place in the world, rituals of transformation that people engage in, respect of ancestors, divinities, spirits, and the created order. From the authors' perspectives, all these beliefs are sources of a living and inspiration arena in which morality is explored and lived. They also allude to some other beliefs in African Traditional Religion worth considering in the religion's connectivity to morality in a broader sense. These are beliefs in magic, witchcraft, and divination. In order to bring practical context to the discussion, the authors draw upon illustrations from some parts of Africa. They then conclude that since African Traditional Religion is not static, it is important to acknowledge that the peoples' beliefs on moral values have been influenced by other interests and factors such as colonialism, European cultural and economic practices, corruption, ethno-religious politics, inter-party rivalries, and democracy.

In Chap. 22, Alloy S. Ihuah and Zaato M. Nor focus on the interaction between African Traditional Religion and African philosophy. The authors commence the chapter with brief definitions of Philosophy and African Traditional Religion. "Philosophy" is defined as a critical activity that is peculiar only to man and instantiates a wave of pondering and reflection on the ideas we live by with the view to finding (an) answer(s) to the perennial problems of humanity. This is what Aristotle declared that it "is the product of wonder."

"African Traditional Religion" is defined as readily constituting the subject of wonder as it is an intrinsic component of Africans' worldview that is understood to present the general picture of the world and the place of man in it. Based on these definitions, the two subjects' interactive dynamics are derivable from the notion that the place of man in the universe is discernable from some important beliefs and ideals, which include, among others, economic, sociopolitical, metaphysical, philosophical, moral, religious, and aesthetics. This is the synergetic relationship between these ideas (Philosophical) and African Traditional Religion that the authors then interrogate. Their arguments are anchored on the understanding that a worldview is either communal or philosophical. They further argue that African Traditional Religion enables African philosophy to make sense of Africans' destiny, reality, and the world they live in. Given this position, they conclude that African Philosophy should be viewed as an essentially metaphysical endeavor. In which case, African reality is ultimately spiritual, thus suggesting African Philosophy is essentially derived from the African peoples' traditional religious worldview.

For Adepeju Johnson-Bashua, in Chap. 23, the focus of discussion is on gender equality and feminism in African Traditional Religion. The author starts by designating gender inequality as one of the prevalent forms of societal problems hindering African societies' progress. She claims this is so because of the rigid customs and traditions of the people. In specific terms, in the author's opinion, the clash between women's rights to non-discrimination and their right to freedom of religious practice are traceable to the intersection of culture, religion, and gender in the context of African philosophy. The chapter then discusses gender relations from the standpoint of African Traditional Religion, highlighting the existing complementary aspects. In doing this, the author discusses features and practices that demystify gender stereotypes that convey African religion as strictly masculine. The conclusion from this submission is that a proper understanding of these features and practices in African Traditional Religion shows no evidence of hindering women from participating fully in contemporary Africa development.

In Chap. 24, David Olali examines intersections in African Traditional Religion, sexual orientation, homosexuality, and transgender. In doing so, the author provides critical engagements of normative assumptions and definitions. Granted that most people in Africa publicly and privately identify as either male or female, Christian or Muslims, he attempts to explore a third option that examines whether traditional African religion has tolerance for sexual orientations or gender categories outside of popularly known and accepted ones. The author explores key factors in historical, psycho-social, and political perspectives that have shaped public and popular perceptions of sexuality and gender in modern Africa. He then identifies and discusses some ideological mis-narratives that have instigated the hyper-sexualization of gender and their consequences in the contemporary global society in general and that of Africa. In addition, Olali interrogates the consequences of systemic violence and other negative actions that have resulted from the discursive and rhetorical lenses of religious tropes against individuals who belong to the category of persons caught in the web of sexual and gender sensibilities. It is important to point out that the author's examination of the issues covers both the pre-colonial and post-colonial African settings. He also uses multiple perspectives derived from African literature and orature in navigating the narratives. In conclusion, the author presents the view that there need to be openings, opportunities, and continuations in conversations around the desire to be human when discussing religion, sexuality, and gender in Africa.

Chapter 25 is titled "African Traditional Religion, Conflict Resolution, and Peaceful Societal Co-Existence." The chapter is written by Noah Yusuf and Raji Shittu. According to the authors, though there is evidence of various intra- and inter-group conflicts arising from socio-economic and political furor in African societies, there are equally mechanisms for their resolutions for peaceful co-existence through strategic features of African Traditional Religion. The authors then set out to expand on this thesis. They begin by first identifying the significant sources of conflict in Africa. These, according to them, include stiff competition for land ownership, chieftaincy tussles, disagreements over family inheritances, and matrimonial squabbles. They then indicate that employing traditional religious tools has been more effective in resolving these conflicts in African communities. The factors responsible for such success are hinged on African spiritual values derived from the consequences that may result from disobeying the resolutions and agreements on the conflicts. Such consequence of disobedience may prove very calamitous for the survival of an individual and the survival of his traditional lineage, including his family, community, and immediate society. The authors also identify and discuss the core settlement features and platforms of African traditional religious conflict resolution. These are the use of shrines, masquerade, oath-taking, truthfulness, forgiveness, appeasement, atonement, and sanctions. Also, identified conflict issues are resolved through pleas, appeasements, fines, and sanctions as pronounced by the deities. In conclusion, the chapter states that because the traditional African method of conflict resolution has been mostly successful, it should be sustained and popularized as a credible platform for resolving conflicts in contemporary African societies.

In Chap. 26, Kweku Nti tackles interaction between African Traditional Religion and Democratic Governance in contemporary Africa. He explains that given the integral nature of African Traditional Religion to culture in its generality, it remains relevant in many societies despite the demonization and denigration during the European colonization era. He also notes that this dynamic is unanimously embarrassed in diverse forms among most, if not all, African ethnic groups or nations. However, to give concrete context to the discussion, the author uses the people of Ghana, a West African nation, as a case study. According to him, in Ghana, the time-honored belief in the Supreme Being through intermediaries such as gods, goddesses, nature spirits, other spirits, and the ancestors, like most foreign religions, are embedded in the Constitution.

Consequently, their recognition and inclusiveness continue in the current democratic dispensation at national functions, and their political expediency is not lost on officials and would-be officials. Their inextricability from the indigenous political system with the king or chief also being considered a priest has made and will continue to make democratic governance officials continue to solicit and seek approval from them. The author is, of course, not oblivious to the potential adverse outcomes when traditional religious democratic strategies are applied. This notwithstanding, the author concludes that the overwhelming successes of adopting these strategies in Ghana's democratic systems are good omens for their adopting and applications in other African nations' democracies.

In Chap. 27, Kweku Nti writes about the connectivity between African Traditional Religion and Economic Development in Africa. The author opens the chapter with the view that African Traditional Religion is endowed with important paradigms of functionalities for economic developments in the communities where it is practiced. According to him, this scenario is made possible by Africans' worldview that such economic development paradigms are accessible through their fear, reverence, and dependence on a powerful otherworldly realm of the ancestors, nature spirits, other spirits, gods, goddesses, and an overarching Supreme Being. In discussing these functional paradigms, Nti uses Ghana as a case study again for context's sake. He points out the situation in Ghana as representative of other African nations where the relevance of indigenous belief systems cuts across a whole slew of sectors, including education, fishing, agriculture, health, land ownership, forest renewal, preservation, and tourism. His thesis is that this religious impact model on all sectors of society's activities is generally self-evident, though sometimes hardly acknowledged across the African nation. Therefore, he concludes that a case can be made for the indispensability of African Traditional Religions both for their cultural nature and, more importantly, for their role in economic productivity in Ghana in particular and across Africa in general.

Chapter 28 is titled "African Traditional Religion, Social Justice, and Human Rights." The author, Samson O. Ijaola, focuses his narrative on issues associated with social justice and human rights in the context of African Traditional Religion. As a background, the author alludes that despite the gap between the ancient and the modern world, there is no disputing the presence of constituents of social justice and human rights in the African past. That indeed, these have always informed Africans' critical perspective and appreciation in evaluating social constructs and their attendant political significance. The author further explains that while African theologians and African humanists are divided on African Traditional Religion being the basis of African ethics, there are strong arguments to support an indispensable relationship between religion and ethics from the African peoples' religious perspective. According to the author, there are lucid indices that the struggle, promotion, and management of ideas of individual rights are recognized and have always been part of African communalists' ideology and structure as reality and enforcement of social justice derived from their religious ethics. The chapter consequently embarks on a discourse by exploring the scholarly works and features of African Traditional Religion in tackling social justice issues and respect for human rights. These features are mainly found in the religion's moral system. This is a system that Africans, particularly those practicing African Traditional Religion, employ to address injustice, moral and financial corruption, violent conflicts, and crimes in their communities. In conclusion, the author submits that neglecting African Traditional Religion is a significant missing link between social justice concerning human rights and their enforcement in contemporary African societies. He suggests that there is a need for the void to be filled.

Eric Ayodele Mason, in Chap. 29, writes on the functional dynamics of the belief and practice of divination in Contemporary African societies. In contextualizing his discussion, the author employs Yoruba Ifa divination as a case study to represent the African society in general. In achieving this, he explores some of the important ways divination functions in the lives of not just the adherents of traditional religion but also the general society—(i) The Cosmological function is employed for attracting the good and avoiding the bad supernatural powers; (ii) Governance function, which is about selecting community and political leaders; (iii) Health function, where divination is used for those seeking a remedy for illness, both physical and spiritual. It is the author's opinion that the function of divination in all these areas of African ways of life usually follows the same pattern or strategic process. Thus, in these cases, divination serves, first, as a diagnostic tool to determine the causes of mal-functioning of expectations or the advent of other afflictions, and second, as a prescriptive tool to provide solutions for the problems diagnosed. Sometimes, it is also used as a preventive tool to guard against calamities for individuals or the whole community. The author then discusses the significance of assessing how divination is accepted in contemporary African societies. He then highlights and discusses examples of occurrences of divination being deployed by governments, NGOs, Western medical professionals, religious practitioners of many religions, and other agencies. In all such cases, divination is considered a valid means to address both individual and corporate issues in the context of African religion's spiritual dynamics.

In Chap. 30, Sarwuan Daniel Shishima writes on the functional dynamics of medicine's belief and practice derived from African Traditional Religion in contemporary societies. The author begins the chapter with a brief discussion on African Traditional Religion's origin and characteristic structure. He further alludes to its holistic impact on every aspect of African life. This, he considers to be true to the extent that it is common to imply that for the Africans, "Life is Religion, and Religion is Life." Within the context of this holistic nature of Africans' religious worldview, medicine's belief and practice become indispensable. The belief and practice of medicine are basically employed as preventive and curative functions in the African traditional health system, comprising both physiological and spiritual applications. Having provided this background, the author expresses his conviction that the belief and practice are still efficacious and functional in contemporary times. This is why African traditional medicine has not been discarded and is still serving the healthcare needs of Africans in the prevention and curing of illnesses. However, the author believes that there is a need for changes to continue to be relevant in contemporary times. Fortunately, the introduction of modern orthodox medicine and interests generated in its complementation with African traditional medicine project a bright future for positive changes. The author concludes the chapter on two notes. The first highlights renewed interest in African traditional medicine by local and international organizations, governments, and Africans who patronize traditional healthcare products to solve their health problems. Second, he calls on the practitioners of African traditional medicine such as herbalists and medicine men/women to improve their services and products to further enhance their efficacy and endear it to the people's generality.

In Chap. 31, Tenson Muyambo writes on the contemporary functional dynamics of African traditional religious festivals. The chapter begins with the author's view that African Traditional Religion is confronted by several twenty-first-century Africa challenges and beyond. The scenario he submits is a by-product of the condescending attitudes that some people have developed toward the religion, in that they argue that African Traditional Religion serves no purpose in a technologically globalizing world. Indeed, their ultimate submission is that the religion is obsolete and should be discarded.

On the contrary, the author argues that African Traditional Religion still plays a significant role in the religiosity of its practitioners and others in society. The author supports this thesis by focusing on the significant position and place of cultural festivals in most African people's lives. According to him, the lives of the adherents and others in society are inundated by festivals celebrating African life's vitality. To illustrate this vitality, the author uses the Ndau Festival of the Arts as an example of how cultural festivals are an essential component of African Traditional Religion that have not only withstood the test of time but also adapted to remain religiously relevant in contemporary times. The chapter then concludes by first discussing the resilience and tenacity that characterize African Traditional Religion because people are born into the religion and not converted to it. Second, it presents the religion's elasticity, flexibility, accommodative as well as its amenable nature. These unique characteristics will continue to make the religion in general and the festivals associated with it enduring and sustainable from one generation of Africans to the other into the future.

The interconnectivity of African Traditional Religion in contemporary settings continues in Chap. 32. In this context, Martina Iyabo Oguntoyinbo-Atere writes on the nature and formats of African Traditional Religion's transplantations into the African Diaspora. The chapter begins with an examination of the meaning of African Traditional Religion and its features. The author then narrates the history and attending factors instigating the transplantations, most especially in Cuba and Brazil. She explores African Traditional Religion's format in these locations, particularly about the assimilations of religious, language, cultural, and social dynamics. In examining these dynamics, the author details and explains their conformity and non-conformity with the "mother" religion on African soil. The chapter concludes with the author examining the study of African Traditional Religion internationally in its Diaspora paradigm and the attendant challenges.

In Chap. 33, Mensah A. Osei discusses the sustainability dynamics of interconnectivity between African Traditional Religion and the cultural, social, and economic experiences in contemporary societies. The author sets out first to show that despite the globalization paradigm and the fact that Christianity, Islam, Science, and Western education have impacted African Traditional Religion, the religion is still a force to reckon with. He believes that what needs to be done is to exploit the influential features of the religion for the good of African societies in particular and the global ones in general. To achieve this goal, the author revisits the definitions of African Religion and the environment within which it operates. He highlights and discusses the various religions' various features, which calls for refinement to be inconsonant with the prevailing realities in contemporary African and global settings. The chapter is concluded with the author discussing how he believes African indigenous religion can be revitalized so that it can be relevant in promoting cultural, social, and economic developments currently and in the future.

Still, on the contemporary developments shaping African Traditional Religion, Danoye Oguntola-Laguda, in Chap. 34, writes on the emergence and functionality of new indigenous religious movements. This chapter's primary focus is to highlight and discuss the dynamics of these movements as paradigms of sustainability of African Traditional Religion as a relevant, functional, and acceptable religious tradition in contemporary African societies. The author opens the chapter detailing some of the challenges confronting African Traditional Religion in present-day African religious spaces. These, as he points out, include lack of scripture and pressure from imported religions, like Christianity and Islam. The author points to the fact that these challenges have been of interest to many scholars who have argued that they posit a future for the religion despite such challenges. The author states his doubt on this and then suggests that the religion's sustainability may depend on the emergence of the New Religious Movements (NRM). From this point, he examines the sustainability of African Traditional Religion and posits the new movements as the agents of solution. The chapter then enumerates the New Religious Movements features, using the Ijo Orunmila indigenous religious movement as a case study. The Movement, according to the author, is a new Yoruba Pentecostal group that combines the liturgy of ATR and Christianity to promote "pristine" African Traditional Religion. Though the author notes some challenges, such as its syncretic strategy, he is convinced that such indigenous religious movements remain the most viable path to the future and sustainability of African Traditional Religion in the contemporary global functional sensibilities.

In Chap. 35, Rotimi Williams Omotoye discusses the interconnectivity between African Traditional Religion and Christianity in their competition for global religious space, particularly in twenty-first-century Africa. For context purposes, the author uses the Yorubá, South-Western Nigeria, and the United States of America as case studies. The former represents Africa, while the latter represents the Western world. According to the author, there is compelling evidence that African Traditional Religion and Christianity are being practiced and studied globally in the twenty-first century. He specifically mentions the United States, though its study was initially resisted, but is now widely studied in many of its tertiary institutions. The chapter concludes by highlighting rapidly developing interest in the practice and study of African Initiated Churches and Pentecostal Churches. With significant input of African traditional religious beliefs and practices, these denominations are contributing significantly to the propagation of Christianity in Africa, the United States, and globally.

Yushau Sodiq discusses the interconnectivity of African Traditional Religion with other institutions—economic, cultural, social, and religious traditions to a close in Chap. 36. His focus here is the interconnectivity between African Traditional Religion and Islam in contemporary religious space. The chapter begins with a background statement describing African Traditional Religion's holistic life involvement for its adherents. It also alludes to their accommodative nature in relating and accepting of other faiths. Unfortunately, religious traditions, particularly Christianity and Islam, took these dispositions as weaknesses when they arrived and propagated their faiths in Africa. The above notwithstanding, the author still believes that African Traditional Religion is continuing to impact both Christianity and Islam. Coming specifically to the relationship between African Traditional Religion and Islam, the author discusses the history of the contact between the two religions, with the advent of Islam in Africa and the conversion of adherents of African Traditional Religion.

Interestingly, as the author points out, these converts have developed a lot of syncretic practices. For example, some of those who carry out African traditional cultural practices and festivals today are Muslims who pray in the Islamic way in public and engage in traditional religious practices in private. Thus, various African traditional cultural systems are not totally discarded in the form of Islam practiced in Africa, though it is re-casted in a new format. Given this dispensation, the author concludes in agreement with Josef Stamer that perhaps, Islam in its traditional African form is entirely a part of the African cultural heritage and thus an African reality. This will eventually ensure mutual understanding, co-existence, accommodation, and tolerance in the interaction between African Traditional Religion and Islam in Africa's contemporary religious space, particularly in general.

Part III: On Pedagogy, Research, and Foundation Scholars

Raymond Ogunade and Grillo Oluwaseun begin the discussions on Part III in Chap. 37. The chapter is titled "Outsider and Insider Study of African Traditional Religion." The authors start with the submission that the debate over this divide of personalities in the study of African Traditional Religion has undergone various evolution stages. They then discuss the ongoing efforts of scholars of African Traditional Religion to identify the classification of scholars who could be so described in the study of African Traditional Religion. The authors express that such a distinction is a blur, overlapping, interface, and cross-pollinating. Consequently, they proffer the argument that to clarify the distinction between the "Outsider" and "Insider" study of African Traditional Religion, there is the need to expunge biological, racial, and geographical sentiments. They conclude the chapter with the suggestion that the same parameters used in the study of other religious traditions, such as Judeo-Christian, be adopted for any meaningful clarification of scholars in the study of African Traditional Religion.

In Chap. 38, Toyin Falola focuses on African Epistemology and its transmission as a form of knowledge. The chapter gives a broader and concrete discourse to several beliefs and practices of African Traditional Religion discussed in some previous chapters of the book. In doing this, Falola argues that African epistemology provides a close linkage between the physical and metaphysical domains. This is demonstrated, especially in the prevalent belief in reincarnation and ancestral worship. He argues that this perspective also explains why Africans ascribe mystical interpretations and meanings to physical phenomenon. This way, according to the author, essential aspects of indigenous African knowledge, that is, the experiences gained over centuries of interactions with the environment, have been enshrined in religious and spiritual edicts, beliefs, and practical activities to maintain social order and the peoples' overall well-being. His conclusion, therefore, is that African epistemology under the paradigms of spiritual worship, medical practice, customary law/taboos, and identity as worldviews are gathered, transmitted, and learned through oral and non-oral sources. During this process, priests, healers, traditional pharmacists, religious heads, elders, and traditional rulers serve as custodians of their sustainability.

In Chap. 39, Toyin Falola continues with the theme of African Epistemology and its transmission. However, in this chapter, he focuses on the indigenous system that provides functional strategies. Usually, the dynamics of the strategies are grounded in the realization of human beings, Africans inclusive, that the interventions of higher powers are needed in different aspects of their lives. These functional strategies in Africa's context are perfected through interactions between the physical and the spiritual in civil existence—the belief in the reality and power of a Supreme Being to influence human affairs has in the course of societal development informed the coordination of social practices around the metaphysical. Thus, through social interaction between Africans themselves and their environment, experiences have been conceived through metaphysical prisms that have evolved into the cultural way of life over time. Indeed, African epistemology's functional strategies and its transmission are based on prisms of African indigenous knowledge systems connected to and expressed in a plethora of fields such as philosophy, anthropology, psychology, medicine, agriculture, education, arts and crafts, music, and literature. The author, in conclusion, uses the examples of the Yorubá, Edo, and Igbo of South-Western and South-Eastern Nigeria to demonstrate the workings of the interconnectivity between the physical and the metaphysical in their beliefs in the Supreme Being and venerations of divinities and deified ancestors.

In Chap. 40, Marcus L. Harvey also focuses on gnostic and epistemological themes in African Traditional Religion. He begins the chapter with the submission that African Traditional Religion is not understood as possessing a vast plurality of dynamic knowledge systems with related but distinct repertoires of ideas and attendant meaning structures in Western circles. According to him, this misunderstanding of the religion's dynamic knowledge system was historically perpetuated by the Portuguese sailors who visited parts of Africa in the fifteenth century and returned home with Feticos. These were African religious implements believed to contain magical properties and often regarded by Europeans as primitive, exotic curiosities imbued with dubious significance. This dismissive Eurocentric sentiment toward Africa, according to the author, continued into the so-called Enlightenment-influenced eighteenth- and nineteenth-century Europe. With the above background, the author then sets out to correct these epistemological misconceptions about Africa and its indigenous religions. First, he addresses questions about the conditions under which something can be known as described by the Greek *gnosko*. That is "having proper comprehension of or acquaintance with," and "seeking to know." This is followed by the question of what such knowing entails in the contemporary, traditional African religious environment. The author then provides answers to the questions by discussing several African religious cosmologies in a broad perspective. Second, he addresses the questions and then provides an epistemological analysis of traditional oral religious discourse, using the Akan proverbs with spiritual references or implications as a case study. In conclusion, he argues that a contemporary sense of what it means to know within a traditional African religious environment can be established by paying attention to two themes.

These are: (i) knowing as an elusive yet adaptable relationship with spirit requiring constant interplay between the ancestral African past and the immediate present, and (ii) knowing as a moral crucible.

Raymond Ogunade and Olorunfemi Dada, in Chap. 41, shift attention to the state of Scholarship in African Traditional Religion on the continent of Africa and its Diaspora. The authors begin the chapter with the description of how scholars of African Traditional Religion have attempted to address challenges facing its study because of the multi-dimensional nature of the religion in terms of culture, language, and application of beliefs. They also mention other kinds of challenges that include the non-availability of written sacred scripture, the appropriate name for the religion, and the faulty notions of the "colonial scholars" toward the religion, particularly their felicitous studying methods. Based on the above background, the authors then discuss the modalities of the study of African Traditional Religion by scholars in the field both in Africa and in its Diaspora. They express the views that such studies, particularly in terms of nature, contents, and dearth, are very concerning. This chapter concludes with the authors' recommendations for improvement in African Scholars' activities and efforts on African Traditional Religion within and outside the border of Africa. Such recommendations include, but are not limited to, first, promoting both research and teaching of the religion in all levels of educational institutions. Second, scholars' establishments on the religion and scholarly journals in the field will encourage and ensure its research visibility and interconnectivity or networking in Africa and the Diaspora.

In Chap. 42, continuing with the theme of Scholarship in African Traditional Religion, Toyin Falola writes, focusing on the global situation. He begins the chapter by prescribing the ethical and methodical guidelines required to study and understand any phenomena, particularly interacting with their sources. However, according to him, it is unfortunate that the study of African Religion, as a component of a larger African culture, has not been exempted from the deliberate misrepresentations of a prejudiced form of scholarship that has not only come to be institutionalized (elevated to dictating conventional methods of knowledge validation) but has in its traditionally unethical interaction with the area compounded the possibility of achieving genuinely representative research outcomes on its religious activities. In addition to the above, there are the customary research challenges peculiar to the area—cultural diversity and linguistic variations, contrasting worldviews, creeds of secrecy, and the absence of corroborative documents. According to the author, all of these challenges make the prospects for an objective evaluation of African religion bleaker. The scenario described above, notwithstanding, Falola submits that African Traditional Religion has, through its dynamism, remained relevant in the face of these onslaughts in the form of institutionalized racism and collaborated criticism from its Abrahamic counterparts. This, as he expresses, should constitute the basis for further research around the topic of African Traditional Religion to provide more understanding and better scholarly information. For this to happen, the author discusses and concludes the chapter with the following recommendations: (i) getting both practitioners and academic interests on the same page by ensuring that the former appreciates the value of having their religion documented for global reach and the generational preservation of their legacy. (ii) establishing a regulatory system that would constitute the required research media to be saddled with disseminating information and document findings across different countries and boundaries. If these recommendations are followed, Falola believes that African Traditional Religion will rise to its full potential as an academic and social resource globally.

Robert Owusu, in Chap. 43, takes up the challenges facing scholars and students of African Traditional Religion in the context of world religions. He begins with a description of how discussions on African Traditional Religion are omitted from books and other literature on world religions. Even when the religion is mentioned, it is usually in passing, without any meaningful or positive details. The author finds these situations unacceptable, given the influence and the population of people associated with the religion in Africa and other global locations. He believes that, as a right, African Traditional Religion should enjoy the same level of recognition, just as other religions such as Catholicism, Judaism, Hinduism, among others. This is because African Traditional Religion has elements that are comparable to those found in other world religions. Indeed, African Traditional Religion possesses the necessary characteristic dynamics that qualify it to be a living world religion. The religion has been in existence for centuries, but it is also active and effective from one generation to the other for Africans. For the author, scholars and students' strategies to be employed with the challenges discussed above should be grounded in conscious and deliberate efforts to reposition African Traditional Religion with new and proper orientations. These efforts should include engaging the study of African Traditional Religion as a major tradition. A major step in doing this, according to the author, is by preserving the vocabulary used by the religion. This makes it possible to research, preserve, and disseminate the meaning of the indigenous idioms, metaphors, and other symbolic expressions. Thus, increasing and making knowledge about the religion available and accessible to scholars and students just like other world religions. And the world will benefit from such knowledge.

Chapter 44 begins the last three chapters of the Handbook, focusing on reviews of Pioneer or Foundation Scholars' contributions in the study of African Traditional Religion. In this chapter, Rotimi Williams Omotoye writes on the works of E. Bolaji Idowu and John S. Mbiti. The author refers to the two as being amongst the first generation of academic giants in African Traditional Religion in Africa. The author gives brief insights into their biographies. The chapter then reviews their contributions to the discipline in terms of the texts they have written and that have been found to be significant in the research, teaching, and learning of African Traditional Religion. Two of such books by E. Bolaji Idowu—*Olódùmarè: God in Yorubá Belief* and *African Traditional Religion: A Definition*—is mentioned. Also, some notables by John S. Mbiti such as *African Religions and Philosophy*, *Concepts of God in*

Africa, and Akamba Stories. Overall, Omotoye submits that these two scholars in African Traditional Religion have significantly impacted the academic study of religion through their numerous published works. Particularly, their interests in studying and writing on African Traditional Religion during the period when most Western scholars and Christian missionaries were hostile to both the study and practice of the religion have been viewed to be spectacular and groundbreaking. This is particularly so because both Bolaji Idowu and John Mbiti were actually Christian Clergies. The author concludes the chapter by noting that by their immense pioneering works in African Traditional Religion scholarship, these two scholars have created more opportunities and windows to study African Religion in Africa by other scholars interested in the field.

In Chap. 45, Olantunde Oyewole Ogunbiyi and Lydia Bosede Akande focus on two other foundation scholars/writers in African Traditional Religion. These are Edward Geoffrey Parrinder and Kofi Asare Opoku—the first being a non-African and the second being an African. The authors examined their contributions against other scholars' backdrop, both earlier and later, on the subject matter of African Traditional Religion. Within the context of a comparative strategy, the authors highlight and discuss these two scholars' works that are primarily considered to be significantly apologetic about the Africans' religion. In this regard, the authors point to acknowledging their works as trailblazing in modern scholarship in the study of African Traditional Religion. Ogunbiyi and Akande conclude the chapter by discussing how Parrinder and Opoku have positively impacted a better understanding of African Traditional Religion. They, however, allude to the fact that building on the foundation laid by Geoffrey Parrinder and Kofi Asare Opoku, as well as other writers and scholars like them, much is still left to be researched and published on the study of African Traditional Religion.

Chapter 46, the last chapter of the Handbook, rounds off the discussion on the reviews of some foundation/modern writers/scholars' contributions to scholarship in African Traditional Religion. Here, Danoye Oguntola-Laguda and Joseph Moyinoluwa Talabi examine the works of Joseph Omosade Awolalu and Peter Adelumo Dopamu. The authors first describe the challenges encountered by early scholars of African Traditional Religion in the face of predetermined biased contents of structures and misconceptions of beliefs and practices by Christian missionaries, foreign researchers, and scholars/writers. It was, therefore, a bold and far-reaching move by scholars such as Awolalu and Dopamu to take up the difficult task of deconstructing the prejudices that had become the face of the study and practice of African Traditional Religion. According to Laguda and Talabi, their works should, more importantly, be viewed as more significant and relevant because both of them were scholars of African descent who lived in Africa and understood the African culture and religion. They both spent decades researching, teaching, and publishing many impactive works on African Traditional Religion. The authors conclude by highlighting and discussing how Awolalu and Dopamu have created an identity for African Traditional Religion in line with its unique structure, mode of worship, perception of the terrestrial and non-terrestrial worlds, among other issues. Through their scholarly contributions, there is no doubt whatsoever that Awolalu and Dopamu, as notable scholars, have created a niche for African Traditional Religion and have situated it in its rightful place of pride among world religions.

Overall, this *Handbook of African Traditional Religion*, through its numerous chapters, aims to speak to students, scholars, and educators of the twenty-first century and beyond. It thus presents African Traditional Religion through the prisms of in-depth understanding of the essential and critical issues that define and situate it within the context and trajectory of transition from the traditional to the contemporary. Apart from all of the above, the most obvious uniqueness of the Handbook is in its comprehensiveness. This makes it an invaluable companion to, first, African and African Diaspora academics/scholars interested in studying African Traditional Religion, particularly as a discipline of twenty-first-century Africa. Second, to students interested in the study of African Religion, who seek to have a single volume addressing most, if not all, religion issues from basic to contemporary engagements. Third, the general reading public seeks first-hand and authentic discussions and debates on the practice and study of African Religion. This uniqueness of the Handbook is further demonstrated by the fact that arguably, it can be regarded currently as the only single volume or Handbook on African Traditional Religion. The depth, breadth, and comprehensiveness of this three-part Handbook and diversity of contributors mark it as a volume of scholarly work whose pedigree may not be available in any published African Religion book/volume so far. Ultimately, the three parts and forty-six chapters of the *Handbook of African Traditional Religion* are written and presented as "scholarly without being pedantic."

PART I

Basic/Essential Features of African Traditional Religion

CHAPTER 2

Origin, Nature, and Structure of Beliefs System

Ibigbolade S. Aderibigbe

INTRODUCTION

Religion is found in practically all known human societies in the world. It is also one of the most important institutional structures that make up the total human social system. There is hardly a known race in the world, regardless of how primitive it might be, without a form of one religion or the other through which the people try to communicate with the divine. This religion becomes inseparable from the total life experience of the people. It thereby permeates into every sphere of the people's lives, encompassing their culture—the social, political, ethical, as well as the individual and societal expectations in their up and down life experiences. As is the case of nearly every other people in the world, religion is invariably the keystone of African culture and is completely enshrined in the people's lifestyles. A meaningful understanding of African Traditional Religion provides the all-important awareness of African customs and belief systems.

Unfortunately, it can be argued that there seems to be no other religion that has been so degraded and misrepresented in the minds of Western audiences as the African Traditional Religion. The religion has been in many circumstances presented as hopelessly savage and "totally" superstitious. This description mainly results from the earliest investigators, writers, and scholars of the religion being overwhelmingly, if not exclusively, European and American anthropologists, missionaries, and colonial administrators. There is no doubt the inadequate knowledge of the African traditional religious beliefs and practices

---

I. S. Aderibigbe (✉)
Department of Religion, University of Georgia, Athens, GA, USA
e-mail: iaderibi@uga.edu

© The Author(s), under exclusive license to Springer Nature Switzerland AG 2022
I. S. Aderibigbe, T. Falola (eds.), *The Palgrave Handbook of African Traditional Religion*, https://doi.org/10.1007/978-3-030-89500-6_2

is responsible for this situation. It is however encouraging today that an increasing number of Africans as "insider' scholars and writers are engaged in valuable researches and publications in African Traditional Religion. Through their efforts, there have been tremendous changes in the content, process, and methodology of reporting the tenets, spiritual values, and satisfaction which are fundamental to African Traditional Religion as in other world religious traditions, such as Christianity, Islam, Buddhism, and others. Also, it is important to point out that these researches have and are having a very significant positive impact on the study and practice of the religion. This is because they have succeeded in highlighting the general truths, concepts, and trends about the religion and at the same time reversing and dispelling the past misconceptions that have been perpetuated about the religion.

Based on the above introductory discussion, the focus of this chapter is essential to identify and discuss the nature, characteristics, structure, and prospect of African Traditional Religion. Consequently, the basic concepts of the religion in terms of characterization of its beliefs and practices will be illuminated. Also, the challenges facing the religion in contemporary global religious space are highlighted with plausible projections about the fate of the religion in the future.

Origin and Nature of African Traditional Religion

African Traditional Religion as the indigenous religion of the African continent is not a religious tradition preached to the African people. Also, they were not converted to it. It originated as, and has remained, a significant part of the heritage of the people that has been in existence for centuries. Indeed, the religious ideas, beliefs, and beliefs of African forefathers have shaped their thought processes and experiences from one generation to the other. Consequently, the origination of the religion cannot be ascribed to a single individual at a specific date in human history as is the case in religious traditions such as Judaism, Christianity, Islam, Confucianism, Buddhism, Hinduism, and many others.

From one generation to the other and over the ages, African people have engaged in religious activities without troubling themselves with the preoccupation of establishing the founder of or giving names for the religion they believed in and practiced. Those who are usually preoccupied by these questions are outsider investigators, who have been only too happy to label the religion with nomenclatures such as paganism, idolatry, fetishism, and many others. Against this background, it is important to do away with such misleading names by replacing them with one that actually describes the true and authentic nature of the religion.

"African Traditional Religion" has been used as the nomenclature for the religion by scholars. This is done not with the purpose of designating the religion as being primitive, local, or unprogressive. On the contrary, the name actually reflects its location in a geographical space and it also underscores its evolution from the African personal experience.[1] In addition, the name is used to distinguish the religion from any other religious traditions, particularly with other religions being practiced in Africa today. These religions did not originate on the continent of Africa. They were "imported" into it. On the other hand, African Traditional Religion is native to Africa and uniquely peculiar to the African people. Therefore, it would be meaningless and useless to try and transplant its origin and peculiarity, through the name it is called, to a different society outside of Africa[2].

Africans regard the religion as a hidden treasure given to them by the Supreme Being as an essential medium of communicating with Him in order to express their worship of Him. This is why it is imperative for non-Africans to first actively participate in the religion in one form or the other, so as to see and appreciate the wealth of spiritual resources embedded within the religion. This is because true nature of the religion cannot be unveiled and understood by mere superficial and casual observations. We believe approaching the religion through just superficial and arm-chair observations, particularly by "outside scholars," without deep knowledge of the experience of the true African spiritual dynamics, has been responsible for the numerous wrong nomenclatures that have been used for the religion. Unfortunately, these misconceptions have led to the notions that Africans have no concepts of God.[3] They have also led to the often derogatory assertions that the religion is ugly and full of demon-oriented superstitions. As a result of these wrongly held notions, the religion is viewed as not possessing the required spiritual components necessary for the salvation of the soul.

Having noted the shortcomings of the "outsider" scholars, we must at the same time acknowledge the significant impression their works have had on laying the foundation for subsequent "insider" scholars who took over from them. For example, scholars in the field of African Traditional Religion, such as E. B. Idowu[4] and Mbiti,[5] have been to some extent successful in correcting a number of erroneous ideas or misconceptions about African Traditional Religion worldviews, particularly as it pertains to its belief systems, thought patterns, rituals, and indeed the African culture generally. Their works fortunately have saved and preserved the true nature of African Traditional Religion as against the erroneous claims of the "outsider" scholars. Through the works of these "insider" scholars, it has become obvious that the true nature of African Traditional Religion can be shown to be the religion is an embodiment of a belief system and functionalism that are lived in everyday life experiences of the indigenous African people.

Ultimately, it should be stressed that a basic understanding of the religion has to be embedded in the full awareness of African unique religious and cultural worldviews. These are fundamentally based on the customs, belief systems, concept of God, relationship with the divinities, spirits, ancestors, and the view of death and the afterlife existence.

CHARACTERISTIC FEATURES

While it is true that African Traditional Religion has no sacred scriptures, it does not necessarily follow that it lacks fundamental religious beliefs and practices. Indeed, the religion showcases significant belief system that depicts the totality of the African beliefs, thought patterns, and ritual practices. Further, the components of this religious system can be categorized into two inclusive paradigms. These consist, first, the major beliefs that are located in a fivefold hierarchical structure of the Supreme Being, the divinities, spirits, ancestors, magic, and medicine. These five major beliefs constitute the basic and unique elements that distinguish the religion from all other religions. The second paradigm is made up of minor beliefs that are essentially derived from the major beliefs. The two paradigms are discussed below, first the five major beliefs in their hierarchical order.

Belief in the Supreme Being

The uppermost belief in the hierarchy is the African belief in the Supreme Being. This is, in fact, fundamental to all other beliefs either major or minor. It is also and is firmly entrenched as in all African religious and cultural consciousness. This is clearly contrary to the outsiders' view that seeks to establish that Africans, as primitive people, are incapable of having any conception or belief of one Supreme Deity. This is well captured by Bolaji Idowu thus:

> *Those who take one look at other people's religion and assert glibly that such people have no clear concept of God or no concept of God at all should first look within themselves and face honestly the question, "How clear is the concept of God to me ..."*[6]

There is no doubt whatsoever that Africans believe in the Supreme Being, whom they recognize and acknowledge as the ultimate object of worship. He is not regarded in abstract terms and neither is He seen as a remote or an idle Deity, who is only preoccupied by His own happiness.[7] On the contrary, the Supreme Being is always and permanently actively engaged in overseeing the day-to-day affairs of humans, whom He has specially created. As the creator of the universe and humans, Africans see Him as the one who brought into existence all things, both in heaven and on earth. These views of the Supreme Being are well reflected in the names and attributes associated with Him. To Africans, He is omnipotent, holy, the creator, and source of all creatures. These creatures are in return expected to be responsible to Him. Also, the exalted position of the Supreme Being is over and above other creatures. This is why all creatures must worship Him one way or the other. The form of worship as seen in different African ethnic groups may be either fully as practiced by the Ashanti of Ghana and the Kikuyu of Kenya or partially as done by the Ewe and Abomey peoples of Togo. However, the Yoruba and Igbo of Nigeria do not have organized cults with features such as temples, shrines, altars, or priests.

This form of worship in no way diminishes the people's belief in his presence and significance. To them, he is believed to be omnipresent. Their idea is that He cannot be not limited to a local shrine or represented in images or symbols. Without any doubt, the Supreme Being has a real existence for Africans and his name and attributes are always in their mouths. The reality is that each ethnic group has its own unique local names for the Supreme Being. Such names are designed to describe his character and emphasize His personal a reality and that He should not be conceived as an abstract concept[8]. This is why Westermann states:

> *The figure of God assumes features of a truly personal and purely divine Supreme Being ... it cannot be overlooked that he is a reality to the African who will admit that what he knows about God is the purest expression of his religious experience*[9].

For example, the Yoruba ethnic group calls Him *Olodumare,* meaning the Almighty God. They also call Him *Olorun* which means, the owner or Lord of Heaven. In terms of attributes, the same Yoruba people refer to Him as *Aterere Kari aye,* meaning the Omnipresent God. For the Igbo ethnic group, the Supreme Being is referred to as *Chukwu* which means the Great Source Being or Spirit. He is also called *Chineke,* meaning, the Source Being who created all things. Among the Akan people of Ghana, this Supreme Being is known as and called *Onyame,* denoting that he is the Supreme Being, the Deity. The Mende of Sierra Leone's name for the Supreme Being is *Ngewo,* meaning the Eternal One who rules from above. There is no doubt that these different names and their meanings from diverse African ethnic groups provide a vivid understanding of the African concept of the Supreme Being, as a real being, the Giver of Life, and the All-Sufficient Deity.

Belief in Divinities

Africans' belief and veneration of divinities constitute a very integral part of the African Traditional Religion. Indeed, the belief is second on the hierarchical structure of the five major beliefs of the religion. The Supreme Being created the divinities for specific functions as his representatives, and as their creator, they cannot exist without him. This relationship between the divinities and the Supreme Being models the sociological dynamics in most African communities. In such communities with kings as the heads are regarded as and can only be approached directly by subjects. The subjects can only do so through other lesser chiefs to the kings. Consequently, the role of the divinities is like that of the lesser chiefs. They act as intermediaries between the Supreme Being and mankind. They are to serve as conventional channels of communication that humans can employ to reach the Supreme Being. With this unique role, divinities enjoy a vital position in African Traditional Religion. This may be responsible for the erroneous submission of outsider scholars that Africans worship the divinities and do not have any concept of the Supreme Being.

Africans see divinities as being real and that each one of them is given a specific function to perform by the Supreme Being. They do this as partakers in the theocratic government of the universe. As intermediaries, the divinities act as a means to an end and never ends in themselves. Thus, the Supreme Being is the end from whom the real and final authority emanates. Consequently, for example, when the Yoruba people bring their prayers and supplications before the divinities, they end them with -ASE, meaning "may it be sanctioned by the Supreme Being."

Different Africans ethnic groups have different generic names for the divinities. For example, the Yoruba call them *Orisa*. Among the Igbos, they are known as *Alusindiminuo*. The name for the divinities for the Akan is *Abosom*. Also, there are numerous divinities in Africa with numbers varying from one ethnic group to the other. Usually, their number ranges between 201 and 1700 in various Yoruba communities.

Another feature of the divinities is that their names most times are derived from their nature or natural phenomena that manifest them. This is why, for example, among the Yoruba, the divinity that was first associated with the wrath of God was called *Jakuta*, meaning "he who fights with stones." This same divinity among the Igbos is known as *Amadioha* and for the Nupe the same divinity is called Sokogba—Soxo's ax.

There are three categories of divinities in African Traditional Religion. The first is the primordial divinities. The divinities in this category are viewed as being in existence from the very beginning with the Supreme Being and actually participated in the creation of the world and human beings. No one knows their origin and in fact such knowledge is beyond human curiosity. For example, one of such divinity in Yoruba belief is *Obatala*. He is believed to have been given the task of creating the human body by *Olodumare*. He is therefore popularly called *Alamorere* (the fine molder). Yoruba people also call him *Orisa-nla*. As an arch-divinity, he is seen as the deputy of *Olodumare*.

The second category is made up of deified ancestors. These are usually humans who performed heroic feats when they were alive. When such people die, they are deified, which means they are no longer just ancestors but divinities. An example of such humans who later became a divinity upon his death is Sango, the deified Alaafin of Oyo. After being defied, He assumed the attributes of *Jakuta*, who was before then divinity for thunder in Yoruba land.

In the third category, we have divinities with expression in natural phenomena. These divinities are usually spirits that are associated with natural forces like rivers, lakes, trees, mountains, forests, and so on. Wherever or the object they inhabit are considered to be sacred. In addition, priests/priestesses are usually custodians of such places or objects, through whom the spirit may be consulted.

Belief in Spirits

The third in the hierarchy of the five major beliefs in African Traditional Religion is the belief in spirits. Spirits are usually described as apparitional beings that make material objects their temporary abodes. In African belief, spirits are considered as being ubiquitous and can therefore make any part of the earth their abode. They are able to do this because they are immaterial and incorporeal beings. In some quarters, divinities and ancestors may be categorized as spirits. However, in such situations, they are distinguished from the class of spirits being discussed here. This is because divinities and ancestors are viewed more positively in their relationships with humans. The difference is in considering divinities and ancestors as "domesticated spirits." Consequently, while divinities and ancestors are respected, venerated, and communicated with by humans, spirits are generally feared and held in awe. Also, spirits are regarded to be synonymous with inimical activities that are detrimental to human's prosperity. This is responsible for human strategy of placarding them so that they would not be inimical to their progress in life.

As mentioned above, spirits sometimes inhabit places such as rivers, hills, water, bushes, and trees. When this is the case, such places become naturally sacred. For example, the Yoruba people believe that the *Akoko* tree (also called Ogilisi by the Igbos) is inhabited by spirits.

Africans divide spirits into groups. For the Yoruba people, there are spirits known as *Abiku,* meaning "born to die children." The Igbo call such children *Ogbanje*. Both ethnic groups regard the children as sadistic spirits with the specialization of entering into the womb of pregnant women so as to be born and die at infancy or at a later date. Such premature deaths certainly bring pain and anguish to the family concerned, particularly as this process may be repeated over and over again if solutions are not found. As a form of solution among the Yoruba people, pregnant women are discouraged from walking in the middle of the day. This is because they believe that this is the time of the day when the evil spirits roam about. If an evil spirit encounters a pregnant woman at this time, it is capable of ejecting the original fetus in the womb of the pregnant woman and substituting it with itself.

In the second group are spirits that are believed to be of dead persons whose souls have not been able to find rest in a spiritual domain for one reason or the other. This may be because when they died, they were not accorded the proper burial rites reposed. Due to this anomaly, the spirits of such dead persons are not allowed or admitted into the cult of the ancestors. Thus, they will continue to roam the earth and trouble the living until amends are made and they are given proper burial rites. Also belonging to this group of spirits are individuals who had engaged in evil and wicked behaviors when they were alive. If they die in such a state of wicked and evil living, they would not be admitted into the domain of the ancestors. Usually, they return to haunt their communities, wreaking havoc, and they have to be appeased.

Witches and wizards who are also considered as evil spirits constitute the third group of spirits. These are generally regarded as human spirits. Consequently, they can be separated from their bodies to engage in errands. Such errands are generally viewed as a perpetuation of evil and wicked acts. When on such errands, the witches and wizards can cause diseases, miscarriages in women, insanity, or deformity in human beings, thus bringing misery, pain, and disorder to individuals or a whole community.

The last group of spirits recognized to be Africans are those considered as anthropomorphic. These spirits are believed to have the same human characteristics such as passions, tastes, and emotions.

Belief in Ancestors

African belief in the ancestral cult is based on the general notion of the dual nature of humans and the world. Both entities are comprised of physical and spiritual natures. The spiritual ones are regarded as extensions of the physical ones. Based on these configurations, Africans strongly believe that the dead continue their existence in the spiritual world. Consequently, the family and communal bonds they enjoyed while in the physical world do not come to an end when they die. They continue to maintain the bonds in the spiritual domain. However in the spiritual domain, they are referred to as ancestors or the living dead. In this state of existence, they remain closely related to the living in the physical world, though they are no longer regarded as ordinary humans. Even when their mortal natures have ceased, Africans still believe that they continue to be part of the family in invisible forms. Such participations however can either be positive or negative contingent on the relationship status of the family or individuals with the ancestors. The combination of these reasons is responsible for why the belief in ancestral cult not only is taken seriously, but also is actually regarded as one of the most important features of African Traditional Religion. Also, ancestors, who are members of this ancestral cult, are seen as agents of cohesion in African communities. They are therefore accorded high respect and honor as predecessors who have experienced the life being lived by those still on earth.

However, it must be stressed that it is not everyone that dies becomes an ancestor. Certain qualifications come into play to determine becoming a member of the ancestral club. Some of the qualifications that must be fulfilled to attain the exalted status of an ancestor are as follows:

First, the dead person must have lived a morally upright life for his lifetime (sometimes young persons who died a heroic death in the service of the community may be exempted from this qualification). Second, he or she must have died an honorable death. This means his or her death must not be as a result of an abominable cause such as an accident, suicide, or a violent or unusual happening and chronic diseases. Third, the person must have been accorded full burial rites by his or her biological children or other members of the diseased family if he or she does not have children. When these qualifications have been met, the dead person becomes an ancestor automatically and is then qualified to receive veneration from living family members or the whole community. Unfortunately, the intensity of such venerations has been erroneously regarded as acts of worship, which Africans reserve for only the Supreme Being. Bolaji Idowu alludes to the important functional roles of the ancestors as follows:

> *To some extent, they are believed to be intermediaries between the Deity or the divinities and their own children; this is a continuation of their earthly function of ensuring domestic peace and the well-being of their community, to distribute favors, to exercise discipline or enforce penalties, to be guardians of community ethics and prevent anything that might cause disruption*[10].

The belief that the dead as ancestors continue to play significant roles in the lives of members of the family who are still alive has resulted in the habit of many African ethnic groups burying the dead in the family compound. This is done in the hope that such dead persons, who are now ancestors, will be able to continue to influence their lives.

Also, as we have mentioned above, ancestors are venerated because they are respected and accorded great honor in African societies. The acts of veneration are performed in different formats. However, they largely include pouring a libation of food and drinks and/or by prayers, by individuals, by family, or by the whole community. They may also be venerated through religious festivals. For example, among the Yoruba ethnic group, there are the *Oro* and *Egungun* festivals that are celebrated in honor of the ancestors as symbolical manifestations of the ancestral cult.

Nearly, if not, all African ethnic groups have one form or other of ancestral cult. A very important feature of such ancestral cult is the religious festival associated with it. It is during such a festival that the ancestor is venerated. For example, the Ashanti of Ghana has the sacred Golden Stool. This is the symbol of their ancestral cult. Also, the Mende of Sierra Leone, the Lugbara of Central Africa, and the Ovambo of Southern Africa, all have ancestral cults with various religious festivals associated with them

Belief in Magic and Medicine

The belief in magic and medicine is the last in the hierarchy of the five major beliefs in African Traditional Religion. Though some have attempted to lump the two terms together, there is need to separate them for a better understanding of the "context" and "content" of the African belief about them. To this end, it would be appropriate to first define the two terms. Magic can be defined or described as a human attempt to access and dominate the supernatural powers for his or her own utilization and ultimate benefit[11] . By so doing, the supernatural powers are manipulated in the human desire to attain a goal through self-effort. However, such manipulations can be used for either positive or negative ends. Man's use of this power could be either positive or negative, depending on objective of the "magician." Medicine, on the other hand, can be described as the science or art of human health issues, particularly in providing prevention, treatment, and cure for illnesses or diseases.

The difference between magic and medicine for Africans is that magic is employed by humans to manipulate supernatural powers to do their biddings. On the other hand, medicine is employed as both material and spiritual means to prevent or cure all forms of illnesses or diseases. This dynamics of the combination of material and spiritual resources in the art of medicine as found in Akan belief about medicine is expressed by R. S. Rattray thus:

"If God gave you sickness, he also gave you medicine."[12]

In line with this consciousness, medicine men/women who are generally known as traditional doctors acknowledge the fact that the source of their power is the Supreme Being. However, they also recognize the divinities as the agents delegated by the Supreme Being to dispense the power to them. They also generally claim that the media of receiving such powers from the divinities are through dreams and or through spirit possession. For example, in Yoruba ethnic group, *Osanyin* is the divinity that is designated by Olodumare, the Supreme Being to oversee the art of medicine.

It is also important to point out that though, Africans generally view magic negatively, there may be situations when it is interwoven with medicine. In such situations, it may be impossible to separate the two. Consequently, the supernatural powers available to both of them may be employed for the purpose at hand.

One other feature of the African belief about magic and medicine, according to Awolalu and Dopamu, is that in some ethnic groups both are called the same name. They point out that, for instance, the Yoruba people call magic and medicine *oogun, egbogi, or isegun*. Also, the Igbo call both *ogwu* and the Akans call them *suman*[13].

MINOR BELIEFS IN AFRICAN RELIGION

There are other beliefs in African Traditional Religion that are derived from its five major beliefs discussed above. These beliefs are referred to as minor beliefs in that they can be regarded as complementing the major beliefs. Some of such beliefs are discussed below:

Belief in the Hereafter

The belief in life after death is also found in African Traditional Religion, just as in many other religious traditions. This belief postulates that human life continues to exist beyond the physical realm. This existence is "lived" in the spiritual realm which becomes "home" to those who have departed from the physical realm. In order to understand this paradox of existence, one must take into consideration the African ontological view that denotes that humans are composed of two elements, the physical and the spiritual. The physical is the human body, while the spiritual is the soul. At death only the human body ceases to exist in the physical realm, while the soul does not die, thereby continuing its existence in the spiritual realm to give an account of its existence in body while in the physical realm. Africans generally call the spiritual realm or domain, "heaven." For example, the Yoruba people capture this human paradoxical continuous existence in the physical and spiritual realms in a popular saying of *Aye loja orun nile*, meaning "the world is a marketplace and heaven is home." As this saying is symbolically understood and implied, a person does not go to the marketplace to sleep there. After concluding whatever transaction he or she must have gone there to make, one necessarily returns home.

It should, however, be understood that not everyone who dies will be admitted into heaven. The qualification for such admission is consequent upon haven lived a morally upright life while in the physical realm.

Belief in Morality

Another minor belief in African Traditional Religion is the belief in morality. To Africans, morality is one and the same with religion. This position stems from the fact that for Africans, every sphere of the life is ultimately associated with religion. This is why Adewale[14] asserts that the ethics (morality) of Africans is religious. That in fact, Africans have a deep sense of right and wrong, and this moral sense has produced customs, rules, laws, traditions, and taboos which can be observed in each society[15].

Africans place ample emphasis on the importance of morality. This is not just for the good of the individuals but also and importantly, for the maintenance of law and order in the community. Also, as we have indicated earlier living a morally upright life is one of the qualifications for becoming an ancestor after death. Also, the importance of the belief in morality for Africans is clearly demonstrated by the prominent place it enjoys in their myths, legends, and proverbs.

Belief in Worship and Veneration

Africans believe very strongly in the act of worship. It is the fundamental component of the human response to the Supreme Being as the inventor of the universe and all in it. Indeed, the core of African Traditional Religion is built around the notion that the act of worship affords humans the opportunity to demonstrate their adoration, respect, and loyalty to the Supreme Being for creating and sustaining them. In this regard, the practice of religion is never complete without the involvement of the act of worship. The acts of worship of the Supreme Being and veneration of the divinities are seen as the panacea for not just attainment of an individual's goals in life, but also and more importantly peace and harmony in the community. This dual role of acts of worship and veneration is consequent upon the fact that they constitute the media of communication between humans, the Supreme Being, and the divinities.

Africans through their indigenous religion have different forms of worship. These may be formal, informal direct, or indirect. Among some African communities, there is the direct/formal worship of the Supreme Being. In such places, there are priests/priestess and altars dedicated to the Supreme Being. In addition, sacrifices are offered to Him directly. On the other hand, there are other African ethnic groups, where there are no religious officials and altars dedicated to the Supreme Being. In such places, the Supreme Being is approached through other direct media or through the divinities.

The veneration of divinities, which has been erroneously misconstrued as worship of divinities by outsiders, is also very important to Africans. The veneration can also be carried at both the individual and communal levels. At the individual level, the veneration is usually done informally by members of a family at the household shrine located in the family compound. The communal veneration of a divinity is usually more elaborate and formal. It is usually carried out in a public shrine. Also, all members of the community are expected to participate in the ceremony led by religious officials, family heads, clan heads, and traditional rulers.

During worship or veneration ceremonies by the whole community, the rituals are usually composed of prayers, songs, libations, invocations, and offerings. In summary, worship or veneration in African Religion is generally regarded as vehicles communication with the supernatural beings so that humans can gain access to all round success in all their endeavors while in the physical domain as a foretaste of what to expect in the spiritual domain.

Sources of Information on African Traditional Religion

Because African Traditional Religion lacks a written scripture like other religious traditions such as Christianity, Islam, and Judaism, information or knowledge about it has to be alternatively sought. Fortunately, other sources have been found to address and make up for the challenge constituted by lack of a sacred scripture. Two of such sources are first, the oral traditions, which are composed of proverbs, myths, pithy sayings, legends, liturgy, everyday speech, songs, and Theophanous names. The second are the non-oral sources, made of features such as works of arts paintings, archeological findings, artifacts, shrines, and other sacred objects. A combination of the features found in these sources has to, a large extent, preserve the religious beliefs and practices of African Traditional Religion.

Oral Traditions

The combination of traditional narratives is regarded as the scriptures of African Traditional Religion. This is because as it has been indicated above, these narratives are employed to preserve and transmit information and authoritative knowledge about the religious beliefs and practices, representing the totality of African traditional worldviews from one generation to the next. In a way, these narratives serve as testimonies of the past for the use of the present and the future. It should be noted, however, that though some of them may be regarded as actual records of past historical events as memorized, others are products of people's creative imaginations. Consequently, some of the narratives are more reliable than others. For instance, proverbs, pithy sayings, and names belong to the first category and are therefore more reliable; myths, legends, and folktales belong to the second and are therefore less reliable. Some African traditional narratives and their functions are briefly discussed below.

Myths

Myths in African tradition are generally employed to explain observable experiences for which there seems to be no available factual or historical understanding. Consequently, myths become the vehicles designed to provide meaningful explanations. Generally, such human experiences have to do with, for example, the origins of the universe and humans. They also seek to provide answers for questions such as, "how human death came about, why it is only women who can conceive, why women must labor before giving birth to children, why humans must labor before eating, and why are there a myriad of different languages in Africa?" Generally, myths are narrated in form of stories in the evenings as a form of recreation before the family go to bed. Apart from being basic explanations for human experiences in the creative order, myths also perform both educational and moral functions. Mythical narratives are employed to teach or instruct the young one in the society, so that they can be knowledgeable about beliefs and practices of the religion. Also, they can serve moral instructional "oral manual" of responsibilities and expectations from individuals in the community. Finally, it is important to indicate that myths should never be seen as historical facts. Rather, they should be seen in the context of explanatory or demonstration stories designed to provide meaningful understanding for observed human experiences.

Proverbs

Proverbs can be categorized in the group of African traditional narratives that are very reliable. This is because they are usually memorized and transmitted in fixed formats that are not subjected to changes as they transit from one generation to the other. This is also responsible for proverbs being regarded as a valuable component of African heritage and major source of wisdom. Also, proverbs provide theological instructions and moral teachings that are considered necessary for the good of the individual and attainment of peace, harmony, and law and order in the community. Further, proverbs are greatly valued by Africans for their metaphysical significance[16] . In addition, proverbs reveal a lot about African worldviews about religious beliefs and practices, particularly as they reference human practical experiences in particular situations. Because of these functional dispositions, proverbs are understandably cultivated as an art form and valued as a demonstration of outstanding delivery of ebullient oratory. This is why, for instance, in Yoruba ethnic group, proverbs are characterized as "horses for retrieving missing words" that are used for conveying and driving home deeper meaning. In addition, proverbs are functional, providing insight into the various attributes of the Supreme Being—as creator, omnipresent, holy, merciful, upright, and the sustainer of both the universe and humanity. In many of such proverbs on the attributes of the Supreme Being, the Akan allude to His transcendent nature with the saying: "If you want to tell God anything, tell it to the wind." The Yoruba reference His benevolence by saying: "God drives away flies for the cow with no tail." The Igbo reference to His omnipotence in the saying: "God has both the yam and the knife, only those whom he cuts a piece can eat."

Names of People
Names are also categorized in the group of reliable oral traditions. This is because names are fixed and depict the same meaning from one generation to another. For Africans, names are given with meaningful indications as to circumstances, parental status, family profession, state, day, or events of birth. Also, in most African countries, the name of the Supreme Being is often made part of the child's name.[17] This is done in recognition and worship of the Supreme Being. For example, the Yoruba people have names such as Oluwatobi (God is great), Oluwaseun (God is victorious). The Burundi also have the name Bizimana, meaning "God knows everything." Africans generally name a child at birth or soon after with various degrees of ceremonial rituals. Such names are considered to portray and largely determine the personality of the child from birth till death and even in the afterlife.

Prayers
Prayers can also be categorized as reliable African oral traditions and are very fundamental to the adoration and worship of the Supreme Being in African Traditional Religion. This is because prayers are the vehicles of direct communication with Him. an essential part of religion. Africans pray to the Supreme Being for different reasons and indifferent forms. Every aspect of human life, in the day-to-day experiences, is captured in relevant prayers reflecting situations, events, and anticipations. Thus, the prayers may be for guidance, blessings, good health, protection, success, and so on. In addition, Africans direct their prayers to divinities and ancestors. However, when this is the case, the intention is to employ the services of the divinities and the ancestors as vehicles to present the prayers to the Supreme Being. The object of the prayers is the Supreme Being in the recognition of his ultimate authority in granting the prayers. African prayers also take different formats; they may be said by individuals as private mode of worship or they may be communal in nature. This happens when the prayers are said together in public place for communal purposes. Generally, African prayers are spontaneous and short by going directly to the purpose of the prayer. Further, there are occasions when Africans as

individuals or as a community pray by themselves directly to the object of the prayers, and there are other times when such prayers are offered indirectly on their behalf. This is usually done by religious officials such as priests (both men and women), rainmakers, chiefs, kings, and sometimes medicine men.[18]

Finally, it is important to stress that for Africans prayers are primarily premised on the belief the Supreme Being is not just the creator but also the sustainer of everything in the universe. Consequently, everything including humans is completely dependent on His goodwill, which can be obtained through prayers. Prayers also function as important sources of information and knowledge about the Supreme Being, particularly in terms of his attributes in His relationship with the created order and human beings.

Non-oral Sources

The second source through which valuable information and knowledge about African Traditional Religion are derivable can be found in different non-oral devices, objects, and places. Some of these are made up of three identifiable forms: (i) artifacts, (ii) wooden masks, and (iii) the sacred institutions.[19]

Artifacts

Different forms of artifacts can be found in most, if not all African ethnic groups. These have come to provide concrete or empirical representations of the beliefs and practices of African Traditional religion. They vividly project African belief and worship of the Supreme Being, devotion and veneration of the divinities, views about the afterlife and ancestral cult as well as other African religious consciousness. Two categories of artifacts can be found in African Traditional Religion. The first consists of objects sourced from archeological findings. In the second category are the products of contemporary artists. A combination of these two derivations has been very instrumental in providing authentic and vital information that may not be available through oral traditions. For example, archeological findings have led to the discovery of the temples and altars of Onyame, the Ashanti Supreme Deity, by R. S. Rattray.[20] There is no doubt that this kind of discovery goes a long way to dispel the notion that Africans did not have any idea about the Supreme Being prior to the arrival of Christian Missionaries. Also, contemporary artifacts that are made up of dance staffs, apparatuses for divination, musical instruments, votive figures, and many other ritual objects are sources of information for practically all aspects of African religious beliefs and practices.

Wooden Masks

Wood Masks are used as covering of the face in order to hide the identity of the person under the mask. This practice is quite widespread in most African ethnic groups as part of religious rituals particularly in celebrating the ancestors. In this context, the mask is used to indicate that the earthly person putting the mask on is an incarnation of the ancestral spirits, who have come to visit the living. Sometimes, the wood masks are used by members of secret societies also to hide their identities in the public. Example of this use of masks can be found among the Ogboni society in Yoruba land and also among the Poro ethnic group.

Sacred Institutions

Sacred institutions are regarded as hallmarks of the beliefs and practices of African Traditional Religion. This is because these institutions are generally the custodians of the fundamental configurations of the religion in its holistic inclusiveness of every aspect of the African ways of life. This is why the institutions are regarded as being sacred. For instance, among African ethnic groups, the traditional ruling institution is both political and religious rolled into one. Consequently, traditional rulers are not just political leaders but also and more importantly partakers in the theocratic governance of the Supreme Being. That is why among the Yoruba people, for example, the traditional ruler called "Oba" is referred to as *igbakeji Orisa*, meaning second in command to the Supreme Beihg-*Oldumare*. For Ashanti, the traditional rulers put on the golden ornaments that symbolize the belief of the people that the Supreme Being is manifested through the sun. By wearing the golden ornaments, the Ashanti traditional ruler becomes the embodiment of the eternal fire of the sun.[21]

Another sacred institution that is popular among some African ethnic groups such as the Yoruba and the Akins is the cult of thunder. Both ethnic groups recognize the ax as the symbol of the judgment of the Supreme Being. The Yoruba then designate Shango as the divinity of thunder who strikes down evildoers with the ax in execution of the wrath of *Olodumare*. It is therefore very usual to find axes in shrines dedicated to Sango. On their part, The Akans call the ax *nyame akuma*, meaning God's ax. Therefore, axes are found in shrines dedicated to *Onyame*, symbolizing his wrath.

African Traditional Religion Status in Contemporary and Future Global Religious Space

Questions have been raised about the status of African Traditional Religion in contemporary setting and also its future sustainability. Such questions are quite understandable given the enormous challenges that have confronted the religion since the advent of Western Civilization and foreign religious traditions, namely Christianity and Islam. While the challenges from these two major "adversaries may be considered to be externally inflicted, there are other challenges that may be considered to have been internally generated by the nature and circumstances of the religion itself." A number of such challenges from both sources are worth consideration. Our focus in discussing these challenges stems from our belief that they are largely responsible for the almost complete "wipe" of the religion on the African Continent. There is also no doubt that this situation has dire consequences for the status of the religion contemporarily and the future that awaits it in the global religious space.

Beginning with the challenges from external sources, a number of them can be identified as follows:

The first and perhaps the most fundamental of the external challenges can be traced to the contacts of the African Continent with other outside continents, particularly Europe. These contacts, unfortunately, began with the unfortunate historic transatlantic slave trade. This human trade witnessed major transportations of Africans into Europe and the Americas. These Africans were of course adherents of the indigenous religion. By transporting this huge number of Africans into slavery led to significant depopulations of practitioners of the religion.

Then followed, or sometimes simultaneously, the contacts with the two religious traditions found in Christianity and Islam. The "evangelical invasions" of these two religions have permanently changed the complexion of religious affiliation on the African Continent. The takeover has become so effective that the African Continent, religious affiliation wise, is today split down the middle by the two religions.

As a third leg of the contacts, the colonial domination, Western Civilization, and education, all rolled into one, have had a profound impact on the decline of the practices of African Traditional Religion among Africans. This is because as it turned out the combination of all of the above produced an "elitist" mentality, whereby practicing Christianity or Islam designates a civilized and educated class. On the other hand, those who practice African Traditional Religion are looked down upon as being as illiterate, uneducated, and uncivilized.

The internally generated challenges to African Traditional Religion are generally associated with sources such as, for example, the massiveness of the continent in terms of geographical dimensions. This understandably makes uniformity of specific aspects of beliefs and practices impossible, even when there is a commonality in general frameworks of such beliefs and practices. This of course denotes an obvious template of diversity in methods and applications of usually commonly held worldviews in different African ethnic groups. This situation is more often than not misrepresented to mean that Africans practice multiple tribal religions. The religion also lacks written documents in form of scriptures as available in other religious traditions. This has expected constituted one other internal challenging factor for the religion. By depending on mostly oral sources as its authoritative sources, most scholars, especially "outsider scholars," are quick to dismiss the claims of the religion as being derived from superstitious and "unintelligible" configurations. There is also the internal challenging factor of the secret nature of the religion. It has been observed that, for various reasons, information regarding fundamental information about the beliefs and practices of the religion are most often than not kept secret by its religious officials and other custodians. When this is coupled with the non-written nature of the religion, vital information providing authentic knowledge of the contents, process, and methods of the beliefs and practices of the religion is lost not only to the present generation but also to the ones in the future.

With the discussion on both the external and internal challenges facing the religion above, the next question to be considered has to do with the implications of these challenges for the future of the religion. To begin with, it should be asserted that these challenges are still ongoing, and they without any doubt constitute active challenges to the overall practice and acceptance of the religion as an authentic religious tradition just as other world religious traditions. So what future awaits African Traditional Religion in the "community of global religious space?"

Our submission is that in spite of the mitigating effects of these external and internal challenges, the religion will continue to have a significant presence in the global religious space in the future. This position is premised on a number of factors and engagements, among others, enumerated below:

First, there have been growing interests and attentions directed to academic and scholarship engagements in African Traditional Religion. Indeed, such engagements are not limited to the African continent but they are found in Europe, the United States, Canada, Latin America, and the Caribbean. Thus, in these places, programs in various forms and levels are offered in both public and private higher education institutions in African Traditional Religion. Also, books, articles in journals, conferences, symposia associated with the religion are now part of widespread engagements in scholarship across the globe.

Second, there are the growing interests and commitments of many African nations to the ideology of African nationalism so as to attain African self-identity. It is obvious that there is no way this objective or mission can be achieved without considering the fundamental African cultural worldviews which are mostly embedded and sustained in the beliefs and practices of African Traditional Religion.

Third, in spite of the seemingly total affiliations of a majority of Africans to the practice of Christianity and Islam, there is still significant and widespread observance of African traditional cultural values among Africans today. Even when they profess either the Christian or the Islamic faiths, they still, one way or the other, continue to observe traditional cultural values in their everyday engagements. However, these traditional cultural values cannot be separated, strictly speaking, from the beliefs and practices of African Traditional Religion, where such beliefs and practices are embedded.

Fourth, there have been significant developments in acculturation, enculturation in the practices of Christianity and Islam by Africans both on the Continent and on the Diaspora. These practical strategies have interestingly incorporated different levels of African traditional religious values. Thus, in one way or the other, these values are now part and parcel of the practices of both Christianity and Islam.

Fifth and lastly for our discussion here, there has been the emergence of African Religion in the Diaspora. Such religions are also referred to as African Derived Religions. These are religions that originated as a result of the transatlantic slave trade. The slaves who found themselves in the Americas devised strategies of syncretic practices of combining basic elements of African Traditional Religion and some elements in different denominations of Christianity to develop new religions. Some prominent ones among these religions that are practiced in the Americas and other parts of the world where there are African people in Diaspora today are Santeria, Candomble, Voodoo, Sango, among many others. Indeed, there is the general belief that these religions will actually be the future of African Traditional Religion.

Notes

1. G. Aderibigbe, "African Religious Beliefs" in A. O. K. Noah, ed. *Fundamentals of General Studies*. Ibadan: Rex Charles Publications. 1995 p. 93
2. J. S. Mbiti, *African Religion and Philosophy*. London: Heinemann Educational Press. 1982. p. 43
3. G. Aderibigbe, *Opp, cit*. p.96.
4. E. B. Idowu, *Olodumare God in Yoruba Belief*. London: SCM Press. 1962.
5. J. S. Mbiti, op. cit.
6. E. B. Idowu, *African Traditional Religion: A Definition*. London: SCM Press. 1973. p.37.
7. P. Baudin, *Fetishism and Fetish Worshippers*. New York: Benzinger Brothers. 1885.
8. E. B. Idowu. *Opp. Cit*.
9. D. H. Westermann, *African Christianity*. London: Oxford University Press 1937.
10. E. B. Idowu. *Opp. Cit*. p. 49.
11. *Ibid*.
12. R. S. Rattery, *Religion and Art in Ashanti*. London: Oxford University Press. 1923.
13. J. O. Awolalu and P. A. Dopamu, *West African Traditional Religion*. Ibadan: Onibonoje Press. 1979.
14. S. A. Adewale, *The Religion of the Yoruba: A Phenomenological Analysis*. Ibadan: Day star press. 1988.
15. J. S. Mbiti, *opp cit*.
16. A. B. Jacobs, *A Text Book on African Traditional Religion*. Ibadan: Aromolaran Press. 1977.
17. J. S. Mbiti, *African Concept of God*. London: SMC Press. 1970.
18. *Ibid*.
19. S. O. Abioye, "African Traditional Religion: An Introduction" in G. Aderibigbe and D. Aiyegoyin, eds. *Religion: Study and Practice* . Ibadan: Olu Akin Press, 2001. P.119.
20. R. S. Rattray, *opp. Cit*.
21. S. O. Abioye, *opp. Cit*.

CHAPTER 3

African Traditional Religion and the Sociocultural Environment

Olutola Akindipe

Introduction

The African Traditional Religion is, perhaps, as old as the continent of Africa itself: it is a religion founded on Africans' unique and indigenous worship of God. Although little was known of the religion prior to the twenty-first century due to the lack of written documentation, scholars believe the religion has been practiced in Africa long before the Europeans' arrival on the continent.[1] The introduction of other religions, like Christianity and Islam, into Africa by Western missionaries and colonial masters led to stiff competition between the African Traditional Religion and its foreign counterparts. In particular, the colonial indoctrination, diversity of language, education, and Western civilization that came with the Europeans led many African Traditional Religion worshippers to renounce the religion and convert to Christianity and other foreign religions. Besides these external oppositions, the decline in the number of African Traditional Religion devotees was further compounded by the challenges inherent within the religion itself, which included the secret nature of the religion, lack of uniformity of worship, and the absence of sacred books.[2]

Despite the aforementioned challenges that stifled the African Traditional Religion's growth and expansion, it remains a potent and relevant force influencing the African outlook.[3] This is particularly true of the African Diaspora in the Caribbean Islands, Brazil, and other regions of the world where the African

O. Akindipe (✉)
Salem College, Winston-Salem, NC, USA
e-mail: olutola.akindipe@salem.edu

© The Author(s), under exclusive license to Springer Nature Switzerland AG 2022
I. S. Aderibigbe, T. Falola (eds.), *The Palgrave Handbook of African Traditional Religion*, https://doi.org/10.1007/978-3-030-89500-6_3

Traditional Religion has spread and has witnessed an increase in the number of worshippers. For example, in the past few decades, many of the converts in these places have been visiting several parts of Africa for religious worship and also to connect with their African heritage.[4] Several books have been written by scholars on African Traditional Religion, and many African Studies Centers or Institutes have been created across the United States and other Western countries.[5] Consequently, this has led to more awareness of the African Traditional Religion through courses being offered by those institutions as well as periodic conferences and scholarly gatherings on the religion.

Critical to the understanding of the African Traditional Religion is the African peoples' worldview—beliefs and assumptions about human nature, life, existence of things in the universe, and general perception of the world from the African perspective.[6] The African worldview, intrinsically, represents who Africans are and it is strongly tied to their perception of self and identity. Generally valued by most Africans, the African worldview explains the presumptions, influences the norms and values, and subsequently impacts the culture of the people. The African worldview, therefore, is hinged on the African culture.[7]

Generally, we do not have a universally acceptable definition of culture. Webster's Dictionary defines "culture" as a set of shared values and assumptions held by a group of people. Culture is the "totality of ideas, beliefs, values, knowledge, and ways of life of a group of people who share a certain historical, religious, racial, linguistic, ethnic, or social background."[8] Culture provides a framework for the way people see the world, process and interpret information and events, respond to situations, and perceive reality.[9] As a dynamic system of values, expectations, beliefs, and practices, culture organizes people's lives and mediates thoughts and actions. Inherent, therefore, within any culture are the values, traditions, and beliefs that influence the behavior of the social group.[10] Every culture is unique and beautiful,[11] and the African culture is by no means an exception.

The African culture could be perceived as the usual ways of living, believing, interacting, and communicating with others experienced by most Africans irrespective of where they live or find themselves.[12] It plays a significant role in the worship and practices of the African Traditional Religion. The rich African culture and heritage, as expressed through the African Traditional Religion, may have contributed to the flourishing state of the religion and the attention it has received. Specifically, the uniqueness, beauty, and grandeur of the African arts and crafts utilized in traditional religious worship and activities may have also aroused public curiosity. Moreover, the current campaign and advocacy for the Africanization of various aspects of the African systems such as education, history, medicine, mental health, politics, and agriculture by scholars, researchers, and politicians may have increased public interest in the religion.

One crucial element of the African Traditional Religion that makes it a "living" and relevant religion is its belief structure.[13] Generally, African scholars and writers hold different opinions on what comprises the belief structure. For example, Edward Geoffrey Parrinder, a prominent African Traditional Religion Scholar, posited that the belief structure of African Traditional Religion is made up of belief in a Supreme God, divinities, ancestors, and charms with its accessories.[14] Percy Amaury Talbot, another proponent of African traditional religion, opined that the religion's belief structure consisted of animism, anthropomorphism, ancestral worship, and polytheism.[15] It is E. Bolaji Idowu's proposition, however, that represents one of the most popular and acceptable belief structures of African traditional religion.[16] This belief structure includes belief in the Supreme Being, divinities, spirits, ancestors, medicine, and magic.

Belief in the Supreme Being

The belief in the Supreme Being is an underlying tenet of the African Traditional Religion. Although many Eurocentric writers initially claimed that Africans began to believe in the existence of God only after their arrival on the continent, yet several scholars have refuted this assumption.[17] Africans' belief in the Supreme Being is revealed in the names given to Him in the African Traditional Religion. The Supreme Being is considered the inventor of both the heavens and the earth. For example, the Yorùbá people call God, *Olorun*, which means the owner of heaven, *Oluwa*, the One who owns us, or *Eleda*, which simply means the Creator. The Bantu of Angola call Him *Suku*, meaning the Creator of the mountains, rivers, sky, and human beings. The Bantu and Sudanese of East Africa call Him *Mulungu*, which means the One who creates or brings into existence.

Belief in Divinities

In the African Traditional Religion, divinities are believed to be spiritual entities that act as messengers or intermediaries between the Supreme Being and humanity.[18] Although the Supreme Being is believed to reign and rule over the universe, He is considered too great or powerful to be directly involved in the daily affairs of human beings. Therefore, He appointed and empowered divinities to act on His behalf. Thus, African Traditional Religion worshippers offer sacrifices and rituals to divinities with the expectation that they will convey them to the Supreme Being. For example, among the Yorùbá, divinities often called *Orisa* are worshipped with the intent that they will transfer the worship to the Supreme Being. Some examples of familiar divinities among the Yorùbá of Nigeria are *Sango, Yemoja, Osun*, and *Ogun*.

Belief in Spirits

Spirits are another group of spiritual beings that serve as intermediaries between human beings and the Supreme Being. There are different spirits, and they can either be nature, animal, or human spirits. Often considered lower in the hierarchy to divinities, spirits are believed to be in charge of the forces of nature such as floods, droughts, or famine. They are worshipped because people believe they are powerful enough to avert natural disasters or protect them from evil occurrences like sickness and pestilence.

Belief in Ancestors

Ancestors are also considered to be intermediaries between the Supreme Being and the living.[19] However, they are believed to be spirits of relatives who died long ago but still dwell among the living in order to help and protect their loved ones. Usually, they are elderly members of the communities who lived and died honorably and have been absorbed into the community's Hall of Ancestors. They were considered, while alive, to have been custodians of the customs, traditions, morals, values, and norms of the society but who upon death assume responsibility of protecting their community.[20]

Belief in Medicine and Magic

These are spiritual practices employed in African Traditional Religion to influence the course of events. Though distinct in nature and usage, magic and medicine are used to meet the spiritual needs of human beings for either destructive or protective purposes. Generally, magic is used to cause individual harm and misfortune. In contrast, medicine is more frequently utilized for its healing properties in treating simple ailments, for its metaphysical powers during rituals, sacrifices, and invocations, curing mental health illnesses, and wading off evil forces that cause sickness, death, and other unfavorable occurrences.

The African society is largely communal. It is a collectivistic culture that encourages interdependence, harmonious living, and the maintenance of the social group. The sociocultural environment exerts a strong influence on what individuals learn and who they become. Adults are respected, revered, and considered custodians of the culture, while children are also valued as essential members of the society. Most African communities are structured around children.[21] The home and society pay great attention to the learning and development of children, especially their acquisition and construction of knowledge. Children also contribute to the economic and financial well-being of the family by helping on the farm, working as artisans, or assisting with household trade. In the traditional African setting, children often carry on the family occupation. For example, children from the lineage of professional drummers learn to drum while those from the family of hunters learn to hunt for animals in the bush. It is the primary responsibility of adults and elders within the family or society to ensure the family occupation is successfully transferred to the next generation.[22]

Similarly, in the African traditional religion, children from the families of priests, priestesses, diviners, herbalists, and fortune-tellers are trained in religious worship and practices. Through interactions and socialization with parents and elders of the family, children imbibe the beliefs, values, and behaviors of the religion. Also, children learn the names of the different religious symbols and artifacts used in religion. They are trained in the use of magic and medicine and how to recite incantations, myths, proverbs, and folktales. For example, the herbalists or chief priests' children often follow the adults into the bush to collect herbs and learn to combine them for treatment purposes. Children are trained to become skillful in the specific area of traditional religion that their families are specialized in. For example, children from the *Ifa* priesthood family may learn how to recite the *Ifa* incantations and consult the *Ifa* oracle to solve clients' problems.

VYGOTSKY'S SOCIOCULTURAL THEORY

The sociocultural theory provides a unique cultural framework for understanding the complex relationship between individuals and their social environment. The theory has been extensively used to study how children learn and develop cognitively in the fields of Education and Psychology. Its applicability extends to several other disciplines, such as Linguistic, Sociology, and Public Health. In this chapter, the sociocultural theory is examined to enhance our understanding of the African Traditional Religion, especially with regards to its continued relevance and sustenance.

Lev S. Vygotsky's Sociocultural theory postulates that the sociocultural environment plays a significant role not only in determining the individual's goals or behaviors but how they are attained.[23] According to the theory, the sociocultural environment is the origin of life's different components, including customary ways of behaving, codes or assumptions, artifacts, and institutions. Culture, therefore, influences an individual's beliefs, values, expectations, and experiential activities.[24] Basically, the theory states that society, through culture, provides individuals with the experiences and tools for procesing information cognitively and for intellectual adaptation. Also, the theory emphasizes a bi-directional relationship between individuals and the sociocultural environment such that the environment influences the individual as much as the individual influences the environment. Consequently, Vygotsky believed any learning that focuses on the individual at the expense of prevailing culture would result in poor cognitive, adaptive, and problem-solving skills. Likewise, learning or education that concentrates on the culture besides the individual would be equally unproductive.

Also, the theory posits that learning and cognition develop within the individual's sociocultural environment at two primary levels—the social and the individual levels. At the social level, the interactions between the individual and society are external and interpersonal, and it equips the individual with the values, norms, and expectations of society. Such social interactions empower individuals with appropriate skills and knowledge to make them acceptable and integral members of the community. According to Vygotsky, interactions at the social level lead to the development of lower structures of cognition which include our reactive attention, associative thoughts and memories, spontaneous or rudimentary conscious processes, and behaviors.[25]

In contrast, at the individual level, the social interactions between an individual and members of the society are deeply processed to become internalized. This internalization results in the formation of more complex and higher cognitive structures that influence thinking, decision-making leading to superior adaptive and problem-solving skills. Vygotsky, therefore, believed that interactions at the social level were instrumental and a presursor to the development of higher cognitive functioning. Vygotsky indicated that advanced thinking and cognitive development are precipitated upon earlier and simple learning acquired from the sociocultural environment, which provides the foundation for superior knowledge and cognition. He believed that from the time children are born, they begin to learn the culture of their society and process information to gradually progress from lower cognitive ability to more sophisticated thinking, reasoning, and problem-solving skills.

Central to the sociocultural theory are several concepts; however, in this paper, I examine just a few of them. They include the concepts of social interactions or interpersonal experiences, the more knowledgeable others (MKO), the zone of proximal development (ZPD), and language as a sociocultural and psychological tool for the transfer of cultural traditions and the development of knowledge and cognition.

Social Interactions

The concept of social interaction refers to the communication and involvement that occur among individuals within a social environment or culture. Vygotsky believed that social interactions are vital for the evolution of the individual as well as society. He posited that social interaction provides children with the opportunities to learn the norms, beliefs, and values of society, and they are the foundation and psychological tools for the development of knowledge, adaption, and intelligence that change society.

The African Traditional Religion's community is the most important aspect of the religion. It consists of individuals who share the same religious beliefs and interact with one another from time to time, especially during religious rituals ad ceremonies. Usually, this community comprises the religious leaders, believers, worshippers, and the general community. The priests, priestesses, healers, diviners, or fortune-tellers are often the religious leaders who perform or officiate at religious ceremonies and activities before a group of followers and the community. For example, the *Sangomas* are spiritual leaders from the lineage of diviners among the Zulu of South Africa. They are healers specialized in the use of herbs and traditional medicine to cure sickness and diseases. They also consult with spirits, divinities, or ancestors to tell people's fortune. The *Sangomas* are chosen by the ancestors and live a life of spiritual dedication to their followers and community.

Whether specially chosen by the ancestors from the community or belonging to some traditional priesthood lineage, children are very involved in the African Traditional Religion practices. They learn and imbibe the religion's values through interactions with parents, other members of the religious community, and observations during religious activities. Some of these social interactions involve participation and engagement in religious practices. For example, in some parts of Rivers State and among the Yorùbá of Nigeria, children participate in the singing and dancing aspects of rituals performed for childless couples to have children.[26] Children are also used to welcome newborn babies during christening or naming ceremony rites.[27] Usually, children are indoctrinated into the religion by having them undergo different forms of herbal, healing, divination, and priesthood training where they are taught to recite incantations and to combine herbs for healing or metaphysical purposes by the religious leaders or apprentices. Furthermore, children are trained to become spiritual mediums for various forms of divination and rituals. These social interactions and socialization of children are, therefore, critical to the continuity of the African traditional religion.

The More Knowledgeable Other

According to the sociocultural theory, children often acquire superior cognitive ability beyond their current capabilities due to interactions with skillful individuals or experts. Vygotsky (1998) referred to these skillful individuals or experts, usually adults or sophisticated peers, as the "more knowledgeable other (MKO)." Adults provide learning opportunities for younger learners beyond their current abilities by tapping their potentials, supporting them, and showing them how to perform tasks. Also, Vygotsky believed sophisticated and trained peers were qualified to be classified as more knowledgeable others because of their unique and exceptional skills and abilities. The more knowledgeable others share their experiences, knowledge, and skills with young learners within their community, thereby providing them with a culturally situated means through which advanced practical knowledge is acquired.

In the African traditional religion, the more knowledgeable others (MKO) are considered individuals who are more experienced in the act of religious beliefs, values, or worship. Usually, they are the religious and spiritual leaders such as priests, diviners, herbalists, and traditional healers. Others are the older and experienced devotees who can teach children and younger members to become integral members of the religious community. Although the religious leaders usually function in a larger capacity as the more knowledgeable others due to being custodians of the religion Older children who have undergone some training are also important more knowledgeable others because they have been trained or acquired specific religious skills that they can easily teach the younger ones. For example, older children inductees can help the new or younger ones to learn the names of different herbs, artifacts, songs, and to recite the incantations. Learning from the more knowledgeable others occurs through guided participation until the younger learners can successfully perform the expected religious practices.

Hence the relevance and continuity of the African Traditional Religion are heavily dependent on the more knowledgeable others who can teach and train the next generation of religious leaders and worshippers.

Zone of Proximal Development

In line with the sociocultural theory, there are several areas of knowledge and skills that children cannot learn or acquire on their own but which they may become capable of with help from others. Young children gradually move from positions where they are unable to perform specific tasks to independently being able to do so by observing and learning from parents, older siblings, teachers, and sophisticated peers. Children's progression from their previous learning capabilities to new levels of possibilities is referred to as the zone of proximal development (ZDP). Coined by Vygotsky, the zone of proximal development (ZPD) is defined as the "distance between the actual developmental level as determined by independent problem solving and the level of potential development as determined through problem solving under an adult's guidance or collaboration with more capable peers."[28] Therefore, the zone of proximal development increases children's skills and empowers them with higher cognitive functioning beyond their current abilities.

As the more knowledgeable others, adults and sophisticated peers in the African Traditional Religion possess the superior knowledge and expertise on religious practices that give direction and guidance to new and younger inductees, thereby significantly impacting their religious zone of proximal development. This growth and development gradually occur under the guidance or collaboration with a more knowledgeable other such that young devotees who were previously incapable of performing a religious task can now do so independently. For example, a religious inductee who could not recite any incantation, consult the oracle, or know which herbs are needed for treatment slowly begins to learn until he/she eventually becomes capable of doing so. The zone of proximal development, therefore, relates to areas of religious learning where specific instruction is given to children to assist them in developing useful and appropriate religious skills and expertise to function independently.

Language

According to Vygotsky, language is the most important sociocultural tool in any society. Although he acknowledged that children acquire and develop language within the sociocultural environment from social interactions with parents, relatives, and other members of society, however, he believed the role of language was greater than being simply for communication. He posited that language served a complex and dual function. First, he noted that language is a tool for the communication and transmission of sociocultural values. This sociocultural function of language does not only involve the individual's power to connect with others but also to influence others through his or her behavior.

Second, Vygotsky noted that language is a powerful tool for intellectual adaptation, critical for human cognition because it influences thinking, perception, and reasoning. Language enables the categorization and interpretation of human reality, thereby providing the medium for further reflection and elaboration of sociocultural experiences. Consequently, it helps individuals in the organization, unification, and integration of behavior for problem-solving. Thus, language bridges the gap between the lower and mental cognitive structure, underlines the internalization of thoughts, and aids the formation of higher psychological processes.[29]

The African Traditional Religion is primarily oral: the nature and sources of its content, information, and knowledge, and modus operandi of religious worship are spoken, or by word-of-mouth, rather than written. Unlike Christianity and Islam each having their sacred books, African Traditional Religion has no sacred scriptures, books, or encyclopedia on which its beliefs and doctrines are documented. Consequently, all that is known of the religion—its concepts, beliefs, and structure—was and is orally communicated and transmitted from one generation to the next, irrespective of the region of the continent or world where it is practiced. To this end, language plays a very fundamental function in the religion's worship and practices.

Similar to other religions, language is the vehicle through which almost all forms of communication and religious activities such as praying, singing, rituals, or performances of rites of passage in the African Traditional Religion occur. It enhances the performance and fulfillment of the religious affairs and goals and also helps communicate religious ideas, beliefs, and values among members of the community. Sessions of religious prayers, songs, myths, proverbs, incantations, and consultations are conducted in the indigenous language. In addition, all the concepts of sociocultural theory, such as social interactions, more knowledgeable others, and the zone of proximal development, are only attainable with the help of language.

Conclusion

Religious scholars have attempted to understand the peculiarity and strengths of the African Traditional Religion that made it survive stiff competition from Islam, Christianity, and other foreign religions to remain ever flourishing and relevant. This paper examined some of the underlying concepts within Vygotsky's sociocultural theory as a means of elucidating the relationship between individuals and the environment in the African Traditional Religion, which may have significantly resulted in the sustenance and successful transference of the religion from one generation to the next.

Usually individuals progress from knowing little or nothing about their religion to learning about its essential aspects and becoming integral members of their religious community. Through social interactions, significant elements of the religion are communicated to the younger members of the community and passed on to future generations. The more knowledgeable others, who are custodians and experts on the religion, train the younger devotees launching them into the zone of proximal development, areas of religious knowledge and skills, unattainable in their independent efforts. All these occur with the aid of language, which acts as the psychological tool that helps to bridge the younger generation's lower and higher mental functioning on religious capabilities. The resultant effect is the making of a people who are firmly rooted in the African Traditional Religion system of beliefs, structure, and practices despite their levels of education, socioeconomic status, and Western civilization, all around the world. Another outcome of the sociocultural environment on the African Tradtional Religion is the raising of individuals endowed with religious intelligence, adaptation, and problem-solving abilities, which works to preserve the traditions and practices of the religion and ensures its successful transfer to subsequent generations. All of these sociocultural tools have successfully contributed to making the African Traditional Religion a very relevant and thriving religion.

Vygotsky's assertion that the sociocultural environment plays an inevitable role in influencing the adaptation and cognitive development of a group of people and that an understanding of the bidirectional relationship between the individual and the social environment is paramount for meaningful progress and development is evident from the sociocultural theory. Invariably, the theory can be viewed as significantly applicable in explaining the sustenance, continuity, and present relevance of the African Traditional Religion, even in this modern times.

Notes

1. John S. Mbiti, *African Religions and Philosophy.* London; Heinemann. 1969.
2. Ibigbolade S. Aderibigbe, "Religions in Africa," In Ibigbolade S. Aderibigbe and Akinloyè A. Òjó (eds.), *Continental Complexities: A Multidisciplinary Introduction to Africa.* San Diego, CA: Cognella Publishing, 2013. pp. 61–84.
3. V. Atta-Baffoe, "African Traditional Religion," In J. Corrie (ed.), *Dictionary of Mission Theology.* Nottingham. 2013. pp. 10–12.
4. Jacob K. Olupona, "The Spirituality of Africa," *The Harvard Gazette*, October 6, 2015. https://news.harvard.edu/gazette/story/2015/10/the-spirituality-of-africa/ (accessed 10/6/2020).
5. Wyatt MacGaffey, "African Traditional Religion," *Oxford Bibliographies*, 25 October, 2012. https://doi.org/10.1093/obo/9780199846733-0064.
6. Molefi Kete Asante, *The Afrocentric Idea* (Philadelphia, PA: Temple University Press), 1987.
7. Chris Barker, *Television, Globalization and Cultural Identities.* Buckingham: Open University Press. 1999.
8. Alean Al-Krenawi, and John R. Graham, eds., *Multicultural Social Work in Canada: Working with Diverse Ethno-Racial Communities.* Toronto: Oxford University Press, 2003.

9. John U. Ogbu, "Minority Status, Cultural Frame of Reference and Literacy," In D. Keller-Cohen (ed.), *Literacy: Interdisciplinary Conversations*, Cresskill. NJ: Hampton Press, 1994. pp. 361–384.
10. D. Parsons, *Djuna Barnes* (Tavistock: Northcote House Publishers. 2003).
11. Chick, 1997.
12. E. O. Ezedike, *African Culture and the African Personality: From Footmarks to Landmarks on African Philosophy* (Somolu: Obaroh and Ogbinaka Publishers, 2009).
13. Aderibigbe, "Religions in Africa," 61–84.
14. Edward Geoffrey Parrinder, *West African Religion*. London: Epworth Press. 1949.
15. Percy Amaury Talbot, *The Peoples of Southern Nigeria: A Sketch of Their History, Ethnology and Languages*, Vol. 2. Oxford University Press, 1926. p. 12.
16. E. Bolaji Idowu, *African Traditional Religion*. London; SCM Press Ltd. 1973.
17. Mbiti, *African Religions and Philosophy*, 1969; Idowu, *African Traditional Religion*, 1973.
18. Benjamin C. Ray, *African Religions: Symbol, Ritual and Community*. Englewood Cliffs, NJ: Prentice-Hall Inc., 1976.
19. Mbiti, *African Religions and Philosophy*, 1969.
20. Osadolor Imasogie, *African Traditional Religion*. Ibadan, Nigeria: Ibadan University Press, 1982.
21. U. R. Onunwa, "Igbo Traditional Attitude to Children. A Religious Interpretation of a Socio-Economic Need," *Africa: Revista Trimestrale di Studi e Decomuntazione dell'Instituto Italiano per l'Africa e l'Oriente*, vol. 43, no. 4.1988. pp. 621–629.
22. Ibid.
23. Lev S. Vygotsky, *Mind in Society: The Development of Higher Psychological Processes*. Cambridge, MA: Harvard University Press, 1978.
24. Vygotsky, *Mind in Society*, 1978; Sternberg, 1985.
25. Derek Hook, Jacki Watts, and Kate Cockcroft, *Developmental Psychology*. (Lansdowne, South Africa: UCT Press, 2002).
26. Onunwa, "Igbo Traditional Attitude to Children," pp. 621–629.
27. Ibid.
28. Vygotsky, *Mind in Society*, p. 86.
29. Ibid.

CHAPTER 4

Metaphysical and Ontological Concepts

Alloy S. Ihuah and Zaato M. Nor

INTRODUCTION

Mankind is perpetually engrossed with investigating the phenomenal world (the physical or the seen world) and the noumena world (the immaterial or the transcendental world) in order to attain meaning as it relates to human existential situation. Mankind is preoccupied with understanding these two worlds because they constitute ontological wonder. Jim Unah explains that "By ontological wonder we mean an extraordinary kind of perplexity ... about the nature of things (i.e. man and the world) in turn gives rise to fundamental questions."[1] Though this situation appears obvious as the two worlds easily inform fundamental metaphysical and ontological questions, some thinkers disclaim this all together. For instance, Immanuel Kant argues that it is an exercise in futility to attempt to make enquiries regarding the noumena or the transcendental realm as the categories of human understanding cannot be applied in the noumena world. To state this Kantian claim differently, mankind can only enquire about things that are known in the phenomenal world. Kant refers to the phenomenal world as the world of things-as-they-appear while the noumena world, known as the world of things-in-themselves, is a transcendental or non-physical world. This is to say that the noumena world is unknowable while the phenomenal world is knowable.

What is implied in Kantian thought is that he acknowledges both the metaphysical and ontological realities. That is, there are things or objects of metaphysical concern and things or objects of ontological interest. While metaphysical realities remain unverifiable, ontological ones are certifiable in

---

A. S. Ihuah (✉) • Z. M. Nor
Benue State University, Makurdi, Nigeria

© The Author(s), under exclusive license to Springer Nature
Switzerland AG 2022
I. S. Aderibigbe, T. Falola (eds.), *The Palgrave Handbook of African Traditional Religion*, https://doi.org/10.1007/978-3-030-89500-6_4

certain cases and unverifiable in others. Certifiable and uncertified here refer to things or objects that are empirically verifiable and non-empirically verifiable, respectively. For instance, being as an ontological concept refers to anything that exists like human being and this can be verified. That is the existence of a human being as a physical reality can never be a subject of disputation. This is because man or human being is an object or being as it appears; it is a physical phenomenon. However, being as being which is taken as the ultimate source of being, that is, taken as being responsible for the source of all being, to Kantian claim, cannot be investigated because it is, a noumena entity, that is, an entity in itself. Thus Kant, in his gnoseology, considers it possible to investigate only aspects of ontology whose features are sense-perceptible. This attitude for sure brings about enormous disservice to humanity as mankind's desire to investigate the holistic meaning of his existence becomes mortgaged. "Man, Zaato Nor aptly notes, is basically concerned with his existence (ontology) knowledge (epistemology) and value (axiology)."

Accordingly, Nor notes that, "Metaphysics investigates into physical and practical things as any other human endeavour concerned about knowledge ... metaphysical enquiry often commences from the foundation of what conceals itself from sense perception, that is, the noumena ... the entity under investigation may have been less distinct, the metaphysical light thrown on it makes it more vivid."[2] It suffices to emphasize at this juncture that mankind's preoccupation with ontology, epistemology and axiology does not rule out science. Science is an entrenched quintessential way of life of man as it is evidenced in its contributions to human ontological life.

However, as Everett W. Hall insightfully notes, "science alone is not enough, life is much more than scientific intelligence, man is incurably metaphysical and instead of being ashamed of that fact, he should openly avow it."[3] To state this differently, the life of man is predicated on what is metaphysical and that which is scientific as it is the collaboration of the two that provides a full meaning of man in his ontology. Joseph Omoregbe corroborates this view, stating that:

> *once we admit that there are some questions about man and the world, which science cannot answer (questions that are vital to human life and which disturb the human mind), then we would appreciate the role and value of metaphysics in our efforts to find answers to th-ese questions beyond the realm of science.*[4]

Omeregbe stresses that "metaphysics goes beyond the realm of sense-perception and positive science as well as the material realm in search of truth (more profound than we can obtain from sense—perception and science) about the world and human life."[5] It is therefore, on the background that 'mankind is incurably metaphysical,' that we commence the clarification of the concepts of metaphysics and ontology within the ambit of African Traditional Religion.

Metaphysics and Ontology

Knowledge precisely as it is based on meaning and understanding implies that concepts, as presented or encoded, must also be clarified for enhanced decoding. In other words, what is said or written must be understood by the listener or the reader as presented. If on the contrary, communication has taken place without its ultimate goal of passing information, giving knowledge and instruction/directive, there will be no assimilation of what has been communicated. It is based on this setting that we advance the elucidation of the afore-mentioned concepts.

Metaphysics

Metaphysics in certain climes and some schools of thought like the logical positivists as nursed by David Hume is all about what is "illusory and sophistry." Hume passionately asks: "If we take in our hand any volume; of divinity or school metaphysics, for instance; let us ask, Does it contain any abstract reasoning concerning quantity or number? No. Does it contain any experimental reasoning concerning matter of fact and existence? No. Commit it then to the flames: for it can contain nothing but sophistry and illusion."[6] This Humean view is subsequently supported by Alfred Jules Ayer in this book: *Language, Truth and Logic*, in which he says that 'the best way to write "finis" to metaphysics is to show that no statement which refers to a "reality" transcending the limits of all possible sense-experience can possibly have any literal significance from which it must follow that the labour of those who have striven to describe such a reality have all been devoted to the production of nonsense.' Put in other words, Ayer is saying that to claim to have knowledge of transcendental reality is a mere literal signification as those who struggle to prove such a reality only labor in vain as all they do is produce what is nonsensical. To Ayer, it is erroneous for metaphysics to claim to give humanity knowledge of reality beyond the material world of science and commonsense. Making a case for the repudiation of metaphysics, Ayer 'sets a criterion of verifiability as the only true test of a proposition's significance.'[7] In other words, metaphysics as a communicator of sophistry and illusion to Ayer and the logical positivists does not convey verifiable or certifiable knowledge and hence, it does not produce genuine knowledge at all. However, this contention is hardly argued and soundly presented as a metaphysical view or position. This is the case: verifiability principle is unverifiable. Besides, as Unah buttresses "one is ever doing metaphysics either directly or indirectly, affirmatively or negatively, constructively or destructively, for a repudiation of metaphysics is not possible without a metaphysics of some sort."[8] In others words, to deny any metaphysical claim takes another metaphysical claim to do that. Unah succinctly clarifies this, saying, "the statement, there is such a thing as reality" and the contrary one, "There is no such a thing as reality"[9] belong to the same field of discourse. This implies that both statements being metaphysical cannot be corroborated or refuted by sense experience or observation.

Thus, arising from the foregoing, Ayer cannot be said to be right on insisting on his verifiable principle. It accordingly follows that Ayer too labors in vain to try to deny that reality exists beyond the limits of sense perception.

Meanwhile, prior to the criticism against Metaphysics and those who share in Ayer's "unverified claim", Panthaleon Iroegbu maintains that other people consider metaphysics as having an inalienable relationship with the following:

1. Dry rationalization;
2. Thrust into discovery of the Great Beyond; or
3. Navigation into ideal world of secret powers; or
4. Abstract speculation; or
5. Analysis of the human mind and language.[10]

However, taking these claims into consideration, which are very distant from the idea and scope of metaphysics, Iroegbu convincingly argues "that these claims are rather affronts to the concept of metaphysics as metaphysics is not or near any of the above mentioned."[11] Having made a disclaimer of the above contention, Iroegbu says that "metaphysics like anthropology, sociology and biology, is science. It is a systematic study of being in its deepest aspects. It is an ordered investigation into the inner side of existence. It unravels the most fundamental contents of being and beings. It radically probes existence in so far as these are knowable. It researches into the prolixities of being and the relationships among them."[12] Thus, in conclusion, Iroegbu patently notes that the end result of metaphysical studies is not occultic premonitions,[13] but rather the discovery of the response to the question of why things are seen to be the way they are and why they are so. To Iroegbu, metaphysics is a conglomeration of the physical and the spiritual, the empirical and the supra-empirical and, accordingly, embraces each particular being, all of being and the being of all. To state Iroegbu's apt submission in less technical way, metaphysics is likened to the behavioral sciences, its study is systematic or ordered in its concern with *being* (ontology) because of its preoccupation with existence. As a matter of fact, the aim of ontology as a fundamental aspect of metaphysics is to bring to the fore, the nature, quality(ies)/attribute(s) of being and beings as well as their relationships. Furthermore, metaphysics is interested in ascertaining the limits of knowledge. Metaphysics in its pure state stands in antagonism to occultism while it provides answers to why things are and why they are so. Thus, it dwells on the physical (phenomena) and the supra-empirical (non-mena). Metaphysics as such is undivorced from investigating being/Being. This would be better illustrated shortly in our consideration of ontology.

The lengthy preamble here is deliberate. It is intended to bring to limelight the claims and disclaims about metaphysics. Recall that our task here is to put the concepts of metaphysics in a proper perspective. Thus, it is incumbent on us to incorporate in this study, the origin, scope, meaning, aim, essence as well as the relationship between metaphysics and other disciplines as they relate to the existence of man in his insatiable quest to know. J. Obi Oguejiofor reminds us that "As rational creatures, human beings are apt to ask questions in quest of explanations of their situation or incomprehensible difficulties in which they find themselves."[14] It is clear from this thought-provoking submission and contrary to Kant that human beings cannot be limited to asking questions about the empirical/material world only but rather to their holistic being or existence which comprises the material and the immaterial worlds. Thus, metaphysics, as one of the core branches of philosophy which also means philosophy itself, is fundamentally primitive in all intellectual discourses.

Etymologically, metaphysics is from the Greek expression *ta meta ta physika biblia*, an expression made by Andronicus of Rhodes who was the editor of Aristotle's treatises. Andronicus while editing Aristotle's works around 70 BC on natural philosophy or physics according to Robert P. Wolff came across some treatises regarding the *physika* (physics or nature) and others relating to non-physics.[15] Andronicus in his wisdom as an editor, while arranging the works, placed the treatises on physics first and the one relating to non-physics came subsequently. Hence, *ta meta ta physika biblia* simply means the treatises or books that came after or beyond those of physics.[16] Wolff, accordingly, stresses that the books became known as the metaphysics while its subject matter was referred to as metaphysics. Understood, etymologically, metaphysics is therefore a science of going beyond or transcending the physical reality of perception. That is, it investigates realities beyond the physical realm. In this wise, Aristotle conceives metaphysics as "First Philosophy; it is the study of *being qua being*. It is a science that investigates the first principles and causes. It studies God as the highest being; a *being* that is both changing and independently existing (theology)."[17] This seminal understanding of metaphysics implies that it is only preoccupied with entities transcending the physical world. Essentially, metaphysics is a branch of philosophy that investigates only the super-sensible objects. To the contemporary conception of metaphysics, it goes beyond this claim. Thus, the traditional claim can at best be accepted as being partially true. To establish the broad nature of metaphysics in the contemporary times, there are three broad and active schools of metaphysics: idealism, materialism and vitalism.

Idealism as a philosophical system maintains that reality is spiritual or simply ideas. To the idealist metaphysicians, all that exist including the physical world is spiritual or immaterial. They contend that matter is a dependent substance and cannot exist on its own but rather depends on spiritual substance.

Idealism is sub-broken down into subjective and objective idealisms. Subjective idealism states that material objects' existence is mind-dependent. In other words, they are the minds' product and cannot exist independent of it. The mind structures them and presents them according to its structuring. Conversely, objective idealism holds that the material world is the self-manifestation of the spiritual reality in a physical form.

Materialism is a philosophical system that admits that matter is the primary substance. To the materialists, all that exist is matter or anything existing, in the long run, can be reduced to matter. Materialism is the direct opposite of idealism, as such, matter is considered as being a reality prior to spirit or ideas. It suffices to note that some materialist metaphysicians acknowledge the existence of immaterial objects but insist that such realities are ultimately objects and ultimately matter.

Vitalism is basically an African metaphysical system that acknowledges the reality of the material and the immaterial universe and accordingly states that reality is made up of matter and spirit. Matter and spirit are two sides of one ultimate reality. Matter and spirit are therefore inseparable.

Thus far, it is no longer contestable that metaphysics preoccupies itself with abstract and non-abstract entities. Be this as it may, Omoregbe maintains that "metaphysics is concerned with essence of things."[18] This goes to say that both abstract and non-abstract entities have their essences and hence the concern of metaphysics. This is what informed Alexus Meinong's definition of metaphysics. According to him, "metaphysics deals with everything thinkable, whether or not it actually exist, whether reasonable or absurd: it is concerned with the totality of the object of knowledge."[19] In other words, metaphysics studies everything real or imaginable to arrive at their essences. Besides studying realities that are abstract or actual, metaphysics also serves as a theory.

In the words of Alfred North Whitehead, metaphysics "is the endeavour to frame a coherent, logically necessary system of generating ideals in terms of which every element of our experience can be interpreted."[20] To put this in different words, for metaphysics to perform its task successfully, it develops logically relevant theories which are employed in the study of what is experienced in order to attain satisfactory interpretation and meaning. It suffices to point out that metaphysics lacks a universally appealing definition like the mother discipline, philosophy.

It is also important to note that metaphysics can be employed speculatively and descriptively. According to Omoregbe, "The former is an attempt to explain the whole of reality in all-embracing speculative system while the letter is a descriptive analysis of metaphysical concepts."[21] But it is worthy to mention that these two approaches are not too easy to separate, one may dominate a discourse but it is not the total absence of the other.

Nevertheless, metaphysics is divided into three subareas: ontology, cosmology and cosmogony. Ontology is the study of being, cosmology is the study of the universe in its totality, while cosmogony is the study of the origin and structure of the universe. We shall now consider ontology in detail.

Ontology

Ontology is drawn from two Greek words *onta* and *logos* which means existence and discourse, respectively. From its etymological source, ontology therefore means discourse on or the science that investigates being or existence. That is, the science of being or the study of being as being. In view of this, ontology makes disclosures about being and being. The term ontology is said to be the coinage of the scholastics. Some writers in the seventeenth century aligned ontology with metaphysics, while others deny this relationship all together. However, we align ourselves with the school of thought that maintains that ontology is a branch of metaphysics that seeks to study Being. According to Martin Heidegger, ontology as a branch of metaphysics is an endeavor which makes being manifest.[22]

Being means *ons* in Latin and in Greek, it is known as *to on*. Despite the Latin and Greek meanings, Panthelon Iroegbu says Being can best be described rather than defined. He states that it is indefinable because to define being is to attribute a specific difference, a quality that distinguishes the defined from other realities. Thus, in Iroegbu's description of being, he says "being is whatever exists, whatever has reality, entity or existence. This could be posited in the universe or outside of it. The reality could be concrete, empirical, notional or meta-empirical. It can be relative or have absolute existence. It may be visible or invisible, potential. It is being in so far as it shares or can share in existence, directly or indirectly, fully or partially, independently or dependently."[23] Stressing this thinking, Iroegbu concludes that ontology as a branch of metaphysics consistently investigates being.[24]

In his *On Being: Discourage On The Ontology Of Man*, Jim Unah by way of the definition says "ontology is the study of what it means to be or what it means to be all."[25] To say this in other words, ontology preoccupies itself with investigating all that exist generally. As a study, ontology embarks on a systematic approach toward the unraveling of being. Thus, Sydney Hook avers that the validity of ontology as a systematic discipline rests on the contention that it gives us knowledge about something or everything which is not communicated in any particular science or all the sciences.[26] Since ontology invokes knowledge about existent and existence, ontology argues that what is revealed is best acquired via the physical phenomena, rational and transcendental means. No doubt, ontology is an all—embracing gnoseology based on the fact that it can take up the investigation of all beings that there are—"seen and unseen, physical and non-physical, corporeal and non-corporeal, etc." The outcome of ontological enquiry is classified as being "exact" or "inexact." Mario Bunge maintains that "Being exact, ontology is either non-scientific: exact tools applied to problems and ideas not controlled by science or scientific: compatible and interacting with science."[27] When ontology is considered to be inexact, Bunge further explains that it is "wooly: pseudo-problems handled with verbal magic" or "clear: genuine problems but no exactness and little science."[28] That is, ontological enquiry is characterized by exactitude and inexactitude, that is, ontological wonder can be determined scientifically and non-scientifically. It suffices to note as Zaato Nor explains "ontology on its own cannot be said to be exact or inexact."[29] The exactness or inexactness is conditioned by the subject-matter or entity under investigation. It is in this context that ontology functions as a communication of "truth" or "falsities." The implication of this is that ontology in praxis could be preoccupied with investigating beings that are scientific-based and those that are nonscientific-based. This is what Unah refers to as specialized or regional ontology which concerns itself with the positive sciences and generalized ontology better known as "transcendental philosophy."[30] According to Unah, "regional ontologies or specialized science ... deal with beings or particular aspects of what—is such as...physics, chemistry, biology...and mathematics, etc."[31] Continuing, he says, "what is left of philosophy after the fragmentation ... deals with Being in general or what—is in totality"; this is how and where *being(s)* and *Being* come to the fore and, subsequently, become the subject matter of ontology.

An Expose of Some Metaphysical Concept

It is in league with the Whiteheadian submission that metaphysics is an activity aimed at fashioning coherent and essential logical system of generating ideas relevant to the interpretation of all human experiences that we commence the exposition of the following metaphysical concepts: God (supreme being) vital force, witchcraft, death, reincarnation and immortality (afterlife or life-after death), freedom and determinism, mind—body (duatity) and concept of person (personhood).

God

For long, Africa has been a subject of negative ascriptions as it received ungratified amount of bashings and scorn from Eurocentric scholars and thinkers, for lacking everything from worldview to intelligence. The early Christian missionaries, anthropologists, ethnographers and even writers negated the African peoples of basic human attributes leading to the conclusion that Africans lacked the idea of God. As erroneous and unjustified as these claims were and are, some people in the West till today cling tenaciously on to them. It suffices to recall one of such experiences as reported by Bolaji Idowu. According to him, "Dr. Edwin W. Smith relates an encounter he had with the environment biographer, Emil Ludwig. Ludwig was curious about what was the business of the missionaries in Africa. ... Smith informed him about Christianity and how Africans were given the saving knowledge of the living, present living God? ...how can this be? Deity is a philosophical concept which *savages* are incapable of framing."[32]

However, contemporary thorough-going researchers even in the Western world have come to debunk these phantom claims all together. The idea of deity, God or Supreme Being is an entrenched belief in Africa. Idowu in his book: *Oludumare: God in Yoruba belief* took a swipe at the dissociation of the Africans from the concept of God[33] by questioning what Ludwig definition of deity is. Idowu sarcastically argues thus: "if he meant by 'deity,' an abstract, intellectual concept, a thing to be attained by ratiocination, then it might indeed be that Ludwig's savages could not frame it. But since the deity of religion and human experience is not an abstraction but a reality, a being, Ludwig's premise is patently wrong, and his conclusion inevitably doomed to grief."[34] Continuing his analytic disclaimer of the likes of Ludwig, Idowu maintains that

> surely, God is one, not many; and that to the one God belongs the earth and all its fullness. It is this God, therefore, who reveals himself to every people to the degree of their spiritual perception, expressing their knowledge of him, if not as trained philosophers or educated theological certainly as those who have had same practical experience of Him.[35]

The informed thinking of Idowu here is that, there is only one universal God who is responsible for all things on the earth and beneath. Thus, God in his benevolence reveals himself to all people such that spiritually, perceptually and expressively such people get to know him not the way the philosophers or theologians may know him. Such people who get to know him not the way the philosophers or theologians may know him, have practical experience of God. He maintains further that people who think and speak in the manner Ludwig thought and spoke either do not know God enough in order to appreciate his divine nature as personal, righteous and loving or that through a subtle intellectual pride, they have arrived at the pharisaical stage of thinking it is not just arguing against Ludwig's ignorance. Drawing heavily from an African paradigm, Idowu advanced the meaning of the Yoruba deity (*Olodunmare*) and his attributes. In his words: "… the Yoruba think of him as one who possesses superlative greatness and fullness of excellent attributes. By calling him *Olodunmare*, the Yoruba acknowledge him to be unique in heaven and on earth, supreme overall."[36] He accordingly identifies nine attributes of Olodurmare as Creator, King, All-powerful, All-wise, all-knowing, all-seeing, judge, immortality and Holiness.

In what appears like a corroboration of Idowu's work, John S. Mbiti maintains that in his field research in Africa which covered more than 300 ethnic groups in Africa (including the traditionally Christian and Muslim communities), without a single exception, people have a notion of God as the supreme being.[37] Sharing in the idea of the universal nature and creator of all things, Mbiti maintains that "Expressed ontologically, God is the origin and substance of all things…, he is outside and beyond his creation… He is personally involved in his creation, so that it is not outside of him or his reach. God is thus simultaneously transcendent and immanent"[38] that is, metaphysically, God can be appreciated transcendentally and immanently based on being in his creation and outside of its physical existence cannot be perceived in the physical world.

In this context God is better regarded as a transcendent being. Immanently, God exists in the universe and also nourishes and sustains all that he has created. In this wise, he comes close to his creatures. Considering the transcendent and the immanent nature of God in African thought, the hierarchical structure of god's created world becomes pertinent to be mentioned. Aderibigbe[39] and Mbiti[40] all attest to this concept of God. He is the creator and author of all things in heaven and on earth.[41] For Mbiti, "God is at the top as the omnipotent; beneath him are the spirits and natural phenomena; and lower still are men who have comparatively little or no power all."[42]

Mbiti like Idowu are clearly advocates of unification theology which talks about the universality of one God. This view needs to be put into proper perspective. Sophie B. Oluwole points out that "to declare the Universality of God is to see him as a being which all things must relate, the creator to which all existences owe their origin as the absolute, he as an object of worship, he is the only true God that deserves praises, reverence and obedience."[43] For sure these attributes cannot be dissociated from religious believers concerning God. This belief has invariably brought about some fundamental questions. Bearing in mind that especially the organized religions which are revealed to particular individuals at particular times in particular place in a particular language, it becomes incumbent to ask: who actually worships the true God, who knows the ideal way to relate to him, which of the doctrines of different religions present God as the only reality to which everybody relates and from whom they expect protection: how can man know him in his true nature? In whose terms do we identify him?[44] These basic questions are predicated on the background of the history of world religions which bears testimony to the possibility of different authentic perspectives of God. For instance, as Oluwole rightly notes Jehovah in the Old Testament chose the Jews as his own people and declared others gentiles to be destroyed.[45] Yet this God in the Bible is identified as the creator of the whole world, Oluwole says, even though Jesus Christ later came and corrected this claim; it is however a question of semantics as he also assumed the title of the only beloved son of God, the only way, the truth and the light to guide the gentiles hitherto left by the created to grope in the dark for centuries, soon after.

In the like manner, Prophet Mohammed also states that he is the true messenger of God. If these two positions are accepted as being true, then it is obvious that chaos or religious intolerance is not an impossibility: Christ—Christianity and Mohammed—Mohammedanism (Islam) will surely claim superiority and will impose itself on the other it considers to be inferior. Reacting to this scenario, Oluwole maintains that "various attempts by different religious groups to establish and propagate their local conceptions of God and to uphold the sovereignty of the Absolute God have resulted to crisis that sometimes lead to wars."[46] The point being made here is that since all religions are product of a peculiar culture as they are revealed in a particular environment in a particular language, such a religion carries in it some cultural elements which define it, and it thus becomes a problem when attempts are made to impose such a cultural biased religion on other people. Oluwole made this point concisely when she says: "Every God worshipped through a particular means and understood in particular ways is necessarily a cultural God-God as seen through the eyes of a specific group of people during a specific era."[47] This goes to buttress the point that religious views are better projected in particular languages, that is languages of founders. The implication of the foregoing is that the general understanding of God as a universal God is rather God as conceived by particular religions and subsequently imposed on the world.

To avoid this situation of imposing a cultural-God from one culture to others, Oluwole is of the view that 'a clear distinction must be made between the universality of God and the Universal validity of a particular religion.'[48] In other words, religious adherents must not confuse the universal nature of God with the universal nature of God as conceived by their religion. This goes to say that the idea of the Universal conception of God must not convey a particular religious undertone. That is, to genuinely talk of a universal, the attributes or qualities attributed to such a universal God must not be traced to particular religions. Religions, especially the organized or the revealed ones, have raised the issue of relativism. As earlier mentioned, the God of these revealed religions identified his messengers or prophets in particular areas and era and accordingly passed his message through them for onward transmission to the rest of the world. According to Oluwole "Every revelation bears evidence of the relativity of each understanding of God. No religious leader successfully escapes the social, political and economic temperament of his era."[49] Arising from these premises, she concludes that local characterizations only become valid and all-attentive when it is recognized that such characterizations have relative significance in man's perception of the absolute.

That is, attributes ascribed to God in the traditional setting of a particular religion help in the understanding of the Supreme Being. For example, among the Tiv people of Nigeria, God is seen as being responsible for everything. For instance, a Tiv person would say: *Aondo ngu noon* literally translated as "God is raining." If the conception of God in Tiv religion is imposed on people of other cultures, or people, for sure, such people will have issues with the idea that it is God that rains. It is not far from this thinking that Oluwole plausibly argues that "The relativity of all religions does not harm the Supreme majesty of God.[50] It leaves intact the basis for all religions." Oluwole stresses that "The Philosopher's effort at reconciling all religious differences by postulating a mathematical God does not reduce all religions to one. The designation God as one universally relevant ontology leaves the various conceptions of God by different religions intact as a reference point." Put differently, though practitioners of different religions have their different conceptions of God, it is important that they keep it strictly to their belief rather than transferring such conception to other religions in order to arrive at a universal God. Rather than see the attempt by the Philosopher to reconcile all religions as being an amalgamation, the Philosopher should be praised for showing distinctively the difference between the cultural-God of religions and God as one universal ontology. This clarification keeps the cultural-Gods of religion untampered with.

Vital Force(s)

Vital force(s), life force(s) or simply force is one and the same thing and is easily equated with what is referred to as being in Western Philosophy. It was placide Tempels, a Belgian Priest, who in his study of Bantu Philosophy identified the concept of vital or life force. According to Tempels, vital force is the reality which, though invisible, is supreme in man.[51] Man can renew his vital force by tapping the strength of other and supreme reality which man exploits to access the potency of other creatures. Going by this ethno-philosophical submission of Tempels, vital or life force is a reality which provides the basic assumptions for the explanation of the ontological, epistemological and metaphysico-religious nature of the African. In a reductionist's thinking, Tempels, even though making reference to the Bantus, says that to the African, all things that exist are life forces even though they are classified in a hierarchical order. They intermingle and interpenetrate. Tempels writes: "All creatures are found in relationship according to the law of a hierarchy ... Nothing moves in the universe of forces without influencing other forces by its movement. The world of force is held like a spider's web of which no single thread can be caused to vibrate without shaking the whole network."[52] Explaining this law of hierarchy, K.C Anyanwu maintains that "God, divinities, ancestors, man, animals, plants, word, knowledge, etc."[53] constitute the qualitative and quantitative vital forces. Vital force theoretically, in the understanding of Tempels, explains everything about the thought of the African and his actions. In the words of Godwin Azenabor, "Life force or vital force refers essentially to the quality of life. Everything experienced is charged with life forces."[54]

As a pacesetter on the intellectual contribution in African philosophy and African metaphysics, Tempels authoritatively declares, "There is no idea of force" among Bantu of "being" divorced from the idea of "force," without the element "force," being cannot be conceived." Tempels' predicament[55] is clearly understood: he wants to demonstrate that Africans like the Greeks have the equivalent of the concept of being.[56]

However, he was quick to point out that the African understanding of force is dynamic while the Western conception of being is static. Azenabor avers that "forces differ in essence or nature-there is the divine forces, celestial forces, animal forces, animal forces, vegetable and even material forces."[57] Nevertheless as earlier adumbrated, these forces maintain an inter-relational and interpenetrating relationship such that "Superior or higher forces can directly influence the lower, while the lower can only indirectly influence the higher or superior."[58] The argued point here is that, in the ontology of life or vital force, there is a perpetual intermingling of forces by superior ranking or inferior ranking. The sure thing is that there is more of an infinite interaction. Thus, "Muntu" (God), according to Tempels, is the source of vital force. It is endowed with intelligence and will and is the active causal force with influence.

Stretching his contribution further, Tempels unveils some characteristics features of Bantu philosophy to include:

- Dynamism: that is, vital forces are dynamic as they are always mobile; interrelating and interpenetrating all things and accordingly non-static. A force is always in relation with other forces.
- Hierarchically structured: vital forces are arranged in an order of hierarchy with God at the summit or apex while divinities, ancestors, man, animals, plants, word, knowledge and so on follow in that order.[59] However, there is an inherent ontological relationship among forces; thus, no force exists in isolation.
- Domineering influence: as structured in the hierarchy of forces, superior force influences the inferior ones. In other words, inferior forces can only indirectly influence the superior force. Nevertheless, there remains a prevailing relationship of influence whether in a descending or ascending relationship which of course is indirectly carried out. This is what Tempels meant when he said in the article titled: "Concepts of wickedness in Bantu philosophy" that all forces are in relationship of ultimate interdependence; "vital influence is possible from being to being."[60]
- Activity and communicability of vital forces: following the dynamism of vital forces as articulated by Tempels, they are considered to be active and communicable. Vital forces can be diminished such that they become greater in influence. Janheiz Jahn in his consideration of the forces from *Muntu, Kintu Hantu* to *Kuntu* says these forces possess vital forces which decrease or increase depending on their position in the hierarchy.[61] Jahn explains that "Apart from some exceptions in the Kintu or frozen forces or unintelligent forces" category where certain trees, Poteau mitan in voodoo and the access way of the loas, etc. are seen as the repository of the deified and therefore superior to man's vital force, the rest are inferior to it'. That is besides Muntu, which is the plural of the word Bantu, and some Kintu (Bintu Singular) regarded as frozen or unintelligent forces which, however, exhibit intelligence in certain identified trees and in the religion of voodooism; the remaining forces are inferior to the forces in the Muntu category.
- Tempels gave another characterization of vital forces as benevolent and malevolent. In their benevolence nature, vital forces could be good, likeable and admirable, loving and so on, while in their malevolent nature assumes the direct opposite of the above-mentioned attributes. Tempels stresses that in their benevolence and malevolence, vital forces though "secrets," "unknown" and even "unseen," have the capacity to intervene, and indeed, they do intervene in events including those that are consciously planned. It suffices to note that this scenario is in absolute tandem with the Tiv people (often referred to as people of Bantu stock as history migration claimed that the ethnic group numbering more than five million have cultural affinity with the Bantu) whose concept of witchcraft connotes both malevolent and benevolent. The traditional Tiv man has absolute belief in witchcraft especially when his plans are punctuated by unforeseen circumstances.

- Potency: in Tempels' consideration of vital force, the idea of potency is deeply rooted. Tempels avers that vital forces can be strengthened or weekend or increased or decreased based on the position they occupy on the hierarchy.

It must be placed on note that according to Tempels these characteristics of vital forces as known or understood are far more matter of experience and of intuition rather than that of a study.[62] This is what informs Azenabor's conviction that "A force is in relation to other forces. This is why lineage and its solidarity had been said to constitute an important aspect of Africanity."[63]

Tempel's seminal work: *Bantu Philosophy* suffered both negative and positive criticisms from philosophers and other scholars. This situation is not out of place. However, as Azenabor rightly notes, "The work of Tempels has become one of those that have tremendous influence on the way most later day African scholars and non-scholars alike, both Africans and non-Africans tend to view, interpret and present the ontologies of African peoples."[64] One of the later day African scholar is Alexis Kagame, a Rwandan Bantu Catholic Priest. Prompted by Tempels' findings, Kagame as a philosopher, anthropologist, linguist and theologian took up the task of validating the claims of Tempels regarding the Bantus.[65] Employing the method of linguistic analysis, he advanced the idea of *being* which he refers to as NTU. NTU is the determinative stem of all forces. In other words, all forces are derivable from the main force NTU. According to Janheiz Jahn, "NTU is a vital force that is traceable to all forces. NTU is being itself the cosmic universal force. … It is the force in which being and beings coalesce."[66] Beyond validating that the Bantus have Muntu, Kintu, Hantu and Kintu forces as stated by Tempels, Jahn moves further to demonstrate that these forces originate from the main force known as NTU. Though the ultimate universal principle, NTU is the determinative stem of all forces. In other words, all forces are derivable from the main force NTU. Though the ultimate universal principle, NTU according to Jahn is not reducible to God. NTU is within all beings or forces and, therefore, does not stand in isolation of beings. NTU is also regarded as the ultimate source from which creation flows. NTU as such is a process which is expressible in the following categories:

1. Muntu: These are intelligent forces. They include human beings, gods, spirits, ancestors, special trees, Poteau-mitan in voodoo, pathways of the gods and so on.
2. Kintu: This category comprises of unintelligent forces like some trees/plants (some trees/plants part of Muntu), animals, inorganic materials, tools and implements and so on.
3. Hantu: The forces under this category are only concerned with space and time, that is, being engrossed with particular places and time, they can alter or change events as planned in particular places at particular times.

4. Kuntu: Forces subsumed under Kuntu are forces of abstract modalities. They are concerned with matters of aesthetics, affection, love, emotions, feelings, laughter and so on.

It is not in doubt here that though Tempels and Kagame are unanimous in admitting that the Bantus have a concept known as vital or life force, they have different understanding of vital force all together; nevertheless, the concept of vital force has remained very critical to African Philosophy and precisely African metaphysics.

Causality

Causality and cause are related terms or concepts. They are both nouns. As matter of fact, cause is written in most cases as cause and effect which oftentimes is referred to as causality. The Encyclopedia of Religion and Ethics Vol. 2 says "cause is an object, event or process in virtue of which some object, event or process comes to exist or occur."[67] In other words in a situation of cause, there is always going to be a certain result. This means that the cause serves as the situation that produces a causality is the causative agent that produces a particular effect. Thus, the concept of causality positively connotes *anything which has a positive influence of any sort on the being or happening of something else*.[68]

In the history of the concept of cause, Aristotle easily stands out as someone who made an elaborate contribution regarding the concept. Recall his four causes: the material cause, the formal cause, the efficient cause and the final cause.[69] David Hume, a British empiricist philosopher also spared some critical thoughts regarding the notion of causality. We are not immediately concerned about what they advocated since the interest of this chapter has no direct bearing on Western thought but rather African thought.

The African conception of causality is best periscope on the background of the African metaphysical worldview, where reality is considered holistically the world, or reality to the African is that it is primarily spiritual.[70] It is on this note that the virtual force discussed by Tempels and Kagame becomes very relevant here.

The Yoruba idea of causality has a Metaphysico-Religious undertone Sodipo in his article: "Notes on the Concept of Cause and Chance in Yoruba Traditional Thought" identifies *Olorun* as "the ultimate cause of all visible processes in the world but the actions and plan of the lesser gods constitute important secondary causes. Human beings seek the special favours of these lesser deities through sacrifice and worship because of the important influence they exert on visible process."[71] For sacrificing to, and worshipping the lesser gods, Sodipe explains that these deities allocate to men or human beings some special powers and protective mechanisms. Meanwhile, sacrifices are not just made, the services of the *Ifa* priests are sought in order to know which god to sacrifice to. Apart from *Olorun* and the lesser deities which constitute one segment of cause in Yoruba worldwide, Sodipo further identifies man's or an individual's *Ori* (the guardian spirit). According to Sodipo, "the *Ori* is the bearer of one's destiny. If a man is destined lucky his affairs usually prosper (barring the influence if witches or an angry god) but if his *Ori* is an unfortunate one, then his affairs are usually ill-fated."[72] It is on this elaborate background that Sodipo embarked on the task of distinguishing between cause and chance among the Yoruba in his theory of causality. In addition, the theory shows how the African and Western (i.e. scientific) concepts of causality differ. According to Sodipo, the Yoruba traditional thinker understands what it means to say that the chances of a Kobo (unloaded) turning up head on a toss is 1 in 2, for he has thrown up, or has seen thrown up, a coin a number of times and has observed that the coin turns head roughly half the number of times and tails the remaining half. Premised on this general understanding, Sodipe recalls a a scenario where one competitor wins and the other loses in a competition for a prize by applying the toss of a coin.[73] In Sodipo's conversation with ten Yoruba people whose views are a reflection of the Yoruba tradition worldwide, only one said the winner won by luck while the remaining said the gods or a god must have ruled in favor of the winner. Sodipo in order to convince his interlocutors to understand, said, "a coin would fall head roughly half the number of times and tails the remaining half, the answer was given that although the coin could on its own fall head or tails, if anything was at stake for man in the fall of the coin, it would fall for the man in whose favour a god is ranged." [74] This succinct submission invariably rules out chance in Yoruba belief. A Yoruba man is not oblivious of the fact of the chances of a kobo falling 50/50, that is, the head and the tail. However, when something is at stake like a prize to be won, many hidden factors come to play or take charge like the gods or a god, in order to determine the outcome. In the words of Sodipo, for these, hidden factors are under the control of the gods and in these situations; it is wise to leave one's decision to divine guidance; the concept of chance plays no part at all."[75]

Sodipo's recourse to the gods or some hidden factors being responsible for the outcome of a tossed coin has been criticized for failing to take the general laws of scientific investigation to its logical conclusion. As such, the question 'how' gives way too soon to the question of why 'here and now.' Besides, it is observed that as soon as the gods take over, the principle of explanation becomes personal. Rather than consider this view as a criticism to Sodipo, it is a proof that his theory of causality is not only understood; it is also appreciated. Sodipo explains this further that "because the principle of explanation is personal, explanations are necessarily given in terms of the motives, which lay behind the events."[76] Recall that the Africans entertain the belief that every individual has his/her personal god *Ori* that gives them protection. This is the situation that gives credence to the principle of personal explanation.

To buttress the principle of personal explanation, Sodipo provides the following analogy:

> The lorry driver who ties a charm to his lorry-seat and a magical object under the lorry's windscreen is not denying or trying to frustrate any of the general laws by

which motor vehicle operates. He knows as well as any scientific man, that of the brakes fail while the vehicles moving at high speed there could be a serious accident: he is aware too that if the accident is serious enough, some passengers could die. But the general laws cannot answer for him the question where and when the brakes will fail, whether they will fail when the lorry is travelling at high or low speed and, should that happen, who of the passengers will be fatally wounded.[77]

Sodipo further explains that the person with a scientific orientation will stretch the application of the general laws further as they could go, and if the answer is not got, everything will be handled over to chance. Contrary to this, he states that to the traditional Yoruba man, even when the general law says it is only 1 person out of the 100 passengers in the lorry involved in the accident that would be saved, the Yoruba man strongly believes that it is the gods and not chance that would decide who survives. Thus, to the Yoruba's, it is certainly worth doing everything possible to be the one who would be saved in the accident even if it means using a charm or making some necessary sacrifices to some god or gods for such a favor. It is this absence of the concept of chance in Yoruba traditional thought that distinguishes it from the concept of causality in an African thought as expounded by Sodipo explains the why, the how and the where of the events.

Witchcraft

The phenomenon of witchcraft and its attendant consequence is not uncommon to the African people and even elsewhere. Mbiti narrates thus:

> Every African who has group up in the traditional environment will, no doubt, know something about this mystical power which often is experienced. Or manifests itself, in the form of magic, divination, witchcraft and mysterious phenomena that seem to defy even immediate scientific explanation.[78]

This goes to say that to the African, witchcraft is integral to his being and that it is a phenomenon that he/she lives with and consciously or unconsciously partakes in. This is the position of Oluwole who defines witchcraft as "a peculiar power by virtue of which some people perform actions which the ordinary man cannot normally perform."[79] Oluwole explains further that the most unique and mysterious characteristic of the power of witchcraft is its ability to affect its victims without any physical contact or application of machine. Witchcraft is simply a spiritual force; it is not seen but is only identified in its manifestations. Witchcraft could be malevolent or benevolent. The power of the malevolent witchcraft is to destroy or cause harm to the victim, while the benevolent type gives protection to the individual. Magicians, sorcerers, witches/wizards and nature doctors are the agents through which the power of witchcraft manifest.

Reincarnation

Conventionally, reincarnation is taken as the rebirth of a dead parent. Unlike the Hindu understanding of rebirth (*Samsara*), where the soul goes through rebirths in order to purify it, A.O Echekwube says reincarnation in the African context "is more reflective of metempsychosis or transmigration, ideas which purports that the soul of the deceased goes to inhabit a new body."[80] Reincarnation in the African context is not construed in the classical sense of the soul being reborn into a body. E. Bolaji Idowu maintains that "the deceased persons do 'reincarnate' in their ground children and great-grand children ... they do 'reincarnate,' not only in one grand-child or great-grant child, but also in several contemporary grandchildren and great-grandchildren who are brothers and sisters and cousins, aunts, and nephews, uncles and nieces, ad infinitum."[81] Idowu stresses that despite this reincarnation, the deceased continues to live in the afterlife while maintaining communion with those family members in the world. The deceased ancestral qualities remain intact despite his reincarnation.

Reincarnation finds justification based on three beliefs. According to Oluwole, "there is family resemblance, the Abiku or Ogbanje Syndrome and memory transfer."[82] Meanwhile, it suffices to point out that a deceased male cannot reincarnate in a female and vice versa. Oracles are usually consulted to know which ancestor reincarnated when a child is three months old. Among the Tiv of Nigeria, the reincarnated child is given the name of the person he/she has reincarnated, that is, *Ngohide* (Mother is back).

Death and Immortality (After-Life or Life-After Death)

The traditional African to a large extent share the Heideggerian conception of human beings 'beings unto death.' It is accepted as what must come to pass in a life of an individual. However, the African consider death as a transition or a gate-value to another world.

According to Awolalu and Dopamu:

> That death is not the final end and does not write <u>finis</u> to the life of man, that death is only a transition from the physical world to the spirit world, and that the deceased is only making a journey from this earth to another place, is seen in funeral arrangement and burial. The corpse is thoroughly washed; it is laid in state in very good costly cloths in preparation for the journey. It is believed that the deceased is being made ready and fit for the next world.[83]

This succinct contribution by Awolalu and Dopamu captures the general belief of the African people. To the African, there are actually good and bad deaths. A good death is a situation where one dies at a ripe old age. It is such a deceased that attracts the funeral or burial rites described above. On the other hand, Awolalu and Dopamu stress that "children and youths who die a premature death, barren women, and all who die a 'bad' death are killed by *Ayelala*, or *Sango* or *Soponno* cannot be accorded the kind of dignified death as described above."[84] In other words, people who die bad deaths suffer discrimination.

Freedom and Determinism

Freedom connotes the capacity of self-determination, that is, the capacity to decide what to do at every given circumstance. However, this thinking may not be very correct in relation to the African understanding. The African, on the contrary, lives in a pre-determined religio-metaphysical world where he is fated or pre-determined in being. Forces are considered as determinants of his fate and actions. Thus, the African is not truly free as it is considered in Western scientific thinking. One's ability to carry out certain tasks may not yield any fruits if the god or gods rise in opposition.

Mind-Body

To the African belief system, there is no independent matter and independent mind. In other words, reality to the African cannot be singly material and singly immaterial. Thus, to talk of reality is where the material and the immaterial are conjoined. Reality as such is the unity of the Spiritual and the Physical. It is in this view that the African treats mind and body.

In the African theory of Vitalism, mind and body are inseparable elements. They are like two sides of a coin. Writing on this, Egbeke Aja says:

> Neither mind nor body is a completely separate and independent entity. Both mind and matter are expressions of some underlying reality that appears as "mind" when we experience it from the inside, or subjectively, and as body or matter, when we view it from the outside or objectively.[85]

An individual in the African context is taken as unified entity or person: Idong sums up this view thus: "in African culture, the soul, spirit and body co-exist as a unified whole but we can refer to each of them as a substance."[86]

The Person (Personhood)

The question of "what is man?", is an interrogave that Africans answered off-handedly. Man, according to Bolaji Idowu man is body, the concrete, tangible thing of flesh and bones which we know through the sense, which can be described in a general way, or analytically by anatomy. Idowu explains that through it, invisible and intangible, it is that which gives life to the body.[87] *Emi* as described causes the functioning of the body. Its presence in the body keeps it alive while its absence leads to death. However, *Emi* is not to be equated with breath. However, *Emi* should not be equated with breath. It should also be distinguished from *Ori* which Idowu describes as *the inner person* – the personality-soul.[88]

Barry Hallen says a person has three major spiritual components:[89]

1. *Emi* (a) refers to the most important element of human make-ups the heart, (b) a spiritual Emi or soul which is of supreme importance because it is imperishable element of human personality.
2. *Emi* is also taken as the element representing human destiny.
3. Emi is also taken to be Ese (foot/leg).

Emi is considered in both physical and spiritual sense as the symbol of power and activity (Hallen).[90] *Emi* is also taken as the vital, life force) by some scholars.

But it is not all about the Emi or Ori that a person is defined in the African context. For you to refer to as a person, the individual must in fact be living an exemplary life. This point is well made by Kirki-Greene in his article "Mutumin Kirki: The Concept of the Good Man in Hausa."[91] In Hausa-land, the fundamental locus of Kirki is of a man's intrinsic goodness, rests in the *hali* his character. Kirki is thus an inner quality, or an accumulation of qualities. This is precisely the concept of personhood adumbrated by Bathista Mondin, when he informs that a person "is a subsistent, gifted with self-consciousness, communication and transcendence."[92] These attributes are also applicable to the traditional African.

With reference to metaphysics, personhood is understood as a foundational typology of reality that incorporates beings that are rational, moral agents, using language and so on. This concept underscores the fact that a human being is exclusive of a particular hair color, or even having hair, or being a particular height or weight. Metaphysics refers to a realm that transcends the physical. This description of metaphysics as the study of the nature of reality in its most basic forms or categories attempts to stimulate the discussion as to whether everything that exists is physical (material), or whether there are two ultimate kinds of irreducible stuff, mind and matter. For those who believe that the mind and/or soul are not reducible to the physical body posit that they are essential to metaphysical personhood.

On the whole, personhood in Africa conceptualizes a man-centered philosophy of life which argues that the dialectics of social engineering is aimed ultimately at achieving true dignity and development of the whole person and every person. Kaunda informs us on this that the human person is above ideology and above institution and so we must continuously refuse to tie him to anything, and that, society is there because of the human person, and whatever we undertake to do, we have got to remember that the human person is the center of all human society.[93]

An Exposé of Some Ontological Concepts

Ontology as earlier discussed is concerned with what it takes to exist or existence broadly. It is on this premise that we shall be considering the following ontological concepts: god, gods, spirits, person, witches, plants and animals (animate objects) and phenomena and objects without biological life). Though some of these concepts have been elaborately discussed under metaphysics, it is imperative to also give them the African ontological slant.

To say that Africans have their ontology is to say the obvious. African ontology, Mbiti rightly notes, "is religious ontology."[94] It is based on the understanding of this religious ontology that African worldview can be better appreciated. Though the African ontology is so construed, "it is extremely anthropocentric ontology in the sense that everything is seen in terms of its relation to man."[95]

Recall that exact ontology is concerned with the study or investigation of the particular sciences such that scientific tools or methods are deployed in the investigation. Inexact ontology, on the other hand, which is in tandem with African ontology views things in the religion-metaphysical context such that the spirit and the mundane are also prioritized.

- God as earlier discussed is regarded by African as an existing being. As pointed out by Mbiti: "God is the ultimate explanation of the genesis and substance of both man and all things. That is why the African man attributes all events to him: good or bad."[96]
- **Spirits:** to the African, the universe as it exists is a spiritual one. Mbiti explains that spirits are beings made up of superhuman beings and spirits of men who died a long time ago.[97]
- **God:** the African believes in the existence of objectives and these deities are very crucial to his own existence.
- Person or human being or man is an existent that maintains a meaningful relationship with both material and spiritual beings.
- Personhood or humanity comprises all humans living and those yet to be born.
- **Animate Objects:** these include plants and animals as well as other objects that have biological life.
- **Inanimate Objects:** these refer to things or objects that do not have biological life and yet exist and are useful to man. It is on this concatenated relationship that the African ontology is predicated. Nothing is taken in isolation. Mbiti avers that this anthropocentric ontology is a complete unity or solidarity which nothing can break or destroy.[98] To destroy or remove one of these categories is to destroy the whole existence including the destruction of the creator which is impossible.

Conclusion

Our consideration of metaphysical and ontological concepts in African Traditional Religion exposes the underlying thought and belief systems of the African people in their traditional environment. It shows how these concepts overlap in the discussion of other concepts. Metaphysical concepts as discussed here tend to dwell on the epistemic understanding of the concepts, while ontology consideration, on the other hand, espouses the conviction of the African based on what exists.

Notes

1. Jim Unah, (ed) *Metaphysics, Phenomenology and Philosophy*, (Ibadan, 1995), 46.
2. Alloy S. Ihuah, (ed) *Studies in Philosophy and Critical Thinking*, (Lagos: Obaroh & Ogbinaka Publishers, 2013), 65.
3. Dogobert D. Runess, (ed) *Living Schools of 20th Century Philosophy*, (New York, 1958), 157.
4. Joseph Omoregbe, *Metaphysics Without Tears*, (Lagos: Jojah Educational Research Publishers, 1999), 134.
5. Joseph Omoregbe, *Metaphysics Without Tears*, 134.
6. Joseph Omoregbe, *Metaphysics Without Tears*, 73.
7. Jim Unah, *Metaphysics, Phenomenology and Philosophy*, 83.
8. Jim Unah, *Metaphysics, Phenomenology and Philosophy*, 80.
9. Jim Unah, *Metaphysics, Phenomenology and Philosophy*, 88.
10. P. Iroegbu, *Metaphysics: The Kpim of Philosophy*, (Oweri: International Universities Press, 1995), 15.
11. P. Iroegbu, *Metaphysics: The Kpim of Philosophy*, 15.
12. P. Iroegbu, *Metaphysics: The Kpim of Philosophy*, 15.
13. P. Iroegbu, *Metaphysics: The Kpim of Philosophy*, 15.
14. J. Obi Oguejiofor, "Is African Worldview Responsible for the African Predicament?" In *Uche*, Vol. 15, 2009: 1.
15. Robert P. Wolff, *About Philosophy*, (New Jersey: Prentice-Hall International Inc., 1989), 373–4.
16. Robert P. Wolff, *About Philosophy*, 373–4.
17. M.K. Munitz, Existence and Logic, New York, New York University Press, 1974: 42–3.
18. Joseph Omoregbe, *Metaphysics Without Tears*, (Lagos: Jojah Educational Research Publishers, 1999), xiv.
19. Mario Bunge, *Treaties on Basic Philosophy*, Vol. 3; *Ontology: The Furniture of the World*, (Holland: D. Reidel Publishing, 1977), 3.
20. Alfred North Whitehead, *Process and Reality*, (New York, Macmillan, 1929), 36.
21. Joseph Omoregbe, *Metaphysics Without Tears*, xiv.
22. Martin Heidegger, *An Introductin to Metaphysics*, (New York, Yale: Yale University Press, 1959), 1.
23. P. Iroegbu, *Metaphysics: The Kpim of Philosophy*, 60.
24. *Metaphysics, Phenomenology and Philosophy*, 60.
25. Jim Unah, *On Being: Discourse on the Ontology of Man*, (Lagos: Fadec Publishers, 2002), 2.

26. Sydney Hook, *The Quest for Being and other: Studies in Nationalism and Humanism*, (Connecticut: Greenwood Press, 1961), 147.
27. Mario Bunge, *Treaties on Basic Philosophy*, Vol. 3; *Ontology: The Furniture of the World*, (Holland: D. Reidel Publishimg, 1977), 7.
28. Mario Bunge, *Treaties on Basic Philosophy*.
29. Zaato M. Nor, Determinism in Tiv Ontological Belief: An Examination of the Question of the Individual's Freedom" in *Essence Journal* "Concepts in African Philosophy", Vol. 6, No. 1, (2009), 23.
30. Jim Unah, (ed) *Metaphysics, Phenomenology and Philosophy*, 25.
31. Jim Unah, (ed) *Metaphysics, Phenomenology and Philosophy*, 25.
32. Bolaji Idowu, *Olodumare: God in Yoruba Belief*, (Ikeja: Longmans, 1996), 28.
33. Bolaji Idowu, *Olodumare: God in Yoruba Belief*, 28.
34. Ibid. Bolaji Idowu, *Olodumare: God in Yoruba Belief*, 28.
35. Bolaji Idowu, *Olodumare: God in Yoruba Belief*, 29.
36. Bolaji Idowu, *Olodumare: God in Yoruba Belief*, 28–29.
37. John S. Mbiti, *African Religions and Philosophy*, (London Heinemann Educational Books 1982), 29.
38. John S. Mbiti, *African Religions and Philosophy*, 29.
39. S. I. Aderibigbe, *Religious Thoughts in Perspectives: An Introduction to concepts, Approaches and Traditions* (San Diego, CA: Cognella, 2012), 125.
40. John S. Mbiti, *African Religions and Philosophy*, 29.
41. S.I. Aderibigbe, *Religious Thoughts in Perspectives*, 125.
42. John S. Mbiti, *African Religions and Philosophy*, 31.
43. Sophie B. Oluwole, *Witchcraft, Reincarnation and the Godhead*, (Lagos: Excel Publishers, 1992), 74.
44. Sophie B. Oluwole, *Witchcraft, Reincarnation and the Godhead*, 75.
45. Sophie B. Oluwole, *Witchcraft, Reincarnation and the Godhead*, 75.
46. Sophie B. Oluwole, *Witchcraft, Reincarnation and the Godhead*, 76.
47. Sophie B. Oluwole, *Witchcraft, Reincarnation and the Godhead*, 76–7.
48. Sophie B. Oluwole, *Witchcraft, Reincarnation and the Godhead*, 78.
49. Sophie B. Oluwole, *Witchcraft, Reincarnation and the Godhead*, 77.
50. Sophie B. Oluwole, *Witchcraft, Reincarnation and the Godhead*, 83.
51. P. Tempels, *Bantu Philosophy*, (Paris: Presence Africaine, 1959), 33.
52. P. Tempels, *Bantu Philosophy*, 41.
53. K.C Anyanwu, "Presuppositions of African Socialism" in *The Nigerian Journal of Philosophy*, Vol. 3, No. 1 & 2, (1983), 50.
54. Godwin Azenabor, *Modern Theories in African Philosophy*, 2010. 39.
55. P. Tempels, *Bantu Philosophy*, 33.
56. Sophie B. Oluwole, *Witchcraft, Reincarnation and the Godhead*, 83.
57. Azenabor, G., *Modern Theories in African Philosophy*, 39.
58. Azenabor, G., *Modern Theories in African Philosophy*, 4.
59. P. Tempels, *Bantu Philosophy*, 41.
60. P. Tempels, *Bantu Philosophy*, 263.
61. Janheiz Jahn, *Muntu: An Outline of the New African Culture*, (Trans. By Grene, M, New York: Grove Press, 1961), 101.
62. P. Tempels, *Bantu Philosophy*, 75.
63. Azenabor, G., *Modern Theories in African Philosophy*, 10.

64. Azenabor, G., *Modern Theories in African Philosophy*, 42.
65. Janheiz Jahn, *Muntu: An Outline of the New African Culture*, 102.
66. Janheiz Jahn, *Muntu: An Outline of the New African Culture*, 101.
67. *The Encyclopedia of Religion and Ethnics* Vol. 2, 1980: 102.
68. P. Coffey, *Ontology Or the Theory of Being*, (London: Longmans, Green and Co., 1918), 210.
69. Joseph I. Omoregbe, *A Simplified History of Western Philosophy, Vol. 1; Ancient and Medieval Philosophy*, (Lagos: Joja Educational Research and Publishers, 1991), 53.
70. C. S. Momoh, (ed) *The Substance of African Philosophy*, (Auchi: African Philosophy Project Publication, 2000), 18.
71. O. Sodipo, "The Nature of Cause and Chance in Yoruba Traditional Thought", in Fadahunsi & Oladipo (ed) *Philosophy and he African Prospect: Selected Essays in Honour of Professor J. Olubi Sodipo on Philosophy, Culture and Society*, (Ibadan Hope Publications, 2004), 81–2.
72. O. Sodipo, "The Nature of Cause and Chance in Yoruba Traditional Thought" 82.
73. O. Sodipo, "The Nature of Cause and Chance in Yoruba Traditional Thought" 85.
74. O. Sodipo, "The Nature of Cause and Chance in Yoruba Traditional Thought" 86.
75. O. Sodipo, "The Nature of Cause and Chance in Yoruba Traditional Thought" 86.
76. O. Sodipo, "The Nature of Cause and Chance in Yoruba Traditional Thought" 86.
77. O. Sodipo, "The Nature of Cause and Chance in Yoruba Traditional Thought" 89.
78. John S. Mbiti, *African Religions and Philosophy*, 194.
79. Sophie B. Oluwole, *Witchcraft, Reincarnation and the Godhead*, 3.
80. C. S. Momoh, (ed) *The Substance of African Philosophy*, 261.
81. Bolaji Idowu, *Olodumare: God in Yoruba Belief*, 209.
82. Sophie B. Oluwole, *Witchcraft, Reincarnation and the Godhead*, 43–4.
83. Awolalu & Dopamu, *West African Traditional Religion*, (Okeja: Onibonoje Press, 1979), 256.
84. Awolalu & Dopamu, *West African Traditional Religion*, 254–5.
85. Aja, E., *Elements of Theory of Knowledge*, (Enugu: Magnet Business Company), 2004), 144.
86. Idang, G.E., "The Mind-Body Problem in African Culture" in Uduigwemen, A.F, (ed) *Footmark in African Philosophy*, (Lagos: Obaro & Ogbinaka Publishers, 2009), 146.
87. Bolaji Idowu, *Olodumare: God in Yoruba Belief*, 179.
88. Bolaji Idowu, *Olodumare: God in Yoruba Belief*, 180.
89. C. S. Momoh, (ed) *The Substance of African Philosophy*, 298.
90. C. S. Momoh, (ed) *The Substance of African Philosophy*, 298.
91. Kirl-Green, Anthony, "Mutumin Kirki: The Concept of a God Man in Hausa", in Momoh, C.S. (ed) *The Substance of African Philosophy*, (Auchi: African Philosophy Project Publication, 2000) 246.

92. Bathista Mondin, *Philosophical Anthropology*, (Urbaniana University Press 2007), 257.
93. Kaunda, K: *A Humanist in Africa*, (Marshville: Abingdon Press, 1966), 103.
94. John S. Mbiti, *African Religions and Philosophy*, 15.
95. John S. Mbiti, *African Religions and Philosophy*, 5.
96. John S. Mbiti, *African Religions and Philosophy*, 16.
97. John S. Mbiti, *African Religions and Philosophy*, 16.
98. John S. Mbiti, *African Religions and Philosophy*, 16.

CHAPTER 5

The Concept and Worship of the Supreme Being

Dorothy Nguemo Afaor

INTRODUCTION

Religion in Africa is pervasive and all-encompassing. It is within the realm of religion that the idea of a Supreme Being is conceived. Due to its insidious nature, religion can be a burdensome word to clarify. This difficulty is in part of the lack of consensus amongst cultural groups about the conception of God or the Supreme Being which is often central in religions. In other words, because of the complex nature of religion, a definition of religion that is both concise and comprehensive as well as universally acceptable is elusive. That notwithstanding, it makes sense to argue that religion is the awareness of the existence of a Supreme Being and it is this awareness that culminates into worship. Interestingly, it is equally discovered that almost all people who follow some form of religion believe that a divine power created the world and influences their lives. In summary, religion seems to be understood briefly as an expression of faith and belief. It is said to be the conscious and subconscious response to the ultimate source of existence referred to as God in whichever name or language.[1]

To cap it up, Metuh asserts that "Religion is an institutionalized system of symbols, beliefs, values, and practices focused on the relationship between God and man, and between men living in society".[2] For the Africans specifically, religion deals with questions of human existence that is deep and serious such as, Why do men suffer? What is the real meaning of existence? And what

D. N. Afaor (✉)
Benue State University, Makurdi, Nigeria

© The Author(s), under exclusive license to Springer Nature Switzerland AG 2022
I. S. Aderibigbe, T. Falola (eds.), *The Palgrave Handbook of African Traditional Religion*, https://doi.org/10.1007/978-3-030-89500-6_5

happens to our souls after death? Thus, African Traditional Religion is heavily centered on important elements, such as rituals, festivals, societies and brotherhoods.

The fact that African Traditional Religion focuses on the society also shows its deep foundation on intersubjectivity of men. As such, African religion contains within its practice, an idea of One Supreme Being. This Supreme Being is approached in collaboration with several other deities or spiritual forces usually symbolized in material insignias representing their presence. Basically, suffice to say that, like the Abrahamic Religions, African Traditional Religion has at its center a Supreme Being who regulates phenomena. The Supreme Being is approachable only through its lesser deities and spirit beings. At the same time, the diversity of deities or spirit mediums explains the multiplicity of religious phenomena in Africa. The relationship between the sacred (for instance, the Supreme Being and divinities) and the profane finds expression in beliefs, worships, creeds and symbols.

THE IDEA OF THE SUPREME BEING IN AFRICA

Virtually all religions conceive an existence of a Supreme Being whose adherents revere and worship. Among the several perspectives, the Supreme Being in every religious worldview is equally considered to be both the inventor and orchestrator of the entire universe. As many as there are ethnic communities in Africa, so there are also varying concepts of the Supreme, though with similar attributes. Within each of these communities, the Supreme Being is granted due respect.

A survey across selected major African ethnic nationalities proves that the concept of the Supreme Being varies greatly but applies to all peoples. Additionally, the Supreme Being goes by a wide range of names that diverges amongst communities. Some of these names can be found below:

Country in Africa	Names for the Supreme Being
Burundi	Imana
Botswana	Modimo, Urezhwa
Ivory Coast	Nyame, Onyabkopon
Mozambique	Muungu
Liberia	Yala
Nigeria	Aondo, Chukwu, Olorun, Owo, Ubangiji, Osowo, Olodumare, Hinegba, Ojo
Cameroon	Njinyi, Nyooiy
Burkina Faso	Na'angmin

The above are the names of the Supreme Being among ethnic groups in Africa; some directly translate only as God while others are descriptive. From this list, it is evident that African communities believe reverently in the idea of Supreme Being as well as hold him in high regard. In every African dialect, there is, at minimum, one name assigned to the Supreme Being. Due to the age of some names, in particular the ones that developed in antiquity, their meaning has been lost. However, in a majority of instances, these descriptive names have unique meanings, and in some languages, there are even up to ten names for the Supreme Being. This demonstrates the level of affection, belief and love the Africans accord to the Supreme Being. Certainly, there are lots of literature about the Supreme Being to show his uniqueness and infallibility among the people.

On one hand, the Belief in a Supreme Being originated from the reflections of people regarding the cosmos. Due to earth's enormity and continuity, as well as the celestial bodies overall, mankind assumed that the universe was governed by a superior, though invisible, mind. Many are convinced that without the Supreme Being, the world would cease to function which caused man to deduce that the universe has a just inventor. On the other hand, the helplessness of humanity in the face of nature placed him at crossroads. Subsequently, his inability to tame natural disaster such as famine, drought, earthquakes, epidemics and, especially, death makes fidgety to search for answers. His limitations made him not only to search for a superpower, but also to believe that his alliance or subjection to this Supernatural force will help resolve his puzzles. On the final analysis, man had no other choice than to turn to the Supreme Being.

Furthermore, the belief in the Supreme Being may have also arisen by the powers of the weather, storms, thunder and lightning and the idea of day and night, the appearance of the stars, moon and sun. These heavenly bodies and powers made people to start having a re-think about a Supreme Being. People depended on heavenly bodies and power for light, warmth, rain and so on. It then became clear that there is an invisible Supreme Being who is responsible for providing man with his needs. People nursed the belief in the Supreme Being and as such, it began to make sense and fit into man's continued attempts to understand and explain the visible and invisible universe. All Africans have ideas about the Supreme Being and the activities in the invisible world. This includes what he does, his human pictures, his nature and the relationship he has with everyone.[3]

The question is, what does Supreme Being do? Certainly, the Supreme Being is regarded as both glorious and might. All these point to the fact that the Supreme Being protects and sustains every visible and the invisible things in the world. Moreover, many people conceive the Supreme Being as a father figure; therefore, it follows that they regard themselves as his children.

Most traditional concepts of the Supreme Being portray it anthropologically as having eyes, ears, nose and so on and that he hears and sees everything. People also describe the Supreme Being as possessing moral attitudes such as mercifulness, kindness, loving and so on. Not only can the Supreme Being be far and near, but he is unchanging as well as all-powerful. Even though the Supreme Being is described as being capable of all tasks, it is interesting to note that he would be ascribed human characteristics, especially since he is not considered human. Such mental image supports our understanding of the Supreme

Being. The mental images also assist the mind to develop a working knowledge of the Supreme Being and help people in communicating their ideas about it.

Aondo: *A Tiv Concept of the Supreme Being*

One of the earliest authors on Tiv religion, Downes R.M, wrote that "*Aondo* is the Tiv name for the above, the firmament that has been described as the vault of heaven with its clouds and stars, its thunder and lightning, winds and rain, cold an heat and this was all that in the same terms as all phenomena as a non-personal power".[4] This description shows that the Tiv people acknowledge, locate or associate their *Aondo* (God, Supreme Being) with the sky, probably a sky Being. All phenomena in the firmament by this understanding are mere products of His handiwork. He is clearly the architect of their creation or existence. Downes, R.M. further stated that:

> This power from above was connected in the minds of the people with other powerful forces that affect the life of man, such as fire, and iron and so was superior to all other powers. The great unknown above is *Aondo*, which in popular allusions consists of iron, possibly because of meteorites. Here the sun arises, proceeds across the sky and sets; it is put in motion by *Aondo*.[5]

The idea here alludes that apart from *Aondo*, the Tiv believe in the existence of lesser forces that are subjected to the supremacy of *Aondo*. *Aondo* has power over all other forces with whom they are interconnected. In the same way, everything that emanates from the sky above, on earth or under the earth is regarded as the *Aondo* power functioning. Similarly, Dzurgba captured that:

> *Aondo* is the Supreme Being. His size is indicated by the firmament and the earth. His power, wisdom, presence, Supremacy and sovereign authority are expressed in nature, functions continuity and mysteries of objects, abstract forces and experiences such as mountains, valleys, thunder, lightning, darkness, sickness and death. All the emanations from the firmament are the functions of Aondo. Thus, God flashes, thunders, rains, shine the sun, darken the earth and blow the wind. God is the primary cause of all events in the universe in general and in human affairs in particular.[6]

Both Downes and Dzurgba hold similar understandings of the Tiv religious conception of *Aondo*. *Aondo* is presented in their view as the sky power that underlies all phenomena in the entire universe. As such, allusions are usually made to God in various maxims. For instance, Downes notes that "when it thunders or lightning flashes, the Tiv will say that "*Aondongukumen*" (God roars), or *Aondonyiar, Aondongu noon* (God is raining)";[7] while Dzurgba reiterates that "Aondo is the creator of the vault of heaven in the sky (*shaabeen*) and the earth, *Tar* which also means the world or the universe".[8]

Another author, Torkula, states that "though *Aondo* is the Tiv word for God—the Supreme Being, the Tiv do not have a personal relationship with

Him. *Aondo* used to live nearer the earth but was forced to retreat into the skies after he was struck by a woman pounding food. There is however a deep acknowledgment of the hand of the Supreme Being (*Aondo*) in the physical setting as in rain (*Aondongu noon*), thunder (*Aondongukumen*), lightening (*Aondongunyiar*) and sunlight (*Aondo ta yange*)".[9]

This understanding differed slightly from that expressed by Downes. This is because Torkula attached anthropomorphic elements to *Aondo* such as body (e.g. eyes, ears, head, etc.) as well as emotions like anger and happiness. This can be seen in his statement above that "*Aondo* used to live nearer the earth but was forced to retreat into the skies after he was struck by a woman pounding food".[10] For one to be hit implies that he/she has a body and, consequently, some sort of emotions. However, other scholars too confirm Torkula's position. For instance, Dzurgba narrates the Tiv religious myth of the early relationship between *Aondo* and the Tiv with anthropomorphic connotations. He stated that:

> From the beginning, God's residence was very close to the earth (tar) and there was a direct communication between God and the people. Thus, the Tiv people could consult with God very easily on matters of interest. The relationship between God and the Tiv was very harmonious and cordial. Life was very good (*uma doo kpishi or tar doo kpishi*). The Tiv will speak of *ya tar* which literally means "eat the earth". But it actually means "enjoy life"...thus, the conditions of life were very good. But a terrible thing happened which destroyed the harmonious and cordial relationship between *Aondo* and the Tiv. On a certain day, a woman was threshing millet (Amine) in a mortal at the back of her house. She raised the pestle too high and it hit God. It hurt God and God was very angry (*ishimavihiAondokpishi*) and God ascended up (*Aondokondoyemsha*). This is the reason God is far away from the people. This refers to the firmament, the vaults of heaven as the residence of God. The direct communication with God was no longer possible. But God created divinities which deal with human affairs.[11]

Furthermore, Atel acknowledges the patriarchal role of *Aondo* in Tiv society and further tried to identify Him as being masculine. He captures that, "the Tiv believed in the existence of a supreme being called *Aondo* (God or the Supreme Being). *Aondo* is conceived as a male and so the Tiv refer to him as *AondoTer* (God Father or God the Father)".[12] Torkula, Dzurgba, Wegh and Atel have acknowledged *Aondo* as having body rather than as a Power, force or spirit, while for Downes, *Aondo* is simply a force in the sky indicated by the firmament.

On his part, Wegh noted that "the association of the Supreme Being called *Aondo* (God) with the sky led Downes to erroneously treat *Aondo* as being synonymous with the firmament and even suggests that the sky is God, just as the sun has being regarded as God".[13] In fact, for him the contrary seems to be the case. The contention here is that certain acts are considered to be Go-acts alone, and one can figure *Aondo* right in the natural phenomenon. For instance, "when it is raining a Tiv man would say that *Aondongu noon* (God is raining)...rain is a symbol of divine presence".[14] By this analysis, Wegh therefore believed that *Aondo* exists in all phenomena of nature and not static or fixed in the sky. *Aondo* is the unseen force guiding all human activities whether those activities be natural or supernatural. Everything at the end will have both its beginning and end in *Aondo*.

Besides, Wang, M.A, in the book *Ieren: An Introduction to Tiv Philosophy*, tries to resolve the contention between Downes and Wegh (i.e. whether Aondo is identifiable with the firmament or not). He first and foremost introduced a distinction between "*Aondo*" and "*aondo*" (i.e. the use of capital initial "A"). He stated that "the word *Aondo* is used in two senses: the first being identified with the sky and the second is the creator ... the difference in the use of the initial letter for the word".[15] He demonstrates that the initial low case "a" as in **aondo** is used to refer to the sky, and the upper case "A" as in **Aondo** is used to refer to the creator God. The conception that has survived to this time is that which is synonymous with the supernatural being and creator. In popular parlance, therefore, *Aondo* is the creator and also referred to as the *Usha* (the above, Lord of the firmament).

From the foregoing, therefore, it is comprehensible that in Tiv religion *Aondo* is unanimously conceived and explained as the Supreme Being responsible for the existence of the universe and all other realities of the world. Although it is not crystal clear, yet on the real nature of God among Tiv, it becomes a matter of contextual analysis. Whether *Aondo* exists as a spirit-force without a body, as argued by Downes earlier, or is embodied and can respond to stimuli as described by Torkula, Dzurgba, Wegh and Atel later are still to be determined or researched.

But on a more rationalized ground, *Aondo* cannot possess a body. First, this position will mean reducing God to a mere human being or superhuman. Second, it will lessen or disqualify some of the attributes to Him such as Immortality and Transcendence because the human flesh and blood are subject to decomposition or corruption. Hence, *Aondo* cannot be reduced to possessing human qualities and attributes, He remains an incorporeal being, a spirit-force that resides in the spirit realm and manifest in the natural phenomena. In Tiv religion also, there are various attributes to *Aondo* in spite of the uncertainties surrounding the knowledge of his real nature. For instance, Shishima, S.D. and Dzurgba, A. has identified some of these attributes to include "God is the Creator, God is Omnipotent, God is Immortal, God is Transcendent, God is Omnipresent, God is Omniscient".[16]

God is a personal being, a conscious being, who knows everything and can reason; He decides, guides, and directs the universe according to His inscrutable purposes. By His divine providence, He directs the destiny of every person, even down to the least creature in the world. More than this, however, Tiv people believe that goodness, love, kindness and mercy are other essential attributes of God. Only things, which are good, pure and noble, can be and are attributed to God.[17]

According to Shishima and Dzurgba,[18] nothing, which is considered bad, impure, or ignoble, can be associated with Him. It is rather absurd, a contradiction, to predicate any evil of God. One cannot ever say that is God is wicked, unjust, deceptive or that He is a liar. Rather, when a Tiv faces a crisis, he wonders why God has permitted it, but finally assumes that it is God's will. In such cases, sympathizers say to the bereaved "Be comforted, God has done His will". Death is the greatest evil in the Tiv people experience, but "God's death" is never questioned and sometimes is even seen as an occasion of great rejoicing. God's moral attributes, His goodness, kindness, mercy, love, justice and so forth, are acclaimed in many proverbs, expressions, and personal names of Tiv people.[19]

Akombo *(deities): Between the Supreme Being and Man in Tiv*

Akombo in Tiv worldview is a very complex phenomenon that deals with the Tiv magico-religious practices that comprise of deities or divinities, cults and spiritual forces. Rupert maintained that, "the origin of the *Akombo* practices amongst the Tiv is very old" (see Note 16). In the Tiv ontological order, *Akombo* appear as the most interactive forces that catch the glimpse of everyone. *Akombo* are the mystical forces that are found in both the animate and the inanimate beings. Since they are forces in spiritual nature, their presence is only witnessed in the various manifestations and emblems. Moti, J.S. and Wegh, F.S. remarked that:

> The Tiv believed that the natural order should function for the good of man, the land as well as the women should be fertile, and human beings should enjoy good health and fortune. To this end, Aondo has given man Akombo (cosmic—natural forces). Akombo are the mystical forces represented in cultic emblems. They are neutral force, being reproductive as well as destructive...the objects that constitute these emblems are part of the material culture, and include pieces of pottery, feathers, and bones of animals (human) or carved images.[20]

There is a general belief that divinities are a derivation of the Supreme Being. They assist him in the control and maintenance of the universe. They can be termed "intermediaries"; they have the attributes and characteristics of God. A host of others considers them to be offsprings of the Supreme Being.[21] This is the idea that Moti and Wegh try to affirm above. However, Utov, C.I and Ioratim-Uba disagree with the submission that God created *Akombo* and handed to man to be used in regulating social order. According to them, *Akombo* were not created by God and therefore have no connection with him; hence, for them this might be a pre-Christian belief or practice.

Obviously, Utov and Uba are seemingly sympathizers of the Christian faith that pays no heed to any negativity in relation with God. Meanwhile, while we may have some concerns for the Christian faith, we must as well address some loopholes to this submission. First and foremost, Moti and Wegh point out the following:

> When the Tiv say that God created Akombo they do not mean that God did this physically and then handed over all the finished products. The understanding here is that God has endowed created order with various forms of potential power and goodness. After all, when God created the world he saw that everything was good...Akombo are linked with therapeutic practice of the Tiv to deal with the needs of life outside technical control. These include disasters, misfortune, illnesses, death and to ensure genral well-being.[22]

Torkula sees *Akombo* as the second basic concept in Tiv Religion after the Supreme Being which can be defined as some unique mystical forces deployed to ensure a balanced and healthy *tar* (community) in which individuals are at peace with each other and the physical components of the environment are regulated and protected from "damage". Each *kombo* (singular of *Akombo*) is represented by an emblem, which could be any relic ranging from a potsherd to a carved piece of wood.[23]

Though an acceptable classification of the whole range of *Akombo* is yet to be done here, the Tiv see *Akombo* in two major categories. Category one is *Akombo a kiriki* (lesser *Akombo*) while category two is *Akomboatamen* (greater *Akombo*). Each ailment and socio-economic component in society has its *kombo* with full compliments of emblem and a structured process of "restoration" (*sorun*) when its foundation is undermined or violated by people who come into contact with it. Each *kombo* has its master whose specialty is in ensuring a viable role for the *kombo* in the community. He does this by "restoring" (*sorun*) the *kombo's* equilibrium if and when it is violated, thus neutralizing the damage that would otherwise have been visited on the violator or even the whole community as the case may be.[24]

Torkula, A.A, in another publication *The Cosmology in Tiv Worldview*, emphasizes the importance of *Akombo* in Tiv religion as a weapon in the hands of the elders to regulate the behavior of members of the community. He emphasized that,

> It is believed to have supernatural powers is used to enforce decisions, ensure societal cohesion and punishment against offenders. Akomboor divinity as a cosmic force or power ensures peace, good health, fertility of the soil and of women. Akombois believed to create wealth and its socio-political and economic importance lie in its application which ensures the stability of the society. Akomboalso checks crime in respect of protected properties or farm produce.[25]

Conclusion

From the discussion above, it is observed that the concept of the Supreme Being is conceived by all Africans. The idea of a spiritual being which created and sustains the universe is a manifest in most human societies around the world. Although it is conceived by all groups, the concept of the Supreme Being comes in different names depending on the ethnic group or language. Hence, the conception of the Supreme Being is not unanimous. In all African cultures, the Supreme Being is the life-giver, the maker of humanity, controller of the universe including the celestial bodies and so on. The devotion to the Supreme Being can be traced through people's thought as well as their worship rituals. Therefore, it is worthy to conclude here that, in spite of a general perspective of a Supreme Being, the conception differs from one tradition, tribal or religious group to the other. Again, some African communities practice a kind of monotheism while others are polytheistic. And finally, the worship rituals relating the Supreme Being vary from one community or locality to another.

NOTES

1. Kitause, R.H. "Moral Decadence: A Challenge to Sustainable Development in Contemporary Nigeria" in *Journal of Sustainable Development* (Vol. 2, No. 1, 2012), 202.
2. Metuh, E.I. *God and Man in African Religion* (London: Geoffery Chapman, 1981), 11.
3. Shishima, S.D. and Dzurgba, A. *African Traditional Religion and Culture* (Lagos: National Open University of Nigeria, 2012), 81.
4. Downes, R.C. *Tiv Religion* (Ibadan: Ibadan University Press, 1971), 17.
5. Ibid.
6. Dzurgba, A. *On the Tiv of Central Nigeria: A Cultural Perspective* (Ibadan: John Archers Publishers, 2007), 175.
7. Downes, R.C. *Tiv Religion*, 17.
8. Dzurgba, A. *On the Tiv of Central Nigeria: A Cultural Perspective* (Ibadan: John Archers Publishers, 2007), 170.
9. Torkula, A.A. *The Cosmology of Tiv Worldview* (Makurdi: Oracle Business Limited, 2006), 20.
10. Ibid.
11. Dzurgba, A. *On the Tiv of Central Nigeria: A Cultural Perspective* (Ibadan: John Archers Publishers, 2007), 175–176.
12. Atel, E.T. *Dynamics of Tiv Religion and Culture: A Philosophical-Theological Perspective* (Lagos: Free Enterprise Publications, 2004), 28.
13. Wegh, F.S. *Between the Continuity and Change: Tiv Concept on Traditional and Modernity* (Lagos: OVC Ltd, 1998), 62.
14. Ibid., 63.
15. Wang, A.M. *Ieren: An Introduction to Tiv Philosophy* (Makurdi: Obeta Continental Press, 2004), 24.
16. Shishima, S.D. and Dzurgba, A. *African Traditional Religion and Culture*, 85.
17. Ibid., 85.
18. Ibid., 85.
19. Ibid., 85.
20. East, R.N. (trans.) *Akiga's Story: The Tiv Tribe as seen by one of its Member* (Ibadan: Caltop Publications, 1939), 205.
21. Shishima, S.D. and Dzurgba, A. *African Traditional Religion and Culture*, 85.

22. Moti, J.S. and Wegh, F.S. *An Encounter Between Tiv Religion and Christianity* (Enugu: Snaap Press, 2001), 25.
23. Ibid., 26–27.
24. Torkula, A.A. *The Cosmology of Tiv Worldview*, 24.
25. Ibid., 26.

CHAPTER 6

Beliefs and Veneration of Divinities

Lydia Bosede Akande and Olatunde Oyewole Ogunbiyi

INTRODUCTION

African Religion is the indigenous religion of the African people. This religion has been a part of their lives from the beginning of time. Their religion is structured on the belief in five pillars of faith. These pillars include belief in God or the Supreme Being, belief in Divinities, belief in Ancestors, belief in Spirits, and the belief in the efficacy of magic and medicine. Out of all these perceptions, the divinities occupy an important position in the hearts of African indigenous religion devotees. These beings have been given many names by various writers such as 'gods,' 'demigods,' 'nature spirits,' divinities, and the like.[1] Among the West Africans, the divinities are given much attention to the extent that if care is not taken, a cursory observer might mistake the worship of the divinities as the totality of the religious consciousness of the people of Africa. The towering figure of the divinities above others in the structure of African Religion has led many earlier investigators to the wrong conclusion regarding African Religion. Emil Ludwig, perhaps considering the overbearing presence of the divinities, concludes that God is a philosophical concept that Africans are incapable of conceiving. Apart from this, many wrong nomenclatures have been used to describe the people and their religion due to what was seen about the divinities and their places of abode. Such obnoxious terminologies include 'idolatry' because of the emblems of worship, 'paganism' as a result of the seemingly unattractive place of worship, and 'withdrawn God,' hinting at the popularity of the divinities and little attention that is given to the Supreme Being of the African people.

L. B. Akande (✉) • O. O. Ogunbiyi
University of Ilorin, Ilorin, Nigeria

© The Author(s), under exclusive license to Springer Nature Switzerland AG 2022
I. S. Aderibigbe, T. Falola (eds.), *The Palgrave Handbook of African Traditional Religion*, https://doi.org/10.1007/978-3-030-89500-6_6

Much has been written about the divinities of Africa both by Africans and by non-Africans. The works of Parrinder are worthy of mention among the non-Africans who have devoted time to the portrayal of Africans and their religious consciousness. Two of Parrinder's works are of particular relevance. In *African Mythology*[2] and *African Traditional Religion*,[3] the issues of the divinities were extensively discussed from the viewpoint of an insider rather than an outsider. His works showcase a turn in the scholarship of African Religion devoid of prejudice and color sentiments. Other writers soon rose to present the case of the African people from the proper perspective. These were Africans who were writing for the Africans about the Africans to the world at large. The people were stooped in Christian theology, a tool that enabled them to research African Christian Theology and, by extension African Religion. Their works are pivotal for the generation of new scholars that were soon to take over from them. They can be regarded as the patriarchs of the African Traditional Religious scholarship. Of this group, only two are mentioned herein. They are John S. Mbiti[4] and E. Bolaji Idowu.[5] These two are chosen for this study because of the scope of this work. The second reason why they merit a place in this work is their sphere of influence coupled with their geographical location. While Mbiti was from Kenya, Idowu was a Nigerian. While Mbiti's searchlight focused primarily on East, Central, and Southern Africa, Idowu's work covered West Africa.

Both wrote eloquently and assiduously in defense of African Religion. Their works can be viewed as polemics in the study of African Religion, especially in the area of divinities. More African scholars have arisen after these, and just a few out of the vast array of writers are mentioned. Among those are such scholars like J. Omosade Awolalu[6] and P. A. Dopamu.[7] Aside from their individual books, both writers have written a book together. The efforts of these scholars dig deeper from their patriarch scholars. The authors of *West African Traditional Religion*,[8] for example, identify the divinities that are worshipped in each ethnic group of West Africa. The work of Jemiriye[9] differentiates God from gods, highlighting the fact that the divinities are subordinate to the Supreme Being. Talking about the divinities, Etuk[10] posits that below and subject to the Supreme Being are arrays of divinities that are highly regarded and worshipped by the people.

THE PLACE OF DIVINITIES IN AFRICAN TRADITIONAL RELIGION

Today, African Traditional Religion is gradually enjoying unprecedented attention among devotees and researchers alike. These have put the religion in a better light, making the religion appealing to those living both in and outside Africa. The religion has been transferred from time immemorial to the present time primarily through oral transmission. The religion is indigenous to the people and often referred to as traditional. It has answered their existential questions until foreign religions arrived in the region to challenge the status quo enjoyed by the people's traditional religion. African religion is based on a structure that recognizes the Supreme Being, who occupies the highest stratum of the ladder. Closely following the Supreme Being are the Divinities, followed by the Ancestors and Spirits, respectively. The belief in magic and medicine occupies the lowest rung of the structural ladder of African traditional religious consciousness. Of all the five, the belief in divinities is given more attention than any other of the entities on the spiritual ladder of the people. It should be noted that belief in divinities varies from one locality to another; therefore, it is unclear as to whether all the ethnic groups across Africa worship one divinity or the other. Nevertheless, divinities are popular among the ethnic groups of West Africa who regard them as the objective phenomenon of their religion. In the eastern part of Africa, however, ancestors are given more recognition than the divinities, though they also venerate the divinities. The divinities, where they are given prominence, are the ones that are most worshipped. They are considered a halfway course to the Almighty. Divinities are believed to be able to provide their worshipper with whatever is demanded. They can protect the people from war and environmental challenges. They can be reached on the land, in the water, and virtually anywhere as they occupy the geographical space of the African people. Divinities are so popular that Awosanmi[11] considers the whole religion of the *Yorùbá* as Orisaism.

Identities and Functions of the Divinities

The idea of the divinities is prevalent among the African people, especially the West Africans. To them, the divinities are the objective phenomenon, not the Supreme Being, and neither are the ancestors. In the elucidation of the Africans' divinities, many scholars and commentators have preferred to describe them by the modern-day governance of individual countries. For instance, Idowu[12] portrays them as members of the cabinet in theocratic governance of the world. These have compared them to ministers in the governance of a nation. In their opinions, the divinities are ministers in the theocratic governance of the world; this assertion is anchored on the notion that God is the Supreme Being of the whole universe. Thus, it is in the attempt at governance that he made them overseers in specific compartments of the authority of the whole world. As messengers, their power and authority were given to them by the Supreme Being, making it possible for them to render services to God and men.

The belief in divinities is entrenched throughout sub-Saharan Africa. These divinities are very popular among the Africans because they are believed to have answers to the prayers of their devotees. They are worshipped because they are believed to provide and protect the people of Africa. It is in light of this that Ray[13] observes that the goddess, Yemoja, gains more devotees because of her benevolence to drowning swimmers, victims of accidents on the waterways, and even fishermen. Oladimeji[14] also speaks of the role these divinities play in conflict resolutions in Africa and among the people. However, these divinities are believed to vary in number. The dominance of divinities or ancestors in an area often determines the population of the divinities or ancestors in that particular area. Where there are many divinities like among the *Yorùbá*, the objective phenomena are the divinities.

On the other hand, the objective phenomena of the peoples of East Africa are the ancestors and local spirits. Therefore, they have a lower number of divinities than in West Africa where the number is greater. There exist a few exceptions to this assertion, however. For example, the Akan citizens of Ghana are people who venerate the ancestors but have a fairly sizeable number of divinities. Parrinder captures the essence of what is being said when he asserts:

> Roughly it may be said that the peoples of Central and Southern Africa have not developed belief in nature gods, whereas many of the leading peoples of West Africa have large pantheons of gods. But some of the Sierra Leone tribes in the Far West regard the ancestors as all-important and have only vague beliefs in other spirits.[15]

In the whole of Africa, the *Yorùbá* ethnic group of Nigeria has the most significant number of divinities. Different Odu corpuses, according to Idowu,[16] have given the number ranging between 201, 401, 600, and 1700 divinities. It is interesting to note here that their perception of the ancestors is not as prominent as the divinities. By extension, the Africans believe that the divinities are known throughout the nooks and crannies of their land. This is what Njoku[17] means when he insists that the phenomenon of belief in divinities is noted everywhere in Africa

From the preceding, it is clear that the divinities are the objective phenomena of the religious consciousness of the West Africans. The Supreme Being is venerated but hardly worshipped, so are the ancestors who are regarded as the living dead. The divinities are the most popular and actively worshipped. They are regarded as ministers within the theocratic governance of the universe. They are burdened with the responsibility of creation, some with justice, and agriculture, to mention a few. Additionally, they are considered to be intermediaries between the Supreme Being and man. They are a means to an end but not an end in themselves. God is worshipped through them, and they are recipients of sacrifices. They have a cult of priests attached to their shrines, grooves, or temples with a large number of devotees.

Categories of the Divinities

The divinities vary in number and responsibilities from one ethnic group to another throughout Africa. The divinities are divisible into three categories[18]— primordial divinities, deified ancestors, and personification of natural phenomena. The primordial divinities are those that are emanations of God. They came forth in consequence of the Almighty. According to Ojo,[19]

> The divinities are spiritual beings. They share aspects of the Supreme Being, inconsequence of which they become gods with a small letter "g." That is why it

is not correct to say they are created. It will be correct to say that they emanated from the Supreme Deity or that they were engendered by Him, brought forth by Him, or came into being in consequence of Him. In other words, the divinities have attributes, qualities, or characteristics of the Supreme Being, and they are, in consequence, off-springs of God.

They were with Him from the beginning of time and were saddled with the responsibilities of the smooth running of the earth. They are the divinities that are believed to have lived in heaven with the Supreme Being. As a result of this, their origin remains shrouded in obscurity, just like the Supreme Being whose origin is also unknown. These divinities were in charge of the creation of the world, the formation of human beings, some were oracular divinities, and others were left in charge of clearing a path to the earth.

The Deified Ancestors occupy the second category of the African divinities. The occupants of this category are those divinities that were once human beings on earth but later died as heroes of their ethnic group. As a result of their extraordinary lives and performances on earth, they became deified after their death. Ordinarily, a person who has lived an exemplary life on earth becomes an ancestor upon death. Thus, a person who has lived an extraordinary life on earth becomes a divinity for that ethnic group. Some of the feats that qualify a person to become a divinity is for saving His people from marauding armies, such as in the case of Moremi of Ile-Ife, or one who had an unusual ability to achieve great things like Sango who could conjure fire to destroy his enemies. Both Moremi and Sango are prime examples from the *Yorùbá*. Usually, a divinity assumes the attributes of another divinity.[20]

The third category of divinities is those that are the personification of natural phenomena. The divinities under this category consist of as many as there are natural phenomena on the land. These Spirits are known to inhabit rivers, streams, caves, forests, mountains, hills, and other natural phenomena available in the African geographical space. In light of this, these places where the spirits inhabit are regarded as sacred places. Such hills and rocks like Oke-Ibadan and Olumo Rocks become the home of the divinities. Usually, the spirits occupying these sacred sites are called by the names of those mountains, rivers, or hills. Annual festivals are also held in honor of these divinities by their adherents.

Awolalu and Dopamu,[21] in their elucidation of the divinities among the West Africans, have attempted a rough categorization of the divinities into different departments. These include:

Arch Divinity: Orisa-nla or Obatala (*Yorùbá*); Ala, Ana, or Ani (Igbo); Olokun (Edo); Egbesu (Ijaw); Obumo (Ibibio); Gunnu (Nupe); Mawu-Lisa (Ewe-Fon); Tano (Akan and Ga); Dugbo (Kono).
Oracle Divinity: Orunmila or Ifa (*Yorùbá*); Fa (Ewe-Fon); Agwu (Igbo); Ibinikpabi (Igbo).
Earth Divinity: Sanponna (*Yorùbá*); Sagbata (Ewe-Fon); Ojukwu (Igbo); Amakiri (Ijaw); Isong (Ibibio); Asase Yaa (Akan); Oto (Edo).

Divinity of Iron: Ogun (*Yorùbá*); Gu (Ewe-Fon); Ta Yao (Ashanti).
Thunder Divinity: Sango (*Yorùbá*); Hevioso (Ewe-Fon); Gua (Akan); Sokogba (Nupe); Amadioha (Igbo); Ogiuwu (Edo).
Divine Messenger: (Trickster): Esu (*Yorùbá*); Legba (Ewe-Fon); Agwu (Igbo).
Water Divinity: Osun, Oya, Olokun (*Yorùbá*); Bosomtwe (Akan); Binabu (Ijaw).

It is worth mentioning that even when the regions or tribes of people speak the same language, divinities vary in numbers from one ethnic group to the other or from one community to the other. For example, a different number of their Pantheon is given by *Ifa* corpus among the *Yorùbá*, where such numbers as 201, 401, 600, and even 1700 were given for their population. However, the number is lower in other ethnic groups across Africa. The reasons for the increase in number may not be unconnected to issues related to migration, development, and cultural contacts forcing a fusion of divinities to form new divinities or nomenclatures similar to the foreign culture that has come to settle within another community. Among the *Yorùbá* and the Ewe, the oracular divinity is *Ifa* and *Fa*, respectively. The combination of divinities in a particular area is known as the Pantheon of that particular place. The Pantheon has an arch divinity as their head. He is the most important of the Pantheon and is usually confused with the Supreme Being. For example, *Orisa-nla* is the head of the *Yorùbá* Pantheon. He rules with the scepter received from Olodumare himself. It must, however, be maintained that the Supreme Being is far above all the divinities.

Worship of the Divinities

Since it has been noted that the divinities are the objective phenomena of the West Africans, it is clear that the divinities are offered worship far above any other spiritual agency in the theology of the people. A look at the liturgical elements indicates the level of veneration the people have for their gods. During worship, the devotees often begin with a libation. Libation is the act of pouring some liquid onto the floor, or onto the emblems of those divinities that are being worshipped. Oftentimes, water, palm wine, spirits, beer, and liquor are liquid items used. Each divinity has its own drink preference, and this is poured on the ground or the paraphernalia of worship. Significantly, the liquid is believed to "soften" the ground and usher the worshippers to the presence of the divinities. Going simultaneously with libation is the invocation of the divinities. This is done by calling upon the divinity that is being worshipped. He or she is called by his or her cognomens, attributes, and praise songs. This is succeeded with an invitation to the worshippers to partake in the ceremony. Next comes the offering. The offerings differ from one divinity to the other through Africa, such as food items like rice, kolanut, yam, or fruits. After the offering, petitions follow next, while songs are accompanied by musical instruments. The songs differ in nature. Songs often come in the form of praises, petitions, expressions of faith on the prowess of the divinity, and sometimes tell the history of the divinity. These songs lead to dancing and merriment. One of the final liturgical acts is the offering of sacrifices. This is a crucial element of the ceremony. Usually, sacrifices that are offered differ from one divinity to the other. Sacrificial items include rams, cows, snails, dogs, and other animals. Often, the entrails of the animals are what are offered as a sacrifice to the divinity. Sacrifices are sometimes for thanksgiving, and it is done when devotees wish to thank the divinities. Votive offerings are made in consequence of an answered prayer that was followed by a vow. Expiation and substitutionary sacrifices are two of a kind that are close to one another. While expiation is to seek forgiveness, substitutionary sacrifices are given as substitutes for the people. There are also preventive sacrifices and foundational sacrifices. Preventive sacrifices are to prevent evils from entering the community, while foundation sacrifices are done when a new town or a new house is to be built.

Objects of Worship, Sacred Abodes, and Religious Personalities

The objects of worship and their habitations of the African divinities have contributed to the religion being misconstrued and misrepresented by earlier writers and commentators. These investigators have concluded that the African people worship a withdrawn god. They have referred to African Religion as idolatry, heathenism, and several other obnoxious nomenclatures. However, a cursory observation of the people's actions, devoid of prejudicial sentiments, would have revealed the truth to these researchers. It is clear that the people are not idol worshippers; instead, they believe that the images they venerate possess the spirits of their known divinities. These divinities can stay or decide to leave their abodes anytime they feel like, and the images become empty. Each divinity has symbols or emblems that are sacred to him or her. These are merely visual representations of the divinities. These emblems and symbols, which are considered sacred to the people of Africa, are kept away from the public. The symbols are sometimes made of wooden materials carved for the purpose of representation. The emblems are kept in various places of worship. The divinities inhabit sacred places that dot the African landscape. They can either be in temples, shrines, or grooves. The divinities are offered worship in these sacred places as they can be communicated to there.

Relationship of the Divinities to the Supreme Being

The divinities are known to be capable of answering the petitions of the devotees. They can give children to those who desire to have children. It is in recognition of this that names are given to children attesting to the fact that the divinities have answered their prayers. Hence, such names like Ogunbiyi, Sagodayo, Esurayi, or Ifabiyi among the *Yorùbá* are given to children due to answered prayers. When the divinities save the people from natural disasters or war, sacrifices are often given to them. However, the divinities are not an end in themselves; rather, they are a means to an end. The implication here is that they have someone who is superior to them in the person of Olodumare. While it is true that they are the objective phenomenon of the people, the Africans do not doubt their position before the Almighty. This can be demonstrated in their sociological patterns. All across the continent of Africa, the King is the supreme ruler and is at the apex of the pyramid. Closely following the King are the Chiefs, the village heads before the common people. It is this pattern that plays itself out in the course of their theological consciousness. The people of Africa view the Supreme Being as the head of the theocratic pyramidal structure, and the divinities as those delegated with myriads of functions. Thus, their authorities are derived from the Supreme Being. In view of this, the divinities are considered to be representatives of God on earth. They are between God and men. Using the *Yorùbá*, as an example, the devotees see them as they see the Chiefs who are expected to take their needs to the King and bring the King's responses to them. That is the reason why the Kings do not usually appear in public. However, when they do, they usually wear a crown that partially covers their faces.

To prove that the divinities are not an end in themselves, the Africans have myths attesting to the divinities' lower position. First, recall that the Supreme Being sent them to the earth to fulfill specific assignments. *Orisa-nla* was sent into the world to create the earth according to the *Yorùbá*, for example. Besides, the story is told by the *Yorùbá* of Nigeria, whereas 1700 divinities demanded that the Supreme Being should abdicate the throne of governance of the universe for them for a trial period of 16 years. God suggested they run it for only 16 days. By the eighth day, things got so bad that they had to petition Olodumare to take back the running of the universe.[22] According to Idowu,[23] the story ended with the divinities celebrating and praising the Supreme Being. Another is the Edo myth that Awolalu and Dopamu succinctly relate in their book, *West African Traditional Religion*,[24] as summarized next.

The myth concerns the Edo ethnic group of Nigeria. It speaks about the beauty contest between Olokun and Osanobwa. On the day of the contest, Osanobwa, the Supreme Being of the Edo people, sent his messenger to invite Olokun, who is a river divinity, to the venue. Once getting out to receive the messenger, Olokun discovered that the messenger was dressed exactly as he/she was. This feat was done several times, and she found that the messenger was always dressed as she was. The messenger of Osanobwa was the Chameleon. Osanobwa accepted defeat because much as she tried, she could not beat the messenger of God. Regarding the relationship between the Supreme Being and the Divinities, Ekeke and Ekeopara[25] has succinctly come up with five reasons to prove the assertion that the divinities are subordinate to the Supreme Being. These include: they are created beings; they are derivations from the Deity; they are given functions to perform in the world; they were functionaries in the theocratic governance of the world; and they are intermediaries between human beings and God.

Conclusion

In African religious consciousness, the divinities exist to add meaning to the life of the devotees and the society at large. While the Supreme Being is regarded as the creator who occupies the highest echelon of the pyramidal structure of the people's religion, the divinities are the most venerated by the Africans. They occupy a place between the Supreme Being and human beings in their quest for answers to life's questions. The words of Ushe[26] are appropriate here:

> The Supreme Being is venerated and not worshipped. The Africans have no temple and an image attributed to Him because He is beyond human comprehension and is unique, showing that there is none like Him. The Supreme Being in African religious belief has so many divinities or deputies who work with Him in the unitary theocratic governance of the universe. They are functionaries and ministers whose duties are to carry out the full instructions of the Supreme Being. They do not have absolute power; their existence is derived from the Supreme Being. They are created as so and are subordinate to God in all matters.

The importance and popularity of these divinities have gone beyond the shores of Africa. They are also worshipped in America and even in Latin America.

Notes

1. C. Emeka Ekeke and Chike A. Ekeopara, "God, Divinities and Spirits in African Traditional Religious Ontology" in *American Journal of Social and Management Sciences*, 2010, ScienceHuβ, http://www.scihub.org/AJSMS. Accessed on February 20, 2019.
2. Geoffrey Parrinder, *African Mythology*. London: The Hamilton Publishing Group Ltd., 1967.
3. E. G. Parrinder, *African Traditional Religion*. London: Sheldon Press, 1976.
4. He wrote several works of which a few will be mentioned.

    J. S. Mbiti, *Concepts of God in Africa*. London: SPCK.1970.
    J. S. Mbiti, *African Religion and Philosophy*. London: Heinemann. 1969, 1975.
    J. S. Mbiti, *Introduction to African Religion*. London: Heinemann. 1975.

5. He wrote several works on African Religion, only a few will be mentioned.

    E. Bolaji Idowu, *Olodumare: God in Yoruba Belief*. London: Longmans. 1962.
    E. Bolaji Idowu, *African Traditional Religion: A Definition*. Ibadan: Fountain Publications. 1973, 1991.

6. J. Omosade Awolalu, *Yoruba Beliefs and Sacrificial Rites*. Essex: Longman Group Ltd., 1979; 1981.
7. P. A. Dopamu, Esu: *The Invisible Foe of Man*. Ijebu-Ode: Shebiotimo Publications, 1986; 2000.
8. J. O. Awolalu and P. A. Dopamu, *West African Traditional Religion*. Ibadan: Macmillan Nigeria Publishers Ltd., 2005.

9. T. F. Jemiriye, *The Yoruba GOD and gods*. Ado-Ekiti: Petoa Educational Publishers, 1998.
10. Udo Etuk, *Religion and Cultural Identity*. Ibadan: Hope Publications. 2000. p. 31.
11. Tunde Awosanmi, "Orisaism, Guest-Faiths and Global-African Spiritual Order: Wole Soyinka's Perspective Creed" in Tunde Babawale and Akin Alao (eds.), *Global African Spirituality: Social Capital and Self-Reliance in Africa*. Lagos: Malthouse Press Ltd. 2008. pp. 197–214.
12. E. B. Idowu, *African Traditional Religion: A Definition*. Ibadan: Fountain Publications, 1991. 115.
13. B. C. Ray, *African Religions*. New Jersey: Prentice Hall, 2009. p. 38.
14. David Oladimeji Alao, "Interrogating the Involvement of Native God's in Contemporary African Conflict Management" in *Global Journal of Politics and Law Research*, European Centre for Research Training and Development, June 2015, Vol. 3, No. 3. pp. 57–71.
15. E. G. Parrinder, *African Traditional Religion*. London: Sheldon Press, 1976. p. 43.
16. E. Bolaji Idowu, *African Traditional Religion: A Definition*. Ibadan: Fountain Publications, 1973. p. 165.
17. F. O. C. Njoku, *Essays in African Philosophy, Thought & Theology*. Owerri: Claretian Institute of Philosophy & Clacom Communication, 2002. p. 28.
18. Sunday Ola-Oluwa Adenrele, "Philosophy of Religion: National Open University of Nigeria: 2009," http://www.africanbelief.com. Retrieved on January 9, 2016.
19. John Olu Adetoyese, "The Present State of African Religion," https://www.biblicaltheology.com/Research/AdetoyeseJO01.pdf. Accessed on July 23, 2019.
20. O. O. Ogunbiyi and L. B. Akande, "Sango: The Religio-Mythical Examination of a Yoruba Deity," in *Kashere Journal of Christian Studies*, Vol 1, No.1, September 2019.
21. J. O. Awolalu and P. A. Dopamu, *West African Traditional Religion*. Ibadan: Macmillan Nigeria Publishers Ltd., 2005. p. 116.
22. O. O. Oladimeji, *African Traditional Religion*. Ilesa: Ilesanmi Press & Sons (Nig) Ltd., 1975. pp. 16, 17.
23. Idowu, *African Traditional Religion*, 1973. p. 159.
24. J. O. Awolalu and P. A. Dopamu, *West African Traditional Religion* (Ibadan: Macmillan Nigeria Publishers Ltd., 2005), 116.
25. C. Emeka Ekeke and Chike A. Ekeopara, "God, Divinities and Spirits in African Traditional Religious Ontology."
26. Ushe Mike Ushe, "God, Divinities and Ancestors in African Traditiona Religious Thought" in *IGWEBUIKE: An African Journal of Arts and Humanities*, Vol. 3, No 4, June 2017. ISSN: 2488-9210 (Online). Accessed on February 20, 2019.

CHAPTER 7

Beliefs and Veneration of Ancestors

Benson Ohihon Igboin

INTRODUCTION

In discussing African concept of the ancestors, we are not concerned about the politically incorrect position such as 'ancestor worship' but rather we are poised to critically examine the traditional fundamentals of assuming ancestor-hood in order to determine whether they are still consistent with contemporary realities in Africa. In any case, ancestors have been defined as the dead whose memory can still be kept among the living. They are those who must have satisfied certain moral and social conditions set by the community before their death. These conditions will be critically examined later in the light of the contemporary realities in Africa. Even though Western scholarship seems to diminish the belief and importance of ancestors, the reality is that in most parts of rural Africa, the belief is still strong. In fact, continuous research has demonstrated that the praxis is truer than the theoretical framework consigning it to the dustbin.[1]

Ancestors are believed to play significant roles in the community they have left behind. The debate over the relevance of the ancestors in contemporary Africa is a controversial one. One school of thought argues that the ancestors are still relevant in societal administration in rural settlements, which have not been completely 'infested' by modernity's machine of devaluation of values, though at different levels in individual communities.[2] The other posits that ancestors have no relevance again, and they should rest in peace, if possible. The latter hinges its arguments on the realities of contemporary social, political, economic, and technological challenges which the ancestors did not

B. O. Igboin (✉)
Adekunle Ajasin University, Akungba-Akoko, Nigeria
e-mail: benson.igboin@aaua.edu.ng

envisage during their earthly lifetime and which they do not have the power to influence or overcome even in their celestial super-state. The pre-colonial and colonial ancestors could not effectively withstand the advent and unfortunate experiences of colonialism respectively. As such, the argument goes, they are imperceptible to them, and therefore, unhelpful in meeting the post-colonial challenges.[3] The third tranche of argument that is the one pursued in this discourse is the reevaluation of the pre-requisites of admission into ancestor-hood. This chapter argues that the prevalent style of life of contemporary elitist Africans can hardly qualify them to be admissible into the communion of, and be venerated as, ancestors. It concludes that there might be no ancestors qua ancestors any more in Africa, unless the preconditions of entering into that state are changed in line with prevailing social realities, but with serious implications.

In achieving this goal, we shall briefly interrogate the concept of tradition, because it is germane to our discourse. Thereafter, we will critically examine the various pre-requisites for admission into the communion of the ancestors of the ancestors; then an evaluation will be made before the final conclusion.

Criteria for Admission into Ancestorship

The idea of a set of criteria for admission immediately suggests that there are people who may not meet them and therefore inadmissible to the communion of the ancestors. A critical question of which literature on African religion and philosophy has not adequately addressed is who set these criteria, the living or the dead? While Ezekwonna[4] seems to suggest that some model might have been set by the ancestors for the living to follow, Jebadu[5] opines that each ethnic group sets up their requirements. But this present enterprise is not concerned very much about that even though it is a worthy field of inquiry. For the moment, we concern ourselves with the basic requirements as have been regarded as 'traditional.'

First, dying at a ripe age is a criterion that anyone aspiring to becoming an ancestor must experience. In other words, a person who dies young is not eligible to be admitted into the communion of the ancestors. This criterion has an exception, depending on the specific ethnic or communal group. As Wambutda stipulates among the Nga of Nigeria even though "only women and men not younger than middle age who die of natural causes may pass on to become recognized ancestors within the patrilineage," when a young person who occupied an important position dies, for example, a young king, he could become an ancestor.[6] This privileged criterion that excludes others ordinarily from becoming an ancestor can hardly be sustained in contemporary Africa, particularly in the urban setting where capitalism and individualism have almost destroyed the communal spirit. As it is now being generally observed, when those who have suddenly become wealthy go to their hometowns, titles meant for 'traditionally' qualified persons may be given away to these young but wealthy ones, whose lineage may also not be connected to such titles.

The idea of age of dying to become an ancestor is a contentious one. Additionally, this would be dependent upon the age-group system of particular communal groups. This writer observes that although the age-group system still operates in many rural areas, the grouping has become a knotty issue and has been bitterly influenced by Western time reckoning. For instance, among the Iuleha of Edo State, Nigeria, it is observed that whereas a 30-year-old person could have been initiated into manhood in pre-colonial era, a 30-year-old person today is far from being initiated. Those initiated in 2013 were well all above 40 years old. In contemporary society where the life span has been put roughly between 45 and 55 years, one wonders whether middle age will not reduce to between 25 and 30 years, which by this reckoning, those within such age bracket are not admissible to ancestor-hood. Well, it has also been observed that 'smart' people join higher age group in order to be initiated into manhood on time. This immediately means that such a person may, by virtue of the age group, at death be regarded as an ancestor. The point must however be made that the foregoing analysis depicts a sense of relativity of age at different times and places.

That an initiated person dies does not automatically also admit him/her into ancestor-hood. In many African settings, people who die leaving either of their parents alive are believed to die a bad death. They are not to become ancestors. In other words, traditionally, a person must live long enough to bury both parents before dying. Assuming a 70-year old person dies leaving behind a parent, the age attainment does not count; it is a wasted life, a bad death. Again, this is despite the burial rites that could have been accorded the person. In many African settings, such a person is not given elaborate burial, but if he or she has left children behind, the deceased could be given a decent burial with funeral rites that could afford the deceased a place in the communion of the ancestors. This contemporary resolve has been contentious in many African settings. This is because in pre-colonial era, such deceased were not to be buried at home but in the evil forest in the first place.

Closely related to the above are those who died unnatural death; they are not regarded as ancestors. Good death is one that is described as peaceful death: in this case, the person's death is not caused by violence (accident), suicide, death during childbirth, death by 'witch-trap,' or smallpox and other diseases as each community may determine. Although the belief in witchcraft is still pervasive, public emphasis has dwindled because of foreign religious and Western influences on law and practice in contemporary Africa. While in 'traditional' Africa, those who died as a consequence of any of these were not buried, they were thrown into the evil forest. Today, there is no smallpox, and those who die by accident are now accorded full burial in the present African communities. Ezekwonna, writing about the Igbo of Nigeria, seems not to resolve the glaring contradictions he props up. On the one hand, he writes:

> As people look at the type of life the person lived before proclaiming or making him an ancestor, they also look at the type of death, whether it was natural or

otherwise. And the accepted circumstances which would warrant making one an ancestor is that one died a natural death after a long life. The contrary would be someone who died unnaturally like in an accident [*onwu ike*] or from a taboo illness. For those who did not die a natural death, it is an indication that they did not live a good community life. Hence, they will not have a befitting burial and will have no place in the community.[7]

On the other hand, Ezekwonna says, "Even when somebody dies in a plane crash and the body is not recovered, people go to the scene of the crash and collect some sand and take it home for the burial. This burial at home has a good moral implication also for the living."[8] The question is whether or not the death by plane crash is not as violent as road accident or when a tree falls on someone leading to death.

Crucial still is marriage and evidence of procreation. In African 'traditional' setting, marriage conferred social, religious, and political recognition and responsibility on a person. There was no room for celibacy, and unmarried person, no matter the age or accomplishment, could never envisage becoming an ancestor. It has even been suggested that, in some cases, a natural eunuch or impotent man could have his wife impregnated by a close kin through a special arrangement in order to raise children for the impotent person. However, such practice was held in utmost secrecy. The thought of one's inability to procreate was harrowing and could lead to committing suicide in communities where such special arrangement was not feasible or acceptable. In this practice of special arrangement (e.g. among the traditional Shona of Zimbabwe), it needs to be emphasized that only blood related person to the potent person, who also agreed to the arrangement, was recognized by the community to raise children for the impotent. Anything outside this brought marital crisis in form of infidelity and bastard children. As it were, bastards were not allowed to inherit property just because they were regarded as non-members of the lineage. Today, impotence can hardly be regarded as an issue. With Assisted Reproduction Technique (ART), Umahi notes that affected people could take advantage of the modern system. According to him,

> Taking advantage of the increasing number of couples afflicted with infertility problems but desirous of children, many young men and ladies whose sperms and eggs are still very healthy are hawking these essential ingredients of procreation at fertility centers in Lagos with the alacrity of street traders selling wares as bread, handkerchief and sachet water, etc.[9]

Although desperation for children can drive people toward test-tube babies, its metaphysical implications are not immediately lost. Even though ART could not have been contemplated in pristine African religious thought, there is the sense in which it still does not fit into the pre-requisites for ancestor-hood. The reason is that most African community-oriented cultures clearly depict that children must be directly traced to the lineage by blood. Adoption of children is also gaining ground in many African societies. The point is that whether through adoption or ART, is the child a blood person whose ontology can be traced to the lineage? This problem is not simple because it is believed that only one's living child can offer acceptable sacrifice to the ancestor in the family. Wouldn't the belief that ousted a 'biological bastard' also apply to adopted and ART children? This customary position seems to have over-ridden modern legal backing of adoption of children.

In traditional African religious culture, being an ancestor required that a man does not only have children, but actually he must have a son at least who will venerate him. The emphasis on male children to succeed the deceased means that those who died though having children who are female may not become ancestors, despite meeting other criteria. Ezekwonna adds that even though a person has many children (male and female), it does not guarantee automatic admission into the realm of the ancestors. According to him, it is not only that one must have children, but one must have had a good relationship with them. This relationship continues after the person must have died through sacrifices promoting the relationship between the dead and the living and as consequence promoting the individual's relationship and the community.[10]

In simple terms, if a person leaves behind at death a disunited, disorganized, and rancorous family, as it is obviously being witnessed today during many burial ceremonies in which children of the deceased publicly disagree or even fight, the cause of which may be traced to the deceased, it implies that the deceased is disqualified from becoming an ancestor. This can mean that the deceased did not live a worthy life by the traditional standard.

According to Stinton, a person aspiring to becoming an ancestor must have lived an exemplarily good life by the standards of the community, demonstrated good characters and behavior in compliance with 'traditional' morality. She adds that a person must practically live a holy life.[11] Biko explicates what is meant by the good life in African setting. According to him, Africans believe in the "inherent goodness of man." This is clearly lived out in the community of interrelated persons. In the community, everybody shares their joys and sorrows together. Actions are primarily directed toward the community good rather than the individuals. The idea of capitalism, which is a fallout of atrophied or rugged individualism, does not arise for the traditional African. Even though progress may be considered slow, the fact is that everyone is carried along in the spirit of communalism.[12] Such virtues as truthfulness, honesty, trustworthiness, liberality, uprightness, and so on characterize the relationship that exists among members of the community. But Ezekwonna believes that the good life is determined also by the number of wives and children and the size of a person's property, and how well he is able to manage or co-ordinate and relate to them.[13] Abanuka underscores that the ancestors are those who have distinguished themselves in "their extraordinary deeds, and so, they are concrete imperishable models who influence the living."[14] In essence, it is their impeccable deeds, volume of past accomplishments and contributions to the welfare and progress of the community that define goodness.

However, it has been said that the means and process by which such achievements are realized must be accounted for. This implies that a corrupt person who has robbed banks or stole public funds and uses such monies to construct hospitals, for example, in the community has not met the criterion of the good life. Since traditional concept of the good life entails that "unaccounted for" wealth is a curse to the community, it stands to reason that many post-colonial Africans who have corrupted themselves may not be eligible for ancestor-hood. Ewelu captures it thus:

> New values have been adopted and canonized. Dishonesty and cheating, fraud and getting away with it have now replaced ancestral moral uprightness and probity. Logic and legal smartness with their quibbling with their nuances of words have banished truth and integrity from traditional values to the archives of antiquarians …. Getting richer overnight without working for it has become the new criterion for achievement. Youths now take on titles such as chiefs by grace of unaccounted-for-wealth, titles that their ancestors merited through years of hardwork and honesty…. Nobody wants to be honest anymore simply because honesty "does not pay". Honesty has no cash values.[15]

Proper burial rites are a sine qua non for admission into ancestor-hood. The importance of a befitting burial cannot be over-emphasized because it is the cord that ritually binds the living with the dead. To be denied a proper burial meant that the deceased was banished or cut off from their earthly members and ancestral communion in the hereafter. Ezekwonna captures it this way: "those who did not meet these conditions [i.e. the first and second burial ceremonies among the Igbo] for proper burial are believed to have been banished to a non-descriptive place that is neither the spirit world nor the earth."[16] Moreover, proper burial entails that the dead are buried in their compound rather than in public cemeteries, which is believed to guarantee connection between the living and the dead. Anyone buried outside their compound is believed to be wandering about and unable to establish a union with the league of the ancestors in the community. Proper burial also means, depending on each community, meeting the traditionally laid down rules and procedures for burial. When there is a breach, it is believed that proper burial has not been accorded to the deceased.

On the other hand, befitting burial would mean that social programs of burial are as elaborate as possible. In this case, the death is announced far and wide to neighboring communities. Although the firing of the cannons has a metaphysical significance, its import is immediately socially established because it announces to the people that a great person has departed. As it was usual, community people would trace the sound to the venue and then participate in the social conviviality that defined befitting burial. Instructively, while the proper burial concerns those the community recognizes to ensure rules and procedures are followed in interring the dead, not everyone present takes part in that process. But for the outward ceremonies, uninvited guests have almost equal rights to enjoy what is served. However, these methods and procedures may not be as sacrosanct today as they were in time past.

Although modern technology affords people the means to announce the death of elders far and wide and easily,[17] with the social media, less effort can be made to announce deaths. In recent times, not only the death of an aged person is announced with pomp and pageantry, but also the death of a child is now being publicly announced by parents. How does one reconcile a situation where parents announced the remembrance of their 13-year-old child on a full newspaper page! A dead child was buried quietly and mournfully in traditional African setting. It should be observed that the corpse of an elder was regarded as very sacred which drew the attention and presence of the other ancestors in the family. This is one among other reasons why an elder's corpse was not displayed openly or buried, in most African societies, during the day. With the arrival of the undertakers, corpses no longer command much awe and reverence. Strangers and children are now in custody of a departing ancestor. Elders who die peacefully are those who die in their room in the presence of their children particularly the first son, assuming they are in good terms. At this point, the dying gives his final instructions as to how he or she should be buried; those who should see his/her corpse and those forbidden from seeing it. The coming of modern hospital has disrupted this sacred space, thus paving the way for the mortuary attendants to give the final bath to the dead, and hand them over to the undertakers in a motorcade in a grandiose parade.[18]

Proper burial implies 'sowing the dead' in the Mother Earth. The earth is thought to be the proper and final resting place of the ancestors even though it is widely believed that they traverse the metaphysical and sensible worlds. Just as the umbilical cord was buried in the earth at birth, the dead is also buried in the earth so that there can be a re-union of the whole being and essence of the dead. The import of burying the dead on the earth during the process of becoming an ancestor cannot be over-estimated. According to Botchway and Agyemang, "the ancestors are regarded as the real owners of land and particular places where the ancestors are buried create a link between the living and the ancestors."[19] The thrust here is that burying the dead in the land is significant for considering the dead as an ancestor.

Recently, however, the Lagos State Government, Nigeria, passed a law that allows for cremation of the dead. By cremation, we mean that a dead person is burnt with fire in a pyre, a practice common to the Asians. "It involves the use of high-temperature burning, vaporization, and oxidation to reduce dead bodies to basic chemical compounds that have semblance of ashes or ground dry bones."[20] In its editorial page, the *This Day* newspaper argues that those who raise cultural and religious eyebrows that such "legal regime...undermines our country's intrinsic values and belief systems"[21] are merely sensational about the law, if not primitive, so long as the law is optional. Apart from the psychological imbalance that cremation may cause for the family members of the cremated, Adewale Adeleke thinks that the metaphysical implications should be given considerable attention. He says: "this is Africa where we have people with different beliefs, superstitions, and traditions that could contradict the idea of cremating corpses."[22] In any case, would a cremated person also become an ancestor in Africa?

The above critique of the prima facie qualifications of becoming an ancestor has demonstrated that many things have transmogrified the traditional concept of ancestorship. Before we attempt an evaluation, I needed to critique though briefly the inculturation hermeneutics that defines Jesus Christ as an ancestor, who the Africans who die in Christ can commune with. According to Jebadu, "African ancestor (sic) are already a constitutive part of the Communion of Saint (sic) taught (sic) of by Catholic Church."[23] Jebadu premises his argument on the assumption that if God in Christianity is the same in African indigenous religion, then Africans who died without hearing about Christ are believed to be in blissful communion with him in heaven. These ancestors, he espouses, must have been "specially saved by Christ" because Christ is the universal savior of humankind. In doing so, the basic criteria set by traditional religious bodies have to be syncretized or jettisoned in favor of the Catholic teaching on the communion of saints. He says:

> While on one hand we need to respect and acknowledge the right of any ethnic group to set up certain requirements to attain ancestorhood, for Christian African ancestral veneration, however, the ancestorhood should be open to all the dead who are believed to have been with Christ in heaven. Either one dies young or in old age, married or unmarried. The dead person still can attain ancestorhood provided he or she has demonstrated a good life during his or her lifetime in the world. They can intercede between God and their living kin. It should be done exactly like in Christian veneration of saints. That is, certain great Christians because of their heroic faith for instance and recognized by the Church through a means of canonization—though they are not recognized by the Church through a canonization—still can become the intercessors of the living Christians, which can fall under the so-called informal devotion.[24]

According to the editors of the (Catholic) *African New Testament and Psalms* in their introduction to the Gospel of Matthew:

> The message of Matthew to Jewish Christians can be a source of enlightenment and strength for African converts. Jesus insisted that he had not come to abolish the Jewish law but to bring it to perfection, and African Christians should realize that this applies also to those genuine values found in African traditional religions and cultures. We must emphasize here the importance of family and community, relationships with the ancestors and the living-dead, and the importance of reconciliation as a contribution to peace. These and other African values are in accordance with the Christian faith. Where there is a need the Christian faith should not hesitate to criticize the negative aspects of African culture in the light of the teaching of Christ. This will often be painful but that is a condition for following Christ. We should realize that anything contradicting the message of Christ cannot be a genuine human value and there is nothing to lose in giving it up.[25]

Ezekwonna does not agree less with proto-ancestor-hood of Jesus Christ. In fact, for him, Jesus "gets a transcendental recognition in which the life of all ancestors depends on him."[26] This position makes Jesus the ground and the activator of the moral life of the Africans. By this, all the ethno-religious conditions of becoming an ancestor are no longer useful because, with the new community that Jesus has founded, one can conceptualize a metaphysical de-territorialization, trans-territorialization, inter-territorialization, and inter-penetration of spaces in line with mundane globalization. This inter-planetary or borderless space makes Jesus to incorporate other ethnic ethical values for the communion of global saints. "As the whole world is his area of operation he (Jesus) accepted the already existing African ethical values and took them even further by allowing them to interact with other values outside itself."[27]

Implicitly, the condition that slaves, unmarried, male-less deceased, violent death, those who die young, improperly buried dead and strangers do not attain ancestor-hood is removed from the African religious metaphysics should the Jesus proto-ancestorship framework be adopted. But the question is: did Jesus Christ consider and fulfill African conditions of becoming an ancestor, if not, is the Catholic Church honoring him with this African status? We may further ask whether all African ancestors believed in Christ. Would Reverend Fathers and Sisters be venerated as ancestors in traditional Africa by their refusal (not inability) to generate life? These questions are important because African vitalogy considers generation of life as guaranteeing continuity in fellowship with the ancestors, but since celibates diminish this vitalogy and ontology, it becomes difficult to conceptualize their admission into African ancestor-hood.

Evaluation

Thus far, we have been able to draw attention to how the traditional prerequisites of becoming an ancestor have been so influenced by modern cultural values and Christianity. Two important questions that have spontaneously arisen are: (1) who qualifies to become an African ancestor in post-colonial Africa, and (2) what measures should we adopt to select them? Teffo and Roux appear to have paved some ways in attempting these interweaving questions. According to them, "metaphysical thinking in the African concept starts from social and moral considerations."[28] This implies that whosoever wants to become an ancestor in the African setting must have been considered socially and morally worthy of it because the attainment of ancestor-hood is the highest honor a person can desire in a 'traditional' Africa. This metaphysical thinking is important because it proffers the basis for the understanding (believing and accepting) analogous and contiguous ontology and vitalogy of the world of the ancestors. That being the case, whoever is qualified to assume this space must of necessity have meant the social and moral criteria of their various communities. Teffo and Roux further argue that there are situations where breaking with traditions is necessary and morally warranted as done, for example, in

South Africa "where traditional ways of doing and judging had to be changed or critically evaluated."[29]

The point here is that the criteria for becoming an ancestor appear to have been generally viewed as outdated and should be reviewed in light of contemporary realities. To insist, for instance, that those criteria are still as sacrosanct as they were in pre-colonial and early colonial periods is to miss the argument. The reality is that the present society has created a spontaneous antithesis that calls for critical attention. In answering the first question, we provide some hypotheses. Who among the following would contemporary Africans accept as ancestors: Nelson Mandela, Sani Abacha, John Mills, Mobotu Sese Seko, Idi Amin, Kenneth Kaunda, Olusegun Obassanjo, Samuel Doe, Charles Taylor, Robert Mugabe, Thomas Sankara, Muammar Ghadafi, Hosni Mubarak, Paul Biya, Ibrahim Babangida, Joseph Kabila, Thabo Mbeki, Muritala Muhammad, Alassane Ouattara, Felix Houphouet-Boigny, and so on? The choice of any of them who should become an ancestor depends on their styles of administration and management of the resources of their countries. This can starkly be judged from their policies and how they have affected the citizens of the nations, and not what they themselves have justified about their administrations. This singular criterion suggestively overrides all other 'primordial' criteria for assuming ancestor-hood.

Down the rung of the ladder, we may also begin to critically evaluate the widespread and scrunching corruption that has decimated the communal spirit of Africa. In pre-colonial Africa, thieves could not attain to the position of ancestor-hood because by implication, without restitution, they were bound to die a bad death and subsequently thrown into the evil forest. The antithesis is whether armed and pen-robbers of contemporary African societies are still qualified to become ancestors. If they are, it is definitely not on the basis of pre-colonial criteria. The same argument goes for African Christians and Muslims or any other foreign religions for that matter. Their belief systems do not rest on the pillar of African religious faith. Therefore, any argument to synthesize these faiths amount to forged convergence. And again, any attempt to believe that the traditional criteria for assuming ancestor-hood are static is a category mistake.

CONCLUSION

We have argued that although the belief in the ancestors is still very strong in Africa, the criteria for assuming that status might have been seriously vitrified by colonial and post-colonial realities: foreign religions, socio-economic and political changes, new legal and moral conditions. Increasing individualism, capitalism, urbanization, and elitism that are eroding the communal values have also significantly adversely affected the traditional criteria for assuming ancestor-hood. These have provided antithesis that appears not to have been critically considered in determining whether or not there would still be African ancestors in the sense in which they were conceived in pristine time. We argued that if the traditional criteria are still being held as sacrosanct as they were assumed to be in the past, they may not be able to meet them. In other words, if the criteria are not adjusted, or rather changed, despite the grubby consequences that may arise there from, the ontology and vitalogy that pristine ancestors offered the African families and communities may be lost totally in a short space of time. However, to change them in order to conform to the present will also mean lowering the cut-off points that would admit every Tom, Dick, and Harry. But the post-colonial vicissitudes are real, and they affect the belief in the efficacy of the moral challenges from the ancestors. Consequently, the relevance and functionality of the ancestors among the elite would depend on either of two options: they either change their way of life to conform to traditional communal ethos that guided African life or adopt criteria that conform to the liberality that defines individualism in capitalist society, both with severe implications.

NOTES

1. John C. McCall, "Rethinking Ancestors in Africa," *Africa: Journal of the International African Institute*, 65/2 (Jan. 1995): 256–270.
2. E. Bolaji Idowu, *Olodumare: God in Yoruba Belief*, London: Macmillan, 1996; John S. Mbiti, *African Religions and Philosophy*, London: Macmillan, 1969; Laureti Magesa, *African Religion: The Moral Traditions of Abundant Life*, Nairobi: Paulines, 1997; Joseph O. Awolalu and Ade P. Dopamu, *West African Traditional Religion*, Ibadan: Onibonoje Press, 2005.
3. Kwame Gyekye, *African Cultural Values: An Introduction*, Accra: Sankofa Publishing Co., 1996.
4. Ferdinard, C. Ezekwonna, *African Communitarian Ethic: The Basis for the Moral Conscience and Autonomy of the Individual—Igbo Culture as a Case Study*, Bern: Peter Lang, 2005, 46.
5. Alex Jebadu, *African Ancestral Veneration and the Possibility of its Incorporation into Catholic Devotion*, Rome: Collegio del Verbo Divino, 2006, 7.
6. Daniel Wambutda, "Ancestors—The Living Dead." In Ade Adegbola, E. A. *Traditional Religion in West Africa*, Ibadan: Sefer, 1998, 129.
7. Ezekwonna, 44.
8. Ezekwonna, 47.
9. Henry Umahi, "Sperm, Female Eggs Now Hawked in Hospitals," *Saturday Sun*, January 23, 2010.
10. Ezekwonna, 50.
11. Diane B. Stinton, *Jesus of Africa: Voices of Contemporary African Christology*, New York: Orbis Books, 2004, 112–113.
12. Steven Biko, "Some African Cultural Concepts," in Coetzee, P. H. and Roux, A. P. J., *Philosophy from Africa: A Text with Readings*, Oxford: OUP, 1998, 27–28.
13. Ezekwonna, 44.
14. Cited in Ezekwonna, 46.
15. Cited in Benson O. Igboin, "Colonialism and African Cultural Values," *African Journal of History and Culture*, 3/6 (July 2011): 96–103.

16. Ezekwonna, 45.
17. Benjamin C. Ray, *African Religious: Symbol, Ritual and Community*, 2nd ed., New Jersey: Prentice Hall, 2000, 103.
18. Benson O. Igboin, "When I Die: The Politics of the Metaphysics of Death." In Chuu Krydz Ikwuemesi, Chidi Ugwu, Christian Agbo (eds.) *Dying, Death and the Politics of After-Death in Africa: Studies of Some Nigerian Communities*, Glienicke: Galda Verlag, 2019, 241–251.
19. De-valera Botchway and Yaw S. Agyemang, "Indigenous Religious Environmentalism in Africa," *Religions: A Scholarly Journal*, 6 (Oct. 2012): 65–80, esp. 72.
20. *The Sun*, July 2, 2013.
21. *This Day*, June 25, 2013.
22. *Premium Times* online, accessed January 28, 2014.
23. Jebadu, 5.
24. Jebadu, 7.
25. Cited in Gregor Schmidt, "The Role of Ancestors and Living-Dead in the Life of Kenyan Christians," Maryknoll Institute of African Studies of Saint Mary's University of Minnesota/USA and Tangaza College, Nairobi/Kenya, 2005, 22.
26. Ezekwonna, 241.
27. Ezekwonna, 242.
28. Lesiba, J. Teffo, and Abraham P. J. Roux, "Metaphysical thinking in Africa," in Coetzee, P. H. and Roux, A. P. J. eds. *Philosophy from Africa: A text with readings*, Oxford: OUP, 1998, 141–142.
29. Teffo and Roux, 142.

CHAPTER 8

Beliefs and Practices of Magic and Medicine

Kelvin Onongha

INTRODUCTION

Belief in the power and efficacy of magic and medicine is foundational in African Traditional Religion (ATR); other beliefs are in God, divinities, ancestors, and spirits.[1] Africans realize that humans are not alone in the cosmos, but there are myriad unseen beings, forces, and agencies that not only affect their existence but also can be harnessed for their benefit. Magic, therefore, entails accessing and controlling the forces of nature for one's own benefit. In other words, there are natural and supernatural forces possessing abilities to make things mysteriously happen, either for good or for evil; the process of exploiting these forces is regarded as magic.

Although Africans believe in the existence of a Supreme Being, the Creator of all, they believe that he has delegated authority to the divinities over various elements of nature. These supernatural beings, the divinities, who are considered more accessible to humans than God, possess immense powers. By appealing to these divinities, humans can therefore access their powers to control their lives, circumstances, and environment.

Besides spiritual beings and deities, which possess the ability to perform the supernatural, Africans in general believe in a powerful pervading force in nature, similar to the Melanesian belief in *mana*.[2] These forces may reside in trees, rocks, hills, rivers, forests, and even in certain animals. For this reason, certain objects in nature are revered, considered sacred, and worshiped to obtain power to serve the worshippers needs. Magic can basically be defined as

K. Onongha (✉)
Adventist University of Africa, Nairobi, Kenya
e-mail: ononghak@aua.ac.ke

"a ritual formula or technique that can be acquired, bequeathed, bought or sold."[3] When contrasted with religion, magic is "seen as the manipulation of spiritual power for human ends, whereas religion involves the worship of spiritual beings for their own sake. In magic the emphasis is on the proper form of the rite, whereas, in religion it is on the intention of the worshipper."[4] Bolaji Idowu, the late renowned Nigerian scholar avers that while the goal of religion is focused on the will of God being done, magic has as its focus the will of the practitioner; the goal being control of one's life, environment, and circumstances.[5]

In general, there are two basic forms of magic—good and bad. While good magic is employed to heal, bless, protect, prosper, and deliver, bad magic is used to hurt, harm, maim, kill, curse, and block or hinder the well-being of others. Some have referred to good magic as white magic and bad magic as black magic—phraseology that some persons today regard as having racist overtones.

Good Magic

All forms of magic essentially entail the intervention or mediation of supernatural beings or powers. Their services are usually sought in times of sickness, or barrenness, for fortune or advancement, promotion, favor, and protection. For healing purposes, the remedies employed may include herbal concoctions prepared after consultation with the ancestors, divinities, or spiritual forces responsible for healing, and laced with incantations to ensure their potency. Barren women seek good magic to bear children for their husbands and thereby secure their status in the home as wives, otherwise, other women able to bear children could replace them. Besides bearing children, having a male heir is crucial to Africans, therefore, for this purpose also, women seek magical assistance.

Farmers, fishermen, hunters, and cattle herders in ancient times relied on magic for improved prosperity in their vocations. In contemporary times, the services of ritual specialists to provide good magic have not abated, rather, the scale and scope of such services have only expanded with time. Businesspersons, politicians, professionals, civil servants, and people in just about every vocational realm are in search of magic to provide advancement in their affairs.

Good magic often entailed charms or amulets prepared from portions of certain animals or plants believed to have powerful *mana*. These charms or amulets may be worn on a person around the neck, wrist, waist, or ankle; however, in certain cases, they are shielded from the naked eye. These charms may also be placed in homes, business places, offices, or cars. They often have been referred to as juju—a name derived from the French word, *jeu*—a doll or toy, something one played with.[6] So strong is the belief in the power and efficacy of magic that whenever a person excels in any endeavor in many parts of Africa, even unto present times, their success and prowess is attributed to the power of their juju.

Charms and amulets are often also used for protection. Hunters of old were feared because it was believed they possessed powerful magic with which they protected themselves as they hunted in dark evil forests, regarded as the abode of evil spirits. The power of their charms not only protected them but also enabled them to return home alive with game after their hunting expeditions. Invariably, hunters in ancient times were also powerful warriors, especially because of the magical powers they possessed. African folklore is replete with stories of heroic warriors who in combat employed magical powers to defeat enemies, escape from dangerous situations, and accomplish great military exploits.

Bad Magic

Another sinister existing form of magic, which leaves a trail of devastation, damage, and destruction with its victims, is known as bad magic. Bad magic manifests in diverse forms—as the evil eye, witchcraft, curses, or voodoo—all of which may result in bodily harm, illnesses, prolonged pain, or death—either instantaneously or progressively. A primary factor underlying the practice of bad magic is generally envy. In communal settings such as Africa, the success or prosperity of any individual over and above the others produces resentment or bitterness, and the desire to bring down that successful person to the level of all others in that community. As studies indicate, this is also the motivation for the practice of witchcraft, and the primary factor underlying witchcraft accusations.[7]

Bad magic is also utilized as a form of revenge or retribution. For instance, among the Yoruba of western Nigeria, husbands suspicious of their wives' fidelity employ *magun*, a form of magical charm that produces painful illness and eventual death of the guilty lovers; similar forms of this charm, also known as *runyoka*, can be found in other regions of Eastern and Southern Africa.[8] In Zimbabwe "the *n'anga* (diviner/healer) is the one who prepares the medicine for the suspecting man to be put in the food or bed of his wife to punish her suspected lover various forms of illness that result in death, if untreated by a traditional healer."[9] The belief in the potency of such charms is widespread in many African countries.

Magic also serves another purpose, to vindicate the innocent and punish the guilty. Among the Yoruba, for instance, the divinity *Esu* was sought as the avenger of wrongs and the executor of justice. Those who appealed for *Esu's* assistance had to be certain of their innocence; otherwise, they could bring upon their own heads the punishment they sought to bring unto others. *Esu* was renowned for returning to the sender retributive justice if such persons were themselves found to be errant. Across the continent, powerless persons often resort to magic in order to obtain the justice they feel they are denied of through conventional means and to find vindication for their cases, or vengeance against their enemies.

Concerning the question of justice, magic does indeed play a significant role. It is strongly believed in some regions of Africa that even the outcomes of court cases can be influenced in favor of a client willing to pay for such services. A *Babalawo* interviewed claimed that he had the power to make a case in the law courts go the way of his client. When asked how he would do this, he balked from sharing the details; however, he claimed that he had done it before and could do it again.

CONTAGIOUS AND HOMEOPATHIC MAGIC

There are essentially two major types of bad magic, namely, contagious and homeopathic magic.[10] Contagious magic works on the principle that things once associated with the victims can be employed in causing harm to them. Such items used for this purpose include finger or toenails, hair, clothing, or any other possessions associated with the intended victim. Recently, there have been in the news reports from West Africa an increase in the theft of ladies' underwear, which supposedly is used in preparing rituals to obtain wealth. When clients in such regions visit a hairdresser or barber, hair clippings are retrieved and given to them to dispose of as they deem fit. This is clearly understood by all because of the fear that such personal articles could be used to perform evil magic against the victim.

Homeopathic magic operates on the premise that whatever is done to an effigy shall have a similar effect upon the intended victim. Ritual experts construct effigies representing their victims and then may strike or insert pins into specific regions in order to cause agonizing pain or harm to the victim. At times, they may shoot or lope off a part of the effigy with the intention of causing severe pain or death to the victim. Another way this may operate is when over a bucket or pool of water the name of the intended victim is called, when the image of such a person appears upon the water surface, the magician would then shoot, strike, or simulate whatever harm was intended upon the victim's image so as to injure, maim, or kill the victim.

MEDICINE

Medicine has been defined as: "The art of using the available resources of nature to prevent, treat or cure diseases. It is the art of restoring and preserving health by means of medicament. Medicine therefore, is both therapeutic and prophylactic (curative and preventative)."[11] It is also true that, "In African belief, medicine is rendered inefficacious and incomplete if it does not involve traditional procedure. Ritual invocations are highly significant in the people's sense of medicine practice. In some societies, great discoveries of cures or new remedies for serious ailments lead some to perform sacrifices to the gods and spirits who are believed to have aided in the revelations."[12]

In some parts of Africa, the expressions used for magic and medicine are similar. This is perhaps because both are associated with the same divinity responsible for those functions, or they entail similar processes such as rituals, incantations, and consultations of the divinities.

Although it has been noted that there is in essence "no semantic distinction between magical medicine and medicine with therapeutic or toxic qualities."[13] African scholars such as Ade Dopamu would disagree with this, stating that Yoruba medicine is not always dependent on magic for it to be effective.[14] This is because certain medicines are essentially plant-based and herbal in composition, depending upon the nature of the illness and its source.

As with magic, there are some medicine that could be produced from just about the same constituent materials, and could serve similar purposes. Such medicine like the charms of the local shaman, "play a most important part as a remedy against sicknesses and as a protection against the evils of witchcraft."[15] So prevalent is the belief in the potency and effectiveness of charms that,

> They are used by people in all walks of life, from the uneducated villager to the university professor, from the lowliest servant to the most powerful politician. Their use constitutes a system of insurance against anything from disease to fire and theft. Full coverage can mean preventing cattle from being eaten by crocodiles, being assured of safety on a journey, making your plants grow, increasing your number of friends, obtaining a promotion at work, or getting your wife to show more love and affection.[16]

Medicine is generally used in the African context to restore depleted vital forces, caused by sickness or disease, "to put things right and to counter the forces of mystical evil."[17] Knowledge concerning this skill and the techniques involved in the preparation of these medicines are transmitted orally from generation to generation. In order to guarantee the potency of these potions, ritual experts, who in many cases perform the same role of magician, and healer, seek the assistance of the divinities through divination to ascertain the cause and cure for each particular condition.

PRACTICE OF MAGIC

In his groundbreaking study of the Tikopia people, anthropologist Raymond Firth describes three main types of the practice of magic—magic of production, of protection, and of destruction—that are also pertinent to the African context. Firth explains that "in a broad sense the aim of all magic is the increase, maintenance or decrease of resources, material or immaterial."[18]

Productive magic is employed by Africans to increase the harvest of the farmer, the size and quantity of game killed by the hunter, the fish caught by the fisherman, and in every vocation people engage in to provide for their livelihood. As the African society evolved, this kind of magic was applied in educational and professional pursuits—to help students excel in exams, workers gain promotion at work, businesspersons thrive in flourishing enterprises, and contractors to obtain large and successful bids. A local diviner once informed the researcher how he could enable his clients, through the use of charms he provided, to dictate the type and size of the contract jobs they desired, entirely on their own terms. That is, whatever the contractor desired he would get, and for the cost he stated. Whoever the possessor of this diviner's charm spoke to, that person would be subject to obey his bidding.

Protective magic serves several different purposes. It is used essentially to protect the lives of the users, but also to secure family or property. Because of the belief that life is fraught with much danger, from spirits, ancestors, divinities, and envious enemies, it was inconceivable that any person would go through life without some form of magical protection. This protection usually came from the wearing of charms or amulets prepared by ritual experts, or using objects considered to possess powerful *mana*. Usually, the vocation of the user determined the kind of protection needed and the divinity that would ensure the safety of the wearer. For instance, warriors in ancient and modern times employed charms, which would make them impervious to metallic objects, while drivers seek magical protection against death by motor accidents.

Destructive magic is the most dreaded form of magic, sometimes referred to contentiously as black magic. This could operate through several different modes such as poison, curses, the evil eye, voodoo, or witchcraft. Ultimately, the desire is to cause hurt, harm, loss, pain, or death to the victim, their family, or property. A primary motive for using destructive magic is envy on the part of an enemy. So prevalent is fear of the enemy in the Yoruba psyche that the Yoruba have a proverb: "It is only the dead man that has no enemy." This proverb has similar expressions among various peoples across the regions of Africa.

Among the Yoruba, Dopamu provides up to eight broad categories of magic that are well-known: these are (1) types of magic against specific types of sorcery—which ward off or prevent the effect of sorcery; (2) types of magic against witches—used to placate or fight witches; (3) types of magic specifically tailored to specific human activities—used to attract customers/bring good luck/secure employment/pass exams/succeed in love or sexual affair, and so on; (4) magic connected with agriculture—produce bountiful increase of crops and herd; (5) magic connected with hunting; (6) magic connected with natural forces—to cause or stop rain; (7) protective magic—against danger, accidents, or misfortune or evil, providing immunity from cuts, bullets, and so on, and even to disappear from danger; and (8) magic connected with diseases and sickness—magical medicine whose processes and ends were therapeutic.[19]

Divination

Where magic is suspected, ritual experts are sought to divine who is responsible for the misfortune.[20] Despite the great regard African chiefs are accorded, diviners appear to hold similar positions of respect, and even dread. Indeed, some state that "The diviner, sorcerer and magician occupied the highest order of place in African cultures."[21] Their roles in ancient African societies commenced at birth and continued to the death of individuals. They served as traditional birth attendants and were often consulted to determine the cause and factors responsible for the death of a deceased person.

Whenever misfortune struck, either personally or communally, it was the diviner who through mysterious arts determined the underlying cause and the remedial pathways to follow for restoration. It was their duty to reveal sometimes through mechanical means, other times through mystical methods who or what was responsible. Some of the mechanical devices utilized included examining the entrails of certain creatures, casting of lots—using bones, sticks, or cowrie shells. In other instances, diviners could mysteriously enter into trances, séances, or become possessed by spirits which enable them to decipher factors amiss responsible for the misfortune.

In ancient times, diviners served not merely as traditional healers, but as priests, counselors, psychologists, and orthopedics of their day. They were indeed the intellectuals of their communities. For these highly demanded roles, the diviners needed careful and comprehensive training. Generally, those who chose to be diviners undertake extensive periods of internship under experienced mentors to gain "the accumulated wisdom of their people."[22] In many cases, such as a few the researcher interviewed, divination was a profession inherited from their parents and forebears who themselves had held such offices for generations. However, it is also possible for an individual who chose this profession to seek training under a respected, experienced diviner. In other instances, some who eventually became diviners were persons who felt called, either by dreams, by visions, or by spirit possession to take such pathways. Although in many cases the office of the diviner is mainly held by men in some African communities, it is not unusual to have women carrying out such functions.

Interestingly, a story featuring a female *sangoma* was reported by the British Broadcasting Corporation (BBC) a few years ago (May 7, 2013). This young lady in her twenties held a regular job as a corporate administrator of a large bank in Johannesburg, South Africa, yet she felt the overwhelming call of her ancestors to this special role.

Despite the fact that in many parts of Africa the ritual specialist combined the functions of healer, diviner, and sorcerer, in some other cases, these offices may be held by different persons.

Contemporary Beliefs of Magic and Medicine

Granted that Africa has now become the home of the fastest-growing major religions of the world, namely, Christianity and Islam, belief in the efficacy and potency of magic and traditional medicine is not in any way on the wane. Scholars of religion in the continent actually report a resurgence of ATR and its associated beliefs and worldview, especially regarding the magical, and medicine. A few factors can be adduced for the worldview continuity witnessed in several parts of contemporary Africa. These include holistic/integrated healing, socio-political conditions, the reaction to globalization, the influence of Nollywood, and the effect of African Pentecostalism.

Integrated Healing

Because in most instances incidents of misfortune are attributable to spiritual causes, the diviner is usually sought to intervene and remedy the situation. Very rarely does the diviner perform his task without seeking supernatural assistance either in the preparation of medicine for the client or in offering the appropriate sacrifice to restore natural or communal harmony between the client and the parties offended. As Alyward Shorter observes,

> Ethnic societies have traditions of integral healing operated by ritual specialists, herbalists, diviners, spirit-mediums and magicians, or any combination of these. These traditional doctors, perjoratively called "witch doctors," continue to flourish in modern, urban situations, though they often take pseudo-scientific titles such as "Professor," "Holistic Healer," "Astrologer," and so on, to gain respectability.... Western medicine concentrates on physical remedies, and departmentalizes other aspects of health. Traditional healers are holistic or integral in their approach to health. In other words they operate on several levels at once.[23]

Also, because "in the spiritual etiology of the African everything is connected with everything,"[24] cosmological interrelationships are critical to dealing with misfortune, medical or magical. Comparing the role of traditional healers with modern medicine, Shorter presents a balanced view of the diviner's work objectively noting,

> At the social level, traditional healers place great importance on the social causes and consequences of sickness and on the experience of misfortune by individuals—even on the healing of the society itself, as is evidenced by rituals of redress. In the Western world social medicine is at its infancy. At the moral and spiritual level, traditional healers identify spirits who they deem to be offended, as well as patronal and alien spirits which are thought to be at work in the patient. They frequently practice as mediums and exorcists. The basic problem with traditional healers is that they resort to magic, and do not distinguish between the magical and therapeutical value of their remedies... They also confuse the levels of healing. For example, a spirit theory of illness tends to mix moral and physical evil, or the healer may apply physical remedies for immoral behavior, such as medicine to prevent a thief breaking into the house.

Socio-political Conditions

Combined with their worldview and religious beliefs, another set of factors ensuring the continued practice and use of magic and medicine by Africans are the socio-political conditions within the continent. For instance, amid the volatile Nigerian political scene about a decade ago, one political group claimed that its local charms and magic could provide "protection against bullets, machete cuts, acid and other bodily harms."[25] Sentiments like these were widely expressed during the independence struggles of most African states as citizens employed charms and magical paraphernalia in their protests and rebellion against colonial rule. During the fight against apartheid in South Africa, some notable African leaders advocated the use of "black magic" to fight against the ruling authorities. It appears obvious then that, "magic is unlikely to fall into desuetude or be relinquished. Rather, magic will continue to suit social circumstances to meet enhanced societal demands."[26] In other words, as long as the worldview of the African remains unchanged, and the societal conditions continue to be challenging the need for magic to address the needs and fears of the people shall endure. Furthermore, the economic poverty and poor social structures prevailing in many African countries leave the masses with few other options than to resort to African magic and medicine.

GLOBALIZATION

One of the unintended consequences of globalization is that around the world it has triggered a re-appreciation for local cultures and a growing sense of nationalism. Many intellectuals and professionals in Africa are heard stating, "There is nothing wrong with our culture, it is a part of our heritage." Along with this is a reemphasis of traditional medical practices. In the countries of Southern and Western Africa, the profiles of *Sangomas* and *Babalawos* are increasing as government officials increasingly engage them in public functions.[27] As African magic and medicine receive increasing airtime on media and the profile of its purveyors grows belief in their efficacy can only appreciate over time.

INFLUENCE OF NOLLYWOOD

The Nigerian movie industry, commonly referred to as Nollywood, which began almost three decades ago has experienced phenomenal growth since its origin. It has become the second largest movie industry in the world, after Hollywood, with an estimated worth at over $5 billion.[28] Its movies are a powerful portrayal of Nigerian culture and lifestyle, and its themes resonate deeply with Africans around the continent and in the diaspora. Among its film genres, which typically reflect strong religious overtones are: "horror, comedy, urban legend, mythic, love and romance, juju/witchcraft, melodrama and historical epic."[29] However, more recently, Nollywood, with the assistance of Africa Magic channels airing Nigerian drama and movies on the popular cable television station around the continent, DSTV, has served a cocktail of magic and the diabolic. Findings from a study on the influence of Nollywood films indicated that the images of magic presented had a strong influence on Nigerian youth, and could result in "the likelihood for them to seek shortcuts in 'magic' for solving their problem (sic)."[30] Whilst the above-mentioned study centered in Nigeria, it is not difficult to imagine that similar results would be obtained if replicated around the continent. The need for magic, against a backdrop of failed institutions and nation states in the sub-Saharan region offers young, and older Africans the promise of escape and a pathway for the attainment of their dreams.

Pentecostalism

African Pentecostalism, apparently an amalgam of Christianity and African Traditional Religious (ATR) beliefs and worldview,[31] is presently the fastest growing, most visible and vocal religious movement in the continent. Similar to ATR, Pentecostalism promotes a magical worldview promising power for miracles, signs and wonders, ecstatic experience of the Holy Spirit, deliverance from witchcraft and the demonic, and protection from evil powers. Curiously, and inadvertently, Pentecostalism has contributed to promoting the quest for magic and the supernatural.

Some *Babalawos* interviewed stated that the growth of Pentecostalism had actually aided their enterprise in two ways: first, more persons than before are desirous of power to experience miracles (or the supernatural); second, some unscrupulous pastors seeking to impress their congregants with their ability to perform miracles visit *Babalawo* to receive the power they display. Whether or not this claim is true, for the pragmatic African more concerned with what works than with orthodoxy, power is power, no matter the source.

Pentecostalism has apparently fanned the flames for the thirst for magic and medicine which has now become a raging, unquenchable fire.

Conclusion

African traditional beliefs and worldview have been orally transmitted from generation to generation keeping alive its myths and its traditions. Along with the efforts to preserve the visible elements of the African culture, has followed the perpetuation of the invisible realm of the worldview, permeated by a powerful spirit realm and belief in the supernatural.

Some have argued that this pre-scientific worldview has left a heavy toll by greatly slowing down the development and technological advancement of the continent.[32] That is, besides the laziness it may have induced in the minds of youth seeking a fast track to immense wealth. Conversely, it may also be argued that the African religious worldview, and especially its beliefs regarding magic and medicine, may have played a role in unparalleled growth of Christianity, and especially Pentecostalism in the continent.

In conclusion, African religious beliefs and worldview provide meaning, and order to the lives of people. In addition, they satisfy people's needs, and assuage their fears, therefore, the belief in the efficacy of magic and medicine may never abate within the continent, not until a complete worldview transformation shall occur.

Notes

1. Bolaji Idowu, *African Traditional Religion* (London: SCM Press, 1973), 139.
2. E. H. Wendland, *Of Other Gods and Other Spirits* (Milwaukee, WS: Northwestern Publishing House, 1977), 28.
3. Aylward Shorter, *African Culture: An Overview—Social Cultural Anthropology* (Nairobi, Kenya: Paulines Publications Africa, 1998), 64.
4. Robert Cameron Mitchell, *African Primal Religions* (Niles, IL: Argus Communications, 1977), 59.
5. Idowu, *African Traditional Religion*, p. 139.
6. J. O. Awolalu, "What is African Traditional Religion," *Studies in Comparative Religion* 10, no. 2 (Spring 1976), p. 7.
7. See Gerrie ter Haar, *Imagining Evil: Witchcraft Beliefs and Accusations in Contemporary Africa* (Trenton, NJ: Africa World Press, 2007).
8. S. I. Fabarebo, "*Magun* in Contemporary Yoruba Traditions," *Africology: The Journal of Pan African Studies* 12, no. 1 (Sept 2018), pp. 190–202.
9. David Simmons, "Of Markets and Medicine: The Changing Significance of the Zimbabwean *Muti* in the Age of Intensified Globalization," in *Borders and Healers: Brokering Therapeutic Resources in Southeast Africa* eds. Tracy J. Luedke, Harry G. West, and Harry West, Georgetown University Press, 2006, p. 79.
10. I. W. C. van Wyk, "African Witchcraft in Theological Perspective," *HTS* 60, no. 4 (2004), p. 1212.
11. P. Ade Dopamu, "Yoruba Magic and Medicine," in *Perspectives in Religious Studies* vol 1, ed. E. Dada Adelowo (Ibadan, Nigeria: HEBN Publishers, 2014), 104.
12. Essien D. Essien, "Notions of Healing and Transcendence in the Trajectory of African Traditional Religion: Paradigm and Strategies," *International Review of Mission* 102, no. 2 (2013), 246.
13. Shorter, *African Culture*, p. 64.
14. Dopamu, "Yoruba Magic and Medicine," p. 104.
15. Wendland, *Of Other Gods*, p. 29.
16. Ibid., p. 30.
17. John S. Mbiti, *Introduction to African Religion* (Long Grove, IL: Waveland Press, 1991), 171.
18. Raymond Firth, "The Sociology of 'Magic' in Tikopia," *Sociologus New Series* 4, no. 2 (1954), p. 100.
19. Dopamu, "The Practice of Magic and Medicine," pp. 110–112.
20. Gailyn Van Rheenen, *Communicating Christ in Animistic Contexts* (Pasadena, CA: William Carey Library, 1991), 217.
21. Dominique Zahan (trans. Kate Ezra Martin and Lawrence M. Martin), *The Religion, Spirituality, and Thought of Traditional Africa* (Chicago: University of Chicago, 1979), 92.
22. Mitchell, *African Primal Religions*, 39.
23. Shorter, *African Culture*, 65.
24. Mitchell, *African Primal Religions*, 55.
25. Dopamu, Ade P. (ed.) "Scientific Basis for African Magic and Medicine: The Yoruba Experience," in *African Culture, Modern Science and Religious Thought* (Ilorin, Nigeria: African Center for Religions and the Sciences, 2003), 447.

26. Ibid.
27. Kelvin Onongha, "Discourse with Diviners: Discipleship Implications for Adventist Missions in Africa," in *Culture, Adventist Theology and Mission in Africa* edited by Sampson Nwaomah, Eriks Galeniece, and Davidson Razafiarivony (Nairobi, Kenya: Theological Seminary, Adventist University of Africa, 2016), 397–398.
28. Dauda Musa Enna, Emmanuel Paul Idakwo, and Olaku Dorothy Akpovye, "The Impact of the 'Magic' in Nollywoood: An Analysis," *The International Journal of Contemporary Research* 5, no. 5 (Oct. 2015), 178.
29. Uchenna Onzulike, "African Crossroads: Conflicts Between African Traditional Religion and Christianity," *International Journal of the Humanities* 6, no. 2 (2008), 166.
30. Enna, Idakwo, and Akpovye, "The Impact of the 'Magic' in Nollywood," 185.
31. Kelvin Onongha, "African Pentecostalism and its Relationship to Witchcraft Beliefs and Accusations: Biblical Responses to a Pernicious Problem Confronting the Adventist Church in Africa," *Journal of Adventist Mission Studies* 13, no. 1 (2017), 48–49.
32. Dirk Kohnert, "Magic and Witchcraft: Implications for Democratization and Poverty-Alleviating Aid in Africa," *World Development: The Multi-Disciplinary International Journal Devoted to the Study and Promotion of World Development* 24, no. 8 (1996), 1355.

CHAPTER 9

Cosmological and Ontological Beliefs

Ibigbolade S. Aderibigbe

INTRODUCTION

African Traditional Religion has quite definitive beliefs about how the universe and the humans in it came into existence. These beliefs are lucidly expressed in the contents of the cosmological and ontological narratives of the religion. The narratives are usually embedded as themes of oral traditions of various African ethnic groups. Indeed, it may be very important to draw attention to the fact that a true or authentic exposition and understanding of the religion will be incomplete without giving adequate considerations to these cosmological and ontological narratives. Indeed, they may be said to constitute the essential starting points in any meaningful discourse of African traditional religious worldview with regard to the relationships between the Supreme Being and humans in particular as well as between the mundane and the spiritual spaces in general. This is because the dynamics represented in the prisms account for the African "theology" of not just the origins of humans (individually and collectively) and the universe itself, but also their envisaged ends ultimately.

The cosmological and ontological narratives described above can be articulated in three thematic discourses of:

1. The creation and nature of the universe
2. The creation and nature of humans
3. The paradoxical dynamics of the relationship between humans and the Supreme Being.

I. S. Aderibigbe (✉)
Department of Religion, University of Georgia, Athens, GA, USA
e-mail: iaderibi@uga.edu

© The Author(s), under exclusive license to Springer Nature Switzerland AG 2022
I. S. Aderibigbe, T. Falola (eds.), *The Palgrave Handbook of African Traditional Religion*, https://doi.org/10.1007/978-3-030-89500-6_9

In discussing these themes, it is also important to point out their overall significance in African traditional religious worldview. This is because they constitute not just the fundamental paradigms of the beginning and end stations of humans and the universe, but also and maybe even more importantly, the "outcomes" of cosmic destinies instituted, sustained, and executed as divine predetermined "journeys" for both humans and the universe.

Cosmological and Ontological Beliefs

Generally, the two concepts are more often than not interwoven in African beliefs, particularly in the dynamics of their expressions. However, they can be approached as separate paradigms of a belief system. This is why it is important to provide basic definitions or explanations of the two concepts here.

Cosmology as a concept is obviously fundamental to African cultural and religious heritage. While it may be argued that this heritage has been characterized by diverse contents and transitions, it is important to point out that the fundamental elements that constitute its subject matter share unique commonalities that cannot be ignored, if objectively considered. Also, it is instructive that the paradoxical prisms of similarities and divergences demonstrated in the cosmological narratives across African ethnic groups should be seen in positive rather than negative connotations. They should, therefore, promote interest and not out of hand dismissal as viable and important African cultural and religious worldviews.

Thus, in order to objectively relate to African cosmological narratives, there is the need to substantially abandon the Western or so-called other world religious traditions' standards of evaluation. This is important so as not to engage in biased dismissal of the narratives as mere anachronistic, unauthentic, and superstitious expressions in comparing them to those of Islam, Christianity, and other popular religious traditions. If this is done, there is the tendency to stereotype what cosmological narratives should look like, particularly in the context of contents, process, methodology, and applications, thereby looking for sophistication, rather than their cultural and religious functionality in seeking answers to questions about origin and end of humans and the cosmos.

To depart from this kind of sensibility, conscious efforts have to be made to objectively evaluate the authenticity of African cosmological beliefs and their configurations. Those who should be trusted with their interpretations should not be "outsiders" to the "life experiences" of the people who believe and cherish these narratives. This is even more compelling in the sense that such outsiders are likely to be more disposed to offering uninformed or misrepresented narratives due to a lack of insightful and detailed research to achieve objective results. Such a research is definitely necessary considering the fact that African cosmological narratives are embedded in very diverse and complex contents and ethnic applications.

On the whole, the main objective of African cosmological narratives can be discerned as themes articulating the totality of African traditional consciousness on the creation of the universe by a supernatural being. These themes are then expressed in cultural and religious expressions that are ultimately applied and lived in diverse formats by different African ethnic groups, where they are sustained from one generation to the other. Also, the narratives are generally quantified, disseminated, and lived through oral and practical agencies such as myths, legends, prayers, proverbs, songs, names, religious festivals, religious ceremonies, and others. John Mbiti vividly captures this very significant dynamics of African cosmological narratives, when he states,

> *It is remarkable that in spite of great distances separating the peoples of one region from those of another, there are sufficient elements of belief which make it possible for us to discuss African concepts of God as a unity and on a continental scale.*[1]

It should also be discerned that for Africans, as clearly articulated in their cosmological narratives, the origination of the universe also incorporates that of the human. This inclusion is fundamentally based on the belief that both the universe and human are products of the same divine creator. This creator is usually projected to be the center of gravity also responsible for the sustenance of the universe and human. Also, known as the Supreme Being, the creator has a special relationship with humans. It can be seen as a paradoxical relationship that started out cordially, but later became strained, due to human misbehavior in different forms that can be found in the myths on creation among different African ethnic groups. The strain in relationship with the Supreme Being resulted in negative consequences for humans. Among such consequences was that humankind lost its privileged position. Consequently, there needed to be reconciliation and return to the relationship with the Supreme Being. That reconciliation path and re-establishing communication for Africans are through the unique strategy of religious worship of the Supreme Being. This is done by the daily practice of religious beliefs. By so doing, humankind, from the perspective of Africans, is able to re-establish and maintain close relationship with the Supreme Being for the continued harmony and order in the universe and the well-being of humankind both as individuals and as communal entities.

African concept of ontology, on the other hand, focuses essentially on the status of the humankind in the created order by the Supreme Being. The main consciousness here is that humankind occupies the center of creation. This dynamics is what John Mbiti attests to by stating:

> *African ontology is basically anthropocentric; man is at the very center of existence, and African peoples see everything else in its relation to this central position of man. God is the explanation of man's origin and sustenance; it is as if God exists for the sake of man. The spirits are ontologically in the mode between God and man; they describe or explain the destiny of man after physical life.*[2]

From this conception of ontology, African religious tradition has no place for the idea that humankind has a generic sinful nature and therefore has to atone for this perpetually as individuals or community. Rather, the relationship between humankind and the Supreme Being is one that is based on being responsible for ones' actions and being ready for the consequences both at individual and at community levels. Indeed, such a relationship with the Supreme Being provides humankind a vantage position to take advantage of employing the services of spiritual forces in attaining both individual and communal well-being in the society. This is a privilege that has paradoxically given human beings an advantage over spiritual forces, even these spiritual forces are higher than humans in the hierarchy. These ontological dynamics has been well-articulated in the Bantu philosophy by Vincent Mulago. His suggestion is that this vividly represents the African traditional perspective.[3] This is also the thought Temple, concerning the same Bantu philosophy. Here, cogently summarizes dynamics of the interactions of power play between spiritual forces and the humans. His conclusion is that the beliefs of other African ethnic groups in employing the services of the spiritual forces as an ontological strategy of gaining access to an earthly life of all round well-being can be found in this Bantu philosophy in all their ramifications.[4] Thus, for Mulago, this ontological permutation indicates the Africans' belief in Humankind being not only occupying the center of the spiritual order created by the Supreme Being but actually fully participating in its functionality and fulfillment. He is also of the view that such roles do not end at death but continue to be enjoyed in the ancestral world.[5] Another way in which ontological dynamics as a strategy of human roles in the operation of the order associated with spiritual forces is the use of the potency of words. For example in the Dogon Cosmogony narrative, everything in the created order is said to be brought about and controlled by words spoken by Mantu, the Supreme Being.

One other African ontological theme in terms of relationship between humankind and the creator is the destiny associated with individuals in their earthly journey of life. Even though this may diversely be applied in different African ethnic groups, there is a commonality of contents, meaning, and understanding. The theme propagates the duration of the time on earth (visible domain), and the destination (invisible domain) is controlled by a destined projection that is usually out of the control of the individual. This suggests an experience of a cosmic journey in which a person is consigned to an existence that is paradoxically shared in a circular formation between the visible and invisible worlds. However, there is a consequential responsibility attached to this cosmic journey. In order to attain the final goal of positive human destiny of becoming an ancestor, an individual is required to live a morally acceptable life during the journey or "travel" in the physical domain. This then guarantees the individual an existence as an ancestor in the spiritual realm. Ultimately, in this context, death becomes the necessary transition "trail" of gaining "citizenship" in the collective immortal abode, known as the ancestral world.[6]

Myths in African Traditional Religion

The study of myths or a body of myths is usually designated as mythology.[7] All cultures of the world have their own myths. These are usually in form of narratives or stories, through which the origins of things and their mystical components are explained. This is why myths are generally considered to be metaphorical by nature. This is from the point of view that they are designed as explanations for events or occurrences, particularly with regard to originations that humans cannot provide immediate or factual understanding. Such understandings seek to address questions associated with human experiences that are captured within the context of cosmological and ontological realities. Examples of such realties include the form of creative activities of the Supreme Being, human relationship with the divine, the mystery surrounding human existence, the stages of human life, and what happens at the end of human earthly life.[8] In sum, when myths are considered holistically, they can be seen as functional media of explanations for the existentialist questions confronting human understanding.

In the same context of the explanation above, myths in African Traditional religious and cultural consciousness serve as prisms designed to make sense of experiences of life that otherwise make no sense through human rational process. For Africans, such experiences would include explanations for the origin of the universe, humans and other living things, suffering, death, and the afterlife.[9] As story narratives, myths were generally told at night in family settings by elders—either parents or others to children and other adults in the family. Though, telling the stories is generally for recreational purposes, they are sometimes utilized to functionally explain and teach the existential realities or experiences of life. When this is the case, telling such stories becomes sources of passing on and sustaining fundamental beliefs about human's relational experience with the created order in the context of both the physical and the spiritual divides. In this context, myths in story narratives provide the much-needed insight to understand people's fundamental cultural and religious beliefs and practices. They thus constitute authentic, dependable, and sustainable sources of knowledge for future generations. However, it should be stressed that the narratives are not usually documented, but rather are processed and retained through oral tradition. The fact that they are products of oral sources evidently makes them to be prone to changes and modifications, particularly, in circumstances in which they have been influenced by other cultures and religious sensibilities.

Given the above explanations about the nature of a myth generally and taken in the context of African perspective of it, one can then give different definitions to the term. This translates to a situation whereby there cannot be the right or wrong or so-called objective single definition of the term myth. Indeed, making such a claim one way or the other would defeat the very fact of the diverse contents, the meaning, interpretations and applications of myths in the contexts of cosmological and ontological traditions of different peoples of the world in general and Africans in particular. Also, it is important to point out that myths as story narratives are not to be interpreted as if they were historical facts or truths that enjoy uniformity of meanings and applications. Indeed, they cannot be seen and accepted as being of the same status of "facts" obtained from laboratory experiments. To do so, accordingly, Shaw will actually make myths to be "untruth."[10]

Based on all of the above, myths should only be considered to be meaningful if they are taken and understood in their rightful roles as complex explanations of religious and cultural "realities" about human existence and subsequent relationships both in the physical and in the spiritual spaces. Within this paradigm, myths are to play symbolic roles as narratives that reflect diverse standards of life experiences and consciousness among different African ethnic groups. Indeed, the ultimate objective of myths here is essentially limited to the attempt of explaining the paradoxical "realities" confronting humankind about the status humans in the world order and the relationship with the supernatural order and the intervention of supernatural beings. This is why different societies or ethnic groups have myths. These myths narrate and explain the cosmic origins as well as folklore detailing ethnic, family, cultural, individual and national events, and heroic exploits. This may be the reason why some have attempted to categorize myths as a form of an ethnic group or family "historical" narratives, rather than mere stories. This line of thought is quite understandable because, mythology as a body of myths can be a fundamental source of knowledge that provides not just edification but more significantly it preserves the sacred and esoteric beliefs and practices of the society or ethnic group from one generation to the other.

In addition, mythology usually serves the purpose of providing validation for the required moral expectations from members of a given community. This guarantees the appropriate consequences of rewards or punishments associated with the actions of the individuals living in the community. There is no doubt that myths, as segments of mythology that are found in different African ethnic group's heritage, oral literature, or ritual drama provide the people with a unique sense of identity and belonging.[11]

We should summarize our discourse above with a definition of the term "myth" that fits our objective here. Such a definition designates or explains a myth as a traditional story, particularly, when it deals with the historical heritage of a people or when it explains the natural or social phenomenon that fundamentally involves supernatural beings or events. It can also be a traditional story that captures historical events that depict the people's worldviews, particularly in explaining their practices, beliefs, or other natural phenomena.[12]

As we have stated and explained above, African myths are almost exclusively devoted to cosmological and ontological story narratives. Sometimes, the themes of cosmology and ontology in them are addressed separately. However at other times, they are combined as a single complementary narrative. When the latter is done, it is seen as cosmogonic strategy. We are adopting the separation strategy here. Thus, the cosmological and ontological narratives are examined separately, providing examples from some African ethnic groups.

African Cosmological Myths: The Creation of the Universe

For African, cosmological myths are designed to explain the creation of the cosmos with all the elements in it such as the sun, moon, stars, the seasons, and all other natural features in it. They also seek to provide the reasons why Africans tend to understand the symbolic categories of the organization of the universe through suggestions of patterns that are responsible for maintaining the balance and harmony of that universe through the narrations of the myths as paradigms of rituals. Indeed, the beliefs which are narrated in the myths are projected as the fundamental groundings necessary for articulating the rites of passage from one cosmic order to the next. Three of such rites are usually identified. These are the rites of separation, transition, and incorporation. Ultimately, the dynamics of these rites are regarded as a fundamental basis of most African cosmological myths.

It is therefore not surprising that cosmological myths are generally regarded as windows through which Africans' beliefs on origins of the universe and its contents are ventilated. It is of course true myths are in most cases unwritten. This has led to some "outsider scholars" to unjustifiably dismiss them as child-like supercilious narratives without any rational groundings and without any meaning or significance. These scholars seem to overlook the fact that these myths speak directly, saliently, and insightfully to Africans and their fundamental worldviews about the why and how of the creation of the cosmos and its maintenance. The most prominent of these is the African firm belief that the Supreme Being is the creator and sustainer of both the universe and everything that constitutes it. The Supreme Being however entrusts the maintenance of the universe to humankind. This is why human beings occupy very important place and are regarded as special creatures of the Supreme Being. One other feature of cosmological myths is that they portray the universe as being made up of two interlocking parts—the visible, which is the abode of humans, and the invisible, which is occupied by the Supreme Being and other spiritual beings. Furthermore, two other fundamental beliefs expressed in African myths are that, first, the creation of the things in the universe was not ex-nihilo—they were formulated from already existing materials; second that the Supreme Being created everything in the universe in partnership with some arch divinities who served as his agents.

African ethnic groups have numerous cosmological myths. Indeed, according to John Mbiti, there are about 2000 of them.[13] Some of the myths have very elaborate and detailed narratives while others do not enjoy such details and are only present limited information. In this case, they usually combine the creation of the cosmos and humans in a single narration.

However, a representative of the first format of cosmological myths narrated in comprehensive details can be found among the Yoruba ethnic group of West Africa. The myths usually give very detailed and informative narration about the process and the agencies of the creation of the universe and everything in it. There are many of these myths in Yoruba oral traditions. Of these, the most popular one in our belief is this one taken from Bolaji Idowu's book, *African Traditional Religion*. Here the creation of the universe is summarized as follows:

> In the timeless beginning, Olodumar, the Supreme Being, lived in the heavens with the divinities. These divinities were many. Among them were Oria-Nla, also called Obatala, Orunmila, and Esu. Each of them deputized for Olodumare. Obatala was deputy for Olodumare in the ordering of things. Orunmila deputized in the area of knowledge, while Esu was the inspector of rituals. Below there was ·a watery marsh. The divinity who ruled over this marshy waste was Olokun. However, the divinities used it as their hunting ground. At this point in time, Olodumare decided to turn the marshy waste into solid earth. The task of doing this was given to Orisa-Nla. Olodumare gave him some loose earth in a leaf packed and a hen and a pigeon which were to spread and scatter the loose earth. Orisa-Nla did as he was told and the marshy waste was solidified. He returned to Olodumare to report the completion of the assignment. Olodumare then sent the chameleon, that was extraordinarily careful and delict in movement, to inspect the work of Oris-Nla and report back to Him. The chameleon made two trips. On the first visit, he reported that the earth was wide but not dry enough. After the second trip, he reported that the earth was now both wide and dry.[14]

The writing stated that the creative activities began in Ife, which subsequently became a holy city for the Yoruba people. Later, they also added the prefix "Ile" to distinguish it from other towns, and give it the status of being the original home of all. This Yoruba myth also provided a calendar for the creative work of the Supreme Being and the divinities. Creation was done in four days. By the fifth day the work was completed and it was designated a day of rest and reserved for the worship of Olodumare, the Yoruba Supreme Being. This is why the Yoruba calendar is made of a four-day week.[15] This is again captured by Bolaji idowu as follows:

> When the work of the earth had been completed, Olodumare again assigned to Orisa Nla the task of planting trees. Four such trees were planted. They are "Igi-bpe" (pa:lffi-tree), "Ire" (silk rubber tree), "Ani" (whitewood), and "Dodo." The trees had juices which would provide drink for man since there was no rain yet. Also, the hen and the pigeon were made to multiply so that there would be food for humans.[16]

African Ontological Myths: Origin, Nature, Status, and Stages of Human and Divine Relationship

As we indicated above in most cases, African ontological myths enjoy distinctive narratives from their cosmological counterparts. Here, they are approached separately in their own rights as stories or narratives giving detailed explanations as answers to questions about the origin of humankind and the initial level of relationship with the Supreme Being, the creator. In addition, the narratives provide insights into the dynamics of the strategies employed by humans to gain back the cordial relationship with the Supreme Being. In most cases, such strategies are quantified and functionalized through the religious beliefs and practices engaged in by the people. The dynamics involved in human religious beliefs and practices, culminating in devoted worship of the Supreme, usually through the divinities, are designed not only to restore and smoothen the relationship between humankind and the Supreme Being; this, of course, is to bring about the much expected individual responsibility of commitment and loyalty to the overall well-being of the entire community so that the individuals in return are guaranteed security, peace, and well-being.

The above quest is largely responsible for the subject matter of African ontological myths revolving around the claims that humans were created by the Supreme Being himself as a special creature. It is also the reason why the Supreme Being is solely credited with inserting the soul into humans and did not delegate it to any of the assisting divinities. In further validating the notion that humans are special to the Supreme Being, the myths usually point out that the Supreme Being ensured that all that humankind would need were created and put in place before they were created. This move ensured that upon creation, humans did not lack any necessities of life. The myths also narrate the circumstances that led to the disruption in the special and close relationship between humans and the Supreme Being at a later stage and the consequences that followed. It is instructive that most, if not all the myths have laid the blame on the disobedience and other destructive acts of humans. In mitigating this unwanted situation, humans have always sought to correct the situation and win back the state of close relationship with the Supreme Being. In achieving this reconciliation, Africans have always employed the strategy of religious observances and upright moral living with the divinities and ancestors as agents of enforcement. One other theme that runs through the myths is that the Supreme Being created humans as couples—man and woman as husband and wife. This definitely accounts for the reasons why Africans subscribe to the belief that marriage is divinely ordained and therefore its sanctity.

As in the case of cosmological myths, there are also numerous ontological myths that can be found in different African ethnic groups. According to Mbiti,[17] there are indeed many versions of such myths and they can be separated into two broad categories. In the first category, there are myths that claim the first humans were created on earth. They were made either from clay, water, or other material. However, in the second category, there are myths that claim that the first humans were created in the heavens and then dispatched to occupy the world.

Just as in the cosmological myths, the Yoruba ontological myths are also very detailed. They provide quite an elaborate description of both the process and agencies of the exercise. A summary of the Yoruba myths definitely serves as a model of African general notion of where and how humans were created. These are described by Bolaji Idowu as follows:

When the earth had been created with food and drink provided, Olodumare decided to create humans. Once again, Olodumare saddled Orisa-Nla with the task of making the physical structure of the human-being. Having completed this work, Orisa-Nla left the bodies in a room awaiting Olodumare to put life into them. However, Orisa-Nla was curious and decided to see how Olodumare would perform the feat. He thus decided to spy on Olodumare. He locked himself in the room where the bodies were. However, Olodumare outsmarted Orisa-Nla and frustrated his plans by putting him to sleep. Olodumare then put the essence of life into bodies made by Orisa-Nla and they became human-beings. Orisa-Nla woke up to find the forms he had made living human beings. He however continued to carry out his duty of forming human bodies -but never the soul that is the source of life. That is why human bodily defects are ascribed to Orisa-Nla. This is also why women venerate him so that their children can have perfect bodies.[18]

Conclusion

In conclusion, it is important to point out that a meaningful understanding of African cosmological and ontological narratives should entail their being evaluated as being fundamental religious and cultural worldviews of the African people. These worldviews as essential components of a unique African consciousness should be approached in proper and unbiased perspectives. It should be realized that the African cosmological and ontological myths, in seeking to provide explanations to the creation of the cosmos and the creatures in it, particularly humans, also allude to the interactions and relationships between the visible and the invisible domains. In addition, the narratives provide the African consciousness that the physical domain and the humans in it are limited and actually depend on the invisible domain and the spiritual forces, including the Supreme Being, who are its inhabitants for their sustenance and well-being.

In addition, it can be argued that the cosmological and ontological myths as paradigms of explanations for the origins of the cosmos and humankind have significant implications and relevance for stipulations on the "end-time" conjugations for both entities. This of course entails the dynamics of the myths' ascribing these origins to direct causal activities of the Supreme Being. Consequently, the myths in a way can be seen as encompassing the notion of the transcendent power of a creator who knows the end even from the beginning. This actually makes sense given first, the theme of human destiny that runs through majority of the myths. Second, there is also the theme of the circular form of existence both for the universe and for humans who occupy it in the myths.

When all these are taken together, one can begin to discern the reasons why Africans largely believe that both the universe and humans came into existence and that they would never end. However, this should be taken with a caveat in the sense that while the spiritual component may enjoy this immortality, it would be misleading and misrepresentative of the African perspective to ascribe the same to the physical component. It should be noted, however, that the physical component is very important and cannot be dismissed as inconsequential. This is because human existence in the physical domain is considered to be meaningful and significant for what happens in the spiritual domain. The connection between the physical and spiritual domains in terms of human occupation of them and the circularity theme of existence are projected by African cosmological and ontological narratives as the divine determination of the "end" from the "beginning." This suggests that the human life that begins its journey in the invisible/spiritual domain continues to live out that existence in the visible/physical domain. He or she then goes back to the invisible domain and again comes back to the visible domain, thus participating in a never-ending circular sequence of existence.

Notes

1. J. S. Mbiti, *African Religion and Philosophy*. New York: Doubleday& co, 1970, p. 38.
2. Ibid.
3. V. Mulugo, "Vital Participation. " in kwesi Dickson and Paul Illingworth eds. *Biblical Revelation and African Beliefs*. New York: Orbis Books, 1969.
4. P. Temples, *Bantu Philosophy* (English Translation, 2nd ed.). Paris: Presence Africaine.
5. M. Jahn, (2004). *Mantu: An Outline of the New African Culture*. Translated by Marjorie Green. New York: Grove Press Inc., 1959.
6. J. S. Mbiti, *African Religion and Philosophy. Opp. Cit.*, p. 39.
7. A. M. Osie "Mythology of Rituals and Sacrifice in African Diaspora Religions," in I. Aderibigbe and C. Medine, eds. *Contemporary Persepective on Religions in Africa and the African Diaspora*. New York: Palgrave Macmillan, 2015, p. 180.
8. Ibid.
9. E. Ischei, *The Religion Traditions of Africa: A History*. Westport: Prager Publishers, 2004, p. 299.
10. A. B. Shaw, taken from Ibid.
11. A. M. Osie, *Opp. Cit.*
12. J. Murray, *Oxford English Dictionary*. Oxford: oxford University Press. & *Merriam-Webster Dictionary* (1828). Springfield: G&C Merriam, 1989.
13. J. S. Mbiti, *African Religion and Philosophy. Opp. Cit.*
14. Bolaji Idowu, *African Traditional Religion*. New York: Orbis Books, 1972, p. 85.
15. Ibid.
16. Ibid.
17. J. Mbiti, *opp. Cit.*
18. Bolaji Idowu, *opp. Cit.*, p. 89.

CHAPTER 10

Liturgy, Rituals, Traditions, Sacrifice, and Festivals

Mensah A. Osei

INTRODUCTION

Festivals are important aspects of African communication systems. According to Ansu-Kyeremeh, any form of endogenous communication system by virtue of its origin, form, and integration into a scientific culture serves as a channel for messages in a way and manner that requires the utilization of values, symbolism, institutions, and ethos of the host culture through its unique qualities and attributes.[1] The objective of this chapter is to examine first, the important features of some West African festivals. Second, the discourse focuses on the historical, religious, and social origins and the impact of globalization on the celebrations today.

SOCIAL MOBILIZATION THEORY

Social mobilization theory is an interdisciplinary study within the social sciences that generally seeks to explain why social mobilization occurs, the forms under which it manifests, as well as potential social, cultural, and political consequences. K.W. Deutsch propounded it in 1953. Deutsch contends that communication plays a major role in molding divergent peoples into a modern nation-state;[2] conversely, groups disunite because of a communicative rupture. Communication reinforces other factors which aid in fostering national consciousness (such as race, culture, geography, fear of common enemies). Deutsch comments that communication only influences a particular segment of the

M. A. Osei (✉)
Clarke County School District, Athens, GA, USA

© The Author(s), under exclusive license to Springer Nature Switzerland AG 2022
I. S. Aderibigbe, T. Falola (eds.), *The Palgrave Handbook of African Traditional Religion*, https://doi.org/10.1007/978-3-030-89500-6_10

population: the mobilized citizenry. According to Deutsch, social mobilization is the name given to an overall process of change that happens to substantial parts of the population in countries that are moving from traditional to modern ways of life.

However, UN Habitat describes social mobilization as a fundamental component of community development. It allows people to think and understand their situation and to organize and initiate action for their growth and development. The document further explains that through mobilization, people can organize themselves to initiate and take collective action for the common goal of championing their own plan and strategy for development rather than being imposed from outside.[3] In Africa, traditional festivals are important platforms for mobilizing the people. Festivals provide opportunity for the elders to pass on folk and tribal love to younger generations. Traditional festivals of many ethnic group anchor the preservation of unique customs, folktales, costumes, occupations, and religious life of the people.[4] Festival is discussed here as a cultural performance, which is scheduled, temporally and geographically bounded, programmed, characterized by coordinated public, private, and heightened occasions of artistic expression.[5] Furthermore, according to Stoeltje, a festival presents opportunities to observe the communicative system of the culture, conveyed through symbolic complex performance events, and serve purposes rooted in group-life. Kuutma[6] opines that a festival performance encompasses the purpose of the articulation of the group's heritage. For writer, activities available in a given festival reflect the concerns of the community, thus providing scenery for expressing particular ethnicity while suggesting personal affirmation, political action, and social revitalization. The author explains that festival facilitates regeneration and enacts social life and it strengthens the identity of the group and its power to act in its own interest; it contributes to the articulation of social issues. The author concludes that festival brings the group together and communicates about the society itself and the role of the individual in it.

Conceptual Clarification

In order to put the chapter in proper perspective it is necessary to understand some vital concepts in African communication system. The concepts are as stated below.

Liturgy

As a religious phenomenon, liturgy is a communal response to the sacred through activity reflecting praise, thanksgiving, supplication, or repentance.[7] In African Traditional Religion, liturgy is considered a customary public worship. It consists of elements like libation, invocation, offering, prayers, and songs.

The term "libation" is derived from the Latin word "Libare" which means, "to take a portion," "to taste."[8] A libation in Africa is a ritual pouring of a liquid as an offering to a god or spirit or in memory of those who have died (ancestors). A prayer is offered in the form of libations, calling the ancestors to attend. The drink/liquid may be palm wine, schnapps, whisky, gin, *akpeteshie* (locally brewed gin), or even water. The idea of pouring out symbolizes destruction, which is found in all forms of sacrifice in Ghana and Nigeria. Libation pouring among the Akan communities in Ghana has three main parts, namely invocation, supplication, and conclusion. The content of the prayer depends many times on the purpose of the occasion for the pouring of libation.[9]

Invocation means calling upon a greater power God, divinities, and spirits for help or their presence. In African traditional religion, the worshippers call upon God or divinities.

Offering: Offerings are usually directed to God, the spirits, and the ancestors. As the items are offered, the officiating priest invokes the recipients of the offering to come and accept the offering. Offering involves the presentation of foodstuffs and other items except animals.[10]

Prayers: Prayers are the most recurrent act of worship through which worshippers can communicate either directly or indirectly with God, the divinities, and the ancestors. It can be done anywhere and at any time. In this act of supplication adherents present their wishes to the invoked spirits, gods, or ancestors to act on their behalf or to have mercy on them.

Songs: Music and religion in Africa act as a singular enterprise. Between the two, there is no separation of sacred and secular, music, vocals, or instruments. Music and dance provide an avenue through which trance and possession can manifest itself within religious ritual.[11]

Drums play a key role in both the song and dance. Music is at the core of African beliefs and practices. Music can convey prayers to specific gods as well as request the spirits to redirect personal actions. For example, in the *atigali* and *blekete* ceremonies in Togo and of voodoo in countries on the coast of the Gulf of Benin, the gods manifest themselves through dance during the trance and during the possession in the ceremonies. So, dance forms the foundation of a physical rapport between human and the divine.

Rituals

According to Freud, ritual serves to discharge repressed sexual feelings, and again ritual or religion generally serves to effect the illusory belief that human beings are one with the world and thus secure in it.[12] To the contrary, suggests Turner, ritual simply expresses the belief, which, moreover, stems from humans' actual experience of unity with the world.[13] Turner is saying not that the belief in unity with the world is true, but that its function is irreducibly religious rather than psychological.

On the one hand, Turner says that ritual serves to alleviate social turmoil.[14] Ndembu ritual may be regarded as a magnificent instrument for expressing, maintaining, and periodically cleansing a secular order of society without strong political centralization and all too full of social conflict. On the other hand, he says that ritual also serves to alleviate intellectual turmoil. As preoccupied as Turner is with what ritual says, he fails to explain how it does so. How ritual releases emotion, he may partly explain, but how it conveys meaning, he does not.

Ritual in African Perspective

In African Religion, rituals are concrete expression of belief and religiously meaningful acts that people perform in appropriate circumstances, usually following strictly prescribed patterns. Prayer, music, and dancing, which are aspect of rituals, enhance the effectiveness of ritual acts.[15] Sacrifices and offerings help to confirm the relationship between the Supreme Being, super humanity, and humanity. Africans make ritual to expiate one for sins committed, show gratitude for blessing received, and to gain permission or license to avail oneself of certain national facilities such as farming and fishing.

Ritual and Its Categories

There are different levels and categories of rituals in African communities with the most common being annual festivals, healing rituals, and rites of passage festivals, all of which exhibit characteristically ritual sayings, artistic imagery, and action (dancing).[16] It is in these situations that libation features prominently in African religious discourse. Adjaye classifies the occasions of libation into three categories: obligatory, preferred, and optional.[17] The obligatory or mandatory are those times that tradition demands that the ancestors be invoked or propitiated. Instances in this category are the ritual calendrical days such as *Odwira*, *Adae*, all "*da bone*" (bad days) days, annual festivals, child naming, marriage, installation and destoolment of chiefs and queen mothers, and war times.

Alphonse Kasongo[18] explains tradition as a concept that is used in comparison to the concept "civilization" which is in turn related to the presence/arrival of Western population in local African societies; "Traditional or traditionalism" would then take a negative connotation as it is opposed to modern or modernism. Nevertheless, tradition is very important in African culture, as it insures the passage of cultural practices from one generation to another.

Tradition takes many different art forms such as music, dance, art, sculpture, and beadwork.[19]

Sacrifice

Most Africans believe that social calamities and cosmic forces, that disturb their world, are controllable and can be 'manipulated' for their own purpose. The maintenance of social and cosmological balance in the world becomes, therefore, a dominant and pervasive theme in African life. They achieve this balance, for instance, through divination, sacrifice, appeal to the countervailing powers of their ancestors against the powers of malignant and non-ancestral spirits, and socially through constant re-alignment in their social groupings.[20]

African people believed that in times of communal crisis such sacrifices would immediately bring positive response, thereby stopping the suffering. Sacrifices are the primary means by which traditional Africans maintain and restore relations with the deity and the community.

In addition to regular sacrifices, Africans perform special purification sacrifices at any time to seek healing from sickness, physical or psychological harm, or moral impurity. Such sacrifices often include killing and feasting on an animal that is blessed and identified with the person for whom the sacrifice is being performed. Slaughtering and cooking the animal carries away the person's sin or sickness.

The following are the different categories of sacrifices in African religion for festivals:[21]

The Thanks-Offering—This type of sacrifice is given to God or the divinity to solicit favors but also in appreciation of the blessings received. It is usually accompanied by feasting where the worshippers and the divinity share a common meal.

The Votive Offering—the worshippers go before the divinity as supplicants to ask for favor and blessings. Like the thanks offering, the sacrifice is made in the midst of dancing, singing, and merrymaking, eating, and drinking.

The Propitiation or Expiation Sacrifice—It is aimed at lessening the wrath of the divinity through the process of self-humiliation because of low or no harvest, protracted illness, famine, sudden death, outbreak of plagues, or epidemics and diseases.

The Preventive Sacrifice

This sacrifice is expected to prevent impending disaster or calamity. It is a means through which the one who offers it expect protection against enemies or the protection of the whole community from disaster. Africans believe the sacrifice can remove evil, calamity and prevent evil or misfortune from occurring.

The Meal and Drink Offerings—This is the most common type of sacrifice and it takes place almost every day at the household shrines, sacred days, and communal shrines. In this sacrifice, any type of food item can be offered and in most cases, the kind of food offered is what the people eat at home. To offer this sacrifice, the leader first pours libation after which the meal is offered to the divinities or the ancestors. The rest of the food is then shared among the worshippers as a sacramental feast through which they enter into communion with the divinity. Sacrifice is primarily a ritual prayer. It allows man to achieve communion with God through mediation of the offering.[22]

Theories of Sacrifice

There are three main theories of sacrifice but time and space will not permit us to discuss it.[23] Briefly, this include the communion, gift, and expiation theories. Robertson Smith popularized the communion theory in 1889[24] fellowship. Renan propounded the gift theory in his book *Histoire d'Israel*. Anthropological writers like Sir Edward Tylor and Herbert Spencer supported it. The theory viewed sacrifice as a gift to a malevolent or a selfish deity. Renan argued that primitive man of whatever race thought of the means of securing the favor of their gods as they also did with men by offering the gods something. The gods, according to the primitive man, were malevolent and selfish. The third theory addresses the union of a god via immolation of a victim that depicts mankind. Its emphasis was on the immolation and shedding the victim's blood. By placing his hand on the victim, man transferred his sins and life principle to the animal. The animal became a substitute for the sacrificer. The theories propounded are not valid because they do not demonstrate the religious significance of sacrifice. In a way, they discuss an unhealthy relationship between God and humanity, but the main purpose in the conception of sacrifice is that it brings people together.

It would be interesting to note that there is occasional "misuse" of some of these practices (such as sacrifices) by individuals in ways that have destructive outcomes (and not really for social mobilization with constructive or positive communal/collective outcomes) but influential tools that can occasionally be prioritized by some people as a means for achieving even mischievous ends.

The practice of Trokosi is a dwindling religious belief practiced by the Ewe people of Ghana. Forms of it are also practiced in parts of Benin and Togo, where the practice is called "voodoosi." According to the religious practice, a young virgin girl is sent to a fetish priest at his shrine where he owns many other girls and women as slaves. This is a form of atonement due to an elder relative's wrongdoings.

The phenomenon of ritual murder has been part of the Ghanaian and South African system of cultural beliefs.[25]

The Akans of Ghana hold a belief that a messenger must accompany a dead chief on his last journey to the land of his ancestors to serve the chief.[26] Another belief system relates to socio-political involving human rights abuse on the acquisition of power and wealth using juju or ritual killing. This involves rituals performed with human blood or body parts.

During the early 1920s in the Belgian Congo, a Christian revival movement was initiated by Simon Kimbangu.[27] He immediately challenged the colonial order by preaching to and healing the local population. The Kimbanguist Church, an African Independent Church born from this movement, considers itself as a tool of identity reconstruction, empowering the believers to express their suffering and challenge the racial inequalities still extant in the post-colonial context.

Traditional Festivals in the West Africa

Traditional Festivals and their celebrations are a welcomed event for both locals and visitors. Interestingly, there are many of them representing all the different ethnic groups of West Africa. Nevertheless, it is possible, despite their diversities, to group the many festivals into different categories such as harvest, migration, purification, and war festivals.[28] Opoku further asserts that a study of the names, modes of celebration, tells much about the origin and the interesting characteristics of West African festivals as well as their relevance. The writer affirms that festival ceremonies have two faces: the private events like visiting the royal mausoleum, and purification rituals like the washing of the ancestral stools are restricted to the chiefs and the court functionaries; there is the public events like the parading of stool regalia, street processions, and durbar of chiefs, together with events such as musical and dancing competitions.[29] The activities of the festivals are spiced with liturgy, rituals, tradition, and sacrifice depending on the nature and purpose of the festival.

Harvest Festivals

In West Africa, most of the harvest festivals usually start in August at the end of the rainy(27) season after the harvest of the main staple crop of an area such as rice, yam, and millet as well as the start of the fishing and hunting seasons.[30] In the Ghanaian context the "Corn—Festival" of the Anyigbe District near Ho, the Rice Festival of the Avatime and Akpafu, all in the Volta Region, the Fordjour Yam Festival of Badu, Wenchi District of Brong Ahafo together with many more held for millet and other grains in northern part of Ghana. The Homowo Festival of the Ga people of Accra is a popular harvest celebration. Homowo means, "hooting at hunger" and the origin is tied to the origin of the Ga people and their migrations to Ghana during which they experienced famine and grew some corn to alleviate it.[31]

Later after gaining a bountiful harvest, they jeered at hunger and instituted the festival as resemblance.[32] Other harvest festivals are the Fetu Afahye of Cape Coast that incorporates the yam harvest and the fishing season.[33]

Exodus Migratory Festivals

In the Ghanaian context, the celebration of the Akwantukese Festival of the New Juaben marks the anniversary of their breakaway from Juaben in Ashanti to their present abode. Worawora in the northern area of the Volta Region also celebrate their Akwantutenten Festival to recall the exodus of their ancestors from Lake Bosomtwe area in Ashanti to their current settlement.[34] Hogbetsotso begins on the Sunday of every November to commemorate the migration of the Anlo–Ewes from their ancestral town, Notsie, in Togo to escape the tyranny of a wicked chief. The migratory aspect of all three festivals is portrayed during the celebration with participants seen carrying their hurriedly assembled possessions. The Kloyo Sikplemi, a festival of the Krobo people of Somanya in remembrance of their forceful eviction in 1892 by the British colonial government from their ancestral home from the Krobo Mountains, together with the Shais from the Shai Hills. The episodes are recalled in an annual pilgrimage in the form of competitive mountain climbing to the top where one can see artifacts of the early settlers.[35]

War

The Asafotufiam Festival of Ada Ghana are celebrated to remember the battles and victories. Held on the first Saturday of August each year, it involves a large-scale musketry event to recall the bravery of past ancestors. The Yaa Asantewaa Festival at Ejisu, near Kumasi, is used to remember the brave Queen mother who in 1900 led the Ashantis to fight the British in their attempt to capture the sacred golden stool (the embodiment of Ashanti unity).[36]

Trans-Atlantic Slave Trade

The Feok Festival of Sandema in the Builsa District of the East Region and the Kabili Festival of Sankana in the Upper West Region of Ghana are celebrated to commemorate the fact that despite the huge odds against notorious slave traders, their ancestors put up as much resistance as possible.[37,38]

Two Events

Yirenkyi[39] and Kemevor[40] share the same views that some festivals may commemorate more than one event. At times, a festival may commemorate more than one event. Both cite examples from the Odwira of Akropong and other Akuapem towns in the Eastern Region and Ashanti of Ghana are a celebration of war and the new yam harvest. They affirm that the war element of Odwira is depicted in the parade of chiefs as they are carried in their palanquins toward the durbar ground. The harvest part of Odwira is found in a ceremony of parading a specimen of the new yam harvest through the town on the second day of the weeklong festival to signal the eating of the previously banned crop.

Religious Purification

The Apoo Festival of Techiman and other parts of Brong Ahafo Region focus on purification.[41] Separate days are aside for the men and women to expose and ridicule wrongdoers in the society, high and low, through songs to shed their bad deeds in the out-going year. The Papa Festival of Kumawu and Nkyidwo Festivals of Essumeja of Ghana are purification events meant to cleanse the traditional state of all negatives of the past year.[42] It also celebrated to assess bravery among the youth, during which the youth amidst the flailing of whips have to struggle in a tense scramble to cut a piece of meat from a sacrificial cow, all intended, especially in the days of rampant wars to identify bold and courageous individuals fit for battle.

Innovative Ones

Dzeradedu[43] discusses innovative festivals. The first in this category is the masquerade Festival of Winneba during which fancy-dressed groups compete in street parades and dancing is about the coming of the Europeans in the fifteenth century. Then the Edina Buronya (Christmas) held on the first Thursday of January by the people of the Elmina to coincide with a Dutch festival but incorporating traditional rituals like invoking the gods and revered ancestors. The Kente festivals of Bonwire in Ashanti Region and Agotime in the Volta Region held to highlight the production techniques of the exclusive handmade textile, Ghana's gift to the world and symbol of excellence in artisanship.

The "Aboakyer" or "animal catching" festival of Winneba[44] highlight a competition between two youth groups to capture a live bushbuck antelope for use in a ritual sacrifice. The essence of the festival is to ensure a healthy environment through the protection of the habitat of the ceremonial animal and by extension other local species as well as the natural environment including the water bodies in the area.

At a few festivals, the entire community congregates to honor and appreciate the Supreme Being, also known as God, other divinities, and their ancestors. The Ogun Festival in Nigeria held between October and November marks the end of the previous year while welcoming the new one. The purpose of this festival is to refortify familial bonds as well as bonds with the community which is why many people travel back to converse with friends and family.

These occasions are used to discuss Development Plans and are utilized to raise funds for community projects such as schools, hospitals, and construction of roads. The Ghana government has created the National Festival of Art and Culture (NAFAC) and the Pan-African Festival of Art and culture (PANAFEST) which are aimed to display various characteristics of the nation's historical and cultural heritage to the rest of the world.[45] (SHEILAH F CLARKE-EKONG, *Journal of Social Development in Africa* (1997), 12(2), 49–60. Traditional Festivals in the Political Economy: The Case of ContemporaryGhana).

Historically, traditional festivals were held in high regard by all members of the community as they play a prominent role in the mobilization of the community. However, recently, Western education and involvement, particularly the involvement of different religious organizations, have minimized the influence of some of these festivals, such as the Egungun and Oro festivals of the Yoruba people. There is clamor in certain quarters that the festivals should be discontinued due to the activities of hoodlums who have hijacked the festivals and turned it into weapon of oppression.[46]

CONCLUSION

From our discussion, there are important features to note about West African festivals. Festivals constitute an essential feature of African culture in West Africans who celebrate one or more festivals periodically. Theses festivals are religious in nature and are associated with the spirit- ancestors. The occupational activities of the people also determine the date of festivals. Not only do West African festivals mark the beginning or end of the harvest seasons but also celebrated for the spiritual and material purification of the whole state. Festivals also feature the role of chiefs as spiritual leaders and to re-assert their authority over their subjects and sub-chiefs. The traditional way of solemnity and awe previously associated with the occasions is slowly taking a backseat now and have given way to merrymaking and financial pursuits. Every festival has had a historical and/or religious origin while some are linked to seasonal changes. However, one thing common in all is that it brings together people from all occupations and offers a sense of belonging for religious, social, or geographical groups. This particular aspect of festivals make the celebrations truly grand. As with everything else, the passage of time, the advent of globalization, and a booming economy have had an impact on the way of our festival celebrations today. Nevertheless, irrespective of whether the festivals are old or new, they convey a message that relates not only to the contemporary local world, but also to the external world far beyond the boundaries of the immediate community. While the festivals' emphasis on the local communities' uniqueness is directed toward local identity, I would suggest, however, that if a festival is to be successful, its local narratives must stand in dialogue with those currently relevant in the outside world.

NOTES

1. Ansu-Kyeremeh Ansu-Kyeremeh, *Perspectives on Indigenous Communication in Africa*. Accra, Ghana: University of Ghana Printing Press, 1998.
2. K.W. Deutsch, *Nationalism and social communication*. New York: John Wiley and Sons, Inc., 1953.
3. UN Habitat, Social mobilization. Retrieved from: www.fukuoka.unhabitat.org/docs/publications/pdf/peoples_process/ChapterIISocial_Molization.pdf, 2016.
4. C. L. Adeoye, Asa ati ise Yoruba. Ibadan: Oxford University Press, 1979.
5. B. J. Stoeltje, "Festival. Folklore, Cultural Performances and Popular Entertainments." Ed. by Richard Bauman. New York, 1992.
6. Kristin Kuutma, Festival as communicative performance and celebration of ethnicity. Folklore (Estonia) May 1998. https://doi.org/10.7592/FEJF1998.07.festiva. Source: DOAJ.
7. K. Agawu, The communal ethos in African performance: Ritual, narrative and music among the northern Ewe (Trans. Evista Transcultural de Musica, 119 Julio), 2007, 3–4.
8. P. Sarpong, Libation. Kumasi (Ghana): Good Shepherd Publishers, 2010.

9. J. Adjaye, Boundaries of self and Other in Ghanaian Popular Culture. Westport: Praeger, 2004.
10. http://projecttopicsforcomputerscience.blogspot.com/2015/05/worship-and-sacrifice-inafrican_7.html.
11. Music around the world Global Encyclopaedia.
12. S. Freud, The Future of an Illusion, trans. W. D Robson-Scott, rev. James Strachey. Garden City, New York: Doubleday Anchor Books, 1964.
13. Turner, V., The Drums of Affliction, Oxford: Clarendon Press. 1968.
14. Turner, V. The Forest of Symbol, Aspects of Ndembu Ritual, New York: Cornell University. 1967.
15. Lugira, A.M. *African Traditional Religion*. New York: Infobase Publishing, 2009.
16. Washington, "Zulu Traditional Healing, Afrikan Worldview and the Practice of Ubuntu: Deep Thought for Afrikan/Black Psychology". In *The Journal of Pan African Studies*, vol. 3, no. 8, June 2010, pp. 24–39. C. Ray, African Religions: Symbol, Ritual and Community, New Jersey: Prentice Hall, 2000.
17. J. Adjaye, Boundaries of self and Other in Ghanaian Popular Culture. Westport: Praeger, 2004.
18. Alphonse Kasongo Journal of Alternative Perspectives in the Social Sciences (2010) Vol. 2, No. 1, 309–322, 309. Impact of Globalization on Traditional African Religion and Cultural Conflict.
19. https://cultureafrico.blogspot.com/2011/03/african-traditions.html.
20. Mbiti, J.S., *African Religions and Philosophy*. Second edition (Oxford: Heinemann Educational Publishers, 1999).
21. Mensah O.A. (2015) Mythology of Rituals and Sacrifices in African-Derived Diaspora Religions. In: Aderibigbe I.S., Medine C.M.J. (eds) Contemporary Perspectives on Religions in Africa and the African Diaspora. Palgrave Macmillan, New York.
22. Oborji, F.A. "In Dialogue with African Traditional Religion: New Horizons". Mission Studies, Vol. 19, Issue 1, 2002, pp. 13–35.
23. Ubruhe, J.O. 1996: A Key to Traditional sacrifice: A key to the Heart of the Christian Message. Journal for Theology in Southern Africa, 95, pp. 13–22, 1996.
24. Evans-Pritchard, E, 1956, 1970, Nuer Religion. Oxford: Clarendon Press, p. 273, 1956, 1970.
25. Masoga A.M.; Rugwiji, A. A reflection on ritual murders in the biblical text from an African perspective Scriptura. Vol. 117, Stellenbosch, 2018.
26. Sarpong, Peter K., Ghana in retrospect: Some Aspects of Ghanaian Culture (3rd ed.). Accra: Ghana Publishing Corporation, 1974.
27. Gondola, D., The History of Belgian Congo. Greenwood Press: Westport, Connecticut, 2002.
28. Opoku, K. A. Religious themes in West African Festivals, In Dialogue and Alliance, Journal of International Religious Foundation, 4 (1), 71–74 1990.
29. https://www.world-festivals.net/ghana/ghana-festivals.htm.
30. Coursey, D.G., & Cecilia K. Coursey. The New Yam Festivals of West Africa. Anthropos 66, no. 3/4 (1971): 444–484. Accessed February 26, 2021. http://www.jstor.org/stable/40457684.
31. Abbey, N.H. (2010). Homowo in Ghana. Studio Brian Communications: Accra, 2010.
32. Opoku-Agyeman. A Festival in Ghana. Ministry of Education: Accra, 1980.

33. Gbadagbe, R. (2012). Aesthetics and Philosophy of the Asogli Yam Festival. Doctoral Theses. KNUST: 2. https://www.ipl.org/essay/Harvest-Festivals-In-Ghana-F3JYY22FC48R.
34. Fosu, K. A. Festivals in Ghana. 2nd ed. Amok Publication: Kumasi, 2001.
35. Opoku-Agyeman, A Festival in Ghana. Ministry of Education: Accra, 1980. http://ghanakey.com/ghana-festivals.html.
36. Kamevor, A. K. Ghanaian Festivals as a resource for At Education. Doctoral Dissertation. KNUST: Kumasi, 2006.
37. Der, B.G. (1998). The Slave Trade in Northern Ghana. Woeli Publishing Services: Accra.
38. Agaasa, L & Hager Ampa-Korsah Feok Festival Costumes: Evolution & Socio-Cultural Importance. Journal of Culture, Society and Development, Vol. 24, 2016.
39. Yirenkyi, 1998.
40. Kemevor, A. K. Ghanaian Festivals as a resource for At Education.Doctoral Dissertation. KNUST: Kumasi, 2006.
41. Yirenkyi, 1998.
42. Opoku, A. A Festival in Ghana. Ministry of Education: Accra, 1998.
43. Dzeradedu, E. Fashion and the Impact on Tong Culture in Ghana. Doctoral Dissertation, KNUST: Kumasi, 2010.
44. Derkyi, E. Aboakyir: The Hunt of the Efutu People. Published by Edusei Derki: Cantonement, Accra, 2010. https://michaelaviel2014.wordpress.com/.
45. Arhin, K., Dickson, K.A. & T.A. Boateng. Kyeremanteng and Culture: The Kyeremanteng Memorial Lectures 1990–1995. Centre for Intellectual Renewal, Accra, 1995.
46. www.Nigerianbestforum.com. (Clarke-Ekong, Journal of Social Development in Africa (1997), 12 (2), 49–60. Traditional Festivals in the Political Economy: The Case of Contemporary Ghana).

CHAPTER 11

African Circle of Life

Segun Ogungbemi

GOD: THE FOUNDATION OF CIRCLE OF LIFE

From my study of African traditional belief, Africans have intuitive knowledge of God. It is like an indubitable mathematical truth to them. The existence of God is responsible for the regenerative nature of human beings. Without God there cannot be any explanation to prove and justify human circle of life. Therefore, the creation of man by God is the basis of human reproduction and without it there cannot be any discourse either biologically or ontologically. Writing about human creation Mbiti explains, "The Lugbara say that God in His transcendent aspect created the first men, husband and wife, long ago. These two bore a son and a daughter who mated and produced male and female children, and so mankind increased upon the earth."[1] Among different names given to God in Yoruba is the Giver of breath, life, and soul. Awolalu writes, "Elemii means the Owner of life. The name, as applied to the Supreme Being suggests that all living beings owe their breath of life to Him."[2] In general, Ogungbemi writes, "In a nutshell, the Yoruba idea of Olorun or Olodumare can be defined as the supreme source of everything that exists, both metaphysically and empirically or otherwise. He is the Supreme Being or the Deity, the eternal, the creative Genius, the Being of beings, the Foundation of morals and principle of justice, the One and the only Supreme and the absolute who controls everything in existence."[3] It is important to note that each ethnic group in Africa has a name for God and conceptions of their relationship with him but generally speaking, scholars and researchers prefer to use the name God or the Supreme Being, among others, as appropriate for the source of African life.

S. Ogungbemi (✉)
Adekunle Ajasin University, Akungba-Akoko, Nigeria

© The Author(s), under exclusive license to Springer Nature Switzerland AG 2022
I. S. Aderibigbe, T. Falola (eds.), *The Palgrave Handbook of African Traditional Religion*, https://doi.org/10.1007/978-3-030-89500-6_11

The nature of this existential life in the primordial existence is ontologically metaphysical. For want of appropriate terminology, it is a form of metaphysical reproduction. That means, the self, a rational being, shares some attributes with God in the lower redefinition of rationality, intelligence, power, superiority, moral, and many other characteristics between Being and being. With the consent of the Supreme Being, the existential beings have the choice and liberty to traverse between the pantheon of the Supreme Being and terrestrial domain of other beings that are not as intelligent as them and at death; it is believed, they can return to him being equal. In other words, the spiritual entity, the soul does not want a total alienation from God while living in the body.

Cosmology of African Circle of Life

We have come to a more complex African concept of humans in a natural world where they live and define themselves from various perspectives of the realities in constantly changing phenomena having left a world order of ontological existence for a universal order. Living in the universal order requires two propositions of knowledge: physical knowledge of survival and spiritual knowledge to connect with the ontological background. But first they have to grapple with understanding of the physical world as it presents itself to their cognitive structure. Zahan explains, "Thus, according to African way of thinking, there is a close correspondence between man and the world. These two entities are like two mirrors placed face to face, reflecting reciprocal images: man is a microcosm which reflects the larger world, the world the macrocosm which in turn reflects man."[4] Without bothering ourselves over Zahan's nuances of African way of thinking, his analogy of man in a bipolar world of existence in which he is encapsulated and only him can explain his relationship with the larger world and the ultimate reality that takes him back to his primordial existence.

In African traditional belief human conjugal relationship for reproduction and meaningful existence are a de facto for a circle of life to be realized. In other words, in my article entitled "Marriage for a Meaningful Existence" in the *Caribbean Journal of Philosophy*, I have argued that human institution of marriage is pivotal to any form of existential achievements. One of the greatest achievements in life in Africa is to have children who are successful and with good character that will bury their aged parents.[5] The aged parents who would have lived according to cultural and moral traditions of their societies, died of natural causes, and buried according to the burial rites are qualified to become Ancestors. The Ancestors who are otherwise called the Living-dead are the dynamics of African circle of life, the great chain of being. It is a life of continuum in an unbroken lineage in the family and clan.

METAPHYSICS OF AFRICAN CIRCLE OF LIFE

So far, I have discussed implicitly that human procreation or reproduction is a composite of body and soul or mind/body relationship and at death the mind gains its freedom and the body remains in its grave. But there is another dimension in this belief that is called a rebirth or reincarnation that explains African circle of life. I am not unaware of mythical stories that are full of contradictions, paradoxes, and confusions on the part of African forebears to unveil their understanding of their daily experiences of the wonders of life and their hopes and aspirations to be with their loved ones that the cold hand of death had taken away. There are, however, similarities in their narratives that I have put together as reasonable representative of concepts that can be generalized as a belief system of African circle of life.

Let me begin this discourse from one of the frontline scholars of African religious beliefs, Mbiti writes, "Belief in reincarnation is reported among many African societies. This is, however, partial reincarnation in the sense that only some human features or characteristics of the living-dead are said to be 'reborn' in some children. This happens chiefly in the circle of one's family and relatives."[6] However, in the *Encyclopedia of Yoruba*, Bayo Omolola narrates, "Reincarnation is variously described as rebirth of the soul in another body, reappearance after death, or beginning a new cycle of death and rebirth after spending some time in the spiritual sphere. The Yoruba have two predominant notions of reincarnation: *akudaaya*, reappearance of a dead person in a different location, and *atunwa*, rebirth of an ancestor.... The second manifestation is derived mainly from belief in the ancestral cult. Here the concept of reincarnation centers on the notion of the human features or characters of the ancestors being reborn in some children."[7] It is customary in Yoruba to give certain names like Babatunde, meaning "father has come back" to a male child and Iyabo, meaning "mother has come back" to a female child depending respectively on the sex of the departed ancestors. This is done most often when the children have certain noticeable biological traits of the ancestors. To the Yoruba such ancestors have reincarnated in their offspring. Idowu explains, "All it appears to establish is the belief in the concrete fact that there are certain dominant lineage characteristics which keep recurring through births and thus ensuring the continuity of the vital existence of the family or clan."[8] Does this explanation resolve the problem of individuals having multiple souls and personal identity? How does the belief resolve the moral implication of reincarnation if the departed ancestor was known to be of good behavior and the reincarnated soul in his family or clan becomes morally bankrupt? Who is to be held responsible for his misbehaviors or misdeeds? It doesn't seem logical or morally and ethically reasonable for the Supreme Being in all his majesty to allow this form of self-replication since the soul of every human being is part of his essence. Besides, given human advancement in biological and scientific knowledge of human reproduction one may question the validity of this belief. Bearing in mind of this view Idowu argues, "It is almost certain that there is no belief in reincarnation in the classical sense among the Yoruba; that is, in the sense that 'Reincarnation' is the passage of the soul from one body to another...the lot of the soul in each being determined by its behaviour in a former life"[9] Summarizing the belief of African circle of life or reincarnation among the Bambara, Zahan writes, "Greatly simplifying things, we can say that at death the spiritual principles of every human being return to God."[10] While that may be true, I believe a contemporary mind has to interpret the concept of circle of life in Africa in accordance with theological reality of human exigencies.

Contemporary Mindset on Reincarnation/Circle of Life

African forebears for centuries have left their religious, scientific, and ethical trademarks grounded in their solitary inwardness of understanding their relationships with the Supreme Being and the cosmos with unbroken chains of spiritual oneness as explicated in the circle of life. There are, however, moral and ethical principles to observe to qualify anyone aspiring to become an ancestor. The belief resonates the sacredness of life no matter human conditions on earth; nobody should end his/her life and if anyone violates it, he/she is not qualified to become an ancestor. It also teaches that human social life or social order is undergirded by divine moral principles.

The hermeneutics of reincarnation is that even though human finiteness makes human beings appear to be physically vulnerable when death strikes, there is a psychological mechanism of hope for a reunion in the hereafter. This is to instill confidence in African mind that immortality is a doctrine of hope and not a doctrine of resignation in the abyss of hopelessness. It is a theological proposition of intimate relationship with God. That is why Mbiti argues, "God is the explanation of man's origin and sustenance: it is as if God exists for the sake of man."[11] Similarly, Zahan argues,

> In my view, in short, the essence of African spirituality lies in the feeling man has of being at once image, model, and integral part of the world in whose cyclical life he senses himself deeply and necessarily engaged.... All of African spiritual life is based on this vision of man's situation and role. The idea of finality outside of man is foreign to it. Man was not made for God or for the universe; he exists for himself and carries within himself the justification of his existence and of his religious and moral perfection.[12]

What one can extrapolate from the arguments of these scholars in a nutshell is that African eschatology and man's relationship with God may appear Otherworldly but in reality, it is essentially this worldly. Is it really true that the ingenuity of African forebears created God? Any answer to this question will probably generate provocative debates depending on one's subjective and objective background. But it seems to me that African traditional religion like any other religions in the world is a human invention in which the soul does not want to alienate itself from God, neither does it want to abandon its relationship with the body. Now, the soul resides in a world of enigma. Therefore, the nature and functions of the soul have to be demythologized.

African ancestors perhaps intended reincarnation as an implicit scientific knowledge of human traits and identity of their descendants, and not as rebirths of any departed forebears. Besides the implicit explanation of human genetic traits that the circle conveys, there is an embedded explicit African religious deoxyribonucleic acid (DNA); it also provides metaphysical and existential understanding that human existence is a circle and death is its spinning wheel. This humanistic study of reincarnation found its expression in African indigenous religion as Zahan argues, "One sees definitively in these conditions that African religion is a kind of humanism, one which, moving away from man only to return to him, seizes in the course of its voyage all that is not of man himself and which surpasses him. This humanism is the basis for an individual and social ethic whose normal development culminates in mystical life."[13] I think the appropriate description is African humanistic religious materialism because it is about man himself, robed in religious materialistic garment to promote and maximize his happiness. And that is what makes the intellectual interrogation of the theology of circle of life worthwhile.

Of course, what I have said so far may not necessarily go down well with those who take a literal study of African indigenous religion because it has not contextualized it within the scope of African spirituality in which Africans are conceived as incurably religious. The beauty of any inherited tradition is to reinterpret it in line with contemporary knowledge of cultural milieu for the purpose of making it relevant as a monumental value to human knowledge production that has to be preserved as a living memory of the way Africans from time immemorial conceived how God has acted in human history. As human knowledge expands due to sociological, psychological, philosophical, scientific, and technological understanding of religious beliefs and provision of modern infrastructures that influence human conducts, our views of religious propositions will continue to be demythologized. Every generation reinterprets its inherited religious beliefs in accordance with the knowledge and values placed on them. In other words, the belief system has to be relevant to the needs and aspirations of the people.

Conclusion

I began the discourse on African circle of life from the perspective of its origin, the Supreme Being. He is the Creator of man and everything that exists and without Him nothing can exist. That the soul of man has capacity to reincarnate is what makes a curious mind to investigate, interrogate, and assimilate its theology. The soul that is the vital force in human body cannot be without a natural constitutional structure. The creation of man has a natural condition of procreation in the universe that is conducive to make him to flourish. By this provision, man has become a dual citizen on earth and in the pantheon of his

Creator. His natural composition is also dualistic, that is, body and soul or body and mind.

While on earth, death threatens his relationship between him and his Ground of being and between him and his family, children, relations, clans, and society. The need for him to relate to both worlds of existence necessitated Africans to develop a theology of reincarnation or circle of life. The concept of reincarnation now becomes the bridge for the soul of alienated man to reconnect with both worlds that he has created in his metaphysical mind.

African forebears rejected the natural science of death and instituted their own form of metaphysical revival known as a circle of life. In their exposition of this belief, paradoxes, myths, contradictions, and confusions became its internal religious logic that the descendants have to unravel in order to understand its existential message. I have in my limited understanding of their religious expression of reincarnation provided a demythologization of it for the contemporary mindset to grapple with and internalize it as humanistic and spiritual materialism in its all ramifications.

As African Ancestors rejected death as the ultimate end of human life by instituting a religious science of circle of life, making life a continuum existence, the present generation should use their ingenious scientific and robotic engineering knowledge to overcome the threat of natural death or any existential form of death. It is a tall order call that challenges African descendants to move beyond their forebears' religious narratives of reincarnation and recognizing the potency of human transcendence; it becomes imperative to harken to the import of this knowledge production and save human beings from the fear of death and the agony of religious abstraction of circle of life because this empirical cosmos is where humans can live and call their own.

Notes

1. John S. Mbiti, *African Religions and Philosophy*. Garden City: Anchor Books Double day & Company 1970, 120.
2. J. O. Awolalu, *Yoruba Beliefs and Sacrificial Rites*. London: Longman. 1979, 11.
3. Segun Ogungbemi, *Caribbean Journal of Philosophy*, 2016, 43.
4. Zahan, 1970, 66.
5. Segun Ogungbemi, *Caribbean Journal of Philosophy*, 2016.
6. John S. Mbiti, *African Religions and Philosophy*. Garden City: Anchor Books Double day & Company, 1970, 215.
7. Bayo Omolola, *Encyclopedia of Yoruba*, 2016.
8. Bolaji E. Idowu, *Olodumare God in Yoruba Belief*. London: Longman 1975, 195.
9. Bolaji E. Idowu, *Olodumare God in Yoruba Belief*. London: Longman, 1975, 194.
10. D. Zahan, The Religion, Spirituality, and Traditional Thought of Traditional Africa. Chicago: The University of Chicago Press. 1970, 136.
11. John S. Mbiti, *African Religions and Philosophy*. Garden City: Anchor Books Double day & Company, 1970, 119.

12. D. Zahan, The Religion, Spirituality, and Traditional Thought of Traditional Africa. Chicago: The University of Chicago Press. 1970, 4-5.
13. D. Zahan, The Religion, Spirituality, and Traditional Thought of Traditional Africa. Chicago: The University of Chicago Press. 1979, 5.

CHAPTER 12

Death, Burial Rites, and After-life

Segun Ogungbemi

EXISTENTIAL DREAD OF DEATH

I remember very vividly the death of a relation in the early 1950s, as if it happened yesterday; the phenomenon of fear that gripped my mind to the extent that I could not enter my father's room alone without the presence of one of my parents. The wailing and groaning of those mourning the deceased terrified me. The fear was like a dark thick cloud unfolding the appearance of the deceased in front of me as if he was ready to snatch me away; and sleeping alone was an enigma of dread in a community where in those days electricity was a rarity or none existent. And when I was eventually able to sleep, getting up to ease myself at night was frightful and when the pressure was unbearable, I asked my father to accompany me to ease myself. I suspected he knew my psychological disposition because he did not ask me to go out alone as he used to do. He got up and led me out. And when we went back to the room to sleep my eyes were wide open while the mind was wondering on the meaning of what has happened. Has death escorted him to another planet earth?

I could not ask my father any questions of what was disturbing my mind because of fear. It was a dead night and no sounds or movements of people. Who was going to unravel the mystic experience of death to me? During the day, it became obvious from the appearances of people around me; and the words of condolences to relations that I was not going to see him anymore? And the existential question in my mind was why was this fear of death? Is my childhood experience of death scare an isolated case in the global world? I do not think so. For instance, the epidemic spread of Ebola virus in some parts of

S. Ogungbemi (✉)
Adekunle Ajasin University, Akungba-Akoko, Nigeria

© The Author(s), under exclusive license to Springer Nature
Switzerland AG 2022
I. S. Aderibigbe, T. Falola (eds.), *The Palgrave Handbook of African Traditional Religion*, https://doi.org/10.1007/978-3-030-89500-6_12

Africa, which also got to some parts of Europe and America between 2013 and 2016 with the attendant response to curtail the scourge, clearly showed human vulnerability to the fear of death.

The world is currently witnessing the most virulent death scare of coronavirus. The social media, TV stations, print media have reported this pandemic ravaging the global world particularly in China, South Korea, North Korea, Japan, Singapore, Italy, Spain, United Kingdom, Germany, America, etc. This has necessitated restriction of movements, closure of boarders, businesses, industries, places of worships, and schools in these countries. The global economy is at risk and if the death threat of the deadly virus is not stopped soon its effects could be scarier than the virus itself. The magnitude of the fear of death is unimaginable and very troubling to human mind.

African Cultural Attitude to Death

From the foregoing, I have shown that one of the first instincts of life that human beings experience is the fear of death. But what is death and what is its significance in African cultural experience? It must be acknowledged that many African scholars and researchers both at home and abroad, some whose works have been cited in this paper, have discussed the subject of death in Africa. But what is death? What is the attitude of Africans to death?

Death

People celebrate life but not death because it is seen as a destroyer and an embodiment of sadness and grief whenever it strikes. However, people and nations rejoice when their enemies die but they don't celebrate death. That is probably why Bolaji writes; "The fact of death is baffling and disturbing question-mark written conspicuously on the face of things. Man has been forced, therefore, since he became acquainted with it, to apply his mind to the question of its origin and purpose."[1] According to Mbiti, "Death is something that concerns everybody, partly because sooner or later everyone personally faces it and partly because it brings loss and sorrows to every family and community."[2] Writing in the same vein, Zahan writes, "Death, however, enjoys the incontestable advantage over life in that it is necessary, for it was not inevitable that life is given, but as soon as it appeared death had to follow. It is fair to say that death seems to be the unavoidable consequence of life."[3] Ajibade also writes, "To the Yoruba, bodily death is not the end of life, but only the inauguration of life in another form, which is called *eyin iwa*–the aftermath of good character. This is because life on earth here itself is seen as a preparation for life after death."[4] There are some fundamental issues raised by these scholars: the question of its origin and purpose, the inevitability of death, and death as transmigration to the world beyond.

All these bother on how Africans have attempted to rationalize their understanding of polarity of human existence and to live with its contradictions; and at the same time create a theology of transcendence, and self-affirmation in the world of the unknown. The proposition of meaning and purpose of death is made explicit in African transition theology. To understand this theology, it is necessary to espouse three different forms of death from the perspective of African religious belief, which are: untimely death, voluntary death that is otherwise called suicide and natural death. It is imperative to mention that ignorance, diseases, misfortunes, poverty, resignations/abandonments, and so oncontribute to these three forms of death in varying degrees in Africa. It seems to me, they are rather uniquely human phenomena.

Untimely Death

It is common experience in human life to see babies, children, young adults, and adults die "untimely" either as a result of accidents, diseases like smallpox, measles, Ebola, and even the current ravaging coronavirus otherwise called COVID-19. Some of these categories of people could even die of natural causes, but in Africa, it is considered untimely and, therefore, not celebrated because it brings sorrow, grief, and pain.

According to African cultural belief system those who die suddenly before the rite of passage as a result of accidents or any form of mysterious occurrences fall within this category of untimely death. There is no unknown sudden death in this belief system. If witches or people of evil machinations are suspected perpetrators of the untimely death of family members in the community an oracle is often consulted to identity them and to determine an appropriate action to take to assuage the agony and grief of their relations and the community at large.

Voluntary Death/Suicide

There are instances of some individuals who decide that life is no more worth living for them and then commit suicide. This form of death is generally not common in Africa but in some instances it has happened. It is not only an aberration to commit suicide but also an abomination and a disgrace to the family.

Natural Death

In African traditional culture the term "natural death" simply means the death of an aged person who has lived to the ripe old age as determined by his people since in most cases until the African interaction with western civilization the actual dates of births were nonexistent. Perhaps, it is fair to assume that it was not part of their culture. They, however, used historical events at the time of birth of individuals to determine the aged among themselves. Some of the aged persons seemed to have premonitions of their death and it was in their practice to have their children around them to bid them farewell ahead of their actual time of death. So when they died in their sleep, it is called natural death.

Ogungbemi writes, "Natural death is therefore not a complete annihilation of man's life. In other words, the death of the aged is never regarded as evil in Yoruba culture because they have lived out the number of years of them by the society."[5] As a matter of fact, "the death of an aged person is an occasion for rejoicing because the person has been recalled home and his children live to bury him."[6]

The import of an age to die of a natural cause, in addition to having lived according to moral and social traditions of the society, qualifies him or her to become an ancestor. The children and the entire family relations have an obligation to give him or her befitting burial rites. One of the first things they do in Yoruba cultural burial rites is the offer a fowl called *adie irana*, for the smooth transition or journey to the world beyond. This is followed with seven gun salutes to signify the death of prominent figures.

The Significance of Burial Rites

In African cultural belief, the physical body is the indwelling of the spiritual substance and when it leaves the body, which is inert, it has to be buried or disposed of in accordance to tradition. The processes taken by the relations and community to dispose the physical body are the burial rites. This practice differs from place to place in Africa. For instance, those who died of untimely death like babies, children, young adults, and so on are quickly buried, as their death is not celebrated. Writing on the Yoruba burial rites, for instance, Awolalu explains, "Circumstances surrounding the death of a person, the age and the social status of the dead are the important factors that dictate the way corpses are treated and the funeral ceremonies are conducted."[7] In other parts of Africa, Mbiti writes,

> Burial is the commonest method of dealing with the corpse and different customs are followed. Some societies bury the body inside the house where the person was living at the time of death; others bury it in the compound where the homestead is situated; others bury the body behind the compound; and some do so at the place where the person was born.... In many areas it is the custom to bury food, weapons, stools, tobacco, clothing, and formerly one's wife or wives, so that these may 'accompany' the departed into the next world.[8]

The corpse of the aged who had lived according to the expectations of his people and died of a natural cause is treated with respect. For instance, in Yoruba society in Nigeria, Awolalu explains,

> Great importance is attached to the washing of the corpse because it is believed that one has to be clean in order to be admitted into the abode of the ancestors. It is believed that if the corpse is not washed in this ceremonial way, it will have no place with the ancestors and will become a wandering ghost, called *iwin* or *iseku*.... After the bath, the corpse is dressed in beautiful and dignifying clothing. It is brought into the sitting room and laid on a well-decorated bed to lie in state.

Music, dancing and feasting begin. There is also the firing of guns outside. The boom of a gun is a sign of respect for the deceased and a means of announcing to the general public that some great event has occurred.[9]

The corpse of the departed person is usually buried in his hometown within his compound or the family compound where other ancestors had been buried. With advent of western culture and some other religious influences in Africa, however, burial rites of the aged are conducted according to his religious affiliation, for instance, if he was a Christian the body is buried in the Church cemetery. Whether the corpse is buried according to African cultural traditions or otherwise, Africans generally believe that death is not the end of life. The physical body that is given befitting burial rites after death, according to African tradition, signifies also a moral appreciation of the service it had rendered to the soul of the departed, before death led it to the final destination; the hereafter. This seems to be the epitome of the existential meaning and purpose of death and the immortality of the soul.

Ancestral Belief/Transition Theology of Ancestors

It is not natural for human beings to live in a world of vacuum. Even though in African religious belief the aged person has been buried and has transited to his final destination, his descendants believe that he is with them and they can communicate with him. This is undoubtedly a manifestation of a psychological state of mind generally referred to as nostalgic feeling. To Africans the departed ancestors have not gone completely from the midst of the descendants and relations. Although gone physically, their spirits are believed to be hovering over them and they can ask for their various needs and wants believing that the ancestors have the capacities to meet them. Professor John S. Mbiti refers to the departed ancestors as "the living-dead."[10] He argues that when the living-dead are no longer remembered by their descendants or there is nobody to pay homage to them, they cease to exist in their memory.

This may be true of his people in Kenya but the Yoruba in Nigeria have a cultural belief of great chain of beings that makes it imperative that even though the descendants of the ancestors have passed away, they still keep the memory alive. The descendants, relations, and communities depending on circumstances venerate the departed ancestors.

When there is an epidemic affecting a community it is a common practice to invoke the power of the Ancestors. Given the contemporary reality of poverty, impoverishment, and human degradation in Africa, why is ancestral power not invoked for help? There is a global threat of coronavirus disease ravaging the world with devastation of lives and human economy; will the spirits of ancestors stop the pandemic when invoked? I believe those who have the expertise will be in a better position to answer these questions. If the ancestors had intervened in such or similar crises in human history in the past, perhaps with appropriate veneration/worship and invocation, it is not unlikely that a similar rescue is possible. Besides, consulting or interacting with the spirits of ancestors by individual collective descendants give religious and psychological soothing in the moments of desperation, frustration, disappointment, and resignation. And when they are happy, and want to demonstrate their appreciations to their ancestor who are believed to be the ones behind their successes and achievements they venerate them privately and sometimes publicly with elaborate celebrations. The theology of African ancestors presents a form of intermediaries between human beings and the Creator, the Supreme Deity. But Mbiti adds, "between men and important, but more distant, forefathers."[11]

Belief in the Hereafter

So far in the explication of belief in death, burial rites, and the hereafter in Africa, it is made clear that death is a necessary and sufficient condition. Without death one cannot talk about after-life. Be that as it may, it is one of the most problematic belief systems in human history that is difficult to unravel because religious concepts of the hereafter, after-life, and heaven cannot be subjected to scientific verification, proof, and philosophical interrogation without antagonism from the adherents of those who believe them to be true. Believers in the religious proposition of the hereafter would probably consider it irreverent to allow the belief in the after-life to undergo the butcher knife of Reason and logic. The geographical location of after-life remains understood by those who understand its religious language-game. To the believers in African religious tradition, the hereafter is the abode of the Creator of everything, that is, the Supreme Being. Therefore, the hereafter is the supersensible world where everyone who has his imprint or the spiritual essence, the soul, resides with him after his/her journey is over in the planet earth.

The Yoruba call it orun *alakeji*, the Hereafter of no return. It is a world of no return because no one has gone there and returned not even the Ancestors. It is the final destiny of the invisible self, the inner mind. According to Mbiti,

> For the majority of African peoples, the hereafter is only a continuation of life more or less as it is in its human form. This means that personalities are retained, social and political statuses are maintained, sex distinction is continued, human activities are reproduced in the hereafter, the wealth or property of the individual remains unchanged, and in many ways the hereafter is a carbon copy of the present life. Although the soul is separated from the body it is believed to retain most, if not all, of the physical-social characteristics of its human life.[12]

Recognizing the complexities in the definitive understanding and indubitable knowledge of what takes place in the hereafter provides a minority view,

> On the whole, however, the Yoruba is definite about the final lot of the good. They go to the Good *Orun*. As they enter through the gates all their relatives and associates who have gone before come to meet them in rejoicing welcome. If a

person was genuinely prosperous and happy on earth, the life in heaven will be for him an enlarged copy of his former happy one. In fact, life in *Orun* is the larger and freer copy of this one, minus all the earthly sorrows and toils, with amenities for peaceful enjoyment considerably enhanced. The choicest benefit of getting to heaven for the Yoruba is that they will become reunited with their relatives and associates who have gone before.[13]

For those who do not live the experience of the theology of African ancestors and what takes place in the hereafter it may appear too simplistic and delusional. However, the intellectual insight of Zahan is instructive, "Tradition for Africans is, then, a means of communication between the dead and the living, as it represents the 'word' of the ancestors. It belongs to a vast network of communications between the two worlds, which embodies 'prayer' offerings, sacrifices, and myths. In this relationship tradition possesses a real originality[14]" The originality of the ancestral transition theology and the metaphysics of the afterlife with seemingly contradictions, paradoxes, and confusions are meant to convey human difficulties in accepting the fact that death ends it all. Ihuah writes, "More importantly, the question of death exemplifies the paradox of human existence. It expresses the limited essence of humans in whom fear of destruction and of nothingness from something abounds, and the inherent burning desire to transcend their limited being and surpass their present existence and become something out of nothing."[15]

PARADIGM SHIFT OF AFRICAN INDIGENOUS BELIEF

Every nation has had its own renaissance when their people began to think or reason for themselves. Western Europe is one of the beneficiaries of their renaissance that has spilled over to the rest of the world in terms of development of revolutionary politics, religious dogma, culture, science, and technology. African forebears left behind a compelling religious solution to the composite fear of death with traditional burial rites to convey a strong message of the significance of human body and the import of hope in the next world, the hereafter that have remained unchallenged for so long by their descendants. It has become imperative to have a humanistic theology in view of modernity without necessarily throwing away the elements that clearly define Africans and their identity. That is what I refer to as renaissance, meaning when African scholars and intellectuals employ rational approach to interrogate traditional belief systems to understand the fundamental principles of life and death, and the purpose and meaning of human existence.

The narratives posit dualistic nature of human life as body and soul in which death causes their separation and the paradox is that both of them are reunited in the hereafter, and life continues as it were on earth. In the case of the Yoruba, the soul acted as humans and the life in the supersensible world is like as it was on earth in which you enjoy your wealth and property like you did on earth.

The myth of this eschatological theology undoubtedly gives an insight to why wealthy Africans are materialistically possessive, domestically authoritative and oppressive because they would like to enjoy their properties, wives, and children, and so on in the hereafter. Is this the reason why African men have many wives and children while on earth? If the forebears would continue to live the way they had lived on earth in the hereafter doesn't it make their fellow human beings to be in perpetual bondage? When would they have their freedoms, rights, and liberty? How would a just Creator sit and watch this horrible practice in his kingdom? A kingdom where there is no justice?

The forebears might not have considered some of the philosophical, moral, and ethical implications of their religious explanation of the end of life after death. Is it not the case that human beings share a common destination with other beings when death strikes? There is no extant evidence that those who have gone to "live in the after-life" have come back to be with their descendants on earth. It is reasonable and logical that a humanistic belief that human beings have no other external world to live after death is undeniable and realistic. Death is the end of all beings, including human beings, and that is the law of nature.

Conclusion

I have presented a general African traditional belief about death as a means to reunite with the Source of human existence, the Supreme Being. The moral compass of this belief is that as earthly human parents desire to have their children around them so also would their heavenly Father, the Supreme Being, the Giver of essence of life, the soul/mind. The problem posed by this belief is that the forebears probably never had an authentic evidence of the existence of the Supreme Deity and a concrete reality of his environment. Their belief was more of a "given" and asking such questions would amount to irreverent behavior.

To our contemporary African scholars, researchers, and intellectuals the need for a paradigm shift is intuitively compelling. Yes, one must have a nostalgic feeling for a departed relation but thinking and believing of reuniting with him or her in an unknown world, in my view, amounts to self-deception.

We must take the bull by the horns and face the true nature of human existence and accept that death ends it all. What we should do while on earth is to live according to the moral dictate of the society and make useful contributions that will impact positively the lives of fellow human beings so that when death comes, the legacy remains as a footprint of remembrance, and that, I believe, is the meaning of immortality.

Notes

1. Bolaji Idowu, *Olodumare God in Yoruba Belief*. London: Longman, 1975: 186.
2. Mbiti, 1970: 195.
3. D. Zahan, *The Religion, Spirituality, and Traditional Thought of Traditional Africa*. Chicago: The University of Chicago Press, 1979: 36.

4. M. O. Ajibade, "Death, Mourning, Burial and Funeral". In Falola, T. and Akintunde A. (eds), *Culture and Customs of the Yoruba*. Austin: Pan-African University Press, 2017: 355.
5. S. Ogungbemi, *A Critique of African Cultural Beliefs*. Lagos: Pumark Nigeria Limited, 1997: 70.
6. Bolaji Idowu, *Olodumare God in Yoruba Belief*. London: Longman, 1975: 187.
7. J. O. Awolalu, *Yoruba Beliefs and Sacrificial Rites*. London: Longman, 1979: 55.
8. Mbiti, 1970: 207.
9. J. O. Awolalu, *Yoruba Beliefs and Sacrificial Rites*. London: Longman, 1979: 55.
10. Mbiti, 208.
11. Mbiti, 1970: 210.
12. Mbiti, 1970: 213.
13. Bolaji Idowu, *Olodumare God in Yoruba Belief*. London: Longman, 1975: 200.
14. D. Zahan, *The Religion, Spirituality, and Traditional Thought of Traditional Africa*. Chicago: The University of Chicago Press, 1970: 48.
15. Ihuah, 2016: 327.

CHAPTER 13

Reincarnation and Eschatology Beliefs

Ibigbolade S. Aderibigbe

INTRODUCTION

The concepts of reincarnation and eschatology are found both in philosophical and religious traditions. The concept of reincarnation, though captured in different forms, basically stipulates the notion of the return of a being that is dead, to live in another body. This, according to Gross,[1] is regarded as a doctrine of circle of existence. Consequently, it is considered to indicate a prism of life after death. Also, this is seen as the point of linkage with the concept of eschatology. Indeed, reincarnation is generally discerned to be central to any meaningful doctrine of eschatology. Eschatology, as a concept, has to do with the questions surrounding the end envisaged for both individuals and the cosmos in which they live.

The interwoven relationship between reincarnation and eschatology has been a fundamental doctrine in many religious traditions. For example, it is found in Asian religions such as Hinduism, Buddhism, and Jainism. It is also prominent in indigenous religions such as the Native American Religion. This interwoven linkage between reincarnation and eschatology is even more glaringly evident in the African traditional religious belief system. Reincarnation is fundamental to the religion's doctrine of circle of life. The implication of this for eschatology in African traditional religious and cultural paradigm of relationship between the mundane and spiritual domains is that reincarnation demonstrates a reality of an end status for the individual.

I. S. Aderibigbe (✉)
Department of Religion, University of Georgia, Athens, GA, USA
e-mail: iaderibi@uga.edu

© The Author(s), under exclusive license to Springer Nature Switzerland AG 2022
I. S. Aderibigbe, T. Falola (eds.), *The Palgrave Handbook of African Traditional Religion*, https://doi.org/10.1007/978-3-030-89500-6_13

The focus of this chapter, therefore, is to examine the concepts and practices of reincarnation and eschatology in African Traditional Religion. This is done in the context of examining the interwoven implications of one on the other as a "theology" of the paradoxical relationship between human existence in the physical world and the "end" destination in the spiritual domain. Additionally, the characteristic dynamics of commonalities and the diverse components of types, processes, expressions, and applications that are found across different African ethnic groups should be taken into consideration. However, before delving into this, it is important to first provide some brief background discourse on reincarnation and eschatology as universal concepts. Such a discourse entails some definitions, explanations, historical sequence, and typologies of applications.

Reincarnation: Definitions and Universal Applications

As a universal concept, reincarnation has been variously defined. Such definitions are invariably based on the forms of reincarnation under consideration. However, there seems to be some common ground stipulating the concept of the acceptance of the notion that a dead being can return to live in another body. This may be human or animals. In agreeing with this general notion, Thomas[2] sees reincarnation as the soul transmitting from one body to another. This often takes place among the same species. However, if the meaning of reincarnation is to be holistically captured even in the situation where there is no belief in the existence of the soul, as in the case of Buddhism, a different kind of definition is more fitting. In this case reincarnation can be defined as "the belief that a person who once lived on earth can be born again."[3] In a way, these two definitions seem to encompass as comprehensively as possible the notion of reincarnation based on the dynamics of migration of an element from an old "organism" into a completely new one.

This universality of the concept of reincarnation definitely attests to the belief in the spiritual reality that characterizes the human existence. Additionally, this is indicative of the human desire for future existence. Thus, it offers the hope of the human manifestation of the reality of the principle possible "rebirths" ensuring eternal existence.

Origin and Some History of Concept of Reincarnation

Some have traced the origin of the concept of reincarnation to three main sources (outside of the African worldview). These are, first, the philosophical traditions of India, second, Greece, and third, the Celtic Druids culture. Where the dispute arises, is in the determination as to if the notion of reincarnation was independently developed or resulted from interactions through cultural contacts and influences.

In terms of historical development, particularly if viewed from the eastern and western perspectives, reincarnation was said to have first been mentioned in the Hindu sacred scripture, the Upanishads about 2600 years ago.[4] Also, two Asian religions, Jainism and Buddhism, with background in Hinduism were credited with forms of the concept in the sixth-century BCE. In addition, the Greek Philosopher Pythagoras has also been given some credit in formulating some elements of the concept during the same period.[5] His claim was that the soul was immortal and that it could occupy another body after death. In fact, part of Pythagoras claim suggested that the returning soul could occupy the body of an animal. This would definitely indicate reincarnation taking the form of transmigration of the soul from one body to the other.

From this period onward, the concept of reincarnation has continued to develop in subsequent centuries until contemporary times. For example, it did form part of the philosophical propagations of Plato. It also enjoyed substantial mention in the Christian tradition of the Middle Ages. The Renaissance movement in the early modern period also witnessed an interest in reincarnation that led to the persecutions and executions of some Christian figures, such as Giordano Bruno.[6] Indeed by the late nineteenth and early twentieth centuries the concept of reincarnation had made inroad into religious sensibilities in the United States, particularly with the arrival and inroad made by the Hindu religious traditions.

It is also important to mention that the concept of reincarnation, as a global phenomenon, has always been part of many world religions. The concept or belief as expression of the dynamics of the relationship between life on earth and the afterlife is of course preserved through different theological doctrines. It has therefore been detailed in different manifestations by different religious traditions and at different periods. This reality definitely points to the fact that the belief in and practice of reincarnation is by no means peculiar to African Traditional Religion. However, the focus of this chapter is its typology and particularly how this interfaces with the concept of eschatology in that religion. These, consequently, constitute our subsequent discourse in the chapter.

Reincarnation: Meaning and Types in African Ethnic Groups

Reincarnation as part of African traditional religious belief system has been manifested in different African ethnic groups. However, while the meaning may be the same across the board, the typologies and applications have usually taken diverse dynamics. Consequently, these ethnic groups have espoused their own diverse versions of reincarnation. For example, some of such groups that may be cited include the Akamba (Kenya), Akan (Ghana), Lango (Uganda), Luo (Zambia), Ndebele (Zimbabwe), Sebei (Uganda), Yoruba (Nigeria), Shona (Zimbabwe), Nupe (Nigeria), Ibo (Nigeria), and Illa (Zambia).

When closely examined the commonality that can be found in their beliefs in reincarnation is usually characterized by the general understanding of the dynamics of processes, types, and applications. However, prominent differences can be noticed in the appellation, particularly with respect to the notions of partial, wholesale, or generational reincarnation.

This obviously is a result of different ethnic groups having different appellations or names for reincarnation manifestations. Generally, the Yoruba people refer to rebirth (reincarnation), in various ways, such as *yiya omo* (emerging forth of a branch, or becoming a child) and *a-tun-wa* (coming anew). Also, the Aboh-speaking people in Igboland call it *inua u'we* (returning to life). This demonstrates that both ethnic groups believe that death is not the end of human life, but actually constitutes an entrance to another life. Consequently, rebirth through reincarnation becomes a spiritual requirement to be a continuous part of human existence.

One other differentiating dynamic in reincarnation manifestations across different African ethnic groups is the typology of contents of the form or process of returning. Generally, two types are noticeable. The first is "partial" returning of an ancestor in one or several individuals that come from the same familial unit. The second is a more comprehensive one that indicates a perpetual cycle of rebirths. This form of returning is usually considered to be generically associated with collective communal spirits of an entire ethnic population. However, the partial manifestation of reincarnation is by far the more popular type among African ethnic groups. Consequently, there is need to give some brief description of it here before proceeding to examples of the application of the concept.

The general features of the belief in partial manifestation of reincarnation are: (1) that such beliefs are associated with the veneration of ancestors; (2) the notion that ancestors can be reborn through their descendants; (3) that the souls of such ancestors can be born again in other bodies—thus death and birth become changing patterns of a web; (4) that reincarnation is possible because the soul as a spiritual force has the capability of existing outside the human body; and (5) that there is a cosmic harmony of existence in time and space. This suggests a meeting point of the circle of births and rebirths. Such a meeting point indicates a situation where only human features or characteristics of the living-dead resurface in a few children. Consequently, the belief holds that the living-dead still continues to enjoy his/her separate existence, which does not cease to exist. As an analogy, this kind of relationship is compared to the one that exists between the sun and the energy it produces. Thus, though, the sun emits energy, it continues to remain hot.

If these characteristics are taken into consideration, it becomes obvious that the belief in partial reincarnation rests on the recognition that a baby identified as the incarnation of a living-dead usually only depicts certain traceable physical features of that person, and not his or her soul. This position is quite understandable because subscribing to the belief in complete reincarnation would be inconsistent with the overall African concept of the continued existence of the living-dead in the spiritual domain of the dead.[7] Consequently, the person who manifests the reincarnation of the living-dead can only demonstrate features, characteristics, or afflatus that are considered dominantly related to that particular ancestor. Indeed, sometimes there is the need to consult a spiritualist to determine who the particular ancestor is so that the identity of the particular ancestor reincarnated is revealed.[8] Thus, if taken purely as a logical deduction, the notion of the same person enjoying existence in two different spheres at the same time makes the thesis of partial reincarnation a viable explanation. Idowu[9] underscores this explanation by suggesting that when a person dies, he or she remains in the afterlife, and that which is reincarnated in the baby are certain identifiable dominant lineage peculiarities. The belief is that as long as these peculiarities continue to be visible through rebirth, there is the assurance that the clan or family will continue to exist.

The other form of reincarnation is comprehensive in nature. This notion depicts the perspective of a perpetual cycle of rebirths that are generically associated with collective communal spirits of an entire ethnic group. Reincarnation in this form is not about individuals but rather about the universal process of cleansing and refining the human soul. The symbol that has often been used for this reincarnation manifestation is that of the experience of dipping a bucket into a deep well. If it does not draw enough water, it is thrown back into the well to draw full measure of water. Taken in terms of the souls being reborn, the belief is that they come and go into the source of life to be filled with goodness that can only be given by the Supreme Being. It is only when the souls attain this status of goodness that they can be said to enjoy finally a successful integrated homecoming. It is only when filled with goodness that it could finally have a successful homecoming and be fully integrated into the afterlife. In such scenario, it is through the coming and going of such souls that they become integrated with the Supreme Being. Consequently, such rebirths of souls should not be regarded as punitive criminality. It is, however, important to point out that the dynamics of these rebirth cycles are not individualistic, but generic, involving the survival strategy of humanity as represented in a given society. Thus, as Shorter[10] suggests, for the African, death becomes a form of rebirth that ensures the continuity of humanity. Shorter further explains how this is so. He states: "the dead are planted and they bear fruit in lives and the procreation of their descendants."[11] Consequently, for example, among the Tiv, when the grave is dug for a burial, it is done in such a manner that when the corpse is deposited in it, it faces the direction of the dead person's natal home.

The above having been said, it is important to briefly mention the fact that belief in reincarnation is generally approached with different understandings that usually result in diverse applications and typologies from one African ethnic group to the other. As there is no way each of these expressions can be covered here, it suffices to summarize two of such typologies. The first is from the Yoruba ethnic group of West Africa, representing the partial typology, and the second is from the Ila ethnic group of southern Africa, representing the universal typology.

The Yoruba Typology

The belief in reincarnation is very central to Yoruba religious culture. It is variously captured in every sector of the people's worldview and articulated in their everyday contextualization of both oral and non-oral traditional prisms of expression—in language, practices, and works of art. In terms of meaning and understanding, reincarnation can be described in different formats among the Yoruba, as in other African society, as the returning of the soul in another body. It can also be described as a form of reappearance after one has died. Another way of describing it as the beginning a new cycle of death and returning and this happens after the dead person must have spent some time in the spiritual domain. The Yoruba descriptions of reincarnation are identifiable in two notions of manifestation—the reappearance of a dead person and the actual rebirth of a dead person. However, the second notion can be further subdivided into two—the rebirth of an ancestor or the rebirth of dead child.

Typically, initial manifestation is in the form of *akudaaya*. This is the Yoruba nomenclature for a dead person that is claimed to have reappeared in a different location from where he or she lived before death. This experience is described concerning a dead person being physically seen in other locations usually by those who are not aware of his or her passing. Such encounter may take place either before or after the burial of the person. The interesting thing about this manifestation of reincarnation is that such a reincarnated person actually continues to live a normal life. He or she continues to engage in the normal sequence of human activities of getting married, having children, having a profession, and socializing without being detected as someone who is actually gone. Usually the Yoruba are of the view that reincarnation in form of *akudaaya* occurs in the cases of people who die before attaining old age and are therefore required to complete their allotted span of life in another location where they would be accepted and treated as normal members of the community.

The second manifestation of reincarnation, in this case the one associated with the Yoruba belief in ancestral cult, centers on the notion of the human features or characters of the ancestors being reborn in some children. This describes the thesis of partial reincarnation that allows the ancestors to continue to have their separate existence. Consequently, even though the ancestors are reborn, they do not lose their continued "personal" existence in the ancestral world. Thus, the descendants in whom they are reborn have only the ramification of the ancestors' *okan*, the part of humans that depicts characteristic features. In fact, the reincarnated ancestor is usually identified in his or her descendant through noticeable similarities in such characteristic features. That is why the Yoruba think that this form of reincarnation is preserved for people who die in ripe old age and are qualified to be ancestors based on the required standards of their exemplary, righteous living on earth.

This form of reincarnation definitely exemplifies rebirth in that it is referred to by the Yoruba as *yiya omo* (turning into a child) or *atunwa* (another coming). This is well reflected in the name given to a child regarded as a rebirth of an ancestor. For example, if the child is a female, she is given such names as *Iyabo* or *Yetunde* (mother returns) denoting a female ancestor. If the child is a male, the names given may be *Babatunde* or *Babawale* (father returns).

The Yoruba usually adopt certain mechanisms in identifying the occurrence and the particular ancestor who has been reborn. It should be noted, however, that the Yoruba restrict the potentiality of reincarnation to only the paternal lineage. Therefore, reincarnated children can only be named after ancestors from the father's lineage. Also, the identity of the reincarnated ancestor can be ascertained through the consultation of Ifa oracle. In addition, the identification can be done through close observation of the looks, mannerisms, and activities of a child both at birth or as the child grows to adulthood. The ancestor can also be identified, for example, if the child displays identical bodily marks and recalls or exhibits characteristic traits as those of an ancestor. In some other situations, the identification occurs if, for example, the child is able to recall the ancestor's past existence, or displays skills that suggest the child is older than his or her age.

The second manifestation of reincarnation as indicated above contains a sub-notion associated with the rebirth of a dead child, known as *abiku* (born to die) by the Yoruba. This manifestation of reincarnation centers on the notion of the existence of a limbo "world" filled with discarnate spirits eagerly seeking a return to terrestrial life. Such spirits are said to dwell in trees such as iroko, baobab, and silk-cotton species.[12] Also, the spirits are attributed with the mysterious powers of being able to replace the original fetus of a pregnant woman and be borne by the same woman and family over and over again. Their ability to keep returning designates them as sources and perpetuators of agony and frustration to the woman and her family. It is usual for an *abiku* to die before reaching puberty—probably within twelve years.[13] The death of *abiku* before puberty is taken to be deliberate and designed to articulate its "indifference to the plight of the mother and her grief."[14]

In order to deter the *abiku* from death after being born again, the child is defaced or mutilated by cutting of one finger, ear, or putting a deep mark in the face or back. Also, if the child still dies, these marks remain and are recognizable when it is reborn. Another way of deterring the *abiku* is to appease it by giving it some pleading names so that it terminates the cycle of rebirth and stays permanently with the family. Such names include Duro-Orike, Durosinmi, Durojaiye, Igbokoyi, Jokotimi, Malomo, Kosoko, among others.

In summary, it is quite obvious that the meaning, understanding, and process of Yoruba belief in reincarnation fundamentally derives from the people's philosophy that gives premium to cosmic harmony. This is ultimately grounded in the recognition of unity of existence that is sustained and subsumed in the circle of birth and rebirth.[15]

The Illa Typology

The notion of reincarnation among the Illa people of Zambia represents the generic type. This type of reincarnation does not concentrate on individual rebirths as discussed in the Yoruba society. The fundamentals of Illa reincarnation consciousness seem to denote that a number of spirits that were given bodies at the point they were created can have other bodies once the body they were created with at the beginning wears out at the appropriate time. However, according to this thesis, there are some exceptions. For example, ethnic divinities and other individuals such as sorcerers, whose rebirths are automatically interrupted, are exempted.

The major characteristics of the Illa type of reincarnation are that first, the reincarnated spirits are gender-neutral. Second, the reincarnated spirits do not have any remembrance of previous lives, earthly or spiritual. Lastly, while such reincarnated spirits animate the body in their lifetime, they are not affected and do not reflect the daily vicissitudes in which they are involved.

In spite of the diverse typologies of reincarnation identified and discussed between the two African ethnic groups above, a thesis of common fundamental trends in doctrine can be advanced. This consists of the agreement that the doctrine of rebirth can be associated with challenges brought by day-to-day experiences and can be seen through the lens of refining of character of humans toward a fullness of life. Taken in this form, reincarnation is approached in African Traditional Religion as nature's strategy of promoting and elevating the spiritual essence of either individuals or generic humanity in the journey toward greater self-consciousness through the fires of multiple life experiences in material or physical existence. Thus, "circular rebirths are regarded to be a spiritual necessity." Indeed, this proclamation that can be symbolized as a golden thread hidden in the coarse fabric of human experience not only depicts the reality of man's inner spiritual nature, but also as "ancient wisdom" deeply rooted in the African Traditional theology of reincarnation. It can also be argued that this is the unique intercession between reincarnation and eschatology in African religious beliefs system. This intercession is what is discussed next as we examine the implications associated with linkage between reincarnation and eschatology in the paradoxical relationship of a reincarnated circle of life and the envisaged end of the individual. However, before this, it is proper to briefly discuss the concept of eschatology in its own right in African traditional religious belief system. This should provide a meaningful understanding of our subsequent discussion on the interwoven relationship between reincarnation and eschatology in African Traditional Religion.

Eschatology in African Traditional Religion and Culture

Universally, the concept of eschatology has been defined in diverse ways and forms representing its different understandings. The beliefs and practices of eschatology have also been explained and approached through diverse prisms of evolving historical developments that have been shaped by different religious cultures and traditions. However, when the concept is viewed holistically, there is the indication that it has evolved in patterns that show unique peculiarities in different religious traditions or cultures. This notwithstanding, there have been noticeable common features in contents, processes, functionalities, and ultimate outcomes of the concept of eschatology in nearly all religious traditions and cultures.

Given the above, a functional and holistic definition of eschatology, apart from the strictly etymological ones, has been offered by Bienvenu Mayemba. He states:

> *Generally speaking, eschatology is the theological doctrine of the ultimate things, of the last or final days, of the world to come, of life after death. It is a theological investigation or a religious quest about the ultimate meaning and the destiny of the world and of human beings. In this sense, eschatology has a teleological dimension. It deals with expectation, with hope, with death, with the future. Its relevance lies on the belief that not everything about human beings is over after death, that death is not human beings' radical end and absolute destination, and that there is something beyond.*[16]

This definition, in our opinion, definitely covers meaning and understanding of the holistic theme or doctrine of eschatological beliefs and practices in African religious tradition. Consequently, it can be postulated that eschatological beliefs have always been part of the African religious tradition. It is also important to note that such beliefs which have been contextualized in various themes can be seen as "theological doctrines" of the religious tradition as part of the rich heritage of the African people. Indeed such eschatological doctrines are quantifiable as existential sensibilities of what constitutes the end for the individual as a historical person on a cosmic journey. This journey is viewed as a circular one in that the end of a historical life actually constitutes the beginning of another one. Additionally, the circular journey is interwoven Xin a framework that involves both the physical and the spiritual spaces of existence. Thus, the circular historical dynamics are essentially captured in the theological doctrine that indicates that while lives of human beings as individuals may come to an end, the human race as a collective of individuals continues to exist in an endless journey. This then suggests that an eternal existence finds concrete expression in the cult of the ancestors. Here the existential cosmic and historical journey is captured in a time frame of the past, the present, and the future that is contextually interwoven and sustained in endless generations comprising of the living, the dead, and future individuals yet to be born. Within this doctrinal consciousness, time is uninterrupted and there is the notion of an everlasting or eternal cosmos.

It should also be noted that with the doctrine of circular life associated with individuals there is no notion of future resurrection of dead bodies in African religious tradition, as found in other religious traditions, such as Christianity. Rather, what obtains is the absolute belief in life after death in the "invisible world." This is seen as a kind of "ancestors' village." It is the domain where those who are qualified by living righteous lives while they were on earth physically congregate to participate in a joyful personal and collective immortality.

However, it must be stressed that an eschatological doctrine based on this ancestral configuration is not about life in the context of future resurrection of the dead. It suffices only in its focus of providing the African people with a veritable potential expectation of the hope of a life that guarantees immortality if lived according to personal virtue, cosmic harmony, collective solidarity as guided by ancestral wisdom. This dynamic of connectivity of ancestral immortality of reincarnated experiences with the projected notion of individual end status constitutes, in our mind, the implications derivable from the doctrines of reincarnation and eschatology in African Traditional religion.

REINCARNATION AS PRISM OF ESCHATOLOGY IN AFRICAN TRADITIONAL RELIGION: THE IMPLICATIONS

After the discourse on the different concepts and practices of reincarnation eschatology in African traditional religious belief system, an examination of the implications of the two on each other in such a system becomes relevant and proper. In doing this, first from reincarnation perspective, it is important to initially delve into the fundamental underlining philosophical and theological sensibilities of African religious tradition in the context of interpretations that have been given to the doctrine of rebirth. Here, it seems that there is, in the tradition, a general agreement in all interpretations of the doctrine of rebirth that suggests a limitation of souls available in a given world space and time. Thus, the notion of rebirth through a process of reincarnation is quite logical if the overall belief in the circle of life is to be sustained. This may be why, for example, the Illa ethnic group in Zambia believes the notion that only a specific number of souls are created and given bodies at the very beginning of human existence. If this is so, then the souls or spirits are capable of living on in the spiritual domain awaiting new bodies. Consequently, it is logical to claim the inevitably of the rebirth of these souls in new bodies. This position of the Illa people, as in many other African ethnic groups, entails two distinctive characteristics of reincarnation as a prism of eschatology. First, that reincarnation is gender-neutral, as they can manifest either in male or female forms. Second, those souls usually have no recollection whatsoever of their previous lives on earth.

Indeed, this characterization of reincarnation through the agency of rebirth posits a reincarnation mechanism that is fundamentally based on nature through a flow of eternal circle of manifested human existence. This "immortality" consists of transitional but successive occupation of both the earthly and spiritual domains that are not subjected to the obstacles of time and space in the quest for the end of both human individuals and the cosmos itself. In this case the suggestion can be submitted that the reincarnating entity should be seen in a spiritual essence that occupies its own time and space of existence after death in the spiritual life but also has the ability to animate a material body in its earth life as the desired end time point. This, therefore, constitutes the eschatological implication.

This ramification of reincarnation mechanism as implication for eschatology is discernible in a number of sensibilities that have become significant parts of African religious tradition located in its formulated beliefs and practices. Some of these are briefly discussed below.

First, in African traditional belief and practice, death and reincarnation are seen as complementary phenomena. Thus, both of them are regarded as necessary processes of existence ensuring that mankind is regenerated, purified, and improved. Indeed, it is usually claimed that it is sometimes necessary for the soul to inhabit healthier bodies in order to overcome diseases.

Second, it is the African position that the human spiritual force is capable of existence outside the human body. This is what portends immortality. This, then, is what defines and ensures continuity of family or ethnic lineage as such immortality is achieved through a process of the ancestors or the generic souls of once-living beings rejoining the communities of their descendants. This is achieved through being reincarnated, particularly, in newborn members of the family or ethnic group. This dynamic is considered to not only be significant but also central to African religious tradition. Not attaining such a status is considered to be humiliating and degrading. This is because such a situation is tantamount to the loss of the possibility of a patrilineal being recycled by playing host to its famous and noble members through rebirths.

Thirdly, in confirmation of the above, reincarnation as an eschatological prism reinforces the African lineage system as spiritual unity for which and in which members are born, exist, die, and are reborn. Also, it depicts a sense in which the dynamics stimulate and establish the all-important support parameters for socio-political healing and religious responsibility that are demonstrated conjunctions in the unity of existence involving the tripartite personalities of the dead, the living, and the unborn in relation to envisaged end destinations. Finally, a meaningfully understanding clearly demonstrates that African belief in reincarnation fundamentally subscribes to an eschatological deterministic view of human existence. This paradoxical connectivity in a way shares and, indeed, may be said to subscribe to the Hebrew fatalistic concept that is succinctly professed in Ecclesiastes 1:9-10 stating, "That which has been is that which shall be and that which has been done is that which shall be done; and there is no new thing under the sun. Is there a thing of which men say, "see this is new?" It has been already in the ages that were before us!"

Notes

1. R. M. Gross, Buddhism After Patriarchy: A Feminist History, Analysis and Reconstruction of Buddhism. New York: State University of New York Press, 1993.
2. N. Y. Thomas, "Transmigration," in James Hastings ed. Encyclopedia of Religion and Ethnics. Vol. xii. Edinburg: T&T. Clark, 1989.
3. Ibid.
4. G. D. Flood, *Introduction to Hinduism*. London: Cambridge University Press, 1998.
5. S. S. Hermann, *Pherekeles of Spirits*. Oxford: Oxford University Press, 2001.
6. W. Boulting, *Giordino Bruno: His Life, Thoughts and Martyrdom*. London: Kegan Paul, 1914.
7. M. Dillon and N. Chadwich, *The Cultic Realm*. London: Weidenfeld and Nicolson, 2009.
8. M. Ara, *Eschatology in the Indo-Iranian Tradition: The Genesis and Transformation of a Doctrine*. New York: Peter Lang, 2003, pp. 9–10.
9. E. B. Idowu, *Olodumare, God in Yoruba Belief*. London: Longman, 1963.
10. A. Shorter, *African Culture and Christian Church*. London: Geoffrey Chapman, 1983, 14.
11. Ibid., 16.
12. T. Mobolaji, "The Concept of Abiku" in JASTOR. 1973. www.jastor.orgstable/33347-54. Retrieved March 20, 2020.
13. Ibid.
14. Wole Soyinka, "Abiku" in Histories of Errancy: Oral Yoruba Texts. https//muse.jhu.edu/article/29669. Retrieved March 20, 2020.
15. I. S. Aderibigbe, "Reincarnation." in Toyin Falola and Akintunde Akinwumi eds. *Encyclopedia of the Yoruba*. Indiana: Indiana University Press, 2016.
16. Bienva Mayemba, (2009). The Nature of Eschatology in the African Ancient Religion: A Category of Deliverance, Promise, Redemption. Posted on escholarship@BC. Chestnut Hill Boston College Library.

CHAPTER 14

Religious Leaders: Priests/Priestesses, Medicine Professionals, and Kings

Danoye Oguntola-Laguda

INTRODUCTION

Leadership has been one of the numerous problems plaguing African institutions in all areas of human engagements. Leaders have often been found wanting to rid themselves of their responsibilities. Religious institutions are no exception in this regard. There have been allegations of misappropriation of funds, sexual abuses, harassments, lying, mismanagement of illness based on falsehoods, and misapplication of medicaments and pharmaceutical prescriptions. The traditional political officeholders, who are supposed to be the custodians of religion and cultural traditions of the people, have appropriated politics into the process of discharging their responsibilities, calling into question their leadership qualities and style. In this manner, kings have compromised their cultural value and relevance in the discharge of their religious duties. In this chapter, I engage the value, meaning, and implications of religious leadership in African Traditional Religion using examples from Yorùbá. This chapter critically examines the anticipated roles of religious leaders with particular reference to ritual leaders—priests, priestesses, medicine practitioners, diviners, herbal sellers, traditional therapists, and political leaders—kings, and chiefs in the economic, social, and cultural lives of the people. This chapter will round up with a look at the expectations of adherents of African Traditional Religion on these categories of religious leaders, especially in contemporary times. The chapter adopts historical and critical methods to analyze current leadership trends

D. Oguntola-Laguda (✉)
Lagos State University, Lagos, Nigeria
e-mail: danoye.oguntolalaguda@lasu.edu.ng

© The Author(s), under exclusive license to Springer Nature Switzerland AG 2022
I. S. Aderibigbe, T. Falola (eds.), *The Palgrave Handbook of African Traditional Religion*, https://doi.org/10.1007/978-3-030-89500-6_14

based on fieldwork carried out in Lagos, Nigeria, during 2015–2018 to determine if the traditional religious leaders are still performing their duties as dictated by traditions and religion(s).

Leadership: A Definition

In simple words or terms, a leader is a person who provides leadership to his or her group, family, community, society, and country. This will suggest that leadership, as a concept, could be defined based on the scope, structure, and objectives of the environment in which a leader is to operate. James M. Burns defines leadership as: "A structure of actions that engages a person to varying degrees throughout the levels and among interstices of social units."[1]

Burns's definition indicates that leaders are agents of the people they lead or represent. It also confirms that there are various levels of leadership that behold some responsibilities and expectations from the leaders by the communities they represent. Julius Nyerere explains the attributes of a leader as follows: "When you are selected to lead your fellowmen, it does not mean that you know everything better than the followers. It does not mean that you are more intelligent than the followers."[2]

The opinion of Nyerere suggests that knowledge is not exclusive to leaders. A leader should, therefore, consider him/herself lucky to be "first among equal." Consequently, the office is a call to duty. The effect of a leader in providing leadership could be measured by the social, economic, political, ethical, and cultural changes that emerge through interaction with the followers by intent and by the satisfaction of their needs and expectations. Thus, leadership and followers have a mutual relationship based on needs, aspirations, and values.[3]

There are three types of leadership often identified by scholars.[4] These are transactional leadership, transforming leadership, and moral leadership. Transactional leadership is a "trading" situation where a person seeking leadership positions gives money or favor in expectation or the support of and loyalty of the followership. This type of leadership is common in political leadership in developing countries like Nigeria and Ghana. In recent elections in the formers, it was alleged in the social and print media (with video evidence) that politicians were buying voters from the electorates. In Ekiti State, Southwest Nigeria, the act was tagged "*Dibo ko se obe*" (Vote and cook soup). Transforming leadership is also a common feature of political governance where the political elite seeks to negotiate power with the electorate with the promise of transforming the society from one position (often negative concerning development) to another. It is a common feature of political leadership negotiations. In the 2015 presidential election, the two leading parties—All Progressive Congress (APC) and People's Democratic Party (PDP)—employed this type of rhetoric in seeking power. The former tagged its policies as "Change" and the latter called it "Transformation."[5] Moral leadership is often associated with ethical, cultural, and religious groups and communities. This is the focus of our study in this chapter. From the above explanations on leadership, I shall define the concept as the process and means for the acquisition of power to lead and mobilize the followers throughout all social classes to advance socio-cultural development and political actions. It should be noted, however, that while political leaders battle for higher-level leadership positions through an electoral process, religious leadership most often inherit, train, or are chosen for leadership based on their experience or selection (by the community).

Religious Leadership

Religion plays a crucial role for many leaders and groups—both in the selection process of religious leaders or elections of political or economic or cultural leaders. However, religion, as a social phenomenon and institution, can be positive or negative depending on how it is deployed. This perhaps informed the opinion of Karl Marx, who suggests that religion is a negative tool often deployed by elites to oppress the poor.[6] On the contrary, Milton Yinger argued that religion has adequate qualities to reengineer social, economic, and political changes to the benefits of humanity.[7] By implication, therefore, I argue that religion could become a social tool with serious implications on leadership as a concept and institution. It should be noted that my view here is subjective, as some people may not subscribe to religion affecting their office as a leader. They may allude to secularization. I have argued elsewhere[8] that even if we live in a secular society, it does not remove religion from our psyche, and its functions (positive) in the society cannot be denied.[9] Scholars like Rodney Stark have argued based on the above[10] that "secularization should be carried to the grave of failed theories" (LEAD Research 2016). While I will not agree with Rodney that secularization has failed, its effect may have waned. There is evidence of religious symbols and tools used by leaders to demonstrate their commitments to religious beliefs and morality. In a LEAD report on a study carried out in German in 2016, it was reported how religion affects the leadership styles and patterns of some Chief Executive Officers (CEOs). The report states that: "A city mayor told us that the cross in his office reminded him to stay humble. A CEO uses an App to remember pause, repose and pray during hectic working hours in the fast paced world … another CEO placed stone on her office desk to remind her of John 8:7: 'whoever is without sin among you let him be the first to cast a stone at her.' This is a physical reminder that it is not only her employees who make mistakes she does too."[11]

Although many CEOs may not use symbols or tools of religion in their daily leadership schedules, they are influenced by their faith in the leadership principles and practices. Thus, the point I make here is that religion influences the leadership styles and practices of many business and political leaders.

Religious leadership suggests a servant leadership orientation where religious leaders are expected to serve their communities. This becomes clear when the transcendental objectives of the leader supersede his/her material aspirations. Our experience in Africa and Nigeria, in particular, is that the situation is to the contrary. Religious leaders now clamor for material aspirations than transcendental objectives like salvation. They desire automobiles, mansions, and influence. A religious leader is indicative of a person like a priest or priestess who provides leadership during religious worship, ceremonies, and rituals. According to P. Adelumo Dopamu and J. Omosade Awolalu, they are "worship leaders who are set apart for the service of God and divinities."[12] These individuals often have advanced knowledge of their religions. They are considered sacred persons and custodians of the history, traditions, and rituals of the religion.

Religious Leaders Among the Yorùbá People of Nigeria

Before we go further, the point should be made that all religions globally and, especially, Africa have their leaders. Whether in Christianity, Islam, Buddhism, or Hinduism, religious leaders abound. These are men and women who provide guidance, direction, and supervision to all their religions' adherents. Our focus here is African Traditional Religion (ATR) from North to South and East to West of Africa where religious leaders are legion. However, the understanding and appreciation of these leaders vary from one community to another. The difference(s) is discernable from the methods of selection, social values, ritual functions, and limitations as dictated by the society and the sacred object(s) of worship. Dopamu and Awolalu refer to these leaders as "worship leaders who are set apart for the service of God and divinities."[13] These leaders are often very versed in the history and traditions of the religion and the divinities they serve. As such, they are considered to be custodians of the religion and the symbols, relics of the divinities, groups, and cultures. Samuel Johnson, describing a priest among the Yorùbá people, captures the metaphysical and physical manifestation of the title of the religious leader as follows:

> When the awareness of the Deity (God) first came upon man, he, became aware at the same time that there was about him an atmosphere different in quality from that of the natural world in which he lives, his common place life ... there was a sharply defined spiritual line of demarcation which could be crossed except with due and adequate precautions. Something happened at the same time in his experience and this put him on his guard by letting him know in terms which could not be mistaken that hew could trespass wantonly beyond this demarcation only at his own peril.[14]

Johnson captures the whole essence of the realization of priesthood on a person among the Yorùbá. However, E. Bolaji Idowu suggests that selection to the priesthood may not have metaphysical dimensions; for him, selection to priesthood could be based on hierarchy and family/societal traditions. He notes that: "The person who succeeds the family priest or town priest is usually the person next to him in rank. He should have been with the priest and should have understudied him by assisting and watching him during conduct of rituals."[15]

Idowu's view is about succession, but it also points to how a person can become a priest or priestess. This is based on hierarchy, experience, and family traditions. In this case, it might not have a divine origin. It could also be by understudying a former/dead priest/priestess; it could also be hereditary. Dopamu and Awolalu created six categories of religious leadership among the Yorùbá.[16] These are Priests/Priestesses, Diviners, Mediums, Medicine men/women, Magicians, and Herbalists.[17] Although these categories are too broad, they can be reduced to four: Priests/Priestesses, Diviners/Mediums, Medicine men/women, and Herbalists Kings.

However, these offices, in contemporary Yorùbáland, could be combined in one person, or one person may have more than one function within these categories. In this chapter, we will concentrate on the priests/priestesses, the medicine professionals, and the king. The priests/priestesses are the official servants of a divinity. They are known as *Baba* or *Iya Orisa*. They serve as a link between the worshippers and the divinities, who are the primary objects of worship.[18] Idowu describes the priests/priestesses as the persons in charge of the shrine and other ritual spaces of a divinity.[19] They get their orders to do things primarily from divination, dreams, visions, and experiences. They are the custodians of the symbols, temple, emblems, and totems of the divinities and also make sure meals and drinks are available not only for worship but for social communion. They offer sacrifices, make offerings, and say prayers to God at the temple or shrine on behalf of the people through the divinities.

The priests and priestesses are often trained. This could be formal or informal. After their training, which could span between three to twenty years, they are commissioned and initiated into their divine duties. The training, in very few instances, could be by apprenticeship. Akintola suggests that the training could be up to twenty years, depending on the apprentice's age.[20] Dopamu and Awolalu suggest three to ten years, especially in the *Ifa* cult.[21] During the training, the apprentice learns the rituals, songs, taboos, dances, and rules as well as regulations of the divinities and their vocation as a priest or priestess. Traditionally, beyond religious leadership, a priest in Yorùbá Traditional Religion is an important social figure who often partakes in the installation of kings and chiefs as well as the funeral and burial of traditional officeholders. They are special guests at community social functions. In the submission of Dopamu and Awolalu, the priests and priestesses: "In general, the priest serves as judges, guidance, and directors with regards to the general well-being of the community in which they live. They may also preside over meetings … and their decisions are always regarded as correct because they represent the divinities."[22] As we shall see in the final section of this chapter, the role(s) of the priests and priestesses in Yorùbá Traditional Religion has changed drastically from what has been discussed so far.

The Kings and Chiefs

The kings are the traditional political leaders of African people. They reign in their communities based on the traditions of the people. They are often assisted by their chiefs, who are often appointed/selected by the king based on the advice of the person's family to be appointed (if it is hereditary). The appointment could also be through divination. As for the king, divination and consultation play crucial roles in the enthronement of a king. In Yorùbáland, which is our main focus, the king is known as *Oba*. He is the vice regents of the divinities—*Orisa* on earth. Thus, his office is sacred, and he commands physical and metaphysical respect among the people. He is known as *Alase Ekeji Orisa*—the deputy of the divinities. His powers are often unlimited. He heads the executive, judiciary, and legislative branches of government. Therefore, he superintends on all matters that concern the society—*oba je lori oun gbogbo*—"the king superintends over all things." His functions also include religious rituals. According to E. Geoffrey Parrinder, the divine rulership of the king is not in doubt as the people believe in divine kingship. Parrinder submits as follows: "Belief in divine kingship appears in the early form of religion, and Hocart suggested that perhaps there never were any gods with a divine king. Before 3,000 B.C., the city kings of ancient Mesopotamia claimed descent from the gods, and the people looked on them as divinely sent redeemers. In Egypt, the king was the son of a god or his incarnate, and there is a theory that these 'children of the sun' established their sway by claiming divine honours and possessing occult knowledge."[23]

Thus, the king among the Yorùbá, like other communities in West Africa, in the opinion of Parrinder, is sacred.[24] Because of the sacredness of the king's office, he is part of religious leaders in society. It should be noted, however, that this is not the situation in all Yorùbá communities. Three examples will suffice here. In Lagos, the *Eleko of Eko* does not perform rituals in the traditional religion of the people, although he is part of the ceremonies, depending on the occasion. However, one of the rituals associated with the *Eyo* Festival is what is known as *Ijo Opa* (burning of the *Eyo* staff). During this ceremony, which is highly ritualistic under the leadership of the leaders of *Awo-Opa*, the king is expected to dance to *Arigo* drum sets seven times around the palace areas in the full glare of the people. Here, the king is a participant, not a leader in religious worship. During the popular *Osun* Oshogbo Festival, the *Ataoja* of Oshogbo, who is the paramount ruler, perform a priestly function as he leads worshippers annually to the *Osun* groove. At the groove, he leads the rituals assisted by the votaries/priests and priestesses of *Osun*. In Ile-Ife, the *Oni of Ife* is not only conceived as a king but also as the chief priest in the worship of *Orunmila*, among other deities. However, in recent times, he does not lead worship but rather partake in the rituals as an adherent; however, without his presence, the ceremonies cannot be performed. These narratives show that the king in Yorùbá can perform priestly functions, but it is not a general practice in Yorùbáland.

Medicine Professionals

This category of people in traditional religion in Africa consists of the diviners, herbalists, magicians, and healers. While we shall not dwell on the interpretation and values of their office, it is important to point out that they are part of the leadership structure in African Traditional Religion (ATR). In Yorùbáland, the medicine professionals are known generically as *Onisegun*. This may not be totally correct as the *Onisegun* only perform the duty of healing. He/she may not be a magician (*Ologun*), herbalist (*Elegbogi*), or a diviner (*Babalawo*). In Yorùbá traditional medicine, the *Babalawo* is a diviner who consults the divinities through *Ifa* to determine the illness of his/her clients. After a consultation, therapies are prescribed, and the patient must see *Onisegun* to make a necessary concoction (*agbo*—an herbal drink from various sources including tree leaves, barks, roots, animated objects, etc.). If the illness is metaphysical, the *Onisegun* provides services in getting sacrificial objects based on the Babalawo's advice. The pharmacologist who sells the herbal materials shall make available the elements of sacrifices. When the sacrifice has been offered, the patient regains his/her well-being and becomes a complete person. However, despite these apparent "separation of power" and duties among medicine professionals, the whole function(s) could be performed by one person. This is the case in contemporary times, as we shall see later.

According to Dopamu and Awolalu: "It is hard to get a medicine man that does not have the knowledge of the properties of herbs or some working knowledge of magic. Thus, medicine men (and women) can also be called magicians or herbalists and vice-versa."[25] The direct implication(s) of this submission is that the "normal" separation in the medicine professionals' duties is no longer visible as they lay claim to knowledge of all areas of medicine in Yorùbáland. However, we must underline the fact that the medicine professionals provide leadership in traditional religion since medicine and healing are integral parts of traditional beliefs and practices. Fundamentally, we must single out the *Babalawo*—the diviner who not only consults for the kings (*Oba*) but must consult for the priests and priestesses when such services are required. Africans, especially the Yorùbá people, are always curious about their lives on earth and their place in the hereafter. Thus, they seek metaphysical explanations for all things that happen in their lives.

Consequently, before and after the birth of a child, before marriages are contracted, before business engagements, during sicknesses, ailments, even after death, the Yorùbá people consult the diviners to determine the causes and effects of events. Consequently, the leadership functions of the medicine professionals in traditional religion are not in doubt. Therefore, a study of leadership in African Traditional Religion will not be complete without a critical study of these medicine men and women.

Religious Leaders in African Traditional Religion in Contemporary Times

The three categories of leaders examined herein are still paramount in the practice of African Traditional Religion in modern times. Although there are modifications and adjustments in the functions and duties of the leaders, in this section, we shall examine the values, functions, and limitations of the religious leaders under a Civil Government that now imposes its will on the traditional institution in Africa. This is premised on the fact that the civil authority now needs to approve the appointment(s) of some, if not all, religious leaders. Interestingly, they pay the salaries of traditional political leaders, such as kings, chiefs, clan heads, and some religious leaders.

Between 2014 and 2018, I studied the structure, values, and functions of religious leaders in African Traditional Religion in Yorùbáland with particular emphasis on the *Ijinla* fraternity, known as *Awo-Opa* and the *Osugbo* in Lagos.[26] The leadership of *Awo-Opa* could be divided into priestly and administrative leadership. The Alagba is the chief priest, while the Olokun is the head of administration. The appointment of Alagba is not hereditary but by consultation of the elders of the fraternity. The decision of the elders must be communicated to the king (Eleko) and his chiefs (Oloye), who are members of the fraternity. It is essential for the king to approve the choice of the Alagba because his office must communicate with the civil authority—state government and the local government—for the office to be gazetted and monthly emolument instituted and paid to the Alagba. With the king's permission, the fraternity, through its "internal mechanism," shall pronounce the offices, and the officers so selected shall celebrate elaborately. They are consequently introduced to the "Council of traditional chiefs in Lagos."

The Alagba leads the initiates in prayers and other rituals of the fraternity. He is in charge of the symbols, totems, and rituals of the group. The Olokun provides administrative leadership with management of the designated meeting place known as *Irele*, the screening of prospective initiates, and the provision of elements of rituals and worship. These officers are joined by other officeholders such as

Priestly class	Administrative class
Alagba	Olokun
Afereji	Togbesi
Adele Awo	Toju Okun
Ominile	Odagba, etc.
Isa Awo	
Awo Gboju	
Oniwata	
Oni ware	
Asole, Elemoso, etc.	

These leaders are expected to provide cohesion. My study reveals that they practice inclusive leadership where all initiates participate in the decision-making process. This is different from the exclusive leadership of Osugbo, as we shall see later. The leaders of *Awo-Opa* always respect the organizational structure of the group. Members of the fraternity must respect their leaders with reverence. Although they have a divine mandate, they always relate with initiates and care for their spiritual and material needs not only through prayers but with group financial support and medications. Therefore, leadership in *Awo-Opa* is about "collective us" rather than leadership mandate.

In the Osugbo fraternity, the leadership structure is different from that of *Awo-Opa*. The Osugbo is headed by the Apena, who is the chief priest. This office could be hereditary or selective based on divination. The ruling house of the fraternity shall provide candidates for the office of Apena, and Ifa is consulted for the choice of the divinities and God. Whoever is appointed is installed as the Apena after due consultation with the Oluwo, the Iwarefa, and the king of the land, Eleko. After due approval, the Apena is installed, and he provides leadership functions in worship and rituals supported by other priestly leaders like the *Gege*. On the administrative side is Oluwo, head of the group. His selection is very strict and based on the traditions of the land. In many Yorùbá communities, the Oluwo of Osugbo is the king. However, where there is a vacancy in the seat of the Oba, the most senior in the Iwarefa (Big Six) becomes the Oluwo. The appointment and coronation of a new king do not change the status quo. This is the situation currently at the Osugbo Ilu Eko. The leadership of Osugbo is exclusive as it claims divine rights. The Apena rules the conclave as he wishes, but with the support of the Oluwo. The two officers often seclude themselves and ignore the organizational purpose of the group; this often backfires. However, it should be stated that the leaders in Osugbo provide moral and ritual leadership. They partake in the decision-making process of the nation. The king often consults them in the decision-making process of the land.

It should be noted that the office of Apena Osugbo is gazetted, and he is on monthly emolument of the local government. He is also the head of all traditional chiefs of Lagos. The Apena is the custodian of not only the conclave, Iledi, but also all traditional shrines in Lagos. All totems and symbols of the *Onile* (the divinity of the group are in his custody). He must, in consultation with the Oluwo, provide ritual elements for the regular worship. The Alagba (of *Awo-Opa*) and Apena (of Osugbo) act as the link between the divinities and the worshippers. They are also the "middle men" between the ancestors (Alasku) and the living. They are important figures who must be part of the material and spiritual functions of the community.[27] They feature prominently during the installation, funeral, and burial of kings and chiefs. In fact, like Dopamu and Awolalu rightly observed, that Alagba and Apena like other Yorùbá priests, "In general serves as judges, guidance and directors with regards to the general well-being of the community in which they live. They may preside over meetings … and their decisions are always regarded as correct because they represent the divinities."[28]

The kings in Yorùbáland perform priestly functions like examples of the Alaoja of Osugbo earlier mentioned. However, there are others like the Eleko of Eko who rarely perform priestly functions. However, Bolaji Idowu informs us that Oni of Ife is Olori Alaworo of Ife (Head of all priests in Ife). It should be noted that the office of the Yorùbá king is now highly politicized. This is the case with the Oba of Lagos, who, in 2014, became political with the statement, "*vote my candidates or perish in the lagoon.*"[29] This statement was issued toward the 2015 general elections in Nigeria. It suggests that the king had become political and no longer neutral in the civil politics of the state. The roles of the king in religious leadership are as discussed earlier, and nothing has changed in their functions. It is impossible to hear of kings in Yorùbáland now who are not initiates of any traditional groups or have renounced membership of such groups due to conversion into Christianity or Islam. Such was the case of Oba Tejuoso, the Osile of Abeokuta, some years back.

Traditional medicine professionals have continued to be relevant in modern times, especially with the continued popularity of traditional medicine as alternatives to Western Orthodox medicine. The medicine professionals are now more organized, appropriating modern medical types of equipment in their practices. Some have even employed trained orthodox nurses and laboratory technicians to help diagnose an ailment before issuing a prescription. The Alagbo (Herbalist) now appropriate the social media and electronic media to advertise their medicaments for more patronage. The Babalawo is still relevant as the curiosity of Yorùbá has not waned. The people, like other Africans, live in a spiritual world dominated by spiritual agents, such as witches and wizards who are harmful to the well-being of the people. They consult for the people on occasions such as marriages, business engagements, leadership selection and appointments, the birth of a child, and so on. The Onisegun is still relevant in the prescription of herbal formulas to treat illnesses such as typhoid fever, malaria fever, erectile dysfunctions, infertility, and mental illness. Many shops are in business in this regard. According to some of the practitioners, the efficacy of their herbal medicine is not in doubt.[30] During one of my observer participation visits to the Oyingbo and Jankara markets in Lagos, patrons of the Elegbogi and Onisegun at the markets confirms the efficacy of the medicine. In the last two decades, Lagos Television, a popular television station, has engaged in the promotion of traditional medicine through its Traditional Medicine Trade Fair at its complex at Ikeja. During my visit to the 2018 Trade Fair, the patronage on the fourth day was over 5000 in attendance. This number excludes the number of exhibitors.

Conclusion

In this chapter, we have discussed and evaluated the values, functions, and traditions of religious leaders, especially in worship, social, and cultural situations. We observed that the priests, priestesses, the traditional rulers, kings, and medicine professionals provide leadership not only in their area of jurisdiction and operations but in the conventional politics of their communities. In recent times, some of these values are declining in relevance while others are on the rise. The traditional priests and priestesses are not as prominent and popular as they were in the pre-colonial and colonial era. At the same time, the kings who during the same period held sway in their communities are now subjected to the whims and caprices of civil leadership. This has reduced their functions and values to their communities. It is not uncommon in recent times to hear of a king facing trial in a civil law court and also remanded to prison. To make themselves relevant, some kings like the Eleko of Eko and Oba Ridwan Akinolu had been involved in civil politics and have become one of the "voices" of the ruling party in Lagos State's All Progressive Congress (APC). The medicine professionals are now very popular, and their relevance in the provision of alternative medicine at a cheaper rate cannot be over-emphasized.

Notes

1. James MacGregor Burns, *Leadership*, (New York: Harper Torchbooks, 1978), 120.
2. Julius Nyerere, "Leaders Must Not Be Masters," in E. C. Eze (ed.), *African Philosophy: An Anthology* (Maiden: Blackwell, 1998), 79.
3. Burns, Leadership, 121.
4. Danoye Oguntola-Laguda, "Religion, Leadership and Struggle for Power in Nigeria: A Case Study of the 2011 Presidential Election in Nigeria," in SHE, *Journal of History of Religion*, University of South Africa, UNISA, vol. 41, no. 2 (2015): 4.
5. *The Guardian Newspaper*, 2015.
6. Blaise Pascal, T. S. Eliot, and William F. Trotter, *Pascal's Pensées*, translated by W.F. Trotter (New York: Random House, 1941), 22.
7. Gerardus Van der Leeuw, *Sacred and Profane Beauty: The Holy in Art* (London: Weidenfeld and Nicholson, 1963), 102.
8. Laguda, "Religion, Leadership and Struggle for Power in Nigeria," 78.
9. Ibid.
10. Rodney Stark, "Secularization, R.I.P.," *Sociology of Religion*, vol. 60, no. 3 (1999): 249–273.
11. A. A. Gumusay, *Religion and Leadership: Ancient Wisdom for a Modern World* (Berlin, Germany: LEAD Research Services, 2016).
12. P. Adelumo Dopamu and J. Omosade Awolalu, *West African Traditional Religion* (Lagos: Macmillan, Nigeria. 1979), 140.
13. Ibid.
14. Samuel Johnson, *History of the Yoruba* (Lagos: C.M.S. Bookshop, 1937), 13–14.
15. E. Bolaji Idowu, *Olodumare: God in Yoruba Belief* (Lagos: Longman Nigeria, 1996), 136.
16. Dopamu and Awolalu, *West African Traditional Religion*, 140–141.
17. Ibid., 141.
18. Ibid., 141.
19. E. B. Idowu, *Olodumare: God in Yoruba Belief* (Lagos; Longman Nigeria, 1996), 139.

20. Akintola, 12.
21. Dopamu and Awolalu, *West African Traditional Religion*, 140.
22. Ibid., 145.
23. Edward Geoffrey Parrinder, *West African Religion* (London: Epworth Press, 1969), 67.
24. Dopamu and Awolalu, *West African Traditional Religion*, 142.
25. Ibid., 147.
26. Oral interview with Asole Bayo of *Awo-Opa*, 2018.
27. Dopamu and Awolalu, *West African Traditional Religion*, 145.
28. Ibid., 147.
29. *The Punch Newspaper*, The Function of Paper, "Punch Editorial Comments," 2014, 15.
30. Oral interview with Erinfolani Raheed, a traditional gynecologist, 2016.

CHAPTER 15

Illnesses and Cures

Kelvin Onongha

INTRODUCTION

The quest for wellness and wholeness is a universal condition that is also obtainable in the African context. Long before the first hospitals emerged in the continent, traditional healers had been engaged in restoring health and treating illnesses within their communities. These local traditional practitioners were held in great awe and respect second only to the traditional rulers because their healing powers were regarded as emanating from their intimacy and devotion to the deities. Hence, healing and religion in the African context are inextricably connected.

AFRICAN TRADITIONAL RELIGION WORLDVIEW

For the African people, wellness, prosperity, and wholeness are quintessential to life. To obtain these, a harmonious relationship is necessary between the individual, nature, the community (the living, the living dead, and the yet unborn), and the spirit realm. Illness, therefore, arises as the result of an imbalance or disharmony between human beings and the other spheres of interaction. For this reason, traditional healers, who are experts in these affairs, are necessary to restore fractured relationships and thus enable ill persons to regain their physical and spiritual vitality.

K. Onongha (✉)
Adventist University of Africa, Nairobi, Kenya
e-mail: ononghak@aua.ac.ke

© The Author(s), under exclusive license to Springer Nature
Switzerland AG 2022
I. S. Aderibigbe, T. Falola (eds.), *The Palgrave Handbook of African Traditional Religion*, https://doi.org/10.1007/978-3-030-89500-6_15

Beliefs About Illness in African Traditional Religion

Illness is "a diminution of the individual's potency, a weakening of the individual's mystical life power";[1] in the African worldview, it is mostly attributable to a spiritual cause. The African cosmos is regarded as saturated with myriad, malevolent spirits, which can cause illness and harm to unsuspecting victims. These spirits, working through various means, can rob the health of their victims either progressively or promptly. The manifestations of these illnesses vary from pains in various parts of the body to infections of the organs and the actual total disruption of the body's organic systems. Before effective treatment of these conditions can occur, it is imperative that the traditional healers first ascertain the source and/or cause of these illnesses. In order to discover who was to blame for the illness, divination was often necessary. Thus, African traditional healers sought the assistance of the divinities for diagnosis of the nature of illnesses and the necessary healing methods to restore health.

Causes of Illness

The germ theory, which explains that germs are the primary causes for illness, is the prevailing concept in the Western world; however, in Africa, the dominant belief concerning the origin of illness is the spirit theory; that is, malevolent spirits are the agents largely responsible for human illness.[2] Despite the conviction that illnesses generally have spiritual etiology, traditional healers do recognize that some conditions may have natural origins. Among the natural causes of illness are: "bad food, bad air and dirty environment," which could result in "anemia, pneumonia, and dysentery."[3]

From his landmark study among the Lugbara people—who are found around parts of Uganda and certain regions of Congo—John Middleton explains, "a man aches and grows thin and so knows that the ghosts have sent sickness to him; he aches in his stomach or in his bones in the early morning and knows that a witch or sorcerer has affected him; he aches in his head and knows a kinsman has cursed him; his wife does not conceive and he knows a grandmother has cursed him; and so on."[4] The Lugbara, like some other African cultures, possessed a coherent means for determining the agents of illness depending upon the nature and region of the body that was affected.

External spiritual causes responsible for illness include the evil eye, curses by older members of a community, the displeasure of ancestors, witchcraft, or the breaking of taboos.[5]

Evil Eye

In some parts of Africa, there is a strong belief that certain persons possess the ability to cast evil spells through the power of their gaze. Simply by glancing at another's property, misfortune could result. Especially vulnerable to the evil eye are young children and pregnant women; the underlying motive for the afflictions caused by the evil eye is generally envy.[6] Although this belief is generally found in Northern Africa and is more commonly seen among Muslim populations, evidence of it has also been discovered in some regions of Ethiopia; among its effects include a wasting disease.[7]

Curse

In oral societies as Africa, curses are greatly feared. Some persons are believed to possess the ability to inflict grave illnesses upon others simply by placing a curse on them. Less than a decade ago, a study by Pew Research indicated that slightly more than one-in-five persons in some countries in East and West Africa surveyed believed in the ability some persons possessed to cast spells using the evil eye or mouth.[8] Evil persons may cause illness and death through curses. Among the reasons elders are respected in Africa is because they are able to curse rebellious or disobedient children, and illness would result. To cure spells or curses caused by the evil eye or mouth, the help of ritual specialists is necessary. They provide the necessary charms to ward off the spells or perform special rites to reverse the curses and restore health.

Displeasure of Ancestors

Another group with the ability to cause illness and misfortune are ancestors. Whenever ancestors are ignored, slighted, or disrespected, they could afflict their descendants with illnesses in order to remind them of their obligations to the living dead.[9] Ancestors desire to be involved in the lives of their descendants and to be offered sacrifices. Neglect in obligations toward them, either during their funerals or during life cycle rituals of the living progeny, could result in illness. As such, sacrifices and rituals to appease the ancestors were usually employed as the procedure for curing the illnesses they may have caused.

Witchcraft

Among the most feared phenomena in the African belief system is the issue of witchcraft. Besides the strongly etched belief in their abilities to kill and eat their victims, witches were also regarded as responsible for painful, progressive illnesses.[10] In more recent times, strange illnesses or mysterious disease conditions have often been blamed on witchcraft.[11] Because witchcraft pertains to the realm of the supernatural, treatment of suspected cases in African traditional religion involved ritual experts. Powerful incantations and rituals are usually necessary to reverse the effect of witchcraft and restore health.

Taboos

The African cosmos is one where religious and moral order is of great significance. The violation of strict communal codes, which taboos served to enforce, could result in grave consequences, including serious illness.[12] Taboos may be grouped into three categories—societal, bodily, and religious.[13] In communal societies, like Africa, morality is more defined by acceptable standards of behavior, and relational conduct, than by other legal or moral codes, such as sin.[14] When taboos have been transgressed and illness results, the assistance of the ritual expert is sought to restore moral or religious order through appropriate sacrifices to appease the offended, whether deities, ancestors, or elements of nature.

Elements of African Traditional Healing

From antiquity, traditional healers have operated in Africa long before the advent of modern medical science or the arrival of the mission hospitals. Indeed, traditional medicine in Africa has produced pharmaceuticals, displayed surgical skills, and conducted specialist training for various conditions and disorders—physical and psychological.[15] There are at least four major functions traditional healing has served in the African continent generally—diagnostic, curative, preventative, and causative.[16]

Diagnostic

Before traditional healers commence their healing duties, they first seek to establish the nature and cause of the illness. Diagnosis, in many cases, entails divination—seeking the assistance of divinities responsible for healing to discern the origin and sender of the condition. Diagnosis was usually twofold—the first involved physical examination and questioning, while the second was divination to determine the spiritual or mystical cause of the illness.[17]

Curative

The range of illnesses that traditional healers often claim to be able to treat is usually quite broad. A few *Babalawo* interviewed confidently claimed that they could cure HIV/AIDS and just about any human ailment. Of course, such conviction was supposedly rooted in their rapport with the spirit world. African traditional healers are renowned for their ability to treat natural, orthopedic, psychiatric, and occultic conditions. In most parts of Africa, four main categories constitute traditional healers. These are traditional birth attendants (traditional midwives), who with the skills and knowledge passed down from generations assist in the delivery and care of expecting mothers and children; bone-setters—versed in the art of setting fractured bones and restoring the use of broken limbs; traditional surgeons—who conduct circumcision and uvulectomy; and therapeutic occultism—employing oracular methods and incantations to bring healing to clients.[18]

Among the natural products employed in healing are water, clay, herbs, salt, and stone. Sometimes, pieces of animal body parts are infused into herbal or natural medicine. These prepared substances may be ingested or applied externally upon the body, depending on the nature and location of the ailment.

Another means by which illness is treated is through the intervention of spiritual agencies involving divination. Employing oracular means, traditional healers entreat the spirits on behalf of their clients to determine the cause of the illness and the best pathway for achieving healing. At times, healers may become possessed by spirit mediums, after which they discover the appropriate remedy to restore the patient's health. Sacrifices and rituals play a significant role in such healing processes.

Preventative

It is generally believed that debilitating illnesses and death can be prevented through mystical means prepared by ritual experts. This is one of the major functions for which traditional healers are sought. For such purposes, amulets and charms made from various portions of animals considered to possess innate power are worn around the body. Also, in various corners of clients' houses, charms may be placed to protect against evil spirits, witches, and malicious enemies.

Illness can also be prevented through the use of powerful incantations chanted by a traditional healer possessed by the divinities responsible for healing. These incantations provide a sort of force field, which inhibit, destabilize, or neutralize evil powers targeting innocent victims.

Causative

Incantations are also employed to reverse curses or suspected sorcery. For conditions such as epilepsy, infertility, and lunacy, incantations are employed with the belief that a more potent power is necessary to expel the evil spirits responsible and cure the victims.

Traditional healers are also sought to provide aphrodisiacs to men who fear they are losing their virility. Younger lovers also patronize traditional healers for love potions to induce partners into marriage or to have sexual affairs with them. Some married women also seek charms or love potions from traditional healers to make their husbands love them more or to have their spouses exclusively to themselves.

TRADITIONAL HEALERS IN THE AGE OF MODERN MEDICINE

The first modern hospitals and clinics established in the African continent were generally by missionaries. Prior to this, the homes of traditional healers had served this function in cases of illness or medical emergencies. Mission medical centers continued to grow in popularity and demand even after the colonial era. Although these mission hospitals met the healthcare needs of a large populace all across the regions, they never came close to eliminating the role and functions of traditional healers. Among the reasons why traditional practitioners have continued to exist and thrive in the face of government and mission hospitals are the magical and resolute nature of the African worldview, the two-tiered worldview of missionaries, persistent witchcraft beliefs, dualistic orientation, cost, holistic approach of traditional healing, and the perceived preeminence of the traditional healing methods.

Magical Worldview

The African worldview has been described as magical because of the conviction that behind every misfortune is a supernatural or mystical cause. As a result, even when a malaria-bearing mosquito bites a patient who becomes ill of the disease, the question that is sometimes asked is, "Who sent the mosquito?"[19] Causation is a pivotal element of the African worldview that must be taken into consideration during moments of crisis, or misfortune, such as illness. The causes of illnesses, which must be determined before they are cured, could be anything from an envious enemy, angry ancestor, witchcraft, the curse of an elder, or the violation of a communal taboo. Because illness is very often attributed to a person or spiritual agent, Western medicine may be regarded as powerless to cure it.

Even after about two centuries of missionary presence in many regions of the continent, the African worldview has remained resolute. Indeed, in recent decades, many testify to the resurgence of this worldview across the continent. Nationalism, considered as a reaction against globalization, is among the factors blamed for this upsurge. Advocates state with powerful rhetoric that the religion and ways of the ancestors are not to be discarded but treasured. Much of the cultural ways that advocates seek to preserve promote this magical, mystical worldview.

Two-Tiered Missionary Worldview

Christian Anthropologist, Paul Hiebert, posits that missionaries who brought the gospel to Africa were creatures of their times influenced by the Enlightenment philosophies of that age. Consequently, they were skeptical of issues related to the spirit realm, such as myths and superstitions.[20] This negative view of African beliefs about the origin of illnesses drove these beliefs underground rather than dispelling them. Unto the present day, there are many African people who draw a line between the kind of illnesses they perceive that Western hospitals can treat and those they believe are within the realm of the traditional healers. During a focus group discussion on the subject of why local diviners are still patronized by Christians even in the age of science, this researcher was informed by some older men in the group that certain conditions could only be treated by going home to the village to consult the traditional healers. In their opinion, the illnesses whose origins are traceable to the villages can only be cured by resorting to the traditional healers.

Witchcraft Beliefs

The belief in witches' existence and power to cause illnesses and death pervade the entire continent of Africa.[21] Witchcraft is believed to be the primary cause for many deaths, ill-health, and even the absence of prosperity among many persons in Africa.[22] Through the casting of spells on their victims, witches are believed to have the power to induce various forms of illness. Witchcraft is perhaps the most dreaded phenomenon for most Africans, and whatever cannot be explained is eventually blamed on it. Because witchcraft is also believed to be adaptable for certain positive endeavors, Western technology and medicine is similarly attributed to this by some Africans.[23]

Dualistic Orientation

A central feature of the African traditional religious worldview is pragmatism, that is, whatever works is what matters. It has been observed on many occasions when African people fall ill, they have no qualms whatsoever about going to "the witchdoctor, the magician, and the diviner, and also to the mission doctor who uses Western medicine,"[24] so long as they get cured. Because it is ingrained in the African peoples' psyche that the *Sangoma*, *Babalawo*, or *marabout* (i.e., the diviner/traditional healer) has the answer to every ailment, even though they recognize the efficacy of modern medicine, they still will resort to traditional healers to augment whatever they consider may be deficient in any of the procedures.

A certified traditional birth attendant and *Babalawo* interviewed revealed that when he has complicated pregnancies to attend to, he first refers his patients to a nearby university teaching hospital to conduct an ultrasound scan of the pregnancy, after which he then will determine the appropriate herbal procedure to apply in order to facilitate safe delivery. For masses of Africans living in poverty, traditional healers are the primary persons they turn to when illness occurs. Despite the visible benefits and progress that modern science and technology have brought to humanity in recent decades, Africans, nevertheless, are hardwired to maintain strong faith in the abilities of traditional healers to cure just about every form of illness—physical, psychological, spiritual, supernatural, or emotional.

Interestingly, although the African worldview is considered holistic, in matters of healing, a dichotomous orientation is evidenced. Commenting on this dualistic orientation, Kirwen observes,

> While many people go to modern medical facilities for treatment due to the influence of Westernization and Christianity, many will seek a second opinion from a herbalist or diviner, while others seek divine intervention through prayers. This illustrates a dual consciousness regarding health and healing. This syncretic approach of management and treatment of illnesses is to ensure the wellbeing of both the physical body and the spiritual component of the person. In cases where it is suspected that the cause of illness is angry ancestors, the community assists

the afflicted person in the performance of correct rituals to ensure that the desired moral order is restored in the community.[25]

Cost

Perhaps the most critical factor as to why many Africans turn to traditional healers when they are ill is that treatment costs appear to be far more affordable. The proliferation of government, mission, and private hospitals and improving literacy rates have indeed led to more confidence in modern medical methods. However, the bills for treatment at these medical facilities, beginning from the purchase of cards, registration, consultation fees, diagnostic tests, treatment charges, and prescription pills, make the total treatment costs for many prohibitive. This is significant in a continent where majority are living way below poverty levels. In contrast, the charges of the traditional healer are often within the range of the local client to arrange payment for, apart from when sacrifices may be needed. Additionally, with the traditional healers, charges may be negotiable.

Holistic Healing

A major inadequacy of modern medicine that has been noted is its preoccupation with physical healing. Other dimensions of illness, such as psychiatry and metaphysical phenomena, are generally compartmentalized and referred to other specialists. Traditional healers, in contrast, are holistic in their approach to healing. Recognizing that illness may result from disharmony in the social and moral order, their therapy also includes measures to restore such broken relationships to facilitate the healing process. One facet of healing that Africans find with traditional healers, which cannot be provided by modern medical facilities, is exorcism. For many African people who believe in the ability of spirits to possess and control humans, the primary recourse they have is traditional healers. Through the art of divination, these healers first seek to determine the root cause of the ailment, after which, through spiritual guidance, they commence the process to exorcize the evil spirits. Traditional healers also treat illnesses due to curses or the displeasure of ancestors, which modern medicine ignores or regards with disdain.

TRADITIONAL ILLNESS AND CURES IN CONTEMPORARY SOCIETY

African traditional religious beliefs still play a significant role in the diagnosis and treatment of illness in the continent, even unto contemporary times. Although it may have been expected that with the progress of modern medical science, increasing literacy levels, and the rapid advancement of Christianity around the continent, interest in traditional healing methods would be on the decline, this is clearly not the case in contemporary Africa. In a study on the

"Trends and Challenges of Traditional Medicine in Africa," Abdullahi (2011) indicates that,

> In countries like Ghana, Mali, Zambia, and Nigeria, the first line of treatment for 60% of children with high fever resulting from malaria is the use of herbal medicine. Carpentier et al. discovered an increasing demand for TM (traditional medicine) in the case of rheumatic and neurological complaints in Burkina-Faso. In Ghana, about 70% of the population depends primarily on TM. About 27 million South Africans (usually the black South Africans) use TM to treat a variety of ailments found out that traditional health care has contributed very significantly to the treatment of *degedege* (convulsions) in rural Tanzania. In some instances, patients use TM simultaneously with modern medicine in order to alleviate sufferings associated with disease and illness. Amira and Okubadejo reported that a significant number of hypertensive patients receiving conventional treatment at the tertiary health facility in Lagos, Nigeria, also used CAM therapies.[26]

Conclusion

It is evident that across the African continent, traditional religious beliefs and practices still hold powerful sway in issues concerning illness and how they are cured. Perhaps what African governments should more actively ensure is that regulatory bodies work closely with local guilds to protect masses from the growing numbers of charlatans claiming to be traditional healers. Also, as these healers become recognized as alternative medical practitioners, better sanitary conditions need to be enforced and regulatory structures established to protect clients from malpractice.

Notes

1. Robert Cameron Mitchell, *African Primal Religions* (Niles, IL: Argus Communications, 1977), 54.
2. Ruby Mikulencak, "Science and Magic Collide in African Medicine," *Evangelical Missions Quarterly* (October 1987), 171–172.
3. Sylvia Osemwenkha, "Disease Aetiology in Traditional African Society," Africa LV, 4 (2000) 583. https://www.jstor.org/stable/40761483?seq=1#metadata_info_tab_contentsAccessed January 21, 2019.
4. J. C. Middleton, *Lugbara Religion: Ritual and Authority Among an East African People* (London: Oxford University Press, 1960), 79.
5. Michael C. Kirwen, *African Cultural Domain: Life Cycle of an Individual* (Nairobi, Kenya: Maryknoll Institute of African Studies, 2008), 50.
6. Gailyn Van Rheenen, *Communicating Christ in Animistic Contexts* (Pasadena, CA: William Carey Library, 1991), 230.
7. Niall Finneran, "Ethiopian Evil Eye Belief and the Magical Symbolism of Iron Working," *Folklore* vol. 114 (2003), 427–428.
8. *Pew Forum on Religion and Public Life*, "Islam and Christianity in Sub-Saharan Africa" (April 2010), 33.

9. John Mbiti, *Introduction to African Religion* (2nd ed.) (Long Grove IL: Waveland Press, 1991), 78.
10. Peter White, "The Concept of Diseases and Health Care in African Traditional Religion in Ghana," *HTS Theological Studies* vol. 71 no. 3 (2015), 2. http://www.scielo.org.za/scielo.php?script=sci_arttext & pid=S0259-94222015000100046 (accessed Feb 7, 2019).
11. Esther P. Archibong, Ebingha E. Enang, and Glory E. Bassey, "Witchcraft Beliefs in Diseases Causation and Health-Seeking Behaviour in Pregnancy of Women in Calabar South-Nigeria," *Journal of Humanities and Social Science* vol. 22 no. 6 (June 2017), 25.
12. Mbiti, *Introduction to African Religion*, 41.
13. David Burnett, *World of the Spirits: A Christian Perspective on Traditional and Folk Religions* (Oxford, UK: Monarch Books, 2000), 76.
14. Paul G. Hiebert, R. Daniel Shaw, and Tite Tienou, *Understanding Folk Religion: A Christian Response to Popular Beliefs and Practices* (Grand Rapids, MI: Baker Books, 1999), 198.
15. Benedict Akpomuvie, O. "The Perception of Illness in Traditional Africa and the Development of Traditional Medical Practice," *International Journal of Nursing* vol. 1 no. 1 (June 2014), 53.
16. Willem Berends, "African Traditional Healing Practices and the Christian Community," *Missiology: An International Review* vol. 21 (1993), 278.
17. White, "The Concept of Diseases," 3.
18. Osemwenkha, "Disease Aetiology," 587.
19. Burnett, *World of the Spirits*, 112.
20. Paul G. Hiebert, "The Flaw of the Excluded Middle," *Missiology: An International Review* vol. X no. 1 (January 1982), 42.
21. Erwin Van de Meer, "The Problem of Witchcraft in Malawi," *Evangelical Missions Quarterly* vol. 47 no. 1 (2011), 78.
22. Elom Dovlo, "Witchcraft in Contemporary Ghana," in *Imagining Evil: Witchcraft Beliefs and Accusations in Contemporary Africa* edited by Gerrie ter Haar (Trenton, NJ: Africa World Press, 2007), 78.
23. Hiebert, Shaw and Tienou, *Understanding Folk Religion*, 150.
24. Ibid., 84.
25. Kirwen, *African Cultural Domains*, 66.
26. Ali Arazeem Abdullahi, "Trends and Challenges of Traditional Medicine in Africa," *African Journal of Traditional Complementary and Alternative Medicines* vol. 8 no. 5 (2011), 115.

CHAPTER 16

Secret Societies: Fraternities, Witches, Wizards, and Sorcerers

Andrew Philips Adega

INTRODUCTION

Secret societies-fraternities, witches, wizards, and sorcerers have one trade in common in African societies and that is the perpetration of evil. They are realities in African cosmology and their activities are not in doubt except for Euro-Americans and neo-Africans who have found a new faith in Christianity. The irony of the matter is that amidst these denials, most Christian ministries and ministers, particularly Pentecostal pastors, spend considerable time organizing crusades to ward off the influence of these realities in their localities.

Secret societies-fraternities, witches, wizards, and sorcerers by classification are grouped under the canopy of mystical powers or spiritual forces. Since these forces or powers perform dysfunctional duties to the societies in which they live, they are found carrying out their activities in discrete or secret and even nocturnal outside the purview of the generality of members of their communities.

In the light of the above perspective, Offiong posits that in the performance of these mystical powers or supernatural forces, the fraternities, witches, wizards, and sorcerers can cause harm, including death to their targeted victims.[1] He adds that the power is purely psychic and that those involved in the art; for instance, witches practice a form of corporeal vampirism by removing the soul of their victim and transforming it into a goat, sheep, or cow (or any animal of their choice) thus, causing a slow wasting disease.[2]

A. P. Adega (✉)
Benue State University, Makurdi, Nigeria

The *Mbatsav* (witches) in Tiv cosmology sell such animals some which may be corpses they have exhumed from the graves to unsuspecting butchers who buy and slaughter such animals and sell to an equally unsuspecting public.[3] As incredible as these may sound, Africans generally believe that they are true and any person who denies the reality of these powers does so at his/her own peril. Similarly, secret societies and fraternities such as the *Poro* operating in Sierra Leone, Liberia, Côte d'Ivoire and Guinea, and the *Okonko* and *Ogboni* among the Igbo and Yoruba of Nigeria have caused the disappearance and or death of many people in the course of their operations.[4]

Secret societies-fraternities, witches, wizards, and sorcerers in African societies have some form of mystical or spiritual power that seems to defy even immediate scientific explanations. They also operate as authentic components of African religion. The chapter examines the activities of secret societies and fraternities in African societies, their role and effect on contemporary African societies, and ways of mitigating the menace. However, it is worthy to note that Africans have also got ways of dealing with these mystical forces in their various communities.

Cleansing Conceptual Cobwebs

The under-listed words, terms, and concepts which appear in this chapter are used with the following contexts in mind:

Secret Societies-Fraternities

The reality of secret societies and some other societies that have secrets is never in doubt. Nwosu perceives the term secrecy to be an ambiguous term closely related to an array of disparate ideas and phenomena, including mystery, privacy, hiddenness, reserves, silence, and unknowability.[5]

He maintains that on the one hand, the word secret is from the Latin *secretum* which means separate or set apart. On the other hand, society is also derived from the Latin *societas* which connotes "fellowship, union, or alliance. Secret refers to a thing or mystery which is not or must be known by other people. ... It is something not properly understood or difficult to understand. Society thus becomes an organization of people formed for a particular purpose".[6]

On the issue of secrecy, Shishima avers that the keeping of secrets is a characteristic of both cults and religions. As a result of this, their inner secrets are kept from the majority and their initiates must proceed through a number of steps or degree of initiations in order to become wise.[7] The above phenomenon is applicable to Islam and Christianity. Citing Anyebe, Nwosu says a secret society is an Association of Men [Women], for a purpose which is neither published nor publicly explained. He further stated that such associations allegedly have no constitutions, no rules and regulations, and no minutes taken at their meetings. Also, their place of meeting is never advertised and they issue no circulars.[8]

Okeke states that Section 35(4) of the 1999 Constitution of Federal Republic of Nigeria defines a secret society as a society or organization not being a solely cultural or religious body that uses secret signs, oaths, rites, or symbols: (a) where meetings or activities are held in secret and (b) whose members are under oath, obligation, or other threat to promote the interest of its members or to aid one another under all circumstance, without due regard to merit, fair play, or justice, to the detriment of the legitimate expectation of those who are not members.[9]

From the above, a secret society can be said to be an organization which is known to exist, but whose members and place of meeting and its general activities are not publicly known. It is a society with a ritual demanding an oath of allegiance to an unknown leader(s) or forces.[10] Secret societies can be classified into two, that is, fraternities comprised only of men and sororities only of women; though sororities also refer to themselves as fraternities.

In the ancient world, Middle Ages and contemporary society, organizations, and institutions that have secrets existed and still exist and are mostly religious. Advancing in on this standpoint, Shishima explains that secret societies have been in existence in Nigeria and Africa before the advent of early colonialism in the country and the continent generally. According to him, they were formed by groups of individuals with the sole aim of seeking ancestral protection by conducting rituals.[11]

It is to be noted that as far as societies in Africa are concerned, there exists a symbiotic relationship between the traditional and modern societies. There are understandings on how they mingle and relate with one another. It is in this respect that the deities play a preponderant role in traditional African societies. Some examples of secret societies and fraternities in Africa include: *Okonko* (Igbo, male) Nigeria, *Ogboni* (Yoruba, male/female) Nigeria, *Poro* (male) Sierra Leone, *oro* (male) Nigeria, *Egungun* (male) Nigeria, *Ekpe* (male) Nigeria, *Zangbeto* (male) Port Novo, *Ndaka Gboya* society (male, Nupe) Nigeria, *Sande* (female, Mende), *Neegee* (male) Liberia, *Osiris* and *serapis* (Egypt), and *Mmou* society (Igbo) of Nigeria.[12]

In addition to the above, there are several secret cults or campus cult groups across various institutions in Africa. In Nigeria, the menace has spread its dangerous tentacles to primary and secondary schools, drawing blood and lives. The first of these cult groups in Nigerian higher institutions was the Seadogs Confraternity also known as the Pirates formed in 1952 at University of Ibadan by the Noble Laureate in Literature, Professor Wole Soyinka and his five friends to fight colonialism amongst other aims.[13] Later, a splinter group emerged from the Pirates thus giving birth to the Buccaneers confraternity (Sea Lords) in 1972.

As this chapter is being documented, there is an array of campus cults in Nigeria, the activities of some which are yet to come to limelight. It is worthy to note as Bewaji does that: "The campus cults represent the embryonic stages of the adult cults which exist in the larger society ... campus cults provide a training (breeding) environment for the adult cults in the larger society".[14]

Witches, Wizards

A witch is a practitioner of witchcraft. The term witch can also be applied to a woman that is skilled in and diligently practices witchcraft. However, in some classifications, while the woman is known as the witch, the man is called a wizard. Ikenga-Metuh explains that this dual classification is also found among the Igbo of Nigeria.[15] He maintains that the act of witchcraft is *Amusu* among the Igbo, the same name with which the female practitioner is known with, while the male practitioners who he says are hard to find are known as *Ajalagba* (wizards). He posits that *Ajalagba* are more powerful and more dangerous than *Amusu*; hence, the saying in Igbo: *Amusu ada ebu Ajalagba*, meaning a witch cannot carry a wizard. Ikenga-Metuh however quickly adds that this scenario has overtones of male chauvinism and is often used by men to remind women who appear to be very forward of their subordinate place in society.[16]

Aside the chauvinism of a male-dominated society, therefore, a witch is a witch, a practitioner of witchcraft, male or female. In contrast, among the Tiv, the female practitioners of *tsav* (witchcraft), that is, *kasev mbatsav* (witches) are more deadly and dangerous than their male counterparts. They are known to have succeeded where the male have failed. They can *wua* (kill) without applying the *ikyehegh* antidote; a substance that is dropped in the nostrils of person who has been killed by the witches to sustain the person to die at a later date. In the view of Offiong, the term witch can be used in two perspectives to refer to an individual. In the first perspective, it may refer to someone who behaves abnormally; that is outside the expected patterns of behavior. This, he says may include people who exhibit excessive meanness, unexplained wickedness, cruelty, great likeness for pains, ills, mischief, misfortune, and sins.[17]

In view of the above attributes, a child may be called a witch if he/she demonstrates such inhumane characteristics. In the second perspective, a witch could refer to a person that the community suspects of practicing witchcraft, a person who has confessed to practicing the art, or a person who has been identified by traditional doctors, spiritualists, or fellow witches to be a witch.[18] Also, Ikenga-Metuh adds that an introvert, who is always internalizing grievances and conflicts brooding over them, will soon discover that her soul begins to leave her body during sleep. The same applies to an introvert, a non-social person, a barren old woman; a wicked boastful person is usually a suspect.[19]

Africans believe that witches are people who possess an inherent power by which they can do anything especially negative things in the world. It is also held that some of the witches acquire the powers for the purpose of protecting their families and children; but the general view is that witches use their powers for evil and anti-social activities.[20] Africans believe that women are typically witches; however, sometimes male witches occupy important positions in their ranks. It also held that while some people are born with the powers of witchcraft, others acquire it. Also, some animals such as dogs, owls, and cats are known to possess the powers of witchcraft.

A person can become a witch through anyone of these means: by inheriting it from the parents, by touching or eating witchcraft substance unknowingly, by purchasing from other witches, by initiation and/or coercion from other witches by having it forced on an individual by demons, and by joining voluntarily.[21] African witches are believed to attack their neighbors and kinsmen/relations rather than distant and unrelated persons.

Sorcerers

Ikenga-Metuh posits that sorcerers are evil men who make medicine to hurt others. He wonders why in some cases people choose to transform the power of herbs, which God has put at the disposal of men to wicked, evil purposes.[22] Parrinder observes that a sorcerer is an evil person, feared and hated. He works in darkness because his deeds are evil. He is someone who deliberately tries to harm his enemies, or those of his clients who have paid him, by evil magical means.[23]

In view of the negative application of their powers to bring harm, pain, and misery on their victims in the community, sorcerers are the most feared and hated people in their communities.[24] No one openly identifies with them, not even close relations. Neighbors strictly and constantly warn their children and wards to steer clear of these wicked and evil men. No one would want to eat or drink from their homes for fear of being poisoned by them. According to Ikenga-Metuh, the Igbo terms, *ndi n'akpa nsi* and *ndi na agwo ajo ogwu* refer to sorcerers, evil men who make one decide to hurt others.[25]

The Reality or Fiction of Secret Societies in African Religio-cultural Beliefs

In recent times the reality or fictional status of secret societies-fraternities, witches, wizards, and sorcerers in African religio-cultural beliefs has been widely debated. The proponents of this debate are Euro-Americans and Africans converts to Christianity and Islam. The basis on which these denials are made hinges on the inability of Africans to scientifically prove the reality of these mystical forces. However, for the Africans the existence of these powers is not in doubt; they are real and not fiction. The belief in these mystical or supernatural forces does not however make the African fundamentally different from the other races of the globe.

Commenting on this phenomenon, Adega notes that African beliefs in these mystic powers may appear incredible, ridiculous, and unbelievable especially in western cycles owing to the fact that they cannot be scientifically verified and can thus not be accorded the status of universal beliefs.[26] Quarcoopome subscribes to the above line of thought when he inferred that the fact that there are no concrete objects in terms of empirical evidence connected to African beliefs and practices does not imply that they are false; the scientific mind would want tangible explanations of a spiritual activity.[27] This is because African science, beliefs, and practices go beyond empiricism to spiritism.[28]

The Role of Secret Societies-Fraternities, Witches, Wizards, and Sorcerers in African Societies

The activities of secret societies-fraternities, witches, wizards, and sorcerers in African societies cannot be overemphasized. While the possessors of these mystical or spiritual forces may also perform some functional roles in African societies; most of their well-known activities are anti-social, dysfunctional, and tilted toward evil. Thus, witches possess a special psychic quality which permits their spirits to leave their bodies while they are asleep to afflict injuries on others or even to eat their souls. A witch therefore uses no medicines, utters no spells, and performs no rites. Her powers are inherent in her personality; she did not have to learn it like learning a trade.[29]

Both sorcerers and witches have the same purpose, namely the devilish intention of injuring their fellow men by occult means. Witches attack their victims in several ways. They may carry away their victim's soul to be shared in their nocturnal meetings. The victim wakes up the following morning feeling week and sick and dies as soon as they eat his/her soul. Ikenga-Metuh reports that once the victim's soul has been shared by the witches, there is no remedy; but since this may be deferred, quick action after an attack may save the victim especially with the co-operation of the witch in releasing the soul of the victim.[30]

Witches and sorcerers can employ a myriad of methods to assault other individuals and their possessions. Among the Tiv, witches and sorcerers have used their mystical powers to kill their victim through *nyiar* and *idyuran* (lightning and thunder); wasps and ants also cause the death of a victim via their strings. The sorcerers could also command a person to appear in a mirror or calabash full of water where the victim is stabbed to death.[31]

Indeed, the activities of secret societies, fraternities, and cults have led to the loss of lives and property in most African societies, especially Nigeria.[32] On a general note, secret societies-fraternities, witches, wizards, and sorcerers use their mystical powers to harm other people, destroy life or property, disrupt the wellbeing of an individual, and change a happy destiny to an unhappy one.[33]

The Functional Role of Secret Societies in African Societies

It is worthy to point out that irrespective of the fact that secret societies-fraternities, witches, wizards, and sorcerers make use of the mystical or spiritual powers in their possession negatively; the truth also be told that they could use these powers in a functional way for the benefit of the society. This said, the activities and roles of witches, sorcerers, and fraternities together with other components of the African traditional religious system provide a descriptive skeleton that elucidates the misgivings that fall onto individuals by revealing what caused these misfortunes in language common in their belief systems. These mystical and spiritual forces thus explain evil persistence as well as the inability of mankind to exterminate it. For instance, witches and wizards can use witchcraft as a means of social control and correcting deviant behavior in Tiv society. As Adega notes, *Mbatsav* (witches) employ *tsav* (witchcraft) for the benefit of the whole community via *tar soron* (repairing the land). He argues that this was the conception of *tsav* before malevolent witches took over the scene in Tiv society.[34]

Not only that, witches can employ the powers of magic and witchcraft medically for diagnosing and curing diseases. For instance, Agbanusi reports the use of magic and witchcraft by some healers to heal fractured bones.

In the pre-colonial time, every person in Mende society—male and female—was in principle initiated into the appropriate school of puberty. A non-initiate was simply not considered as a mature person, whatever the age. The initiation in the bush school which could last as many as seven years was based on gender roles.[35] The *Zangbeto* secret society in Port Novo also serves as an initiation society for young men as well as representing the spirits of the dead.

Furthermore, the *Ndako Gboya* secret society of the Nupe's major task is the administration of justice and punishment on women suspected of witchcraft. The suspected witch was taken to the bush and made to scratch the ground with her bare fingernails. If after a while blood appears under her nails; she was proven a witch and executed or made to pay a hen fine.

Another secret society is the Oro society. This society is usually assigned the responsibility of not only protecting the community but also punishing evil doers through execution after being condemned by the Ogboni society.[36]

The above attributes of secret societies affirm the assertion that the secret societies in Africa were implemented in order to command the people. From the foregone, it can be conveniently argued as does Agbanusi that secret societies-fraternities, witches, wizards, and sorcerers have some mystical or spiritual powers which could be used either positively or negatively, but more often used negatively. He laments that it is in line with this thinking that sometimes we hear people remark, regrettably though, that while the "white man" exhibits his own witchcraft in innovations and in the production of superior technological equipment, the "black man" exhibits his in mischievous acts.[37]

THE EFFECT OF SECRET SOCIETIES, WITCHES, WIZARDS, AND SORCERERS ON THE AFRICAN SOCIETY

The effect of secret societies, witches, wizards, and sorcerers on the individuals and African societies cannot be overemphasized. There is no gain stating the obvious fact that one is not able to quantify these impacts. Secret societies, witches, and sorcerers have left a trail of deaths, injuries, harm, bewitchment, terror, and fear on the Africans. Among the Tiv of Central Nigeria for instance, some individuals have gone on self-imposed exile due to the fear of witches, leaving their compounds desolate and unoccupied. Since the Tiv are farmers, the mass exodus of youths from their villages has created the problem of hunger as the youthful population escapes to towns and cities. This has brought the Tiv economy sagging and crumbling on its knees. When this scenario is put in contrast to the economic recession in Nigeria, the magnitude of suffering now being experienced is horrifying.[38]

African societies will remain underdeveloped because of the above outlook. Also, witchcraft paraphernalia like *Imborivungu* (owl pipe), *pool* (ancestral relics), and *ibiamegh* (prosperity cult) have caused the spillage of human blood and loss of lives in the process of reactivating and retaining their efficacy.[39] Regarding the effect of sorcerers on the Tiv, there is a general sense of insecurity owing to the reckless application of *ci bibi*, *chigh ki bo*, and *vue chi* (poisons) by the *mba kaan chi ki bo* (sorcerers) who administer these substances in their victim's drinks, food, seats, doors, or pathways to cause them harm and death. This has made many a Tiv discrete on their movement and in whose company they socialize.[40]

Generally, secret societies, witches, and sorcerers have disastrous effects on African societies because they constitute: (1) a threat to the people's lives, their property, land, and economy (2) they are used in perpetrating injustice in the land and (3) they are used in taking from others what belongs to them.[41] Secret societies also have no boundary as to who they target in so much as their interest is under threat. In view of this, Nwosu reports that in western Igbo land, a religiously induced violence orchestrated by the *Ekumeku* secret society unleashed terror on the activities of the Christian missions, raiding mission establishments in Igboland between 1896 and 1904.[42] In response to the mystical or spiritual forces of secret societies, witches, wizards, and sorcerers, Africans in desperate bids to protect themselves from coming to harm have resorted to the use of charms, amulets, and various types of medicines, either taken directly (orally) or through incisions and the use of bracelets, charm belts (*bende*), finger rings, and other protective articles placed in secluded places in the house or in the field. All these secure a feeling of safety, protection, and assurance.

In addition to the use of diviners and medicine men who provide antidotes to the menace of these mystical powers, the Tiv organized anti-witchcraft movements to rid their society of witchcraft. Some of these anti-witchcraft movements include: *Haakaa/Namakea* (1929), *Ijov* (1912), *Inyamibuan* (1939), *Igyar yo* (1948), and *Korchan* (1979). The role of contemporary anti-witchcraft movements like *Nyamor*, *Anyamkwase*, and *Gande chihi* and some priests of the Catholic Church like Revd. Frs. Hyacinth Alia, Matthew Dzer, John Atoba, Stephen Suega, and Christopher Utov also made inroads at combating the evil activities of witchcraft and witches in Tivland.[43]

Reports from several parts of Africa also indicate that witches are not treated with kid gloves. As a matter of fact, persons found to be guilty of witchcraft are burnt alive. This same fate befalls witches in some different areas of the world. In Igbo land, witches and sorcerers are not buried; their corpses are thrown into the evil forest/bad bush, *ajo ohia* (Ikenga-Metuh, 128). It is often said that change is the only permanent thing and undoubtedly change has brought to bear its influence on African beliefs in secret societies-fraternities, witches, wizards, and sorcerers. Most Africans now tend to hold the erroneous belief that these mystical forces are mere fictions and downplay their influence on their lives. The agents of change include Christianity, Islam, western education, and globalization.

Mitigating the Menace of Secret Societies-Fraternities, Witches, Wizard, and Sorcerers on African Societies

From the foregone discussion, the chapter in view of the negative use of the mystical powers of secret societies, witches, wizards, and sorcerers calls on Africans to deemphasize on the acquisition, application, and use of the negative side of these mystical powers. This is because these mystical powers breed no good fortunes for anyone. Their activities are characterized by evil, pain, hurt, misfortune, fear, ill-luck, illness, and death. A society which is shrouded in these forms of misfortune can never develop. Thus, the activities of secret societies, witches, and sorcerers should be discouraged. Instead of breeding evil in society, they can channel their activities into productive ventures, for instance, in seeking for a cure of diseases like Ebola and HIV/AIDS that have no known cure for now. Furthermore, traditional rulers who are custodians of culture and in whose domain the witches, sorcerers, and members of secret societies reside can openly speak out against this evil practice to deter others from joining these groups.

Again, Islamic and Christian clerics can preach on these ills; members from their congregation known to engage in these evil practices should be sanctioned or ex-communicated to deter others from such negative practices. While these practices are spiritual and difficult to prove scientifically, law enforcement agencies can also prosecute those who are suspected or fingered as witches, secret cultists, and sorcerers with appropriate legal sanctions applied. Medicine men and women should also be encouraged to produce licit medicines only to enhance the safety of society.

Conclusion

This chapter has examined the reality or otherwise and activities of secret societies-fraternities, witches, wizards, and sorcerers in African society. The outcome of the examination reveals that fraternities, witches, wizards, and sorcerers exist. They are real and they use their knowledge of mystical and spiritual forces negatively on the members of their society. Their evil practices have produced illnesses, bewitchment, ill-luck, loss of lives, and property. In some instances, Africans have gone into self-exile out of fear of these spiritual forces, thus, depopulating their villages and bringing about economic hardship and hunger. To ward off the influence of these mystical powers, Africans have resorted to the use of protective articles like charms and amulets. The chapter notes that in an environment riddle with fear and uncertainty, no society can have hope of developing. The valuable time Africans spend running after medicine men/women for protective charms can be put into good use in bringing about developmental ideas for Africa. Evil should never be allowed to strive at the detriment of good. Evil must be condemned in all its forms and ramifications for the overall good, development, and wellbeing of society.

Notes

1. D. Offiong, "Witchcraft among the Ibibio of Nigeria", In Arthur C. Lehmann and James E. Meyer (eds), *Magic, Witchcraft and Religion; Anthropological Study of the Supernatural*, Palo Alto and London; Mayfield Publishing. 1985. P. 153.
2. Ibid., p. 153.
3. A. P. Adega, "African Beliefs in Magic, Witchcraft and Sorcery", In S.D. Shishima (eds), *The Traditional Religions of the Benue People: A Research Report*, Makurdi: Selfers Academic Press. 2008. P. 75–78.
4. http://projecttopicsforcomputerscience.blogspot.com/2015/05/secret-societies-in-african-socieites.html.
5. U. P. Nwosu, "The Theory and Practice of Secrecy in Okonko and Ogboni Societies", *AJACS*. 2009. P. 5.
6. Ibid., p. 5.
7. S. D. Shishima, *Campus Cultoculture in Nigeria*, Makurdi; Obeta Continental Press. 2009. P. 29.
8. U. P. Nwosu, Op. Cit. p. 7.
9. C. U. Okeke, *Secret Cult in Schools: A Spiritual Affair*, Abagana-Anambra State; GEM Publications. 1999. P. 2.
10. Ibid., p. 8.
11. S. D. Shishima, Op. Cit. p. 11.
12. http://projecttopicsforcomputerscience.blogspot.com/2015/05/secret-societies-in-african-socieites.html.
13. S. D. Shishima, Op. Cit. p. 51.
14. C. Bewaji, "The Menace of Campus Cults!!", *International Christian Digest*, 6, 1. 2004. P. 4.
15. E. M. Ikenga, *God and Man in African Religion*, Enugu; Snaap Press. 1999. P. 129.
16. Ibid.
17. D. Offiong, "Witchcraft among the Ibibio of Nigeria", In Arthur C. Lehmann and James E. Meyer (eds), *Magic, Witchcraft and Religion; Anthropological Study of the Supernatural*, Palo Alto and London; Mayfield Publishing. 1985. P. 151.

18. Ibid., p. 153.
19. E. M. Ikenga, Op. Cit. pp. 129–130.
20. http://www.nairaland.com/4350537/introduction-african-traditional-religion-witchcraft.
21. A. P. Adega, Op. Cit. p. 71.
22. E. M. Ikenga, Op. Cit. p. 127.
23. E. G. Parrinder (1968). E. Geoffrey, *African Traditional Religion*, London; SPCK. P. 117.
24. E. M. Ikenga, Op. Cit. p. 127.
25. Ibid.
26. A. P. Adega, Op. Cit. p. 50.
27. T. N. O. Quarcoopome (1987). *West African Traditional Religion*, Ibadan; AUP. P. 152.
28. Ibid., p. 151.
29. Ibid., p. 129.
30. E. M. Ikenga, Op. Cit. p. 131.
31. A. P. Adega, Op. Cit. pp. 73–77.
32. S. D. Shishima, Op. Cit. p. 86.
33. www.nairaland.com/4350537/introduction-african-traditional-religion-witchcraft.
34. A. P. Adega, Op. Cit. p. 79.
35. http://projecttopicsforcomputerscience.blogspot.com.
36. http://projecttopicsforcomputerscience.blogspot.com.
37. A. Agbanusi (2016). "Witchcraft in West African Belief System—Medical and Social Dimension". *Mgbakoigba Journal of African Studies*, 5, 2. P. 199.
38. A. P. Adega, Op. Cit. p. 80.
39. Ibid., p. 80.
40. Ibid., p. 114.
41. Enya Edwards, et al., prezi.com/ignrseid49/origins-of-sorcery-and-witchcraft-in-Africa.
42. Ibid., p. 8.
43. A. P. Adega, Op. Cit. pp. 80–81.

CHAPTER 17

The Role of Women in African Traditional Religion

Atinuke Olubukola Okunade

INTRODUCTION

To delve into the topic of women in African traditional religion, one would need to know what African traditional religion means. The African traditional religion, or traditional beliefs and practices of African people, is a set of highly diverse beliefs that include various ethnic religions.[1] Generally, these traditions are oral rather than scriptural.[2] It includes belief in higher and lower gods, including a supreme creator, belief in spirits, veneration of the dead, magic, and traditional African medicine. The role of humanity is generally seen as a harmonizing nature with the supernatural.[3] Before other religions such as Christianity, Islam, and Judaism penetrated throughout Africa, African people were cognizant and recognized the existence of a God, who was a Supreme being of sorts that was greater than all things, whose worship is by way of utterances mainly, and not meditative and comes in many forms, such as sacrifices and offerings, prayers, invocations, blessings and salutations, and intercessions.

Women hold vital roles in these traditional practices, and the internal gender traditions and dynamics are pronounced. There are many goddesses, priestesses, female diviners, and other figures, along with their male counterparts.

A. O. Okunade (✉)
Lagos State University of Education, Lagos, Nigeria

© The Author(s), under exclusive license to Springer Nature Switzerland AG 2022
I. S. Aderibigbe, T. Falola (eds.), *The Palgrave Handbook of African Traditional Religion*, https://doi.org/10.1007/978-3-030-89500-6_17

Roles and Status of Women in African Traditional Religion

Just as women's contributions toward the social, economic, political, educational are evident in society, so are their roles becoming imperative in religious spheres. In African traditional society, there is little to no significance given to gender issues which is a result of the belief that these roles, both in the family and in society at large, are granted to every individual. The campaign of "feminism" was not necessary because each gender had its traditional role in society's development. It was believed that women's roles were interdependent to men's, which minimized the campaign for gender equity. Each role, regardless of who performed it, was considered equally important because it contributed to the fundamental goal of community survival. So were the roles of women in serving and worshiping the gods, divinities, and deities of the land. In essence, these traditional ideas insinuated that Africans, in traditional indigenous societies prior to colonialism, fulfilled specific roles to sustain their societies. In traditional African society, African women are capable of a power that secures society together. Moreover, women are instrumental in the perseverance of the familial unit in African society. Leith Ross says that,

> Culturally, African women were the transmitters of the language, the history and the oral cultures, the music, the dance, the habits and the artisan knowledge. They were the teachers and were responsible for installing traditional values and knowledge in children. Men were also essential in the transmission of knowledge to the youth because they had a different type of knowledge of the earth and environment, and of ceremonies and traditions that were performed exclusively by men.[4]

Leith stresses that women had extensive knowledge of the natural environment. They were the gatherers, which means that their communities depended on them to provide nourishment, or they would face starvation.[5] Cognizant of their roles in spiritual matters, indigenous women in Africa also held vital knowledge of herbs and medicine that ensured their communities' survival. They were the healers. To buttress this view, Jone Hafkin and Hanson Bay emphasize that women were treated with unparalleled respect because of their peculiar role in procreation.[6] As "creator of life," they were charged with the sacred responsibility of caring for the next generations' needs. Because of this, they can be regarded as the originator of the idea that is now known as "sustainable development." Afusi says in every society, the most important aspect of life and survival was a family.[7] The women are often the backbone of the family in traditional Africa. The African family has always been characterized by strong women who usually held pertinent positions in the family.[8]

Women were the dominant figures in prehistoric Africa. Selected women controlled the spiritual systems and often held positions of leadership in African Traditional Religion.

These positions require special religious services and may not be seen or known by all society members except the initiates and dedicated individuals or families whose hereditary roles are to be part of the rites and rituals. Their spiritual offices included being oracles, mediums, seers, and advisers; they maintained the religious activities' calendar, and were powerful enough to lift curses from the accursed. This is so because religion is not location-based; neither is stage-based; rather, it is life. Their spiritual dominance accorded women respect in the society.

In her article, "Motherhood in African Literature and Culture," Remi Akujobi analyzes the place and role of women in African tradition and religion and interrogates the place of motherhood in the production, circulation, and consumption of items in African tradition. She viewed motherhood as sacred as well as a powerful spiritual component of the women's life. To her, motherhood is defined as an automatic set of behaviors and feelings that are switched on by pregnancy and birth of a baby. The experience is profoundly shaped by social context and culture. According to Akujobi, motherhood is also seen as a moral transformation whereby a woman comes to terms with being different in that she ceases to be an autonomous individual because she is one way or the other attached to another, her baby.[9]

Motherhood takes on several meanings in various societies. These meanings often have a cultural and religious undertone to them; seen as a sacred, spiritual path to be taken by women. In Africa, motherhood is considered as a God-ordained role.

Although motherhood is vital in African society, not all women experience motherhood. Childbearing is not the factor that determines a motherly role in society. It is womanhood that qualifies the female members of the society for the roles. Though, childbearing confers some spiritual power on the woman over her children. For instance, in Iyuku, a community in Estakor west of Edo state, when a mother tells a child that "I will bring out my breast," it means a lot as this is enough to caution any erring child. The power in the breast is so significant in the sense that everyone is considered to have suckled the mother's breast. The breasts signify blessings and nourishments. It is believed that a woman's curse is more potent when she curses with her breasts exposed. No child will be so stubborn to the extent that he/she will not dread the mother's breast.[10]

Hafkin and Bay emphasize that women were treated with unparalleled respect because they were viewed as being closer to the creator than men were.[11] This is because women themselves had the ability to create because they were able to give birth. In every society, the most important aspect of life and survival is a family. The women are often the backbone of the family in traditional Africa. They possessed the power that binds society together. In fact, the existence and survival of the family depended a great deal on the African women.[12]

Additionally, men were also vital in helping young people acquire knowledge which was facilitated due to men exclusively holding different types of ceremonies and traditions. Women had extensive knowledge of the natural environment; they were the gatherers, which meant that their communities depended on them to provide nourishment, or they would face starvation. For centuries, women were doctors without degrees, barred from books and lectures, learning from each other, and passing on experience from neighbour to neighbour, mother to daughter.[13]

Medicine is a component of women's heritage; it is their birthright. Despite the fact that men occupy the dominant role in African society, women play essential roles in the traditional healthcare system. These roles extend from the homes where women are often the household authorities on herbal remedies, to practitioner levels as herbalists and highly organized women societies that focus on disease prevention and cures.[14] Women's roles in family healthcare are central, as they are the primary coordinators of healthcare for their children. They shoulder responsibility in the family to select their child's doctor, take them to a doctor's appointment, and arrange for their child's follow-up care. They also help manage their partners' health needs, and approximately one in ten women are taking care of an aging or a chronically sick relative, often a parent.[15] Traditionally, women are the custodians of various nutritional, medicinal, and cultural needs of the family. They know the best type of foods to prepare for the particular health needs of the family, the right taste and preservation of plants and food for the future needs of the family with indigenous knowledge acquired through oral and non-oral methods, from informal and formal education they acquired from their parents, community, and society. They are knowledgeable in the use of herbs as preventive and curative to illnesses. Traditional African women view herbs as spiritual allies and intrinsically essential foodstuffs as well as medicines. The use of herbs as preventive medicine has contributed to the reduction of infant mortality, malaria, and measles being the major diseases that kill infants, especially in rural areas.[16]

Besides their indigenous knowledge in health affairs, the roles of women in religious affairs are spiritual imperatives. Most times, men are seen outwardly playing religious roles in most festivals, whereas, in the inner chambers, women of spiritual substance have played foundational roles before the outward shows that the community beholds. These women are knowers, seers, and advisers, and they had the power to place and remove curses.[17] For instance, festivals are the peak of worship celebration in honor of ancestors, deities, and divinities, such as *egungun* (masquerade) and *oro* festivals, of Yorùbá Southwest Nigeria. Commonly, well-dressed senior women who attend these festivals sing and dance during these celebrations. In the *egungun* festival, the role of the most aged woman (an initiate), known as *Iya Agan*, is very crucial; she has a similar status to *Alagba* (male head of the *egungun* cult). Without her pronouncing the commencement of the *egungun* festival, the masquerades cannot come out. She does this by breaking the *Agan*, which is a typical spiritual noise that spreads throughout the community. The men will now seek for the *Agan* until seen and then give it back to *Iya Agan* for purposes that are more spiritual. While all these are going on, other women will be singing melodious songs, and preparing different types of foods, especially the frying of beans cake throughout the period, which usually lasts seven days. *Iyalode*, who also has the same status as *Ajana oro*, the male spiritual leader of the *oro* cult, performs similar ritual practices. Notably, women are not allowed to see *oro*; however, the *oro* rituals and outings cannot commence without the women leading the *oro* out with the appropriate songs. The women's voices, led by the eldest woman initiate, prompts the *oro* procession and alerts the community of the *oro* outing and ritual session. The women's singing accompanied by ritualistic dances warm the hearts of the gods.

Women are also viewed as spiritual "sources of danger" because of the "polluting nature of blood," due to the special significance of blood. The blood of menstruation and childbirth is considered pollution, and the unclean women have to be separated from the "clean" women during rituals and some special religious sessions. Menstruating women are not allowed to take part in all the sessions that abhor such presence.[18] This natural state of women has conferred special treatment on them in traditional African society.

In Yorùbá mythology, *Osun*, the goddess of the Osun River and the only woman deity within the sixteen major deities (*Orisa*), is believed to be an immensely powerful woman. Osun's role is to shield the people as well as bless the women with fertility. The annual festival takes place during August and is visited by a myriad of people all over the world who visit Osun State, Nigeria so that they may attend and participate in the famous two-week-long festival. *Arugba*, a virgin maiden who aids people in communicating with the river deity, is the main attraction of the festival as well as the one who leads a procession of devotees to offer sacrifices to the river. There cannot be any festival until a virgin is found to take the role of *Arugba*. Mbiti (1991: 2–3) submits that women play a significant role in the religious activities of society by offering prayers for their families in particular and the community in general. During prayer, the woman brings before God her family and hands them over to God, believing that He will keep away all evil from them.[19] She also offers a prayer for sick children, addressing it, especially to the departed members of the family who are believed to have intermediary influence in carrying the supplication to the Almighty God. Here, the religious consciousness of women and care for the community is exhibited. The physical and spiritual world mingles here in a harmony of going and coming. The woman depicts here a deep sensitivity towards the invisible and spiritual realities. It is clear that women both participate in society's religious activities and make their own contributions to the spiritual welfare of their lives, their families, community, and society. The prayers are a small window that opens unto their spirituality, which indeed is the spirituality of all human beings. As they share with God in the great mysteries of passing on life, so they share also in giving human life a spiritual orientation.[20]

Within African traditional religion, spirit possession grants provisional respect to women in some contexts; however, under other circumstances, it can extend indefinite social benefits to women. Spirit possession refers to the belief in the ability of intangibles, gods, or spirits to seize control of the human body. This belief is not constrained to African traditional religion, but rather, it exists in many religions including Christianity, Buddhism, as well as others. While dependent on the cultural setting, spirit possession is thought to be either voluntary or involuntary, beneficial or detrimental. Within these belief systems, it can be observed that women are more likely to believe in spirit possession than their male counterparts. Spirit possession may transpire due to music, drumming, or medicine. The possessed individual speaks for the spirit. Regardless of the duration, possession signifies a bond with the spirit, and the possessed are called brides. The bonds make possession an ecstatic and enjoyable experience. Even though possession is often described as a marriage between the spirit and the possessed individual, possession remains a symbolic act because there is no physical or genital activity involved, although the sense of pleasure or suffering is real. Possession can also be a violent event, especially possession by the god *Sango* who mounts a person as a horse.[21]

Possession ends when the spirit departs, but the phenomenon of possession remains a constant feature of the spiritual life of the individual. Spirit possession is important because the spirit that controls the devotee communicates messages to the community through the individual.

Over thousands of years, indigenous people have developed an intimate relationship with their ancestral lands and ecosystems in which they live and form their territories. These people groups have entrenched their own systems of knowledge innovation, and practices relating to the cultivation and protection of these lands and their biodiversity. Sacred and natural sites are embedded in their territories as places of cultural, ecological, and spiritual significance. The rituals and ceremonies associated with this underpin their customary laws and governance systems.[22]

Sacred natural sites cover a wide range of natural features such as mountains, hills, forests, groves, rivers, lakes, lagoons, caves, islands, and springs. Additionally, these sacred sites may vary in size from miniscule individual trees to an entire mountain range. They are predominantly terrestrial but are also found inshore marine areas, islands, and archipelagos. Furthermore, these sites can be located in temples and shrines as well as incorporate other important religious entities, for example, pilgrimage traits.

Inherent is the belief that women are custodians of acceptable African traditional beliefs and behaviors. Women are likely to have spent their time handling spiritual obligations and ceremonies where sacred places acted as a myriad of things, such as ceremonial grounds for keeping ritual objects, a safe house for the abused women, and other general services. Besides, they instruct and socialize younger female members of the household, such as daughters, daughters-in-law, and younger sister-in-law into the rituals of their religion. These women were oracles, spirit mediums, knowers, seers, and advisors.

African people are known for their spiritualism and love for religion. Therefore, we can see how dominant female energy in the spiritual sphere helped to ensure that women were respected in society.[23]

In terms of macro-political organization, in the past, most African societies had a dual sex political system, which allowed for substantial female representation and involvement in governance and administration. The position of Queen Mother gave women prominent and political authority in running the nation. In most cases, the queen mother was older than the king was and biologically related to him.[24] Among her essential roles is to ensure the well-being of the women and children of the nation. The queen mother is in charge of childbirth, coming of age, the rite of passage, and many other ceremonies. A significant role that the queen mother, and sometimes the wife of the king, has is that of either selecting or endorsing the king's successor.[25] Women directly ruled many African nations, and this was an exception rather than the rule.

Even though colonialism had a profound negative impact on African women's social role, there are still a plethora of women who persevered and who can still inspire us today. We can conclusively say that the status of women in society often is an outcome of the interpretation of religious texts and the cultural and institutional setup of religious communities,[26] thus ensuring the continuity of domestic religion. Unmarried girls, others by married women, and some by widows perform some of the rituals.

Goddesses in African Traditional Religion

Throughout Africa, bodies of water such as seas, rivers, lakes, and lagoons are regarded as deities' habitats. Therefore, these natural phenomenons are often treated with high reverence; sometimes even being worshiped and honored with shrines and specially appointed priests and priestesses. It will not be out of place to state that African traditional religion is feminine. This is because deities and goddesses are numerous in Africa in a way that survival of both tangibles and intangibles lies in the roles of women. Deities that have men as the Chief priests still utilize women for vital roles during worship sessions. Some of these goddesses and their imperatives to the societies are explained below.

Yemoja

Yemoja, the most prominent of the river divinities among the Yorùbá in Southwest Nigeria, is seen as the mother of numerous river deities. She is also the mother of fish and the giver of children. Yemoja is the African goddess of the ocean and the protector of pregnant women. She is the patron deity of pregnant women. Yemoja embodies all characteristics of motherhood, caring, and love. This maternal source of the divine, human, animal, and plant life is most widely symbolized by the ocean.[27]

Oya

Other prominent river goddesses like *Oya*, the goddess of the Niger River, are believed to be the companions, or one of the wives of *Sango*, the god of thunder. She is so fierce and terrible that no one can look upon her. Oya is often identified with the wind that blows when no rain follows. Oya is the favorite wife of Sango, the only wife who remained true to him until the end, leaving Oyo with him and becoming a deity after his death. She is the goddess of the Niger River, which is called River Oya (*odo Oya*), but she manifests herself as the strong wind that precedes a thunderstorm. When Sango wishes to fight with lightning, he sends his wife ahead of him to fight with the wind. She blows house roofs off, knocks down large trees, and fans the fires set by Sango's thunderbolts into a high blaze. When Oya comes, people know that Sango is not far behind, and it is said that without her, Sango cannot fight.[28]

Oba

Oba (goddess) in Yorùbá mythology is the first wife of *Sango*, the third king of the *Oyo* Empire, and the Yorùbá god of thunder and lightning. *Oba* is said to be an *Orisa* of the river. She was the daughter of Yemoja and one of the consorts of Sango. She is the sanitarian goddess of the river, which figuratively represents the flow of time and life. Turn to her for assistance in learning how to go with the flow or when you need to inspire some movements in sluggish projects or goals.[29]

Otin

Otin, the goddess of defense, is similarly personified in the River of Otin. Her power extends to the protection of people against pending danger. She is thought to bestow prosperity, good health, and longevity upon her adherents. She is a warrior who defended her people and continues to fight for her followers. Her actions as a female deity are recognized in high regard. As Jacob Olupona and Olajubu Oyeronke explain, "Otin is an example of a goddess who exhibits leadership qualities and braveness."[30]

Aje

Aje is among the loved *Orisa* out of the 401 gods that are worshiped in Ife, Osun State, Nigeria. She is the goddess of wealth, and she also provides sufficient wealth and greater economic benefits for whoever worships her. Aje is the daughter of Olokun; nevertheless, Olokun himself respects Aje, which is why she is referred to as *Aje Olokun*. It is essential to praise Aje before anyone can get favor from *Olokun*. This is because Aje is the only daughter of *Olokun* and *Olokun* loves her dearly. *Aje* can be found in waters, and this was the source of spending cowries before the advent of present currencies. All the following foods are what *Aje* accepts as offerings: ekuru, bananas, beans, and *oyin* (honey), among others. All these could be the main reason why all you see about *Aje* is white clothes and cowries, and all must be clean.[31]

Modjadji

Modjadji is the South African goddess of rain whose spirits live in the body of a young woman. The Balobedu people of South Africa consider her a key figure, as she can start and stop the rain. The rain queen has been around for the longest time, and it was only in the sixteenth century that her spirit decided to dwell in a woman.[32]

Nana Buluku

Nana Buluku is a prominent deity famous in most West African nations. She also has different names in various tribes. Nana Buluku is worshiped as the mother goddess. Her image is that of an older woman who is thought to be the creator of the world.[33]

CONCLUSION

Throughout history, women have played an essential role in maintaining society's stability, progress, and long-term development. African societies believe that religion is a way of life and that it must be exhibited in the day-to-day behavior of the citizenry. The natural potentials of women are thereby recognized as being essential to their families, community, and society. Though their roles are primarily recognized in the social, political, economic, and cultural spheres, their presence and status are pertinent to religious activities and practices. In the religious sector, women occupy a key role in mankind's progression reinforcing their significant status in society. They are not seen as being inferior to men because they can take care of their allotted responsibilities of life. The primary duty of a woman is to preserve the human race, as we have seen in the roles played by various goddesses mentioned herein. There is a great deal of variance in this dimension from the extremely traditional gender role stereotype of women as homemakers to the modern notion of women as key breadwinners for the family.

NOTES

1. Molefi Kete Asante and Ama Mazama, *Encyclopedia of African Religion* (Thousand Oaks, CA: SAGE Publications, 2009), 124.
2. John S. Mbiti, *Introduction to African Religion* (Portsmouth, NH and London: Heinemann Educational Books), 1991, 2–3.
3. William St. Clair, *Imperialism and Traditional African Culture* (Cambridge: Cambridge University Press, 1994), 27.

4. Leith Ross, *African Woman* (New York: Macmillan Publishers Ltd, 1967), 34.
5. Ibid.
6. Jone Hafkin and Hanson Bay (eds.), *Women in Africa: Studies in Social and Economic Change* (Stanford, CA: Heineman, 1976), 59–60.
7. Oseni Taiwo Afusi, "An Introductory Evaluation," *Journal of Pan African Studies* vol. 3, no. 6 (2010): 229–238, 18.
8. Bina Agarwal, *Socio-Economic Background of Traditional African Family System* (New York: Oxford University Press, 1970), 75.
9. Remi Akujobi, "Motherhood in African Literature and Culture", *CLCWeb: Comparative Literature and Culture,* vol 13, no. 1 (2011):11.
10. Ibid.
11. Hafkin and Bay, *Women in Africa*, 59–60.
12. Ibid.
13. Leith Ross (1967), 34.
14. Sekuru Friday Chisangu is the Founder and President of the Zimbabwe National Practitioners Association. www.kaiserfamilyfoundation.com.
15. "[O]ver one in ten women are taking care of an aging or chronically sick relative, often a parent," Kaiser Family Foundation, www.kff.org.
16. Dr. Margaret Uyouyou Ugdoma, "Availability and Use of Indigenous Knowledge Among Rural Women in Nigeria," *Library Philosophy and Practice* (e-journal), 2014, http://digitalcommons.unl.edu/libphilprac/1167 (accessed November 9, 2020).
17. Marion Kilson, "Women in African Traditional Religions," *Journal of Religion in Africa*, vol. VIII, facs. 2 (1976): 133–143. https://www.jstor.org/stable/i271866.
18. Kenneth Kojo Anti, KKAnti: *Women in African Traditional Religion*, http://www.mamiwata.com/women.html (Zugriff:30.01.2010).
19. Mbiti, *Introduction to African Religion*, 2–3.
20. Marion Kilson, "Women in African Traditional Religions," 133–143.
21. "Africa Religion and Possession," https://science.jrank.org/pages/11039/Religion-Africa-Religion-Possession.html (accessed November 9, 2020).
22. The rituals and ceremonies associated with this underpin their customary laws and governance systems; *see* www.earthfoundation.org.
23. Kilson, "Women in African Traditional Religions," 133–143.
24. Stacy Ann Wilson quoted Sacks (1979) on page 168: Identity, Culture and the Politics of Community Development. Stacy is a Lecturer in the Department of Government and Research and a Fellow at the Center for Leadership and Governance at the University of West Indies, Mona.
25. Ibid.
26. Klingorova, K. (2015): Genderové rozdíly ve vybraných světových náboženstvích. In: Doboš, P., Honsnejmanová, I. [eds.]: Geografický výzkum: Prostor ve své transdisciplinaritě. Brno, Masarykova univerzita (in print).
27. Kennet Kojo Anti, *Women in African Traditional Religions* (Presentations prepared for the Women's Centre Easter Washington, 2010). www.manniwata.com.
28. Oya is believed to be the companion, or one of the wives of Sango, the god of thunder. *See* www.journeyingtothegoddess.com.
29. Migene González-Wippler, *Santeria: The Religion* (Llewellyn Worldwide Limited, 1994). *See also* www.journeyingtothegoddess.com.

30. Oyeronke Olajubu and Jacob K. Olupona, *Women in the Yoruba Religious Sphere* (McGill Studies in the History of Religions, a Series Devoted to International Scholarship, State University of New York Press, 2003).
31. Facts about the goddess of wealth by Gbenga Olowu. *See* www.braintrusthub.com (accessed 5/16/20).
32. Julie Kwach, *see* www.briefly.co.za (accessed 5/21/20).
33. Ibid.

CHAPTER 18

Arts, Music, and Aesthetics

AdeOluwa Okunade

INTRODUCTION

The true identity of any society can be reconstructed through its belief systems, which are an integral part of its arts. Unfortunately, the continent of Africa suffered a significant loss in the spheres of arts, science, technology, and religion. These areas are keys to the identity of a nation or society. The significant loss came through the hospitality doors of Africans and, perhaps, their quest for knowledge. Scientists are always inquisitive and observant, even in the face of risks. The African people became inquisitive at the glance of the Europeans and opened its doors for them. One of the most significant risks the continent took was "closing of eyes" when receiving the Northern hemisphere citizens. No matter the mixed blessings that the arrival of the Europeans in Africa has brought, the fact still remains that it is easier to destroy than to build. What takes a second to destroy may take a millennium to rebuild.

The emergence and the activities of the Caucasians in Africa gave birth to versions of the history of Africa mostly authored by uninformed and cerebrally myopic cultural scientists. To date, efforts are still ongoing in portraying Africa accurately. The continent has suffered an identity crisis and lost most artifacts that could have been used to authenticate its history. The 1897 loot by the British to their museums are strong evidence of this. In Peju Layiwola's words, "1897 was the year the nascent British imperialism invaded the ancient empire of Benin, sacked its traditional government and monarch Ovonramwen (ruled c.188–1897) and looted its largely bronze and ivory, art works over a schism

---

A. Okunade (✉)
University of Port-Hacort, Port-Hacort, Nigeria
e-mail: adeoluwa.okunade@uniport.edu

© The Author(s), under exclusive license to Springer Nature Switzerland AG 2022
I. S. Aderibigbe, T. Falola (eds.), *The Palgrave Handbook of African Traditional Religion*, https://doi.org/10.1007/978-3-030-89500-6_18

that seems more orchestrated."[1] To get these works repatriated has been a tug of war. This experience is not only in Britain but scattered all over Europe and part of the Americas. The presence of Africa is felt more in these two continents, not through human migration alone (forced or voluntary), rather through its arts and religion, among other knowledge icons. The heterogeneous nature of Africa is also reflected in its diverse religious traditions that even in the same traditions, there are variations.[2] To capture these African religious beliefs and practices under one umbrella, African scholarship covers them with African traditional religion.

In this chapter, I will briefly factualize the theme from the spheres of the concepts of what the key words—arts, music, aesthetics, and religion—are in traditional African society. The symbiotic concept of the key words may also appear in a web form in the text. The word "arts" has been appropriated in many facets of life whereas it is necessary to zero in on a precise meaning within different contexts. Is it visual arts, poetry, literature, or language grouped in modern scholarship as one of the arts disciplines or architecture as the case may be in some other reasoning and intellectual terrains? In traditional African society, dance, movement, drama, poetry, singing, and other related arts are integral parts of what modern education views as music. This is why it is argued that "music" as a word does not represent the concept in Africa; rather, it is viewed either as musical arts in the classroom or "play" in meaning. The "play" here is not a mere play but a serious play that comprises education, therapy, and other valuables for both cerebral and physiological aspects of life. To comprehend this within this chapter, musical arts shall be used as the underpinning focus wherein music is being discussed. This is used to represent the actual activities that this concept means in the traditional African society.

The littered definition of "music" in most classrooms and textbooks is the "combination of sound in a way that pleases the ear." The shortfall in this definition is that it looks at sound alone, and therefore, considers such absolutely as what should be regarded as music. Both tangibles and intangibles are the constituents of "music" in Africa. Singing, dancing, movement, miming, sculptures, costumes, hairdo, painting, poetry, and history, among others are entailed in the original appearances of this activity that we find in the classroom as music in modern education. Because of these constituents, the "musical art" concept as it should be has made the subject a real art. Traditionally, entertainment has not been the primary aim of music in African society. The entertaining flavor of this stage production is for memorization and retention purposes. Music in African society is for valuable societal education. It is used to sermonize on ethos, norms, ethics, and other traditions of the society. Though music for music's sake or entertainment purposes was not disallowed nor non-existent, it was only a marginal concern in terms of societal beliefs and recognition.

Humanity is the bedrock of living in every sphere of life in traditional African society. The communities are religiously and socially bonded with respect for lives and properties. The religions were not there for profit-making neither did the arts belong to any particular individual. For generations, the religion was lived; it was a way of life, and all the facets of arts belonged to the community. Wellness of the communities is the paramount aim of all members of the community, which, therefore, behooves on every member to make contributions to the growth and development of the society. Any activities that would not benefit the entire society were not acceptable in traditional African society. The copyright of all beneficial activities belonged to the entire society, as it was believed that services are rendered for humanity's sake and not for personal reasons. Artists or *artistes* see themselves as part and parcel of the society that must be recognized for their contributions to society. Success is measured through the level of contribution to society and not the volume of wealth acquired through such services. The innate joy experienced in delivering the service is what makes the *artiste* a successful person. The services are rendered at different events in the society, of which religious activities are paramount. Because, recently, studies on religions in Africa are evolving, several postulations thereby abound. The true identities of African traditional religion can only be verified through oral sources and non-oral sources via objects and other activities. In visual arts, for example, objects with strong symbolism are embedded and encoded in religious arenas. Totems, dance, poetries, folktales, folklores, stylized movements, and a combination of all these are a core aspect of worship. Through any of the belief structures of African traditional religions, these "ingredients" mentioned are an integral part of all. There are three prominent belief structures marshaled out by scholars from different perspectives. P.A. Talbot cultured a four-element structure of polytheism, anthropomorphism, animism, and ancestral worship. In E.G. Parrinder's perspective, the four structures comprise the Supreme Being, Chief Divinities, divinized ancestors, and charms and amulets. Bolaji Idowu has the most popular and acceptable five hierarchical structure. These are the Supreme Being, divinities, spirits, ancestors, magic, and medicine. Within each of the five structures, the arts play an integral role.

The word "aesthetic" connotes beauty in a hurry instance. Its philosophies and theories are usually based on visual appearances that are visible in structure, alignment, and coordinates. Meki Nzewi cautions, however, that searching for aesthetics in the African artistic milieu with an exogenous mental-cultural background perceives vanity as beauty, whereas traditional Africa assesses beauty in terms of experienced merit or virtue.[3] In traditional African society, external or exterior beauty does not represent the needed aesthetics; instead, the message, norms, virtues, and ethos are found in the arts. The arts could be visual, tangible, or intangible.

African arts are not to be taken, therefore, as art for art's sake, especially when it goes along with the sacred entity of the society. When it is art for art's sake, as it is as an art product in many societies, the emphasis is an exhibition of superficial aspirations of creativity. Here, intentions matter a lot to the traditional African society. Religion and festivals is an avenue where creativity, which encompasses arts, is the best avenue to determine the level of aesthetics and its meaning in Africa. This is expressed thus:

The philosophy of arts in indigenous African societies prescribes that aesthetics is to be perceived in the contexts of creative intention and its practical outcome Creative intention primarily aims to demystify existence through the performance of the mystifying, critical to which is aspiring for humaning and humane objectives. Extra musical arts objectives then inform the choice of objects and personnel for performance as well as the rationalization of the tangibles and intangibles of creative intention.[4]

The aesthetic spheres in African traditional religion premised on the attendant arts (attendant arts—music visual arts, objects, etc.) are those artistic exhibitions with utilitarian characteristics and contemplative narratives. This lasts longer than mundane or ephemeral aesthetics that dwell on physical beauty, sweetness before the eyes, spectator's momentary satisfaction, and individualism glorification. This chapter, therefore, examines the components of the music and its symbiotic relationship with religion, arts as in visual arts (and objects) as an integral part of religion, and the roles both play in building lasting aesthetic values in the African traditional religion.

Music in African Traditional Religion

One of the avenues of experiencing full musical activities in traditional African society is festivals. Festivals are always lacquered with appropriate music at all levels. Some are in three stages—pre-festival, the festival proper, and post-festival. Initiations and cultural rites are other avenues. Music used in worship or special worship occasions is not incidental but an integral part of the whole. While modern scholars and contemporary narratives will bring demarcation of traditional sacred and secular festivals in discourses, it is pertinent to align with the facts that hardly can one find a festival that is not sacred. All festivals have a varying underlying degree of sacredness. It might be attached to a deity, an ancestral spirit, or some degree of myth surrounding it. The impulse of this is to correct the impression of scholars whom most times paint African festivals as an avenue of mere merrymaking.[5] Each festival is boldly focused on the sustainability of humanity and humanness of the members of the society. Oyin Ogunba (1978) writes, "But when one watches an African festival, which is the chief physical and metaphysical representation of African religion, the dominant impression is often found to be humanistic rather than religious."

The music performed during these festivals makes use of other arts in representing the motif of the festivities. Religious or non-religious, a typical gathering of worshipers or other cultural assemblies in the traditional African society exhibits two perspectives of ideational and theatrical spheres.[6] The ideational entrenches principles, philosophies, and norms in the focus, while the theatrical unfolds as events in a time–space structure. At both levels, music (as in musical arts) occupies prominent roles. The religious festivals consist of two layers of ceremony; one is absolute sacredness while the second is "secular." Music propels both layers and dictates the steps and activities to be taken by the religious conductors and the worshipers and spectators where necessary. Here, the spectators are not mere spectators who have just come to take the role of an eye witness account; rather, they are members of the community whose consciousness is alert to the importance of the religious outing and ceremonies. To properly give accuracy to the importance and role of music in African traditional religion, musical arts theater is best used as a graphical and objective description and adjective to qualify the artistic presence. Musical arts theater is part of the imperatives in the festivals (religious/worship or non-religious). Some aspects of the festival demand specially trained musicians who must know the tenets of the religion. Some families are specially designated for such purpose in most communities. For example, the dùndún ensemble, which is the most common ensemble of the Yorùbá people of Southwest Nigeria, has its record of having its members belonging to the specialized family of *Ayan*. Akin Euba records that:

> *Each dùndún drummer typically belongs to a family in which drumming has been practised for several generations past. A drumming family includes not only a drummer and his children but also his brothers and their children, all of whom usually live in the same compound or at least same neighbourhood.*[7]

The musicians do not only belong to the same biological family group; they also perform together in ensembles at various and necessary events. The musicians make necessary sacrifices or rites before going out for performances. For the core parts of religious worship or festivals, music or musical arts theater is the core activator of every stage of the events. It directs the steps of the key leaders—the priests and priestesses. The musicians, having knowledge of the stages required in the worship, know what rhythm and when to perform such that it will allow the events to go smoothly. To summon participants out and for communal participation at various levels, the musicians change the music to announce such participation. The embedded aesthetics of these actions are that community members honor the land and the importance of the festival as it relates to their survival in terms of communal living of brotherhood. It reinforces the unity that is expected of the community. Okunade shares that

> "In *Agà* festival of the Gbágùrá people, one of the ethnic groups of the Yorùbá Southwest Nigeria, the festival reminiscences their survival during inter-ethnic wars of the 18th century.[8] The festival is said to remind them of the unity that was exhorted during the war, which made them to survive it and still remains in their different places of abode. Where shrines or sacred spots dedicated for worship or sacrifices exist, the qualified members of the community who are initiates either by belonging to the dedicated families or by special initiation are the only ones

who take part in the rites before coming to the public glare for full participation of members of the community."

However, musicians are allowed because their special status and services are part of some of the rites at the "inner chamber." Sometimes, the music may be performed *a capella*, wherein the musicians stay meters away from the sacred spots to usher the worship coordinators—priests, priestesses, and announce the public participation of the community members, respectively.

African traditional religion is brilliantly a combination of the worship of God, veneration of deities, and ancestral spirits.[9] Some ill-informed scholars have replaced veneration with worship, making it appear as if Africans worship the deities or ancestral spirits in place of God the supreme. Some religions venerate their beliefs to reach God the supreme through certain mediums as an intermediary in reaching the Almighty for both worship and veneration. Music is used to keep both flowing in actualizing the ultimate aim of the focus of the events. Through "hot rhythm," psychical transformation takes place.[10] This is what most authors regard as spirit possession. I have decided to use "psychical transformation" to distinguish this ecstatic state from the negative notion of spirit possession used in Christianity. During the worship of *Sàngó*, the god of thunder known among the Yorùbá of Southwest Nigeria, the psychical substantiation is instigated through the hot rhythm of the music. A similar experience happens at the *stambeli*, a ritual healing music of the aborigines of Tunis.[11]

It is a thing of interest that in as much as there are variations in worship styles from one locality to another, one still finds the essential common traits and functions of music in the variations. My visit and experience at the Camdomble Worship Center in Salvador, Bahia, Brazil reveal that the structure of music in the worship of the gods that were exported during the enslavement of Africans to the Americas still have strong and visibly similarities with what is obtainable at the root, despite the "alterations" or variations. It shows that African traditional religion in the diaspora still maintains the function, structure, and form of music in traditional African society. With the variations, a robust common denominator is that the intensity of the music, most times during the worship sessions, generates a state of altered consciousness that connects the subject with supernormal realms. This is where the intangibles make due contact with the tangibles. The music used in African traditional religion as a singular construct unifies the theoretical and experiential peculiarities of music, which involves dance, dance drama, and mystical drama, reinforcing the atmosphere of the worship or festival to create a spiritual ambiance within the environment. There are peculiar instruments dedicated or attached to a particular god or deity. Among the Yorùbá of Southwest Nigeria, the entire cosmology is unified by *Ifá*, the divination system based on the interpretation of the verses of *odu*, a large body of religious, social, and philosophical knowledge. While many ensembles take part during the festival, there are still particular instruments dedicated to the worship. These are *agogo* (bell), *Àràn* (pot drum), and *Ìpèsè* (tripartite drum). Bàtá drums are used as the official music instruments for the worship of *Sàngó*. However, other instruments appear and are welcome, especially during the parts that involve the members of the community as participants and spectators. This is one of the modern experiences in contemporary Africa. One finds more of *dùndún* ensembles performing at this stage. This stage brings the full aesthetics of the essence of the religion, which creates more social bonding among the community members.

Arts in African Traditional Religion

The word "arts" connotes several meanings and implications in many discourses. The extent of its usage is even found in the sciences: "The art (s) of Science." Academic disciplines with scientific study concerning day-to-day living are also grouped under "Arts," with Humanities as a synonym in most cases. Because of its usefulness, wider coverage, therapeutic nature, problem-solving mechanism, other wellness of humans, and relevance to life, arts have become an integral part of religion, which human beings use as one of the means to solving problems encountered in the world. The arts here refer to visual arts-objects as part of religious spectacles in Africa. My intention, therefore, is using symbols and iconography as tools of the discourse primarily. The transcendental effort in getting closer to God through worship or veneration—desire an object (or objects)—may convincingly relax the spirit of the worshipers and lets them know that they are in the presence of a "being" who is greater and far above the mortals. Agberia points out that "This is identified clearly on the floor of the shrine by some objects, natural or artificial, in which it implies a worshipper or priest can enter into a more immediate relationship with Òrìsà (a Yorùbá word for God- sic)…, image he designates it an icon, implying the material manifestations of the spirit and the vessel through which Spiritual content with men are released."[12]

The presence of the icons at the place of worship is part of the convincing phenomenon to the devotees that the powers of the intangibles are there to intervene in their requests in the form of thanksgiving or supplication. These icons and images are an expression of pre-conceived objects, both tangibles and intangibles, filled with meanings and interpretations. They become either the physical or the spiritual imagining supernormal reality. Some of these artistic images may be designed on some special and dedicated music instruments or other paraphernalia of worship. They may be images representing certain spirits, and some icons are also found hanged or positioned strategically at worship venues. Òjó views objects as acts, relationships, or linguistic formations that stand for a multiplicity of meanings.[13] This suggests that a symbol can have several meanings and implications. It may further suggest that it is only the faithful or devotees of a particular worship that can give accurate meanings to symbols. Nabofa sees objects as an overt expression of what is behind the veil of perception.

Conclusion

Arts and music activate spirituality in African traditional religion, while spirituality pervades life. The symbiotic relationship between Arts/Music and African traditional religion remains the bedrock of its aesthetics. The ascendancy of the religion may not be as visible and widespread as Christianity and Islam, but its presence cannot be overlooked or ignored. For example, the worship of the *Ifá* divination in Yorùbáland of Southwest Nigeria takes place weekly in a modern building with a signboard "*Ijó Orunmila*"[14] (Congregation of Orunmila). The aesthetics in African traditional religion is not premised on the mundane philosophy of fancies, and packaging, rather it is premised on the benefits accrued to the society in terms of norms, ethos, and other societal values. Emphasis is on the inner beauty, which produces the outward character or behavior, and ultimately shapes society.

Notes

1. See Peju Layiwola's *Benin1897.com: Art and the Restitution Question*. Retrieved October 24, 2020, from http://benin1897.com/benin.php.
2. See Aderibigbe, Ibigbolade Simon in "Religions in Africa" in Aderibigbe Ibigbolade and Akinloye Òjó (eds.), *Continental Complexities: A Multidisciplinary Introduction to Africa* (San Diego, CA: Cognella Publishing, 2013), 63.
3. See Aderibigbe, Ibigbolade Simon in "Religions in Africa" in Aderibigbe Ibigbolade and Akinloye Òjó (eds.), *Continental Complexities: A Multidisciplinary Introduction to Africa* (San Diego, CA: Cognella Publishing, 2013), 63–65.
4. Nzewi, Meki. *A Contemporary Study of Musical Arts: Informed by African Indigenous Knowledge Systems*, Volume 4 (South Africa: Compress www.compress.co.za 2007).
5. Nzewi, Meki. *A Contemporary Study of Musical Arts: Informed by African Indigenous Knowledge Systems*, Volume 4 (South Africa: Compress www.compress.co.za 2007).
6. Ogunba, Oyin. "Traditional African Festival Drama," in Oyin Ogunba and Abiola Irele (eds.), *Theatre in Africa* (University of Ìbàdàn Press, 1978).
7. See Aderibigbe, Ibigbolade Simon in" Religions in Africa" in Aderibigbe Ibigbolade and Akinloye Òjó (eds.), *Continental Complexities: A Multidisciplinary Introduction to Africa* (San Diego, CA: Cognella Publishing, 2013).
8. Euba, Akin. *Yorùbá Drumming: The DùnDún Tradition* (Lagos: Elekoto Music Center, 1990).
9. Okunade, A. A. "Ijó Ìwòsí in Àgùrá Palace, Abeokuta." African Notes (Journal of the Institute of African Studies, University of Ìbàdàn 29:1&2, 2005), 65–76.

10. Falola, Toyin. *Culture and Customs of Nigeria* (Westport and London: Greenwood Press, 2001).
11. Falola, Toyin. *Culture and Customs of Nigeria* (Westport and London: Greenwood Press, 2001), 8.
12. Falola, Toyin. *Culture and Customs of Nigeria* (Westport and London: Greenwood Press, 2001), 9.
13. Agberia, John-Tokpabere. "Iphri Sculptures as Icon and Images of Religious Worship among the Urhobo people of Nigeria" (Unpublished Doctoral Dissertation, University of Port Harcourt, Nigeria, 1998).
14. Òjó, E.C. "Symbols as Means of Communicating Religious Concepts in Urhobo Traditional Society," in G. G. Darah, E. S. Akama, and J. T. Agberia (eds.), *Studies in Arts, Religion and Culture Among the Urhobo and Isoko People* (Port Harcourt, Nigeria: Pan Unique Publishing, 2001); Dr. Abel Adeleke, a Chief lecturer at the Department of Music, The Polytechnic, Ìbàdàn gave a brief idea of this congregation.

CHAPTER 19

Oral and Non-Oral Sources of Knowledge in ATR: Orality and Secrecy Ethos in the Yoruba Traditional Religion within the Latin American Diaspora

Félix Ayoh'Omidire

INTRODUCTION

Téléni lawo ori ẹni
Ìgbàṣòòrò lawo ilẹ̀ẹ́lẹ̀
Alápàndẹ̀dẹ̀ lo kólé silẹ̀,
Ti ko kanlẹ̀, ti kò kan omi
A difa fun Oyẹgolu,
Ọmọ iwarèfà n'Ífẹ̀
Ti baba oun iya rẹ̀ kú,
ti won fi silẹ̀ ni rewerewe
Ohun orò dé, won ni ki Oyẹgolu waa ṣe
Oyẹgolu tu puuru ṣẹ́kún,
O ni rewerewe lohun wa,
Ti awon obi oun foun ṣaye lỌ, ó ní
S'omi ni nkọ́kọ́ tasile ni, èmi ò mò,

Félix Ayoh'Omidire is Professor of Brazilian and Afro-Latin-American Studies in the Department of Foreign Languages, and Director of the Institute of Cultural Studies at Obafemi Awolowo University, Ile-Ife, Nigeria.

F. Ayoh'Omidire (✉)
Obafemi Awolowo University, Ile-Ife, Nigeria

© The Author(s), under exclusive license to Springer Nature Switzerland AG 2022
I. S. Aderibigbe, T. Falola (eds.), *The Palgrave Handbook of African Traditional Religion*, https://doi.org/10.1007/978-3-030-89500-6_19

Isoro òrun, ẹ gba orò mi ṣe!
S'ótí ni nkoko ta silẹ̀ ni, èmi ò mọ̀,
 Isoro òrun, ẹ gba orò mi ṣe!...
(Odu Ifá OlOgbón méjì)

The *Odù Ifá* in the above epigraph speaks directly to knowledge acquisition and transmission in Yorùbá Traditional Religion (YTR). As the *odù Òtúrúpọ̀n méjì*, aka *OlOgbón méjì*—two knowledgeable men—points out, knowledge and knowledge transmission represent a major quest and, indeed, a mark of respect and leadership in Yorùbá Traditional Religion as in other religious traditions worldwide, notwithstanding whether the religion in question belongs to the so-called religions of the book or the African Traditional Religions whose hallmark is the oral transmission. The possession of knowledge is considered a fundamental distinction between human and non-human communities inasmuch as it is knowledge about human beings, animals, and material nature that makes it possible for mankind to master and dominate the universe. It is thus not surprising to have philosophers equate knowledge with power.

In African Traditional Religions, as in every other religion, knowledge is the fundamental element that guarantees the link between human beings and the divine. Indeed, one can safely affirm that religion is, to a great extent, based on knowledge, despite the doctrinarian affirmation that faith is supposed to be a blind trust in the powers of the divinity. Faith and belief are only possible because the believer 'knows' that the deity has the power to make things happen in his or her life. More importantly, this knowledge is premised on the assurances of getting the deity to respond to the needs of human beings based on the ability of the latter to know how to please and compel the deity to act in their favor through supplications, praise, offerings, and so on. For human beings to get such a result, they must have an intimate knowledge of the nature and culture of the deity in question: their names and how to evoke them; their tastes in terms of what foods, drinks, and other material gifts to offer the deity; and their laws and commandments, that is, what he or she loves and what he or she abhors. It is those who possess the totality of this knowledge on a particular deity that eventually form the ranks of the priesthood. That is precisely the reason for the anguish and dilemma of the subject in the above epigraph, *Oyegolu*, who is at a loss concerning the order of the ritual he is expected to perform in place of his deceased parents, who always offered such rituals on behalf of the community but who, apparently were not able to transmit the full knowledge to their son before they died. However, even though *Oyegolu*, the protagonist in the *odu Ifá*, felt insufficient in his knowledge of the liturgy of the deity, his knowledge of the benevolence of the *irúnmolès*[1] gave him some consolation, hence his trusting plea: "*Isoro òrun, ẹ gba orò mi ṣe!*" (you priests of the outer world, please make perfect my ritual performance).

While religions all over the world took their roots and formation from the basic 'knowing' relationship between the human and the divine, the different stages of human evolution has made it possible for different religions to create diverse modes of accessing the knowledge about the divine through the development of complex liturgical structures that seek to systematize the acquisition, use, and transmission of the knowledge about the divine. The classical structure most commonly referenced is that of the so-called religions of the books, that is, Christianity, Islam, Judaism, and other world religions whose history, tenets, practices, liturgical cycles, doctrines, and dogmas have been laid down in well-ordered books to be followed by adherents who come into, and grow in the 'knowledge' of the divine through regular reading and sharing of the laws of their deity as laid down in his divine scriptures. The hierarchy of such religions is thus based on the different levels of the authority and competence of individuals to read and interpret the scriptures.

The vast majority of African Traditional Religions does not belong to or are not considered as religions of the book based on the absence of established written compendiums of their history, doctrines, and dogmas controlled exclusively by a formalized priestly class.[2] For such religions, access to knowledge about the divine is gained through a combination of modes which may include but are not limited to the predominantly oral. This chapter analyzes the different forms of knowledge acquisition and transmission in African Traditional Religion with a specific emphasis on the Yorùbá Traditional Religion as originated in West Africa and its extended life among various categories of adherents in diverse societies of Latin America and the Caribbean, specifically in countries like Brazil, Cuba, Trinidad, and Tobago.

A Word on Yorùbá Traditional Religion

The traditional religion of the Yorùbá people of West Africa has been a favorite object of study by different generations of scholars since the earliest contacts of Western scholarship with indigenous Africa. Pre-colonial and colonial agents, such as the British Colonel A.B. Ellis in his 1894 publication titled *The Yorùbá-Speaking Peoples of the Slave Coast of West Africa,* have been credited with some of the earliest written attempts at documenting the Yorùbá traditional belief systems for a Western (European) readership.[3] Diversely referred to as *èsìn ìbílè, èsìn àbáláyé, èsìn ìsèdálè* or *isèse,* the Yorùbá traditional belief system is comprised of elements of ancestral worship known as the *egúngún* and other related practices, the *Òrìṣà* worship system with its elaborate pantheon of more than 600 deities, and the oracular system characterized by the *Ifá-Orunmila* and other related divination sciences. Each one of these belief systems has their own peculiar and elaborate structures of forms and contents that can be acquired and transmitted through diverse modalities. Western scholarship among the Yorùbá people has created a rich array of literature on virtually every imaginable aspects of the Yorùbá belief systems with the works of native and specialist scholars, such as Wande Abimbola, Ifayemi Elebuibon, Lijadu, Epega, Bolaji Idowu, Omosade Awolalu, and a host of others forming what has today become the core of Yorùbá Traditional Religion classical literature.

Much has been written on the transition of Yorùbá Traditional Religion to the Americas, a historic process produced predominantly during the infamous slave era when enslaved Africans and their indentured cousins transplanted their religious and spiritual belief systems to societies in Latin American and the Caribbean regions. In the case of the Yorùbá, the forced migration of the *Òrìṣà*, *Ifá*, and *Egúngún* traditions to that region led to the emergence of Afro-Latin religions such as *Candomblé* and its diverse modalities and offshoots (Xangô, batuque, Xambá, umbanda, etc.) in Brazil; *Santería* or *La Regla de Ochá* in Cuba; *Sango* and other related traditions in Trinidad and Tobago[4] and their expansion into other parts of the continent within what has been termed the second and third waves of the *Òrìṣà* migration cycles, respectively.[5]

For obvious reasons of social (and racial) contexts and power relations, language policies, and cultural hegemony among others, the process, and structure of the transmission and acquisition of the knowledge on the Yorùbá deities in the diverse Latin American and Caribbean locales vary from one society to another, although there are patterns of similarity in the options adopted. The subsequent segments of this chapter are dedicated to some of the modalities of the acquisition and transmission of religious knowledge within the context of the three major Afro-Latin religions in the regions—Brazil, Cuba, Trinidad and Tobago.

ORAL HISTORY AND THE FOUNDATION OF YORÙBÁ TRADITIONAL RELIGION IN THE LATIN AMERICAN DIASPORA

Candomblé, Sango, and Santería

The mystery shrouding the origin and etymology of most of the key terminologies and nomenclatures by which Yorùbá Traditional Religion operates in the Diaspora attests to the adversities encountered by the earliest proponents of these traditions within the slave societies of Latin America and the Caribbean. In the case of Brazil, for example, oral historiography of the *terreiros de Òrìṣà* (Orisa Temples) emphasizes how the founding priests and priestesses were forced to operate clandestinely to avoid persecution and harassment from the White slave oligarchy and the Catholic clergy who were always quick to condemn any spiritual practice at variance with the Catholic faith as heresy and idolatry. Within the charged environment of the Catholic inquisition campaigns of the seventeenth and eighteenth centuries, practitioners of such commonplace spiritual and trado-medicinal[6] practices like herbal healing of simple ailments were often dragged before the *inquisition* tribunals, which handed down draconian judgments such as burning at the stake to the presumed offenders. Many were the enslaved and manumitted African healers and *calundu*[7] priests in rural Brazil who suffered such a fate.

It was therefore expedient for priests and priestesses of Yorùbá Traditional Religion in Brazil to maintain not only absolute secrecy about their rituals but also camouflage their religious sessions under the different Catholic Brotherhoods known as *irmandades*, just as their Cuban counterparts who hid their African religious lores under the *cabildos de nación*, which allowed them some measures of ethnic expressions during the regular festivities in honor of the popular Catholic saints whose colorful liturgies and festive calendar were imported by the White elites from the Iberian peninsula into Latin America and the Caribbean regions. I have advanced elsewhere as my contribution toward unraveling the mystery surrounding the terminology *Candomblé*, officially adopted today as an umbrella term to describe organized Afro-Brazilian religious traditions, especially the Yorùbá-derived *ketu-nagô* tradition, which has its roots in Bahia, that the term probably derives from the Yorùbá expression *nkan-to-mbẹ* (kan-dom-blé).[8] This, I argue, would be a perfect subterfuge within the Yorùbá tradition of ẹnà (slang or coded language) commonly used among the Yorùbá people to refer to issues among those 'in the know' without the *ògbèrì* (non-initiate; incidentally, called *oberi komo* in Brazil) suspecting what is going on. Thus, one can imagine how, in those turbulent days of clandestine Òrìṣà worship in Bahia, words would be passed around in hushed tones among the enslaved population to invite the initiated to an Òrìṣà worship session at a designated place and time for them to adore *nkan-to-mbẹ*.[9] A message that would be understood unambiguously by those in the know because, as the Yorùbá adage goes: *àsọtì òrò níí jẹ́ kíní àná nkọ́?* (it is only when two people are in the know that one can say to the other, "could you give me that thing of yesterday?"). It is thus safe to presume that, like other African religious traditions transplanted unto the American Diaspora, Yorùbá Traditional Religion heavily relied on orality and oral transmission of knowledge and practices right from its earliest periods.

ORALITY, KNOWLEDGE, SECRECY, AND POWER IN THE YTR TRADITIONS OF THE DIASPORA

This segment focuses on how knowledge about the Yorùbá Traditional Religion is conceived, understood, sourced, and negotiated within the Òrìṣà communities of the Latin American and Caribbean Diaspora. It is, however, instructive to note that when we refer to knowledge in Yorùbá Traditional Religion within the Brazilian *Candomblé*, Cuban Santería, or Trinidadian *Sango*, it must be borne in mind that such knowledge is not entirely limited to purely religious or ritual knowledge. This is because the peculiarities of the adverse environment and hegemonic relations that kept the cultures, language, and traditions of the enslaved populations of Africans in the Diaspora as a dispossessed and marginalized culture elicited in them the necessity of 'sacralising' in the form of routine deification in virtually every aspect of their daily life. Every original concept and practice remembered from Africa, be they names, epithets, orikis, songs, myths, tales, legends or stories (personal or collective), or even recipes for ordinary, everyday food and material cultures, become ritualized elements to be sourced, manipulated, and transmitted with utmost liturgical respect in order to guarantee its survival and perpetuity. A good example is what came to be known as the principle and concept of *acaracentrismo* of Bahia, whereby *àkàrà*, a typical everyday delicacy in Yorùbá quotidian diet, became a protected patrimony with highly referred religious credentials in Brazil.[10]

This takes us to the issue of knowledge, secrecy, and power in Yorùbá Traditional Religion in the context of Afro-Latin-American societies. Ethnographic researchers in *Candomblé, Santería,* and *Sango* religions have revealed the re-invention of very elaborate and intricate religious hierarchy within the Afro-Latin religious circles. It is expedient to evoke here the re-invention of the Yorùbá family structure of *ilé* or *agbo-ilé*, which gave birth to the analogous *ilé axé* (Orixá Temple) in Brazil and its counterparts in Cuba and Trinidad simply called *Ile* in Cuba and *Ile Ijùbà* in Trinidad, headed by a father or mother figure known as *babalorixá, babalocha,* or simply *baba* or their female *iyá* counterparts (ialorixá, ìalaxé).

These figures became the pivots of all Yorùbá traditional religious knowledge in their communities, sharing their leadership roles and powers with their immediate lieutenants, such as the *iyá kekere, iyá moro, iya basse, ogan, equedis,* and *ebomes* in the case of the Brazilian *Candomblé*.[11] As custodians of knowledge, they determine who to empower with such knowledge, when, how, and how much of such knowledge to release. Of course, the type of knowledge also determines the level and modalities of its transmission. For example, quotidian knowledge mostly related to names and naming of objects and situations that are not considered sacred can be transmitted freely among all categories of members of the *ilé*. This is the kind of knowledge that late *iyalorixá* Maria Bibiano do Espírito Santo, popularly known as *Mãe Senhora Oxum Muiwá*, classified as "*da porteira para fora*," that is, common knowledge that can go out of the *ilé axé* to be shared with the larger Brazilian society. Such knowledge includes names of the *Orixá* (Ogum, Iemanjá, Oxalá, Omolu, Nanã, Iansã, Oxum, Dadá, Erinle, Exu, and Oxossi), some songs, myths, and legends related to the Orixá and, ultimately, to some popular Afro-Brazilian heroes and heroine figures such as Zumbi, Dandara, Gangazumba, and Akotirene. Others include common nomenclatures in the Yorùbá language that depict the Afro-Brazilian worldview and values, a champion among which is the Yorùbá word and concept known as *àṣẹ*, spelled in Brazil as *axé* and in Cuba as *ache*.[12]

These categories also must include the preservation, adaptation, and transmission of Yorùbá tales culled mostly from the oracular repertoires of *Ifá* and *erindinlogun* lores that relate to the exploits of fictive and real *Orixá* characters as they tackle existential issues. Mestre Didi, a foremost *egúngún* priest in Bahia, pioneered the transformation of this rich material, which used to circulate purely as restricted ritual narratives within the *ilé axé* communities into literary materials that he began publishing in the late 1940s as *Contos nagôs, contos crioulos da Bahia,* and *contos afro-brasileiros*.[13] Others like Agenor Miranda Rocha[14] and Mãe Beata de Yemanjá[15] have made significant contributions to this literary genre in Brazil while the legacy of the great Cuban ethnographer Lydia Cabrera, author of many ground-breaking narratives on the *Lucumi* (Yorùbá) worldview, endures today in classical Afro-Cuban *Lucumí* tales like *Kariochá*, *El monté*, and *Yemayá y Ochún*.

A more complicated approach is observed when the type of knowledge involved borders on ritual knowledge, commonly referred to as *awo* (secret) in Yorùbá. First, this kind of knowledge can only be accessed through formal initiation into the priesthood of the tutelary deity identified as the 'owner of the head' of the individual. One peculiarity of the process of initiatory rites in the Diaspora is that it is much more secretive, rigorous, and elaborate than in the Yorùbá homeland. To retake the Brazilian example, the process of becoming an *iaó* initiate (from the Yorùbá concept of *iyàwó òrìsà*) is a long, drawn-out process, which starts from the level of a postulant known within Brazilian *Candomblé* circles as *abiyan* who is expected to spend a long period first as an observer who is himself or herself under observation by senior members of the *terreiro*, who would make recommendations to the *iálaxé* or *babalaxé* of the temple to approve basic initiatory rites that may include *banho de folhas* (ritual bath with macerated leaves), *lavagem de contas* (ritual sanctification of beads), and the ultimate *bori*, the rite of appeasement/consecration of the *ori* (inner head or personal deity) of the individual concerned after due oracular consultation using the *jogo de búzios* (the sixteen cowries).

The elaborate stages of initiation rites in *Candomblé*, *Santería*, and *Sango* traditions have been studied and analyzed from various perspectives by diverse specialists since the time of the pioneer Ethnographers and Anthropologists like the Herskovits couple, Roger Bastide, Pierre Verger, William Bascom, and Lorenzo Turner among many others. One aspect that is often emphasized by all is secrecy and the power associated with the possession of ritual knowledge within the established hierarchy of all Yorùbá religious traditions in the Diaspora.

Castillo registers the centrality of orality, secrecy, discretion, and observation to access this kind of ritual knowledge in the Brazilian *Candomblé*.[16] One of her informants whose name she gave as Sandra, an *equede* (a kind of ritual assistant to an *iyawo* under *Òrìsà* possession) explains that emphasis is placed on the gradual acquisition of knowledge via the preferred medium of orality and participatory observation at *obrigações* (ritual ceremonies) in the temple:

> Everything is done as if the individual is ascending a set of stairs. At each stair level one learns, acquires experience, and at each ritual held for your saint (orixá), you earn more responsibilities. The responsibility is enormous, for you to learn, and transmit to others such knowledge that is permitted to transmit to other individuals according to their initiatory age and also learn to keep the secret. Because ritual secrets must be protected at all cost, or else, in no time, one might get to a situation whereby people who do not have the initiatory age or experience to become *pai-de-santo* (head of an orixá temple), who don't even have the required number of years of initiation, go about opening their own temples and beginning to shave people's heads.[17]

Selective Writing, Knowledge, Secrecy, and Power in the Initiation Process: *Os Cadernos de Fundamento*

Castillo pointed out the relationship between the preferred oral method of knowledge acquisition in the *Candomblé* tradition, and power relations among individual members and the different *terreiros* and the quest for 'quicker' knowledge through recourse to selective liturgical literature. I argue for a revision of the role and position of a *Babalawo* (*Ifá* priest) in the typical Yorùbá society by looking beyond the classical translation that is common in the Diaspora whereby they are called "father of secret" (*pai do segredo*). My argument is that—looking at the long years of training that is required for an individual to acquire the complex knowledge and competence to become a *Babalawo*—considering the intricate process of learning by heart the 256 *Odù Ifá* volumes of the *Ifá* Corpus, acquiring knowledge about the plants, animals, and other material objects that are required in the propitiatory and healing processes, memorizing the hundreds of *Ifá* poems known as *ẹsẹ ifá* that make up each one of the 256 *Odù Ifá*, it is obvious that the 'secrecy' aspect, though of paramount importance in the protection of the ethics and practice of the art and science of the *Babalawo*, is not enough to describe his role and position solely. Rather, he must be seen as the Yorùbá organic intellectual per excellence. This is borne out by many of the epithets of *Orunmila*, the exponential deity of *Ifá* who is saluted in his *oriki* as "*akéré-f'inú ṣ'Ogbón, òpìtàn Ilẹ̀-Ifẹ̀*" (the young man full of wisdom, expert in the history of *Ilẹ̀-Ifẹ̀*). The *Babalawo* is thus a doctor-pharmacist, a surgeon of sorts, a historian, a literary artist, a philosopher, a biologist, and so on all rolled into one. He sources his knowledge from such diverse origins as memorization of verses taught by his master, participation at ritual activities within the *Ifá* collegiate system, quest for, and acquisition of knowledge through the barter of the *àṣẹ* or life forces of the animals he sacrifices to the different deities to renew and augment his own *àṣẹ* and mystical power, the knowledge he acquires through his daily interaction with unseen forces such as the *ajogun* (malevolent forces) and the *aládìmú* (benevolent forces), including the special category known to all *Babalawo* as *àrònìmàjà, a-kOmO-n'Ifá-ojú-àlá* (the wise ones who teach one the secret knowledge of *Ifá* via the medium of dreams).

The acquisition or presumed possession of similar ritual knowledge on the rites and rituals of the *Òrìṣà* tradition by individuals in the Diaspora is invariably viewed as a mark of ritual seniority and superiority. One additional peculiarity that characterizes the Diaspora tradition in this respect is the mastery of African languages used in ritual activities in the African Traditional Religions in the Diaspora. In most cases, the Yorùbá language, in its diverse Diaspora versions and dialects, such as the *nagô* in Brazil, *Lukumí* in Cuba, and *Yarriba* in Trinidad, play a central role. The greater the mastery of this language by an *Òrìṣà* priest, *Santero*, *Babalawo*, or *Oriate* in the Diaspora, the greater his prestige among his peers. Such knowledge is, in turn, respected by the entire community who would seek out such individual priests and patronize their temples in large numbers, thus forming around such an individual an extensive network of *filhos-de-santo*.

In the case of Brazil, the historiography of *Candomblé* is replete with the records of many *babalorixás and iálorixás* of the *queto-nagô* (Yorùbá) traditions who became nationally respected as the guardians of the 'purest' and most authentic forms of African religious ethos and praxis. Some of them even had among their admirers and ritual clients ministers and members of the Brazilian federal executive cabinet. Notable priestesses in that category included the afore-mentioned *Mãe Senhora Oxum Muiwá* (Maria Bibiana do Espírito Santo), supreme priestess of the Ilê Axé Opô Afonjá temple located in Bahia who had a large followership among ministers, intellectuals, scholars, writers, and famous plastic artists in the 1950s and 1960s. Her example was followed in the 1970s and 1980s by Mãe Menininha do Gantois, popularly referred to as the Oxum Mother of Brazil, to whom many popular musicians dedicated specially composed songs such as the famous *oração a Mãe menininha do Gantois* (eulogy to Mãe Menininha do Gantois) rendered by Gal Costa and Maria Bethânia in a 1988 album.

However, as pointed out by Castillo, in the quest for the intricate African ritual knowledge in the Diaspora with its rich attendant rewards, it is not uncommon to have situations whereby some individual priests or temples would seek alternative sources of ritual knowledge to accelerate their progression on the ritual and social ladder. While most temples frown upon the indiscriminate acquisition of ritual knowledge through the unsupervised consumption of anthropological and ethnographic literature produced mainly by non-initiates, some temples recognize and give a silent assent to the acquisition of knowledge to be gleaned from the secret notebooks kept by most *Candomblé* priests and priestesses. Castillo analyzed, within this ambit, the practice common to some temples in which the leadership kept a notebook known as the *caderno de fundamento* (ritual information notebook). In such *cadernos* are recorded some ritual data and personal information considered sacred and of utmost importance. Such booklets are kept in so much secrecy that most members of the *terreiro* are completely ignorant of their existence. Lydia Cabrera also mentioned the existence of something similar among Cuban *Lucumí* priests who refer to them as *libretas*.

It is interesting to note the kind of knowledge recorded in such *cadernos*, which ranges from records of oracular sessions to names of plants and their usage, particular messages received from an *Òrìṣà* during the *xirê* ceremony. Others are records of myths, sacrificial elements, some ritual prayers, *oriki* (praise names) of *Òrìṣà*, and even songs which are carefully copied into such *libretas* so that they can serve as *aide mémoire* to their owners who alone understand the codified order in which such ritual diaries are compiled.[18] When such *cadernos* change hands or ownership on the occasion of the death of the priest-owner, those into whose possession they fall are considered as the legitimate inheritors and successors of the original owners.[19]

The classic example of such *cadernos* was the legendary manuscript known as *Caminhos de Odu*, whose origin was traced to the leaders of the Ilê Axé Opô Afonjá in the 1920s, migrating between the mother temple in Bahia and its offshoot in Rio de Janeiro.[20] The content of this particular *caderno* consisted of some seventy Afro-Brazilian versions of the major *ese ifá* used in the *erindinlogun* (sixteen-cowry oracular corpus) common among Òrìṣà priests. The content was later published in a book form, first in 1982 by a German Yorùbáphile Professor in the then-University of Ife, Wilfred Feuser, and a Brazilian diplomat José Mariano da Cunha under the title *Dilogún: Brazilian Tales of Yoruba Divination* discovered in Bahia by Pierre Verger,[21] while Agenor Miranda Rocha, a babalorixá from Rio de Janeiro also published another version of the book as *Caminhos de Odu* in 1998.

Material and Non-material Objects in the Transmission of Knowledge: indumentárias, colares, emblemas *(*opaxorô, adja, ipele, ojá, alákàá*)*

One other transmission mode of Yorùbá traditional religious knowledge consists of the knowledge rooted in the material culture of the Yorùbá and its manifest modalities of expression. These range from dressing codes and ritual insignias to drum rhythms and coded languages employed in the quest for spiritual and ritual power. One of the most powerful memories carried over from Africa to the New World was the language and idiom of colors representing the different African deities. While Òrìṣàs of the Obatala family are generally called *orisa funfun*, thanks to their association with the color white—*aṣọ àlà* (white garment), *ṣéṣé ẹfun* (white) beads, *eyín erin* (ivory), other Òrìṣàs are associated with 'hot' colors—red, black, indigo, and so on. In the Yorùbá Diaspora, these color codes came to occupy the central stage in the preservation and transmission of ritual knowledge. In fact, the Òrìṣà colors became an active element in the codification of Òrìṣàs identity among initiate *candomblecistas* and *santeros* in Brazil and Cuba, respectively. In the face of ruthless persecution of all forms of African spirituality in the slave enclaves of the Americas, which made it impossible for practitioners of African traditional religion to build elaborate alters to their deities, the genius of Yorùbá traditional religion invented what came to be known in Cuba as *la sopera*, whereby porcelain dishes are used as recipients of the *àṣẹ* of each Òrìṣà—white for *Obbatala*, yellow for *Ochún*, red for *Changó* and his conjoint *Oya*, indigo for *Oggun*, green for *Ochossi* and *Orula* (*Orunmila*). This made it possible for individuals to keep the *Ọta* (spelled *otan* in Cuba) and other sacred objects of their tutelary deity inconspicuously displayed on open shelves in their living rooms without arousing the ire of inquisitive police or other agents of racial persecution and religious intolerance. The same goes for the use of colored beads known as *eleke* in Cuba and *contas* in Brazil.

Indeed, over time, Òrìṣà beads have become a distinct idiom of the Yorùbá peoples' traditional religious knowledge in the Diaspora. Apart from the distinct color associated with each deity, the volume, length, and number of beads worn by an individual during a typical *Òrìṣà* ceremony—known as *xiré* in the Brazilian traditions and *bembe* within the Cuban *Regla de Ocha*—can be used to determine the level of the individual within the *Òrìṣà* hierarchy, such as whether they are *babalarixá/iálorixá, equede, iaô* or *abiã* within the Brazilian *Candomblé* tradition, or *Babalawo, Oriate,* or a recently initiated *Santero* within the Cuban *Lucumí* rites.

Knowledge Acquisition Through Myths, Tales, and Music: suyere, rezos, cantos, oriquis, *and* patakines

Perhaps, the most significant source of general knowledge of the Yorùbá Traditional Religion in the African homeland and the Diaspora are *Òrìṣà* songs, praises, prayers, myths, and legends. It is always interesting to see how much information and knowledge about a particular deity can be gleaned from his praise names, oriki, songs, and myths, which usually form part of the invocation and worship of such deities. A typical example is an Afro-Brazilian myth, which explains the account of how the sacred palm-kernel known as *ikin ifá* comes to represent the oracular memory of *Òrúnmìlà* through which Exu 'speaks' and instructs the *Babalawo* during a Yorùbá divination session. The myth was published by Mãe Beata de Yemonjá in a book she succinctly titled *Caroço de dendê: A sabedoria dos terreiros,* which bears the telling subtitle *como ialorixás e babalorixá passam conhecimentos a seus filhos* (how *ialorixás* and *babalorixás* transmit knowledge to their godchildren). Here is a translation of the opening paragraph of the myth as adapted by Yemonjá:

> When the world was created, the *caroço de dendezeiro* (palm-kernel) was given an enormous responsibility by *Olorum,* that of keeping within its hard shell all the secrets of the world. In the world of the Yoruba people, keeping secrets is considered the greatest talent with which *Olorum* could endow a human being. That is why all palm-kernels that possess four 'eyes' (tiny holes on their conical surface) are considered the ones with the greatest oracular powers. Such (*ikins*) are able to see the four cardinal points of the universe in order to reveal how things are, and relate with *Olorum.* No other entities are allowed to know such secrets. This is to prevent discord and disharmony. It is through this formula that the world could know its moments of peace. There are palm-kernels who only possess three eyes, but those ones were not given the responsibility of keeping the secrets of the universe.[22]

A close analysis of this myth cannot fail to reveal the message of the author, who is instructing her readers and *filhos-de-santos* on the supreme oracular and epistemological importance of the *ikin ifá,* the sixteen sacred palm-nuts which are used by the typical Yorùbá *Babalawo* for divination purposes. It is interesting to note that the author, Mãe Beata de Yemonjá, a highly respected Afro-Brazilian *Òrìṣà* priestess belongs to the generation and indeed, the clan of *Bahian ialorixás* of the ketu-nagô tradition which, since the late 1940s, have come to jealously defend and actively protect the conservation and transmission of power within the *Òrìṣà terreiros* only in the hands of the venerated priestesses who saw themselves as the direct descendants and sole successors of the three legendary founders of the *Candomblé da Barroquinha*, reputed to have been the first organized Yorùbá religious temple in the Americas.

Within the active historiography of the Brazilian *Candomblé* tradition, the descendants of the three major temples that evolved from the primordial *Candomblé* formation credited to the three emblematic nagô-Yorùbá priestesses—*Iyá Adetá, Iyá Akalá, and Ìyá Nasso*, namely the successive ialorixás of the three major *ketu-nagô* temples that occupy the preeminent position in Bahia and Brazil till today known respectively as *Terreiro da Casa Branca do Engenho Velho* or by its nagô-Yorùbá name Ilê Axé Iyá Nassô Oká. *Ilê Iya Omim Axé Iyamassé*, otherwise known as *terreiro do Gantois*, and *Ilê Axé Opô Afonjá*, are said to have decided during the formative years of the temples not to surrender the power and supreme ritual leadership of their temple to men. This has been analyzed variously as an apparent attempt to live up to the reputation arrogated to them by a certain North American Anthropologist, Ruth Landes, who, after a brief stint of field research in the *Candomblé* world of Bahia, came up with the idea in her 1947 book that Bahia was indeed *The City of Women* (*A Cidade das Mulheres*)[23] where homely and uneducated Black women who were otherwise invisible in a typically male-dominated society such as Bahia and Brazil, possess enormous spiritual power over men within the *Candomblé* tradition. One of the means by which the *ialorixás* intended to maintain their hegemony and power was through a systematic exclusion and prevention of *Babalawos* trained in the use of *ikin ifá* to share power with them in the *terreiros*, preferring instead to concentrate oracular power in the hands of the *ialorixá* who cast the *erindinlogun* (the sixteen-cowry tradition) for all the divination needs of the *terreiro* communities.

It is, therefore, emblematic that Mãe Beata de Yemonjá should present in her myth the *caroço de dendé* (*ikin ifá*) as the only oracular instruments capable of 'keeping' and revealing the secrets of the universe, thus (in)directly underlining the efficacy and superior value of the *Ifá* divination processes that employs the sixteen sacred palm-nuts above the *Òrìṣà dídá* version of the oracular tradition which favors the medium of the sixteen cowries (*erindinlogun*).

Notes

1. The Yorùbá people refer to the numberless deities who populate the *Òrìṣà* pantheon as *irúnmolè*, a term that suggests their countless number.
2. More and more scholars are wont to argue these days that the extensive corpus of the oracular texts of the *Ifá* divinatory system among the Yorùbá more than qualifies this African religion to be considered also as a religion of the books, even though the book in question has always been an oral compendium. (*See* Ayoh'Omidire, 2005, 2019).

3. Ellis, A. B. (1894). *The Yorùbá-Speaking Peoples of the Slave Coast of West Africa*. Chicago, University Press.
4. Cros-Sandoval, M. (1975). *La Religión Afrocubana*. Madrid: Plaza Mayor.; Cros-Sandoval, M. (2006). *Worldview, the Orichas and Santería: Africa to Cuba and Beyond*. University Press of Florida. Bastide, Roger. (2000). *Le Candomblé de Bahia* (Rite Nagô). Paris–La Haye. Mouton (1958) Plon.
5. Ayoh'Omidire, Félix. (2009). "The Yoruba Atlantic Diaspora—Brazil, Cuba, Trinidad and Tobago," in Tunde Babawale, Akin Alao, Félix Ayoh'Omidire, and Tony Onwumah (eds.), *Ensino e divulgação da história e da cultura da África e da Diáspora Africana (Teaching and Propagating African and Diaspora History and Culture)* (pp. 305–326). Lagos: Centre for Black and African Arts and Civilization (CBAAC).
6. The term 'trado-medicine' is commonly used in Nigeria, Ghana, and some other African countries to refer to what western or the so-called orthodox medical system has grudgingly come to refer to as 'alternative' medicine.
7. *Calundu*, an African religious tradition from the Congo-Angola region was one of the earliest expressions of African spirituality in Brazil.
8. Ayoh'Omidire. (2009). "The Yoruba Atlantic Diaspora—Brazil, Cuba, Trinidad and Tobago."
9. In Yorùbá, *nkan-to-mbẹ* literally means "that which exists."
10. Ayoh'Omidire, Félix. (2003). "CarnavÁfrica à la Baiana de Acarajé: of the Uses and Abuses of Africanity in Bahia" (Anales del 8°. Congreso Mundial de la Tradición Yorubá), Edición en CD-ROM, La Habana, Cuba; Ayoh'Omidire. (2009). "The Yoruba Atlantic Diaspora—Brazil, Cuba, Trinidad and Tobago."
11. By far, the most intricate and complete model of the Yorùbá communal structure, the Brazilian *Candomblé*, shall be taken as the representative model for all other Yorùbá Traditional Religions to be analyzed more systematically in this chapter, with more examples drawn therefrom than from the other two centers of Yorùbá traditional religion irradiation in Latin America and the Caribbean, namely Cuba and Trinidad. This is with a view to save time and space within the scope of this study.
12. Martínez, M. F., and V. P. Potts. (2003). *El ashé está en Cuba*. La Habana: Instituto Cubano del Libro, Editorial José Martí; Ayoh'Omidire, Félix. (2008) "The Yorùbá Àṣẹ as a Social Capital among Afro-Diasporic Peoples in Latin America," in Tunde Babawale and Akin Alao (eds.), *Global African Spirituality, Social Capital and Self-Reliance in Africa* (pp. 287–298). Lagos: Malthouse Press Limited.; Ayoh'Omidire. (2009). "The Yoruba Atlantic Diaspora—Brazil, Cuba, Trinidad and Tobago"; Ayoh'Omidire, Félix. (2010). "Mestre Didi e a oralitura nagô-iorubana no Brasil," in Juana Elbein dos Santos (Org.), *Criatividade Âmago das Diversidades Culturais: A estética do sagrado* (pp. 157–173). Salvador: Communitatis Mundi/SECNEB—Sociedade de Estudo das Culturas e da Cultura Negra no Brasil.

Ayoh'Omidire, Félix. (2014). "Àse in Contemporary Yoruba-African and Latin-American Literary and Popular Cultures," in George Àlàó (ed.), *Voyage à l'intérieur de la langue et de la culture yorubá – Journey into yorùbá language and culture (en l'honneur de Michka Sachnine)* (pp. 31–53). Paris: Éditions des Archives Contemporaines.
13. Ayoh'Omidire. "The Yoruba Atlantic Diaspora—Brazil, Cuba, Trinidad and Tobago"; Ayoh'Omidire. "Mestre Didi e a oralitura nagô-iorubana no Brasil.";

Ayoh'Omidire. (2015). Mestre Didi: Nago Tales and the Re-Invention of Literary Genres in Afro-
Brazilian Literature. *Ibadan Journal of European Studies*, No. 14, 15 & 16, pp. 238–265.
14. Rocha, Agenor Miranda. (1998). *Caminhos de Odu*. Rio de Janeiro: Pallas.
15. Yemonjá, Mãe Beata de. (2002). *Caroço de dendê: A sabedoria dos terreiros (como ialorixás
   e babalorixá passam conhecimentos a seus filhos)*. Rio de Janeiro: Pallas, 1997, 2nd Edição.
16. Castillo, Lisa Earl. (2008). *Entre a oralidade e a escrita: A etnografia nos candomblés da Bahia*. Salvador: EDUFBA.
17. Castillo. *Entre a oralidade e a escrita: A etnografia nos candomblés da Bahia*, 35. Shaving of the head is one of the high points of Orixá initiation in the Diaspora. An individual owes total allegiance to the babalorixá or iálorixá who shaved their head during initiation rites.
18. Castillo. *Entre a oralidade e a escrita: A etnografia nos candomblés da Bahia*, 90.
19. Another of Castillo's informants mentioned that the *caderno* is one of the first things that people go for immediately when they learn that a respected ialorixá or babalorixá has passed on, suggesting that many people do go to ruthless ends to lay their hands on such a booklet as they believe the *caderno* is a priceless means of acquiring ritual knowledge and power.
20. Castillo. *Entre a oralidade e a escrita: A etnografia nos candomblés da Bahia*, 96.
21. Feuser, Wilfred, and Cunha, José Carneiro da. (1982). *Dilogún: Brazilian Tales of Yoruba Divination*. Lagos: Centre for Black and African Arts and Civilization. A fuller version of this book was published by the Centre for Black and African Arts and Civilization in 1982.
22. Yemonjá, Mãe Beata de. (2002). *Caroço de dendê: A sabedoria dos terreiros (como ialorixás e babalorixá passam conhecimentos a seus filhos)*, 97.
23. Landes, Ruth. (1947). *The City of Women*. Albuquerque: University of New Mexico Press, 1994. This pseudo-feminist theory of Ruth Landes, indeed, became a powerful motif and a decisive factor in the general configuration of the internal arrangement of most Bahian *Candomblé* temples since the 1950s with many documentaries seeking to 'document' this peculiar Yorùbá traditional religious tradition which, at some strategic moments, created the impression that the Yorùbá culture operated under some form of matrilineal tradition.

PART II

Contemporary Interconnections: Contents and Discontents

CHAPTER 20

African Traditional Religion and Religious Ethics

David Olali

INTRODUCTION

This study has one aim, and it is not to show that Africa has an ethical system. That should be obvious enough to anyone who cared to know; Africa does not need to prove its culture to Europe or America. Those artifacts stolen from African "villages" and sitting in display glasses, decorated without remorse as educational resources and evidence of European victories and progress, could speak about the minds that made them! This study also does not entail a preoccupation with pontifications on the preferred ethical system for the world. For to attempt that would almost certainly imply a repeat of a historical miscalculation. The result of privileging one culture as superior to another as barbaric does not fall too far from the commencement of terrorism.

This study marries scripturalization—the process of becoming "scripture"— with what and how it means to *mean* among the various peoples of Africa. The study deploys ethics as a sub-theme of religion. And by religion, let it be clear, this study does not, and it would not, imply the colloquialized designations and demarcations that take place when the major faith systems—à la Abrahamic belief systems—are being discussed. While such collocations have facilitated understandings of religion as a concept in human society, they have also directly increased confusions and problems for the vast majority of people who may not be inclined to *read religion critically*.

D. Olali (✉)
Comparative Heritage Project, Atlanta, GA, USA
e-mail: david.olali@comparativeheritage.org

As used in this chapter, religion becomes a major socio-political qualifier for why human beings exist. Thus, religion, here, reifies all the rationale for human activities and inactions in society, particularly with regards to developing social networks, communications, communities, nations, systems, as well as the political arrangements that emerge from such intelligent organizing. Here, the assumption is, rather than continuing to live under brutish conditions, human beings began to develop systems that may be likened to checks and balances. Thomas Hobbes (1904: 84) had this in mind when he desired to show the warring factions during the English Wars the benefits of social ethics of existence in order to save the English from life that would perpetually be "solitary, poor, nasty, brutish, and short."[1] But, unlike English/Western ethics, which hinges on the secular, African ethical systems transcend the physical reality, pointing to beyond the corporeal and worldly existence. Perhaps, it is for this or a similar reason that David Robinson and Douglas K. Smith question the logic "in the incorporation of a 'universal religion' into an African society."[2]

As a Method—Disruptions

When it comes to African ethical systems, we must also draw close to African religions to understand the peoples' worldviews. That will entail outright jettisoning, or at least minimizing foreign influences in our interpretations of what we see, hear, or perceive about Africa and her ways of life. As E. S. Atieno-Odhiambo states, "African vision of reality that informs the political, historical, philosophical, value-ethical, and epistemological fields of concern."[3] While referencing other forms of traditional religions in Africa, the Yorùbá religion shall, for two reasons, be the main traditional religion for this study. The first and primary reason is that "the Yoruba are an important ethnic group mainly occupying Southwestern Nigeria."[4]

The second reason is more relevant to the topic of this chapter because it connects to the foundation of the religion of the people. According to E. Bolaji Idowu, African Traditional Religions are based on a five-level hierarchy.[5] This structure consists of belief in God, belief in divinities, belief in spirits, belief in the ancestors, and belief in magic and medicine.[6] Ethics in African Traditional Religions are founded on human beings' understanding of the dynamic nature of their roles and relationship and responsibility toward themselves and others in society, but especially their responsiveness to the demands of *Olodumare*, the Supreme Being, or God.[7] As Ben Knighton puts it, "there are no languages, which have not expressed a meaning of 'God.'"[8] According to the Yorùbá cosmology, God is the head of, and over all, other creations and existence.

In *The Sacred Void: Spatial Images of Work and Ritual Among the Giriama of Kenya*, David Parkin notes that the spiritual world is consulted and spirits of the dead propitiated "when things go wrong in the homestead."[9] The idea of collaborating with the spirit over things that "go wrong" in the world is one way to say that existence is a continuum for Africans, which means that although the dead are no longer physically present, they continue to play their roles as ancestors whose new, translated, and elevated status grants them special privileges to be able to perform certain extraordinary feats on behalf of the living.

Ethics, Logics, and Power Imagines in Empire

Most popular media images about Africa convey a rampant barbarism, of peoples who are atavistically portrayed as perpetually ethnic or village dwellers: lovers of chaos who live under the brutish rule of fatalism. At best, we read or hear about the conditioned admixture of hopelessness in the teeming millions of African peoples who await the flippant performance of White magnanimity, to salvage what is left of their situations, often with the high-pitched chord of Western deliverance!

That classic objectification of Africa, remastered on television screens for the remodeled reveling of American and European audiences, viewed on *CNN* as a sampling of the other, or on *FOX News* networks as embodiments of divinely disdained dwarfs, who, suffering from a predominantly primordial curse of Noah, need the pity, and thus the Whitened experience, of evangelical Christianity, or be condemned to the new mercies of Muhammadans. This is an image of Africa known to many Euro-Americans. Racism rostered on the rims of Western intellectualism—perhaps Joseph Conrad's *Heart of Darkness*, first published in 1902, facilitates some understanding of the public sentiment which Europe and America had entertained, sustained, or inherited throughout their histories.[10]

Celebrated as an iconic scholarly production in Conrad's oeuvre, there hardly would any imperialist failure to see how the author's intellection aided and guided the perpetuation of slavery and colonialism's savagery, beginning with the people of the Congo. Frederick R. Karl expresses a similar thought, stating "Heart of Darkness is possibly the greatest short novel in English, one of the greatest in any language, and now a twentieth-century cultural fact."[11] To a considerable extent, Karl's position is justified because he expressed what might rightly be considered a consensus about Africa and such considerations commonly associated with Black people, whether in eighteenth-century Europe or twenty-first-century America. Continuing, Karl authoritatively asserts that, "Like all great fiction, [Heart of Darkness]_sic involves the reader in dramatic, crucially difficult moral decisions which parallel those of the central characters, here Marlow and Kurtz."[12] Well, the problem is while Conrad had not much difficulty flagging an entire continent as a site of "darkness," thereby sanctioning the violent discourse of imperialism, Samet Güven proposes that "the real purpose of Conrad is that he wants to remind the inadequate attention his citizens pay for the natives, since they are no more than a creature of a cannibal for the Europeans."[13]

Eloise Knapp Hay's piece unmistakably recognizes a foreboding danger in not calling out the lasting and damaging effects which a work of literature such as *Heart of Darkness* is capable of inflicting on the mind.[14] Conrad's depiction of Africa as a dark site that is in great need of European light becomes problematic because pre-history research, which "originated in France around 1860," provides evidence to the contrary.[15] Recently corroborating the significance of looking back to Africa in search of useful recommendations for the future survival of humankind, Stephen Jay Gould has pointed out that "all events (at least preceding the origin of Homo erectus) occurred in Africa."[16]

Hay goes specifically to state that: "If we put together all that Conrad said about impressionism, we see three fairly distinct phases in his attitude: the first in his disgust at a collection of impressionist paintings in 1891; the second when he met Crane and gave qualified praise to his art in 1897, soon afterwards writing his Preface to The Nigger; and the third at the end of his life when he curiously reversed himself—after years of denigrating the movement—and began to aim for the same effects that he had earlier questioned."[17]

Hay's argument can be used to understand how Conradian impressionism in the *Heart of Darkness* could have been an emanation from the author's conscious or sub-conscious self. Essentially, the consciousness of depth creates an appreciation for impressionism—or its implied deniability—in subtle, subcutaneous, and sprawling dimensions such that privileged human agents ingratiates the will against reason. In their book, *Humanistic Reasoning and Cognitive Science*, Keith Stenning and Michiel van Lambalgen narrated the story of "the Kaluame, a Polynesian people who live in small warring bands on Maku Island in the Pacific."[18] In their story, the manner in which "Kaluame 'big men'—chieftains—yield" is consistent with a specific logic of consent. Whereas, Kurtz, one of Conrad's main characters in the *Heart of Darkness*, leaves Africa or Africans no room to negotiate an alternative. In and according to Conrad's *Heart of Darkness*, Africa had no choice than to fall before the allure and almightiness of European episteme of violence!

Conrad, like many imperialists, whether they wear the garb of globalism or tout nationalism's insignia, could not fathom Africa as anything other than primitive because he followed and flowed with what is recognizably a logic of empire: racism and violence. Otherwise, how could any serious scholar miss the contributions of Africa to human civilization? After all, it was in Africa, specifically in Egypt, not a stretch from the Mediterranean Basin, where "the bonds between the divine and secular realms governed social and moral life."[19]

Given the willful and schooled combo racism and ignorance of the like of Conrad, Chinua Achebe's "An Image of Africa" simultaneously appears and transcends a riposte.[20] That Conrad's characters, like "the young fellow from Yonkers, perhaps partly on account of his age," "the other person being fully my own age," or "that erudite British historian and Regius Professor at Oxford, Hugh Trevor Roper," required "a trip to Africa to encounter those things" considered to be superstitious and old customs of humankind, to be remembered of what the evolutionary past looked like was either stunningly unbelievable or unforgivably racist![21] According to Achebe, although book publications about Africa have appeared in great numbers and volumes, Conrad's *Heart of Darkness* occupied a special place. While to the ordinary onlooker, Conrad has done great justice to the reality of the world as he knew it in Africa, Achebe almost certainly sees beyond the letters into the furtive mindset of Conrad's pen. Thus, contrasting Conrad with other authors on the subject of Africa, he is of the view that Conrad, on the other hand, is undoubtedly is one of the great stylists of modern fiction and a good storyteller into the bargain. This is why his contribution should be seen as falling into another class of permanent literature as found in The *Heart of Darkness*. Indeed, *the work has been listed by a* leading Conrad scholar as being "among the half-dozen greatest novels in the English language."[22]

In *Envisioning Africa: Racism and Imperialism in Conrad's Heart of Darkness*, Peter Edgerly Firchow writes that "Anyone relying solely on the evidence of *Heart of Darkness* would be led to believe that there were only three company stations of any consequence along the whole length of the Congo at the time the story takes place."[23] Conrad's masterpiece holds sway as an important and accurate piece of literature in shaping opinion and discourse among European and American circles. Citing some works by Arthur Conan Doyle, Hilaire Belloc, and Basil Temple Blackwood, to name a few, as examples of acclaimed writer-historians who believe that *Heart of Darkness* meets a special stylistic threshold that gives it a unique qualification to occupy the status of literary magistrality, Firchow supports the idea that Conrad does not stand as a loner in his racist attitude toward Africa. For instance, Hilaire Belloc and Basic Temple Blackwood conceived a solution for the "native mind," should s/he constitute an obstruction to their imperial penetration.

> Blood understood the Native mind.
> He said: 'We must be firm but kind.'
> A Mutiny resulted.
>   I never shall forget the way
>   That Blood upon this awful day
>   Preserved us all from death.
>   He stood upon a little mound,
>   Cast his lethargic eyes around,
>   And said beneath his breath:
> 'Whatever happens we have got
> The Maxim Gun, and they have not.'[24]

Locked in on the allure of Conrad's book of over a hundred years old, Phil Mongredien confesses that: "It is tempting to see *Heart of Darkness* as a masterfully constructed parable on human nature (witness Apocalypse Now, Francis Ford Coppola's film adaptation, in which the action was transposed to south-east Asia) but as historian Adam Hochschild has pointed out in King Leopold's Ghost, about the king's rape of the Congo, Conrad himself was quite clear that it was based on specific events he had witnessed."[25]

The Euro-American otherization of Africa, and consequently of African people, hinges on the privileges that only imperialism's racist ideology could confer a status, which not only endorses rhetorical violence but also authorizes the promotion of continent-scale mutiny and pilfering. For Roger W. Smith, the predisposition to perform such destructive violence, the scale of which Conrad's characters represent constitutes a genocide.[26] Furthermore, to think that Arthur Conan Doyle who, in *The Professor Challenger Stories*, identified the natives as "brutes" *merely* engaged in some trendy or even a literary stylization *sui generis* misses the surrounding opportunities to deftly interrogate the implications of the characters' performance of the authors' ideas. Not unlike Conrad, Doyle, Belloc, and Blackwood recognized that their use of impressionism generates fanciful yet subtle intersections with the empire's projections.[27]

Conrad is by no means alone in his stereotypical thinking about Africa, which has conveniently been *taxonomized* into an ethnic *other*. Firchow observes that "Conrad's fiction tended in this respect to be subtler and more balanced than that of most other writers of the period."[28] The point being emphasized from the foregoing is that it would be difficult, not impossible, to associate any significance to epistemologies that come from a particular location or region once the location has been labeled as incapable of producing human beings who are worthy of progress and development. After all, do Europe and America not pride in the idea that their civilization hinges on their individual and corporate abilities to govern their lands and regions by themselves, without requiring the interventions of external forces?

How does the preceding discourse about European and American intellection affect ethics in Africa? Or, put another way, what nexus is there between African Traditional Religion, ethics, and European perceptions about Africa? First and foremost, answering these questions satisfactorily would have necessitated—or at the least, meant—revisiting variations in geopolitical perceptions and how each region has historically perceived each other. Hence, starting in the middle of some of the major events in African history paves proper perspectives for sustained interest.

Consequently, if the assertion of earliest European scholars that Africa had no history, no past, no record-keeping methods were, for the sake of argument, to be given some validation, how then would African say that she has control over developments and progress in her domain? The fact that European standards for reasoning, science, and knowledge systems saturate the educational and public and private sections in many African countries should not be viewed to mean that these instruments of the West organically triumphed over peoples who once were *barbarians* and *brutes*. Rather, the discovery of Peter and Paul or Mary and Martha in a Bassambiri in Nembe in Nigeria or a Gabriel in Kutama, Zimbabwe conveys a history impregnated mostly through the coerced coitus between European imperialism and the unsolicited textualization of indigenous peoples and cultures across Africa. Pre-contact era African peoples and cultures were led by non-complex lifestyles based upon transmittal of information through various means other than via writing as it is presently known in modern times.

The Fallacy of Mission Civilisatrice

Dominant thinking among Europeans ignored complex imports of a procedure, which James Harvey Robinson terms *The Humanizing of Knowledge*. Robinson thinks that for knowledge to become acceptable, first, it must seem "good."[29] Unfortunately, this fallacy of public popularity of an idea turns out to be to the undoing; that an idea is regarded as fashionable or acceptable does not make it preponderantly ethical or "good." Thus, from the very beginning, colonialism's assumptions to the superiority over not just the cultures and religions of those to be colonized but its aggressive pursuit and promotion of policies, which terrorized Black people, profoundly weakened the moral and ethical basis of its proponents.

Winfried Georg Sebald's *The Rings of Saturn* uses the character of Konrad (for Conrad) to reflect on the making of the man who, in another century, would become the target of Achebe's racism accusations. Speaking through his character, Konrad, Sebald explains that:

> At that time, the Congo had been but a white patch on the map of Africa over which he had often pored for hours, reciting the colourful names. Little was marked in the interior of this part of the world, no railway lines, no roads, no towns, and, as cartographers would often embellish such empty spaces with drawings of exotic beasts, a roaring lion or a crocodile with gaping jaws, they had rendered the Congo, of which they knew only that it was a river measuring thousands of miles from its source to the sea, as a snake coiling through the blank, uncharted land.[30]

Sounding eerily familiar to the description which Conrad himself gave through his character on the journey through the River Congo in the *Heart of Darkness* as follows: "It had ceased to be a blank space of delightful mystery—a white patch for a boy to dream gloriously over. It had become a place of darkness. But there was in it one river especially, a mighty big river, that you could see on the map, resembling an immense snake uncoiled, with its head in the sea, its body at rest curving afar over a vast country, and its tail lost in the depths of the land."[31]

The unmistakable connection between Sebald's and Conrad's descriptions accentuates the presence of impressionism to new realms of believability. As Zayn Kassam puts it, "little value is given to the symbiotic relationships indigenous people encountered."[32] For instance, in giving additional details to the "uncharted land" that appeared on the map in the "gloomy office," which Albert Thys, the managing director for the Société Anonyme Belge pour le Commerce du Haut-Congo occupies, Sebald observes that: "Since then, of course, detail had been added to the map. The white patch had become a place of darkness. And the fact is that in the entire history of colonialism, most of it not yet written, there is scarcely a darker chapter than the one termed The Opening of the Congo."[33]

Right inside *The Opening of the Congo*, a euphemistic allusion to the entry of colonial masters into the native lands of Africa, discourse presents an opportunity for engagement with the imports and implications of such opening—or put in direct colonial scripting—for discovery. This *Opening* had, in Sebald's words, the intention "to open up the last part of our earth to have remained hitherto untouched by the blessings of civilization."[34] Sebald also notes that the intent of King Leopold was good as at 1886 when the Société set forth its "exemplary venture."[35] Well, as history recorded, the brutish reign and rule of Leopold left, by Sebald's calculations, no fewer than five hundred thousand dead.

One wonders why as civilized, educated, advanced, and progressive as Europe was, or claimed to be at that time, with all the written histories and records on civilization, government, and psychology, one would have assumed that it should have been difficult to fathom the dangers in giving one man that much power! For the Société and the larger to have looked on while millions of Africans perished, while Africa lost precious artifacts, artworks, gold, and natural resources toward the development of Europe and America require much intervention in terms of what religion means. For instance, the pilferage and destructions that Africa suffered at the hands of Europe and America would not be possible without the foundational blessings of the religion that birthed "civilisatrice mission."[36] And some of the worst aspects which this mission fulfilled included the institution of "hierarchies of subjects and knowledges."[37]

Tradition Versus Modernity and Comparative Religion

W. E. B. DuBois blames the corruption of the black person's ethical system on the ills of enslavement. Consequently, for DuBois, the mind of a black religious person became corrupted because "his religion became darker and more intense, and into his ethics crept a note of revenge, note his songs a day of reckoning close at hand."[38]

Mircea Eliade leaves a note of caution on the adventure of comparative religion. The eminent historian of religion writes: "The rare historians of religion who have wanted to integrate the results of their researches and mediations in a philosophical context have contented themselves with imitating certain fashionable philosophers. In other words, they have compelled themselves to think according to the model of the professional philosophers. And this is a mistake."[39]

In interrogating "tradition" and "modernity" as these terms relate to African Traditional Religion or the religions of peoples of African descent, Peter Lancelot Mallios's interview with Edward Said on contrapuntalism comes in handy and I take some liberty to utilize some lines:

> [T]he most high-minded intentions and ostensibly without any vested national or private interests. Exalted personages representing the aristocracy, the churches, the sciences, industry, and finance attended the inaugural meeting, at which King

Leopold, patron of the exemplary venture, proclaimed that the friends of humanity could pursue no nobler end than that which brought them together that day: to open up the last part of our earth to have remained hitherto untouched by the blessings of civilization. The aim, said King Leopold, was to break through the darkness in which whole peoples still dwelt, and to mount a crusade in order to bring this glorious century of progress to the point of perfection. In the nature of things, the lofty spirit expressed in this declaration was lost from sight. As early as 1886, Leopold, now styled Sovereign de l'Etat Indépendent du Congo, was the sole ruler of a territory on the second longest river on earth, a million square miles in area and thus a hundred times the size of the mother country, and was accountable to no one for his actions. Ruthlessly he set about exploiting its inexhaustible wealth, through trading companies such as the Société Anonyme Belge pour le Commerce du Haut-Congo, the soon legendary profits of which were built on a system of slave labor which was sanctioned by all the shareholders and all the Europeans contracted to work in the new colony. In some parts of the Congo, the indigenous people were all but eradicated by forced labor, and those were taken there from other parts of Africa overseas died in droves of dysentery, malaria, smallpox, beriberi, jaundice, starvation, and physical exhaustion. Every year from 1890 to 1900, an estimated five hundred thousand of these nameless victims, nowhere mentioned in the annual reports, lost their lives. During the same period, the value of shares in the Compagnie du Chemin de Fer du Congo rose from 320 Belgian francs to 2,850.[40]

Armed through ideologies of racism and power, imperialism and colonialism have battered life and living among simple folks, thereby complicating relations and relationships to create new complex layers of socio-cultural, economic, and political categories. In his article that was supposed to be a reflection on the life and work of Sebald, Eric Homberger writes that the historian "delighted in using the 'real' world as a springboard for meditations upon writing, history and the inner life."[41]

What Conrad saw in the Congo burnt in his soul for eight years until, within a few months, he ran off this most haunting of novellas. Some of its power comes from its eloquent denunciation of the conceit behind colonialism and some from the harrowing thought that humanity has actually behaved like this. But its real power for me is that when I next pick it up, I know I will feel something new.[42]

In "Secular Interpretation, the Geographical Element, and the Methodology of Imperialism," Edward Said writes that "It is in this spirit of releasing heterogeneous sources of knowledge and agency from the grip of the disciplines of colonialism that this volume resists disciplinary boundaries and geographical enclosures."[43] Holding a contrary position from that of Achebe, Samet Güven writes that "it can be said that *Heart of Darkness* is different from traditional Victorian novel since the novel leads the readers to think realistically and reflects the truth of colonialism imposed by England in Africa."[44]

Therefore, ignoring the psycho-social and historical impressions which a work of literature such as Conrad's has had on the subjugation of African peoples or even under the guise of being a great work of English literature would continue to come with a costly price. Otherized through writings and literature that were, for all intents and purposes, produced to justify the superiority of text-wielders or people(s) of books, Africa had for a long time emerged and remained in the image which Europe and America desired it to assume. In other words, there have been sustained and intentional efforts to give Africa a bad name. That dark christening process served and continues to serve the interests of the Global North. Popular narratives from Europe and America make it seem as though only bad things ever come out of Africa.

Kaisa Kaakinen's "Introduction" in *Comparative Literature and the Historical Imaginary: Reading Conrad, Weiss, Sebald* weaves a fine narratological tapestry that provides neatly historicized "episodes from the early life … Konrad Korzeniowski" that implicates Conrad's connection and attraction to the Congo.[45] Dark "episodes," in Conrad's formative years, would eventually shape his view of the world—with colossal consequences for the future of ethics on the people of Africa who soon would commence on the axial-initiated journey of self-hatred and Whited identities through the emergence of modernity, producing the ongoing questioning of Africa's capacity for ethics and thus knowledge productions.

Notes

1. Thomas Hobbes, *Leviathan* (London: Cambridge University Press, 1904), 84.
2. David Robinson and Douglas K. Smith, *Sources of the African Past* (New York: Africana Publishing Company, 1999), xiv.
3. E. S. Atieno-Odhiambo, "From African Historiographies to an African Philosophy of History." In *Africanizing Knowledge: African Studies Across the Disciplines*, eds. Toyin Falola and Christian Jennings (London: Routledge, 2017), 14.
4. Fernand Leroy, et al., Yoruba Customs and Beliefs Pertaining to Twins, 2002: 132.
5. E. Bolaji Idowu, *African Traditional Religion: A Definition* (Ibadan: Fountain Publications, 1973).
6. *Ibid.*, 137–202.
7. E. S. Atieno-Odhiambo, "From African Historiographies to an African Philosophy of History," 14.
8. Ben Knighton, "The Meaning of God in an African Traditional Religion and the Meaninglessness of Well-Meaning Mission: The Experience of Christian Enculturation in Karamoja, Uganda." In *Transformation*, 1999:16:4, 120.
9. David Parkin, *The Sacred Void: Spatial Images of Work and Ritual Among the Giriama of Kenya* (New York: Cambridge University Press, 1991), 207.
10. Joseph Conrad, *Heart of Darkness* (1902).
11. Frederick R. Karl, "Introduction to the 'Danse Macabre': Conrad's 'Heart of Darkness.'" *Modern Fiction Studies*, vol. 14, no. 2, 1968, 143. See also Mohit K. Ray, *Joseph Conrad's Heart of Darkness* (New Delhi: Atlantic Publishers, 2006); Peter L. Mallios, *Our Conrad: Constituting American Modernity* (Stanford University Press, 2010); Sven Lindqvist, "'*Exterminate All the Brutes*':

One Man's Odyssey into the Heart of Darkness and the Origins of European Genocide" (New York: New Press, 1997); Royal Roussel, *The Metaphysics of Darkness: A Study in the Unity and Development of Conrad's Fiction* (London: Hopkins, 1971); Scott Denham and Mark McCulloh, (eds.), *W. G. Sebald: History, Memory, Trauma* (Berlin: W. de Gruyter, 2006); Christopher John Chivers, *The Gun* (New York: Simon & Schuster, 2010); Ronald Robinson, John Gallagher, and Alice Denny, *Africa and the Victorians: The Official Mind of Imperialism*, 2nd ed. (London: Macmillan, 1983), 2–3.
12. *Ibid.*, Karl, "Introduction to the 'Danse Macabre'," 143.
13. Güven, "Post-Colonial Analysis of Joseph Conrad's Heart of Darkness," 82; Clare Clarke and Lindsay Scorgie-Porter, *An Image of Africa: Racism in Conrad's Heart of Darkness* (New York: Routledge, 2017).
14. Eloise Knapp Hay, "Joseph Conrad and Impressionism" in *The Journal of Aesthetics and Art Criticism*, Vol. 34, Iss. 2 (1975).
15. Gloria K. Fiero, *The Humanistic Tradition, Book 1: The First Civilizations and the Classical Legacy*, Sixth Edition (Boston: McGraw Hill, 2011), 2.
16. Stephen Jay Gould, *The Structure of Evolutionary Theory* (The Belknap Press of Harvard University Press, 2002), 960.
17. *Ibid.*, 138.
18. Keith Stenning and Michiel van Lambalgen, *Humanistic Reasoning and Cognitive Science* (The MIT Press, 2008), 154.
19. Fiero, *The Humanistic Tradition, Book 1*, 45.
20. Chinua Achebe, "An Image of Africa." In *The Massachusetts Review*, vol. 18, no. 4, 1977, pp. 782–794. JSTOR, www.jstor.org/stable/25088813. Accessed 9 May 2020.
21. Chinua Achebe, "An Image of Africa." In *The Massachusetts Review*, vol. 18, no. 4, 1977, pp. 782–794. JSTOR, www.jstor.org/stable/25088813. Accessed 9 May 2020.
22. *Ibid.*, 783.
23. Peter Edgerly Firchow, *Envisioning Africa: Racism and Imperialism in Conrad's Heart of Darkness* (Lexington: The University Press of Kentucky, 2000), 63.
24. Hilaire Belloc and Basil Temple Blackwood, *The Modern Traveller* (London: Edward Arnold, 1898), 41.
25. Phil Mongredien, "Heart of Darkness by Joseph Conrad—Review." *The Guardian*, https://www.theguardian.com/books/2011/jan/23/heart-of-darkness-conrad-review (accessed May 09, 2020).
26. Roger W. Smith, "Human Destructiveness and Politics: The Twentieth Century as an Age of Genocide." In *Genocide and the Modern Age*. Edited by Isidor Wallimann and Michael Dobkowski, (New York: Greenwood Press, 1987), 20–40.
27. Arthur Conan Doyle, *The Professor Challenger Stories* (London: John Murray, 1952), 41.
28. Firchow, *Envisioning Africa*, xiv.
29. James Harvey Robinson, *The Humanizing of Knowledge* (New York: George H. Doran Company, 1929), 19.
30. Winfried Georg Sebald, *The Rings of Saturn*, trans. Michael Hulse (London: Harvill, 1995), 117.
31. *Ibid.*, Conrad, *Heart of Darkness*, 5.

32. Zayn Kassam, "Considerations of Development in Malaysian Borneo." In *EnviroLab Asia* (2017) Vol. 1: Iss. 1, Article 5. Available at: http://scholarship.claremont.edu/envirolabasia/vol1/iss1/5, 9.
33. Ibid., Sebald, *The Rings of Saturn*, 117
34. Ibid., 118.
35. Ibid., 118.
36. Tunde Adeleke, *Unafrican Americans: Nineteenth-Century Black Nationalists and the Civilizing Mission* (University Press of Kentucky, 1998), 9.
37. Gyan Prakash, "Introduction: After Colonialism," in *After Colonialism: Imperial Histories and Postcolonial Displacements*. Edited by Gyan Prakash (Princeton University Press, 1995), 3.
38. W. E. B. Du Bois, *The Souls of Black Folk*, 100th Anniversary Edition, "Foreword" by Charles Lemert, "Introduction," Manning Marable, "Afterword" Cheryl Townsend Gilkes (London: Routledge Taylor & Francis Group, 2016), 107.
39. Mircea Eliade, Comparative Religion: Its Past and Future. In *Knowledge and the Future of man: An International Symposium*. Edited by Walter J. Ong, S.J. (New York: Holt, Rinehart and Winston, 1968), 252.
40. Peter Lancelot Mallios, "What is Contrapuntalism? An Interview with Edward Said on Joseph Conrad, in *Cultre.Pl*. December 1, 2017. https://culture.pl/en/article/what-is-contrapuntalism-an-interview-with-edward-said-on-joseph-conrad (accessed May 09, 2020); See also Pinar Bilgin, "'Contrapuntal Reading' as a Method, an Ethos, and a Metaphor for Global IR," *International Studies Review*, vol. 18 no. 1 (2016), 1–13; Mahmoud Darwish, "Edward Said: A Contrapuntal Reading: Translated by Mona Anis. In *Cultural Critique*, No. 67, Edward Said and After: Toward a New Humanism (Autumn, 2007), 175–182; Mark Millington, "Transculturation: Contrapuntal Notes to Critical Orthodoxy," *Bulletin of Latin American Research*, vol. 26, no. 2, (2007) 256–268; Geeta Chowdhry, "Edward Said and Contrapuntal Reading: Implications for Critical Interventions in International Relations," *Millennium: Journal of International Studies*, vol. 36 no. 1 (2007) 101–116; Tony C. Brown, "Cultural Psychosis on the Frontier: The Work of the Darkness in Joseph Conrad's 'Heart of Darkness,' *Studies in the Novel*, vol. 32, no. 1 (Spring 2000), 14–28; Jennifer Lipka, "The Horror! The Horror!": Joseph Conrad's Heart of Darkness as a Gothic Novel," *Conradiana*, vol. 40 no. 1 (2007) 25–37; Fetson Kalua, "Locating the Ambivalence of Colonial Discourse in Joseph Conrad's Heart of Darkness," *Current Writing: Text and Reception in Southern Africa*, vol. 26 no. 1 (2014) 12–18.
41. Eric Homberger, "WG Sebald: German writer shaped by the 'forgetfulness' of his fellow countrymen after the second world war," *The Guardian*, December 17, 2001. https://www.theguardian.com/news/2001/dec/17/guardianobituaries.books1 (assessed May 9, 2020).
42. Tim Butcher, "Book of a Lifetime: Heart of Darkness, By Joseph Conrad," *Independent*, January 25, 2008, https://www.independent.co.uk/arts-entertainment/books/reviews/book-of-a-lifetime-heart-of-darkness-by-joseph-conrad-773538.html (accessed May 09, 2020).
43. Edward Said, "Secular Interpretation, the Geographical Element, and the Methodology of Imperialism," in Gyan Prakash, *After Colonialism: Imperial Histories and Postcolonial Displacements* (Princeton University Press, 1995), 12; See also David Denby, "The Trouble with 'Heart of Darkness': Is Joseph

Conrad's novel a critique of colonialism, or an example of it?," *The New Yorker*, October 30, 1995, https://www.newyorker.com/magazine/1995/11/06/the-trouble-with-heart-of-darkness (accessed May 09, 2020).
44. Samet Güven, "Post-Colonial Analysis of Joseph Conrad's Heart of Darkness" in *Journal of History Culture and Art Research*, 2013/07, Vol. 2; Iss. 2, 86.
45. Kaisa Kaakinen, "Introduction: Comparative Readings in the Twenty-First Century." In Kaisa Kaakinen, *Comparative Literature and the Historical Imaginary: Reading Conrad, Weiss, Sebald* (Cham: Springer International Publishing: Palgrave Macmillan, 2017), 1.

CHAPTER 21

Traditional Religion, and Morality in Society

Dauda Umaru Adamu and Amidu Elabo

INTRODUCTION

While it is true that the idea of morality is universal to all human societies in the world, each community has managed to develop ethical systems that resonate with its cultural milieu. For example, in Western societies, the moral order is designed within a cultural setting that caters to the realities of the individual. However, in Africa, morality is rooted in communal values and hardly atomizes the individual from society's collective existence. To adequately address this study's core aims, the chapter is divided into four broad sections, each exploring various aspects of the study's purposes. The first part concentrates on the definition, nature, and sources of African indigenous ethics and, concurrently, presents the historical study of African indigenous ethics by reviewing the existing literature. The second section unpacks African indigenous cosmology to create a context in which to situate the discourse of African morality and society. The third section delineates the content and nature of African day-to-day social practices by using indigenous cosmology as an epistemic lens. The final part concludes by highlighting the main points and shed light on the future challenges African ethics may encounter.

D. U. Adamu (✉)
Gombe State University, Gombe, Nigeria

A. Elabo
Princeton Theological Seminary, Princeton, NJ, USA

© The Author(s), under exclusive license to Springer Nature Switzerland AG 2022
I. S. Aderibigbe, T. Falola (eds.), *The Palgrave Handbook of African Traditional Religion*, https://doi.org/10.1007/978-3-030-89500-6_21

African Indigenous Cosmology and African Ethics

In pre-historical and pre-colonial African societies, the awareness of the indigenous spiritual order or sacred regime formed the basis of a moral community.[1] Such consciousness about the efficacy of the supernatural was so profound that it vested the moral principles of the African communities with social and political relevancy.[2] The concept of separation of the sacred from the secular was an idea that was not rigorously discussed as it was articulated in other societies. The debate continues today as to whether the notion of separation of religion from secular society is relevant to African societies, a view which some would argue is unthinkable. Before the advent of Islam and Christianity, indigenous ethical and religious values served as the fundamental source of identity formations and the regulation of most African societies. The gravity of penalties for violating given moral codes makes it impossible for an individual's self-interest or personal identity to threaten the stability and general welfare of the community. Under the regime of the ancestors, the moral framework is configured to enable inward propensities not only to be pro-communal but also inhibits anti-moral tendencies that may incur the wrath of the gods. Nonetheless, the next discussion delineates the nature of the African indigenous worldview.

The majority of sub-Saharan African indigenous religious worldviews are made up of two cosmic worlds—the physical and the spiritual realms.[3] The material universe, with its multiple facets, which includes the sky, the land, and water (as well as all inhabitants), are all fundamental dimensions of how the African indigenous worldview is constructed and structured. Thus, while the physical realm of creation is made up of different cosmic entities, flora and fauna, and the human race, it is also co-habited by disembodied beings of all categories. In most African indigenous societies, certain places are recognized as the residence of supernatural emissaries and classify as sacred. It is impossible to separate the spiritual realm from the material realm; such dichotomy is artificial to African indigenous socio-cultural existence. For example, most African indigenous societies believed that the canonized spirits of ancestors continued to exist among their living family members and the community. According to Ogbu Kalu, "Each space dimension is imbued with divinities (principalities), territorial spirits (powers), and a host of minor spirits (localized to specific professions, places, objects, for instance, a river, a hill, a stone, and so on). ... On the whole, the human world is inhabited precariously by a spirit of good or evil while human being manoeuvre to tap the resource of the."[4]

It is interesting how Ogbu exposed the connections of various spiritual beings to different spatial forms. As demonstrated below, in most Nigerian societies, the geography, topography, and ecology are central to the formation and sustenance of ethnic cosmology, rootedness, and identity. While we may disagree with the British Anthropologist Robin Horton on his theory of conversion in Africa, his work, however, demonstrates the microcosmic configuration of most Nigerian ethnic societies.[5] However, Horton failed to foreshadow the resilience of the lesser categories of beings other than the Supreme Being in the African peoples' worldview that continues to shape contemporary African Christian theologies and the sociological existence of most Africans in present times.[6] Thus, it is germane to give a bird's eye view of the spiritual component of the African worldview.

First, the supernatural realm is inhabited by the Supreme Being, the divinities, and the ancestors. At the top of the hierarchy of the African indigenous category of beings is the Supreme Being, who is the creator of the universe. According to most African indigenous mythologies, the Supreme Being is believed to possess various attributes, including all-powerful, all-knowing, and all-present.[7] Traditionally, given that the Supreme Being is *remote* to the day-to-day existence of most African indigenous societies,[8] he is approached and worshiped through intermediaries such as the deities and ancestors.

The pantheon of divinities created by the Supreme Being is the next category of beings in the hierarchy of African indigenous cosmic order. The Supreme Being created the deities (pantheon of gods). In Yorùbá cosmology, there are over 1400 Yorùbá divinities. The most famous ones among them are *Obatala* (arch-divinity), *Ogun* (deity of iron), *Yamoja* (deity of all oceans), and *Sango* (deity of thunder).[9] According to the cosmic narrative of sub-Saharan Africa, the gods are both celestial and terrestrial deputies of the Supreme Being. They rule the different realms of material and non-material worlds. The deities wield power to serve as administrators of the various material domains of the universe like the stars, moon, sun, sea, forests, mountains, rivers, earth, wind, thunder, wars, and wisdom. They also act as liaisons between human beings and the Supreme Being. In this capacity, they are regularly consulted through elaborate rituals and divinations to either seek divine favors or find explanations for space-time events. They also, on the one hand, have the powers to bless when cultural norms and customs are obeyed, and on the other hand, they can curse when traditions are violated. Specific rituals and sacrifice must be made to forestall the rage of the gods. Most scholars have demonstrated how every African society has developed a "wealth of techniques for approaching and manipulating" the gods.[10]

Following the beliefs in the Supreme Being and divinities are the belief in ancestors. Spirits of dead family members who, in their lifetime, satisfied the moral and cultural standards of the community become canonized as ancestors. To install the soul of a departed ancestor and usher him into the spiritual world, certain elaborate ceremonies must be carried out by his progenies. After canonization, the ancestors automatically assume several cosmic duties and diplomatic functions. First, in most African indigenous societies, ancestors play the roles of intermediaries between their living family members and the Supreme Being or gods.[11] Secondly, ancestors as disembodied entities maintain continuous surveillance over their family members to make sure they are safe, and every need of their living family is met. Thirdly, they act as the custodian of morality and customs of the African society. While ancestors are benevolent spiritual beings with the powers to be gracious to, as well as, prosper a faithful community, they also reserve the powers to enforce divine justice on the society that violates cultural norms and taboos. The wrath of the ancestors, like the wrath of the gods, is appeased when the offenders are identified and the required sacrifices offered. Ancestors, more than the gods, are easily accessible and are the closest link between the supernatural world and the physical world.

At the bottom of the African hierarchy of beings are magical forces. They include but are not limited to sorcerers, witchcraft, herbalist or medicine men, diviners, and magicians. There is a consensus among members of most African societies that men can master the arts to manipulate supernatural powers and use it for good and bad. With such expertise comes the African primal belief in the existence of neutral cosmic energy running through all facets of nature and creation known as the "vital force."[12] Such impersonal force is neither inherently bad or good, neither is it positive or negative. However, it can be harnessed and used for either good or evil. For Turaki, "the source of this impersonal or (mystical) mysterious power is not always known but attributed to the activities of higher 'mysterious' powers."[13] As a "primal power," deposit of the vital force is contained in everything ranging from plants, geological entities, animals, and humans. Turaki notes that "the potency, efficacy and the durability of such 'inhabited' impersonal powers vary from object to object."[14] He noted that the "medicine men and women, diviners and seers" have crafted different methods to harness the vital force to make magic charms, medicine, incantations, and amulets, among others.[15] The question to ask is: What constitutes the nature of African indigenous morality, and how does this morality operate in societies that are under the tutelage of such cosmology?

The answer to the above question introduces two separate schools of thought on the nature of African indigenous ethics. The first school of thought, referred to as the theological approach, includes scholars like John S. Mbiti, Bolaji Idowu, Geoffrey Parrinder, R. S. Rattray, and A. B. Ellis, among others. While it is significant to mention that most of these scholars are religious leaders, missionaries, and colonial ethnographers, they espoused a moral system that is rooted in a divine source or religious cosmology. In his book, *Olodumare: God in Yoruba Belief*, Emanuel Bolaji Idowu noted that "our view is morality is the fruit of religion and that, to begin with, it was dependent upon it. Man's concept of the deity has everything to do with what is taken to be the norm of morality."[16] For Idowu, the African indigenous "moral universe" is substantively religious. A "Deity" is the ultimate arbiter of what is determined to be right or wrong. Philosophers like Kwame Gyekye, Kwasi Wiredu, and Thad Metz rejected such supernatural rendition of African indigenous morality and espoused a critical and social constructivist understanding of African peoples' morality. They postulate that the substance of African morality is a function of the African peoples' sense of socialism, welfare, humanism, and personhood. In their view, the production of African morality is entirely independent of any metaphysical order outside the boundary of the material world, and it is not subject to the administrations of disembody entities. Therefore, it will be germane to explore this debate further to unpack the nuances of the discussion and find areas of consensus as a way forward.

Supernatural Origin of African Indigenous Morality

The principal claim of this school of thought is that African indigenous morality originates in the supernatural realm. In other words, Africa's structure is developed around the belief in, and the realities of, the supernatural world and its ability to influence humans' material existence. In their view, the African indigenous golden maxim that states *I am because you are and because you are, I am* was construed as a governing principle of life holding members of African indigenous societies accountable to the Supreme Being, gods, and the ancestors. For these groups of scholars, the humanization or de-religionization of this principle is entirely out of alignment with the African indigenous cosmic essence, and it is therefore alien. Thus, reducing the nature of African morality to sociological forces or as the product of humanist aspirations offers an insufficient understanding of African ethics and does not address certain teleological questions beyond mundane realities. For instance, Idowu could hardly understand "why this 'mass' which is called society should be so keen on its preservation."[17] This rhetorical question was not intended to derogate the position of social constructivists, but it is a critic of Emile Durkheim's concept of morality and religion.[18] However, in a way, it also implicitly questions the social constructivist position by raising the concern that any moral order that is a product of human "intersubjectivity" and rationality lacks the fixity to stabilize any society. Idowu appears not to be satisfied with the idea of human agency as a reliable basis for the production and appropriation of morality. He drew extensively on biblical sources, Christian literature, and indigenous Yorùbá cosmology to argue that "morality is the fruit of religion."[19] Seeing God as the source of morality, goes further to assert how such "provides an unchallenged authority for morals."[20]

In his paper, *A Rejection of Humanism in African Moral Tradition*, Molefe is fully persuaded that "the best account of the foundations of morality in the African tradition should be grounded on some relevant spiritual property—a view that [he] call 'ethical supernaturalism.'"[21] Molefe rejected the humanistic perspective because "African indigenous ethics must cohere with a holistic and supernaturalist tenor that often characterizes African indigenous ontology, which in turn demands we accord moral status to some aspects of the environment, like animals, for their sakes."[22] A fundamental implication of the humanist rendition of traditional morality that irritates the supernaturalist is the implicit atheism or agnosticism it espouses. Thus, shifting creative agency away from the supernatural to human beings is completely unacceptable for the "ethical supernaturalists." Idowu cautioned that any effort to separate morality from religion would have "disastrous consequences."[23] For scholars likes Idowu, Mbiti, and Molefe, the material redefinition of morality does not sit well with the African indigenous world outlook. Molefe argued that "'holism' I am referring to the claim social (human), natural (environment) and spiritual (God, ancestors, and spirits) communities are interdependent and interrelated."[24]

The above convictions on the religious or theological origin of African indigenous morality stem from the belief that the African people are deeply religious and intensely fascinated with the spiritual. The possession of such enchanted imaginations by the people has led many scholars to argue that African indigenous moral order is innately rooted in religious beliefs. The majority of African people believe that the Supreme Being and his intermediaries wield power to punish any community that violates the "rules of engagements" that exist between the spirit world and the physical world.[25] They argue that the spirit world is not one abstract and remote existence; instead, it is real. As mentioned earlier, the spirits and men co-exist together, and some rules define the interactions between them.[26] For instance, the gods are expected to bless the lands for it to yield a bountiful harvest, prevent deserters, diseases, and sickness, and bless human reproduction, among others. Human beings, as members of society, must keep cultural and social taboos, pay homage to the various categories of beings, offer sacrifices to the gods and ancestors, perform rituals and sacred ceremonies, among others.

The balance of this relationship is what translates to a peaceful and harmonious existence in African indigenous society. The failure to maintain this equilibrium signifies increased misfortunes and disaster. African indigenous religion, through its theology of the Supreme Being, generates holy dread in the hearts and minds of their adherents. The fear of the gods induces a punitive consciousness in believers not to derail from ethical standards. In most African indigenous communities, the gods and the ancestors wield such a formidable power they do not hesitate to use it when there is any failure on the part of the members to keep moral requirements. It takes true repentance followed by sacrifices to them and other ritual observances to appease their anger and avert doom on the community. For the likes of Idowu, African indigenous morality cannot exist independently of divine favor, which permeates both the consciousness and day-to-day lives of most African indigenous communities.

Humanist/Social Constructivist Grounding of African Ethics in Local Cultures

Bewaji argues that the claim of "Africans are in all things religious and that religion is the basis of their morality misses the relationship between religion and morality," and "boldly affirm the wellspring of morality and ethics in African indigenous societies is the pursuit of a balance of individual, with communal, wellbeing."[27] Most scholars in this category believe the hub of African indigenous morality is socially constructed and a derivative of the African indigenous sense of personhood.[28] They espouse that the ontology of African indigenous morality has no supernatural properties but derives from the material existence of most African indigenous societies.[29] For them, there might be a close relationship between African indigenous morality with indigenous religious cosmology, but it does not mean it is religious. In other words, African ethics did not originate from the religious world, but it is socially constructed and stems from the African idea of humanism or personhood. The majority of these scholars argue that the breaking of a "specific rule of conduct" is not based on "the flouting of some divine or absolute law of the universe."[30] One of the primary rationales that African morality is not the function of religion, according to these scholars, is because folk religions are not revealed religions like Islam and Christianity. Gyekye points out that: "A morality founded on religion is thus a necessary concomitant of revealed religion. Since the African indigenous religion is not a revealed religion, there is no way by which the people would have access to the will of God contains elaborate moral principles upon which a coherent moral system can be erected."[31]

Kwame Gyekye is right that African indigenous religions are not revealed religions like Islam and Christianity. However, the claim that African people were unable to decipher divine moral code as a result of the absence of a real religious source of revelation not only simplified the nature of traditional religion but naively construe revelations as the sole criterion for morality. This also means one should dismiss the entire religion of African indigenous societies as not religious because they were not revealed or had revealed texts or founders like in Christianity and Islam. It also implies a worldview to pass as religious; it must involve the spiritual or the realm beyond the natural where disembodied entities generate a non-material outlook for it to be religious. However, extensive documentation from both African and Western scholars of indigenous religions affirms how African indigenous religious worldviews were constructed from other sources. Some of these sources include myths, legends, music, shrines, proverbs, names of people, stories, folklore, and aspects of life, among others.[32] Also, the language of a "coherent moral system" used by Gyekye tends to expose how the academic reflections of these local scholars are a function of a Western influence or the deployment of the west epistemic lens to analyze African indigenous ethics. Such an attempt to construct African morality independent of the African indigenous religious worldview might suggest or imply that traditional religion is civil religion. Thus, it seems that the postcolonial interpretation of the African Traditional Religion ultimately essentialized the essence of the religion as communalistic and humanistic, which is devoid of theological significations.

Scholars have argued that one of the cores of the African philosophy of ethics is the tenet of communitarianism that seems to permeate almost all African societies. The principle postulates that individual actions do not exist in isolation. Instead, they are often influenced by other members of the community and have an effect on the entire community and also have profound social ramifications.[33] Members of some African societies would argue that an individual's behaviors can put the community in danger. Therefore, it is common to hear members of some communities argue that one *exists for all, and all exist for one*. Supporters of this view of communal social relations would argue that these beliefs about the influence of shared communal values have contributed immensely to the peace and social integration among the African people and their attitude toward the rest of the world. It instills values that inhibit selfishness and egocentrism. It prevented individualism, which seems to be the hallmark of Western civilization and the root-cause of self-assertion and the ego-driven world where "dog must eat dog" to survive almost at all costs. In Africa, morality is rooted in communal values and hardly atomizes the individual from society's collective existence. Religion and ethics are tied to the everyday lives of the African people, and some think that they are inseparable. One can understand how and why an act is "ethical" in a given African milieu through religion. To comprehend African ethics, there should be a readiness to do what Emile Durkheim says: "Every time that we undertake to explain something human, taken at a given moment in history—be it a religious belief, a moral precept, a legal principle, an aesthetic style or an economic system—it is necessary to commence by going back to its most primitive and simple form, to try to account for the characteristics by which it was marked at a time, and then to show how it developed and became complicated little by little, and how it became that which is at the moment in question."[34]

Greetings and the Respected Positions of Elders

Greeting someone when people meet in formal or informal settings is a cardinal aspect of African peoples' lives. It tells the community who one is, whether respectful or not, and it is a bottom-to-top thing. While everyone is expected to greet other people, the younger ones are supposed to greet their elders first because they have a prominent place in African culture. They are repositories of rules and regulations with which communities are governed; they are consulted, and their words carry weight like the laws.[35] Chinua Achebe, in his book, *Things Fall Apart*, explains the pre-colonial African societies and the colonial period using the figure of Okonkwo to illustrate how powerful African elders were.[36] Despite the fame and power of Okonkwo and the honors he brought to the community, the elders forced him to reluctantly kill the captive-turned adapted child of Okonkwo, a boy who grew up in his house. This illustrates how powerful elders were/are in African societies. Every culture has its unique greeting pattern. Some portrait to the ground when greeting their elders, for example, the Yorùbá of Southwestern Nigeria bend or kneel down. This is in no way an abuse of human rights or punishment; it is inherited from the ideals of the founding fathers of each society. Some societies do not encourage younger ones to look straight into the eyes of elders when greeting or talking to them and must use respectful terms, such as, if communication is in English, words like Sir or Ma. These greeting cultures are imbibed in children right from childhood by their families. The family is considered the first agent of socialization that enables children to learn all they need to act as members of society. However, these cultures have been affected by urbanization, modernization, democracy, education, migration, and so on, as shall be discussed later.

Some African people who have migrated to other continents have seen their ethics misunderstood and misinterpreted when it comes to the use of respectful terms. In 2018, an online version of the *WMBFNews* reported that "Parents in North Carolina are seeking answers after they say their 10-year-old son was punished by his teacher for addressing her as ma'am," a situation which traumatized the child.[37] Situations like this call for awareness of different cultural ethics. It is worrisome if someone acting with the intention of being respectful ends up being punished; this is indeed traumatizing. Though she warned him several times as contained in the report, why the child could not adapt quickly can be understood through John Taylor's argument, as described by Waje. He says: A person who migrated to a new environment "has his roots in a particular soil; he cannot be transplanted to a different soil without feeling the change very deeply; and if he is left with his root in no soil his personality will become weak and unhappy and sick."[38] If the teacher was aware of this, what happened could have been eschewed.

Some practices, which in some societies would be considered courteous, are seen as part of the fabric of morality. For example, in some African communities, it is expected that every morning before children go out to begin the work of the day, they should first greet their parents and elderly siblings before leaving the house. When they are out of the house, it is expected that they will display similar attitudes to other elders as this speaks well of the type of discipline they receive at home. Also, they normally do not do so while walking or doing something else; they are expected to pay attention like Tamarion's parents who displayed this form of upbringing thus: "Wilson and Bryant [Tamarion's parents] said their children were taught to refer to elders as "ma'am" and "sir," and that Tamarion was not trying to be disrespectful."[39] African parents do this as a way of instilling in their children good character, which they consider as a framework for a successful life.[40] However, the issue here is: How do these ethics survive in a modern society known for individualism? How can a child who is working in a place where he/she is being paid per hour for a job done, a child who can be fired if he/she does not concentrate on his/her job, be able to exhibit this upbringing without challenges? Transforming and adjusting to a new culture is part of everyday life and comes with challenges. But as Munro says, "Humans from birth learn much by imitation. They are predisposed to copy."[41] This is mostly what becomes of a migrated African.

African Communication and Interaction: Respect, Impartiality, and Reciprocity

To understand how the people of Africa communicate and interact among themselves, it is necessary to realize that Africans are vibrant people who express themselves with great exuberance through the clapping of hands, stamping of feet, the ringing of bells, beating of drums, singing, and dancing. These gestures are part of their religious and meaning-making activities. This quest for ethics and morality that celebrates life in a community is one reason that the African people convert to Christianity seceded from the churches to form their independent churches. Passion for vibrancy exists in almost every sphere of their lives; this includes how they communicate and interact. Studies demonstrate how this social web and communalism were misinterpreted by colonial scholars. For instance, John Welsh claimed that Africans could not live as people of commonwealth that they lived like a beast, and without religion and law.[42] This claim goes contrary to what we know of Africa's sense of community and the social relations which have held African communities together for centuries. The idea that African people lacked the communal and, by implication, the moral sensitivity to live together was also extended to political life. Birks, a colonial officer who visited the Waja communities in Northeastern Nigeria, even out of mere impression reported that the people could not live under the same native authority because of the way the topography (hill and plain) of the area as that time.[43] This is over sixty years since he made that declaration, and the people are still united together. Before the arrival of the colonial administrators, the people of Southern Gombe demonstrated that they could interact together through the joking and trading relations they had; they were able to coordinate their Trade by Barter businesses even before the introduction of the European cash, an indication that their traditions promoted concepts of what was socially and economically acceptable, hence they had a strong sense of moral order.[44] Reciprocity, impartiality, and respect were codes that enhanced such interactions among these peoples. Munro argues that reciprocity "reminds everyone that we are all in this together";[45] it builds trust and brings about exchange of technology and so on. He further noted that impartiality, which has been seen as neutrality, is more than being neutral; it is a virtue of judgment, key to how moral judgments are made. Trade by Barter cannot function effectively among people who are not reciprocal, and this allows for communication, interaction, and respect among a group of people, as demonstrated by the people of Southern Gombe.[46]

The ethics of communication in African societies vary according to these circumstances. Communication in Africa is both verbal and non-verbal (gesticulation) and occurs in different situations. When one is in the midst of elders, it is not wise to jump into a communication that he/she is not invited to. He or she is to remain quiet, listen, and learn from the wisdom of the elders unless there is an invitation by the elders to the younger one to participate in the conversation. Even when the younger one is invited into the discussions, there is a limit to what the person can do and also how the person can do those things. The velocity of the voice also matters. You are not expected to point your finger at someone when communicating as this is an indication of disrespect; no long-lasting direct eye contact with the elders too; if it happens, it should not be persistent. Therefore, if one communicates with an African man who avoids eye contact, he should not be mistrusted; that is his way of life. However, this is not the case when you are with your age mates. While you are not supposed to be rude to them, there is some form of freedom when you are with your peers. Gossip, slander, abuses, lies, and insults are not welcome during communication. Intermittently, communications are intercepted with moments of euphoria characterized by meaningful shouts, laughs, clapping of hands, stomping of feet, head nods, dancing, handshakes, and, in some cases, singing! This kind of moment shows how friendly and peaceful they are in communicating. People who interact this way are always keen to know what is going on with a member whom they have not seen for some time. Typically, they do have specific spots in neighborhoods where they meet and participate in these social activities; for example, in Northern Nigeria, it is referred to as a *Majalisa* (meeting spot). This is a place where like-minded individuals arrange specifically to meet and interact. Sometimes, people purchase food or other items and share among themselves to quench their hunger as they partake in discussions. These kinds of ethics have helped the African people to overcome the life of individualism that has characterized the modern era.

COURTSHIP, MARRIAGE, PROCREATION, SURROGACY, AND FAMILY

The Asymmetric Argument, which argues that bringing somebody into existence is always wrong, makes no sense to the African people.[47] Waje Kunhiyop writes: "The home is a key institution that shapes individuals and society. If families are distorted, so is the whole society."[48] According to Waje, marriage, courtship, divorce, infertility, death and widowhood, sexuality and procreation, domestic violence, love pleasure, and companionship are important ethical issues to consider in African courtship, marriage, and family matters.[49] Waje, referring to John Taylor, explains how important community is in African peoples' life:

> *Every man is born into a community. He is a member of a family and he grows up inheriting certain family characteristics, certain property, certain obligations; he learns certain family traditions, certain patterns of behavior, and certain point of pride. In the same way, also, he is a member of a particular clan, tribe, and nation, and this will give him a particular culture and history, a particular way of looking at things, probably a particular religion. It is in such way that every other human being belongs to his own environment. He has his roots in a particular soil; he cannot be transplanted to a different soil without feeling the change very deeply; and if he is left with his root in no soil his personality will become weak and unhappy and sick. Men and women who do not live in a community and feel that they really belong to it are not completely human. Something essential is missing, something which God has ordained for them as necessary for their true life.*[50]

This quote explains the roles of the families and the communities in African ethics. Traditionally, when it comes to the matrimonial issue, the people of Africa frown at what is today commonly referred to as "move-in," a situation whereby an adult male and a female start to live together without being married. Though some African couples are beginning to live that way, it was not part of traditional ethics. Every African parent wants their daughter to marry a man that will take care of her more than the way they (the parents) do. In an ideal African situation, it is expected that at approximately the age of thirty, a woman should be married, all things being equal. If such a lady's peradventure is predestined by God to live for ninety years, it indicates that the majority of her life will be spent with her husband and not her parents. Therefore, parents want their daughters to marry hardworking, sincere, and upright men who respect laid-down societal norms. In this type of setting, there is no provision for "move-in" arrangements; it must be marriage. According to Waje Kunhiyop, marriage "is a type of union of a man and a woman that God established at creation."[51]

In early traditional African societies, marriages began with courtship, which could last for as long as six raining/farming seasons (six years). In some communities, the man would work on the lady's father's farm. The inability to endure this requirement and length of time meant that one was not man enough to take care of a woman. Thus, this type of arrangement gave them ample time to understand themselves better. To understand African principles about courtship and marriage, one needs to be familiar with African life cycle rituals. African Rites of Passage are more than just helping members of a community to manage fear and anxiety. African people do not interpret their practices in psychological terms. For an individual, the rites begin from birth (a period of celebration) and end with death (a mourning period). They are more than managing any anxiety; they are moral and religious obligations. Between birth and death, there is the separation and the incorporation of rites. Knowing them will help in comprehending African indigenous ethics on courtship, hard work, and marriage.

In traditional African societies, one must attain adulthood before getting married. Adulthood and marriage are part of a whole life cycle ritual. This begins from conception (pregnancy). For the sake of an unborn child, the mother undergoes place, time, labor, dietary, and sight ritual restrictions such as avoiding areas believed to be the abodes of evil spirits, for example, forests, tamarind trees, and streams. This is to prevent evil spirits from possessing or replacing the child in her womb. She is restricted from seeing horrible things (ghosts, horrific animals, masquerades, etc.). There are times in a day, twilight, and mid-day whereas she is not allowed to go out of the house; these are times as conceived by the people when evil spirits perambulate within society. The pregnant women are restricted from eating certain foods and also from doing hard labor. After the women give birth to the child, there is a naming ceremony which, according to Quarcoopome, humanizes, individualizes, and socializes a child. At a particular age in life, the child is taken to the shrine for initiation; after initiation, there is a ritual that transforms the child into adulthood, eventually marriage, and death.[52] Traditional marriage systems have their ethics or rules inter-woven with the religion of the society. It begins with courtship.

Courtship and marriage are not meant for teenagers who are not mature to make consequential decisions; this type of relationship is between two adults, a male, and female. Traditionally, the woman and the man must have gone through the rite of passage that marks their transition from childhood into adulthood. At that point, it is anticipated that the woman has learned how to cook, respectfully talk to her husband, and must have obtained sex education from her mother. The males, in some communities, must endure some forms of hardships like sleeping on a bare floor, being threatened in the bush at night, and must have learned the family trade to be qualified for adulthood. These rituals prepare the boy for manhood and the girl for womanhood. After courting and marrying each other, African societies expect a moment of celebration after nine lunar calendars. The hope is that by this time, the wife would have conceived and given birth to a child. Procreation has an essential place in African life. According to Waje Kunhiyop, the concern of the traditional African man is not the number of wives he marries, but whether the marriage will produce a male child who will maintain his linage and remember him as an ancestor.[53]

Failure to do so calls for alarm, and people may tend to interpret it in diverse dimensions, for instance, attributing it to may be a promiscuous life before marriage, or as a result of punishment or curse by her parents or the ancestors (the ancestors are considered to be custodians of the moral values of society who also punish people for contravening societal norms). This is in objection to the Asymmetric Argument, which argues that bringing somebody into existence is always wrong.[54] The African societies fume at promiscuous behaviors, whether as married or as singles. Sex must be performed within the ambits of the norms. As such, the current situations in the world where there are a wide variety of dating websites (with naughty images), or websites where married women or desperate single mothers visit to look for male suitors that match their interest to satisfy their sexual desire instantly without entering into a relationship; or sites where opposite sexes sign up to chat naughtily between themselves without necessarily knowing each other, is morally wrong in traditional African societies. On televisions, social media networks, in public spaces, or even in secret, African cultures do not condone nudity, and this is why some aspects of the human rights are condoned.

A significant debate in African societies today concerns same-sex marriage, which many people oppose on the grounds that such sexual relations are not tolerated in African moral practices. This remains a crucial debate as some people call attention to the human rights implication of denying same-sex couples the right to marry. However, Africans tend to link disparate things together for the sake of their moral arguments. Therefore, pornography, same-sex marriage, and gender transplants are rejected in Africa. It does not mean that there are not people who like pornography or like partners of the same sex, and changing one's gender does not exist. Nevertheless, some members of the society want those beliefs and practices abolished or criminalized. In traditional African societies, such people would not be allowed access to the position of ancestors as a good moral life was a requirement.

Democracy has watered down this practice as people can bribe their ways into key positions in society. Although Africans promote procreation, there are certain forms of procreation that are prohibited, especially the ones before marriage or outside it, which many times are accidental. Community elders encourage the people to stay away from certain practices because beliefs and practices that promote social ill-health also affect a person's social wellbeing and may require treatment with traditional medicine. Some communities view procreation and virginity differently; the *Bace* of Plateau State in Nigeria is a good example. These people had a practice called *izne*, which did not place importance on the idea of virginity. A lady was expected to have a child, which she would leave behind with her family before getting married.[55]

Surrogacy is another ethical issue to consider in African ethics. The concept of a human being in African cosmology, which somewhat influences recent generations, makes it almost impossible for surrogacy and cloning to have a place. The indigenous religions of Africa, as noted earlier, view the human being quite different from the Greco-Roman world and, if I may add, Western concepts of it. Wilson and Luke argued that surrogacy has been in practice right from the Old Testament period when Abraham and Sarah used Hagar to bear a child for them.[56] Because technology was not used to transfer Ismael into the womb of Hagar, we think what happened here is not surrogacy as being talked about in its modern sense! However, among the Waja of Nigeria, the idea of a traditional form of surrogacy without technology existed right from the pre-colonial times and still looms today. Modern surrogacy is said to have become available with "'[t]he first test tube baby' in 1978, who was conceived through in vitro fertilization. Surrogacy thereafter became more 'widely available [and] prevalent' in the 1980s."[57] It is preferred to abortion and is not executed the same way as the one practiced and backed by laws in the contemporary time. Kathleen Hoeger et al. state that:

> *This, they say, is practiced in various ways such as "medication to grow multiple eggs, retrieval of eggs from the ovaries or ovary, insemination of eggs with sperms, culture of any fertilized egg (embryos), placement ("transfer") of one or more embryos into the uterus, and support of the uterine lining with hormones to permit and sustain pregnancy." There are additional methods employed at some moments (cases) such as "intracytoplasmic sperm injection (ICSI) to increase the chance for fertilization, artificial hatching of embryos to potentially increase the chance of embryo attachment ('implantation'), and cryopreservation (freezing) of eggs or embryos."*[58]

According to Wilson and Luke, in vitro fertilization can be full or partial. In partial surrogacy, the surrogate mother's eggs are fertilized through artificial insemination by the would-be father; it is also "the easiest, cheapest, and safest."[59] In this type of surrogacy, the surrogate mother has an equal "biological connection with the child." In full or gestational surrogacy, "both the sperm and the egg of the intended parents are implanted in the surrogate mother, severing her biological connection with the child."[60] Surrogacy is performed using "modern reproduction technologies" (MRT), which assist in human reproduction.[61] While modern surrogacy is done with the help of technologies, the indigenous African societies where it was practiced relied on magic. In both cases, there is the challenge of how the ancestry of this surrogate child can be determined. How could the early African societies use the lunar calendar to determine when a child would be born through the MRT method? How could the child observe the transformational rituals and celebrate the naming ceremony to the acceptance of the people in rural communities where traditional African ethics are being preserved without the child suffering from prejudice? These are challenges that surrogacy faces in Africa.

CONCLUSION: CHANGING TRENDS IN AFRICAN ETHICS

Wariboko argues that temporality has germane repercussions for ethics, and that ethicists will ignore it at their own risk, and that every social system struggles between *momos* and *kairos* as it passes through chronic time.[62] "Nomos is the historicized and contextualized situatedness and the limit of a particular social existence in time", while *kairos* allows for temporalities.[63] That is to say, *nomos* is conservative, while *kairos* is liberal. Contemporary Africans, at home or in the Diaspora, are locked between *nomos* and the *kairos*. *Kairos* comes with the human's ability to recognize, name, and be faithful to when something they never foresaw emerges in society.[64]

Colonialism, education, democracy, and migration (in the *kairos*) have collapsed the sacred and moral canopy that bound Africans in their societies together. Democracy enhanced the ascendency of the individual with the power of not just to vote, but to vote in private. The ascendency of the individual happened[65] together with the emergence of secularization, which is the social and psychological marginalization of religion; it is the moment when non-religious narratives were used to explain human existential problems as against the traditions that relied on religious narratives.[66] Democracy introduced the Fundamental Human Rights, which becomes the greatest weapon that suppresses African moralities. Many African people who accept the claims of human rights still practice—what some in other parts of the continent and worldwide might be called a confusing position for—supporting human rights but rejecting gay rights. Africans who want to see gay rights eliminated argue that Africans would not be dealing with these issues were it not for the influence of colonialism, education, and democracy. Those who support gay rights in the name of human rights might evoke Emile Durkheim, who consents that as societies develop, some elements of the early tradition are retained. Durkheim says: "Every time that we undertake to explain something human, taken at a given moment in history—be it a religious belief, a moral precept, a legal principle, an aesthetic style or an economic system—it is necessary to commence by going back to its most primitive and simple form."[67]

William Parson talks of how the child at the early stage of his life with his parents considers the dictates of his parents as facts which must be believed and obeyed without questioning them. He refers to this as an *idealization*. As the child keeps growing up (i.e., becoming an individual), he begins to question parts of the dictates—de-idealization.[68] This sequence of transformation applies to African moralities. We want to create an understanding that people are not only predisposed to copy from contemporary scenes but also their primordial traditions. Therefore, the current changes in Africa and the peoples' ethics do not mean that they have completely lost touch with their founding fathers' moral precepts. Here, we illustrate using some events among the Waja on how African ethics have been impacted by changes. Before and even after the advent of colonialism, Christianity, Islam, Western education, and democratic dispensation in the Waja communities, the people were known for carrying weapons (against external aggressors) or ritual sticks (against hunger) only on one occasion when facing a common enemy; they never used weapons against themselves as aggrieved persons only retrieved from the rest of the people to form their own settlements (for those in the plain areas where there was enough land) or moved to live among different people entirely (for those in the hilly areas with compacted land space).

NOTES

1. John S. Mbiti, *Introduction to African Religion* (London: Heinemann International Literature & Textbooks, 1975), 180.
2. Emanuel Bolaji Idowu, *God in Yoruba Belief* (Longmans, 1962), 145.
3. Rebecca L. Stein and Philip Stein, *The Anthropology of Religion, Magic, and Witchcraft – Pearson EText* (Routledge, 2015), 207.
4. Ogbu Kalu, as cited in Jacob K. Jacob Obafemi Kehinde Olupona, *African Spirituality: Forms, Meanings, and Expressions*, vol. 3 (The Crossroad Publishing Company, 2000), 56, (Crossroad Publishing, 2001), 3.56.
5. Robin Horton, "African Conversion," *Africa* 41, no. 2 (1971): 85–108.
6. See Jacob K. Olupona, *Beyond Primitivism: indigenous Religious Traditions and Modernity* (Psychology Press, 2004).
7. John S. Mbiti, *Introduction to African Religion* (London: Heinemann International Literature & Textbooks, 1975), 40–45.
8. Joseph Adyinka Olanrewaju, "The Relationship Between People and Supernatural Beings in Yoruba Traditional Culture," Journal of Adventist Mission Studies, vol. 5, no. 2 (2009): 41–49. https://digitalcommons.andrews.edu/jams/vol5/iss2/6/.
9. E. Bolaji Idowu, *Olodumare: God in Yoruba Belief* (Longmans, 1966), 71–107.
10. Horton, "African Conversion," 101.
11. Joseph Adyinka Olanrewaju, "The Relationship Between People and Supernatural Beings in Yoruba Traditional Culture," 41–49.
12. Roland Hallgren, "The Vital Force. A Study of Àse in the Traditional and Neo-Traditional Culture of the Yoruba People," *Lund Studies in African and Asian Religions*, vol. 10, 1995, http://www.diva-portal.org/smash/record.jsf?pid=diva2:312571.
13. Yusufu Turaki, "Africa Traditional Religious System as Basis of Understanding Christian Spiritual Warfare," *Lausanne Movement* (blog), August 22, 2000, https://www.lausanne.org/content/west-african-case-study.
14. Ibid.

15. Ibid.
16. Idowu, *Olodumare*, 145.
17. Ibid.
18. See Emile Durkheim, *The Elementary Forms of the Religious Life*, trans. Joseph Ward Swain M.A. (CreateSpace Independent Publishing Platform, 2014).
19. Idowu, *Olodumare*, 146.
20. Mbiti, *Introduction to African Religion*, 1975, 175.
21. Motsamai Molefe, "A Rejection of Humanism in African Moral Tradition," *Theoria* 62, no. 143 (January 1, 2015): 59–77, 59.
22. Ibid., 59–60.
23. Idowu, *Olodumare*, 176.
24. Ibid., 64.
25. Laurenti Magesa, *African Religion: The Moral Traditions of Abundant Life* (Orbis Books, 2014), 57–74.
26. Ibid., 72.
27. John Ayotunde Isola Bewaji, "Ethics and Morality in Yoruba Culture," 2007, 396. https://doi.org/10.1002/9780470997154.ch32.
28. Kwame Gyekye, "African Ethics," in *The Stanford Encyclopedia of Philosophy*, ed. Edward N. Zalta, Fall 2011 (Metaphysics Research Lab, Stanford University, 2011), https://plato.stanford.edu/archives/fall2011/entries/african-ethics/.
29. Ibid.
30. Ibid.
31. Ibid.
32. Mbiti, *Introduction to African Religion*, 1975, 19–27.
33. Chinua Achebe, *Things Fall Apart* (New York: Penguin Books, 1994).
34. Durkheim, *The Elementary Forms of the Religious Life*, 6.
35. Samuel Waje Kunhiyop, *African Christian Ethics* (Grand Rapids, Mich: Zondervan, 2008), 9.
36. Achebe, *Things Fall Apart*.
37. "Child Was Punished for Calling His Teacher 'ma'am,' Parents Say," accessed December 28, 2020, https://www.wmbfnews.com/story/38958764/child-was-punished-for-calling-his-teacher-maam-parents-say/.
38. Ibid.
39. "Child Was Punished for Calling His Teacher 'ma'am,' Parents Say."
40. Ibid.
41. Donald J. Munro, *Ethics in Action: Workable Guidelines for Private and Public Choices*, vol. 3 (Chinese University Press, 2008), 49.
42. Umar Habila Dadem Danfulani, "African Religions in African Scholarship: A Critique," *African Traditions in the Study of Religion in Africa: Emerging Trends, indigenous Spirituality and the Interface with Other World Religions*, 2012, 344.
43. Laiman, Victor. *The Waja People of Gombe State in Nigeria*. Zaria: Joda, 2003.
44. Ankruma, N. H. *Reconstructing African Past: Sources and Prospects of Tangale History*. Jos: Ehindero, 2005.
45. Munro, *Ethics in Action*, 3: 48.
46. Ibid., 3:9–10.
47. David Benatar and David Wasserman, *Debating Procreation: Is It Wrong to Reproduce?* (Oxford University Press, 2015), 40.
48. Kunhiyop, *African Christian Ethics*, 190.

49. Ibid.
50. Ibid., 67.
51. Ibid.
52. Theophilus NO Quarcoopome, *West African Traditional Religion* (African Universities Press, 1987), 112.
53. Kunhiyop, *African Christian Ethics*.
54. Benatar and Wasserman, *Debating Procreation*, 40.
55. Achato, Elizabeth. Virginity among the Rukuba (Bace) in the Traditional Society and Modern Christian Girls: A Comparison, Student Long Essay, 2017, 2–3.
56. Shriya Luke Richardson Wilson, "Surrogacy—Laws and Medical Ethics," *International Journal of Scientific & Engineering Research* 3, no. 7 (2012): 1.
57. Ibid., 1–2.
58. Ibid.
59. Richardson Wilson, "Surrogacy–Laws and Medical Ethics," 1–2.
60. Ibid., 1–2.
61. Ibid., 2.
62. Wariboko, Nimi. *Ethics and Time: Ethos of Temporal Orientation in Politics and Religion of the Niger Delta* (Lanham, MD: Rowman & Littlefield, 2010), 4.
63. Ibid.
64. Ibid.
65. Jonte-Pace, Diane, and William B. Parsons, *Religion and Psychology: Mapping the Terrain* (London: Routledge, 1st edition, 2001), 3–4.
66. Ibid.
67. Durkheim, *The Elementary Forms of the Religious Life*, 6.
68. Ibid., *Opt Cit.*, 3.

CHAPTER 22

African Traditional Religion and African Philosophy

Alloy S. Ihuah and Zaato M. Nor

INTRODUCTION

Religion and philosophy have a longstanding relationship dating back to antiquity. Philosophy like religion is a human activity and therefore a social phenomenon. Man is completely locked up in religion and philosophy. Religion has to do with worship, supplication, deity, God, altar, Priest, piety, body of beliefs, monk, temple and adherent, and so on. *The Penguin Encyclopedia* defines religion as "the body of beliefs and practices by which man expresses his attitude to any superhuman power in whose existence he believes."[1] Religion evolved from mythology while philosophy in turn, evolved from religion. Unlike mythology which is less patronized in the contemporary period, religion and philosophy are areas of study that command enormous attention by scholars. Philosophy is traditionally understood as "a quest for wisdom and an attempt to provide a vision of the world that is systematic and clear, in which the

---

Alloy S. Ihuah is Professor of Philosophy at Benue State University, Makurdi, Nigeria. He researches and teaches philosophy of science, epistemology, and African philosophy.

Zaato M. Nor is Associate Professor of Philosophy at Benue State University, Makurdi, Nigeria. He researches and teaches metaphysics, contemporary ideologies, and African philosophy.

A. S. Ihuah (✉) • Z. M. Nor
Benue State University, Makurdi, Nigeria

© The Author(s), under exclusive license to Springer Nature Switzerland AG 2022
I. S. Aderibigbe, T. Falola (eds.), *The Palgrave Handbook of African Traditional Religion*, https://doi.org/10.1007/978-3-030-89500-6_22

connections between significant facts are made manifest. It is a search for first things and last things for the first principles and their ultimate implications."[2]

However, the understanding of the association between philosophy and religion as outlined here readily fits the occidental perception. As a critical study, philosophy seeks to understand reality, dialectically by asking and answering questions on such matters as; what ultimately is reality, what is the right way to live, and how can we know these things, using reason from an objective point of view. Conversely, religion seeks not only at understanding, but also, and even more, at living through faith with or without understanding the faith-based issues at hand. While philosophy is rational, religion is faith-based and subjective. African Traditional Religion (ATR) or African indigenous religions (AIR) or Traditional African Religions (TAR) and African Philosophy like the Oriental World Religions and Philosophy are fundamentally intertwined as philosophy is taken to have an intrinsic relationship with religion. Thus, ATR is taken as the foundation of African Philosophy. Like Hinduism, Buddhism, and even Confucianism, ATR has three basic discernible components namely: Religion, Philosophy, and Culture. However, ATR can be teased out to provide so much more. This is because ATR is predicated on African metaphysical worldview. Olusegun Oladipo defines worldview as "a general picture of the world and the place of man in it."[3] This broad picture has been lucidly captured by T.U. Nwala when he says, "Traditional African Philosophy is said to be contained in oral literature and general culture (in rituals and social institutions)."[4] Consequently, ethnographic studies, works on traditional religions, art, symbols, myth proverbs, and so on provide the raw materials from which scholars have tried to give systematic accounts of such traditional philosophy. Traditional African Philosophy as such is basically a worldview that informs some important beliefs or ideals, that is, economic, socio-political, philosophical, moral, religious, and aesthetic. Thus understood, African Philosophy, arising from the foregoing, is richly founded by the raw materials provided by ATR and African worldview. For as rightly observed by Bertrand Russell, "to understand an age or nation (or a people), we must understand its philosophy because the circumstances of men's lives do much to determine their philosophy and their philosophy does much to determine their circumstance."[5]

A Labyrinth of African Traditional Religion (ATR)

Africans particularly Sub-Saharan Africans are branded as people who are notoriously and non-repentantly religious. This assertion is borne out of the fact that Africans were indigenously religious as they were committed to the practice of African indigenous religions (AIR) prior to their contact with Europeans (Christianity) and Arabs (Moslems) which were more organized with founders and spiritual leaders. African Traditional Religion (ATR) in the words of Segun Ogungbemi "is the religion of our forebears which is passed from one generation to another. Some of the beliefs in this religion concern God, divinities, spirits, ancestors and the place of man in the universe, worship, witchcraft, sorcery and magic, initiations, morality, death and immorality and so on."[7] This goes to demonstrate the overwhelming influence of ATR in the life of the African people. John S. Mbiti explicitly captures this overbearing influence thus: "Because traditional religion permeated all the departments of life, there is no formal distinction, between the sacred and the secular, the religious and the non-religious, and between the spiritual and material areas of life. Wherever the African is, there is his religion."[6] Religion simply is the way of life of the African people. Apart from a few religions like, the *Ifa*, a religion practiced among the Yoruba people of Nigeria that has its written corpus, majority of ATR are without scriptures. However, as Moses D. Gbadebo aptly notes the "basic tenets of TAR though not written exist. They are neatly written in the hearts of their adherents ... doxological names, prayers, legends, myths, riddles, parables."[7] Gbadebo further explains that it is through these channels that the TAR is passed on from generation to generation.

ATR believe in the Supreme Being that he is the creator of everything which he in turn has absolute control and power to exercise on. ATR acknowledge the seen and the unseen forces, that is, the physical and the spiritual and consider both as being aspect of one reality. To ATR, existence is one homogenic reality. All existing things interact in a harmonious manner. In ATR, the supreme being does not compel people to worship him neither does he impose a demand on his subjects to go out and evangelize and even convert people. Besides, ATR are not domineering or conquering religions. As such, they are peaceful and tolerant religions. The adherents have no cause whatsoever to become fanatical or fundamentalists. ATR also take cognizance of the inhabitants of the physical (material) and the spiritual worlds. The material world is the abode to material objects while the spiritual or immaterial world is home to spiritual entities. According to Gbadebo, "it is believed that the world of the spirit is inhabited by God, gods, (deities or divinities), ancestors and spirits in a hierarchical order. They ... interact with the physical world to help and protect those in the world."[8]

Suffice it to state at this point that to the African, all things that exist whether animate or inanimate, are life forces. This metaphysical conceptualization of the African worldview has been thoughtfully captured by Zaato Nor thus,

> whatever can be known now or later, or thought of to exist now or which may manifest later which can be sensually or otherwise perceived, is a life-force or spirit. ...Which does not exist in isolation ... but exist in a hierarchical order, interrelating and interpenetrating other worlds. Under African ontology, what is seen and known now or later and what is unseen and unknown now or later constitute what is known now or later constitute what is known as life-forces or spirits. These life forces exist in a harmonious relationship and are therefore, constantly interrelating and interpenetrating each other despite their hierarchical ordering.[9]

K.C. Anyanwu outlines the qualitative and quantitative hierarchical structure of these life forces thus: "God, divinities, ancestors, man, animals, plants, words, knowledge, etc."[10] In alignment with Anyanwu and buttressing this structural ordering, Janheinz Jahn maintains that "there exist four categories of life forces: *Muntu, Kintu, Hantu* and *Kuntu*, which he refers to as the four categories of African Philosophy." Meanwhile, Jahn points out that these forces are the product of *NTU*.[11]

According to Jahn, "*NTU* is *Being* itself, the cosmic universal force. … it is that force in which being and beings coalesce."[12] That is, all the forces have an element of *NTU* in them be it *Muntu*—Intelligent forces, *Kintu*—Frozen Forces, *Hantu*—Space and Time and *Kuntu*—Abstract modalities. From Anyanwu's submission and as it is clearly elaborated by Jahn "everything there is must necessarily belong to one of the four categories and must not be conceived as a substance but a force."[13] Thus, "*Muntu* is represented by human being(s), *Kuntu* by thing(s), *Hantu* by place and time while *Kuntu* is represented by abstract modalities)." This being the case, ultimately *NTU* simply means God or Being. Consequently, Jahn concludes that "NTU is the point from which creation flows."[14] *NTU* as such could be likened to a propeller that stimulates the motion of things. This point has been well elucidated by Ihuah when he says, "God is seen as the originator and sustainer of the human being: the animals and the plants and the natural phenomena constitute the environment in which the human being lives."[15]

In an explanation of the workings of the forces based on the hierarchical order, Anyanwu maintains that "the higher the position of a force on the ladder of superiority, the more domineering influences it has on the lower forces. But this is not to say that the forces at the bottom of the ladder do not influence those at the top."[16] For instance, human being (*Muntu*) as an intelligent force (just as words considered to be inferior to human beings) do participate in the forces with superior vital force.

It can thus be argued that these cultural ideas are the building blocks of African belief in the existence of forces. Kwame Gyekye passionately resonates this thinking in his work: *African Cultural Values: An Introduction* as quoted by Peter Oni "To be born into the African society is to be born into a culture that is intensely and pervasively religious."[17] This intensity and pervasiveness is not in terms of ATR being polytheistic. For instance, E. Bolaji Idowu maintains that "there are some divinities that are closest to *Oludumare* (Supreme Being or God in Yoruba) from the beginning in creative and executive function."[18] Idowu accordingly identifies "*Orisa-nla, Orunmila, Ogun, Esu, Sango (Oranfe, Jakuta) Sonponna*"[19] as being principal divinities with regard to their relationship to *Oludumare*. He concludes that the identified deities are prominent because they are believed to be charged with vital functions and they are universally recognized and worshiped by the Yoruba. Thus, in Yoruba religion, *Oludumare* delegates certain aspects of his responsibilities to certain divine functionaries in religious expression. This attitude in Yoruba religion appears to be the general dogma of the indigenous religions of the African people.

A Maze of African Philosophy

Philosophy in traditional parlance is the critical evaluation of the ideas (religious, economic, political, social, scientific, etc.) we live by. It seeks to clarify and organize concepts and issues in an explicit and systematic manner such that all the relevant interrelations become easily discoverable. Thus, philosophy embarks on an enquiry to determine the basic principles underlying things and at the same time their ultimate consequences. This view of philosophy being very broad encompasses African philosophy. The thinking that man is man everywhere such that all human beings in space and time are the same though true, their experiences and belief systems may differ. The implication of this is that though Africans, Europeans/Americans, Asians, and so on may differ in terms of experiences and beliefs, they are humans. However, there are some basic questions arising from this claim: do all humans share the same experiences, beliefs, and worldview? Without any equivocation, the emphatic answer is no.

Again, are some humans inferior to others? Do Africans have a philosophy/history/civilization, and so on? Are Africans capable of rational/critical thinking? These questions and related ones were and are still being answered derogatively by Europeans and Americans and other races that consider themselves as being superior with regards to Africans. Meanwhile, it suffices to state that it is these questions and other related ones that prompted a perspective in African philosophy. To the advocates of this position, African philosophy is fundamentally a response philosophy which projects the African experiences, beliefs, people, and worldview as they differ from other people. To demonstrate that Africans cannot be inferior to any race or people, the advocates of this view disclaimed the claim by European/Americans that Africans are inferior as they argue to the contrary that Africans are as rational as they are also critical.

To launch a pointed discussion regarding these concerns and others, J. Obi Oguejiofor maintains that "African philosophy is therefore a hermeneutics of African cultures."[20] However, the synonymic between philosophy and culture must not be construed that African philosophy is synonymous with African culture. Culture as Edward B. Tylor presents it and as quoted by John W.T. Gbor is "the complex whole which includes knowledge, belief, art, morals, law, custom, any other capabilities and habits acquired by man as a member of the society."[21] This synonymic conceptualization of culture brings to the fore the perception that symbolic elements inhere in African culture which a creative genius can structure African Philosophy. This is the position subscribed to by A.F. Uduigwomen as he says, "African philosophy has its roots in culture."[22] It is therefore not out of place to describe African Philosophy as African Cultural Philosophy (ACP) connoting African outlook, conceptual model of reality that enables the owners of the culture to understand and develop a strong sense of belonging to a community of shared values and beliefs, religious, political, economic, social, morals, and so on. Thus, ACP sums up the outlook of the African on the created world. It is more so to the African conception of reality as submitted by African religion and culture.[23] It is summed up here that, in thoughts, in action, and in words, philosophy underpins the African world and to deny this fact is to deny Africans humanity.

It is premised on this background that it becomes pertinent to advance a few definitions of African philosophy on the anchor of hermeneutics of African culture, African condition/experience, and even peculiarities. Prompted by this understanding, Uduigwomen patently notes that "African philosophy is adapted to explain reality from the African perspective."[24] In what appears as a re-echo of this view, J. Olubi Sodipo unequivocally states that "when you say African philosophy you are drawing attention to the aspect of philosophy which arises from a special problem and the unique experience of the African people."[25] This thinking finds elaboration in Oshita O. Oshita. According to him, "African philosophy is the outcome of the reflection on the fundamental question of philosophy as they impinge on a distinctively African experience."[26] It is glaring thus far that by the nature of African philosophy, reality as conceived and understood, is interpreted and transmitted by the African worldview. Nor insists here that "African philosophy is conscious and deliberate philosophical attempt adopted as an urgent necessity to address the African in his ontology as someone who, in spite of humanness, harbors experiences and encounters experience that may not be compared to mankind elsewhere. More so, he upholds a world view that is distinctively his."[27] Nor stresses that "to contemplate studying his thoughts and beliefs without adopting a philosophy that captures his ontology amounts to a disservice to him." This is what informs the conviction that African philosophy is synonymous with a world view.

As earlier adumbrated by Oladipo, worldview is like a big mirror which captures the whole of reality as it includes man and his role in the broad picture. Oladipo identifies two sides of a worldview. According to him, "there is a communal worldview which is usually unconscious and non-rational and philosophical worldview which is conscious and theoretical."[28] From Oladipo's explanation, a communal worldview is concerned with the collective experience of a people which in turn is the product of interaction between them and nature and among themselves. Based on the nature of communal worldview as explained, it is unconscious and non-rational. Furthermore, Oladipo avers that this kind of worldview "generated by the empirical conditions of life and experience handed down from generation to generation is usually acquired by the individual through a process of socialization and it is usually validated by a heavy reliance on tradition and authority."[29] In other words, communal worldview on its own is a dogmatic worldview which is blindly accepted by the people as an inheritance. Nevertheless, Oladipo says, communal worldview influences actions of the professional philosopher as it provides the intellectual framework within, which, things or phenomena are perceived, felt, and transformed.

On the flip side, the philosophical worldview according to Oladipo "is both systematic and prognostic."[30] He says, "it is systematic in so far as it attempts to provide a categorical scheme within which various components of culture and their interconnections can be interpreted and prognostic because it also offers society or mankind some alternatives to its current mode of being."[31] Oladipo adds that in the prognostics function, philosophy is regarded as the thought of its time as it critically examines the intellectual foundations of society just as it generates explanatory schemes that illuminate problems in the society in their varying degrees of complexity. This means that philosophical worldview is a critical theory which challenges the prevailing situation in order to advance new and better ways of handling issues. Accordingly, Oladipo emphasizes that philosophical worldview "serves to provide the context of ideas within which particular choices and preferences in the realm of action—economic, political, scientific and even religious—are made."[32] African philosophy as such when considered from a philosophical worldview could therefore be referred to as a critical theory which challenges the prevailing descriptions and conceptions of Africans and, consequently, offers new hermeneutical interpretation of them in space and time.

Consequent upon the understanding that African philosophy as a philosophical worldview which is systematic and prognostic, Anthony O. Echekwube introduces three core principles: principle of harmony, the principle of symbolism, and the principle of participation.[33] Echekwube argues that "since metaphysics is an all-embracing discipline that investigates "Being as Being, *Ens in Quatum Ens*"[34] in its totality, it views the universe in its components parts; God, deities, Heaven, Human Communities, Inanimate objects, and so on. African Philosophy as such could proceed from metaphysical principles to tackle its most pressing religio-socio-politico-economic problems." This situation as far as Echekwube is concerned calls for the introduction of the basic principles of African Philosophy. He maintains that by familiarizing oneself with the main characteristics of African Philosophy, it will equally project the worth of those attributes as they will contribute to a more meaningful global civilization and to the attainment of universal harmony through peaceful coexistence. Thus, in his explanation of the principle of harmony or homogeneity, Echekwube says, "it searches for the unity of all existent beings. The multifarious nature of the universe is conceptually one in the African worldview as there is no clear-cut distinction between the spiritual and the physical."[35]

To the African, reality is taken as a homogenous cosmogonic view. He stresses that with the principle, it becomes easy to resolve problems in African Philosophy as well as religious systems. He adds that with the principle of harmony, "it is easily understood why action and energy and purpose are applied to both animate and inanimate objects."

On symbolism, Echekwube maintains that it "is an interpretation of an object in order to make it signify that which it is not."[36] For instance, among the Tiv people of Nigeria, when a chameleon blocks one's path as he/she walks on the way, it is regarded a symbol of bad omen. Aylward Shorter maintains that "a symbol represents an objective cultural reality which has psychic implications for the members of a particular culture."[37] In other words, symbols are of significance to people of different socio-cultural groups. People of a particular culture are the ones to give meaning to particular objects or things as it relates to them. For instance, people of other cultures may not find any symbolic significance about a chameleon blocking their path or a bird flying past them on a lonely road. For the African therefore, man and nature are interdependent variables. Man relates to and uses nature for his own good. If and when a man construes his leadership of nature as manipulator who dominates nature, he destroys himself and the entire earth. This point has been lucidly adumbrated by Ihuah thus, "Man and nature are important to each other although nature exist for the good of man and remains so. ... man is what he is because he lives in the company of others and in harmony with nature."[38] The argued point here is that interaction remains the basic principle of participation of the elements that inhabit the environment; therefore, any conception of our environment that perceives only ourselves and our dispositions is necessarily flawed from the point of view of essential human nature. Echekwube illumines this principle of participation metaphysically that every cause has an effect and the effect participates in the perfection of the cause.[39] He explains that by the principle, it is common knowledge to find trees bearing the likes, human parents bearing children who are like unto themselves. In the same vein he stresses that creatures exhibit the qualities of their creator.

ATR as a Practical Manual for an African Philosophical Discourse

Prior to engaging in the discussion proper, it would not be out of place to highlight some basic features of ATR even though some have been presented earlier.

- ATR is the religion that evolved from the culture of the African people and it is transmitted from generation to generation by oral tradition and practices.
- ATR in other words are indigenous religions. ATR have no founders and no written scriptures.
- ATR acknowledge God as the Supreme Being even though the Supreme Being has inalienable divinities.
- The Supreme Being is variously addressed depending on a particular ethnic group. For example, the Tiv people of Benue State Nigeria refer to Him as *Aôndo*, the Yoruba call him *Olorum* or *Oludumare*, to the Igbo people, He is *Chineke* or *Chukwu*. Hausas refer to him as Obangiji.
- No African Traditional Religion has a symbolized image of the Supreme Being.
- The divinities in ATR are assigned special responsibilities by the Supreme Being.
- Human beings can penetrate the Supreme Being through the divinities by offering sacrifices to them.

- The Supreme Being is the creator of everything—seen and unseen.
- ATR have channels of transmitting its beliefs, worship, and sacrifices.
- Worshipers of ATR believe that the world of the spirit as inhabited by the Supreme Being in the hierarchical order interacts with the physical world for the protection of the living. That is, the world of the mortals and the world of the immortals. However, there is an interrelation and interpenetration of these worlds.
- ATR is a peaceful and tolerant religion.
- ATR do not seek to conquer or convert worshipers of other religions nor do they make mockery of other religions.

Informed by these unique features of ATR, Mbiti maintains that "to African people, man lives in a religious universe, so that natural phenomena and objects are intimately associated with God. They do not only originate from Him, man's understanding of God is strongly colored by the universe of which man is himself a part."[40] This goes to explain the bond between man and the Supreme Being and by extension, all that He has created. It must be emphasized here then that it is this quality of African culture, a religiously based culture which conceptual model of reality is religiously based, and from which every other life index finds its bearing.[41]

ATR and African philosophy are both man and society-centered. As such, they can be referred to as forms of social consciousness. These phenomena are social in many respects: Philosophy as a critical theory is a product of a philosophical worldview while ATR is a product of African culture from which African Philosophy in its prognostic and rational context emanates. African philosophers today, like the ancient Greek philosophers who sanitized the mythological worldviews of Homer, are in the process of systematizing the religious worldviews of the African by demythologizing the cosmological concepts of ATR. This is made possible through the systematic and prognostic approaches of African philosophy. It may not be out of place to conclusively reason that, Africa is both the heartland of religious practice and philosophical rationality. The deconstructive effect of philosophy and reason on African Traditional Religion has made the African to be deeply involved in a dialectic between reason and not only their own subjectivity, and their own tradition, but also the subjectivity and traditions of others.

Ramose B. Mogobe simplifies this with the birth of an African indigenous philosophy which he tagged Ubuntu.[42] For him, Ubuntu is the root of African Philosophy; the wellspring flowing with African ontology and epistemology. The understanding here is that African Philosophy is rooted in human fellow-feeling and or relationships. "To be a human *be-ing* for the African is to affirm one's humanity by recognizing the humanity of others and, on that basis, establish humane relations with them".[43] Momoh may have anticipated this essentially existential philosophy when he suggests the adoption of "standard topics for the investigation this indigenous African philosophy as follows: *God, Man, Spirits, and Ancestors.*"[44] There are several other topics like *life, society, leadership, spiritualism, worship, obedience, eldership, followership, mysticism, occultism,* and *divination* combined to define the substance and philosophical foundation of African Philosophy.

In yet another symbiotic relationship between African Philosophy and ATR, they both impact on the ontology of the African. As a matter of fact, they are indispensable to the life of the African people. They seek to enlarge human experience socially and spiritually. They are considered as quintessential media through which the African people appreciate reality which to them is essentially spiritual.

Now granted that reality is primarily spiritual, it means African philosophy gravitates from ATR and African metaphysics. Thus, Echekwube and Momoh observe that ATR provides a reservoir of topics, area perspectives for African philosophical discourses. African philosophy is desperately interested in the life of the African just as ATR. In the same manner, they are both concerned with the human spiritual culture of the African. It is the preoccupation with the African spiritual culture that African philosophy becomes manifest as it employs metaphysics to investigate the claims of ATR. In this context, African philosophy may be taken as a philosophy of ATR which seeks to examine religious concepts, discourses, religious worldview, claims, justifications, and arguments advanced on their behalf. This understanding of African philosophy could best be taken as a second-order activity that is ordered to advance beneficial effects of the African society. Knowledge of environmental thermodynamic and electromagnetism in African solar system has for instance been made possible by ancient African sages. Through repeated observations and simple projections of the past trends into the future, it was possible for the Yoruba of Nigeria to make impressively accurate predictions of sunrise, sunset, lunar phases, positions of the stars, relative movement of the earth, sun, and moon. Olaitan chronicles this painstaking thinking when he says

> Observations of the early Yoruba of the disease called *Sagbadiwere* (the symptom of which includes temporary loss of direction) which their observation could occur during the period of intense solar activities, a result of being victim of wrath of the sun … has been explained within the context of contemporary physics.[45]

He explains further that the Yoruba knowledge of other solar phenomenon and activities variously housed in their traditional knowledge and beclouded by their religious beliefs and practices can be illuminated through this same process of observing nature. This, he says, enables the Yoruba to project past trends into the future, thus making impressive correlations and predictions of their observations. The foregoing largely informs the thinking that apart from the synergetic relationship between ATR and African philosophy, ATR provides the basic raw materials for philosophical activities. It is thus with the hermeneutic aid of ATR that concepts such as witchcraft, reincarnation, determinism, freedom, fatalism, life-after death, and ghost and death are articulated and subsequently, investigated in African philosophy. Alloy Ihuah suggests that

African intellectual culture can be explicitly presented in oral texts, that is, names, songs, rituals, proverbs, folktales, visual arts, and so on.[46]

Conclusion

This essay demonstrates the synergy between ATR and African philosophy. Both phenomena are of immediate concern to the African as they constitute social phenomena leading to a social consciousness. Engaging African philosophy from the background of a systematic and prognostic understanding, ATR serves as a rich resource which provides the necessary raw materials for African philosophical activity (ies) especially in the area of metaphysics. As a critically engaging endeavor that concerns itself with the way in which the indigenous peoples' of Africa, past and present made and make sense of their destiny and of the world in which they live, African Philosophy informs the entire ideas that the Africans live by, inclusive of their indigenous religious and scientific ideas. Our conclusion is that the combined symbiotic power of ATR and African Philosophy underlies the widely recognized African philosophic view of the wholeness of the universe. The desire to soar with unwearied passion until they grasp the true nature of being/things as they really are, African philosophers have combed their humanistic heritage (largely a metaphysical one), to make their ontology and epistemology meaningful. This is made possible through a reconstructive dialectics between African philosophy and African Traditional Religion; this perhaps explains the unity in diversity that brands African religions.

Notes

1. Sir John Summerscale (Ed), *The Penguin Encyclopedia* (Baltimore: Penguin Books, 1965), 50.
2. A. J. Minton, *Philosophy: Paradox and Discovery* (New York: McGraw-Hill Book Company, 1976), ii.
3. O. Oladipo, *Philosophy, Literature and the African Novel, (Dialogue in African Philosophy)* (Ibadan: Option Books and Information Service, 1993), 2.
4. T.U. Nwala, "The Concept of Traditional African Philosophy", in Maduabuchi Dukor (ed), *Essence Journal: African philosophy and Pathology of Godhood and Traditionalism*, vol. 2 (2005), 21.
5. S. Ogungbemi, "Rationality and African Traditional Religion", in Segun Ogungbemi (ed), *God, Reason and Death: Issues in Philosophy of Religion* (Ibadan: Hope Publications, 2008), 91.
6. J. S. Mbiti, *African Religions and Philosophy* (London: Heinemann Educational Books, 1969), 2.
7. Moses D. Gbadebo, 'God and Ethics in Traditional African Religion and Philosophy', in Maduabuchi Dukor (ed), *Essence Journal: African philosophy and Pathology of Godhood and Traditionalism* (Vol. 2, 2005), 144.
8. Moses D. Gbadebo, "God and Ethics in Traditional African Religion and Philosophy", 145.

9. Zaato Nor, "Elements of African Philosophy" in Alloy S. Ihuah (ed), *Philosophy and Logic for Beginners* (Makurdi: Obeta Printing and Publishing, 2010), 135.
10. K. C. Anyanwu, "Presuppositions of African Socialism", in the *Nigerian Journal of Philosophy*, Vol. 3, Nos. 1 & 2 (A *Journal of the Department of Philosophy*, University of Lagos, 1983), 50.
11. J. Jahn, *Muntu: An Outline of the New African Culture*, Trans by Marjorie Grene (New York: Grove Press Inc., 1961), 101.
12. Jahn, *Muntu: An Outline of the New African Culture*, 101.
13. Jahn, *Muntu: An Outline of the New African Culture*, 101.
14. Jahn, *Muntu: An Outline of the New African Culture*, 101.
15. A. S. Ihuah, "African Humanistic Heritage", in Alloy S. Ihuah (ed), *Philosophy and Human Existence: Critical Essays in Philosophical Discourse* (Saarbrucken, Germany: LAPP Lambert Academic Publishing AG & Co, KG, 2010), 138.
16. K. C. Anyanwu, "Presuppositions of African Socialism", 50–51.
17. Peter Oni, "African Culture and Religious Terrorism: A Critical Examination", in *Or-Che Uma: African Journal of Existential Philosophy* (Vol. 4, No. 1, March/April 2013), 14.
18. E.B. Idowu, *Oludunmare: God in Yoruba Belief* (Ikeja: Longman Nigeria plc, 1996), 68.
19. Idowu, *Oludunmare: God in Yoruba Belief*, 68.
20. J. O. Oguejiofor, *Philosophy and the African Predicament* (Ibadan: Hope Publications, 2001), 199.
21. J.T. Gbor, *The Tiv Concept of Culture and Tiv Cultural Values* (Makurdi: Centre for African Culture and Development, 2006), 1.
22. A.F. Uduigwomen, "Philosophy and the Place of African Philosophy", in A. F. Uduigwoman (Ed), *Footmarks on Africa Philosophy* (Lagos: Obaroh & Ogbinaka Publishers, 1995), 7.
23. Ihuah, "African Humanistic Heritage", 148.
24. Uduigwomen, "Philosophy and the Place of African Philosophy", 7.
25. J.O. Sodipo, Interview in *The National Philosopher*, in annual magazine of the National Association of Philosophy Students, NAPS, University of Ife, (UNIFE) Branch (Vol. 1, No. 1a, 1983), 6.
26. O.O. Oshita, "The African Experience and Western Philosophy", in A. F. Uduigwomen (Ed), *Footmark on African philosophy* (Lagos: Obaroh Ogbinaka Publishers, 1995), 139.
27. Ihuah, "African Humanistic Heritage", 130.
28. Oladipo, *Philosophy, Literature and the African Novel*, 2.
29. Oladipo, *Philosophy, Literature and the African Novel*, 3.
30. Oladipo, *Philosophy, Literature and the African Novel*, 3.
31. Oladipo, *Philosophy, Literature and the African Novel*, 3.
32. Oladipo, *Philosophy, Literature and the African Novel*, 4.
33. A. O. Echekwube, "The Basic Principle of African Philosophy", in Maduabuchi Dukor (ed), *Essence Journal: African Philosophy and Pathology of Godhood and Traditionalism*, Vol. 2. (2005), 3.
34. Echekwube, "The Basic Principle of African Philosophy", 3.
35. Echekwube, "The Basic Principle of African Philosophy", 4–5.
36. Echekwube, "The Basic Principle of African Philosophy", 6.
37. A. Shorter, *Revelation and its Interpretation* (London: Gregory Chapman, 1985), 9.

38. Ihuah, "African Humanistic Heritage", 149.
39. Echekwube, "The Basic Principle of African Philosophy", 8.
40. Mbiti, *African Religions and Philosophy*, 48.
41. Ihuah, "African Humanistic Heritage", 149.
42. R. B. Mogobe, *African Philosophy through Ubuntu* (Harare: Mond Books, 2002), 42.
43. R. B. Mogobe, 2002, 42.
44. C. S. Momoh, "Problems on African Philosophy", in C. S. Momoh (ed) *The Substances of African Philosophy* (Lagos: African philosophy Projects Publications, 2000), 19–20.
45. H. M. Olaitan "Environmental Thermodynamic and Electromagnetic Effect in Yoruba Solar Physics", *Journal of African Philosophy and Studies*, vol. 2, no. 3 (1999), 1.
46. A. S. Ihuah, "Philosophy in African Oral Texts", in *Journal of African Philosophy and Studies* (Auchi: African Philosophy Projects Publication, 1999), 1.

CHAPTER 23

African Traditional Religion, Gender Equality, and Feminism

Adepeju Johnson-Bashua

INTRODUCTION

Gender discrimination is ramped within a majority of the established religions. The status of women in religion is a composite of many variables, often casually independent of each other. Consequently, a woman's status may be low or near equality in one and may surpass that of men in another. Thus, the generalization that gender inequality is a prevalent practice in all societies of Africa is baseless because each religion has its unique parameter for measuring the status of women. Contrary to the unequal gender relations in the vast majority of religions, African traditional religions view gender relations as complementary to one another. Despite this vantage position, they hold on the religious sphere, a careful examination of African society reveals a male-dominated society where women are subservient to men.

An examination of women's status in African society reveals a set pattern of thoughts that is intricately connected with peoples' cultural worldview. African culture has set a mold of beliefs and values for women, which are not taken lightly neither are they negotiable. Gender relations in Africa have a bearing on familial lines, which assigns roles to both sexes and makes the household duties a woman's principal responsibility. Traditionally, an African woman is one who should devote all her energies toward the "physical and spiritual well-being of her family." This traditional role ascribed to women in African society has made gender equality a difficult task to achieve. The ideology that women must be

A. Johnson-Bashua (✉)
Lagos State University, Lagos, Nigeria

submissive to their husbands, their community, and the Supreme Being is regarded as the most significant barrier to freedom of self-actualization. This belief is strongly supported by religion, which clearly shows that the status of women religiously is no different from the cultural status quo. This study presents African religious stance on gender as diffused liberalism, which exalts women, on the one hand, presenting them on equal status to men while, on the other hand, requires them to be submissive to their leadership roles.

Theoretical Framework

According to Mbiti, African cosmological accounts often submit that God, the Supreme Being, created the world and the first humans as male and female though the exact methods differ from one locality to another.[1] Their cosmologies and rituals display a generally positive attitude, which gives both genders secular and religious power. This negates the belief that African religion supports the cultural belief that women were created inferior to men and, therefore, should be treated as subordinates. This view is buttressed by Akyeampong and Obeng, citing the Asante of Ghana, whose concept of gender roles is hinged on the belief that power is available to all persons irrespective of gender. This belief is reinforced in the predominance of the matriarchal family dynamics of the Asante.[2]

In the African religious sphere, biology does not always predetermine the capabilities and responsibilities of men and women; rather, it becomes a space for engagement by both genders to showcase their spiritual endowment and competence. The socio-cultural context can often assign gender roles to men and women in ways that reinforce and perpetuate complementary dependency. This has become a space in which African women are seriously harnessing to prove their relevance in a male-dominated world. Unfortunately, the status women occupy in African society is premised on claims of innate predispositions. Society's conditioning and stereotyping can result in undermining the capability of women and girls to perform a myriad of tasks resulting in fixed role expectations ascribed to them by society. This is aptly described by Gloria Chuku: "Everything about her socialization as a girl was built around marriage and procreation. The girl was taught how to cook and provide domestic services to her husband. She was also trained in her mother's trade or sent away as an apprentice to learn other trades that would enable her to take care of her children when the time comes."[3]

The degree of religious independence women enjoy in the ritual space of African traditional religion, if extended to other spheres of life, is believed will serve as a significant stage in bridging inequalities and fostering self-esteem and well-being in male-dominated society. This chapter addresses the issue of gender inequalities through examining the impact of cultural repertoire in the religious sphere, which allows for the exploration of gender, can contribute to women's empowerment in African societies. The methodology for this study is phenomenological, historical with data from books and oral interviews.

Status of Women in African Society: An Overview

Despite Africa's exposure to civilization and modernization, there is still a firm belief in cultural and religious practices that shapes their worldview. Africans still hold to the prism that women are subservient to men in all ramifications. The traditional laws are more favorable to men, while it is stringent on women. For example, cases where women are sentenced to death based on adultery or pregnancy outside of marriage, while the men involved were acquitted for lack of evidence.[4] It is safe to conclude that African women are born into societies where they are often powerless to change their own realities nor attain their full potentials based on lopsided laws. The status of African women will always be low compared to men based on their subjection to rigid cultural practices which place them in a disadvantaged position such as early marriage which truncates their education, inheritance laws which deny females of any inheritance, widowhood practices that deny women social and economic rights, female genital mutilations, and the preference of male above female children. The continued invocation of culture, sexuality, and religion in order to treat women unequally is under constant well-grounded criticism by human rights activists and feminist movements who have identified them as discriminative and demeaning.[5] In African societies, the glaring gaps between men and women, which makes it difficult for women to perform to their full potential, can be examined from two interlocking perspectives classified as the private and public space.

In the private space, based on the socio-cultural pattern of Africans, the girl child is owned from birth until her death, first by her family and then by her husband, leaving little or no room for personal desires and choices. Total submission to the wishes of her parents and husband at all times makes her the ideal woman, which the Yorùbá refer to as *Obirin rere*. Fatherhood gives her father the right to make decisions on her behalf, while the act of marriage gives the husband full ownership of the woman.[6] In situations where a bride price is paid, this gives legitimacy to his ownership of the woman both in body and estate, and this is why the African woman usually refer to their husbands as my master as in the context of a master-servant relationship.[7] Society teaches her to be submissive in all situations to her husband for this will ensure the success of their marriage even if it is an abusive relationship.[8] This mentality has helped fuel domestic violence, which takes many forms, including physical, sexual, emotional, and mental claiming the lives of many women.[9]

Furthermore, the traditional division of labor places more workload on women compared to men. Women usually saddled with the responsibility of household tasks such as cooking, cleaning, and childcare. They are also responsible for a good portion of the agricultural work, thereby contributing their quota to the upkeep of the family. Women perform heavy arduous tasks to secure their family's subsistence; simultaneously, this binds them to domestic servitude and allows them little or no time to pursue any personal ambition. Despite all the efforts put in by the woman to sustain the home, this does not guarantee that she will inherit any property after the death of her husband despite the fact that she has been his lifelong partner. However, while she cannot inherit, she could be inherited after the demise of her husband by any of her husband's relations based on the belief that traditionally wives of the deceased were part of his property.

Another problem women face in the private space is their inability to control their sexuality; within the confines of the bedroom, sex is exclusively the prerogative of the husband. In providing a justification for this, African sexual rules are considered as concluded issues handed down by religion and society. Thus, there is no flexibility for change or modification. Consequently, any attempt to challenge or alter these established gender norms is perceived as a threat to accepted norms and may inspire social anarchy. This makes it difficult, if not impossible, for many African women despite civilization to express themselves sexually among their pairs and, most importantly, to their spouses. This often leads to sexual frustration in many marriages. Indeed, the few who are bold enough to raise and discuss the subject are viewed with suspicion and mistrust. They are usually labeled with derogatory terms by both men and women in society. Obviously, with the advancements in civilization, the big burden placed by sexual tradition on African women has become inimical to the evolution of African sexuality, particularly in the area of the candid discussions on sexual issues between couples (which helps to enhance sexual relations). It has also denied African women worthy self-esteem compared to their male counterparts since they are dominated sexually. Therefore, sexuality, in this sense, cannot be regarded as pleasurable or expressions of love. If there is any pleasure to be derived at all, it is for the husband. Thus, the role of women in marriage is to satisfy their husband's sexual gratification unconditionally and to produce children. Any deviation from this norm is faced with stigmatization.[10] This has led to sexual frustration for many women who are suffering in silence.

Limitations on women's functions in public space are also based on local gender constructs, claiming that women are supposed to be seen and not heard. Politically, the history of African women in governance is a composite of many variables. For example, in pre-colonial Africa, women enjoyed a favorable status. In this era, they were not marginalized for their sexuality and thus attained high political positions in a patrilineal society. Therefore, they functioned at different levels politically: there were kings such as *Yeyenisewu* in Ado-Ekiti who ruled in the sixteenth century, *Eye Aro* in Akure who ruled in the fifteenth century, and *Queen Amina* from the fifteenth to the sixteenth centuries.[11] Numerous female chiefs were deeply involved in traditional governance. For example, in the old Ibadan kingdom, the title of *Iyalode* was created in the 1850s to reward Madam Subuola, who used to assist the warriors.[12]

Arrival of colonial masters, this marked the beginning of the fall of African women. Colonial politics and statutes were clearly sexist and biased against women. Their powers were continuously eroded as few women were offered political or administrative positions; this led to opposition; most famous of this was the Abeokuta women's revolt in Nigeria, also known as the Egba women's tax riot.[13] The revolt was slightly successful as this led to the appointment of three women into the house of chiefs in the 1950s: Western House of Chiefs—Chief (Mrs.) Olufunmilayo Ransome Kuti, Eastern House of Chiefs—Chief (Mrs.) Margaret Ekpo, and Chief Mrs. Janet Ekpo. After independence, the first and second generations of African administrations largely failed to return traditional powers to women but instead chose to solidify the status quo established by colonialists. Despite many oppositions by women, the chauvinistic tendencies of their male counterparts have made it nearly impossible for them to have any meaningful impact in governance to date. This was particularly evident in the Nigerian situation during the military rule, where women were completely denied any position of authority in governance. In this era, women have come to the realization that bridging the wide gap in political inequality is essential to the formation of a democratically sustainable society that aspires to social justice and human rights. Hence, they have intensified their demands for inclusive governance. Because women are aware that politics decided the distribution of resources, they also know that women's exclusion from political life results in their interest that of their children would not be adequately represented.

Educationally, a large percentage of African women are illiterates. The cultural perception of women, by both men and women, has often prevented the advancement of women. Parents' low response to formal education of their daughters is based on the conception that they are minors in society. It is believed that the only form of teaching a woman needs is embedded in cultural education, which is aimed at character development, development of intent and physical skills, preparation for motherhood, and promotion of cultural heritage.[14] It is mostly assumed that educating women would make them too independent, which could alter the cultural perception of who and what is expected of them in society. It is culturally accepted that the basic responsibilities of women are to look after the house, bring up children, and cater to their husband's needs; anything short of this is regarded as anti-womanhood.[15] This stereotyped role assigned women by religion, culture, and society at large encourage the impression that education is exclusively the men's prerogative. Though this stance is gradually shifting and girls are increasingly getting some limited education; however, boys, typically, are afforded more of a claim on the limited educational opportunities. For example, in most rural communities where there is extreme poverty, domestic and family demands are primarily placed on girls and women. They are regarded as valuable assets for making money through informal economies such as petty trading, subsistent farming, and early marriages.[16] Consequently, their parents cannot afford the luxury of them attending school when they are expected to be in the marketplace. In situations where the girl child is compelled to attend school by the government, they are made to combine schooling with housework, and it usually results in poor performance at school. This situation places them in inescapable domestic servitude and allows them little or no time to acquire formal education. Stromquist describes this gloomy situation aptly when he said: "The existence of intensive domestic work, coupled with conflictual family dynamics, renders literacy an unattainable dream for a large number of women and even a dream for some of their children, particularly their daughters who early in life tend to be assigned the same domestic roles their mothers perform."[17] The lack of education usually results in low self-esteem.

Economically, the poor financial capabilities of African women have also contributed to their low performance publicly. Despite being the primary contributors to the economics of the continent, the majority of women are living below the poverty level. Generally rural women undertake tasks that involve food productions. Some of these include fetching of water, gathering of firewood, and so on. However urban women are not usually involved in these kinds of tasks because of industrialized dynamics that tend to favor the employment of men rather than women. Also the dynamics of food production is also different from the rural situation. Consequently, even when women are the producers of the food, men are more often than not, the agents of making the food available to the public.

Also, the practice of men requiring women to give up their income has remained substantially in most parts of Africa. For example, in Northern Nigeria, in complaisance with Islamic law, women are required to stay at home. Consequently, they hardly have access to earning incomes with exception of some of them who engage in small scale trading.

In the Southern part of Nigeria, laws are more liberal compared to the North whereas women are allowed to work but often divide their time between trading and farming. In employment, they are concentrated in semi-skilled and unskilled and low-paid jobs. The elite women who wish to improve their legal and economic status must expect to lose honor, and respect.[18] Because of the limited educational opportunities afforded to women, there are few women in the professional/white-collar sector; rather, women often resort to low-paid manufacturing work. Not only is their sexism in job advancement, but there are cruel consequences if women challenge this sexism. Additionally, male professionals receive more respect, even from female practitioners. Consequently, women have lagged behind men economically, and this has greatly affected their participation in politics. However, just as much of the Global South, circumstances are slowly but surely advancing for women in Africa. More women are joining the formal sector of the economy (especially the public sector), more women are acquiring management positions, more women are entering into fields dominated by men, and more women are self-employed.

Religiously, in this respect, the women's leading in rituals, especially with regard to the life cycle, such as birthing, puberty, marriage, funeral, and mortuary rights, cannot be overemphasized. This makes the religious sphere one of the long-established institutions in which African women have substantive control. Within the religious sphere, women's leadership skills and knowledge are created, validated, and transmitted. Women who officiate such as priestesses, spirit mediums, and prophetesses are quite common in African traditional religion. Acting in this capacity, they can act as seers for their communities. The Yorùbá ritual song below shows the extent of female power in African traditional religion.[19]

> Ka ma de pe obirin o mawo
> Awo mejilelogun l' obirin mo
> Meji to le lori e re e t' okunrin
> Gbogbo ogun yooku t' obinrin ni
> We should not say women are un-informed about esoteric cults.
> They are initiated into twenty-two (esoteric) cults
> Only the last two are known to men
> The remaining twenty belong to the women fold.

There is a consensus that women's status in contemporary Africa is in need of dire improvements. However, it would be unjust to accuse African indigenous cultures of maintaining gender discrimination for two basic reasons: firstly, gender relations in Africa is not a rigid practice of female inferiority as portrayed by many feminist authors both Western and African, citing the traditional Igbo society of Southeast Nigeria as a case study.[20] Secondly, culture is not static, but rather it is dynamic though it can be conservative.[21] For example, women in urban areas are gradually resisting oppressive cultural practices through feminist movements and human rights groups.[22] Taking into consideration how these women respond to gender inequality may help generate an even more nuanced understanding of the dynamics of culture concerning how gender ideologies operate in practice, thus avoiding the portrayal of women as hopeless victims of patriarchy.

STRUGGLE FOR GENDER EQUALITY IN AFRICAN TRADITIONAL RELIGION

Within institutionalized religions, gender discrimination is extremely prominent, especially if it is left undisturbed or tackled. It is no gainsaying that the male domination of religion constrains women's role within any given religion, both in their doctrine and ability to be officeholders. Perhaps the most significant problem is that most women, especially in Africa, do not engage in the effort to make changes by challenging the status quo of being consigned to subordinate roles in the society. It is important that religion and women's rights should not be seen as being mutually exclusive so as to avoid the danger of perpetual gender discrimination. A situation that gives all the power to men to the disadvantage of women, particularly in paradigms of gender roles. This kind of arrangement can only encourage and enhance women not being acknowledged and unprotected.

In recent times, the status of women in African traditional religion is continuously evolving to a more prestigious stance. Women are conscious of the need to play not just complementary roles alone but become crusaders of a new religious heritage befitting the new world order.

The following are ways in which women are demanding a paradigm shift. First, female practitioners are more emboldened in demanding equal recognition from their male counterparts on the premise of divine provision. The recognition given to women by the Supreme Being since the inception of the world means that they hold a valuable status that men are expected to respect. Female suzerainty at the creation of the world is attested to in *Odu Osa Meji*, where it is said that *Olodumare* gave woman (*Odu*) control on the condition that she use her enormous powers with care and discretion. *Olodumare* also compelled that whatever may happen, men should always incorporate women in all their endeavors.[23] The divine superiority of women is also reinforced in *Odu Irete* through the cosmogonical marriage of *Orunmilla* to *Odu*, who is believed to hold the knowledge of the oracles and divination. It is *Odu* who gave *Orunmilla* the "*Awo*," which is the secret power to control the "*Ase*."

This is the primary reason why women are included in all ritual cults; even those described as strictly masculine cults have at least one powerful female member. A classic example of this is the Egungun cult, where the *Alaagba* and *Iya Agon* (male and female titles) share the equal status of authority. The realization that women are fundamental to their success and, if sidelined, can be a hindrance to their progress both physically and spiritually is a germane tool employed for gender advocacy and equality.

The dual personality ascribed to women is also a negotiating factor for gender equality. Africans believe that women can be both cool and hot at the same time. Her outward calm nature is never mistaken for cowardice but rather serves as a covering for an inner masculine aggressiveness, which is only displayed when threatened or provoked; hence the Yorùbá adage "*esu lobirin*" meaning "women are tricksters like Esu." This unpredictable and contradictory nature makes men wary of them at all times. This belief is corroborated by *Odu Ifa Osetura*:

> Akere finu sogbon
> Ni oruko ti an pe Ifa iran
> Ija gidigidi ko kan agba
> Eniti Olorun ba ni agba
> Baba lama pe
> Adifa fun Osetura ti o ma ti kere
> Gba agba lowo olodunmerinlogun
> The small one whose mind is full of wisdom
> Is the name we call Ifa iran
> Violent scuffles has nothing to do with old age
> He who the god's ordain as elder we call father
> Ifa divination was performed for Osetura
> Who performed a fatherly role despite his small age.[24]

The *Odu* specifically says that if women are not given honor and respect, then they can be angry and destroy the world. If a woman wants to capture power from a man, she can use 201 tricks that are intrinsic to all females and an additional 50 tricks, after which man's power will be theirs if they desire it. The lives of all males are in the hands of women. If a husband is to succeed, it depends on the wife. The success of the family also depends on her. The *Odu* warns that men should not devalue women. The socio-cultural pattern of the people also corroborates this from the homefront in husband and wife relations. In African society, women after long years of marriage become the bedrock of the home. This is in recognition of her endurance and tenacity at holding the home intact despite all odds. At this stage, she metamorphosis from an ordinary wife (*iyawo*) to *iya wa* (our mother) and is addressed personally by all members of the family, including the husband as *ma'ami* (my mother).

The natural fear that men have for women when it comes to secrecy is another area women are exploiting in the struggle for power.[25] Africans perceive a fundamental difference characteristically between males and females in the ability to conceal secrets. For example, the Yorùbá stress this distinction in the adage "*Inu obirin jin*"; this simply means "women are more secretive than men." This belief is buttressed by the *Odu Ifa Ogbe Iwori*. This secretive nature of women can be negatively and positively utilized. It can negatively be deployed when a woman, particularly a mother, curses a person. On the other hand it can be positively manifested through the blessing pronounced by a woman, particularly, a mother. For example, it is believed that the power of a mother to evoke blessings or curses upon her children by the virtue of motherhood is a very potent force. This is why Africans regard mothers as a "god." This belief is typified in the Yorùbá adage "*orisa bi iya kosi*"; therefore, children are expected to accord their mothers the same respect given to the gods. Her mystical powers can also be used negatively when operating as a witch. This mystical power is greatly dreaded in African society. It is believed that when angered, they unleash their wrath of destruction on their victims resulting in all forms of maladies. Their wrath can only be placated after sacrifices are made unto them.[26] The secretive nature of women is a primary manifestation of feminine power.

From the above, it is obvious that African women in the new world are poised to put gender equality on the religious agenda. When and only when women begin to characterize their own identities and rejecting traditionally accepted views, they will be able to spur positive changes. The belief that women should be seen and not heard is not in tandem with the cosmogonical plans of the Supreme Being for African religion. Ultimately, African women want the opportunity to fully utilize their skills and capabilities to enhance the religion.

African Traditional Religion and Gender: Benefits for African Women

One of the adverse effects of colonization is the introduction of Western culture, which is opposed to African culture. Western culture introduced the separation between the secular and religious, while in African society, all institutions derive their validity from religion. In pre-colonial Africa, women enjoyed the exalted status given to them by the Supreme Being. They featured prominently in every sector of society. There was no discrimination on the basis of gender. Consequently, the status of women today in African society is a product of foreign culture/mentality.

In all cultures and societies, religion is a prominent influence. Its power is not limited to monolithic religious communities but extends to pluralistic societies and those known as secular nations, like Nigeria. In third world countries like Nigeria, the role of religion cannot be overemphasized. Indeed, religion can serve as a means of copping with all forms of life hardships at the individual level. Also it can provide the opportunities for the resistance of corrupt and ineffective leaders in government. Thus, religious institutions play a vital role in the cultivation and realization of all rights, not merely religious rights.[27]

Unfortunately, when it comes to gender equality, this is not the norm. Many religions, including African traditional religion, are increasingly paying lip service to the concept of gender equality; they do so within the limited concept of complementary roles for men and women and deny the applicability of substantive gender equality.[28] The reality is that, while the roles are seen as reciprocal, men and women are only equal with regard to dignity and not in status. Despite this, African women enjoy some level of independence when compared to other religions.

In the African religious sphere, the realm of ritual has proven versatile for displaying, to no small extent, favorable feminine gender construction. This is because when it comes to spiritual matters, roles are not dependent on gender delimitations. Instead, the emphasis is placed on personal inspiration orchestrated by divine selection as the true source of power and authority rather than institutional hierarchies.

Also, the fluidity of the ritual space regarding gender construction confirms the limitless opportunities women enjoy. For instance, legendary goddesses are known to possess "wives" (devotees, votary maids, and mediums), just as certain gods do. Some community rulers are considered to be "wives" of their affiliate deities, who may be perceived as male or female.[29] The ritual space is a veritable tool that African women are seriously harnessing to prove their relevance in a male-dominated world. Women skilled in religious matters usually command respect and admiration from society, just like their male counterparts. Aspects where they feature prominently are displayed during worship, rituals, and liturgies, aesthetics as well as musical functions, thereby injecting life, fire, and beauty into religion. It is a common sight in many African societies to see women function in leadership roles, healing practices, spirit possession, fertility rites, goddess worship, and divination practices.[30]

Secondly, the western liberalization of sexuality and its primary role fails to represent African society's traditional logic. African women are increasingly aware of the beneficial impacts of traditional religion in shaping their perceptions of sex and sexuality in the face of modernization and globalization. The African status of women, which Europeans consider as servile and dominated, is an actual part of the ideals of our culture. It confirms the African preference for areas of specialization reserved for women and men assigned by the Supreme Being.

In exercising the powers associated with these roles, African women transcend the confines of just being "legal minors" under the male's subjugated control. Seen from this perspective, it is usual to hold the view that while men hold to political authority, women have the mystical authority.

Also, while one cannot deny the practice of mistreatment of women in African societies and the claim that this is in keeping with African traditions, it must be stressed that this is not limited to African culture. The ill-treatment of women is an issue that cuts across cultures and people. Stigmatizing African culture for this may be regarded as unfamiliarity with the culture, a misunderstanding of the culture, or abuse of the African culture. In many parts of Africa, it is believed that discrimination against women based on gender is wrong and they should be treated with respect. There are many proverbs, myths, and legends that buttress this view but most importantly, the *Ifa* corpus which illustrates *Olodumare's* stance on male and female relations. *Odu Osa meji* describes a scenario indicating that women were not endowed with power by Olodumare when they arrived on earth. Consequently they were being mistreated by men. At this point, the women began to ask questions and decided to go back to Olodumare for redress. Olodumare, in having compassion on them, gave them the power of witchcraft. This power was considered to be greater than any power possessed by men. However, Olodumare admonished the women not to misuse the power. That is the power that many women now use.

Similarly, African women have rigidly resisted the European permissive expression of sexuality, which has distorted the traditional role of sex in this day and age. For example, African traditional religion forbids the arbitrary use of sex and sexuality. Africans' contact with Western societies, which veered between careful and elaborate analyses of sexuality, has so far failed to entice Africans into engaging in a similar expression of their sexuality. This is basically because sex is regarded as a spiritual act only to be engaged in by married couples and expressed purposefully for procreation. Consequently, it would be difficult, if not impossible, for Africans to legitimize homosexuality, which has been legalized in many societies of the world. The religious ideals of African religion provide a haven against such demands. Thus, African sexual rules are considered as concluded issues handed down by religion and society; this inhibits any room for change or modification. All endeavors to seek, to challenge, or to reform established gender roles or norms are regarded as forbidden and would erode society's set pattern. Many old traditions and customs relating to sexuality have tended to endure. This makes Africa a prime example of how traditional culture continues to impact aspects of sexuality despite modernization. African society, based on its religious mentality about sex, forbids adultery, homosexuality, masturbation, lesbianism, incest, and all other sexual acts that defile the sanctity of sex. They are not only regarded as sexual immoralities, but they are also conceived as a sin against God and society at large. This means that African sexuality is one of the most respected worldwide for its sanctity. African women are benefiting from the ideals of African religion in an age when sexuality and its relevance are being so distorted.

CONCLUSION

At present, it is clear that women have been denied an equal right to religion as a result of the operation of patriarchal religious creeds and power structures. However, it is established that in African traditional religion, women can be legitimately empowered since they do not have one gender identity given the multiple roles they play in the religion. This corroborates the flexibility of gender constructs in African religion and the perception that gender is different from sex. Therefore, those advocating for gender equality and citing African religion and society as an example need a paradigm shift in their argument. It is not enough to say that African women's position in society is in need of improvement without making efforts to understand the fundamentals of the people's socio-cultural pattern. For example, in many parts of Africa, gender relationships can be equal, unequal, or complementary. Consequently, for African traditional religion, the image of subordinate, passive, and vulnerable women is not applicable. Instead, one is left with the image of strong, courageous, independent, and hardworking members of society whose roles are complementary.

NOTES

1. John Mbiti. *Introduction to African Religion.* Ibadan: Heinemann Educational Books, 1991.
2. E. Akyeampong, and Pashington Obeng. "Spirituality, Gender, and Power in Asante History." *International Journal of African Historical Studies* vol. 28, no. 3 (1995): 481–508.
3. G. Chuku. "Nwanyibuife Flora Nwapa, Igbo Culture and Women's Studies," in Gloria Chuku (ed.), *Igbo Intellectual Tradition: Creative Conflict in African Diaspora Thought.* New York: Palgrave Macmillan, 2013.
4. Y. Akinseye-George. *Justice Sector Reform and Human Rights in Nigeria.* Abuja: Centre for Socio-Legal Studies, 2009.
5. Ibid.
6. R. Arisi, "Cultural Violence and the Nigerian Woman." *African Research Review* (2011): 39–60.

7. The Yoruba women refer to their husbands as "*Olowo Ori Mi*" meaning "the one who paid my bride price."
8. T. Aluko, "Keeping the Feminist Goal Alive in the 21st Century: An Assessment of the Impact of Policies and Initiatives in the Nigerian experience." *Journal of Arts and Culture* vol. 1, no. 1 (2006): 19–23.
9. B. O. Lawal, "African Traditional Education: Nigerian Experience," in Gabriel Oguntomisin and Edo Victor (eds.), *African Culture and Civilization*. Ibadan: GSP, University of Ibadan, 2005.
10. Sanday Peggy Reeves. *Female Power and Male Dominance: On the Origins of Sexual Inequality*. New York: Cambridge University Press, 1981.
11. T. Makinde, "Motherhood as a Source of Empowerment of Women," in Toyin Falola and Ann Genova (eds.), *The Yoruba in Transition: History, Values and Modernity*. Durham, NC: Carolina Academic Press, 2007.
12. T. Falola, "The Political System of Ibadan in the 19th Century," in Ade Ajayi and B. Ikare (eds.), *Evolution of Political Culture in Nigeria*. Ibadan: University Press Limited, 1984.
13. Judith Byfield. *Taxation, Women, and the Colonial State: Egba Women Tax Revolt*. Duke University Press, 2003.
14. B. O. Lawal, "African Traditional Education: Nigerian Experience," in Gabriel Oguntomisin and Edo Victor (eds.), *African Culture and Civilization*. Ibadan: GSP, University of Ibadan, 2005.
15. H. A. Adetunji, "Re-Orientating the African Woman Today," in Akintude Dorcas (ed.), *African Culture and the Quest for Women's Right*. Ibadan: Sefer, 2001.
16. E. D. Ojo, "Women and the Family," in Lawal Nasiru et al. (eds.), *Understanding Yoruba Life and Culture*. Trenton NJ: Africa World Press Inc., 2004, 63.
17. N. Stromquist, "Women and Literacy: Promises and Constraints." *Media Development* vol. 1, no. 1 (1990): 17–102.
18. Christine Obbo. *African Women: Their Struggle for Economic Independence*. London: Zed Books, 1980.
19. Dimeji Ajikobi. *What Does An African New Woman Want?* Lagos: Ark Publications, 1999.
20. Ify Amadiume. *Male Daughters, Female Husbands: Gender and Sex in an African Society*. London: Zed Books Ltd., 1987.
21. I. Ronald, and E. Baker. "Modernization, Cultural Change, and the Persistence of Traditional Values." *American Sociological Review* vol. 65, no. 1 (2000): 19–51.
22. GADN (Gender and Development Network). *Achieving Gender Equality and Women's Empowerment in the Post-2015 Framework*. London: GADN, 2013.
23. P. Verger. "Grandeur et decadence du culte de Iyami Osoronga (ma mere la sorciere) chez les Yoruba." *Journal de la Societe des Africanistes* vol. XXXV, no. 1 (1965): 141–243, 143.
24. Axosu Agbovi. *Iwe fun Odu Ifa: Ancient Afrikan Sacred Text*. Kilombo Restoration and Healing Publications, 2013.
25. Jacob Olupona (ed.), *African Traditional Religions in Contemporary Society*. New York: Paragon House, 1991.
26. Jacob Olupona. *African Spirituality: Forms, Meanings, and Expressions*. New York: The Crossroad Publishing Company, 2000.

27. Johan D. Van der Vyver and John Witte (eds.). *Religious Human Rights in Global Perspective: Legal Perspectives.* The Hague: Kluwer Law International, 1996.
28. Essam Fawzy, "Muslim Personal Status Law in Egypt: The Current Situation and Possibilities of Reform Through Internal Initiatives," in Lynn Welchman (ed.), *Women's Rights and Islamic Family Law: Perspectives on Reform.* London: Zed Books Ltd., 2004.
29. Matory Lorand. *Sex and the Empire That Is No More: Gender and the Politics of Metaphor in Oyo Yoruba Religion.* Minneapolis: University of Minnesota Press, 1994.
30. David O. Ogungbile. *African Indigenous Religious Traditions in Local and Global Contexts: Perspectives on Nigeria, A Festschrift in Honour of Jacob K Olupona.* Nigeria: Malthouse Press, 2015.

CHAPTER 24

African Traditional Religion, Sexual Orientation, Transgender, and Homosexuality

David Olali

INTRODUCTION

Religions that are indigenous to the ancestors and peoples of Africa are known as African Traditional Religions. These religions convey the ways of life of the people, their belief systems concerning relations of things, including ontological realities, their attitudes about and mannerisms toward worship of deities, spiritual and earthly correspondences, and their epistemologies about known and unknown phenomena. Charles Kimberlin Brain, a South African researcher, stopped short of acknowledging that the cave people engaged in forms of religious worship. The Rhodesian-born paleontologist Brain interprets materials (ceramics, rock paintings, etc.) discovered in Drakensberg as well as other data collected on the cave dwellers, whom he spent over fifty years studying in his well-researched book, *The Hunters or the Hunted?* only to note that: "the ritual aspects of the paintings are emphasized."[1] This aside-like statement seems to erase much of the symbolisms that African rituals convey intentionally.[2]

Two decades after the publication of *The Hunters or the Hunted?*, the Official Custodian of South Africa's nation brand, known as "Brand South Africa," in April 2013, published a newsworthy item with the title "Swartkrans Gets Heritage Plaque" on its website. This publication at least demonstrates some level of consciousness about the heritage or "history" of South Africa and recognizes the importance of the work of Dr. Charles Kimberlin Brain.[3] Yet, in the

---

D. Olali (✉)
Comparative Heritage Project, Atlanta, GA, USA
e-mail: david.olali@comparativeheritage.org

© The Author(s), under exclusive license to Springer Nature Switzerland AG 2022
I. S. Aderibigbe, T. Falola (eds.), *The Palgrave Handbook of African Traditional Religion*, https://doi.org/10.1007/978-3-030-89500-6_24

ideology-driven bias against Africa, Brain does not stand alone in the willful ignoring of the presence of religion among African peoples.

A "successful" work that celebrated the natural "inferiority" of Africa-descended peoples was an eight hundred-page book entitled *Types of Mankind*.[4] In exemplifying the classic mannerism by which enthusiasm's fire engulfed Euro-Americans (plural) in epiphanic, euphoric celebration of the ascendancy of the racism preponderant in *Types of Mankind*, the authors virtually excised any residue of remorse or shame in their revelry with White bigotry, nearly sealing off chances that contemporary Africans would be rescued from an uncritical acceptance of *mission civilastrice*, and producing a failure in the many missed opportunities to engage the now-historic and not undocumented credentials of "the new world religions."[5]

The uncritical acceptance of Westernized soteriological ideology arrives with devastating discursive consequences against the heritage of Africans. Although Europeans succeeded in dispossessing the African people of their rights, the moment soon came whereby new consciousness about the same African peoples activated memories of their histories and heritages to overcome slavery's psychology.[6] Thus, once fully ensconced in and driven by ideology, research about the subjects of religions, gender qualifications, cultural tropes, identity representations, sexuality, and power ought to be regarded with measured scoops of suspicion. This suspect attitude, to delay judgment until further notice, materializes in this interrogation of religions, gender, and sexuality in Africa, particularly because of the foreignness and strangeness in the meaning of quizzing of the ancient symbolism encoded within the spiritual worlds of African peoples. As Michael Y. Nabofa writes, manifestations of these symbolic "expressions can be seen in religious emblems, ideograms, rituals, songs, prayers, myths, incantations, vows, customary behaviour and personifications."[7] Nabofa expressly states that "research, a careful and meaningful study of the religious significance of certain ritualistic elements and behaviour enables us to understand and appreciate the more why certain things are treated in some special way by the believers, and thus helps to deepen our knowledge of that very faith."[8] Given the prominence of religious rituals within African communities, it would therefore be hard-pressed to think that research done on any African tribe for a period up to half a century failed to reveal dimensions of religion and spirituality! Thanks to C. K. Brain.

Redefinitions and Clarifications Concerning Religions and Gender in Africa

Being simultaneously important and symbolic domains within Africa, emerging discourse redraws ideological battle lines around gender, sexuality, and power relations. With religion as the subtext of these culturally framed realities, dynamics of the political sooner than later unveil themselves both in subtle and often surreptitious ways, particularly with the growth and waves of westernization disguised as globalization. In turn, the development and waves which manifest as interactions, interconnectivities, and interdependences produce internationalizations of and resurgences in old and new(er) trends and the transplanting and transference of systems from one environment to another. One area where such localization and domestication of habits has gained ascendancy is through the vocalizing of gender and sexuality topics across the continent. And in Africa, religion, being a social, cultural, and political institution, facilitates the production of silence around the subject of sex.

Consequently, any serious, critical, comparative engagement of the phenomenon of religion and its apparatuses across Africa, including the issues, which religion implicates in its wake, requires at least a two-prong broad approach: the pre-contact and the post-colonial. While the purpose of this categorization involves a rapprochement that would trigger analysis of the presence of religion on the continent, its final ideal does not entail an establishment of a moment of innocence before the first arrivals of westerners. Besides serving as useful analytical foundations for examining religion in Africa, these broadly defined taxonomies could facilitate a historical positioning of sexuality and gender. Yet, whether the era in conversation began and ended in some pre-science moment or only emerged after the emergence of a Barak Obama, one clear fact is that there is a glut in the literature on the presence and potentials of religions among Africans on the eve of western colonization. The post-colonial moment had arrived for Africa, but not before it had occasioned a rupturing in epistemologies and meaning frames for the subalterns.

The writings of John S. Mbiti are good starting points. *African Philosophy and Traditional Religions* and *Concepts of God in Africa* are two very important and ground-breaking books.[9] Affirming some of the issues that Brain's research failed to "see," one reviewer noted that Mbiti "is primarily concerned with belief and ideas, with forms of worship and with religious office."[10] Not only does this view state what ordinarily was obvious within the landscape of African spiritualities, but this position also recognizes the innate capacity of Africans to produce and articulate religion as "an idea" because that, in part, holds the promise that the African, who in the disruptive and oftentimes destructive avalanches of axial movements, might gain the respect s/he deserves as a whole and complete human being. Consequently, in the assessment of Sir Edward Evan Evans-Pritchard: "Dr. Mbiti is an African and naturally wants to show traditional African religions in a favourable light. He is also an Anglican clergyman and, therefore, formally committed to certain dogmas and rituals, which may not correspond too well to some African ideas and practices. On the whole, the author has managed, with skill and tolerance (and I suppose some unexpressed reservations), to reconcile his sympathy with African religions and his vocation in a faith whose missionaries are trying to get the Africans to abandon them."[11]

Evans-Pritchard notes a possible clash between African religious systems and those "introduced" by European and American missionaries. That clash over whether there can be compatibility between African religions and Christianity could also imply—as a veil for the normative supremacy of the missionary religions—that religions in Africa connote the evolutionary and cultural inferiority of the African people. With the presence of racism and ethnic discrimination against minorities, nonetheless, Mbiti successfully paved the way for future African scholars and scholars on African religions toward a firm academic foundation that would lead to a codification and referencing of African Traditional Religion as a university subject of study. Jacob K. Olupona of Harvard Divinity School describes Mbiti's scholarly representations brilliantly:

> In every generation, there rises a mwalimu, someone who completely transforms the pace and trajectory of a scholarly tradition. The bravery and brilliance it takes to accomplish such an enormous task are not only rare but are bound to leave a mark on scholarship forever. Such scholars pave the way for those who will come after them, encouraging them to follow in their footsteps and build on the foundation they have laid. Mbiti was one such scholar, and his research and teaching have irrefutably shaped the academic study of African religion as we have come to know it today.[12]

Evans-Pritchard's assessment indicates a key trajectory in the West's understanding of history and establishes the premium that western epistemology places on a culture of textualization. As a result, this is why missionaries and scholars of western orientations and training used their observation of an absence of "texts" on African Traditional Religions to erroneously settle for an interpretation and lack of writing, and thus civilization existed in pre-contact Africa.[13] From this misjudgment emerges the assumption that variation between genders among communes in Africa automatically indicated oppression and injustice. Hence, the characteristic narratology that fails to fathom the meanings and symbolism encoded within indigenous African religions and cultures "produce the contemporary construction of a diminished and deracinated African personality."[14] Therefore, a meaningful study of African religions and culture, including the socio-cultural structures they produce, would do well to invest in the psychology of humanity because presumptuousness around knowledge claims invariably misleads the researcher into the thick forest of ignorance, and in the words of Victor Turner, make "comprehensible many of its seemingly bizarre components and interrelations"[15] among the issues which the missionaries tried to get Africans to abandon. Unfortunately, one aspect where the needed humility and patience had long been missing in many western scholarship and activisms is gender.

Restating the Issue

Whether or not Africa has religion has never truly been at issue. Neither has the crux of scholarship on Africa been sufficiently preoccupied with gender affairs around the continent. Debates that center attention solely on these issues, without locating their interrelatedness, or to use a more apt concept, intersectionality with other dominant and overriding issues, from pre-contact to modern Africa, at best, even if unwittingly, recycle the wheel of western hegemony and dominance. To deploy Gayatri Chakravorty Spivak, when it comes to issues surrounding gender and sexuality in Africa, it is almost certain that "Some of the most radical criticism coming out of the West today is the result of an interested desire to conserve the subject of the West, or the West as Subject."[16] After all, the western idea that Africa should maintain gender "equality" does not simultaneously place on the table autonomy for African nations to control their own cultural and political destinies without western encroachment. The question to ask then is: If "gender equality" only implies the making of Africa synonymous to Europe and America on those terms alone, without a desire to see the complete and total emancipation of Africa form the vestiges of the transatlantic slave trades and colonization, what sort of equality of gender and sexuality rights are these western systems advocating for Africa? Mbiti's contributions resonate here. Once again, Olupona writes thusly:

> Mbiti was committed to expanding the lens through which Africa, its peoples, its knowledges, its religions and its culture were studied, and he stayed so committed until his final breath. Mbiti was ahead of his time. He sensed the danger in compartmentalizing African systems of knowledge and articulated a kind of unity between African thought systems espoused through philosophy and African spirituality. His most famous book, "African Religions and Philosophy" (1969), opened the way for the study of religions and philosophy in African, European and North American universities. His numerous publications have become durable classics in the fields of African Christianity and theology and continue to be staples in classrooms where African religious traditions are taught.[17]

From the classroom to city hall, discourse concerning traditional religions in modern Africa has suffered in two significant ways. At the hands of westerners (missionaries, colonizers, activists, etc.), the image of Africa assumes one of monstrous barbarism, criminality, and retrogression, a site of darkness, mandatorily in need of a western soteriology. This attitude subsists into modern times in the form of proselytized or "educated" Africans. The second way whereby indigenous religions suffer comes through the efforts and activisms of Africans themselves. Ironically, the suffering created as a result of this is worse than that created by foreigners. This condition is illuminated in the Yorùbá proverb: "*ti ogiri ko ba lanu alangba kole raye wobe*" (translation: it will not be possible for a lizard to crawl into a wall without a crack or hole in it). Fueled through a conscripted desire that is descriptive of the objectified penchant toward consumption of foreign "ideas" as the ideal, the prototype "civilized African" saturates the post-colonial ego with religious and cultural "produces" grown on soils of westernization as spoils of axial conquests. Collectively, these manners in the sufferings of African Traditional Religions metastasize into veritable denials of agency to Africans, the projection of a subordinated cultural status, and establishments of paternalistic relationships, with Euro-America sitting at the helms of the global serfdom.

Sources for African Traditional Religions

Post-modern ideations about text, textuality, and textualization limit westerners' understanding of literacy beyond their immediate epistemological and ideological borders. Hence, cultures where the people did not possess "a book" were immediately judged negatively. William Albert Graham assesses that "no orally communicated word carries the kind of legal, scholarly, or administrative authority for us that a written or printed document does."[18] Would this, therefore, indicate for Africa and Africans that the outright absence of "printed documents" equals the absence of documentation about religion and other social-cultural realities? Given the mode through which most people transmit memories about their culture's history, it would be an error to assume that the absence of written books or documents on religion, gender, and sexuality meant that these phenomena were not present or that their manifestations to indicate that the Western world bequeathed them to modern Africa.[19]

Sadly, in many contemporary African societies today, the inability of an individual to read and write in the English language works to the former's disadvantage. As a result of the limited understanding which the early westerners had when it came to the meanings and appurtenances of literacy and education among African peoples, the former was unable to "fully read" or "accurately interpret" many of the realities which they encountered among the indigenous peoples. Language gaps impeded smooth communication and furthered tensions between the invasive emissaries and local chiefs. Besides the foregoing, early European and American travelers on the continent arrived with a biased mind; the welcoming receptions that the local peoples accorded them became some of the worst mistakes of Africa's ancestors.[20] The African ancestors were punished with slavery and colonialism over their "crime" of believing in the Whiteness of "truth" that got housed in a book. Yet, displays of post-colonial frenzy among proselytized Africans hardly prevent them from consulting the religions of their ancestors during moments of crises.[21]

Sources of African Traditional Religion are the sites, sounds, and locations in which peoples of African descent visit to invoke autochthonous identity.[22] These sources could be spiritual or earthly, structured, or unstructured. Broadly speaking, sources for the study of African Traditional Religions are distinguishable into two aspects: non-physical sources and physical sources. Within the non-physical category are myths, language, legends, stories, liturgies, songs and hymns, pithy sayings, proverbs, riddles, idioms, adages, names, beliefs, customs, and systematic recitals; while the physical category include rites, rituals, ceremonies, sacred spaces, sacred symbols and objects, and music and dances. Strictly speaking, these classifications form useful lenses that facilitate, for scholars and activists alike, great insights about the African people, their socio-political worldviews, as well as the types of relationships that are culturally permissive or even condemned. Take the language as an example. Among Africans (Yorùbá, Igbo, and Azande), language is a very formidable window unto "seeing" and knowing gender portraitures and the imaginaries of sexualities within a specific socio-cultural milieu.[23] Therefore, just as the rich histories among the earliest ancestors of humankind wielded enormous human's truths about some of the oldest civilizations on earth, knowledge systems in Africa hold certain clues that can yield up for the searcher possibilities, presences, and prevalence of gender and sexuality themes to bring present societies out of the drama of discourse.

Origins of Gender and Sexuality

The sources for African Traditional Religions convey gender and sexuality relations. Ifi Amadiume chronicles two myths of the origins of gender found among the Nnobi and Nri peoples.[24] In both myths, assumptions about the sexuality of each character invariably generate gender roles in society. In nearly every instance of similar tales, narratology serves the same role as written would in text-based cultures. Absence, misplacement, or displacement of holy texts around the social and political landscapes, wherein meaning production occurs, does not impede the meaningfulness in relational transactions.

Conversely, apart from what evolution and religio-cultural myths teach and human biological compositions, no one really knew how human beings arrived here on earth. According to Donald E. Thomas, Jr., "one pair of inherited chromosomes, the sex chromosomes, determines whether we are born male or female."[25] Usually, at birth, a child gets one sex chromosome from the father and another (one) sex chromosome from the mother. "The X-chromosome is the female chromosome, and the Y-chromosome is the male chromosome."[26] This is the known science of biology, and this is what sex variation means. Of course, while there are circumstances in which the "normal" does apply, homosexual behaviors are not recent.[27] Those exceptions, rather than being the rule, are medically known as abnormalities.[28] In the United States, sex, gender, and sexual orientations are considered highly politicized.[29] The language which uses an individual's genitalia, chromosomes, and biological makeups to describe them refers to their sex. Viewed as human rights among Euro-Americans, debates on gender and sexuality (often pluralized) have significantly "progressed" among these westerners.[30] Gender and sexuality encounters among westerners reveal interesting dynamics with a growing array of choices: lesbian, gay, bisexual, transgender, pansexual, aromantic, asexual, non-binary gender or genderqueer, cisgender, and two-spirit.

Besides the fact that gender as an idea relates to the roles that society assigns to individuals, politics complicates this role assignment process in ways that reveal a normalization of oppressive regimes.[31] That politics, which begins at a specific point in time from the local domain, eventuates into a global phenomenon testifies to human creativity and ingenuity.[32] Scholars and activists invoke visual, legal, and psycho-emotional authorities as foolproof evidence to justify their positions. African scholars and activists are not staying off the ring as there are, more than ever, growing sexuality and gender battles drawn up along conservative and liberal perspectives. Africans who have attained "advanced" status in Euro-American indoctrinations tend to believe that traditional Africa is bogged down with myths and superstitions, implying that "progress" ought to be forward-looking. It seems to acquiesce with the idea that gender and sexuality are matters which society should have no say about; that determinations and judgments concerning gender and sexuality should be the prerogative of the individual. This individualistic interpretation stems from a post-modern, post-colonial, and post-scripture reading of human agency.

Nearly all traditional societies in Africa possess myths that help them navigate daily social and political existence when it comes to gender and sexuality issues. These are often contained alongside stories or origins of human beings. As a result, gender and sexuality myths in Africa correspond to the lived realities of the peoples. Hence, the expectation of outsiders that Africa needed to adjust its gender and sexual orientations to fit into the outside world is partly unrealistic and paternalistic; the idea that gender orientations outside of the "normal" were importations seems to perpetuate the subjugation and undermining of the sexual dexterities and innovations among African peoples. In his article "African Theology," John Mbiti criticizes those who give certain yardsticks of expectations for African theology. Writing, Mbiti says, "he does not accept this orientation to theology: it assumes that we theologize to make our theology heard by other people who will do something to us or about us. The motivation of such a theology is false and untrue to the real nature of theology."[33]

Mbiti's critique is valid and relevant toward certain positions of conservatives and liberals, who use western, textual-styled, cave paintings and/or certain cultural or military practices among some tribes (e.g., the Azande) as evidence that African culture endorses sexuality and gender forms outside of the male-female dichotomy.[34]

A Yorùbá traditionalist/Ifa Priest Dr. Ifabunmi O. Adewale, who doubles as Secretary of the International Congress of Orisa Tradition and Culture, and author of *Introduction to Ancient Yoruba Systems*, reveals that pre-contact Yorùbás were advanced in matters sexual and sensual.[35] Dr. Adewale notes that two Yorùbá religious groups that showcase sexuality and gender are Osun and Ogun worshippers. While Osun epitomizes sensuality, Ogun is sexual, Dr. Adewale points out. Idioms, proverbs, and pithy sayings are among these religious formations. Femininity is to Osun as masculinity is to Ogun; among the panegyrics of Osun are the following:

> *otoriileke oba waon ni orun toogun*
> *otoriide werewere bawon lowo gbogboro*[36]

In the above couplet, the praise song is delivered in honor of an Osun adherent, whose necklaces adorn her neck in a sensual manner. According to Dr.

Adewale, although Eweri moje was one among Ogun's many wives, there is no place in the *Ifa* corpus where homosexuality is mentioned, let alone endorsed. Also, it is true that beings in the spiritual world have capabilities to have sexual relations with women, particularly during the night, in their sleep; it is in the *ijaala*, a music of Ogun's cognomen, that sex, sexuality, and sexualization become most obvious. Mention is made of pubic region and the hairs therein (*irun obo to réwa titi*). Additionally, in praise of the virginal, Ogun followers would sing "*isale obo, ko somi lasaan lowo elepan l'oti se*" (a penis is responsible for a watery virginal). Dr. Adewale compares Ogun-Osun sexuality-sensuality to an opening scene in *Coming to America*, where naked women bathe for Hakeem the prince inside a swimming pool at the palace.[37] Similarly, says Dr. Adewale, "women bathe for Ogun, dry him up, and paste camwood all over his body (Osun's role), cook for him (*amala* and *gbegiri*) before he dances the baata."[38]

While the Osun and Ogun deploy lewd language in the expression of sensuality and sexuality, the Yorùbá people generally mention sexual points on the body with reservations. Secrecy surrounds issues of sex.[39] Careless or even causal jokes about it is regarded as indecent talk (*isokuso*).

A Few Remarks

In many contemporary African settings, denunciation and outright condemnation meet any expressions of sexuality that transgresses against the norm. What is commonly seen, known, and/or publicly considered sanctioned and thus accepted as an African consensus is that African Traditional Religion does not support sexual relationships besides the male-female binary.

While the position that those "who think that homosexuality was alien to Africa are not enlightened enough regarding Africa's history of sexuality" is partly accurate, at least when juxtaposed with the idea in Professor Ebun Oduwole's rendition of the *Òdù Otúrá Gorì-ìrete*, which implied that homosexuality was naturally "a threat to heterosexual marital institutions and procreation,"[40] inference could be drawn that the phenomenon existed. It might also be read as a "simultaneous affirmation of difference as a dimension of power and resistance."[41] Yet, the locus of the African peoples' moral standing on issues of religion, gender, and sexuality does not have to come from a western understanding of social and political culture or their foundational epistemologies of textualization.

Notes

1. Charles Kimberlin Brain, *The Hunters or the Hunted?: An Introduction to African Cave Taphonomy* (University Of Chicago Press, 1983), 50.
2. Clifford Geertz, "Ethos, World-View, and the Analysis of Sacred Symbols." In *The Antioch Review*, vol. 74, no. 3, 2016, 622–637; Clifford Geertz, *The Interpretation of Cultures: Selected Essays* (Basic Books, 1973).

3. See also *UNESCO Region: Fossil Hominid Sites of Sterkfontein, Swartkrans, Kromdraai, and Environs*, https://whc.unesco.org/uploads/nominations/915bis.pdf, 99.
4. Josiah Clark Nott and George R. Gliddon, *Types of Mankind* (London, Philadelphia, 1854).
5. The challenge I propose here is that Africans "re-read" the terms of reference for the world religions, especially Christianity and Islam: whence and how they originated. Knowing that the average individual, being "normal," and in the daily race for survival, spends little to no time investigating intangible subjects or investing resources in philosophical exercises.
6. Bénézet Bujo, *Foundations of an African Ethic: Beyond the Universal Claims of Western Morality* (Nairobi: Paulines Publications, 2003); Valentin Dedji, "The Ethical Redemption of African Imaginaire: Kä Mana's Theology of Reconstruction." In *Journal of Religion in Africa*, vol. 31 no. 3 (2001): 254–274.
7. Michael Y. Nabofa, "Blood Symbolism in African Religion." In *Religious Studies*, vol. 21, no. 3 (September 1985), 389.
8. Ibid.
9. John S. Mbiti, *African Religions and Philosophy* (London: Heinemann, 1969); John S. Mbiti, *Concepts of God in Africa* (London: S.P.C.K., 1970).
10. Jean Buxton, "African Traditional Religion and Concepts of God in Africa, by John S. Mbiti: A Review." In *Man*, New Series, vol. 5, no. 4 (December 1970), 721–722, Royal Anthropological Institute of Great Britain and Ireland: http://www.jstor.org/stable/2799144 (accessed: August 05, 2016).
11. Edward Evan Evans-Pritchard, "Review of 'African Religions and Philosophy' by John S. Mbiti." In *Journal of Religion in Africa*, vol. 2, Fasc. 2 (1969), 214–215.
12. Jacob K. Olupona, "A Tribute to Mwalimu John Mbiti, Patriarch of African Philosophy and Religion Studies." In *Religion News Service*, October 31, 2019, https://religionnews.com/2019/10/31/a-tribute-to-mwalimu-john-mbiti-patriarch-of-african-philosophy-and-religion-studies (accessed May 17, 2020).
13. O. Oko Elechi, *Doing Justice Without the State: The Afikpo (Ehugbo) Nigeria Model* (Taylor & Francis, 2006), 98. See also Alexander Ives Bortolot, "Ways of Recording African History." In *Heilbrunn Timeline of Art History*. New York: The Metropolitan Museum of Art, 2000–. http://www.metmuseum.org/toah/hd/ahis/hd_ahis.htm (October 2003); Ralph A. Austen, ed., *In Search of Sunjata: The Mande Oral Epic as History, Literature, and Performance* (Bloomington: Indiana University Press, 1999); Mary Nooter Roberts and Allen F. Roberts, eds., *Memory: Luba Art and the Making of History*, Exhibition Catalogue (New York: Museum for African Art, 1996). Jan Vansina, *The Children of Woot: A History of the Kuba Peoples* (Madison: University of Wisconsin Press, 1978); Kwame Anthony Appiah, *In My Father's House: Africa in the Philosophy of Culture* (1st paperback edition 1993. ed.) (New York: Oxford University Press, 1993).
14. Jawanza E. Clark, *Indigenous Black Theology: Toward an African-Centered Theology of the African American Religious Experience* (New York: Palgrave Macmillan, 2012), 1.
15. Victor Witter Turner, *The Ritual Process: Structure and Anti-Structure* (Symbol, Myth, and Ritual Series) (New York: Cornell University Press, 1977).

16. Gayatri C. Spivak, "Can the Subaltern Speak?" In *Marxism and the Interpretation of Culture*, edited by Cary Nelson and Lawrence Grossberg (London: Macmillan, 1988), 24; Gayatri C. Spivak, *Can the Subaltern Speak?* (Basingstoke: Macmillan, 1988).
17. Olupona, "A Tribute to Mwalimu John Mbiti."
18. William Albert Graham, *Beyond the Written Word: Oral Aspects of Scripture in the History of Religion* (Cambridge: Cambridge University Press, 1988), 9.
19. Michael Tosin Gbogi, "Contesting Meanings in the Postmodern Age: The Example of Nigerian Hip Hop Music." In *Matatu* 48 (2016), 353.
20. Vincent L. Wimbush, *The Bible and African Americans: A Brief History* (Minneapolis: Fortress Press, 2003). For some frightening futuristic descriptions, see also Diedrich Westermann, *The African To-Day and To-Morrow* (London: The International African Institute by the Oxford University Press, 1949).
21. Hance A. O. Mwakabana, ed., *Crises of Life in African Religion ad Christianity* (Switzerland: The Lutheran World Federation, 2002), https://www.lutheran-world.org/sites/default/files/DTS-Studies_Crises_of_Life-200202.pdf (accessed May 18, 2020).
22. Molefi K. Asante and Abu S. Abarry, *African Intellectual Heritage: A Book of Sources* (Philadelphia: Temple University Press, 1996); Donald B. Redford, *The Oxford Encyclopedia of Ancient Egypt* (New York: Oxford University Press, 2001).
23. Ibid.
24. Ifi Amadiume, *Male Daughters, Female Husbands: Gender and Sex in an African Society* (London: Zed Books, 2015), 28–29.
25. Donald E. Thomas, Jr., *The Lupus Encyclopedia: A Comprehensive Guide for Patients and Families* (Baltimore: Johns Hopkins University Press, 2014), 49.
26. Ibid, Thomas, Jr., *The Lupus Encyclopedia*, 49.
27. Richard Krafft-Ebing, *Psychopathia Sexualis*, With Especial Reference to Contrary Sexual Instinct: a Medico-Legal Study, translated by Charles G. Chaddock (Philadelphia: F.A. Davis Co., 1893); Anna K. Schaffner, *Modernism and Perversion: Sexual Deviance in Sexology and Literature, 1850–1930* (Basingstoke: Palgrave Macmillan, 2012), 69; Louis-Georges Tin, *The Invention of Heterosexual Culture* (Cambridge: MIT Press., 2012); Karen E. Lovaas and Mercilee M. Jenkins, *Sexualities and Communication in Everyday Life: A Reader* (Thousand Oaks: SAGE Publications, 2007).
28. David Sue, Derald Sue, Diane Sue, and Stanley Sue, *Understanding Abnormal Behavior*, 10th Edition (Belmont: Wadsworth/Cengage Learning, 2013); Anders Agmo, *Functional and Dysfunctional Sexual Behavior: A Synthesis of Neuroscience and Comparative Psychology* (Ann Arbor: ProQuest, 2011); Ronald J. Comer, *Abnormal Psychology* (New York: Worth, 2010).
29. Strong Medicine, "The Diversity of Sex, Gender, and Sexual Orientation." In *YouTube*, October 23, 2017, https://www.youtube.com/watch?v=2yM_P6WdRJU (accessed May 18, 2020).
30. Katy Steinmetz, "Beyond 'He' or 'She': The Changing Meaning of Gender and Sexuality." In *Time*, March 16, 2017, https://time.com/magazine/us/4703292/march-27th-2017-vol-189-no-11-u-s/ (accessed May 15, 2020); "Sexual Orientation and Gender Identity Definitions." In *Human Rights Campaign*, https://www.hrc.org/resources/sexual-orientation-and-gender-identity-terminology-and-definitions (accessed May 8, 2020).

31. Taiwo Oloruntoba-Oju, "A Name My Mother Did Not Call Me: Queer Contestations in African Sexualities," 3. Unpublished paper.
32. Mircea Eliade, *A History of Religious Ideas, 1, from the Stone Age to the Eleusinian Mysteries* (University of Chicago Press, 1978); see also Robert N. Bellah and Hans Joas, *The Axial Age and Its Consequences* (Cambridge: Belknap Press of Harvard University Press, 2012); Shmuel N. Eisenstadt, *Jewish Civilization: The Jewish Historical Experience in a Comparative Perspective* (Albany: State University of New York Press, 1992); Jóhann P. Árnason, Shmuel N. Eisenstadt, and Björn Wittrock, *Axial Civilizations and World History* (Leiden: Brill, 2005); Peter Spry-Leverton and Michael Wood, *Legacy: The Origins of Civilization* (Silver Spring: Athena, 2010); Iain W. Provan, *Convenient Myths: The Axial Age, Dark Green Religion, and the World That Never Was* (Waco: Baylor University Press, 2013); Christopher Peet, *Practicing Transcendence: Axial Age Spiritualities for a World in Crisis* (Cham: Palgrave Macmillan, 2019); Benjamen Franklen Gussen, *Axial Shift: City Subsidiarity and the World System in the Twenty-first Century* (Singapore: Palgrave Macmillan, 2019).
33. John S. Mbiti, "African Theology." In *Worldview*, vol. 16, no. 8, (August 1973), 37.
34. E. E. Evans-Pritchard, "Sexual Inversion among the Azande." In *American Anthropologist*, vol. 72, no. 6, 1970, 1428–1434.
35. Ifabunmi Adewale, *Introduction to Ancient Yoruba Systems* (North Carolina: 2017); "Interview," May 13, 2020.
36. Ibid.
37. Eddie Murphy and Nile Rodgers. *Coming to America* (Miami: CPP/Belwin, 1988).
38. Adewale, "Interview." See also Paul Marshall, *Praisesong for the Widow* (New York: G.P. Putnam's Sons, 1996); Robin Brooks, "Manifestations of Ogun Symbolism in Paule Marshall's Praisesong for the Widow." In *Journal of Africana Religions*, vol. 2 no. 2 (2014), 166–183.
39. Chief Oludare Olajubu, "References to Sex in Yoruba Oral Literature." In *The Journal of American Folklore*, (April–June), vol. 85, no. 336, (1972), 152–166, http://www.jstor.org/stable/539246 (accessed May 19, 2020);
40. Babajide Olugbenga Dasaolu, "On Efficient Causation for Homosexual Behaviours among Traditional Africans: An Exploration of the Traditional Yoruba Model." In *Bangladesh Journal of Bioethics*, vol. 9 no. 2 (2018), 35.
41. George J. Sefa Dei, "Local Cultural Resource Knowledge: Identity, Representation, Schooling, and Education." In *Ethnic and Cultural Dimensions of Knowledge*, edited by Peter Meusburger, Tim Freytag, and Laura Suarsana (New York: Springer, 2016), 122.

CHAPTER 25

African Traditional Religion, Conflict Resolution, and Peaceful Societal Co-existence

Noah Yusuf and Raji Shittu

INTRODUCTION

Virtually all human societies are characterized by varying forms of conflict ranging from intra- and inter-group conflict, religious, ethnic, and political conflicts along with disputes generated by prevailing climatic and social realities.[1] The significant sources of conflict in Africa revolve around stiff competition over land, chieftaincy tussle, and discord in personal relationships, disagreements over the inheritance of family property, murder, and matrimonial fallouts, among others. Empirical pieces of evidence have shown that most of the sustained conflicts in Africa are products of the failure of the foreign-imposed legal systems, which revolves around litigation to resolve such conflicts.[2] As argued in the Institute of Chartered Mediators and Conciliators Training Manual, the search for solace within litigation is often disappointing not because the court is indifferent to the problems presented but because the interpretive outcome of such court judgments are often adversarial rather than retributive while such outcome does not optimally promote interpersonal post-litigation friendship but enmity.[3] Such a formal adjudicative judicial process is also overloaded and overburdened with case hangovers because of the delay in the dispensation of justice.

Litigation is also very formal with difficult and technical comprehension challenges for most uneducated Africans to understand and interpret. Due to the above disadvantages inherent in litigation, many conflicts in Africa are now

N. Yusuf (✉) • R. Shittu
University of Ilorin, Ilorin, Nigeria

© The Author(s), under exclusive license to Springer Nature Switzerland AG 2022
I. S. Aderibigbe, T. Falola (eds.), *The Palgrave Handbook of African Traditional Religion*, https://doi.org/10.1007/978-3-030-89500-6_25

being resolved using traditional African mechanisms of conflict prevention, management, and resolution, which started in the pre-colonial days. The traditional method of conflict resolution has mostly been documented to be effective, less costly, mutually benefitting, empathic, and respected, while the decisions emanating from the traditional method revolves around the consensus approach of a "give" and "take" resolution outcome that is rooted in accommodation.[4] The traditional method of conflict resolution is willingly binding on all parties not because the parties are being forced to obey the judgment outcome but mainly because the identity and survival of such individual are linked to the survival of his or her traditional social variables, including their family, community elders, traditional leaders, and traditional religions as credible agents of resolving conflicts for peaceful societal co-existence. Thus, those who resolve their conflicts through the traditional methods have confidence in the process, and the actors, including the elders, chiefs, and religious priests are ready to submit themselves to the judgment of the above constituted authorities.[5]

Also, in resolving disputes through the traditional African methods of conflict management, the principles of equity and social justice, which is primarily entrenched in African customs and traditions, are upheld as the main factor responsible for the peaceful social organizations established by the earlier African political and traditional leaders before colonialism while different traditional conflict resolution methods exist with variation across African cultures.[6]

In Africa, some religions, especially Islam, Christianity, and African Traditional Religion, are very central to peace, security, and spiritual advancement of the people as the adoption and application of their doctrinal tenets uphold social justice and unite the people for the development of different segments of the society.[7] Religion teaches people to live in harmony with their fellow human beings and to evade greed and corruption. It is also a fundamental pillar for good governance, fairness, justice, and equity in order to promote and sustain peace and security as political leaders are asked to swear by their religious scriptures before assuming offices with the promises of governing with the fear of God while also promoting fairness and equity to all.

Religion, by nature, detests violence, cheating, and acquisition of wealth through illegal and ungodly means, which promotes conflictive existence. As a matter of fact, religion is the very foundation of societal morality and sustainable peace. Religion regulates the conduct and behavior of people in society and preaches vital virtues needed in sustaining a nation towards peaceful co-existence. Religious sermons are preached in churches and mosques with specific reference to citations from the Bible and Qur'an to modify the behavior of the people positively to bring about peace and security in society. The missionaries who brought Christian religion to Africa and Nigeria, in particular, made Religious Education and Moral Education compulsory to all students, and this helped to reduce social vices and crime rates, most especially in the 1950s and 1960s, thus promoting peaceful societal co-existence. However, immediately after the Government took over mission schools in the mid-1970s, moral decadence such as stealing, prostitution, financial crimes, which undermined peace and security, became very pronounced in Nigeria.[8]

While Christianity and Islam have dominated the doctrinal religious space with many African adherents, African Traditional Religion still permeate most societal activities. It is difficult to divorce major spheres of life, especially politics and dispute resolutions, from religion. For example, a ruler in traditional African society is both the political ruler of his community and the Chief Priest.[9] This phenomenon is particularly noticeable among the Yorùbá community, where the *Oba* (King) is referred to as *Igba Keji Orisa* (*Eledumare*) (Next in rank to the Supreme Being) and he is also regarded as *Olori Awon Awoo* (a leader among the priests).[10] Apart from resolving disputes among adherents, the African Traditional Religion promotes security and good governance by not condoling stealing, injustice, immorality, and dishonesty amongst political leaders. In traditional Yorùbá society, there is the concept of *agogo eewo* (the forbidden gong). When sounded, criminals, evil-doers, adulterers, lawbreakers, and robbers shivered with terror because they expect to die soon.[11]

In pre-colonial African societies, crime was considered harmful to the gods. This collective consciousness was enshrined in the traditional doctrinal laws of public and private crimes. Such transgressions, which were tried by the gods, included certain forms of abuse, incest, witchcraft, and treason while the traditional religious Judicial Council, which is comprised of a council of religious interpreters, interprets the god's decisions on the cases that are referred to them. There is equally the invocation of supernatural forces to expose all forms of criminality with dire consequences of disgraceful death from such gods, including a heavenly strike from the god of thunder. Olaoba Olufemi has shown clearly that oath-taking, which was one of the extra-judicial doctrinal methods, usually assisted the judge or adjudicators in locating the guilty parties in cases referred to them.[12]

This chapter examines the contributions of the traditional African religions to conflict resolution in Africa and its effects on peaceful societal co-existence. The objectives of this study, which relied on secondary data, were to investigate the critical features of conflict resolution mechanisms in African Traditional Religion and examine the methods of conflict resolutions in selected African traditional religions from the Yorùbá, Ibo, and Tiv traditions, which have a rich traditional religious culture of conflict resolution. This chapter also discusses the effects of traditional religious conflict resolution mechanisms on peaceful societal co-existence.

Conceptual Issues

Conflict takes various forms and dimensions in African societies. It is significant to note that conflict is difficult to define from the perspective of the African people. It seems to be part of the excitement for networking relationships, whether negative or positive. Consequently, conflicts are in the magnitude of rages, rifts, misunderstandings, family and market brawls, skirmishes and wars, public insurrections, and assaults. It also includes chieftaincy and boundary disputes. These storms of conflicts are widespread in Africa.[13] Conflict, as an element of social interaction, has been defined in various dimensions. Some writers note that a conflict situation emerges when two or more parties cannot agree on an issue. The parties to such conflict may not necessarily be the government or nation-states. In an incompatible stage among nation-states, every party involved seeks to achieve specific objectives, such as additional or more secure territories, security, and access to markets, prestige, alliances, and the overthrow of an unfriendly government.[14] The study of conflict in Africa has not always been mindful of the need to consider the interaction of local and international factors in the evolution of conflicts between African nations. African conflicts are not susceptible to prediction, although it can be explained. Overt manifestations of conflict are seldom unremitting, even in relationships between rival cultures.[15] Conflict is a particular relationship between states or rival factions within a state, which implies subjective hostilities or tension manifested in subversive economic or military hostilities.[16] Conflict can be described as a condition in which an identifiable group of human beings, whether tribal, ethnic, linguistic, religious, socio-political, economic, cultural or otherwise, are in conscious opposition to one or more other identifiable human groups because these groups are pursuing what may be incompatible goals.[17] More importantly, conflict arises from the interaction of individuals who have partially incompatible ends. The ability of one actor to gain his end depends, to a significant degree, on the choice or decision that the other party will make. Conflict could be violent, uncontrollable, dominant or recessive, resolvable or insolvable under various sets of circumstances.[18] Conflict is said to be inevitable in human beings' social relationships wherever crucial resources are in contention.

Isaac Olawale Albert has argued that there is nothing wrong with conflict; it is a critical mechanism by which the goals and aspirations of individuals and groups are articulated.[19] It is a channel for a definition of creative solutions to human problems, and a means to develop a collective identity. The repercussion of conflicts between person-to-person, group-to-group, community-to-community, state-to-state, or nation-to-nation rarely ceases with the termination of overt hostilities. However, conflict can solve contentious issues between nations, or it can further exacerbate them. In any case, the consequences of conflicts are usually felt for some time after a war ends.[20] Wadama Wadinga described African conflicts as a phenomenon that is frequently brushed and dismissed as being chaotic or worthy of some vague pity or humanitarian concern, but rarely of any in-depth political analysis. Wadinga added that the divide and rule policies of colonial administrators assured the docility of different ethnic groups, and this shielded them from the menace of insurrection.[21]

Review of Relevant Literature

Essentially, conflict resolution in traditional African societies provides an opportunity to interact with the parties concerned while promoting consensus-building, social bridge reconstructions, and enactment of order in society[22] The most typical methods for this purpose include, among others, the use of the council of elders, kings' courts, and open market assembly. Other traditional conflict resolution techniques include mediation, adjudication, reconciliation, negotiation, and cross-examination. Rather than offering ineffective resolutions such as those achieved in litigation settlements in a court of law, these traditional techniques provide superb support for peaceful co-existence and harmonious relationships during post-conflict.

As discussed by Adelodun Ibrahim in the traditional African society, conflict may generally exist whenever or wherever incompatible events occur and may result in a win-lose outcome.[23] The resolution, transformation, and management of conflict may, however, produce a win-win situation too. Truth is a covenant logo that disputants or parties in conflict must not miss. In contemporary African society, nobody cares about the truth. If Africans have to put the falling apart together, their original values must be revisited. Conflict is as natural as the concept of peace contrary to the global or universal conception. Africans have particular ways of conceptualizing conflict. Traditional definitions of "conflict" regard it as a struggle over values and claims to scarce status, power, and resources in which the opponents aim to neutralize, injure or eliminate their rivals[24]. However, conflict may generally exist wherever or whenever incompatible activities occur and may result in a win-lose outcome. The resolution, transformation, and management of conflict may also produce a win-win situation.[25]

It is important to emphasize that conflict management in general and conflict resolution, in particular, are almost entirely determined by our understanding of the composition of a conflict and not only by symptoms.[26] In some African societies, indigenous law is derived essentially from customs and traditions. Unlike some Western societies, literacy was not strictly defined by knowledge of written word but included verbal art and remembrance. While the Yorùbá's legal traditions were typically undocumented, these traditions were preserved and survived due to continuous performance.

The traditional society presented an atmosphere conducive for enduring performance.[27] As posited by the author, the Yorùbá people derived their sources of adjudication from the wisdom and traditional knowledge of their forebears, which were always dramatized. Olaoba confirmed that the elders sit under a tree and talk until they agree; the elders (old age or seniority) are considered as the force behind order and decorum in traditional society.[28] This indicates that elders, within the Yorùbá culture, are the powerhouse of wisdom and knowledge. Cases of fighting among adolescents or young people were in the past accorded an impromptu settlement by the passers-by who normally ensured restoration of peace and harmony.[29]

There existed various community associations and guilds saddled with the responsibility of maintenance of peace and order in marketing operations, including stealing, debt, and fraud. In certain circumstances, gods and ancestors (the living dead) are called upon, their spirit invoked, and everyone, especially the disputants, are reminded of the aftermath of their wrath if they refuse to tell the truth. In the markets and the palace (court), a spirit is present. The spirit could be malevolent or benevolent.[30] In Africa, there were levels or phases of conflict resolution; there were dispute resolutions at the inter-personal or family level, the extended family level, and village or town level (chief in council). These tiers represent the political units making up the community. The smallest unit called *Idile* (nuclear family) is headed by a Baale. The next unit is the *Ebi* (extended family headed by Mogaji), the most influential or usually the eldest person in the Ebi. The extended family includes all people who have blood ties. The last tier of the units is the quarter, which comprises several family compounds headed by a Baale (the chief-of-ward/quarter) while the head of the household includes the man's immediate family of wife or wives and children[31] cases resolved by Baale include conflicts among co-wives, brothers and sisters, truants, and street fights involving his children and his foster children or dependents. Conflicts solved immediately include minor issues, such as scolding the troublemakers and appeasing whoever was offended. The Baale is required to visit the offended person, even to thank him/her for accepting a peaceful resolution of the conflict. It is the duty of Baale to call together his household and warn them to desist from making any more trouble.[32]

The court imposed no fine. However, appeals could be made from one court to the second court, which is the court of the ward-chief (*Ile-ejo ijoye Adugbo*). This court tried civil cases. It could not try the criminal cases, but it had the authority to conduct a preliminary investigation into criminal cases before transferring them to the king's court (*Ile-ejo Oba*).[33] Baale (chiefs) also controls the relationship between members of his family and outsiders. Such cases can threaten the survival of the entire lineage or ward. Once the matter is resolved, the emphasis is placed on how good neighbourliness can be achieved and preserved. Land disputes, lack of good care for women and children by the husband, infidelity by the women, and disputes over inheritance are the commonest in this category.[34]

However, dispute resolutions by the Chief-in-Council (*Igbimo Ilu*) in Yorùbáland were the highest traditional institution. In the pre-colonial era, the Council had the power to pass a death sentence on any offender brought before it. The Court of the King was the highest court. It was also the last court to which appeals could be made, but among Egba and Ijebu, however, the Ogboni court seemed to be the last court of appeal.[35] A woman is traditionally expected to be on her knees and to offer the traditional greetings unless the chief instructs her to stand up. A man has to start by prostrating, which is a way of offering a traditional greeting. Whatever judgment is given is accepted. In the traditional judiciary system in Yorùbáland, fines of damages are not usually awarded by the mediators in civil cases. The utmost aim is to restore peace by settling disputes amicably. As such, restoration of harmony is what is paramount in the traditional judicial system. Sometimes, however, mediators award simple fines as a deterrent to the occurrence of particular anti-social behavior. This may be demanded in the form of kola nuts or local gins, both of which have ritual significance. Some of the kola nuts are broken and passed around for everyone to eat to celebrate the resolution of the conflict. The drink is also passed around for all to taste. If no gin or palm wine is available, ordinary drinking water can be used. In some traditional settings, the palm wine or gin is used to pour libation to the gods and ancestors of the people involved in the dispute. These actions help to reinforce the terms of reconciliation.[36]

Chibuzor identified the methods of conflict resolution in the traditional African societies as follows: mediation, adjudication, reconciliation, arbitration and negotiation, and employing extra-judicial devices and usage of legal maxims to persuade or convince the disputants about the implication or otherwise of their behavior.[37] These methods have been effective in traditional African society. Mediation is an old method of conflict management surrounded by secrecy. It involves the non-coercive intervention of the mediators(s), called third-party either to reduce or go beyond or bring the conflict to a peaceful settlement. Olaoba (2002) described mediation as a method of conflict resolution that had been so critical to traditional society. The mediators usually endeavoured that peace and harmony reigned supreme in the society at whatever level of mediation. This is also usually couched with the dictum of "no victor no vanquished," as buttressed by the maxim,[38] *Bia ba be'eran wi K'a si tun beran wi*. If we apportion blame to the guilty person, we must do the same to the other party in a conflict. Mediators are sought from within the communities or societies of the parties concerned. Due to their cumulative experiences and wisdom, elders are regarded as trustworthy advisors all over Africa. Their roles depend on traditions, circumstances, and personalities accordingly.[39]

These roles include pressurizing, making recommendations, giving assessments, conveying suggestions on behalf of the parties, emphasizing relevant norms and rules, envisaging the situation if an agreement is not reached, or repeating the agreement already attained.[40] In traditional African society also, adjudication involves bringing all disputants in the conflict to a meeting, usually in the chambers or compounds of family heads, quarter heads, and palace court as the case may be. The dialogue was linked with the adjudicatory processes in traditional African societies.[41] Reconciliation was the most significant aspect of conflict resolution. It is the end product of adjudication. After the disputants have been persuaded to end their dispute, peace was restored. This restoration of peace and harmony has always been anchored on the principle of "give a little and get a little," an indication for the disputing parties to give concessions. A feast was usually organized to confirm the readiness of the conflicting parties towards reaching points of compromise.[42] As a characteristic of traditional African society, the conflict resolution method uses arbitration. Authority figures are the ones allowed to practice the reconciliation function and form binding judgments when they are mediating between opposing parties; however, the aim is not to simply render a judgment, but to bring about reconciliation between the two parties.

The relationship between the authoritative figures and the community is cushioned by community representatives who advise them.[43] The secret of negotiation is to harmonize the interests of the parties involved. Thus, even when the conflict involves a member against his or her society, there is an emphasis on recuperation and re-insertion of errant members back into their place in society. The recovery of a dissident member can just as well be seen as the restoration of the harmony and integrity of the community, the assertion of value consensus, and social cohesion so that the management of the conflict favours the concerns of both parties.[44] In traditional Yorùbá society, peace was negotiated. An apology for wrongs done to individuals and the entire community was a feature of negotiation. Such apology was channeled through the Yorùbá elders, compound heads, and chiefs of high caliber in society. It was done on the representative level or through quasi-representation. The *Babaogun* (patron) played the role of a representative in the sense of conflict resolution.[45] Conflict resolution provides an opportunity to interact with the parties concerned, with the hope of at least reducing the scope, intensity, and effects of their disputes. During formal and informal meetings, conflict resolution exercises permit a reassessment of views and claims as a basis for finding options to crisis and divergent points of view. Those who organize conflict resolution exercises or meetings usually constitute a third party in a triangular arrangement and consist of traditional rulers, such as kings and chiefs. Conflict resolution in plural societies can be quite complex, principally because of the determinate effects of culture and language symbolism.[46]

According to Kevin Avruch and Peter Black, "it is quite dangerous to relegate culture to the background in conflict resolution."[47] Although culture is a marker of social differences, it should be regarded as an obstacle to conflict resolution in multi-ethnic/multi-cultural societies. Cross-examination is an important mechanism employed in the process of conflict resolution in traditional African society. It was a means of weighting evidence through cross-checking, and corroborating the facts of the conflict.[48] In the Yorùbá maxim, a good sense of justice is associated with cross-examination, which is expressed as follows: *Agbejo enikan da, agba osika* (wicked and iniquitous is he whose judgment is based on the evidence of one party to a case). Consequently, in traditional African societies, particularly Yorùbáland, in conflict resolution, undue favour toward the disputants was discouraged. The extra-judicial methods took the form of ordeals and the invocation of supernatural forces to expose all sides of the conflict. Olaoba has shown clearly that oath-taking, which was one of the extra-judicial methods, usually assisted the judge or adjudicators in locating areas of weaknesses in the conflict. Aside from the iron object (sacred to the god of iron) used for oath-taking, the Yorùbá people also use an *apasa* (weaving instrument), *iru* (chiefly scepter), royal shrine, or religious sanctuaries. The wrath of the gods is used for eliciting facts of the dispute. Such gods as *Sango* (god of Thunder), *Yemoja* (goddess of the river), and *Ayelala* (guardian of social morality) are used to ascertain the veracity of the story told by disputants.[49]

Adeloju discusses the level of interaction and inter-religious harmony between the Christians, Muslims, and African Traditional Religions, describing them as being very cordial during their early years.[50] As noted by the author, the African religion exhibited a high degree of accommodation and hospitality to the adherents of other religions. This assertion is justified by the tolerance of the Aerialists society to the Christian and Muslim missionaries despite the intimidation manifested in the missionaries' disdain for rejection of virtually anything associated with African religions.

Adigun finds mutual relationship and cooperation between the Muslims and Christians than their bilateral relationship with the traditional African worshippers, especially in the South-Western part of Nigeria.[51] Some of the harmonious relationships are noticeable in the area of social celebrations as religious differences are often put aside by both adherents when it comes to celebrations like naming ceremonies, house-dedications, marriages, funerals, and burial rites whereas both Christians and Muslims dine together and exchange gifts and pleasantries despite their diverse religious affiliations. Christians and Muslims also enjoy mutual tolerance and co-operation in business transactions where both adherents freely patronize each other. The author notes further that there is tolerance and expression of inter-religious harmony during the observation of major Christian and Muslim religious festivals as families, friends, and neighbors of the two religious affiliations celebrate with one another. In some families, both the Christmas and Ramadan festivals often serve as avenues for a family reunion irrespective of their religious differences, while inter-religious marriages between Christians and Muslims are common, especially in South-Western Nigeria, thus extending the bond of cordiality among the adherents of the two religions. Despite their cordiality in Nigeria, which has largely promoted inter-religious harmony, the two religions are intolerant in the area of doctrinal understanding as the adherents of both religions often provoke one another by openly condemning each other's religious beliefs and practices, especially in sermons, thus, leading to inter-religious disharmony in many instances. The review of relevant literature herein finds that there are advantages of the traditional methods of conflict resolution in Africa, which include accommodating, pleading, compromise and collaboration, soft bargaining, and restorative justice, which mends rather than destroys cordial relationships.

Theoretical Framework

This study relies on the Conflict Transformation Theory as its basis for explanation. As posited by Morgan, the conflict transformation model represents the transformation of conflict issues from confrontation to collaboration by first transforming human thoughts and mindsets towards greater positive understanding, especially amongst the warring parties[52] Such a transformational strategy is also tilted towards building the culture of permanent peace in the minds of the conflicting parties. The conflict transformation state is thus a process of changing incompatibility to compatibility, hatred to love, disharmony to harmony, amongst others. There are about five stages of conflict transformation processes to achieve peace.[53] These are actor, issue, institutional, legal, and structural transformation stages. The transformation strategy for conflict actors focuses on the positive changes in the behaviour and the attitude of such actors in order to drop their confrontational attitudes for collaboration to bring about peace in a troubled community. Issue transformation processes focus on transforming conflict issues from their point of disagreement to compromise by changing their hard-line positions on conflict issues and interest for softer and consensus bargaining processes.

The institutional transformational stage of conflict represents a positive alteration of the performances of social, institutional structures that provides services to the public from their previous poor performance ratings for better and optimal performance. The legal transformation process refers to rules transformation, which removes the obnoxious laws that made people rebel. The structural transformation of conflict represents a credible transformation of each of the transformational stages but with a special interest in their inter-stage collaboration for effective conflict transformation owing to the observation that conflict might not be adequately mitigated even where a particular stage had been successfully transformed while neglecting other stages. The conflict transformation theory is very relevant to this study because the essence of the traditional African methods of conflict resolution revolves around collaboration, a consensus approach to peace-building, and plea bargaining, leading to restorative justice and peaceful co-existence in society.

Features of Conflict Resolution Mechanisms in African Traditional Religion

A typical African religious conflict resolution mechanism is typically distinguished with the principles of equity and justice, and is customs ingrained in the fiber of African customs and traditions. Thus, while the Western countries relied on the police to detect crime through torture during the pre-colonial period, several African societies relied on oath-taking and divination to curtail crime.

The core platforms and key features of conflict resolution mechanisms in African traditional religions include a religious shrine, oath-taking, religious festivals, truthfulness, and sanction. The shrine is the center of reconciliation, mediation, and appeasement of African traditional religion, while simultaneously providing a medium of arbitration. When a person threatens the life of his neighbour or has injured him, the two are brought to the shrine, where conciliation is carried out within the confines of restorative justice, and the wounded party is treated with medicines at the shrine.

The masquerade also constitutes a reconciliation platform between the disputing parties because whatever is his pronouncement, it is considered to have come from the heavenly god since the masquerade himself is considered as traditional indigenes of the world beyond. The intervention of the masquerades aids villages in regulating their concerns because they are also involved in cases relating to spiritual matters, such as witchcraft and poisoning. Oath-taking is another central character of conflict resolution through the traditional African religion to establish the truth and discourage dishonest attitudes and evil actions. Additionally, African traditional religious societies commonly prevented, managed, and resolved conflict through oath-taking, mostly at the shrine of a powerful deity, over an instrument that acted as a medium for contacting the deity. Moreover, to avoid shame or even death, the repercussions of taking on oath on fabrications was widely taught and known. The celebration of religious festivals serves to foster peace, solidarity, harmonious living, and respect for others among the people. The festivals usually involve rituals and sacrifices offered to the deities and ancestors for peace and security. Reciprocity equally fostered peaceful co-existence and, consequently, eliminated the likelihood of conflict and wars.[54] Sanctions and punishments are also a critical feature of African traditional religion towards conflict resolution: Erring individuals and families who contravened religious tenets and traditions are sanctioned with appropriate punishments. This measure was meant to prevent all antisocial misconducts such as stealing, willful murder, incest, abuse of elders, willful damage to property, lying, bearing false witness, poisoning, and rape. It was also largely believed that deities could inflict sanctions through accidents, sickness, death, famine, poverty, misery, barrenness, and loss of children, in addition to societal exile, ostracism, fines, compensation, restitution, and the rendering of an apology.[55] The mediator, arbitrator, and judge must also be truthful before the god, while the presence of the ancestral forces may coerce or force the offenders to tell the truth.

METHODS OF CONFLICT RESOLUTION IN SELECTED AFRICAN TRADITIONAL RELIGIONS

The methods of conflict resolution in African traditional religions are very rich and effective. Some examples are provided through the instrumentality of the Yorùbá, Ibo, and the Tiv traditional religions in Nigeria. Among the Yorùbá peoples, who live in the South-Western part of Nigeria, indigenous religious law derives essentially from customs and traditions. Although the religious dogmas of the Yorùbá are largely unwritten, their preservation and survival were done through practical applications to make them relevant and easily understood. Thus, the Yorùbá people derived their sources of adjudication from the wisdom and traditional knowledge of the forebears. In certain circumstances, including the exposure of the criminals, gods, and ancestors (the living dead) are called upon, their spirit invoked, and everyone, especially the disputants, is reminded of the aftermath of their wrath if they refuse to tell the truth. As mentioned earlier, in the markets and the palace (court), a spirit is present, and such spirit could be malevolent or benevolent.[56] Occassionally, mediators distribute small fines in the hopes that this would dissuade specific anti-social behavior as demanded by the gods.

Next to be discussed is the Igbo traditional society. Apart from the iron object (sacred to the god of iron) used for oath-taking, the Yorùbá people also use *apasa* (weaving instrument), *iru* (chiefly scepter), royal shrine, or religious sanctuaries to seal the judgment as pronounced by the gods. The wrath of the gods is used for eliciting facts of the dispute. Such gods as *Sango* (god of Thunder), *Yemoja* (goddess of the river), and *Ayelala* (guardian of social morality) are used to ascertain the veracity of the story told by complaintants.[57]

The Igbo traditional religious institution for conflict resolution is called *Agbara* (local deities or oracles). Warnings of impending dooms for any recalcitrant disputants are often received through the chief priest of *Obinze*, the messenger of *Alanlwn* (big Earth deity), saying that they see an impending blood flow, insisting that there must be no bloodshed and that the dispute must be settled peacefully. Disputes are eventually resolved through oath-taking, which centers on the declaration of no more war, a peace treaty, and the performance of a cleansing ritual called *Ikomue*. Most communities do come with their respective representatives and local deities (oracles) to be sworn to in the presence of gods and all people present. The oath, which is binding on every indigene of the participating communities, was taken to the effect that the contracting parties accept peace, and there would be no more war and bloodshed between the warring communities. Violators of this oath face the wrath of the deities and the ancestors, who, in the presence of god, constitute the source of moral sanctions and peace guarantors. This first oath-taking process usually relaxed tension in the war-torn area and paved the way for their processes that brought about final peace.[58]

After the first oath process, a second oath takes place, in which the disputants are invited to the deity shrines, where the representatives of each community arrive with a big he-goat, some kola nuts along with a symbol of their own community's deity and its chief priest (*Ezemmoo*). After reading the oath's contents, each community appointed one representative to take the oath on its behalf and in the presence of its deity.[59]

Tiv is an ethnolinguistic group or nation in Central Nigeria. The 'Swem' Oath or Covenant is the traditional religious method of conflict resolutions among the Tiv. It revolves around the Swem, which is an Oath or Covenant: The name 'Swem' refers to the "past transitional habitation of the Tiv ethnic nation."[60] However, "the Tiv Swem oath or covenant was the highest oath of faithfulness and truth and the demonstration of one's innocence in the ancient Tiv nation."[61] As succinctly put by M. Msue, the "Swem oath was a Covenant of faithfulness and truth and nothing but the truth."[62] Therefore, U Bumun Swem or U Hemben Swem, both represented the ways of swearing upon the

Swem Oath. U Bumun Swem was to swear upon the Swem Oath, to stand for and tell the truth and nothing but the truth. U Hemben Swem, on the other hand, was to demonstrate disputants' faithfulness, truthfulness, and innocence before the whole world by releasing the Swem pot to drop and break into pieces. To swear to a Swem oath or to break the Swem pot was not a casual or joking exercise, but a most solemn and serious undertaking and a matter of life and death.

From the above examinations, the features of traditional religious conflict resolution in Nigeria are largely characterized by spiritualism involving incantations, curses, witchcraft, and oath-taking. It also involves sacrifice and libation brought before the traditional and spiritual leaders, including the fetish priests, custodians of deities, herbalists, and soothsayers. For example, one party may invoke a curse by using the name of a river or a deity to harm another person for perceived wrongdoing. Once the afflicted party realizes, through divination, that they have been cursed, the accused is requested to reverse or remove that curse by performing the necessary rituals at the appropriate fetish/shrine and going through the necessary religious purification. It is also common to invoke an oath during conflicts. A litigant may swear an oath to support his/her claim. When that happens, it is expected that the other party, if innocent, will also swear an oath against that claim. In that case, the contending parties having sworn the oath have to go to the paramount chief, fetish, river, among others to perform the necessary rituals and settle the dispute. However, failure to respond to an oath is perceived to be an admission of guilt until reversed by the custodian of the oath (e.g., chief/fetish priest).[63]

Traditional healers, diviners, herbalists, and spiritual healers/seers also play an important role in the traditional religious conflict resolution mechanism at the individual, family, and community levels. They are a medium between the living, the ancestors, and God.[64] Traditional/spiritual healers may use herbs, animal sacrifices, and water to perform rituals to resolve conflicts between the living and their ancestral spirits. Traditional healing may be a strictly private family affair or an open community function, depending on the issues involved.[65] Conflicts arising from witchcraft are usually resolved between the traditional healers and the affected parties. A person may choose to revenge the evil that has been done, or just strengthen/protect themselves against similar fetish attacks in the future. Traditional healers are frequently sought on critical issues, including various kinds of conflict in the community. Thus, the role of traditional religions, especially in helping to identify suspected criminals and resolving conflict, cannot be over-emphasized.[66]

There are operational similarities in the three traditional religious methods of conflict resolution examined above as they all showcase the importance and contribution of religion to peaceful societal co-existence. Thus, the processes focus on reconciliation, stability, harmony, and safety while it attempts to reconcile individuals and groups based on traditional doctrinal norms and practices. Thus, the traditional religion has become part of the modern governance and administration systems. Though enshrined in the indigenous cultures, they function as regular parts of national governance and are recognized and accepted and used by the governments as many government officials do swear at a shrine to be loyal to political godfathers, while disputes resulting from non-fulfillment of promises between the two parties are sometimes resolved at the shrine.

In contemporary times, there is high respect for the traditional religious authorities and institutions. Generally, in many instances, the conflict resolution process is transparent, publicly performed, and the evidence, discussions, and solutions are open to all. More so, the affected individuals and families find a traditional healer to either reverse or protect them against any curses that may have been pronounced on them by their enemies. However, in Ghana, traditional priests are allowed to hear and resolve spiritual conflicts, and their decisions are respected.[67] The major difference between the traditional religious methods of conflict resolution is the peculiarity of their traditional weight.

Effects of Traditional Religious Conflict Resolution Mechanisms on Peaceful Societal Co-Existence

In the typical African conflict resolution through the religious mechanism, the principles of equity and justice, which are entrenched in the customs and traditions of the people, are upheld, thus promoting peaceful co-existence. It is a general belief in traditional African society that there is no award for winning an argument. As such, the result of conflict resolution is to accommodate all parties involved in the dispute through genuine collaboration by all, in the search for effective compromise. In doing so, unnecessary competition is avoided because the ultimate aim of conflict resolution is an amicable settlement by persuasion, mediation, adjudication, reconciliation, arbitration, and negotiation, not necessarily reverting to the use of force or coercion.[68]

In typical African traditional society, religious socialization through festivals, such as the Osun Osogbo festival in Nigeria is an important factor in conflict resolution, as those settled at the riverbanks end up being friends rather than foe. African children are raised to consider that a quarrel or a fight with others is a quarrel or a fight between blood and ancestral relations. Thus, it becomes imperative to avoid injury and harm, as well as avoiding situations of always trying to win at any cost, thus promoting oneness and unity of the society. The African traditional religious conflict resolution mechanism performs a healing function in African societies as it provides an opportunity for the examinations of alternative positive decisions to resolve differences. Conflict resolution through the instrumentality of the African traditional religions promotes consensus-building, social bridge reconstructions, and the re-enactment of sustainable peace and order. The traditional religions take into account the cultural setting and the social context of every dispute in order to find a lasting solution based on the prevailing customs. It looks at the history of preceding events that led to the conflict. And while concentrating on the conflict itself and the process of resolving it, it takes optimal interest on how such resolution outcome would promote peace in the society. A wider interest is taken than one which just includes the disputing parties; possible consequences for others in their families and social network are also taken into consideration while the potential effects of such relationship and interests are envisaged to not undermine social cohesion.[69] It was also found that the traditional principles of tolerance, accommodation, fairness, the sanctity of human life, absolute condemnation of the spilling of human blood, genuine apology and forgiveness, justice, humility, a culture of peace, true reconciliation, agape love, impartiality, neutrality, and trust-building were deeply ingrained in the African traditional religious methods of conflict resolution. Conflict resolution mechanisms within the confines of traditional religion perform a healing function in African societies. It provides the service of restoring such society to its original state of piety and crime-free entity and a pure state of sanity in which the world was created. Moreover, the essence of dispute settlements and conflict resolutions through the African traditional religion is to remove the root-causes of the conflict; reconcile the conflicting parties genuinely; to preserve and ensure harmony, and make everyone involved in the resolved conflict happy and be at peace with each other to set the right milieu for societal production and development; to promote good governance, law and order, to provide security of lives and property, and to achieve collective well-being and peaceful co-existence within the African societies.[70]

Conclusion

The traditional religious method of conflict resolution has remained a credible mechanism with a fantastic outcome for the people of Africa. Such an outcome is largely premised on restorative justice, which mends rather than destroys relationships between the disputants while promoting society's peaceful co-existence among Africans. As mentioned earlier, it is a general belief in traditional African society that there is no award for winning an argument. As such, the end result of conflict resolutions through the African religious doctrine is to accommodate all parties involved in the dispute through genuine collaboration to search for effective compromise. In doing so, unnecessary competition is avoided because the ultimate aim of traditional religious-induced conflict resolution is an amicable settlement by persuasion, mediation, adjudication, reconciliation, arbitration and not necessarily reverting to the use of force or coercion at all costs, or at any cost.

Notes

1. Yusuf, N *Traditional African Conflict Resolutions, Strategies and Peacebuilding Models: Lessons for the Diaspora* (Paper presented at the 2019 BICAID Conference on Africa and its Diaspora. (Athens: University of Georgia, November, 2019).

2. Burgan, 2009; Charles, 2014; Adelodun, 2015.
3. Chartered Institute for Mediators and Conciliators, *M ediation Skills Accreditation and Certification* Training (Abuja: ICMC, 2019).
4. Attah-Poku, A. "African Ethnicity: History, Conflict Management, Resolution, and Prevention (Lanham, MD: University Press of America, 1998), 106; See also Olaoba, 2012, and Charles, 2014.
5. Attah-Poku, *African Ethnicity*, 106.
6. Yusuf, *Traditional African Conflict Resolutions*, 3.
7. Charles, 2017, 6.
8. Ibid.
9. Dopamu, A.P, "African Religion (Afrel) and National Security in Yoruba Perspective," In M. A. Folorunsho et al. (eds.), *Religion and National Security* (Ijebu Ode: Alamsek Press, 2006).
10. Awolalu, 1987.
11. Dopamu, "African Religion," 2006.
12. Olaoba, 2009.
13. Olaoba, O B., "Ancestral Focus and the Process of Conflict Resolution in Traditional African Societies," In Albert Olawale (ed.), *Perspectives on Peace and Conflict in Africa in Essays in Honour of General (Dr) Abdul Salam A, Abubakar* (Ibadan, Oyo: Institute of African Studies, 2005), 140–151.
14. Omotosho, M., "Evaluating Conflict and Conflict Management: A Conceptual Understanding in Africa," *Journal of International Affairs and Development*, vol. 9, no. 1 & 2 (2004).
15. Robert, G., "*Political Conflict on the Horn of Africa* (USA: Praeger, 1981), 3.
16. Quincy, W., "The Escalation of International Conflicts," In C. Smith (ed.), *Conflict Resolution: Contributions of Behavioural Science* (London: Notre Dame Press, 1971).
17. Ibid.
18. Omotoshi, "Evaluating Conflict and Conflict Management," 2004.
19. Isaac, O.A, "*Introduction to Third Party Intervention in Community Conflict* (Ibadan: PETRAF/John Archers Publishers, 2001).
20. Robert, *German: Political Conflict on the Horn of Africa*, 3.
21. Wadama W., "Post-Colonial Conflict in Africa: A Study of Richard Ali's City of Memories," *International Journal of Arts and Humanities*, vol. 2, no. 4 (2013), 319.
22. Adebayo, 2013.
23. Adelodun, 2016.
24. Otite and Albert, 2001.
25. Kotze, D., "Issues in Conflict Resolution," *African Journal on Conflict Resolution*, Vol. 2, No. 2 (2002), 77–86.
26. Olaoba, **O. B.**, "The Traditional Approaches to Conflict Resolution in the South-West Zone of Nigeria". *Nigerian Army Quarterly Journal, Vol. No.1 (2002), 14.*
27. Abel, R., "A Comparative Theory of Dispute Institution in Society". *Law and Society Review, Vol 2, No.3* (1973), 16.
28. Ajayi, A.T., and Buhari, L.O. "Methods of Conflict Resolution in African Traditional Society". *African Research Review*, Vol. 8, No 1 (2014): 138–157.
29. Ajayi, A. T., "Methods of Conflict Resolution in African Traditional Society", *African Research Review*, Vol. 8, No 2 (2014), 8.

30. Albert, I.O., Tinu A, George, H, and Wuyi, O, "*Informal Channels for Conflict Resolution in Ibadan,* Nigeria", Institute Francais de Recherche en Afrique, 1995).6.
31. Anyacho, U, "Traditional and Western Mechanism of Conflict Management: A Case of Aguleri and Umuleri Crisis, Anambra State", *Ph.D. dissertation,* University of Port Harcourt,(2017). 18.
32. Ayitte, G., "*Indigenous African Institution*", *Irvington-on-Hudson. (New York*: Transnational Publishers, 1991), 15.
33. Crocker, H. and Pamella A., "*Managing Global Chaos*". Washington: Institute of Peace *(1996), 7.*
34. Dauda, G. K., "Indigenous Conflict Resolution Method among Fulbe of Adamawa State", University of Maiduguri Public Lecture Series(2009), 9.
35. Ibid.
36. Hirschi, T., "Causes of Delinquency", California: University Press, 1969), 22.
37. Dauda, 2009, 6.
38. *Ibid.*
39. Ademowo, J., "Conflict Management in Traditional African Society", (2015) Available at: <https://www.researchgate.net/publication/281749510> [Accessed 20 September 2020].
40. Ayittey, G., 'African Solutions, African Problems, Real Meaning', (2014) Available at: <https://www.panafricanvisions.com> [Accessed 21 September 2020].
41. Ibid.
42. The Kom Heritage Foundation, "*A Short Cultural History of the Kom People*". Bamenda: Destiny Prints, 2014), 33.
43. The Kom Heritage Foundation (2014) op. cit., 38.
44. Nkwi, P., "*Traditional Diplomacy: A Study of Inter-Chiefdom Relationships in the Western Grassfields, North West Province of Cameroon,"* (Yaounde,: University Publication, 2016), 64.
45. Adam, A. M., "Inter-group Conflicts and Customary Mediation: Experience from Sudan," *African. Journal on Conflict Resolution"* Vol.2, No.2, (2000), 13.
46. Bennett, T.W., "Human Right and the African Cultural Tradition Transformation", African Journal of Conflict Resolution Vol 3 No 2 (1993), 32.
47. Bright-Brock, U., "Indigenous Conflict Resolution," African. Institute of Educational Research, University of Oslo (2001), 8–11.
48. Kotze, D,. "Issues in Conflict Resolution", African Journal on Conflict Resolution, Volume 6, No.2 (2000), 77–86.
49. Poku, H., "African Ethnicity; History, Conflict Management, Resolution and Prevention", (New York: University Press, 1998), 106
50. Ibid.
51. Isaac, O. A., "Introduction to Third Party Intervention in Community Conflict,"(Ibadan: John Archers Publishers, 2001), 8.
52. Ibid.
53. Poku, 1998, 6.
54. Omotosho, M., "Evaluating Conflict and Conflict Management: A Conceptual Understanding in Africa", Journal of International Affairs and Development, Vol.9, No 1 (2004), 5.

55. Jannie, M.O., "Conflict Resolution Wisdom from Africa," African Centre for the Constructive Resolution of Disputes (ACCORD South Africa (Johannesburg: Natal Publishers, 1997), 7.
56. Ibid.
57. Oguntomisin, G.O.," The Processes of Peacekeeping and Peace-Making in Pre-Colonial Nigeria," (Ibadan: John Archers, 2004), 10.
58. Olaoba, O. B.," The Traditional Approaches to Conflict Resolution in the South-West Zone of Nigeria". *Nigerian Army Quarterly Journal, Vol. No.1,. (n.d.), 22–37.*
59. Olaoba, O.B., "Introduction to Africa Legal Culture," (Ibadan: Hope Publications, 2001), 1–2.
60. Olaoba, O. B., "The Town Crier and Yoruba Palace Administrator through the Ages". (Ibadan: John Archers, 2002), 16.
61. Olorunsola,V. A., "The Politics of Cultural Sub- nationalism in Africa". (Lagos: Anchor Books, 1972), 18.
62. Ibid.
63. Olaoba, 2002, 13.
64. Quincy, W., Ed." The Escalation of International Conflicts," In Clajelt Smith *Conflict Resolution: Contributions of Behavioural Science.* (London: Notre Dame Press, (1971),16.
65. Ibid.
66. Olaoba, 2002. 12.
67. Widnga, W., "Post- Colonial Conflict in Africa: A Study of Richard Ali's City of Memories," International Journal of Arts and Humanities, Vol.2 No 4 (2013), 10.
68. Ibid.
69. Omotoshi, 2004, 8.
70. Wadama, 2013, 11.

CHAPTER 26

African Traditional Religion and Democratic Governance

Kwaku Nti

INTRODUCTION

African societies developed enduring philosophies and concepts of the world around them, their place in it, the meaning of existence, being, and some such deep issues, with all these dynamics filtered through the idea of the physical and the spiritual. Various manifestations of these belief systems across the continent underwent egregious demonization and denigration from the middle of the nineteenth century with the influx of Western Christian missionaries. Yet among these societies, including the Akan, especially the Fanti, indigenous African religious thought remain "Emintsimadze," literally, an established and enduring force almost in the same manner as the earth or even the universe itself in which all things have their existence. These religious or other-worldly concerns continue to play crucial covert and overt roles in all aspects of the peoples' private and public lives. Like many others, traditional religious systems from the era of the Scientific Revolution onward were described as mindless and irrational, especially in the estimation of advocates of the separation of State and religion principles who advocated, banishment; but the religions survived that assault, lingered, and now seem to claw back into mainstream thoughts and actions in subtle ways.

Generally, the larger Akan group of Ghana subscribe to a dualist worldview; that is, the physical and the spiritual, with all their respective complete set of hierarchies and specially recognized intermediaries including priests,

K. Nti (✉)
Georgia Southern University, Savannah, GA, USA
e-mail: knti@georgiasouthern.edu

© The Author(s), under exclusive license to Springer Nature Switzerland AG 2022
I. S. Aderibigbe, T. Falola (eds.), *The Palgrave Handbook of African Traditional Religion*, https://doi.org/10.1007/978-3-030-89500-6_26

priestesses, diviners, mediums, and medicine men and women.[1] While this category is the most undisputed mediator between the two worlds, sometimes the top echelon of the indigenous political system in certain ceremonies also function as priests; hence, in most cases, the chief, for instance, becomes not only a political figure but also a religious personality imbued with an unquestionable ritual status.[2] All these indigenous officials in their various capacities fit the apt description as curators and purveyors of the indigenous religious culture.[3] The mediators, as well as other practitioners, of the indigenous religions at various times and situations supplicate or appeal to the Supreme Being, supernatural beings, gods, goddesses, nature spirits, spirits, and the ancestors not only on their own behalf but also for the *Ɔman* (or indigenous state), nation-state, rulers, clan (or *Ebusua*) family, and others. This intercession is done bearing in mind a salient principle and pervasive belief in the traditional religious set-up that upholds the spiritual world as being more powerful than the physical, and therefore able to impact or influence the latter.

Blatant efforts in Ghana at reclaiming and celebrating the indigenous culture after the missionary and colonial onslaught also resulted in a subtle re-enactment of certain aspects of the traditional religions at some public ceremonies. The movement or advocacy for reclaiming aspects of the indigenous culture, and therefore facets of the traditional religions obviously took inspiration from the Akan Sankɔfa philosophy.[4] This idea expresses the view that it is hardly an anathema to re-claim, re-tool, or re-appropriate a discarded practical and meaningful aspect of the culture of a people. These tendencies became systematic, especially during the Provisional National Defense Council military regime from the end of 1981 to the beginning of the current democratic dispensation in 1992.[5] Be that as it may, robust precedents even took place during the First Republic when the first President, Kwame Nkrumah, made one of the sons of the former paramount chief of Akropong, F. W. K. Akuffo, Kwesi Boafo Akuffo the state *Ɔkyeame* or linguist given his impressive and popularly acclaimed skill in the indigenous art of public speaking.[6] He added a touch of indigenous religion and culture to state ceremonies with extensive customary poetry recitals and appellations while offering the traditional religious prayer.

Constitutional Provision

The current Constitution promulgated in 1992 pontificates on the nature of the relations between the State and religion. Article 17 (2), in a mandatory manner, establishes an essential element of secularism in Ghana that respects the equality of all persons of any religious inclination with the stipulation that "a person shall not be discriminated against on grounds of gender ... ethnic origins, religious creed, social, or economic status." Furthermore, Article 21 (1) (b) and (c) establishes the general fundamental freedoms of the citizenry, including religious freedom in the following provisions: (1) All persons shall have the right to freedom (b) freedom of thought, conscience, and belief which shall include academic freedom, and (c) freedom to practice any religion and to manifest such practice. In chapter six of the Directive Principles of State Policy, Article 35 (1) outlines the political objectives of the Constitution for the State to promote the integration of the people with the statement that "Ghana shall be a democratic state dedicated to the realization of Freedom and Justice; and accordingly, sovereignty resides in the people of Ghana from whom the government derives its power and authority through this constitution." In furtherance of the preceding, Article 35 (5) establishes as one of the duties of the State the promotion of integration of the people of Ghana and prohibits any form of discrimination in the following words: "The State shall actively promote the integration of the peoples of Ghana and consequently prohibit discrimination and prejudice on the grounds of place of origin, circumstances of birth, ethnic origin, gender or religious creed, or other beliefs." Furthermore, Article 56 forbids Parliament from enacting laws to impose one religion or political party on the people of Ghana in the following terms: "Parliament shall have no power to enact a law to establish or authorize the establishment of a body or a movement with the right or power to impose on the people of Ghana a common program or set of objectives of a religious or political nature."

In the face of this critical mass of provisions, the Supreme Court of Ghana observed the absence of ambiguity in the guarantee of the freedom of religion as it stated in no uncertain terms, "the wordings are explanatory, simple, and easy to appreciate their import and admit of no ambiguity."[7] According to the Court:

> The combined effect of the spirit and letter of these provisions guarantees the fundamental freedoms of the citizen including the right to practice any religion and to manifest such practice. By the letter and spirit of these provisions, religious pluralism and diversity which are features of a secular state are clearly recognized and thereby discrimination on any ground is prohibited. By the Directive Principles of State Policy in Articles 35 and 37 the State is to actively promote, within reasonable limits; and facilitate the aspiration and opportunities by every citizen to their fundamental freedoms as a way of ensuring national cohesion.[8]

Given its opinion that a Constitution mimics the history of a people as well as reflects their aspiration, the Supreme Court observed that the government must recognize "the existence and importance of religious identity and affiliation in the Ghanaian society and encourage their open and lawful expression at national events."[9]

Thus, various governments at different periods in the annals of this country have countenanced or allowed the inclusion of traditional religious practices in conjunction with others such as Christianity and Islam at certain major national functions in the spirit of inclusivism. This all-embracing stance has caused some scholars to doubt the extent to which Ghana upholds the separation of State and religious principles. The Ghanaian situation, to some of these scholars, especially given the foregoing constitutional provisions, is not a matter of whether there ought to be any relationship between these two entities, but rather what should be the nature and extent of that interaction. Hence, they describe the country as more of a religiously plural than that of a secular one. In their view, this labeling's legal effect is that religion is inextricably embedded in public life.[10] The State-Religion dynamic, as enshrined in the Constitution, is one that falls well within the ambit of the functions of the central government. A corollary view comes up in the Supreme Court ruling in *Bomfeh* versus *Attorney General*, in which, among other complaints, the former accuses the Government of Ghana of "excessive entanglement" in religion. The ruling in its preamble refers to a 1980 Court of Appeal sitting as the Supreme Court. Again, it stipulates that a national Constitution "mirrors the history of the people" and their "basic aspirations." Both assertions are reified with the explanation that historically, Ghana as a nation has recognized the importance of religious identity to its peoples and, again, has encouraged their "open and lawful expression" even at national ceremonies. Further, the ruling avers, "the Constitution ... while secular in nature, affirms and maintains the historical, cultural, and religious or atheist character of Ghanaian society." In a matter of fact manner, the ruling emphasized that "obviously, secularism in the context of the constitution must be understood to allow and even encourage state recognition and accommodation of religion and religious identity."[11]

Undoubtedly, the Constitution does not explicitly preclude the government from supporting, assisting, or cooperating with religious organizations. Rather, it precludes the State from hindering freedom of worship, religion, and belief and discriminating on the ground of religion. Groups and peoples are all guaranteed the right to "subscribe to the religious belief and faith of their own choosing without interference ... by the State." The State then is free to lend support to a religious group if it will be for the good of the nation. Therefore, freedom of religion and religious tolerance are core values not only in constitutional democracies but also in pluralistic societies that are undergoing the manifest complex processes of integration and national cohesion.[12]

TRADITIONAL RELIGIONS: MANIFESTATIONS AND EXPRESSIONS

Pursuant to the spirit of religious inclusivism, and because of the ubiquitous element of political expediency, one key practice that underpins all the manifestations and expressions of African Traditional Religion, that is libation, has been performed at state functions and other political gatherings.

Libation: State Spaces and Political Places

The pouring of libation is the most visible and definitive form of prayer in the indigenous sense. As much as libation is done by certain recognized leaders within the traditional scheme of things because it constitutes an art of poetry, other individuals or adherents of this belief are not prohibited from that performance.

At the highest level of State functions in Accra, the capital city, two major traditional religions are offered—that belonging to the Ga, whose land hosts the seat of government, and that of the Akan, who constitute nearly half the population of Ghana. While the former is performed by the *Wulɔmei*, the traditional chief priest, the Akan libation might be done by an accomplished *Ɔkyeame* or traditional linguist from one of the nearby indigenous states. Libation as a form of prayer, supplication, invocation, solicitation, plea, or appeal to several entities within the traditional spiritual world, in a hierarchical order starts with the Supreme Being all the way down to the ancestors. It is performed to the accompaniment of the pouring of a slew of liquids from plain water to assorted alcoholic beverages on the ground.

Alcohol casts itself as a metaphor for power because it encapsulates a spectrum of dynamics. Given its nature as a sharp mood-influencing fluid, alcohol remains a potentially dangerous substance, and yet as a liquid possesses the power vital for communication with the spiritual realm.[13] This religious or ritual use of alcohol hinges on its perceived potential to invoke the spiritual world and thus create a pathway for the physical to confer with it. In line with the social and religious belief systems of the Akan, the supernatural forces that inhabit the spiritual realm could be accessed in a powerful manner through alcohol. The typical Akan libation commences with a plaintive call upon the Supreme Being at the apex of the spiritual space. He is referred to metaphorically as "*Twereduampong*" or "*Onyankopong*," meaning the great tree on whom one can trustingly lean and the great friend, respectively. In a meaningful personification, he is *Kwame*, an intimation of the belief that he came into existence on a Saturday.[14] Because the Supreme Being does not drink, the alcoholic beverage is merely presented or shown to him, which in the Akan language is stated, "*Yɛkyerɛ wo nsa nso wo nnum nsa*." He is then praised for his greatness, power, wisdom, and creative abilities. Although individuals can worship him, the traditional religious systems hinge on the principle that this Supreme Being, at the apex of the spiritual hierarchy, cannot be communicated to directly by ordinary mortals except a bottom-up approach through a chain of intermediaries. The performer then turns his or her attention to the mother Earth, Earth goddess, or *Asaase Yaa*, who indeed is given a portion of the drink.[15] From this point onward, the supplicants work their way along the hierarchy calling upon the other spiritual beings until they get to the ancestors. In a national setting, the names of the early generation of leaders or the founding fathers who played prominent roles in the struggle for independence and succeeding generation of heads of state are invited to have their portion of the drink. Among other pleas, the *Ɔkyeame* or linguist beseeches the "*Nananom*" for health, wisdom, and prosperity for the nation.[16] Additionally, those who lead the libation always pray for the abatement of evil and even for the instantaneous elimination of the agents thereof.

Festivals and Ceremonial or Working Visits

Yet another exemplification of the mutual patronization between governments and the traditional religions occurs within the context of annual festival celebrations across the country. Although festivals fall plainly within the cultural, historical, political, and social category, aspects of its overt and largely covert underpinnings make them indubitably religious. Long before the public celebrations marked by drumming, singing, dancing, cultural displays, parading of different groups, kings, chiefs, and queen mothers, initial esoteric religious practices take place often for longer periods. These rituals are purposely for cleansing and purifying the primary or principal actors and the various sites earmarked for the upcoming public celebrations. During these times, the prominent rituals include sacrificing cows and sheep and the indispensable libation pouring. To celebrate the climaxes of these festivals across the country, albeit at different times, the traditional political authorities, mainly at the larger paramount level, do invite the president, the vice president, their representatives, government officials, regional ministers, members of Parliament, members of the Diplomatic Corps, and the various political parties. And for political expediency, these invitations are honored not only with respective delegations but also with the presentation of assorted gifts in cash and in-kind as varying forms of support and patronage.

Alternatively, the embodiment of the national political establishment often makes approaches or overtures toward the traditional religious systems indirectly through kings, chiefs, and queen mothers. This is justifiably so because, in the indigenous scheme of things, these offices are not only political but also religious. In this sense then, the occupant is a king or chief and priest simultaneously. In view of this religious status, the occupants are at certain times within the traditional calendar to perform some rituals for the stability, peace, and cohesion of their respective societies. National political officeholders who seek renewal of their mandate and other political office aspirants directly or indirectly solicit the approval, blessing, and recommendation of these kings or chief priests who are viewed as the embodiment of the long-departed ancestors and therefore inextricably connected to the spiritual sphere.

Additionally, aspects of traditional religion come into play if the president, ministers of state, government officials, and political party representatives pay ceremonial or working visits to the indigenous political and traditional authorities. At the durbars or gatherings on these occasions, libation performance becomes a recurrent factor during which the "*Nananom*" are invoked to ensure graceful and fruitful deliberations for the prosperity of the traditional area and the nation in general. It is not uncommon for these visiting national political actors to, again, offer gifts of assorted local and imported alcoholic beverages as the major vectors of the libation process.[17] After the drink is poured out to the ancestor and the other spiritual entities, the rest is passed around for willing individuals at the gathering to partake in small quantities.

Those who do not drink alcohol are even expected to pour their portion out on the ground as a burlesque of the actual libation process.

The theme of African Traditional Religion runs through all indigenous protocols and practices. To this end, the plethora of drumming and dancing performed at these gatherings hardly remains a spectacle of entertainment only, but also an element of invocation of the spiritual world. Adowa, Kete, *Fontɔmfrɔm*, Asafo, as well as other royal or courtly music are played, especially, by the master drummer or *Kyirema*, as among the Fanti; who knows the common rhythm of traditional songs and further showcases his ability to create drum poetry and other esoteric sound fusions powerful enough to communicate with the world of spirits in the air, land, and the water bodies. These skills, essentially, create the right ambience for the occasion and a great sense of expectation as the physical world communes with the spiritual and, again, as the living celebrates that enduring sense of interaction between them.

THREATS AND REDRESSING OF GRIEVANCES

While the traditional religions of Ghana have commendable roles toward the advancement of democratic governance, there are few instances where some potential adverse traits crop up. Inherent in these religious practices is the overwhelming belief in the power that the spiritual world possesses over the physical, with the conventional thought that the fortunes and destinies of the latter are subjected to the whims and caprices of the former for good and evil ends. Some practitioners of these religions have exploited this lingering fear factor as means of threats to perceived and real adversaries alleged to have made defamatory, false, or unsubstantiated statements or some such utterances deemed injurious to the character of the complainant, reputation, or social status. Given the perception that the wheels of justice turn slowly; and worse still that sometimes justice is sold to the highest bidder, some aggrieved people resort to threats of taking accused persons to shrines or groves of certain gods, goddesses, and other spirits known not to hesitate in administering instant justice. There is also the threat of the use of libation to call on the ancestors, spirits, and elements to invoke adverse outcomes on detractors. These perceived enemies and detractors could also include government or political party officials.

Another interesting dimension of the adverse use of traditional religious beliefs and practices is the threat of nudity on the part of women. As in all indigenous religions across Africa, and indeed across the world, women are deemed relatively spiritual and, therefore, sensitive to that realm. The female body biological functional processes, especially the reproductive cycle, are deemed as important reflections of nature or the larger natural processes in terms of renewal and recreation. Consequently, most societies regard women as being close to the divine and quite responsive to spiritual systems. Hence, it is not uncommon to find that in some Ghanaian communities, the category of people deemed to have the capacity to communicate with the spiritual world or act as intermediaries are dominated by women as mediums and spiritualists, among others. While it is healthy and commendable for men to see the nakedness of their wives, it is not proper when they see the bodies of strange women. To have a group of women, either totally or partially nude, charge at a man or men is bad because it is deemed an ignominy, and one smacking of ill-omen; indeed, in the Akan language, it is "*musuo.*" In view of this generally held perception, some women's groups, particularly market mummies, petty traders, and others in that category, who see themselves as unfortunate victims of certain central government policy implementations have found it necessary to threaten officials with a nudity march; that is, if their grievances are not addressed. It is a threat that is seldomly invoked, given its serious implication for all parties involved. Often, its invocation draws the government or the concerned officials to the negotiation table.

The interconnectedness of the indigenous political system to the African Traditional Religions again manifests in situations when government officials or political party activists incur the displeasure of some kings, chiefs, and their council of elders. The likelihood of that grievance going a long way to affect the political fortunes of the accused persons either locally or nationally would often compel them to smoke the peace pipe with the aggrieved indigenous political leadership. Because these kings, chiefs, queen mothers, and their council of elders can make their people vote against the offending government or party officials, the concerns emanating from these threats would, in most cases, compel the latter to make a formal indigenous apology. It is this form of expressing regret and making amends that bring the traditional religion dynamic into the equation. Some of the requisite items for this ritualized process of apology include but are not limited to local alcoholic beverages, imported drinks, sheep, and cows. These are mainly used for the cleansing of both the offender, the offended, and their stools or thrones; and for the appeasement of the gods, goddesses, as well as the ancestors. These processes include but are not limited to the pouring of libation—a recurrent practice in the indigenous traditional religions, and the sacrificing of animals.

Conclusion

With constitutional underpinnings, traditional religious beliefs remain surefooted and possess the solid groundings to endure in their relevance to the current democratic governance efforts. These bases have granted some aspects of traditional religious practices, especially the pouring of libation, recognition at national events and ceremonies, as well as festivals with the patronage of government officials, while their inextricability from the indigenous political system also endows them with some influence over the democratic political elite. Threats of the adverse use of traditional religious beliefs and practices also make politicians conduct themselves decorously around indigenous political officeholders. Thus, when the unfortunate happens, they are quick to undergo a ritualized process of apology.

Notes

1. The Akan constitute the largest of the various ethnic groups, occupying an equally great territorial extent from the middle to the coastal belt. Some of the major Akan groups included the Ashanti, Fanti, Denkyira, Ahanta, Assin, Guan, Bono, Ahafo, Akyim, Akwamu, Kwahu, Akwapim, Sefwi, and Nzima.
2. Kofi Abrefa Busia, *The Position of the Chief in the Modern Political System of Ashanti* (London: Frank Cass, 1968).
3. The Summary of Report of Final Results of the 2010 Population and Housing Census indicates that 71.2% of the population profess the Christianity faith, 17.6% refer to themselves as Moslems, and 5.2% adhere to the various traditional religions. Another 5.2% denied any religious affiliation whatsoever. However, a small group of people, that is the remaining 0.8%, identified with other small religions such as the Bahai Faith, Eckankar, Buddhism, and Hinduism. In all these statistics, it is important to point out that structure of the Census did not make room for and, therefore, did not account for those who claim to be Christians and still do believe in aspects of the tenets of the traditional religions as well.
4. Literally "*San kɔ*" is go back and "fa" take it.
5. *Sankɔfa yɛ nnkyi* as in the Akan language.
6. He worked as a Research Assistant at the Center for National Culture and at the Department of Linguistics, University of Ghana, Legon. After the end of the First Republic, he came back into national prominence in the 1980s and 1990s during the Armed Forces Revolutionary Council (AFRC) and the Provisional National Defense Council (PNDC) eras.
7. In the Superior Court of Judicature in the Supreme Court, Accra—A.D. 2019 Writ No. J1/14/2017, January 23, 2019: *James Kwabena Bomfeh Jr. (Plaintiff)* vs. *Attorney General (Defendant)*, p. 12.
8. Ibid., 13.
9. Ibid., 17.
10. Christopher Y. Nyinevi and Edmund N. Amassah, "The Separation of Church and State under Ghana's Fourth Republic," *Journal of Politics and Law* vol. 8, no. 4 (2015), 287.
11. In the Superior Court of Judicature in the Supreme Court, Accra—A.D. 2019 Writ No. J1/14/2017, January 23, 2019: *James Kwabena Bomfeh Jr. (Plaintiff)* vs. *Attorney General (Defendant)*, p. 18.
12. Dr. S. K. B. Asante, Constitutional Lawyer, traditional ruler, and Paramount Chief of Asante Asokore, Address at the S. H. Amissah Memorial Lectures, Topic: *The Constitution of Ghana and Freedom of Religion: Challenges and the Way Forward*, at the Wesley Methodist Church Cathedral, Koforidua, March 22, 2017.
13. Emmanuel Kwaku Akyeampong, *Drink, Power, and Cultural Change: A Social History of Alcohol in Ghana, c. 1800 to Recent Times* (Oxford: James Currey, 1996), xxi, and 8.
14. Kwame is one of the several Akan common names derivatives from the days on which individual boys and girls are born. So, from Sunday to Monday, boys and girls have their respective sets of names.
15. In Akan mythology and philosophy, the Earth or *Asaase* is female, a great goddess at that, who was born or created on Thursday, hence the name *Yaa*.

16. *Nananom* is a generic term that refers to the totality of the hierarchical entities in both the spiritual and the physical world; with respect to the latter, it might also include both the living and the dead.
17. The idea of gift-giving at palaces and with the indigenous system hinges on the Akan concept that one does not have to go to these places empty handed, "*Yɛ nnfa nsa paen nnko ahinfie.*" A corollary concept is "*Ade ko ahinfie a ennsan nba,*" meaning a gift that goes to the palace is never returned.

CHAPTER 27

African Traditional Religions and Economic Development

Kwaku Nti

INTRODUCTION

Belief systems, whether philosophical, economic, social, or religious, as part of the super-structure of societies, have historically impacted inherent tendencies to make life better, richer, and fuller. African communities fall within this general category, and for Ghana, among other belief systems, the role of the traditional religions in its economic development cannot be justifiably overlooked.

Development as a dynamic in human societies could be considered from various perspectives, including but not limited to, the personal and the national perspectives. With respect to the former, it might border on issues such as capacity-building, know-how, creativity, self-discipline, responsibility, and other related matters. At the national level, among other things, it includes "capacity for dealing with the environment. However, this capacity for dealing with the environment is dependent on the extent to which that group of people understand the laws of nature (science) or the extent to which they put that understanding into practice by devising tools (technology), and how work is organized."[1] In this sense then, all societies and peoples across the face of the earth "have exhibited that tendency towards independently increasing their ability to live a more satisfactory life through exploiting the resources of nature."[2] In an aptly enduring apologetics for African Traditional Religions, Walter Rodney observed that: "Traditional African practices exist in great variety, and it should also be remembered that both Christianity and Islam

K. Nti (✉)
Georgia Southern University, Savannah, GA, USA
e-mail: knti@georgiasouthern.edu

© The Author(s), under exclusive license to Springer Nature Switzerland AG 2022
I. S. Aderibigbe, T. Falola (eds.), *The Palgrave Handbook of African Traditional Religion*, https://doi.org/10.1007/978-3-030-89500-6_27

found homes on the African continent almost from their inception. The features of traditional African religions help to set African cultures apart from those in other continents; but in this present context, it is more important to note how much African religions had in common with religion elsewhere and how this can be used as an index to the level of development in Africa before the European impact in fifteenth century."[3]

Expatiating on the preceding argument, he had this to say: "Religion is an aspect of the superstructure of a society, deriving ultimately from the degree of control and understanding of the material world. However, when man thinks in religious terms, he starts from the ideal rather than with the material world (which is beyond his comprehension). This creates a non-scientific and metaphysical way of viewing the world which often conflicts with the scientific materialist outlook and with the development of society. African ancestral religions were no better or worse than other religions as such."[4] Along these lines of reasoning, the relevance of African Traditional Religions to significant aspects of life, including economic development, is a familiar theme in Ghana, as in many other countries across the continent and elsewhere.

Component of Educational Curricula

Societies worldwide do possess established bodies of knowledge relevant to their welfare and development that all members for the realization of those ends ought to know. This endeavor pertains to knowledge creation and dissemination in order to raise a functional and productive population. In Ghana, the recognition given to the relevance and usefulness of traditional religions, among other disciplines, is reflected in their inclusion in the educational curricula, especially in the area of intellectual and moral development. When member states of the West African Examinations Council collectively required the General Certificate of Education Advanced Level (G.C.E. A Level) as a pre-requisite for entry into their respective universities, African Traditional Religions featured prominently as a component of the Religious Studies option. While it remained an option for some students at this level, all first-year university students (freshman year), at least in the University of Ghana, had to take courses in African Studies with a heavy element of traditional religions underpinning the various aspects during the First University Examination (F.U.E.). The mandatory requirement of a pass to proceed with the rest of their years of study evidently attests to the significance attached to these that permeate the various societies in subtle ways. Ultimately, these courses are structured to impart a basic, yet comprehensive, understanding and appreciation of the African religious worldview to students.

LAND: RELIGIOUS RESOURCE IN DEVELOPMENT PROJECTS

The Supreme Court of Ghana, in a recent ruling, unanimously reiterated the time-honored collaboration between "the State and religion" that had contributed to the socio-economic growth of the country.[5] For all intents and purposes, the country's traditional religions cannot be conscionably excluded from that equation. In this instance, the judgment specifically referred to the role of Christian and Islamic missions in the establishment of educational institutions, medical facilities of varying degrees of operation, agricultural projects, and other related contributions. According to the judgment, "in some remote areas of Ghana, it is the religious bodies that pioneered the establishment of schools and health facilities before the State ventured in those areas."[6] It is necessary to point out the instrumentality as well as the indispensability of the indigenous political and traditional religious authorities in order for these developments to happen. The prominence of their facilitation is reflected in the release and allocation of land in their respective jurisdictions for many of those projects to be accomplished. In this context, the indigenous conceptualization of land is relevant to appreciate the enormity of their contribution.

Among Ghanaian communities and societies, land does not only constitute an exclusively economic and political resource but also has crucial cultural and religious significance. However, its essence and meaning, like other diverse African cultural practices and institutions, exhibits some considerable degree of fluidity and dynamism. Generally, the land remains a communal property, and the right to occupy, farm, or develop a piece or section derives from the recognition of the membership of an individual in a family, clan, or society. Thus, when the colonial authorities formulated a policy to take over some lands and endeavored to ensure its implementation, the people touted these indigenous conceptualizations as justifiable cause to oppose those various attempts as constituting a clear violation of their time-honored property rights. As a religious resource, land has immense implications for the people of Ghana as it connects them to their ancestors in a variety of ways. Bequeathed by their departed and venerated forebears, land retains some degree of elevation as an equally inalienable revered resource.

Ancestors obtained their land from a variety of ways, including original settlement, war, and bloodshed. The sanctity of these various modes of acquisition enjoins the living to treat and regard land in the same manner as they would the ancestors and any other family heirloom. If any land was inappropriately given away or ended up in wrong hands, the ancestors viewed this as an infraction that would certainly incur their displeasure. Furthermore, land remains the sacred resting place of the ancestors and could, therefore, not be given away. The practice of libation, a time-honored communication mechanism, amounts to affirming the importance of land in their relationship with the ancestors. Moreover, the ancestors, in their beneficence, are thought to bestow treasures embedded in the land to their descendants. To this end, the various peoples of Ghana had cogent reasons not to relent in their bid to prevent the colonial government from getting the Crown Lands Bill passed. These conceptualizations of land, especially its underlying religious implication, more than anything else, reveal the sacrificial extent of its release for public development efforts.

Traditional Religions, Health, Wellness, and Productivity

The person and position of the indigenous healer, deeply embedded in the traditional African religions, are consequential for issues of health and productivity. While a few might be ordinary healers and a good number of them go by titles, such as *Enninsifuɔ* or *Abosomfuɔ*, both undergo long periods of training in the traditional pharmacopoeia. Ultimately, they possess a deeper understanding of the available flora and fauna, their inter-relationships with the spiritual world, and how both impact human health and wellness. While the ordinary indigenous healers might gain their expertise from serving or being close to a well-experienced elder in the clan, the *Enninsifuɔ* or *Abosomfuɔ* will necessarily have to come into that knowledge after long periods of apprenticeship at the shrines or groves of certain gods and goddesses. These categories of traditional healers, in the past, long before the introduction of Western medicine in the country, played an enormous role in the diagnosis, treatment, and management of all manner of diseases such as malaria, yellow fever, skin infections, infertility, bone fractures, pains, aches, and many other related afflictions. They also treated ailments that affected children. The proof of their relevance and respect for their knowledge of herbs inheres in the current efforts by government and international agencies to help systematize their operations against a critical background of inadequate medical facilities, and worse yet, the unhealthy doctor-to-patient ratios across the country. The Government of Ghana, through the instrumentality of the Ministry of Health, and some Western biomedical practitioners saw the need to revamp efforts at systematizing, sanitizing, and subjecting traditional medicine to measurable as well as explicable scientific preparation and administration. The groundswell of these efforts hinged on the World Health Organization's (WHO) World Health Assembly meeting in Geneva that established the "Working Group on Traditional Medicine" in May 1976. This program of action followed the publication of the report of a joint UNICEF/WHO study.[7] The mobilization and training of individuals involved in traditional medicine and traditional healing, including traditional birth attendants, became the way forward for primary healthcare services upon interests expressed by member states. The World Health Organization propagated the idea of promotion and development of the various traditional or indigenous systems of medicine.[8]

To this end, the World Health Organization proposed a collection of all available data on traditional healers and indigenous systems of medicine, including survey and research findings, studies of traditional practices, as well as training programs for traditional healers, and indigenous practitioners. All the available information, according to the organization, must be analyzed for the determination of the relevance of traditional healing to the primary healthcare needs of the population. Additionally, it recommended a field study of existing systems of traditional or indigenous medicine, and most importantly, suggesting the main directions for action regarding the training of traditional healers and their utilization in the public biomedical health system. For the proper integration of these two systems, Western biomedical personnel such as physicians, nurses, midwives, and related health workers also had to undergo orientation courses in the services and application of simple technology in the work of the indigenous practitioners. All these efforts became necessary to foster a realistic approach to traditional medicine to enhance its contribution to primary healthcare, explore its merits considering modern science to maximize inherent useful and effective practices as well as to discourage harmful ones.[9]

For the successful implementation of these recommendations, member states had to reformulate their respective national health policies to reflect provisions concerning traditional medicine, mechanisms for the coordination, and better utilization of the useful elements of traditional medicine in their healthcare systems. The requisite administrative machinery had to ensure effective planning, utilization, and supervision of practitioners of traditional medicine.[10] Finally, the World Health Organization recommended multidisciplinary investigations on systems of traditional medicine, paying particular attention to laboratory and clinical elements in the identification of effective remedies that comprise medicinal flora, fauna products, as well as mineral substances. Additionally, the organization advised that investigations be conducted on the psychosocial and anthropological aspects of traditional medicine and other healing methods, with priority being given to developing useful local resources such as herbs in the production of medicines, where necessary.[11]

In Ghana, Robert Bannerman, a physician, became the secretary of the National Working Group in their dealings with the Primary Health Care Training for Indigenous Healers (PRHETIH) program while facilitating their deliberation with the Ministry of Health and the World Health Organization. These efforts culminated in the establishment of the Center for Scientific Research into Plant Medicine, at Akropong, under the directorship of Dr. Oku Ampofo. The attempts at integrating traditional healing and Western biomedical health systems resulted in practitioners in both areas, sometimes referring cases to the facilities of each other at the regional and district healthcare levels.[12] The significance of the totality of these endeavors speaks to the relevance of healthcare to economic development, that is, securing a strong and healthy labor force for sustainable development. In this regard, therefore, the role of traditional medicine and its connection to African Traditional Religion cannot be denied.

Taboos, Prohibitions, Productivity, and Natural Regeneration

Across communities in the coastal and hinterland regions of Ghana, the exigencies and practice of traditional religions, to some extent, impact productivity. In fishing and farming communities across the country, Tuesday is traditionally isolated as a day on which work is prohibited in those fields. No one must go to sea, "*kɔ pu*," or "*fow pu*" on Tuesdays or "*Binada*." In rural areas, farmers are not supposed to enter the forest to weed or "*dɔ*." The conventional indigenous religious thought behind these work prohibitions refers to this day as the period when the spirits or nature spirits are out and about, so there existed the high risk of a defiant individual encountering them. This explanation is part of the many indigenous religious taboos. The alternative scientific explanation that never came up for discussion hinged on rest for the individual and nature. Both the sea and the forest will not be disturbed as that will enhance a kind of natural regeneration. On this day in the fishing communities, fishermen will mainly mend their fishing nets and fix canoes that need to be worked on. Also, government officials on policy dissemination missions directly to some such communities choose days like this. Productivity in the fishing sector generally increases the next day when the fishermen go back to work.

The Akan traditional month that revolves around a forty-day calendar culminates in the performances of several rituals, some of which include *Awukudae* and *Akwasidae* observed specifically on Wednesday and Sunday, respectively. On these days, the departed elders and chiefs—collectively referred to as the ancestors or *Nananom* as well as their various black stools—are venerated. These days are traditionally observed as holy. The prohibition of work on farms during *Awukudae* releases the labor of men and women together toward what is generally referred to as *Amandwuma* or public work within the traditional state, which constitutes a crucial element in rural development efforts. On this day in these parts of the country, men and women help with the maintenance or construction of school buildings, markets, borehole water supply systems, roads, rural electrification efforts, and other related projects. Labor could also be channeled into public sanitation in the community, clearing paths to rivers, wells, and other places. As and when called-for, some of these Wednesdays are devoted to public education campaigns by government agencies, Non-Governmental Organizations (NGOs), civic organizations, or immunization exercises for children.

Other prohibitions, emanating from traditional religious practices that impact economic development to some extent, are the idea of groves and shrines. These traditional sacred spaces are deemed to be abodes of gods, goddesses, spirits, nature spirits, and the ancestors. In view of their religious significance, most of these places pass as forbidden areas for ordinary mortals except for the traditionally recognized intermediaries between the seen and unseen worlds. The upholding of these sacred spaces mimics the same significance as national forest reserves in their contribution to natural resource renewal and preservation, both of which are inextricably linked to development. The lingering profound fear of retribution from some of these vindictive deities and spirits is enormous enough to bar unauthorized persons, thus essentially keeping these sacred spaces intact, and significantly adding to the percentage of untouched as well as untouchable forest belt.

Marketing of Religious Artifacts

The pervasiveness of traditional religions in African cultures also has a measured presence in the field of art, particularly in the making of drums, masks, fertility dolls, and other related artifacts that have appreciable demand within the tourism sector. From the pouring of libation before the taking down of trees, the casting of iron, the actual carving, to the carved abstractions, many of these processes tend to be ritualized. Some masks are considered religious artifacts because they constitute abstract representations and abodes of the ancestors and spirits, and people who avidly uphold indigenous beliefs venerate them. The simple *Akuaba* fertility dolls among the Akan are deemed to have the power to induce pregnancies, especially among women who desire that condition and have them in close proximity to their bodies. All these artistic pieces essentially become veritable objectification of the convergence between the seen and unseen worlds. The enduring foreign interest in "exotic" African artifacts has created an emerging market for tourists, and other local and distant clientele. These traditional religious artifacts abound in the Art Center Markets in Accra, Aburi, Kumasi, and other cities across the country, contributing some modest capital injections into the economy. These markets have benefited from generous patronage in recent times because of the several projects and programs in Ghana that target the African Diasporas, or peoples of African descent globally, including the continent itself.

Conclusion

Undoubtedly, the far-reaching and inescapable influence of African Traditional Religions in all the manifest sectors cannot be denied. Their silent but robust impact on economic development as pertaining to intellectual and moral development, land ownership as well as utilization, health, wellness, productivity, natural resource renewal, and preservation, including markets for religious artifacts, collectively and in varying degrees of effectiveness, accentuate the relevance of traditional religions to the economic development of the African continent.

Notes

1. Walter Rodney, *How Europe Underdeveloped Africa* (Baltimore, MD: Black Classic Press, 1972), 4.
2. Ibid.

3. Ibid., 35.
4. Ibid.
5. In the Superior Court of Judicature in the Supreme Court, Accra—A.D. 2019 Writ No. J1/14 /2017, January 23, 2019: *James Kwabena Bomfeh Jr. (Plaintiff) vs. Attorney General (Defendant)*, 17.
6. Ibid.
7. Djukanivic, V. and Mach, E. P., (ed), *Alternative Approaches to Meeting Basic Health Need in Developing Countries* (Geneva, Switzerland: World Health Organization, 1975).
8. Official Records of the World Health Organization, WHO No. 243, *The Work of WHO 1976–1977 Biennial Report of the Director-General to the World Health Assembly and to the United Nations* (World Health Organization, Geneva, 1978), 44.
9. Ibid., 45.
10. Ibid.
11. Ibid.
12. Kwasi Konadu, *Our Own Way in this Part of the World: Biography of an African Community and Nation*, (Durham, NC: Duke University Press, 2019), 185–187; for instance, illustrates this phenomenon in great detail using the life of ɔbosomfuɔ Kofi Dɔnkɔ who was a popularly acclaimed traditional healer in the Takyiman traditional area in the Bono Region. Konadu writes: By 1981, Kofi Dɔnkɔ and other traditional healers involved in the PRHETIH program had renamed the project "*Abibiduro ne Abrorɔfuduro Nkabom Kuo*" that is African Traditional Medicine and Western Medicine Integrated Group. … An April 1981 report prepared by Mary Ann Tregoning of the Holy Family Hospital, an Anthropologist Dennis Warren, Peace Corp volunteers, and PRHETIH field coordinators, G. Steven Bova and Mark Kleiwer also suggests … the traditional healers … not passive receptacles. Rather … approached the one-way flow of Western medical knowledge with tact and from their own self-understandings. The PRHETIH sessions on medicinal herbs … enthusiastically received. While organizers of the PRHETIH project envisioned a health revolution wherein traditional healers could be used in national health delivery systems within and outside of Ghana, the healers' rebellion against their prescribed role and the pejorative view held by the Ghana Ministry of Health against them placed the project organizers and their backers in a precarious position. Kofi Dɔnkɔ led the revolution not only in how traditional healers practiced their evolving craft but also in the ways in which healers and biomedical practitioners worked toward the health of the communities in which both served, albeit from different epistemologies. … The Holy Family Hospital received an average of 300–350 patients a day, but the 44 traditional healers who received primary health training were an integral part of the twenty six percent decrease in the outpatient department and of the more than eighty percent drop in the number of diagnoses of malaria, gastroenteritis, respiratory tract infections, and skin diseases by the department in 1981.

CHAPTER 28

African Traditional Religion, Social Justice, and Human Rights

Samson O. Ijaola

INTRODUCTION

Discourse in African Traditional Religion (ATR), social justice, and human rights find its mooring in the scholarly views on religion and morality. African Traditional Religion, though often regarded as an indigenous religion, spreads beyond Africa across the Atlantic. The religion affords spiritual mooring and cultural identity for its teeming adherents through its interconnections between the supernatural and the existential experiences of people. It provides and promotes the ethical basis for harmonious relationships, consequent upon which human rights and social justice are encouraged. While social justice is based on moral ideologies (a choice of what is good as opposed to what is bad for the generality of people), human rights translate the moral ideologies to prerogatives and make them binding on the community or the leadership of society. Brigid M. Sackey describes social justice as "a common concept that revolves around the ideas of a just society, equal opportunities, and the general well-being and freedom of human being."[1] He also notes that this concept is engrained in the traditional religious beliefs for Africans and its aim is to synchronize various communities in steady and harmonious social relations.[2] Along the same vein, Patrick Kofi Amissah connects social justice to traditional religion, giving the instance of Ghanaian communities, where the idea of justice is associated with social regulations anchored on the Supreme Being.[3] Inarguably, religion affords us the knowledge of our forebears and the

S. O. Ijaola (✉)
Samuel Adegboyega University, Ogwa, Nigeria

© The Author(s), under exclusive license to Springer Nature Switzerland AG 2022
I. S. Aderibigbe, T. Falola (eds.), *The Palgrave Handbook of African Traditional Religion*, https://doi.org/10.1007/978-3-030-89500-6_28

appreciation of the trajectories of social justice by highlighting its effects on ethical principles and behaviors of adherents. Similarly, religion accentuates how social justice has religious implications in the manner it is being administered or not.[4] Almost all religions in their different shades articulate the notion of social justice and human rights through their various doctrines and practices; such as expressed in their views, management of common resources, defense, and care of the helpless, advocacy for sanctity of human life, fairness, equality, participatory politics, and inclusive economy.[5]

From the pre-colonial to the post-colonial era, African Traditional Religion has found its own way of expressing social justice and human rights concerns. A critical reflection on the resistance to colonization in various African nations is indicative of the ferment for social justice and recognition of African beings' human rights, which colonialism jettisoned. As African philosophies such as Ubuntu philosophy were displaced for Eurocentric ideologies such as individualism, the idea of social justice becomes more complicated. African culture was infiltrated by the Western worldview and changed the African societal structure, including family, politics, and economy. The fears of the 'policegods' and ancestors in traditional Africa were replaced with policemen and western armaments. In this way, fundamental philosophical underpinnings and mechanisms that ensure fairness, equality, and human dignity were replaced. This chapter discusses the ethical framework of African Traditional Religion for social justice and human rights, and interrogates it as an agency of social justice and human rights. Also, the participation of the religion in contemporary struggles for social justice and human rights is examined.

Ethical Framework of Social Justice and Human Rights in ATR

Social justice and human rights are intricately linked, and both are social constructs that emerged in the nineteenth century to engender purposeful discourse and actions toward social progress. While both concepts evolved during post-World War II, their underlying ideas and properties such as fairness, equality, recognition of inherent human dignity, and freedom have existed in relation to social progress and social order in human society long before the modern political constructions. Social justice and human rights ensure an egalitarian society in which individual matters, with their rights recognized and protected, as well as encouraging and enforcing a decision-making process founded on justice and honesty.[6] Therefore, this section of the chapter examines the inherent ideas found in the nineteenth-century concepts of social justice and human rights in African Traditional Religion.

Africans have been described to be docile bodies for anything religious. Thus, religion is considered to have permeated the entirety of their human life, be it economic, marital, social, and political. A religious experience in the views of the African people does not end as merely providing spiritual connections; it must improve their psychological, emotional, cultural, and social relations. The idea of social justice and human rights in social relations borders on ethical principles. Ethics is subsumed in philosophy, and it is concerned mainly about the right demeanor and good life. While its scope is beyond the mere notion of analyzing right and wrong, it deals with the philosophical conception of good, right, and duty. The moral view of what is right or wrong and what is defined as a good deed or bad character in society also provides the framework for its ethics.[7] The ethics of society is also enshrined in what is certified as satisfying social relations, individual viewpoints, and forms of behavioral patterns that conform to societal goals such as harmony, progress, justice, and fairness. Moral principles evolved from human societies and impacted the ideas of social justice and human rights because "they respond to basic human needs, interests, and purposes."[8] They also influence human interactions as it tethers power relations and management of economic resources within a social system. The idea of ethics in relation to social justice and human rights also connects to religion. The influence that religion has on the development of a society's ethical principles is proportional to the extent the people believe in the principles and essential elements of that religion. Not surprisingly, it is held that "an ethics without religion lacks depth and strength, so does religion without ethics."[9] Religion, as defined by Emile Durkheim, is "a unified system of beliefs and practices relative to sacred things, that is to say, set apart and forbidden, beliefs and practices which unite into one single moral community, called a church—all those who adhere to them."[10] The context in which Durkheim used the term "church" is instructive for this chapter. "A Church is not fraternity of priests. It is a moral community formed by all the believers in a single faith, laymen as well as priests."[11] Durkheim further opines that history has proven, over time, that there is no religion without a Church—adherents. "Sometimes the church is strictly national, sometimes it passes the frontiers; sometimes it embraces an entire people (Rome, Athens, the Hebrew), sometimes it embraces only a part of them ... sometimes it is directed by a corps of priests, sometimes it is completely devoid of any official body."[12] The high point here is that religion only attains its full inspirational authority when it affects the totality of human life through a transformational moral relation that conforms to a common way of life.

African Traditional Religion, in a way, is the religion, philosophy, and science of Africans and most of the African nations as a church, especially before the advent of the Christian and Muslim missionaries. Linked with it are communal principles and strong kindred spirits. Thus, it was constituted as a national religion for various African nations in the pre-colonial era. Little wonder, John Mbiti describes the African people as "extremely religious."[13] While 'ethics' and 'adherence' are by themselves essential elements of religion, a religion gains more acceptability when other factors such as the belief in supernatural beings are well conceptualized and strengthens moral subjectification.

Following Tylor's theory and classification of religions, the anthropologists' evolutionary approach to religion disparages African Traditional Religion as animism or totemism, placing it at a lower stage of religious development or, at best, a higher stage as polytheistic religion but not monotheistic. Along the same vein, the morphological classification as well as Mircea Eliade's division considered African Traditional Religion as nature religion or higher nature religion (polytheism) and traditional religion; but neither as ethical religion nor historical religion (which are at par with monotheism), respectively, unlike Judaism, Christianity, Islam, and Buddhism.[14] The common criteria for categorizing a religion as historical or ethical or monotheistic include mainly the revelation vouchsafed by a Supreme Being, sacredness placed beyond the visible sphere, spirituality unconnected to emotions and significantly, ethical standard objectivized in the person of the Deity, and intellectual engagement in the religion evident in some sort of revolution.[15]

Belief in supernatural beings in African Traditional Religion includes the Supreme Being or the Deity, divinities, ancestors, and other spirits. The belief in supernatural beings is a common element held virtually in all living religions of the world. African theologians like Bolaji Idowu, John Mbiti, J. Omosade Awolalu, and P. Adelumo Dopmau, however, reacted to Western analysis and classification of African Traditional Religion as animism or polytheistic religion. These African theologians disagree with the western view, which rejects African Traditional Religion as a monotheistic religion because it is clearer that the religion has a lucid concept of one Supreme Being, who is well distinguished from other supernatural or superhuman beings.[16] Bringing to fore the idea of the Supreme Being in African Traditional Religion suggests that religion can be referred to as a moral source and participates in social progress. Thus, it is a revealed religion, though it has no founder.[17] It is significant, therefore, that African morality materializes from the power relationships that exist between God and the 'church', whom the latter worship directly and indirectly through other divinities. In African religion, there is a strong connection of deity-sacred-ethic, which influences the peoples' behavioral patterns. Thus, African concepts of morality are considered to materialize from the interactions between human beings and God and other supernatural beings.[18] It is, therefore, averred that African ethics are derived "from the sanctions or commendations attaching [to] … the infringement or observance of [social] norms,"[19] which result from interactions with the Deity and the divinities. "With the Yorùbá, morality is certainly the fruit of religion. They do not make an attempt to separate (the) two, and it is impossible to do so without disastrous consequences."[20] For example, *Emitai*, the Supreme Being in Diola religion, affords revelations that border on the ethical behaviors relating to social justice and human rights through the prophets.[21] The Diola religion does not only reinforces the inherency of ethics in African Traditional Religion but further depicts the idea of revelation bestowed by a Supreme Being. John S. Mbiti opines that "It is believed in many African communities that their morals were given to them by God from the very beginning," and this provides an unchallenging authority for their moral principles.[22]

One critical point that connects the element of belief in the Supreme Being or other supernatural beings to ethics vis-à-vis social justice and human rights is the idea of God as the king and ruler, which depicts the idea of a divine rule and the supreme judge who dispenses perfect justice in African religion. Bolaji Idowu, recognizing the morality derived from the social phenomenon theory of common sense principles, argues in favor of authority-based morality. For Idowu, "morality is basically the fruit of religion and that, to begin with, it was depended upon it. Man's concept of the Deity has everything to do with what is taken to be norm of morality. God made man; and it is he who implants in him the sense of right and wrong."[23]

Against the view of African theologians championing divine revelation as the basis of African ethics is the African humanists' view. It is essentially important for humanist ethicists to negate any idea of divine revelation or institutionalization of African Traditional Religion. While they recognized the Supreme Being as distinct from other divinities, they attached him to neither moral impositions nor worship systems, but referential behavior to the one who can be trusted. Thus, African humanists' view of African Traditional Religion is that of an intellectual religion with its predisposition to reason as the ground for morality. This suggests that "the content of both spiritual and intellectual revelations on the idea of God can be divided into human and divine projections, because it is through rational human agents that divine and spiritual notions are communicated and transmitted … if religion is discerned by human reason, the question arises as to why human persons are not figured out as representative and leading part of that intelligible revelation."[24] Similarly, Godfrey Wilson argues that the ideas of social behavior linked with moral virtues are not articulated in sacred terms and clearly independent of religion among the Nyakyusa of East Africa.[25]

Kwasi Wiredu, in his study of Akan religion, opines that morality and their indigenous religion are independent of each other, and ethics as the common good is based on what is defined to be in harmony with human interests.[26] Therefore, "the will of God, not to talk of that of any other extra-human being is logically incapable of defining the good."[27] Kwame Gyeke buttresses this position, noting that since what is considered moral as human conducts in society are directed mainly by social ideologies and normative principles, arguments in favor of African Traditional Religion as the source from which African morality stems is contra-distinctive because it is a non-revealed religion whose divine truth is not a preserve of an individual who could translate himself or herself to an initiator.[28] While this idea of African Traditional Religion as a non-revealed religion is controversial, Gyeke's argument is self-contradictory because social ideologies and normative principles should neither favor revealed nor non-revealed religions; especially, if ethics is just an important element acquired by religion through the transposition of typifying moral standards to a conceptualized deity by the adherents; a construction of moral principles found suitable in human relations by principal devotees and ascribed to the deity believed in a religion.[29] Thus, the best of virtues observed in human relations became canonized in religion. This implies that morality is first a bottom-up ordering value affair uploaded to a God up there or out there, which religious people look up to for their self-ordering in the world.[30] However, the African ethicists' position differs from such Freudian powerful 'father figure and of projection' because Africans regard the Deity, other forms of beliefs in their religion and morality as both ontological and epistemic reality of the people, which Sigmund Freud defines as illusory.

The arguments of both African theologians and African humanists, however, afford an intersection. The development of morality, such as observed among the Akan, Nyakyusa, Banyarwanda, and Mende with social ethics independent of their traditional religions, did not suggest that African Traditional Religion is not relevant to moral principles or vice-versa. It is also difficult to submit that African Traditional Religion, as a non-revealed religion, is incapable of developing morality inherently since a 'nature religion' cannot be morally neutral because nature itself embodies some moral virtues. For instance, virtues such as self-discipline and prudence can be learned from ants, as shown in Proverbs 6:6, "Go you sluggard; consider its ways and be wise!"[31] The Psalmist says:

> The heavens declare the glory of God; the skies proclaim the work of his hands ... they have no speech. They sue no words; no sound is heard from them. Yet their voice goes out into all the earth, their words to the ends of the world. ... The law of the LORD is perfect, refreshing the soul. The statues of the LORD are trustworthy, making wise the simple.[32]

Behavioral scientists have also observed that nature teaches us some virtues, which are not peculiar to homo-sapience. Altruism, for instance, has been observed in social animals. Thus, linking morality to the Deity in African Traditional Religion is a possibility either as revealed or non-revealed religion. Projecting morality as the preserve of religion may suggest that homo-sapience, an advanced social being, cannot develop virtues better than social animals, which do not have a religion. Therefore, it can be argued that African ethics were developed from complex phenomena and experiences even in the pre-colonial period. While African Traditional Religion has its unique ethical principles, it cannot be the only source of African ethics. Nevertheless, if the Supreme Being is regarded as the creator in African Traditional Religion, it is inarguable that as there exists the law of nature as shown in science, so also there must be moral law for human beings (encoded in human conscience and nature). Hence, if African Traditional Religion is argued to be a nature (non-revealed) religion, its moral codes found in human interactions only emanates from human nature. Consequently, African Traditional Religion has an inherent ethical framework for promoting social justice and human rights.

The Instrumentality of ATR in Social Justice and Human Rights

For fairness, equality, and respect of other human rights to be achieved among their people, various African communities in pre-colonial Africa are structured so that harmonious relationships are cultivated through the instrumentality of religion. This section of the chapter discusses the Supreme Being and other superhuman beings. They serve as judge(s) and surreptitiously punished offenses or openly dispense justice based on the gravity of the offense(s) of the individual(s) or community. Also, the communitarian ideology built on their religious beliefs provides the ground to nurture and instill disciplines in persons to accept and live according to the standards of society.

Supernatural Beings Agency

The belief in supernatural beings is central to the African peoples' daily living. Their aspirations and fears are the primary reasons the community aligns themselves with ethical principles aimed toward social justice and observance of human rights. In his reflection on S.G. Williamson's student's comment who bemused that "in olden times, there were no policemen and no need for them, the gods were policemen,"[33] Ogbu Kalu connects African ethics and social order in the pre-colonial period to the belief in the justice dispensed by the gods.[34] The divinities often appear to be no-nonsense beings, always eager to dispense and enforce justice once ethical principles associated with them are breached, or offenses in the communities are reported to them. *Shango* or *Jakuta* (god of thunder) as known among the Yorùbá, Edo, Cuba, Brazil, Trinidad, and Tobago, or as *Soko-egba* among the Nupe, or *Amadioha* among the Igbo is known to as enforcer of justice by publicly shaming offenders, especially by striking thieves or other evil perpetrators with a special stone (called *edun ara* among the Yorùbá). More so, he would carry the culprits by wind to the public square with the item stolen placed on them. *Sango* forbids robbery or stealing, deceit, and harming among his devotees, so he defends people against such evil persons.[35] Thus, "Jakuta represented the wrath of God, the scourging and cauterizing of evil by fierce justice."[36] *Ogun* (god of iron) and one of the divinities in West Africa, known as *Gu* in Haiti, has incredible power so much so that hunters, warriors, surgeons, and other metal associated professions do not only revere but fear him.[37] He is considered an aggressive god and could be merciless in dealing with evil perpetrators such as thieves, betrayers of trust, or those defiant to communal covenants through a ghastly accident with major harm to the physical body or outright death as punishments. The African people, especially in the pre-colonial era, strongly believe that the ancestors can inflict them with sicknesses, ill lock, curses, and death if they trespass against the community's ethical expectations. Ogbu Kalu opines that the ability to sustain social order, politically, economically, and socially in traditional Africa was only possible through solicitation to values and powers of their religious belief.[38] *Ogun* is known to help and support any fight in the course of justice for the right of the people. Ama Mazama notes that "in an environment where Africans were subjected to cruelties and tortures of all kinds, on a constant basis, a divinity like Ogun became quite necessary and significant. In fact, Ogun is intimately associated with the Revolutionary War in Haiti, which took place in the nineteenth century. It is said that Dessalines and Toussaint L'Ouverture, two major players in the war, both served Ogun and were in turn protected and guided by him."[39] *Ayelala* (a goddess that dispenses justice and perfect morality) is known to inflict evildoers, and defend victims of injustice in West Africa.

Most divinities associated with African Traditional Religion are ambivalent. They have the capacity to help people achieve good purposes and equally afflict them when they violate the ethical regulations that promote social justice and human rights in the community where they are being referenced. Some dreadful deities like *Sopona* (lord of the earth among the Yorùbá) or *Ojukwu* among the Igbo are believed to have powers to kill evil people who commit heinous crimes in secret. Victims killed by *Ojukwu* do not receive a normal burial[40] because the divinity's wrath against them ensures only a burial that makes them exemplary to the community.

While the Supreme Being, as known in African Traditional Religion, has different local names in various African communities, he is known with common attributes among them. One such common attribute is that he is a judge. His dispensation of perfect justice is shown in different expressions of the people or panegyrics to him. The Yorùbá, for example, refer to him as *Oba, Adake-da-jo*, the King that executes justice quietly.[41] The perfect justice of God indicates both his control over the universe and his involvement in human affairs to ensure fairness, recognition of peoples' rights, and retributions at every level and in all spheres of human engagement. Robert M Baum alludes to this in his analysis of social justice, a Western concept that exists as "*cashumaye*, a term that means all things good, a correct relationship with the Supreme Being known as *Emitai*, and as a result a peaceful and harmonious life" in Diola.[42] Whatever violations against the well-being of the people are considered an abomination among the Diola and punishable by *Emitai*. This includes the illicit quest for wealth or power and robbing people of their inheritance, engagement in the slave trade, and other actions or inactions against social justice and human rights.[43] The spirit shrines also inflict wrongdoers with specific infections, such as leprosy, a punishment associated with theft, which could affect not only the thief but anyone who aided or benefited from the theft and corruption.[44] More so, they believe the Supreme Being takes into account the good deeds of individuals, which will account for their forms and place in the after-life.[45] Thus, belief in supernatural beings in African Traditional Religion serves as a mechanism for the enforcement of ethical principles and harmonious relationships necessary for promoting social justice in many African communities, even in the post-colonial era.

COMMUNITARIANISM

While scholars are divided on the nexus between communitarianism and individualism in Africa, the connection between African religion and the various perspectives of communitarianism elicits interesting debates. The disparate arguments over communitarianism are always supportive of human rights and social justice and do not necessarily rebuff the role of African Traditional Religion in their promotions and enforcement. This is because, in most African communities, social justice is viewed as a divine obligation toward individual members[46] since the idea of perfect justice is attributed to the Supreme Being. Inarguably, there is an obvious interconnectedness among traditional government, judiciary, and religious belief both in pre-colonial and most rural communities in post-colonial Africa. The sacred authority was and is being conferred on their leaders to execute justice and promote the rights of individual persons. Thus, African communitarianism hinges on ontologies and epistemologies and serves as an essential instrument through which social justice and human rights are enforced and inculcated into the members. Communitarianism in Africa is structured to begin with family, home, clan/kinship, and the main community. Members of a community at each level of the structure include the living, living dead (ancestors), and non-living sacred places. Scholars like John S. Mbiti and Ifeanyi Menkiti link the idea of ancestors in African Traditional Religion to communitarianism, emphasizing that African ontology appreciates the co-existence of some supernatural beings such as spirits and ancestors with people in their various families, clans, and communities. The ancestors are referenced and regarded as the invisible third parties in human relations. Their established ethical regulations are preserved by invoking them to ensure justice. This idea of 'policegods' among men fosters and strengthens communitarianism in most African communities.

African communitarians are divided on the idea of individual rights to the radical and moderate school of thoughts, with African theologians like Mbiti and Menkiti on the radical side and the Akan humanists—Kwasi Wiredu and Kwame Gyeke on the other side. While the radical school subdued individual rights in community rights, the moderate identifies the collective rights that recognize individual rights. Famakinwa and Matolino advocate that moderate communitarianism is not diverse from the radical communitarianism which Kwame Gyeke attempts to criticize. "Their claim is that both versions treat the issue of individual rights the same way—that is, both versions recommend that communal duties be fulfilled even if they clash with individual rights."[47] Hasskei M. Majeed, however, condemns the position of both Famakinwa and Matolino on the ground that the similarities highlighted between radical and moderate communitarianism are based on misinterpretations of various concepts discussed by the two sides.[48]

Nimi Wariboko, in his analysis of the Kalabari, his native people, argues in favor of moderate communitarianism, noting the reality of the co-existence of individualism and communalism in the Kalabari community. The unique ontology (human nature, body, heart, and spirit-soul) and epistemology (including their adventures into commerce and creativity for survival) of the people from a nuancedly humanist approach of transimmanence allude to moderate African communitarianism, which Wariboko conceptualized as Agnostic communitarianism—"an attitude and a position that speaks to the intense and relentless struggle of individualism with the weight of communitarianism on one hand and the struggle of communitarianism against the fires of individualism that want to melt and erode the established structures of the community on the other. Agonistic communitarianism is the artful irruption into communitarianism of individualism."[49] Thus, Wariboko posits that ethics and social justice for egalitarian African communities in either the pre-colonial or the colonial era are not necessarily connected to religion. For him, "Traditional Africans, adherents of African Traditional Religion (ATR), like Christians are not 'always' able to be selfless, to consider the community and its welfare before their own. Such advocates of African communitarianism are as wrong as the Christian ethicists who hold that the arc of the ethos of Christianity inviolably bends toward communitarianism."[50] Inarguably, the moderate African communitarians reject the radical communitarian view that seemly depicts the African people as lacking the ability to merge faith and reason and presents Africans as a docile body to their religion or painting them as divine bodies.

Criticizing the African philosophers, M.E.S. van den Berg notes that notions on human rights from radical and moderate African communitarianism are not sufficient proof that social justice is intrinsic in communalism. While the radical or extreme communitarian view, common with most African philosophers, is based on the hypotheses that the objectives, norms, and well-being of a community are ultimate and prevailing in the matter of ethics and social justice has been subjected to more criticism because it is more inclined to various ontologies; the African humanists' moderate communitarian, on the other hand, misconstrue human dignity enshrined in communalism for the respect of individual rights that guarantees social justice.[51] Thus, communal interest in the extremists' views yet become supreme, regarding the welfare and morality, making individual persons and their interests docile to the community as well as being the yardstick in which individual rights are measured or recognized from the moderate's perspective.[52] While there is evidence in the revisionist literature that communitarianism and individualism co-exist in Africa as against the extreme communitarians' position, which canvases communalism as the only context for human rights and social justice, the claims that human dignity, individual rights, and social justice are based on African humanism also fall short on the ground of conspicuous sexism against women, social class, serfdom, an outcast that exists in some African communities.[53] Whereas M.E.S van den Berg concludes that communitarianism and individualism actually co-exist in Africa, he argues that neither of them is supportive of individual rights like liberalism.

It is, however, important to note that the essence of communitarianism is to ensure harmonious relationships among people, which begins by learning the ethics of the community from the dos and don'ts of the clan and the family. This is important because it is believed that the prosperity of African communities depends on harmonious social affairs and spiritual relations with the Supreme Being, divinities, and ancestors. The 'Ubuntu' ideology provides an example of sustained communitarianism through African Traditional Religion. Ubuntu is a Zulu word expressed in the apothegm, *umuntu ngumuntu ngabantu*, meaning "a person is a person through other persons."[54] Dirk J. Louw argues that while humanism in Western understanding is religiously biased, Ubuntu, which depicts African humanism or communitarianism, is sturdily religious. In Louw's words:

> For the Westerner, the maxim "A person is a person through other persons" has no obvious religious connotations. He/she will probably interpret it as nothing but a general appeal to treat others with respect and decency. However, in African tradition this maxim has a deeply religious meaning. The person one is to become "through other persons" is, ultimately, an ancestor. And, by the same token, these "other persons" include ancestors. Ancestors are extended family. Dying is an ultimate homecoming. Not only the living must therefore share with and care for each other, but the living and the dead depend on each other. ... In African society there is an inextricable bond between man, ancestors and whatever is regarded as the Supreme Being. Ubuntu thus inevitably implies a deep respect and regard for religious beliefs and practices.[55]

Among the Diola, it is believed that the spiritual world rewards good human conduct with abundant rain, harvests, children, and general prosperity, and punishes adverse conduct with drought, famine, infertility, and misfortunes.[56] The harmonious social relationships in communitarianism are dependent on ethical principles that ensure equal opportunities, respect for human dignity, well-being, and peaceful co-existence. While it is arguable that there was a skeptic view of communitarianism in pre-colonial Africa, it is obvious that in contemporary Africa, both individualism and communitarianism co-exist and function in the promoting and enforcement of social justice and human rights.

THE STRUGGLE FOR SOCIAL JUSTICE AND HUMAN RIGHTS IN POST-COLONIAL AFRICA

There are several responses to the need for social justice and human rights in modern society through various governmental and non-governmental organizations. This is not unconnected to the various social and economic needs of people all across the globe. People seek both protection of their rights as persons and justice when their rights are violated. They want fairness in the administration of their shared resources, guaranteed well-being, and peaceful co-existence. Religious groups and organizations are equally involved in advocacy and agency for social justice and human rights in various African communities and beyond. This section of the chapter focuses on how African Traditional Religion has participated in social justice and human rights struggles in contemporary Africa.

Undoubtedly, the influence and significance of African Traditional Religion suffered tremendously from both colonialism and missionary activities in Africa. The social disharmony among Africans resulting from Western liberal individualism, aided by colonial administrators with the support of the missionaries, created major moral problems for the people of Africa. Traditional political authority and justice systems through the agency of the traditional religion were demonized, many Africans converted to new religions, and very few adherents have African Traditional Religion. A sample of religious demographics in Africa indicates a dismal population of Africans who are adherents. As of 2012, there are 93.2% Christians, 2.0% Sunni Muslims, 2.5% claims no religious affiliation, 0.7% Jehovah witnesses in Rwanda.[57] South Africa had 82.0% Christians, 7.1% adherents of African Traditional Religion, 5.4% agnostics, 2.4% as Hindus, 1.7% Muslims, 0.5% Baha'is, 0.3% Buddhists and atheists, 0.2% Jewish, and 0.1% interreligious individuals as of 2010.[58] In Nigeria, there are 51.6% Muslims, 46.7% Christians, and 0.9% African Traditional Religion adherents as of 2013.[59] Despite the very low percentage of adherents of African Traditional Religion in the population of most African States due to conversion to Christianity or Islam, the religion still plays a functional role in the promotion of human rights, fairness, and well-being of not just its adherents but other members of the society.

Recent scholarly works on the need to invoke the oath-taking system of the traditional religion into the justice system in Nigeria, and at the assumption of public office by politicians and political appointees, are geared toward ensuring the promotion of human rights and social justice. Financial corruption in Nigeria, which depicts gross mismanagement and theft of common resources by a privileged few, evinces the nonchalant attitude of public officers to the well-being of the people. The various places and ways corruption is being perpetrated in Africa defy the moral theologies of popular missionary religions. Little wonder, David Cameron, the former prime minister of the United Kingdom, in a tête-à-tête with Queen Elizabeth II says that "We have got some leaders of some fantastically corrupt countries coming to Britain … Nigeria and Afghanistan, possibly the two most corrupt countries in the world."[60] With the obvious failures of government agencies to deal with corruption, Eghosa Osa Ekhator argued for the need for customary courts in Nigeria to be saddled with the responsibility of hearing criminal matters and other crimes related to metaphysical and traditional religious matters and, where swearing on oath by means of traditional religious means (such as the invocation of *Ayelala*, a goddess that dispenses justice and protects morality) can be done especially for public office holders in Nigeria.[61] Itohan Mercy Idumwonyia and Solomon Ijeweimen Ikhidero observe the Benin traditional justice system's resurgence in modern Africa due to its affordability and effectiveness in the administration of justice.[62] The Benin traditional justice system further gained more acceptability among the Edo people as the cumbersomeness and the high cost of arbitration in English courts increase in Nigeria.

Many African countries are re-vamping their traditional justice systems to ensure that individuals or groups are not denied their human rights in society. For example, the rejuvenation of Gacaca, the traditional justice system of the Rwandans, addresses the matters of genocide that took place in the country. The Government of Rwanda introduced a retributive structure into the restorative intent of the old Gacaca with some other new imports to hear genocide matters.[63] The traditional Gacaca is headed by Umwani, the king, who is regarded as an incarnate of *Imana*, the Supreme Being in the pre-colonial era. However, the traditional aspect of Gacaca began to wane in the 1920s through the activities of the colonialists and missionaries that resulted in the conversion of several Rwandans. Gacaca, therefore, represents a concept built on the agency of the traditional religion but which has lost its potency due to Christianity and Western judiciary ideologies. Not surprisingly, there are contradictory claims on the effectiveness of the modern Gacaca in determining some of the genocide matters.[64]

African Traditional Religion became part of the post-Civil War reconciliation from 1994, which is meant to restore respect for human rights, rejuvenate social capital and healings through harmonious relationships among the Gorongosa in central Mozambique. Through the gamba spirit possession that aimed at evoking the truth about responsibilities of various victims during the war.[65] "Magamba spirits bear witness to the violent events that occurred during the civil war. If these spirits are to be dealt with successfully, the violence of the past cannot be overlooked. There is a need to engage with the past, to find out what injustices were done, to acknowledge the wrongdoing and to repair the damage."[66]

The modern Gacaca in Rwanda and the Magamba spirits in the Gorongosa raise questions about African humanists' and African theologians' communitarian views. While both cases above provide examples of social justice and respect for human rights through their communitarian ethos, they also point to a relationship between faith and reason. African Traditional Religion is not opposed to reason; they rely on each other to birth an egalitarian society. Undoubtedly, African Traditional Religion has endured the overriding influence of the missionary religions to remain relevant in the enforcement of social justice and the promotion of human rights in modern Africa thanks to human rights, too. The enduring legacies of African Traditional Religion, through its adherents in contemporary African communities, are only possible because human rights ensure individual rights in most African countries and other nations. In this way, African Traditional Religion continues to maintain and reconstruct ancient legacies in the struggle for social justice and respect for human rights.

Conclusion

The basis for social justice and human rights can be found in African ethics connected to African Traditional Religion. The idea of a Supreme Being and other divinities in the religion provides an ethical source and agency for the social justice in African communities both in the pre-colonial era and in the post-colonial period, since it survives as a living religion with adherents beyond Africa. African ethics, as an agency for human rights and social justice, are not limited to revelations in African Traditional Religion because the religion in its various shades embraces even virtues from nature and human experiences. Thus, communitarianism can be seen to hinge on the African Traditional Religion's ethical and agency to pursue the goals of social justice and human rights enforcement. While the Gacaca justice system in this chapter shows how African Traditional Religion bequeaths legacies for modern Africa, even when the supernatural contents are unenforced in Magamba, the spirits provide rejuvenation of the justice system associated with the religion as it was in the pre-colonial period.

Undoubtedly, injustice associated with moral and financial corruption, conflicts, and other criminal acts is alarming in modern Africa. This is not unconnected to the heavy disposition and predilection of most Africans to the missionary religions, which condone misdemeanors under the preaching of grace without punishment. This coupled with liberal individualism, eschew African communitarianism that checks excesses on the strength of the 'police-gods' associated with African Traditional Religion. It is quite obvious, therefore, that modern Africans should appreciate and imbibe the ethical values and agencies of the Supreme Being and supernatural beings in African Traditional Religion to promote and enforce social justice and human rights.

Notes

1. Brigid M. Sackey, "Colonialism," in Michael D. Palmer and Stanley M. Burgress (eds). *The Wiley-Blackwell Companion to Religion and Social Justice* (West Sussex: Blackwell Publishing Limited, 2012).
2. Ibid.
3. Patrick Kofi Amissah, "Religion and Social Justice in Africa," in Nimi Wariboko and Toyin Falola, *The Palgrave Handbook of African Social Ethics* (Cham: Palgrave Macmillan, 2020).
4. Michael D. Palmer and Stanley M. Burgress (eds). *The Wiley-Blackwell Companion to Religion and Social Justice* (West Sussex: Blackwell Publishing Limited, 2012).
5. Ibid.
6. Karien Stronks, Brigit Toebes, Aart Hendriks, Umar Ikram, and Sridhar Venkatapuram, *Social Justice and Human Rights as a Framework for Addressing Social Determinants of Health. Final Report of the Task Group on Equity, Equality and Human Rights Review of Social Determinants of Health and the Health*

Divide in the WHO European Region. (Denmark: World Health Organization, 2016), 6.
7. Kwame Gyekye, "African Ethics," *The Stanford Encyclopedia of Philosophy* (Fall 2011 Edition), Edward N. Zalta (ed.), https://plato.stanford.edu/archives/fall2011/entries/african-ethics/.
8. Ibid.
9. Editorial, "Ethical Religion," *The Biblical World*, vol. 38, no. 5 (1911), 293.
10. Emile Durkheim, *The Elementary Form of Religious Life: A Study in Religious Sociology.* Trans by Joseph Ward (Mineola, NY: Dover Publication, 2008), 47.
11. Ibid., 44.
12. Ibid., 44.
13. John S. Mbiti, *African Religion and Philosophy* (London: Heinemann, 1969).
14. Charles Joseph Adams, "Classification of Religions," *Encyclopaedia Britannica*, 2020, Online, https://www.britannica.com/topic/classification-of-religions (Accessed 07/07/2020).
15. Ibid.
16. Namawu Alhassan Alolo, *African Traditional Religion and Concepts of Development: A Background Paper* (University of Birmingham, International Development Department, 2007) https://core.ac.uk/reader/1633008.
17. J. Omosade Awolalu and P. Adejumo Dopamu, *West African Traditional Religion* (Onibonje Press, 1979).
18. Namawu Alhassan Alolo, *African Traditional Religion and Concepts of Development: A Background Paper* (Working Paper No. 17, Religions and Development Research Programme, University of Birmingham, UK, 2007).
19. Emeife Ikenga-Metuh, *Comparative Studies of African Traditional Religions* (Onitsha, Nigeria: IMICO Publishers, 1987), 243.
20. Bolaji Idowu, *Olodumare: God In Yoruba Belief*, rev. ed. 1996 (Ibadan: Longman, 1962), 150.
21. Robert M. Baum, "Africa Religion and Social Justice among the Diola of Senegal, Gambia, and Guinea-Bissau," in Michael D. Palmer and Stanley M. Burgess (eds.), *The Wiley-Blackwell Companion to Religion and Social Justice* (West Sussex: Blackwell Publishing, 2012).
22. John S. Mbiti, *Introduction to African Religion* (Nairobi: Heinemann, 1989), 175.
23. Odowu, *Olodumare: God In Yoruba Belief*, 150.
24. Irene Omolola Adadevoh, "A Humanistic Explication of the Transcendental Implications of Segun Ogungbemi's 'Belief in God'," in Segun Ogungbemi, *God, Reason and Death* (Ibadan: Hope Publications, 2008), 51.
25. Godfrey Wilson, "An African Morality," in Simon Ottenberg and Phoebe Ottenberg (eds.), *Cultures and Societies of Africa* (New York: Random House, 1960), 348.
26. Kwasi Wiredu, "The Moral Foundation of an African Culture," in P.H. Coetzee and A.P.J. Roux, *The African Philosophy Reader* (London: Routledge, 2005), 338–339.
27. Ibid., 339.
28. Gyeke, "African Ethics," https://plato.stanford.edu/archives/fall2011/entries/african-ethics/.
29. Walter Goodnow Everett, "The Relation of Ethics to Religion," *International Journal of Ethics* vol. 10, no. 4 (1900), 479–493, 481.

30. Everett, "The Relation of Ethics to Religion."
31. Proverbs 6: 6, NIV.
32. Psalms 19: 1, 3–4, 7, NIV
33. Ogbu Kalu, "God as Policemen: Religion and Social Order in Igboland," in Jacob K. Olupona and Sulayman S. Nyang, *Religious Plurality in Africa Essays in Honour of John S. Mbiti* (Berlin: De Gruyter, 1993).
34. Kalu, Ogbu, "God as Policemen: Religion and Social Order in Igboland."
35. Idowu, *Olodumare: God In Yoruba Belief.*
36. George Bradon, "Shango," *Encyclopaedia of African Religion* (Thousand Oaks, CA: Sage Publications, 2009), 612.
37. Ama Mazama, "Ogun," *Encyclopaedia of African Religion* (Thousand Oaks, CA: Sage Publications, 2009), 482.
38. Kalu, "God as Policemen."
39. Mazama, "Ogun," 482.
40. Awolalu and Adejumo, *West African Traditional Religion.*
41. Ibid.
42. Baum, "Africa: Religion and Social Justice."
43. Ibid.
44. Ibid.
45. Ibid.
46. M.E.S. van den Berg, "On a Communitarian Ethos, Equality and Human Rights in Africa," *Alternation* vol. 6, no. 1 (1999), 193–212.
47. Hasskei M. Majeed, "Moderate Communitarianism is Different: A Response to J. O. Famakinwa and B. Matolino," *Journal of Philosophy and Culture* vol. 6, no. 1 (2018), 4.
48. Ibid.
49. Nimi Wariboko, "Between Community and My Mother: A Theory of Agonistic Communitarianism," in Nimi Wariboko and Toyin Falola, *The Palgrave Handbook of African Social Ethics* (Cham: Palgrave Macmillan, 2020).
50. Ibid., 152.
51. van den Berg, "On a Communitarian Ethos, Equality and Human Rights in Africa," 193–212.
52. Ibid.
53. Ibid.
54. Augustine Shutte, *Philosophy for Africa* (Rondebosch, South Africa: UCT Press, 1993), 46.
55. Dirk J. Louw, "Ubuntu: An African Assessment of the Religious Other," Philosophy in Africa, (Accessed on 20 July, 2020), from https://www.bu.edu/wcp/Papers/Afri/AfriLouw.htm#top.
56. Baum, "Africa: Religion and Social Justice."
57. National Institute of Statistics of Rwanda (NISR), *Fourth Population and Housing Census, Rwanda, Thematic Report 2012 Socio-Cultural Characteristics of the Population* (Kigali: NISR, 2014).
58. "South Africa's People," in *Pocket Guide to South Africa* (Government of South Africa, 2011/2012). (Accessed 29/01/2020) 12, from, https://www.gcis.gov.za/sites/www.gcis.gov.za/files/docs/resourcecentre/pocketguide/004_sas-people.pdf.

59. World Fact Book, "Nigeria," (Accessed 29/07/2020) from, https://www.cia.gov/library/publications/the-world-factbook/attachments/summaries/NI-summary.pdf, 2019.
60. BBC News website "David Cameron Calls Nigeria and Afghanistan Fantastically Corrupt" (Accessed 29/07/2020) from, https://www.bbc.co.uk/news/uk-politics-36260193.
61. Eghosa Osa Ekhator, "Traditional Oath-Taking as an Anti-Corruption Strategy in Nigeria," in Akogwu Agada (ed.,), *Combating the Challenges of Corruption in Nigeria: A Multidisciplinary Conversation* (Awka: Black Towers Publishers, 2018).
62. Itohan Mercy Idumwonyia and Solomon Ijeweimen Ikhidero, "Resurgence of the Traditional Justice System in Postcolonial Benin (Nigeria) Society," *African Journal of Legal Studies*, vol. 6, no. 1 (2013), 123–135.
63. Bert Ingelaere, "The Gacaca Court in Rwanda," in Luc Huyse and Mark Salter (eds.), *Traditional Justice and Reconciliation After Violent Conflict: Learning from African Experiences* (Stockholm: International Institute for Democracy and Electoral Assistance, 2008), 25–59.
64. Ibid.
65. Victor Igreja and Beatrice Dias-Lambranca, "Restorative Justice and the Role of Magamba Spirits in Post-Civil War Gorongosa, Central Mozambique," in Luc Huyse and Mark Salter (eds.), *Traditional Justice and Reconciliation After Violent Conflict: Learning from African Experiences* (Stockholm: International Institute for Democracy and Electoral Assistance, 2008), 61–83.
66. Ibid., 70.

CHAPTER 29

African Traditional Religion and Contemporary Functionalism: Divination

Eric Adewuyi Mason

INTRODUCTION

Divination, as a discipline and area of academic study, is broad and very complex, particularly when considering the practices across the various cultures that employ divination. It is beyond the scope here to consider divination practices across all cultures, so this work confines itself to a single case. A tremendous amount of knowledge about the subject, however, can be gleaned from studying one expression of divination, which can be used to make some generalizable statements about the field. Here, Ifá divination is the primary case, paying specific attention to the functions that Ifá divination plays in the societies in which it operates and among the peoples who use it; this will include the Yorùbá people in Nigeria and those in the African Diaspora who use Ifá divination as a way to navigate their lives. Ifá divination includes all associated art, practice, paraphernalia, literature, and so on. However, this chapter adopts the expanded meaning of Ifá divination that Kola Abimbola provides when he observes that "there are two divination processes associated with Ifá. The full Ifá divination system, which has 256 books (each book having between 600 and 800 poems) and the system known as Ẹ̀rìndínlógún (sixteen cowries). Ẹ̀rìndínlógún condenses the 256 books of the full Ifá divination into 16 books."[1]

E. A. Mason (✉)
University of Georgia, Athens, GA, USA
e-mail: Eric.Mason@uga.edu

Some argue that divination is primarily concerned with forecasting the future or telling one's fortune; however, Ifá divination serves several important functions as we will explore. The first function is the cosmological function of how Ifá divination aids one in living an optimal life in a world besieged by the conflicting drives of the good, bad, and neutral supernatural powers. The second function is governance, how Ifá divination aids in the selection/election of monarchs or heads of state. Governance can also include how heads of state use divination in managing political and social affairs. And finally, we describe the ways Ifá divination is used in the healthcare function. Ifá is used as an essential tool in all facets of healthcare in Yorùbáland and the African Diaspora.

Jacob Olupona observes that "in traditional and contemporary Yorùbá culture and society, the Ifá divination system occupies a vital role in ordering and regulating the social and moral order," using "social and moral order" as a catchall for all social and cultural institutions, and, for the sake of this study, all societal functions.[2] In the hope that no violence is done to Olupona's conception of "Yorùbá culture," this study uses the expansive definition that Kola Abimbola (2006) provides when he opines, "if cultural identity is intimately bound to a people's way of life, then Africa, or at least Yorùbá culture, is everywhere the world over," referring to Yorùbá religious practices in Cuba, Brazil, the United States, and elsewhere.[3] Therefore, this work treats the use of Ifá divination, sixteen cowries, and full Ifá divination, collectively, and gives equal weight to all people who use it no matter their ethnic identity or geographic location.

Cosmological Function

The Yorùbá cosmos envisions many natural and supernatural beings who operate from moral, amoral, and immoral positions. The Òrìṣà, who is responsible for the architecture, building, and sustaining of the cosmos, along with ancestors, human beings, animals, and nature itself, uphold the moral order. The Àjẹ́, inaccurately translated as witches, are amoral, pursuing their own ends using whichever means suit the situation. The *Ajogun* are immoral, insistent on the ruination of anything the moral agents devise. Thus, divination serves as a means of navigating the minefields inherent in such a cosmic war since "Ifá is the mouth-piece of the divinities and the ancestors. It is through the Ifá divination system that human beings can communicate with the divinities and the ancestors. Without him and his system of divination, human beings would find it difficult to reach the heavenly powers and tap their resources of divine power in the hours of need."[4] An example of this occurs within the Ifá divination literature, a vast collection of oral poetry describing the conditions and results of ancient supplicants who had gone for divination in the distant past, divided into 256 Odù (or chapters). This story from Odù Ọṣẹ́ Ìrètè describes a time when Ikú (Death), the leader of the evil *Ajogun*, appeared nightly in the dreams of a man named Jègbé and killed his wife Jégbọ̀. Jègbé went to the divine, as one would do when presented with this kind of situation. The diviners gave

Jẹ̀gbẹ́ a specially-prepared switch to beat Ikú should Ikú return, which Jẹ̀gbẹ́ did. This story makes clear that Ifá divination guides human persons in fighting back against the malevolent powers.

Similarly, a person can run afoul of the benevolent powers. One story in Odù Ọyẹ̀kú Ọkànràn describes when the monarch of Ìpọrọ̀ went to the divine and was told that someone in his household was engaged in behavior that offended the Òrìṣà. The monarch attempted to get the person to stop and make the appropriate offerings, but the person refused and was struck dead. The poem demonstrates that the benevolent supernatural powers have requirements that human persons must abide by or they will face serious consequences. Because Ifá divination operates as a mouthpiece of the Òrìṣà, one learns how best to navigate the Òrìṣà's requirements.

Governance Function

One practical use of divination is in governance—the selection of leaders and the execution of policy decisions. As any society can attest, leadership selection is fraught with many pitfalls and potential false starts. Those responsible for choosing a new monarch among the Yorùbá in Nigeria, even to this day, use Ifá divination to ensure the best person is chosen. Divination is woven into a complex political process, as described by John Pemberton and Funso S. Afolayan in *Yoruba Sacred Kingship: "A Power Like That of the Gods."* A new *Orangun* (name of the title of this monarch) was being elected for the city of Ila from among the candidates who were proposed by the royal families eligible to propose one. Pemberton and Afolayan observe that:

> Once the ruling house and the Alasan have reached a decision on a candidate, the Alasan conveys the news to the Afobaje, who conduct their own investigation into the worthiness of the candidate. When they are satisfied with their findings, they meet with the Olori Awo and the Aseda to consult Ifá and learn whether the candidate is acceptable to the ancestors and the orisa, gain some insight into the nature of his reign, and determine what sacrifices must be made to assure a propitious reign. It is possible that the consultation of Ifá may result in a candidate's rejection. If this occurs, then the royal house must present another candidate. Ifá may also pose a warning regarding a candidate and reveal the need for frequent rites of divination to discover what sacrifices must be performed and to whom throughout his reign.[5]

The selection process of a good leader is paramount. In the case above, we see Ifá divination used in a democratic approach to put the final stamp on the candidate. This process is democratic since it requires candidates to be proposed rather than creating a hereditary dynasty based on succession by the older son as practiced in Europe.

The Yorùbá in Nigeria is not the only group that employs Ifá divination for leader selection. It is apparent even among various groups in the Yorùbá

(African) Diaspora. Luis Nicolau Peres observes the succession of religious houses, called *terreiros*, within Candomblé, an Afro-Brazilian expression of Yorùbá religious culture. Peres writes that "the famous diviner or *olowo*, Agenor Miranda Rocha, ninety-four years of age, was invited from Rio de Janeiro. On May 30, 2002, ... after examining the cowry shells of Ifá, he appointed Dofona Zaildes Iracema de Mello ... as the new *doné*," head of the *terreiro*.[6] Ifá divination legitimized the installation of Dofona Zaildes Iracema de Mello.

However, even more important than leader selection is the policymaking uses of Ifá divination. As Pemberton and Afolayan point out above, Ifá divination will be used throughout the administration of the *Orangun*, prepping him/her for potential issues in the future. A good monarch is expected to consult Ifá throughout his/her reign both annually and when major issues arise. The annual New Yam Festival of the monarch of Ilé Ifẹ̀, the Oọ̀ni and the New Yam Festival of Ifá is a good example of how Ifá divination is used annually for policymaking. Jacob Olupona describes one such festival, occurring sometime in the late twentieth century.[7] As is customary during the festival, the messages of Ifá are delivered to the Oọ̀ni, providing him with advice to better reign. In this case, the Oọ̀ni was given two policy initiatives: (1) work to prevent turbulence or war in the kingdom, and (2) develop diplomatic strategies among the other monarchs to prevent the denigration of traditional practices.[8]

Health Function

Perhaps health is the greatest function that divination serves. Wande Abimbola presents three things that human beings search for: money, children, and long life with good health: where he opines that health is the greatest of the three.[9] Wande Abimbola continues by writing that "In the traditional Yoruba society, Ifá priests were the physicians, psychiatrists, historians, and philosophers of the communities to which they belonged."[10] Given these important professions—physician and psychiatrist—this work shall give more attention to the discussion of health function examining areas of healthcare that the diviners provide.

In George Simpson's fascinating study of one Yorùbá city, Ibadan, in *Yoruba Religion and Medicine in Ibadan*, he shows the extent that practitioners of various religions, including Christianity and Islam, use divination for health purposes. Simpson interviewed between 230 and 280 Yorùbá people in the areas surrounding Ibadan. He determined that roughly 33 percent of respondents consulted with diviners or used similar spiritual technology, with 63 percent of Muslims and 46 percent of Christians having done so. In short, Simpson observes that "the majority of ... informants consult diviners or use magical protection or do both," and given the nature of the study itself, it is clear that these consultations are primarily about health and health outcomes.[11]

George Simpson (1980) quotes an extensive passage from Raymond Prince's article, "Indigenous Yoruba Psychiatry," that provides Prince's proposed healthcare selection sequence, which Simpson's study contradicts. The validity of Prince's sequence is not being argued here, only the presence and importance of divination and the remedies it specifies to improve healthcare outcomes. Prince writes that someone who goes for Ifá divination may be advised to "make a sacrifice to the witches, his double, his ancestors or one of the òrìṣà, take certain medicines or use certain magical devices for protection against sorcerers, witches or bad spirits; change his place of abode ... change his occupation ... change his character ... become an initiate into one of the òrìṣà cults." There are a host of other potential remedies to prescribe, including many medicinal preparations, some of which are called òògùn and others are called *Ifá*, depending on the method of preparation.[12] Additionally, many of the rituals that Prince mentions include herbs intended to address many physical, emotional, and spiritual ailments.

As physicians, Ifá diviners must know cures and treatments for a host of illnesses. Therefore, some comprehension of illness is necessary to properly understand the full services that diviners provide to patients/supplicants. Anthony Buckley describes the causes of illness among the Yorùbá in Nigeria that he studied in a fairly succinct manner, and this work attempts to be more concise than that. While Buckley named the machinations of "witches," "bad medicine," and an Òrìṣà as causes of illness, we think it advantageous to describe the illness as "natural," meaning ailments that follow bodily or other processes in the world with no external supernatural influences or "supernatural," meaning some supernatural power such as the "witches" Buckley describes, or an Òrìṣà is the source of the illness, as well as any "natural" occurrences of illness that are influenced by a supernatural power.[13] This concise definition of "illness" makes it more manageable to discuss the uses of Ifá divination in healthcare. Kola Abimbola says much the same as we do when he writes that:

> Yorùbá traditional medicine ... is not just interested in getting rid of symptoms; it is interested in identifying and removing the causes of illness, just as much as it is interested in maintaining holistic balance. But there is also a spiritual dimension to the treatment offered by the Yorùbá herbalist (called oníṣègùn—literally, this name means "medicine maker"). So, in their efforts to restore holistic balance in the patient, the oníṣègùn will also be interested in finding the spiritual causes of illness (if there are any), just as much as s/he will be interested in restoring spiritual balance in the patient (if necessary).[14]

Ifá diviners are essential to the Yorùbá Traditional Religion communities around the world. Simpson notes that "nearly all of the traditional Yoruba healers ... rely mainly on some type of divination in diagnosing illnesses of their clients, and a divinatory technique may also be used in determining the appropriate treatments."[15] The use of divination in this regard is to be expected for diviner-physicians. Divination reveals not only the causes of the illness—whether the illness has a natural or supernatural source—but also where the illness fits within the current life of the supplicant, encouraging adjustments in the supplicant's life to bring it back into balance. This idea about balance highlights a critical understanding of disease revealed by Buckley. Buckley notes that "normally, the diseases contribute to the body's health, each one, at least in principle, having a defined role. However, the diseases may become 'too much' or 'too powerful' in the body."[16]

Mental Health

While it is true that as Ifetayo Ojelade observes, noting Kola Abimbola in her work, that Yorùbá Traditional Religion does not separate physical health from mental health, it is important to denote this distinction to understand those in the Yorùbá Diasporic Religious communities living in the Western world where this distinction is more pronounced.[17] From a Yorùbá Traditional Religion perspective, diviners "are consulted for a variety of issues without specifically separating out mental health concerns."[18] Yet, Ojelade also observes that "a growing number of African Americans drawn to indigenous healing systems" seek the counsel of Òrìṣà priests and diviners "when addressing mental health concerns," themselves accepting the mental health distinction while acknowledging that the source of the mental disturbances may be supernatural.[19]

In addressing the concerns of supplicants, diviners use Ifá divination as a "diagnostic tool," determining the best path in dealing with the mental health issues, if any are determined to exist. As mentioned above, concerning physical health concerns, the prescribed remedy may be some changes in behavior or character, or offerings to an Òrìṣà. The diasporic diviner may also advise the supplicant to seek additional help from a mental health provider such as a psychiatrist or counselor. The reverse may also be true, that a mental health professional recommends that a client seek divination if indeed that client subscribes to any of the Yorùbá-derived religious traditions. Ojelade provides a case that is included herein.

Ade, a young African American boy, required the services of a counselor. The counselor was aware of the religious preferences of the boy and his father, Mr. Cotton.

> The counselor shared her assessment that Ade could benefit from psychodiagnostic testing by the school psychologist. She also noted Mr. Cotton's interest in pursuing divination from an Ifá priest. The two agreed that divination should occur first and coincide with family therapy. However, Mr. Cotton did not have access to a local Ifá priest. The counselor had established relationships with local priests, the child's school counselor, and school psychologist. She assisted the family in coordinating care for Ade.[20]

It is obvious that the use of Ifá divination and Western mental health practices can co-exist and even complement each other. Based on Ojelade's research, it is certain that more of this cooperation is occurring in the United States. In an article by Oluyomi Esan and colleagues, "A Survey of Traditional and Faith Healers Providing Mental Health Care in Three Sub-Saharan African Countries," it demonstrates that several African countries, Nigeria among them, are attempting to integrate traditional healers, including diviners, into the healthcare system with some special emphasis in mental health.[21]

Conclusion

Ifá divination is used in many areas of life in Africa. Across the world, divination is used in leadership selection and policymaking, in large and small ways. Among the Yorùbá of Nigeria and Brazil, including the small groups of Ifá practitioners in the United States, Ifá divination plays a vital role in selecting leaders. Divination is also used to set by-laws and ethical standards. We continue to see Ifá divination integrated into established Western healthcare systems. Both the governance and health functions operate in a delicate dance with the cosmological functions as supplicants seek to alleviate any negative impact that the supernatural powers may have in their lives.

Notes

1. Kola Abimbola, *Yoruba Culture: A Philosophical Account*. (Iroko Academic Publishers, 2006), 37.
2. Jacob Olupona, *City of 201 Gods: Ilé-Ifè in Time, Space, and the Imagination*. (Berkeley: University of California Press, 2011), 177.
3. Abimbola, *Yoruba Culture*, 23.
4. Wande Abimbola, *Ifa Divination Poetry*. (New York; London; Lagos: NOK Publ., 1977), 14.
5. John Pemberton and Funso S. Afolayan, *Yoruba Sacred Kingship: "A Power Like That of the Gods."* (Smithsonian Institution Press, 1996), 79.
6. Luis Nicolau Parés, *The Formation of Candomblé: Vodun History and Ritual in Brazil*, 189.
7. Olupona does not provide an exact date for the festival. It is possibly around the same time as the Olojo Festivals he attended in 1993 and 1995. But we can presume it occurred after 1981 as Professor Wande Abimbola gives 1981 as the year he was installed as *Awise ni Agbaye*. Professor Abimbola, as *Awise Agbaye*, was present at the festival.
8. Olupona, *City of 201 Gods: Ilé-Ifè in Time, Space, and the Imagination*, 197.
9. Abimbola, *Ifa Divination Poetry*, 34–35.
10. Ibid., 11.
11. George E. Simpson, *Yoruba Religion and Medicine in Ibadan* (Ibadan University Press, 1980), 125.
12. Abimbola, *Yoruba Culture*, 47.
13. Anthony D. Buckley, *Yoruba Medicine* (Clarendon Press, 1985), 25.
14. Abimbola, *Yoruba Culture*, 79.
15. Simpson, *Yoruba Religion and Medicine in Ibadan*, 97.
16. Buckley, *Yoruba Medicine*, 32.
17. Ifetavo I. Ojelade, Kenja McCray, Jeffiey S. Ashby, and Joel Meyers. "Use of Ifá as a Means of Addressing Mental Health Concerns Among African American Clients," *Journal of Counseling & Development* vol. 89, no. 4 (2011): 406–12, 408.

18. Ibid., 409.
19. Ibid., 410.
20. Ibid.
21. Oluyomi Esan, John Appiah-Poku, Caleb Othieno, Lola Kola, Benjamin Harris, Gareth Nortje, and Victor Makanjuola, "A Survey of Traditional and Faith Healers Providing Mental Health Care in Three Sub-Saharan African Countries," *Social Psychiatry & Psychiatric Epidemiology* vol. 54, no. 3 (March 2019): 395–403, 395.

CHAPTER 30

African Traditional Religion and Contemporary Functionalism: Medicine

Sarwuan Daniel Shishima

INTRODUCTION

Health is paramount and of utmost concern to humans and animals. It is a state of being free from physical or psychological disease, illness, malfunction, wellness. This explains why the human being can go to any length to secure his/her health and wellbeing. In this respect, medicine and religion are both devoted to the welfare of the individual. This explains why in the orthodox and Pentecostal churches of Christendom, healing masses and crusades are organized intermittently for the healing of those with infirmities.

The scenario above finds credence in African Religion which employs African Traditional Medicine for safety, health, and wellbeing of its adherents. For a long time, Africans have had to rely on African Traditional Medicine as a recipe to their health challenges. This is because orthodox hospitals and other health facilities are either non-existent or in dilapidated shapes and most often, mere consultancy rooms.

In this situation of want, African Traditional Medicine or alternative medicine comes in handy to bridge the gap. This makes true the assertion by Gbenda that an estimated 80% of the Nigerian population living in the rural areas depend on African Traditional Medicine for their health needs. In addition to the above, some ailments like *kwambe* (whitlow), *ishombon* (fractures) heal better when treated in traditional healing centers.[1] This implies that in most cases, illnesses that defy a cure in orthodox hospitals are quickly brought to traditional medical practitioners for prompt attention and remedy.

S. D. Shishima (✉)
Benue State University, Makurdi, Nigeria

© The Author(s), under exclusive license to Springer Nature Switzerland AG 2022
I. S. Aderibigbe, T. Falola (eds.), *The Palgrave Handbook of African Traditional Religion*, https://doi.org/10.1007/978-3-030-89500-6_30

It is worthy to note that even as humanity edges deeper into the twenty-first century, African Traditional Medicine has retained its efficacy and is still being patronized as earlier explained. The functionality of African Traditional Medicine is therefore not in doubt. This does not, however, take away the truth of the matter that several changes have also been brought to bear on the practice and dispensation of African Traditional Medicine (ATM). The chapter examines these challenging issues affecting the wider acceptability of ATM by the generality of Africans and non-Africans with a view to charting a way forward.

Conceptual Clarification

The following concepts which appear in this are explained thus:

> African Traditional Religion: Also known as African Religion, and African Indigenous Religion. It is the Religious traditions of the Africans which originated and developed on the African soil by the forebears of the Africans. The Religion preceded the Arabian import of Islam and the Western European import of Christianity.

Towing this line of thought, Ajima and Ubana posit that African Religion is: "The system of beliefs, practices, rituals and symbols through which the Africans relate with the sacred, make meaning of reality as a whole and cope with the ultimate experience of their lives."[2] They further explain that it is the indigenous beliefs and practices of the African people and is described as indigenous because it is the beliefs and convictions which originated and are nurtured as well as sustained by Africans, on African soil, or carried out of Africa by Africans. The Religion is called African by virtue of the fact of its origin and practices. It is thus, the traditional religious heritage of the Africans, handed down from generation to generation.[3]

African Religion is characterized by specific beliefs, myths, symbols, and rituals which make up the religion. On the structure of African Religion, Anyacho provides a hierarchical structure comprising God (the Supreme Being), divinities, spirit beings, cult of ancestors, and the practice of magic and medicine.[4]

Basically, not being a revealed Religion or religion of the books, African Religion is written on the hearts of the Africans and observed by them in their day-to-day living and interactions with fellow humans and their environment. Ikenga-Metuh makes a categorization of the sources of African Religion in the following manner: (i) sacred institutions, (ii) oral institutions, (iii) myth, (iv) proverbs/riddles, and (v) names.[5]

African Traditional Medicine (ATM): This is also known as folk medicine, alternative medicine. Generally, medicine is any substance which is used in the treatment, prevention, and cure of an illness. Borokini and Lawal making a statement on this concept averred that: African Traditional Medicine (ATM) is the alternative or non-conventional modes of treatment often involving the use of herbs in a non-orthodox manner as well as the process of consulting herbalists, mediums, priests, witch doctors, medicine men/women, and various local deities when seeking a solution to diverse illnesses.[6]

According to them, African Traditional Medicine (ATM) includes herbal medicine, bone setting, spiritual therapies, circumcision, maternity care, psychiatric care, massage therapy, aromatherapy, homeopathy, and the likes.[7] The medicine is tagged traditional in the sense that it is based on knowledge, practical experiences, and observations handed down from generation to generation, either verbally or in written form, from African forebears.[8]

Mbiti points out that African Traditional Medicine is made from plants, herbs, powders, bones, seeds, roots, juices, leaves, liquids, minerals, charcoal, and animal substances.[9] Shishima broadly categorizes African Traditional Medicine into: (i) Good medicines are socially approved medicines which are used for socially approved goals, that is, to cure and prevent diseases, wade off witches, attract some fortunes, or wade off some misfortunes.[10] (ii) Bad medicines are socially disproved medicines or medicines used for socially disapproved goals, that is, to kill, harm someone, or bewitch a neighbor. Irrespective of this twofold classification, it is worthy to note that for the user, medicine is medicine so far as it meets his/her goals.

African Traditional Religion and African Traditional Medicine: Birds of the Same Feathers

If the assertion that birds of the same feathers flock together is anything to go by, the relationship between African Traditional Religion and African Traditional Medicine cannot be overemphasized. African Traditional Medicine (ATM) draws from the pool of African Traditional Religion (ATR). It is in the light of this perspective that Anyacho noted that: The practice of ATM is hard to separate from African Traditional Religion because medicine men are also religious authorities. Many of them are priests of divinities who in the cause of preparing medicine, worship and make their client worship their divinity. Again, spirits, ancestors, and divinities not only give knowledge of medicine to the medicine men [women], but also guarantee the potency and efficacy of native medicine.[11]

Thinking along the same line, Shishima observed that the traditional religious practices are a unique integration of beliefs found in most African societies. According to him, Africans have a subtle orchestration of notion about God as a prime source of healing.[12] Similarly, the notion of medicine, disease, illness, and healing among Africans is thus very often associated with the people's worldview. This scenario is demonstrated in the African value system such as social conduct, myths, rituals, and healings. In this respect, in Africa, the basis of medicine is Religion.[13]

African Traditional Medicine is believed to have come from the Supreme Deity and operates through tutelary divinity or spirits. Idowu explains that the lines of thought above find relevance with the Nupe in the preparation and administration of medicine where the name of God (*Soko*) and other divinities are mentioned. This means that medicine is applied with reference to God.[14]

This makes Nupe medicine without augmentation with the traditional procedures become automatically inefficacious. This explains why ritual invocations have significant roles in *Cigbe* (medicine) practice among the Nupe. Thus, whenever the *cigbe-ni* (doctor) discovers a new remedy, he/she must first perform a sacrifice, saying these words: "*Soko*, the medicine that has been prepared here it is. May the medicine be successful, I am sacrificing to *Kpara*, I am sacrificing to *tswana malu*, I am sacrificing to *tswako Dzana*."[15]

The Tiv also belief that *Ka Aondo a ne icigh ki been angev ye* literary meaning it is God who gives the recipe for any medicine that heals. In this respect the Tiv make incantations of thanksgiving to *Aondo* acknowledging that without his help the attempts of man are futile. For the Yoruba people the divinity of medicine is Osanyin, who is also associated with the oracle divinity, called Orunmila. This divinity is designated with all knowledge about leaves and roots with regards to their uses to cure illnesses.

The emblem of Osanyin is usually kept in a room in a puppet form which the priest manipulates by means of ventriloquism (the art of speaking without moving one's lips). As the priest makes consultations, he addresses the tutelary divinity in supplication tone thus: Father of children (our father), prepare medicine for us. We (children) have no medicine.[16] The Igbo also affirm that medicine can be used for defensive purposes.

From the foregone, it is apt to state the obvious fact that Religion remains a crucial component in the examination of any phenomenon in Africa, especially as relates to the issues of health, healing, and medicine. Therefore, medicine is an important aspect of the African Traditional Religion. African Traditional Medicine covers both natural healing agencies and the invocation of ritual or spiritual influences that are thought to be associated with them.[17]

This sub-section has conscientiously tried to examine the link between ATR and ATM and has established that by its nature, ATM derives its strength and appeal, not just from its efficacy, but also from the worldview of the African people. This is in direct contrast to the Cartesian paradigm of western medicine by which the world is viewed in purely physical terms and the body as separated from the mind. The African view of the world and disease is broader; it encompasses the physical, psychological, and spiritual realms.[18] Medicine is thus, an integral part of ATR and cannot be divulged from it.

The Impact of Change on African Traditional Medicine

There are no two ways regarding the fact that before the advent of orthodox or science-based medicine, African Traditional Medicine which draws its vitality, potency, and efficacy from the pool of African Traditional Religion was the dominant medical system for millions of rural-based Africans who constitute over 70% of the entire population of the people. However, the advent of

Europeans on the African coast generated a dramatic turning point in the trajectory and practice of this ancient tradition and culture.

For instance, during the colonial era, attempts were made to outlaw traditional medical practitioners such as diviners, medicine men/women, and healers. In their place, orthodox hospitals, dispensaries, and clinics were established and doctors, nurses, and other paramedics were employed to man these health centers and cater for the health needs of the Africans. This standoff continued after independence with African converts to Christianity maintaining this hardline approach.

Despite this hostile disposition to ATM from various quotas and the attempt to cajole Africans to abandon their culture and medicinal practice in lieu of orthodox medicine, the plot did not succeed due to the efficacy of traditional medicine. Globalization for instance has created awareness about the efficacy of traditional medicine. Through Information Communication Technology, it has been possible for the rest of the world to know that traditional medicine is not barbaric, fetish and irrational as the colonialists had painted it. It is now possible to verify the claims by traditional healers to ascertain whether they are true or false. For instance, Professor Charles Wambebo, head of Nigeria's National Institute for Pharmaceutical Research and Development, reported preliminary clinical data on a Nigerian herbal medicine that seems to increase CD4 cell counts and leads to improvements in HIV related illnesses. CD 4 cells help protect the human body from infections (qtd. in Wikipedia, Traditional African Medicine).

Consequent upon the above, the Nigerian Government has encouraged research in Traditional Medicine as the Nigeria society of pharmacognosy has been saddled with the task of investigating into traditional medicine with the aim of developing its products to meet international standards. Also, the National Association of Traditional Medicine Practitioners has emerged to unite practitioners of Traditional medicine across the country. Not only that, the National Agency for Food and Drug Administration and Control (NAFDAC) have a mandate to register traditional medical products of proven safety for human consumption and healing. At present, Traditional Medical Practitioners are now allowed to advertise their products and services via trade fairs where they display their products and attend to patients.

Again, Traditional Medicine in Nigeria has to a great extent been demystified. Through enhanced capacity to meet and interact with the practitioners, some have begun to come out and explain in detail their herbal medicines and therapies, procedures and sources. This interaction has greatly improved the quality of academic and scientific research. The results are very impressive as many medicinal materials that were hitherto unknown, have now uncovered, examined and found to be quite effective in the cure of management of certain disease conditions. Thus, Traditional Medicine is gradually becoming a practice involving western-trained academics, medical practitioners, scientists, and even Christian clergy.

It could be remembered, through globalization, Traditional Medicine practitioners are able to market their products across international boundaries. They now package their products and sell across the continent, thereby making their way into the global scene. This has improved the packaging of traditional products as they are now properly packaged in containers like glass bottles, plastic paper, and polythene bags.

African Traditional Religion and Contemporary Functionalism: Medicine

The scenario above takes us to the functionalism of African Traditional Medicine even in contemporary times. This clearly shows that ATM is not only just in good working order, but it is useful, serving a purpose and fulfilling its functions. The reason for this turn of events is not farfetched. This is because while orthodox medicine may be successful in advanced countries of the west and Americas, the same cannot be said of its positive impact in most of the developing countries including Africa where hospitals, doctors, nurses, and other medical facilities are difficult to come by.

In addition to the above, Ajima and Ubana assert that several ailments and sicknesses exist that orthodox medicine and personnel cannot cure hence, they are ignorant of their causation and diagnosis. All these are referred to as traditional medicine for solution.[19] Among the Tiv, *loho*, *kwambe*, *dagi* (whitlow), *ishombon* (fractures), *iyav mbu moron* (swollen stomach), *akpiti* (arthritis), and *usu* (shingles) heal better with Tiv Traditional Medicine (TTM).

Furthermore, poor roads, rough terrains, and transportation systems compel Africans to travel long distances sometimes on foot, bicycles, motorcycles, or pulled in carts to reach overcrowded hospitals. Africans also spend considerable time on queues to see a doctor; while in the process of carrying out several prescribed laboratory tests, most african patients loose their lives.

Moreover, the African would always want to know the cause of his/her sickness hence he/she beliefs that a person does not just become sick but could have been afflicted with a disorder from his/her ancestors, spirits, and God for having disrupted the social equilibrium. This makes the African unable to take precautionary measures to ward off these misfortunes. Again, the equipment used are often of poor quality which affects the outcome of results and impairs the quality of treatment.

It could be remembered that orthodox medicine is quite expensive for an average Nigerian citizen who lives below the poverty line and is unable to get the basic necessities of life. Orthodox medicine also alienates the African from his/her culture and he/she does not get the proper spiritual healing that their culture seeks, and that which is required by traditional ideology.

In direct contrast to the hiccups that Africans face in accessing orthodox medicine, Borokini and Lawal point out that ATM has several advantages over orthodox medicine (OM). These include:

1. There is little or no pathogenic resistance to traditional formulation hence many herbal recipes are usually polyherbal formulations; it becomes very difficult for any parasite or pathogen to develop resistance to it.
2. ATM is accessible, acceptable, and affordable.
3. ATM is a potential source of new drugs, a source of cheap starting products for the synthesis of known drugs, or a cheap source of known drugs.
4. The proliferation of high and rising proportions of fake and adulterated synthetic drugs makes a lot of Africans to crave for ATM or natural products.[20]

It is with respect to the numerous advantages of ATM and its potentials of affordability and accessibility as a health system for the majority of the rural population of Africa that the African Union (AU) declared the years 2001 to 2010 as a decade for African Traditional Medicine with the goal of making safe, efficacious, quality, and affordable traditional medicines available to the vast majority of the African people.[21] It is in this regard that ATM compliments Orthodox medicine (OM).

It could be recalled, both health and life constitute a single continuum. Thus, the need to maintain life in its wholeness becomes paramount. The African perception of sickness is wholistic. Thus, their approach to healing is multidimensional. The traditional doctors operate at different levels: physical, psychic, social, religious, emotional, and so on. Indeed they operate at several levels at once. This is perhaps the greatest strength of their approach.

According to J.V. Taylor, a man's wellbeing consists only when he maintains a harmonious relationship with the cosmic totality.[22] Thus the disruption of this harmony at any level can result to disease. The malfunction could be at the spiritual level, moral level, or social level. It could be psychological or ontological. It could be simultaneously at all levels. Thus, sometimes the physio-biological manifestation of an illness may only be a symptom of a deeper moral or mystical problem. Thus, once you limit the diagnosis of an ailment to the physio-biological level, you have not helped the patient. This explains why some patients simultaneously take treatment from both orthodox and traditional medicine men. Therefore, traditional medicine has continued to be functional because it is wholistic.

Challenges of Traditional Medicine

Having stated the above, it does not, however, mean that ATM does not have its hiccups and or challenges. Cashing in on this situation, Anyacho is quick to enumerate the following inadequacies of ATM. According to him, these amongst others, include the fact that ATM is shrouded in secrecy as traditional medical practitioners shroud their knowledge and do not easily make their art known to others. Most often, when the practitioners die, they go with their art/knowledge.[23]

Also, the hygienic condition of the environment in which ATM is prepared cannot always be guaranteed. For instance, Apenda and Adega point out that the consultation and referral rooms of most medicine men/women and healers serve as their sleeping huts which they share with other family members and their chickens and goats.[24] This makes the place unkempt and sometimes filthy. Therefore, there is the need for improvement in this regard.

Furthermore, specialization is a problem as one traditional practitioner prepares medicines for diverse illnesses. There is also the absence of medical laboratory tests.[25] Danfulani adds that the challenge of dosage, quality/quantity and standard control in the procurement and preparation of ATM; use of human saliva as part of medical recipe, un-sterilized razors and blades, crude implements for surgery and circumcision cast aspersions on ATM.[26]

Suggestions

In view of the discussion above, the chapter makes the following suggestions geared toward enhancing traditional medicine practice in Nigeria and Africa generally for its overall acceptance by the generality of Africans and beyond:

1. There is the need for the documentation of traditional medical recipes to forestall the prospect of losing them especially with the death of practitioners. It is therefore a thing of joy and a welcome development, the report from Borokini and Lawal that the National Agency for Food and Drugs Administration and Control (NAFDAC) in Nigeria has recorded over 275 herbal medicines in its green pages publications as of the year 2011.[27] The number may have grown beyond the 275 above seeing that it is now seven years since that documentation.
2. Traditional medicine should be de-mystified to attract more patronage
3. Public spirited individuals and non-government organizations can come into assistance in the provision of structures to serve as clinics, consultative/referral rooms with staff to take care of such places to enhance hygiene.
4. The regulations and strict monitoring of street hawkers of traditional medicinal products should be sustained to curtail abuse and unregulated use. The problem of the abuse of codeine cough syrup in northern Nigeria is a sad episode to recount.
5. Traditional medicine practitioners should be trained properly and specialization encouraged. Healers, medicine men and women should not be jack of all trades in matters of medicine just because they need money.
6. NAFDAC should also make haste in establishing a traditional medicine agency to export and showcase the potentials of traditional medicine from Nigeria.
7. Specialized research centers dealing with traditional medicine should be established by the governments in Nigeria and Africa in general to pioneer research into traditional medicine.

8. Above all, there is the need to integrate ATM with OM to complement each other most especially where one proves inadequate.

Conclusion

The chapter has examined the issue of African Traditional Religion and functionalism-medicine. It is the position of the chapter that ATM has come to stay despite several attempts to cajole Africans to abandon the practice with an array of objections and uncomplimentary campaigns against it in the past and present times. ATM has remained firm in spite of sustained attacks from the agents of globalization, western education, and Christianity. Another challenge is also noticed from industrialization, urbanization, and climate change which have negatively affected and shrunk the number of medicinal trees and recipes.

Despite these challenges, ATM has strived in modern times because of its accessibility, availability, and cost effectiveness. ATM similarly takes care of both the spiritual and physical components of the African person, thus, bringing about satisfaction and restoration of the person to complete health.

Furthermore, despite the hiccups apparently noticed with ATM, it has also made remarkable achievements as drugs are now stored in sachets or bottled. Other areas include the use of razors on individual patients, use of hand gloves, scissors, establishment of herbal hospitals and the hospitalization of patients and improvements in bone setting, and so on. Also, many traditional medical practitioners regulate the dosage of the medicine to be taken by using small glass cups and calabashes.

The assertion by Professor Adeoye Lambo in 1979 that "we made an evaluation, a programme of their work (ATM) and compared with our own (OM), and we discovered that actually they were scoring almost sixty percent success in their treatment of neurosis; and we were scoring forty percent. In fact, less than forty percent adequately captures the functionalism of African Traditional Medicine (ATM) in contemporary Nigeria and Africa in general."[28]

Notes

1. Joseph Sarwuan Gbenda, African Religion and Christianity in a Changing World: A Comparative Approach. Nsukka: Chuka Educational Publishers, 29, 2006.
2. Ajima and Ubana, 2.
3. Ajima and Ubana, 2.
4. E. O. Anyacho, Essential Themes in the Study of Religion (2nd ed). Obudu-Cross River: Niger Link, 244–255, 2005.
5. E. Ikenga-Metuh, Comparative Studies of African Traditional Religion. Onitsha: Imico Publishers, 12–28, 1987.
6. T. I. Borokini and I. O. Lawal, "Traditional Medicine Practices among the Yoruba People of Nigeria: A Historical Perspective". Journal of Medicinal Plants Studies 2.6, p. 20, 2014.

7. T. I. Borokini and I. O. Lawal, "Traditional Medicine Practices among the Yoruba People of Nigeria: A Historical Perspective". Journal of Medicinal Plants Studies 2.6, p. 20, 2014.
8. T. I. Borokini and I. O. Lawal, "Traditional Medicine Practices among the Yoruba People of Nigeria: A Historical Perspective". Journal of Medicinal Plants Studies 2.6, p. 2, 2014.
9. J. S. Mbiti, African Religions and Philosophy. London: Heinemann, 1969.
10. S. D. Shishima, African Religion: A Bird's Eyeview. Makurdi: Obeta Continental Press, 89–90, 2014.
11. E. O. Anyacho, Essential Themes in the Study of Religion (2nd ed). Obudu-Cross River: Niger Link, 253, 2005.
12. S. D. Shishima, African Religion: A Bird's Eyeview. Makurdi: Obeta Continental Press, 94, 2014.
13. S. D. Shishima, African Religion: A Bird's Eyeview. Makurdi: Obeta Continental Press, 94, 2014.
14. S. D. Shishima, African Religion: A Bird's Eyeview. Makurdi: Obeta Continental Press, 201, 2014.
15. S. D. Shishima, African Religion: A Bird's Eyeview. Makurdi: Obeta Continental Press, 94, 2014.
16. S. D. Shishima, African Religion: A Bird's Eyeview. Makurdi: Obeta Continental Press, 94, 2014.
17. Ajima and Ubana, 2.
18. S. D. Shishima, "African Traditional Medicine and Globalisation: The Nigerian Experience". In Aderibigbe, I.S. Omotoye, R.W. and Akande, L.B. eds. Contextualising Africans and Globalisation: Expressions in Sociopolitical and Religious Contents and Discontents. USA: Lexington Books, 110, 2016.
19. Ajima and Ubana, 4.
20. T. I. Borokini and I. O. Lawal, "Traditional Medicine Practices among the Yoruba People of Nigeria: A Historical Perspective". Journal of Medicinal Plants Studies 2.6, p. 28–29, 2014.
21. B. Stanley, "Recognition and Respect for African Traditional Medicine". Canada's International Development research Centre (CIDRC). 13th February, 2004. http://www.idrc.ca/en/ev-55582-201-1-DO_Topic.html. Accessed September 18, 2018.
22. J.V. Taylor, The Primal Vision. London: SCM Press, 67, 1969.
23. E. O. Anyacho, Essential Themes in the Study of Religion (2nd ed). Obudu-Cross River: Niger Link, 253–254, 2005.
24. A. Z. Apenda, and A. P. Adega, "Constraints and Challenges in Traditional Healthcare in Nigeria: The Tiv Perspective". Olayemi Akinwumi et al. (eds). African Indigenous Science and Knowledge Systems: Triumphs and Tribulations. Abuja: Roots Books and Journals, 363, 2007.
25. A. Z. Apenda, and A. P. Adega, "Constraints and Challenges in Traditional Healthcare in Nigeria: The Tiv Perspective". Olayemi Akinwumi et al. (eds). African Indigenous Science and Knowledge Systems: Triumphs and Tribulations. Abuja: Roots Books and Journals, 254, 2007.
26. U. H. D. Danfulani, "Cosmology and Healing: Models of Interpretation of African Disease Aetiologies". ATE: Journal of African Religion and Culture, 1, p. 15, 2010.

27. T. I. Borokini and I. O. Lawal, "Traditional Medicine Practices among the Yoruba People of Nigeria: A Historical Perspective". Journal of Medicinal Plants Studies 2.6, p. 29, 2014.
28. A. Z. Apenda, (2010). "Towards Nigeria Healthcare Delivery in the 21st Century: Prospects and Challenges for Traditional Medicine". ATE: Journal of African Religion and Culture, 1, p. 84.

CHAPTER 31

African Traditional Religion and Contemporary Functionalism: Festivals

Tenson Muyambo

INTRODUCTION

African Traditional Religion is a contested nomenclature whose arguments are beyond the purview of this chapter. However, it is prudent to state that the middle term "traditional" has been dropped in some instances and "indigenous" adopted instead. This is necessitated by the negative permutations that are associated with the word "traditional." Nevertheless, this chapter uses "traditional." We are alive to the arguments therein. Joseph Omosade Awolalu is instructive when it comes to the use of the word "traditional." He argues thus:

> We need to explain the word "traditional." This word means indigenous, that which is aboriginal or foundational, handed down from generation to generation, upheld and practised by Africans today. This is a heritage from the past but treated not as a thing of the past but as that which connects the past with the present and the present with eternity. This is not a "fossil" religion, a thing of the past or a dead religion. It is a religion that is practised by living men and women.[1]

The continued use of the term "traditional" in this chapter is informed by Awolalu's arguments. From this understanding, the word "traditional" is well-meaning and well-intentioned whenever used by scholars who are mostly Afrocentric as opposed to the Eurocentric ones. African Traditional Religion, as summed up by Awolalu, "when we speak of African traditional religion, we

T. Muyambo (✉)
Great Zimbabwe University, Masvingo, Zimbabwe
e-mail: tmuyambo@gzu.ac.zw

© The Author(s), under exclusive license to Springer Nature Switzerland AG 2022
I. S. Aderibigbe, T. Falola (eds.), *The Palgrave Handbook of African Traditional Religion*, https://doi.org/10.1007/978-3-030-89500-6_31

mean the indigenous religious beliefs and practices of the Africans. It is the religion which resulted from the sustaining faith held by the forebears of the present Africans."[2]

This conceptualization of African Traditional Religion (ATR) has been under the spotlight in twenty-first-century Africa. This is necessitated by the condescending attitudes some people have developed toward the religion. One of the significant challenges ATR faces is, its critics argue that African Traditional Religion serves no purpose in a technologically globalizing world. As such, the efficacy of African Traditional Religion is often doubted. While skeptics believe that African Traditional Religion is becoming obsolete, this chapter argues that African Traditional Religion plays a significant role in its practitioners' religiosity. The chapter demonstrates the significance of African Traditional Religion by focusing on the position and place of festivals in the lives of the practitioners of African Traditional Religion. The lives of the adherents are inundated by festivals that celebrate the vitality of African life. To illustrate this vitality, a Ndau people's festival, the Ndau Festival of the Arts (NdaFA), celebrated every September of every year among the Ndau, is used as an example of how festivals are an essential component of African Traditional Religion that have not only withstood the test of time but have adapted to remain religiously relevant to the contemporary times. This chapter celebrates the resilience and tenacity that characterize African Traditional Religion. It argues that African Traditional Religion, as expounded in festivals, is a religion that people are not converted to but are born into. It permeates all aspects of their lives.

Festival: The Concept

According to Oluwatosin Adeoti Akintan, "festivals are celebrations of important events in every society which bring together people from all walks of life."[3] Arvind P. Nirmal is of the view that festivals are an important aspect of any religion. This implies that festivals are of a religious nature.[4] George T. Basden argues that festival is nothing but a *fête* with dancing, music, feasting, and the general manifestation of pleasure and enjoyment with congratulations for the years past and good wishes for the years ahead.[5] Festivals, according to Famuyiwa, are periodic recurring days or seasons of gaiety or merry-making set aside by a community or clan for the observance of sacred celebrations, religious solemnities, or musical and traditional performances of special significance.[6] The above conceptualization of festival shows that festivals are characterized by celebration and merriment. African life is celebrated in many ways, and festivals are one of them. Central to festivals is merry-making, where life is celebrated with aplomb. The celebratory atmosphere punctuated by dancing, singing, and drumming provides festivals with a certain level of licentiousness. According to E. Bolaji Idowu, when Europeans saw these vivacious celebrations, they rubbished most African cultural fecundity as "fetish," "primitive," and "backward."[7] Using an Afrocentric lens, this chapter argues that festivals are the *axis mundi* of African religiosity. The chapter demonstrates this by discussing a festival among the Ndau people of Chipinge in south-eastern Zimbabwe. The festival has become an annual celebration that is now on the national calendar of events. The festival is code-named Ndau Festival of the Arts (NdaFA)

Theoretical Framework and Methodology

This study utilizes the Afrocentric paradigm as a theoretical framework to understand African festivals' functionality in twenty-first-century Africa and Zimbabwe by extension. Scholars who have popularized Afrocentricity as a theory are Molefi Kete Asante and Maulana Karenga.[8] Afrocentricity rose as a reaction to Eurocentrism, which "universalised European aspects of culture, communication, philosophy, education, rhetoric, linguistics, history, psychology and anthropology."[9] The condescending attitude toward ATR, particularly African festivals, has its roots in Western ideologies and epistemologies. African Traditional Religion and its elements such as festivals have been denigrated as no religion and practices from a Western perspective. This pushed, and is still pushing, African Traditional Religion to the periphery. The Afrocentric approach becomes handy as a corrective and a critique paradigm meant to counter the European meta-paradigm, which denied and still denies the agency of festivals in people's religious matters. As both a corrective approach and critique, the Afrocentric paradigm counters the Eurocentric predominance in matters that are African and sensitizes African people to realize that they are not only religious in their own rights but proud practitioners of a living religion, including their participation in festivals.[10]

The author of this study collected data from interviews with elders, NdaFA participants, the NdaFA's founder, Kusasa, and other NdaFA board members. Participant observation was also adopted in collecting data where, as a Board Member, I participated in organizing the festival and, at the same time collecting data as the festival took place. The data collection process occurred during the annual festival celebrations from 2014 to 2017.

The next section focuses on African festivals' functionality as an expression of ATR by examining the Ndau Festival of the Arts (NdaFA), a Ndau festival whose participation in is for all and sundry. African Traditional Religion is not on the demise but is on the resurgence, thanks to its believers and practitioners who have revived the practice of festivals in their variant forms.

Ndau Festival of the Arts (NdaFA)

The Ndau people are an ethno-linguistic group found in the South-Eastern part of Zimbabwe. They are predominantly in the Chimanimani and Chipinge districts of the Manicaland province.[11] The NdaFA is a festival for the Chipinge ethnic group, although the Chimanimani Ndau people also grace the occasion as well as Ndau speaking people of western Mozambique. NdaFA is the brainchild of a Ndau young man in his early forties, Philip Kusasa Bangira. The man is a culturalist and values what it means to be African and Ndau in particular. Having realized how the Ndau culture was fast losing its grip on the Ndau youth and some elders, Philip Kusasa decided to promote the Ndau culture in its entirety by coordinating activities meant to encourage the people to wholesomely embrace their culture. This includes the Ndau language, as a carrier of culture, Ndau folklores, traditional medicines, Ndau indigenous knowledge, songs, and dances. He, together with other culturalists, identified a place in Bangira village in the chief Musikavanthu area where he built a cultural center. He erected traditional huts, planted traditional trees, and decorated the huts with artifacts that range from traditional beads, bows and arrows, clay pots of various sizes, and many other ornaments that display deep Ndau heritage. The place is located in Chikore area of Chipinge District, a mission founded by the American Board of Commissioners for Foreign Mission (ABCFM), renamed the United Church of Christ in Zimbabwe (UCCZ).[12]

Before discussing the themes that emerged during my fieldwork, it is prudent to summarize the objectives behind NdaFA as narrated by Kusasa during the interview. The objectives include *inter alia*:

- To preserve the Ndau cultural values;
- To create recreational space for the people;
- To promote cultural tourism;
- To publicize Ndau culture to other cultures worldwide;
- To promote the documentation of indigenous knowledge;
- To conscientize the local people of the need to protect, promote, and preserve indigenous knowledge of the Ndau culture.

From the above objectives, the NdaFA, right from the onset, is clear about its mandate: the resuscitation, promotion, and preservation of the Ndau culture for several reasons. The NdaFA is premised on the African Renaissance Studies agenda.

NdaFA as a Social Identity Indicator

Identity is an African ethos that is central to African Studies. The Ndau, in particular, engage in activities that portray who they are.[13] Thus, the Ndau festivals are not empty happenings but rich events that celebrate the Ndauness of the Ndau people in particular, and the Africanness of the African people in general. This theme recurred during my fieldwork. In an interview with Mr. Philip Kusasa Bangira, NdaFA's founder, it came out clearly that NdaFA is organized to allow the Ndau people and even those who participate in the events to celebrate and appreciate their identity and fight very hard to preserve it. One interviewee concurred when she shared that the Ndau people are proud of their identity, and to ensure that this does not become extinct, NdaFA, through dance and performance, revitalizes the Ndau identity. In a different study by Tenson Muyambo a Ndau practice *shupa* which is a traditional herbal medicine, both provides primary health care for the Ndau and acts as an expression of Ndau identity.[14]

Similarly, Alexa Delbosc views social identity as a motivator in cultural festivals.[15] For him, identity is "how people identify themselves as a unique individual, different to the rest of the world."[16] Social identity motivates people to rally behind each other during cultural festivals. Through participant observations, I discovered that the NdaFA is predominantly about the Ndau people and their indigenous knowledge. To illustrate this, during the festival, I heard people complaining of *Jerusarema*, a Zezuru dance that certain schools display at the festival. One elder candidly expressed her displeasure. She stated that "the *Jerusarema* dance was not Ndau and hence had no place at the festival." Without wanting to sound tribalistic, the elder had a point. If the festival is meant to celebrate and showcase the Ndau culture, the *Jerusarema* dance has no place at the festival, for no one identifies with it. It is a "foreign"[17] dance, and displaying it at the Ndau festival defies logic. If it is displayed, it must be made clear that it is not Ndau but added to provide diverse entertainment at the festival.

The close affinity displayed by the Ndau people at the festival sums it up. The dances, songs, language, dress code, drumming, drum types, and artifacts displayed are predominantly Ndau. One interviewee stated that "this festival *ngeye va Ndau veiita zvechi Ndau chavo* [is for the Ndau performing their Ndau culture]." The festival, though attended by both the Ndau and non-Ndau people, creates a predominantly Ndau aura.

NdaFA as Social Cohesion

Festival events are liminal periods when people come together as a group, renew their relationships, and strengthen their cohesion. Heerden points out that liminality is a period of experimentation and reflection.[18] The NdaFA is a platform where the Ndau people meet and reflect on their culture, which is not only under siege from globalization and modernity but is threatened by a host of factors. The festival is a rallying point for the communities to take stock of their culture and map the way forward in ensuring that their culture continues to exist, possibly, undiluted.

That NdaFA is a social cohesion for the Ndau people is indisputable. It was found out that it brought Ndau people from various backgrounds together, where the Ndau bond finds expression. It was also revealed that festivals provide not only the opportunities to fellowship together but also, and more importantly, to celebrate the culture of the people. This allows the young to mingle with the old and symbiotically learn from one another.

Delbosc seems to concur with this, as he also found that social networking is the most common motivation for community members to attend cultural festivals.[19] The togetherness displayed during the NdaFA preparations is testimony to a community that coheres. Tasks are allocated to members who carry them out with a business acumen that surprises many observers. Food is donated from the community as well as utensils that are used at the festival. Some members go out of their way to provide accommodation to visitors from outside Ndauland. The local schools transport their students to the festival. Things just flow, and the festival's level of organization is excellent. Various committees pool resources together, and the common saying is *vaNdau toita zviro zvedu pauNdau hwedu* [We, the Ndau, are doing our things in our Ndauness]. This is said with pride, pride meant to reinforce the need to be conscious of one's culture.

NdaFA as an Education Tool

Given how the indigenous forms of education have been marginalized, the NdaFA offers a platform where education, in its various forms, is offered to children, especially those of school-going age. This is where the Ndau people, through the festival, educate their children about their heritage. It was observed that apart from teaching children about their culture, efforts are made to start by teaching them the Ndau language as a carrier of the Ndau culture. Despite being recognized in the Constitution of Zimbabwe Amendment (No. 20) Act 2013, the Ndau language has remained marginalized. The Constitution clearly states that "The following languages, namely Chewa, Chibarwe, English, Kalanga, Koisan, Nambya, *Ndau* (emphasis mine), Ndebele ... are officially recognised languages of Zimbabwe" (Constitution of Zimbabwe Amendment (No. 20) Act 2013: 17). The Constitution goes further to state that "The state and all institutions and agencies of government at every level must ensure that all officially recognised languages are treated equally" (Constitution of Zimbabwe Amendment (No. 20) Act 2013: 17). Of note is that the Constitution requires the state to promote the use of all the languages used in Zimbabwe, and by so doing create the necessary conditions for their (languages) development. However, the Constitution's provisions have remained a talk show with no clear-cut policies being implemented to achieve them. Having noted how marginalized the Ndau language is, Emmanuel Sithole discusses the need to intellectualize the language from being a dialect into an "official" language.[20] Despite the challenges therein, as a result of the colonial onslaught on local languages, Sithole believes officializing Ndau is achievable. The social discrimination and inequality, according to Nhlanhla Mkhize and Nobuhle Ndimande-Hlongwa, need to be shaken off. This can only happen when cultural festivals turn into education platforms, especially for the youth.[21]

Observations are that the NdaFA has taken upon itself to educate the youth about the Ndau language. Quite instrumental in this aspect is Muzi Mlambo, a University of Zimbabwe Lecturer, who, with the assistance of an indigenous knowledge scholar, Pindai Sithole, administers a Ndau language competition in spelling, essay writing, and poetry at the festival. Winners get their school fees paid for one year and there are different awards, and various prizes on offer on the day of the festival. This has not only increased interest but also a sense of pride in the Ndau language. The language is normally shunned in schools where students and teachers alike speak Shona; a language claimed to be a result of many dialects. Yet, it is predominantly Zezuru and Karanga, dialects of the ruling elites. With the introduction of the language competition at the NdaFA celebration, the Ndau language is gaining prominence among some students, though it is not yet examinable despite the recognition by the Constitution. Muzi Mlambo not only hosts the language competition at NdaFA events but also distributes Ndau literature to schools and students. For the first time, the Ndau language is finding its way into academia. This is premised on Beban Chumbow and Julian Dakin's perspective on the language question and national development in Africa.[22] They have argued that no foreign language is as efficient as the mother tongue in transmitting knowledge. Herbert Vilakazi also places a premium on the mother language when he argues that students whose mother tongue is not the medium of instruction in higher education are at a disadvantage. This points to the efficacy of the use of the mother language in people's livelihoods.[23]

The festival also showcases some of the artifacts that the Ndau use. These include mats, bows and arrows, and traditional medicine like *mungurahwe*.[24] The youth and schoolchildren attending the festival are taken through the traditional huts built there and shown the various Ndau traditional artifacts. The students take down notes as guides explain these traditional displays. There are also beads that women exhibit as part of their dressing code. Students are taught how the beads, for instance, are made, their functions in sexuality, and many other teachings.

NdaFA as a Potential Tourism Attraction

Another area that could see festivals becoming sources of people's livelihoods is in the tourism sector. Inasmuch as festivals are indicators of social identity, social cohesion, and tools for education as discussed above, observations at the NdaFA indicate that most traditional artifacts are the envy of many. I recall one incident at the 2014 festival when the former permanent Secretary of the then Ministry of Rural Development, Promotion and Preservation of National Culture and Heritage called for the elderly Ndau women to prepare as many beads as were possible for the next festival for buyers to purchase. She made it abundantly clear that the beads, apart from being souvenirs of the vitality of the Ndau dress code, could be sources of income for the Ndau women.

The various artifacts on display at the NdaFA are sources of attraction. There is a local artist who makes excellent designs using ordinary locally available material, such as rapoko grains, that are very attractive to the eye. Members of the provincial team led by the Manicaland Provincial Administrator, now known as the Provincial Development Coordinator (PDC) were very much attracted to the artist's work. They commended the artist for his excellent work and advised him to find a market for his products.

Ezenagu Ngozi and Olatunji Tabitha agree that "traditional festivals act as a hook to attract tourists."[25] As such, traditional festivals like the NdaFA attract visitors "who spend money within the community, enhancing the local economy and supporting the local economy."[26] This is a missing link that the NdaFA can explore in order to commercialize its displays and performances such that it realizes revenue. This tourist attraction dimension is not explored and is an avenue for the incoming generation. Since tourism relies heavily on the natural environment, the preservation of indigenous vegetation around the NdaFA event is quite conducive for tourism to thrive. The forest nearby also provides scintillating scenery for visitors. The forest, which is well kept, provides an ambiance for tourist attraction. To illustrate how the NdaFA can become a source of tourism revenue for the local Ndau people, insights are presented from Ngozi and Tabitha:

> In addition, tourism is instrumental to preserving local culture and tradition of the community. During cultural festivals, tourists/visitors have a unique chance to interact with the local community, thereby gaining a deeper experience of the ambience, customs and local cultures. This enhances the resident's pride and promotes the preservation and cultivation of the local culture. Through this medium, visitors get acquitted with the local traditions and customs thereby leading to its preservation. In this vein, festivals act as a medium through which a destination's image can be improved by offering prime opportunity for tourists/visitors to get to know the local culture and experience the essence of the place.[27]

The citation above illustrates that traditional festivals are functional even in twenty-first-century communities. The festivals are indicative of pride and celebration for the peoples' culture, and a potentially vital source for tourist attraction and entertainment for the local people. Traditional festivals usually take place during times of less work in the fields. For the Ndau people, the NdaFA is celebrated in September of every year.

It would not be very sensible to give the impression that all is well with African festivals. Experience has shown that African festivals have come in combat with the world's homogenization agendas of globalization, or rather a glocalization, whereby the whole world is becoming a localized village. This project has not only brought stiff competition but also power dynamics where certain practices and beliefs are given prominence over others. This has resulted in the peripheralization of most African festivals. Thanks to works from international organizations such as UNESCO, The World Bank, and many vigorous advocacy activities from culturists, festivals still express African existentiality. Their (festivals) exuberance unsurprisingly still sustains as evident in the NdaFA case in point given above.

Conclusion

The chapter concludes that African festivals are relevant in twenty-first-century Africa despite the vilification by colonialism, modernism, and globalization. From an Afrocentric perspective, I posit that the Ndau Festival of the Arts, as one of many African celebratory festivals, still has a place in society and is significant in the lives of the African people, the Ndau in particular. The festive events are far-reaching, contributing to the African peoples' preservation of their heritage, culture, language, artisanship, and indigenous knowledge as an identity indicator, a social cohesion asset, an education tool for children, and a potential source of annual income if its tourist attraction is explored. African Traditional Religion, via cultural festivals, among others, has withstood the test of time, and it is a religion that is not bound by space and time. It is ubiquitous.

Notes

1. Joseph Omosade Awolalu, "What Is African Traditional Religion?" *Studies in Comparative Religion*, vol. 10, no. 2 (1976): 1.
2. Ibid.
3. Oluwatosin Adeoti Akintan, "Traditional Religious Festivals and Modernity: A Case Study of Female-Oriented Cults Annual Festivals," *Ijebuland of South Western Nigeria* vol. 3, no. 4 (2013): 267.
4. Arvind P. Nirmal, "Celebration of Indian Festivals," In J. B. Taylor, ed., *Primal World*. Ibadan, Nigeria: Daystar Press, 1976.
5. George T. Basden, *Niger Ibos: A Description of the Primitive Life, Customs, and Animistic Beliefs and Customs of the Igbo People of Nigeria* (London: Frank Cass, 1966).
6. J. Famuyiwa, "The Role of Traditional Festival and Modern Festivals of Arts and Culture in the Promotion of Cultural Education in Nigeria," *Journal of The National Commission for Museums and Monuments*, vol 1 no. 1 (1992).
7. E. Bolaji Idowu, *African Traditional Religion: A Definition* (London: SCM Press Ltd, 1973); John S. Mbiti, *African Religions and Philosophy* (London: Heinemann, 1969); Awolalu, "What Is African Traditional Religion?".
8. Tunde Adeleke, *Case Against Afrocentricism* (Jackson, MS: University Press of Mississippi, 2009).
9. Molefi Kete Asante, *The Afrocentric Idea* (Philadelphia: Temple University Press, 1998), 19.
10. F. Sibanda, "Discrepancy Between the Legality of the Death Penalty and the African Religious Heritage in Zimbabwe," In M.C. Green, R.I.J. Hackett, L. Hansen, and F. Venter, eds., *Religious Pluralism, Heritage and Social Development in Africa* (Stellenbosch: Con-RAP, 2017).
11. T. Taringana and P. Nyambara, "Negotiated Cultural Identities? Missionaries, Colonisation and Cultural Transformation in Chipinge, 1894–1965," *Chiedza, Journal of Arrupe Jesuit University*, vol. 20, no. 1 (2018): 45–59; Tenson Muyambo, "Indigenous Knowledge Systems of the Ndau People of Manicaland in Zimbabwe: A Case Study of Bota Reshupa" (Unpublished doctoral dissertation, University of KwaZulu Natal, South Africa, 2018); E. Konyana, "When Culture and the Law Meet: An ethical analysis of the interplay between the domestic violence act and the traditional beliefs and cultural practices of the Ndau people in Zimbabwe" (Unpublished doctoral dissertation, University of KwaZulu Natal, South Africa, 2016).
12. C. J. M. Zvobgo, *A History of Christian Missions in Zimbabwe, 1890–1939* (Gweru: Mambo Press, 1996); R. Matikiti, "Christian Theological Perspectives

on Political Violence in Zimbabwe: The case of the United Church of Christ in Zimbabwe" (Unpublished doctoral dissertation, University of Zimbabwe, Harare, 2012); R. S. Maposa, "Christianity and Development: A History of United Church of Christ in Zimbabwe and the Emergence of a Theology of Liberation, 1965–2005" (Unpublished doctoral dissertation, University of Zimbabwe, Harare, 2013); Muyambo, "Indigenous Knowledge Systems," 2018.
13. MacGonagle 2007; Maposa, "Christianity and Development," 2013; Muyambo, "Indigenous Knowledge Systems," 2018.
14. Muyambo, "Indigenous Knowledge Systems," 2018.
15. Alexa Reynolds Delbosc, "Social Identity as a Motivator in Cultural Festivals," *Visitor Studies*, vol. 11, no. 1 (2008): 3–15.
16. Ibid., 5.
17. The *Jerusarema* dance is not imported from outside Africa but is a Zimbabwean dance. Its foreign import in this cited case is that it is a Zezuru dance among the Ndau. Zezuru is a tribe different from the Ndau tribe. Hence, imposing the dance on Ndau cultural festivities is not only unethical but unfortunate especially at an event meant to promote and showcase a Ndau cultural festival. It is therefore foreign among the Ndau for they do not identify with it hence my use of the term "foreign."
18. Heerden, 2011.
19. Delbosc, "Social Identity as a Motivator in Cultural Festivals," 3–15.
20. Emmanuel Sithole, "From Dialect to "Official" Language: The Intellectualization of NDAU in Zimbabwe," Department of African Languages (Unpublished PhD Thesis, Rhodes University, South Africa, 2017).
21. Nhlanhla J. Mkhize and Nobuhle Ndimande-Hlongwa, "African Languages, Indigenous Knowledge Systems (IKS), and the Transformation of the Humanities and Social Sciences in Higher Education," *Alternation* vol. 21, no. 2 (2014):10–37.
22. Beban Sammy Chumbow, "The Language Question and National Development in Africa," In Thandika Mkandawire, ed., *African Intellectuals: Rethinking Politics, Language, Gender and Development* (Dakar and London: Codesria Books, 2005); See also Julian Dakin, Brian Tiffin, and H. G. Widdowson, *Language in Education: The Problem of Commonwealth Africa and the Indo-Pakistan Sub-continent* (London: Oxford University Press, 1968).
23. Herbert W. Vilakazi, "A New Policy on Higher Education," A response to Minister Kader Asmal's Proposals on Mergers and Transformation of Institutions of Higher Education (Unpublished MA Thesis, 2002).
24. This is a traditional herb that is sweet but has medicinal functions. *Also see* Muyambo "Indigenous Knowledge Systems," Chap. 5.
25. Ezenagu Ngozi and Olatunji Tabitha, "Harnessing Awka Traditional Festival for Tourism Promotion," *Global Journal of Arts Humanities and Social Sciences* vol. 2, no. 5 (2014): 45–46, 54.
26. Ibid., 54.
27. Ibid.

CHAPTER 32

African Traditional Religion and Diaspora Transplantations: Nature and Formats

Martina Iyabo Oguntoyinbo-Atere

INTRODUCTION

The traditional religions of African people are referred to as African Traditional Religion. This religion was transported by the people of Africa who were dispersed to other nations due to slavery or other movements. The term "Diaspora" was originally used to describe the colonization of Asia Minor and the Mediterranean (800–600 BC). The word "diaspora" is from two Greek words *dia* "through" and *speirein*, "to scatter, or sow," implying being dispersed from an original center. These Africans in Diaspora had to transplant their religion in a new location in which they found themselves. In the process, the characteristics of the religious practice back in Africa faced some challenges. The peoples' religious practice on the new land was distinct from what was expected or intended. This chapter discusses whether there has been conformity to that which was practiced back in Africa and distinguished from their actual experience. For this work, the social action theory and symbolic interactionism[1] are used.

SOCIAL ACTION THEORY AND SYMBOLIC INTERACTIONISM

Max Weber defined "sociology" as the study of social action—when a performed action takes account of other members of society, it is a social action.[2] Weber believed that to understand what social action is, one must understand

M. I. Oguntoyinbo-Atere (✉)
Adeleke University, Ede, Nigeria
e-mail: martina.atere@adelekeuniversity.edu.ng

© The Author(s), under exclusive license to Springer Nature Switzerland AG 2022
I. S. Aderibigbe, T. Falola (eds.), *The Palgrave Handbook of African Traditional Religion*, https://doi.org/10.1007/978-3-030-89500-6_32

the meanings and the motives behind human behavior. One can only interpret the meaning given to actions by the actors themselves. This can be demonstrated through the notion that motives can be understood, when one puts himself or herself in the position of the person displaying a particular behavior.

Symbolic interactionism implies that "human behaviors are largely governed by internal processes by which people interpret the world around them and give meaning to their own lives."[3] It is believed that people have a "self-concept" or an image of the kind of person or people they are, and they tend to act in accordance with that concept.

George Herbert Mead was regarded as the founder of symbolic interactionism. He is of the view that human thoughts, experiences, and conducts are essentially social.[4] If this is accepted, then it can be assumed that human interactions are expressed through symbols that are embedded in language. This, however, does not suggest that social roles are fixed as they are constantly open to modifications as they go through the dynamics of interactions.

Mead's view of human interaction sees humans as actively creating the social environment and being shaped by it. Individuals initiate and direct their own actions while at the same time being influenced by the attitudes and expectations of others in the form of the generalized other. The individual and society are regarded as inseparable, for the individual can only become a human being in a social context. In this context, individuals develop a sense of self, which is a pre-requisite for thought. They learn to take the roles of others, which is essential both for the development of self and for cooperative action. Without communication in terms of symbols whose meanings are shared, these processes would not be possible. Humanity, therefore, lives in a world of symbols that give meaning and significance to life and provide the basis for human interaction.[5]

How is African Traditional Religion domesticated outside Nigeria? We must understand that transporting religion to other places is itself a social action. In projecting it, there is also social action. The objects and other things used for worship represent one aspect of the religion or the other. This is symbolic interactionism, being in agreement and relating to God and man through their symbols.

African Traditional Religion and Sources

We get to understand African Traditional Religion through both oral and non-oral devices. Information about African traditional religions is passed down orally, from generation to generation. Initially, most of the practitioners of African Traditional Religion were not literary people. The device used to preserve and transmit the beliefs and practices of the religion was mostly oral. Proverbs, names, and pithy sayings were memorized and passed down from generation to generation. According to Abioye, the aforementioned were more reliable than myths, legends, folk tales, and daily speeches that may be distorted.[6]

Myths are stories told to describe the genesis of explain the origin of existence. Among the Yorùbá, for instance, the myth of creation has it that the "earth was without form and void" when *Olodumare* (God) decided to create the earth.[7] It is told that *Orisa-nla*, the arch divinity, was sent by *Olodumare* to perform the assignment of creating the earth. Some Yorùbá people often sing the following song to back up the creation job of *Orisa-nla*.

Orisanla ni ma sin
Emi soju semu
Orisa nla ni ma sin

I will worship Orisa-nla
The one who made the eyes and nose
I will worship Orisa-nla.

Some myths are recited like prayers, and they give authentic information about African Traditional Religion. Among the Fon is a belief in a dual deity, *Mawu-Lisa*. It is said that *Mawu-Lisa* formed the first human being with clay and water.

Proverbs are held in high esteem among the Yorùbá of Nigeria and Africans in general. From proverbs, a lot is revealed about God. These proverbs are rich in meanings and theological expressions with moral significance.

Names—In the names of African Traditional Religion's worshipers, beliefs are expressed. Their faith in the gods they serve is also portrayed. For example:

- *Eeegunleti*: Translation: The masquerade has listening capacity.
- *Ifaponle*: Translation: I am honoured by the Ifa oracle.
- *Sangomuyiwa*: Translation: *Sango's* gift.
- *Fakoya*: Translation: The Ifa oracle has fought for us.

Prayers—Prayers are made to God, the deities, and the ancestors. This is a special way of communication by the adherents of African Traditional Religion to the creator. Whenever there are challenges, the African people turn to God for help. Unfruitfulness is a matter of serious concern among Africans, so petitions are made to God (*Olodumare*, through his representatives, *Ogun, Sango, Osun*, and *Oya*, among others). Prayers are not bound by any time or place. Prayers are usually short and direct, although there are exceptional cases of long prayer sessions. Libations are poured for effectiveness, especially at the beginning of the day or new ventures. Additionally, prayers are professed for protection, healings, and solutions to all problems of life.

Artifacts, wooden masks, and neolithic emblems—Man's dependence on God and his agents is expressed artistically. Through archeological excavations, some discoveries have been made revealing our people's history, their belief, and practices. Works of art are found in places of worship for divination, musical instruments, and ritual paraphernalia. Masks are worn by masqueraders to portray their ancestors. Stones are found in the shrines of *Sango* (minister of justice) as a cultic object. *Sango* is believed to be the thunder divinity, *Jakuta*, meaning, "one who hurls with stone"[8] while in the shrine of *Ogun*, metals are found, symbolic of his office as the god of iron.

THE SUPREMACY OF *OLODUMARE* IN AFRICAN TRADITIONAL RELIGION

In African Traditional Religion, God is supreme. This Deity does not operate at the same level as the divinities. He is far and above all. Africans see this God as the immortal (*aiku*) king of the universe (*oba gbogbo aye*) and creator of the whole world (*Eledaa, aseeda*). *Olodumare* or *Olorun*, the Supreme Being, He is the creator, the one who brought the divinities into being. Everything on earth and heaven can be attributed to Him. He is the king, all-wise, all-knowing, all-seeing, immortal, and holy God. *Orisa-nla* is said to be the oldest among the divinities. There have been several suggestions as to the number of divinities. Some have suggested one thousand seven hundred. Other suggestions are one thousand four hundred and forty divinities, six hundred, and four hundred. In Ile-Ife alone, we are told that two hundred and one of them were originally represented in the Ooni's Palace.[9] Among the ministers of *Olodumare*, the key ones are *Orisa-nla*, the deputy in terms of creative and executive function.

Orunmila is the oracle divinity. *Ogun* also ranks high in status among the divinities of Yorubaland. He is the god of iron who demands justice and fair play. *Sango* was a historical figure who eventually became venerated and exhibited the wrath of *Olodumare*. Some of these gods and goddesses inhabit rivers, hills, and trees. *Osun*, for instance, inhabits a river. Connected to the divinities are the ancestors, known as the living dead. Their cult is referred to as the *Egungun* (masquerade). When masquerades appear during festivals, it is believed that the ancestors have visited. The Yoruba also believe in magic and medicine; they also emphasize character and a good relationship with others in the community. When things go wrong, divination and sacrifices may be performed for restoration to take place. Therefore, maintaining a connection with the spirit world is essential to the adherents of African Traditional Religion.

Santeria

Several of the slaves in Cuba brought their African religions to the new world. These were officially condemned by the Roman Catholic Church as witchcraft. The slaves had to worship their gods secretly or identify them with Catholic Saints.

> Eventually popular religion became a syncretistic blend of African and Catholic elements. The best known was Santeria, which arrived with the Yoruba people. It is a monotheistic religion whose God, Olodumare, is seen as the creator of the Universe. Humanity's personal God—an aspect of Olodumare—is Olofi. God's power or Energy (a she) is mediated through Orishas, spirits who personify vari-

ous natural forces or human interests. The ceremonies reflecting African roots, make use of ritual music, dance, and sacrifices. Four basic ingredients are involved—water, herbs, cowrie shells, and stones—plus offerings to the Orishas such as fruits, foods and animals.[10]

According to Braun, Yoruba Orishas were identified with Catholic saints as listed below.

Oggun (representing work, brute force, raw energy, arguments, war) with St. Peter (head of the church).
Orunla (representing wisdom, patience, holy divination, herbal knowledge) with St. Francis of Assisi.
Babalu–Aye (representing cure of illness, compassion for those with broken or missing limbs, beggers) with St. Lazarus (A beggar in Luke 16:20).
Chango (representing fire, thunder, lightning, passion virility, raw power) with St. Barbara (Chango was able to escape from enemies waiting for him outside his doorway by dressing as a woman).
Obatala (representing purity) with Our Lady of Mercy.
Yemaya (representing the sea, life, sustenance) with Our Lady of the Regla.
Eleggua (representing fate, justice, healing, divination) with St. Anthony of Padua (a great doctor of the Catholic Church), known for his knowledge of the Bible.[11]

According to Oguntoyinbo-Atere, a few changes occur in the names of gods and goddesses from the way they are called in Yorubaland. In the Cuban case, Sango became Chango, Oshun became Ochun, Yemoja became Yemeja, cladenogenesis takes place.[12] The orishas were clothed with Catholicism. Santeria is the new African religion of the oppressed people. Having found themselves in a foreign land, they began to seek new ways of expressing their belief and new ways of communicating with the divinities.

In the concept of illnesses and healing among the practitioners of Santeria, medical explanations are not given to ailments. For example, viruses are not considered as causes of diseases, rather illnesses are seen as a product of sorcery caused by tense social relationships. Thus, to them, healing can only be accomplished when there is a good relationship with divine beings and spirits.

> For this to be properly done consultation is made with an espiritismo an individual with skills in Spiritism. The Spiritists reconnected the Africans of Yoruba origin with their once lost relationship with the living dead. Today in Cuba one can find in the home of a Spiritist a boveda, a table covered with a white cloth. On top of it, there are usually photographs of departed family members, a crucifix, dolls, and glasses of water. The dolls represent spiritual guides, and each glass represents a particular muerto, often a deceased family member.[13]

Therefore, worshipers are encouraged to have a good interpersonal relationship with one another, knowing that problems do originate from irregular or ethically unacceptable behaviors. Oppression is discouraged to ensure the safety and security of "those within African societies in the Diaspora," and several rituals are also performed to sustain the wellbeing of the people.[14]

A look at a group of drummers in Oyotunji Village, South Carolina, is necessary here. Oyotunji Village was founded by Oba Oseijeman I, born Walter King of Detroit, in 1970. The purpose was to provide a geographical and cultural space to experience African culture for African Americans in the United States. This is patterned after the culture of Yoruba in the Southern part of Nigeria. Oba Adefunmi I, the founder of Oyotunji Village from Detroit, Michigan, was said to be the first African American to be initiated into the cult of Obatala in Matanzas, Cuba in 1959.[15] After initiation, he went to Harlem, New York, and founded a Lucumi temple. There, several people were introduced to Orisa devotion and Yoruba cultural practices. It was after this that he went and founded Oyotunji Village. The cultural and social life in Oyotunji Village, though African, were not necessarily Yoruba in origin. A lot of visual arts displayed throughout the village is said to be of East or Central African origin. The serpent deity worshiped during their annual festivals is said to have Dahomean origins.

Oyotunji Village is usually visited by Orisa devotees during their annual festivals to give talks and conduct workshops, thereby training others on the various aspects of Orisa devotion. "There is also a thriving online community that allows for Orisa devotees from around the world to discuss, debate, share, and exchange ideas and practices."[16] Even though they believe in the Supreme Being, *Olodumare*, whose habitation is far above, they do not worship Him directly but focus on the worship of *orisa* who have been variously numbered at 200, 401, 800, and more. This is also buttressed by Olupona in his discussion of Ile-Ife as the city of 201 GODS. Ile-Ife, the cradle of the Yoruba, known for the worship of Orisa in South Western part of Nigeria.[17]

In Oyotunji Village, there are three primary phases of a typical festival: a *bembe*, the night before the festival day, the *Egungun* (masquerade) parade on the day of the festival, the appearance of the *Oba*, and concluded by another *bembe*. "The *bembe* is a ritual where drummers and singers play specific rhythms and sing specific chants for each individual orisa."[18] They also have *egbe* (groups) for the different *Orisa*. Most importantly, here, is the society of drummers who reside in Oyotunji Village or the nearby communities of Beaufort, Sheldon, or Savannah. This group is usually present at the festival events to perform most especially for the worship of influential deities like *Sango*, *Oya*, and *Ogun*. Talking about drumming in Oyotunji Village, South Carolina, Townsend met one of the drummers named Olafemi and has this to say about him.

> Olafemi is fairly typical in regards to demographic descriptions of the drummers at Oyotunji. He is an African-American male in his early twenties who was born in Beaufort, South Carolina, located approximately twenty miles from the Village.

He is also typical of many of the younger drummers in the community in that he represents a new generation of "Yoruba revivalists" (Clarke); he was raised in the culture of Oyotunji Village as the son of two members of the community who both joined in the early years of the Village's formation... Oyotunji Village positions itself as a representation of Yoruba culture and society in a transnational, deterritorialized setting in the United States.[19]

Music and dance comprise a prominent element of African Diaspora religious practices. This is a replica of the ritual performances of the practitioners of traditional religions in Africa. Ibigbolade S. Aderibigbe states that "for the African, music and religion are seen as a singular enterprise."[20] A combination of singing, drumming, and dancing produce trance-like performance, and spirit possession takes place. The Spirits are invited through drums, songs, and dance to inhabit humans, temporarily. During this time, there is a relationship with the metaphysical world. Prominent in the *Santeria* tradition, the role of drumming and dance in the *bembe* festivals cannot be overemphasized. In these festivals, the *orishas* are honored, and prayers are made to them. Sometimes, animal sacrifices are performed, and the blood is applied to the heads of the sick people for restoration of health. It is believed that the life of the animal is used to appease an angry *orisa* and to replace the life of a human being. Whether there is eco-justice in this action is food for thought.

Candomble

When African slaves were taken to Brazil, the official religion of the Brazilian Empire was Roman Catholicism. However, African slaves brought their religions, and Brazil moved from "Catholic monopoly" to contemporary religious diversity.[21] Candomble developed with vital elements of Yoruba and Ewe-Fon ritual organizations' language and mythology. Candomble is Brazil's most influential Afro-Brazilian religion. It mixes Catholicism and Yoruba traditional religion, which is characterized by gods and goddesses called *orishas*. These Yoruba slaves took their religions to Brazil as they did in Cuba.

> In Brazil, these orishas are divided into seven divinities with defined functions. Some are represented as saints of catholic religion or a natural element, and each has a symbolic color. They are (a) Oxala the supreme authority of Candomble represented in the form of Jesus Christ as the sun, and his color is white. This must be a reference to Orisa-nla in Yoruba religion. (b) Ogun is seen as the Lord of war, who overcomes obstacles and difficulties. He is represented in the form of Saint George on his horse. He is also represented by himself. The colors are red, white and green. (c) Xango is the orisha of justice. Myth has it that he had three wives—Oxum, Yansa, and Oba. He is represented in the form of Moses, holding the ten commandments, and his color is brown.[22]

Candomble, like Santeria, is a religion of the oppressed originating from African slaves who felt the need to connect spiritually to their origin. The worshipers initially operated underground until much later in the 1970s, when they no longer needed police permission to hold public ceremonies. Before this time, they hid their *orishas* under Catholic saints for worship. According to Okunade, Candomble itself means music and dance in honor of the gods.[23] Through songs, every area of life is exhibited. In Yoruba theology, for instance, the supremacy of *Olodumare* is presented in the following lyric.

> Ile n ja oun Olorun
> Olurun l'oun l' agba
> Ile l' oun l' egbon
> N' tori eku emo kan
> Ojo ko ko ro mo
> Isu p'eyin ko ta
> Agbado ta' pe ko gbo
> Gbogbo eye ku tan l'oko'
> Igun ngb' ebo r'orun

> Earth has a contention with Olorun
> Olorun claims to be older;
> On account of one emo (brown) rat,
> Rain ceases and falls no more,
> Yams sprout but do not develop,
> The ears of corn fill, but do not ripen,
> All birds in the forest are perishing,
> Vulture is carrying sacrifice to heaven.[24]

The lyric is from a myth that shows the superiority of *Olodumare* over the earth. Things only became normal after *Olodumare* has received a propitiation sacrifice that the earth sent with apologies. *Olodumare* is the one who has the final say on all things. The orisha was brought forth by *Olodumare*.

Candomble religion is mostly defined by ritual dance, spiritual healing, divination, possession, and sacrificial offerings.[25] All these things are embedded in the Yoruba tradition. It has been found that many of these Yoruba traditional practices faded away as families became scattered in Brazil. However, to a large extent, they still remain connected to their spiritual background, which was "life" to them. The Yoruba creation myth implies that *Olodumare* created the universe and its inhabitants before ordering the *orisas* to put everything in the proper positions. Another point to be observed is that the spiritual and material works are exact duplicates.[26] It implies that whatever happens to a man in the natural world is connected to the spiritual world. It becomes clear that the spiritual controls the physical. Like the belief structure in Santeria, it is also established in Candomble that to have a peaceful existence on earth, the individual must be connected to the spiritual world. This is different from the secular Western's belief, which separates religion from all spheres of life. Within the system of Candomble, "this separation causes an unbalance, a disequilibrium, in the workings of day-to-day activity which can lead to illness, financial ruin, marital feuds, or simply the smallest accident".[27]

Examples suffice that a person's destiny may be altered for the worse by "Omo Araye" (children of the world). This phrase is used to describe those who are vested with evil powers like witches and those in secret cults who manipulate spiritually to destroy the destinies of others. Hence "Alagemo teer-ekange, who came to this world and was confronted with Ogun omo araye pleaded, Eje n jise ti Olodumare ran mi" (Let me fulfill the mission committed to me by Olodumare).[28]

> E ma pe mi nip e e pagbe
> Kagbe o too di a laro igbo
> E ma pe mi ni ipe e paluko
> Ka luko o too d' olosun egan
> E ma pe mi n' ipe e p' oburo
> K'oburo o too d' alawirin eye ninu oko
>
> Do not telepathise me as you did agbe
> So that agbe became the Indigo-coloured one of the forest,
>
> Do not telepathise me as you did aluko
> So that Aluko became the cam wood-coloured one of the wilderness,
>
> Do not telepathise me as you did oburo,
> So that oburo became the vagrant-babbler of the groves.[29]

Telepathy is one of the deadliest weapons used by the evil ones. An individual who is persistently having misfortunes can be said to be afflicted by *Aye*. This is further corroborated by Bolaji Idowu.

> Bi e r'aye, esa f'aye
> Bi e r'aye, e sa f'aye
> Isese w'aiye ijimere dudu,
> Aye naa lo t'aso ijimere b'epo
> A r'aye naa lo p'ogidan
> Ogidan oloola iju,
> Bi e r'aye, e sa f'aye
>
> If you encounter aye, flee from aye
> If you encounter aye, flee from aye
> The primeval ijimere was black
> This aye it is that soaked ijimere's clothes in palm oil
> This aye it is that slew Ogidan
> Ogidan the surgeon of the wilderness
> If you encounter aye, flee from aye.[30]

The fact that the spiritual controls the physical, adherents of Africa Traditional Religion in Africa and the Diaspora try to establish or re-establish, as the case may be, a spiritual connection necessary for a steady balance. In the case of Candomble, rituals either in the form of small or elaborate ceremonies are conducted. This is necessary so that the needed power and energy to deal with life's problems are supplied. Sometimes, dancers are brought in to help solve life problems. Initiation takes place, and in the process, the initiate has time to himself to reflect and avoid distractions. Sacrifices are also performed, and the blood of a bird is applied to the forehead of the initiate. Another important feature of Candomble is spirit possession, such as when the spirit of the *orishas* manifest in the worshipers in the course of singing, drumming, and dancing. Candomble can then be seen as a way to gain honor, self-esteem, and solid grounding in a foreign land.[31] It is the adherents' ways of worshiping the Supreme Being and finding solutions to their problems.

We must note with emphasis that the beliefs and practices of Africa Traditional Religion have not been systematically arranged in a single book like the scriptures of the Western religions. However, attempts are being made by academics at home and in the Diaspora to document the various facets of Africa Traditional Religion. Examples of such efforts are *Religion Study and Practice* edited by Gbolade Aderibigbe and Deji Ayegbonyin,[32] *Religion and Society in Nigeria: Historical and Sociological Perspectives edited* by Jacob K. Olupona and Toyin Falola,[33] *City of 201 Gods: Ile-Ife in Time, Space and the Imagination* by Jacob K. Oluponna,[34] *Africa: Our Times and Culture* edited by Egbe Ife,[35] *Contemporary Perspectives on Religions in Africa and the African Diaspora* edited by Ibigbolade S. Aderibigbe and Collins M. Jones,[36] *West African Traditional Religion by* J. Omosade Awolalu and P. Adelumo Dopamu,[37] *Olodumare: God in Yoruba Belief* by Bolaji Idowu,[38] and the current work by Ibigbolade S. Aderibigbe and Toyin Falola in 2020 bringing together about fifty contributing authors for *Palgrave's Handbook of African Traditional Religion* is commendable.[39]

INTERNATIONALIZATION OF AFRICAN TRADITIONAL RELIGION THROUGH THE ACADEMIA

Academic migrants constitute as a part of Africa's Diasporas. Africa and its Diaspora have been built alongside as well as shaped by continuities, changes, and ruptures.

> Diaspora is a state of being, and a process of becoming, a condition and consciousness located in the shifting interstices of "here," a voyage of negotiation between multiple spatial and social identities. Created out of movement—dispersal from a home land—the Diaspora is sometimes affirmed through another movement—engagement with the home land. Movement, it could be argued then, in its literal and metaphorical senses, is at the heart of the diasporic condition, beginning with the dispersal itself and culminating with reunification. The

spaces in between are marked by multiple forms of engagement between the Diaspora and the home land, of movement, of travel between a "here" and a "there" both in terms of time and spaces, of substantive and symbolic concrete and conceptual intersections and interpellations.[40]

The academic examination of African Traditional and African Diaspora Religions has garnered a great amount of curiosity. The presence of seasoned academics and researchers in African Traditional Religion at the global level is a pointer to this religious dynamism. This makes it clear that Africa Traditional Religion is not local. Currently, African Traditional Religion is taught by scholars of international repute in several universities around the world. Thus, Africa Traditional Religion is considered as a global religion on both the national and international arena. Worthy of note are Jacob K. Olupona, a Professor of African Religion at Harvard University, and Ibigbolade S. Aderibigbe of Georgia, among others.

The Inseparability of Yoruba Language, Culture, and African Traditional Religion

The language of a society is an integral part of its cultural and social heritage. As such, African language, culture, and traditional religion are inseparable. It came as no surprise to the people of Africa that the Brazilian Government introduced a compulsory study of African History and Yoruba Language into their primary and secondary school curriculum.[41] Therefore, the importance of culture and, by extension, of the language of any given society to the development of that society in every ramification cannot be overemphasized. Anthropologists working on African Traditional Religion would be wise, when working on the local language of the people, to properly understand the sources like myths, parables, divination, songs, values, virtues, and history of the people. This will enhance the understanding of African people's religious background. Greater knowledge of the historical background will propel an excellent pathway to a successful future.

Conclusion

In the contemporary world, some individuals are of the opinion that there are two virtually unrelated forms of the religion, an actual religion as practiced in Africa, Cuba, Brazil, Haiti, and in some other settlements in South America and the evil or imaginary religion which is said to be created for Hollywood movies, exhibiting violence and bizarre rituals. This may not necessarily exist in reality.[42] With the diverse religious practices of the African Diaspora, some scholars have wondered whether an "authentic Africanity" can be maintained. How possible is that with the international character of these religious practices? It must be understood that there are individuals who are not of African descent but are adherents of African Traditional Religion. Despite the differences in these religions in diverse settings and contexts, some similarities exist; there is the main God with intermediaries between Him and man. They believe in spirit/god possession, the offering of sacrifices to the gods, the use of altars, ancestor veneration, and worship, among others.

The migration of Africa to the Americas and Diasporan Africans to Africa, which existed during the Slave Trade era and persisted after its abolishment facilitated cultural flows between South America and Africa. The religious beliefs, rituals, and values of the people are usually inseparable. Even though the African-derived religions have been referred to as "religions of the oppressed" and "religions of protest," they were also ways of refashioning their culture, retaining and recreating their identities in new and often not too hospitable contexts.[43] Therefore, African-derived religions did not remain static but had to incorporate practices and beliefs from other religions. Apart from the cross-fertilization that took place among the enslaved Africans, having come from different ethnic groups and parts of Africa, the differences in their migration to the Americas also accounted for the peoples' various sources of religious creativity and transformation.

Notes

1. Michael Haralambos and Martin Holborn, *Sociology Themes and Perspectives.* (London: Harper Collins Publishers Limited, 2013), 885.
2. Ibid., 885.
3. Ibid., 885–86.
4. Ibid., 885–86.
5. Ibid., 979–80.
6. S. A. Abioye, "African Traditional Religion: An Introduction," In Ibigbolade S. Aderibigbe and Deji Aiyegboyin, eds., *Religion Study and Practice.* Lagos: Olu-Akin Publishers, 2001, 187–91.
7. Ibid., 187.
8. Ibid., 191.
9. E. Bolaji Idowu, *Olodumare: God in Yorba Belief.* (Longman Nigeria Plc Revised and Enlarged edition, 1996), 64.
10. Theodore A. Braun, *Perspectives on Cuba and Its People.* (New York: Friendship Press, 1999), 25.
11. Ibid.
12. M. I. Oguntoyinbo-Atere, "African Derived Religions in Diaspora: An Overview," In Carolyn M. Medine, Ibigbolade S. Aderibigbe, and D. Hans, eds., *Contemporary Perspectives on Religions in Africa and the African Diaspora* (New York: Palgrave Macmillan, 2015), 122.
13. Umesh Patel, "Finding Home in a Foreign Land," In Carolyn M. Medine, Ibigbolade S. Aderibigbe, and D. Hans, eds., *Contemporary Perspectives on Religions in Africa and the African Diaspora* (New York: Palgrave Macmillan, 2015), 167.
14. Ibid.
15. Colin Townsend, "Drumming for the Orisa: (Re)inventing Yoruba identity in Oyotunji Village," *Student Anthropologist* vol. 3 no. 4 (2013): 46. Walter King

was a non-Hispanic African American initiated as a Santero. He changed his name to Oba Efuntola Nana Oseijerman Adelabu Adefunmi 1. See also Robert Y. Owusu, "Socioreligious Agencies of Santeria," In Carolyn M. Medine, Ibigbolade S. Aderibigbe, and D. Hans, eds., *Contemporary Perspectives on Religions in Africa and the African Diaspora* (New York: Palgrave Macmillan, 2015), 203.
16. Townsend, "Drumming for the Orisa," 46.
17. Jacob K. Olupona, *City of 201 Gods. Ile-Ife in Time, Space and the Imagination.* (University of California Press, 2011).
18. Townsend, "Drumming for the Orisa," 47.
19. Ibid., 49–50.
20. Ibigbolade S. Aderibigbe, "Religious Traditions in Africa: An Overview of Origins, Basic Beliefs and Practices," In Carolyn M. Medine, Ibigbolade S. Aderibigbe, and D. Hans, eds., *Contemporary Perspectives on Religions in Africa and the African Diaspora* (New York: Palgrave Macmillan, 2015), 14.
21. Patel, "Finding Home in a Foreign Land," 169.
22. Oguntoyinbo-Atere, "African Derived Religions in Diaspora," 122.
23. AdeOluwa Okunade, "Arts and Music in African Derived Diaspora" In Carolyn M. Medine, Ibigbolade S. Aderibigbe, and D. Hans, eds., *Contemporary Perspectives on Religions in Africa and the African Diaspora* (New York: Palgrave Macmillan, 2015), 128.
24. E. Bolaji Idowu, *Olodumare: God in Yoruba Belief*, 46.
25. Patel, "Finding Home in a Foreign Land," 169.
26. Ibid.
27. Ibid., 170.
28. Idowu, *Olodumare: God in Yoruba Belief*, 188.
29. Ibid.
30. Ibid., 190.
31. Patel, "Finding Home in a Foreign Land," 171–72.
32. Ibigbolade S. Aderibigbe and Deji Aiyegboyin, eds., *Religion Study and Practice.* (Lagos: Olu-Akin Publishers, 2001).
33. Jacob K Olupona and Toyin Falola, eds. *Religion and Society in Nigeria. Historical and Sociological Perspectives.* (Ibadan: Spectrum Books Ltd., 1991), 31.
34. Oluponna, *City of 201 Gods*, 2011.
35. Egbe Ife, ed., *Africa: Our Times and Culture* (Ibadan: Oputoru Books, 1999).
36. Carolyn M. Medine, Ibigbolade S. Aderibigbe, and D. Hans, eds., *Contemporary Perspectives.*
37. J. Omosade Awolalu and P. Adelumo Dopamu, *West African Traditional Religion.* (Ibadan: Onibonoje Press & Book Industries, 1979).
38. Idowu, *Olodumare: God in Yoruba Belief*, 1996.
39. Ibigbolade S. Aderibigbe and Toyin Falola, eds., *Palgrave Handbook of African Traditional Religion* (Palgrave: In process).
40. Paul Tiyamba Zeleza, "Africa and its Diaspora: Remembering South America." John Hopkins University Center for African Studies, Working Paper Series No. 13.
41. "Brazil Adopts Yoruba as Official Language," The Nigerian Voice, https://www.thenigerianvoice.com/news/27029/brazil-adopts-yoruba-as-offcial-language.html.

42. "African Traditional Religion," Wikipedia, https://en.m.wikipedia.org/wiki/Africantraditionalreligion.
43. Paul Tiyamba Zeleza, "Africa and its Diaspora," 13.

CHAPTER 33

African Traditional Religion and Sustainable Cultural, Social and Economic Dynamics

Mensah A. Osei

INTRODUCTION

Culture, as Jesse Mugambi opines, has six main pillars.[1] The pillars are politics, economics, ethics, aesthetics, kinship and religion. However, religion, he contends, is the most conspicuous element of the African heritage. It permeates all areas of human life. Meaning that religion defines their cultures, their social life, their politics and their economics. Nevertheless, religion intertwines with and shapes the traditional way of African life at the same time. The intent of the chapter is, first, to examine the definition of African tradition and its unique characteristics. Second, the discussion focuses on the relevance and applications of African Traditional Religion (ATR) in modern development.

Awolalu attempts a definition of African religion. He notes that when we speak of African Traditional Religion, we mean the indigenous religion of the Africans.[2] Forebears have handed down religion from generation to generation to the present generation of Africans. African Traditional Religion cannot be regarded as an outdated practice of the past, but rather a religion that modern-day Africans have embraced through their lives and practice.

M. A. Osei (✉)
Clarke County School District, Athens, GA, USA

African Traditional Religion (ATR) as a Misnomer?

The impression is that the concept "traditional" has a Christian prejudice. The objective is to describe the African spirituality as "archaic, ancient, old-fashioned, outdated; hence irrelevant."[3] Consequently, some scholars have argued that it should be called "African Religion." In this discourse, it will describe the original and native religions of the African people. According to Gathogo, African religion deals with their cosmology, ritual practices, symbols, arts and society. As a way of life, it is about African culture, which relates to their worldview or cultural milieu.

The term "African Traditional Religion" is used in two complementary senses. In most publications, African religion is commonly referred to as the African Traditional Religion (ATR). It encompasses all African beliefs and practices that are neither Christian nor Islamic. The expression is also used almost as a technical term for a particular religion of such beliefs and practices, one that purports to show that they constitute a systematic whole—a religion comparable to Christianity or any other "world religion." In that sense, the concept was new and radical when it was introduced by Parrinder in 1954 and later developed by E. Bolaji Idowu and John S. Mbiti.[4] These scholars intended to challenge the status-quo handling of the African people due to the historic negative nature of this approach by removing words such as "heathenism," "primitive" and "paganism." This phrase is, however, a controversial description of the African religiosity. African religion is thus an integral part of the African peoples' ethos and culture.

Olupona[5] and Gathogo[6] listed some facts about African religion. We shall dwell on their sources. In general, (i) African indigenous religion cultivates the whole person, for example, African religion permeates all departments of life; (ii) it provides people with a view of the world, for example, the views of the universe; (iii) it answers some questions that nothing else can, for example, unlike science it has no limitations; (iv) it provides humanity with moral values by which to live, for example, it tells us right and wrong, what is good and evil, just and unjust and virtue and vice; (v) it gives food for spiritual hunger, for example, it provides spiritual insights, prayers, rituals, ceremonies, sacrifices and offerings, dedication, devotion and trust in God among other religious discourses; (vi) it is a means of communication, for example, through prayer, sacrifice, common myths, legends, morals and views; (vii) it pays attention to the key moments in the life of the individual, for example, birth, initiation, puberty, marriage and death; in so doing, it shows the value/concern of the individual; (viii) it celebrates life, for example, they dance life, ceremonize and festivize—thereby affirming life; and (x) it shows people their limitations, for example, that life is short, temporal hence the need to depend on the Creator.

Gathogo[7] offers the sources of African religion. Among other things the primary sources include shrines, sacred places, religious objects, rocks, hills, mountains, caves and under certain trees. Africa has a plethora of rich resources in the form of rituals, ceremonies, festivals and rites of passage, dance, proverbs, wise and pithy sayings, names, appellations, attributes of people and places, praise names, wood carvings, art and symbols, myths and legends, masks, wood carvings, ivory and stones. Religious beliefs and customs also constitute important sources of African religion. These include the concept of God, ancestors, birth, death, life after death, magic and witchcraft. Religion in Africa, therefore, permeates the lives of Africans. African religion includes shrines or sacred places and religious objects such as rocks, hills and mountains; Gathogo further describes other primary sources of African religion. The sources include under certain trees, caves and other holy places. Other sources are rituals, ceremonies and festivals of the people (e.g., childbirth, naming, initiation, marriage, funerals, harvest festivals and praying for rain). Incorporated in Gathogo's sources are art and symbols—for example, wood, stools, calabashes, stones, sticks, pots, handicrafts, domestic animals and human bodies, also in masks, wood carvings, ivory and stone, music and dance, proverbs, riddles and wise sayings—names and attributes of people and places, myths and legends. African traditional sources are also found in beliefs and customs. Beliefs cover topics such as God, spirits, birth, death, the hereafter, magic and witchcraft. In all aspects of life, as religion, in the African indigenous context, it permeates throughout the lives of the people.

African religions demonstrate a perfect link between the living and the world of the dead. The living pay the ancestors cultic attention to maintain peaceful relationships and influence the life of the surviving descendants. From the above it can be said that although there are no written sources, oral literature abounds in African religion. These sources permeate arts, political discourse and social structure. Olupona avers that unlike other world religions that have written scriptures, oral sources form the primary sources of indigenous African religions. He argues that the oral sources are inextricably interlinked into all spheres of life—arts, political and social structure, and material culture. For him, the oral nature of these traditions allows for a great deal of adaptability and variation within and between indigenous African religions.[8]

IS IT AFRICAN RELIGIONS OR AFRICAN RELIGION?

It is generally accepted that there are many religious systems. It is, therefore, impossible to talk of one type of religion as being uniquely African. There is diversity in religious concepts and practices in Africa and it will, therefore, be correct to talk about different African religions (plural).[9] Mbiti argues that although the religious expressions in Africa are multiple, the philosophy underlying religious life is singular.[10] Krüger and colleagues point out that the religions of Black Africa are similar enough to talk of African religion in a generic sense and share a sufficient number of characteristics.[11] There seems to be a coherent philosophy underlying the different expressions of religion in Africa. The expressions may vary, but remain an expression of the peoples' basic beliefs.[12]

Characteristics

Although varied in outward appearance, African religions display similarities. There have been many attempts to describe African Traditional Religion according to its main characteristics. Turaki lists the following main characteristics: (i) belief in a Supreme Being, (ii) belief in spirits and divinities, (iii) the cult of ancestors and (iv) the use of magic, charms and spiritual forces.[13] Krüger et al. identify the following three common traits of African religions that enable scholars to talk of African religion (singular): (i) belief in a Supreme Being, (ii) the realm of spirits and (iii) a unified community.[14]

Mndende,[15] however, has contested Mbiti's[16] assertion of African Traditional Religions in the plural. She argues that it should be referred to as "African Religion," since no religion is monolithic but people look at the common features. Mndende contends that we never hear people talking about "Christianities," "Islams," "Hinduisms" and so on. For her, since we hardly talk about Zulu Religion or Xhosa Religion—African religion is one.[17] Mndende[18] affirms while there are differences in some of the customs, there is a common theme that captures the people's beliefs and practices. This central theme is the universal belief in the Supreme Being as an integral part of African cosmology and practical religion. In the words of E. Bolaji Idowu, "we find that in Africa, the real cohesive factor of religion is the living God and that without this one factor, all things would fall to pieces."[19] According to Idowu, it is against this background of an identical concept that we can speak of the religion of Africa in the singular.[20]

THE PLURAL CONTEXT IN "DOING" AFRICAN RELIGION

We must acknowledge that any religious discourse in Africa will have to be done within the context of pluralism in the social and religious areas since Africa is full of multiple faith traditions. The dominant ones are African (indigenous) religion, Christianity and Islam. Even within the traditional religions, John Mbiti rightly notes that traditional religions are not universal: they are tribal or national.[21] Gathogo[22] also avers that geographically each religion is located and found among a group of people. Since African religion is not missionary one, traditional religion cannot be spread to another locality. However, that does not mean religious ideas cannot be transmitted to another tribal group. Historically, such ideas are transmitted through migrations, intermarriages and conquests. Each religion is bound and limited to the people among whom it has evolved. One traditional religion cannot be propagated in another tribal group. This does not rule out the fact that religious ideas may spread from one people to another. Moreover, such ideas spread spontaneously, especially through migrations, intermarriages, conquests and expert knowledge being sought by individuals of one tribal group from another. Traditional religions have no missionaries to propagate them, and one individual does not preach his (or her) religion to another.

That Christianity, Islam, Science and Western education have had a huge impact on African Traditional Religion cannot be underestimated. A considerable number of people, particularly Western-trained Africans, have openly refused to follow and identify themselves with African religion. Regarding this issue, Olupona[23] posits that while those who identify as practitioners of traditional African religions are often in the minority, many who identify as Muslims or Christians are involved in traditional religions to one degree or another.

In addition, he says Traditional African religions are not stagnant but highly dynamic and constantly reacting to various shifting influences such as old age, modernity and technological advances. Lupine concludes that while many Africans have converted to Islam and Christianity, African religion still informs the social, economic and political life in African societies.

In addressing change in African religion, Rosalind Hackett[24] argues that it is not the complete religious system that changes but rather concepts, practices and symbols. Citing Robin Horton,[25] she continues by noting that when the enormity of the world enters into a small community, the local spirits are first to be devalued. Instead, the community focuses more on the Supreme Being and places more importance in one place. Others claim that the cultic, collective or calendrical aspects diminish first. This is because the community suffers a loss of identity and power. However, according to these writers, important rites like healing, divination and magic keep their importance as they continue to be helpful in the challenges of a changing world. According to Hackett, the main waves affecting the change of African religion are universalization, modernization, politicization, commercialization and individualization.

What Is Sustainability?

The definition of "sustainability" is the study of how natural systems function, remain diverse and produce everything it needs for the ecology to remain in balance.[26] It also acknowledges that human civilization requires vital resources to sustain our modern way of life. Modernity has not put a total stop to the influence of indigenous African spirituality. According to Olupona,[27] modernity has not adversely affected the impact of indigenous African spirituality. He explains that because of the pluralistic nature of African traditional religions, African spirituality has the tendency to adapt to change and consequenttly has succeeded in absorbing the merits of other religions. For Olupona the accommodating nature and the absence of a uniform doctrine and lack of written text or codes allow it to be amended and influenced by other religious ideas, religious wisdom and modern development. This allows it to more easily be amended and influenced by other religious, religious wisdom and modern development.

Modern Application

Due to the dynamism of African religions, it is not difficult to understand their modern-day relevance and applications in that they present a worldview that has collectively sustained, enriched and given meaning to a continent and numerous other societies for centuries through their epistemology, metaphysics, history and practices. Rosalind Hackett[28] speaks of a process of revitalization of traditional religion in Africa as a manifestation of religious diversity and dynamism in Africa. Hackett has posited the following five: the tendency of universalization, modernization, commercialization, politicization and individualization. Hackett holds that the tendency toward universalization is tantamount to an effort to increase the attractiveness of African community religions and to increase their reach outside the particular group where a specific religion first came into existence. Under the influence of so-called world religions (notably Islam and Christianity), the concept of a Supreme Being has developed quite markedly, at the expense of local deities and spirits. An example of this may be seen in the Nigerian movement known as "Godianism" that demonstrates an attempt to restore worship of the "God of Africa." Godianism can be viewed as a philosophical reflection on African traditional religious customs in such a way as to acquire universal relevance.

Moreover, traditional African religions have gone global. Olupona argues that the transatlantic slave trade led to the growth of African-derived religions in the Americas, such as Candomblé in Brazil; Santería in Cuba, the Dominican Republic and Puerto Rico; *Shango* in Trinidad and Grenada; and *Vodun* in Haiti. Furthermore, many in places like the United States and the United Kingdom have converted to various traditional African religions, and the importance of the Diaspora for these religions is growing rapidly.[29] African religions have also become a major attraction for those in the Diaspora who travel to Africa on pilgrimages because of the global reach of the tradition. The survival of African religions in the Diaspora is testimony of their resilience to their staying power.

Culturally, the tendency toward modernization takes various forms. Gerrie ter Haar[30] uses Hackett to illustrate this assertion. He cites a classic case, which was created in 1997 in Nigeria. A traditional shrine was created by a group of academics at the University of Ile-Ife. This shows how in a university setting people can practice traditional worship and compete with mainline churches and other religious groups. Gerrie ter Haar[31] cites an example of the modernization of traditional religious expressions as the creation, in 1977, of a traditional shrine by a group of intellectuals on the campus of the University of Ile-Ife (Nigeria). This implies, in practice, that on the university campus, the possibility exists to practice traditional worship, alongside the existing facilities for worship in the Christian chapel and the Muslim mosque.

Gerrie ter Haar cites another example of the tendency toward the politicization of traditional from Hackett (32). For him religion is often encountered among government and political leaders as a means of buttressing their power and authority. In Ghana, for example, government leaders pour libations during official ceremonies when new schools or hospitals are opened and new projects are commissioned. In addition, governments advocate for the inclusion of African Traditional Religions as a core content subject in the general education curriculum.

In West Africa, the West African Examination Council has papers on African religion in the West African School Certificate Examinations. The scholarly study of African religions at the colleges in Africa and the Western world has also contributed to its survival. Gerrie ter Haar also discusses how African religions are linked to royal authority to influence the selection and installation of royals. Other examples cited by Gerrie ter Haar are the appeal to secret societies and the use of rituals of the enthronement of traditional leaders in Ghana, Swaziland or Uganda. The examples here illustrate how religion and politics merge to consolidate or maintain the traditional balance of power.[32]

From an economic standpoint, Hackett discusses commercialization as a process in which some features of indigenous religions are assembled or produced and merchandized to promote the important ideas, elements inherent in them. Some of these ideas and symbols include the propagation of African art and healing methods that relate to sickness and healing in the African setting. This is also a classic case of religious appropriation by people considered outsiders. This woman acted as a priest and officiated at annual religious festivals in honor of the river-goddess Osun.[33] In the economic sphere, Hackett talks about the tendency toward commercialization as part of a process whereby particular elements of traditional religions are, as it were, manufactured, that is, developed into products and offered on the market for sale. The explicit aim is to promote significant aspects of African religious traditions by spreading ideas and symbols derived from them. This may find expression, for example, in the propagation of African art or of traditional healing methods, which connect to traditional ideas of sickness and other manifestations of evil.

Olupona argues that the emphasis on health, wealth and procreation is very important in African religions. Dopamu[34] adds that it is when a man is in good health that he can fulfill his social functions as well as his moral obligations. According to Olupona, this explains why Africans have devised pragmatic responses for healing, commerce and general well-being of their own religious leaders and devotees of other religions.

In African societies, where healing involves not just the curing of diseases but also the protection and promotion of human beings' physical, spiritual and material well-being, traditional healers represent hope and destiny in their respective communities. In certain places in Africa, they are the major or only source of health care, and that makes them very important.

Features of African religion

In the Akan society, one avenue to achieve balance of harmony and morality is to appeal to people to observe their customs and traditions including taboos since these are significant. One major means by which social harmony and morality can be achieved, thus ensuring development in traditional Akan society, is through the application and enforcement of taboos, which are inextricable attributes of African religions.[35] Hackett[36] addresses the tendency toward individualization. The emphasis here is person-centered approach in which individual rites replace public rituals. Hackett cites a popular ritual of divination in West and South Africa. The practice of divination is to help adherents to know their future. These diviners read the will of the spirits and pass it to the people. In times of epidemics, drought or anything that threatens the stability of the various societies, the priest/priestess consult the spirit to determine what to do to avert the situation. Divination is also used as an aid to success in business, for football matches or for students faced with exams. For the adherents the rituals give them a psychological boost. Related to the above is Hackett's argument on the tendency toward individualization that marks a shift from a public-oriented approach to a more person-centered one. Individual rites are increasingly taking the place of public rituals, a development that clearly reflects the times we live in.[37] An example of this can be found in the field of divination, a popular ritual with a crucial role in the traditional religion of West and South Africans that aims at discovering the individual's destination. Divination is very well adapted to the requirements of believers in situations such as ailments, death or misfortune. Nevertheless, divination also finds application as an aid to success in business, for football matches or students faced with exams and so on. On such occasions, people frequently summon the help of a traditional religious specialist, a diviner or marabout, whose role in Africa in many ways bears comparison with that of a psychotherapist in the United States. Celebrations and rituals keep indigenous religions alive.

Women play important roles in the traditional religious sphere. They function as herbalists and diviners. These positions are held by both males and females—both illiterate and educated. One can add that preponderance of women in these areas may be a subtle way for women to be on their own and for that matter to assert themselves in a male chauvinist world. It is no wonder that feminist scholars have drawn from these traditions to advocate for women's rights and the place of the female in African societies. Women play a key role in the practice of these traditions. There are many female goddesses along with their male counterparts.

The traditional approach of indigenous African religions to gender is one of complementarity where males and females need each other. Extant literature of success stories debunk the conventional mentality that the role of the woman is in the kitchen.[38]

The tacit support of enlightened husbands challenge men who never want to see their wives go high. One would, therefore, read about a woman whose ambitions were bolstered by her own husband even when conventional expectations had risen against their moves.

Magessa (2002)[39] contend African religions have always paid attention to individuals and the community. He calls it "the moral traditions of abundant life". Awuah-Nyamekye[40] asserts that indigenous African religions contain a great deal of wisdom and insight on how human beings can best live within and interact with the environment. For him because of the prevailing ecological crisis indigenous African religions have a great deal to offer to both African countries and the world as a whole. Further, he argues that the traditional Akan people believe that humans have utilized their environmental resources to survive the vicissitudes of life. The implication is that environmental consciousness is an integral part of Akan's people worldview. Awuah-Nyamekye explains why the Akan people have devised tough measures to ensure the conservation of their environment. Akan people place the role of water in sustainable development in their environment. Among the Akans, it is forbidden to defecate near a river. It is also taboo to farm near watersheds or the primary source of a river. The objective is to avoid a situation where the river is not exposed to the direct rays of the sun. It was perceived that exposure to direct rays of the sun can lead to excessive evaporation resulting in the river becoming dried up. Given our current impending ecological crisis, indigenous African religions have a great deal to offer to both African countries and the world at large. In the perspective of the traditional Akan people, human beings were made to live in the world by means of the resources available in their environment. This means that environmental consciousness is part of the traditional Akan peoples' view.[41] Thus, they have stringent measures in place to ensure the conservation of their environment. They know that water is certainly one of the essential elements in sustainable development. In traditional Akan society, it is a sin (taboo) to defecate near a river. It is also a sin to farm near watersheds or the primary source of a river. This injunction is certainly meant to ensure that the river is not exposed to the direct rays of the sun, which can lead to excessive evaporation and thereby the river becoming dried up.[42] This is the Africans' way of ensuring a constant flow of water to the river.

Another measure used by the Akan people (and, in fact, throughout traditional Africa) to ensure environmental conservation is the institution of sacred groves. In the traditional Akan worldview, the Supreme Being, the gods, the ancestors and other spirits are believed to serve as "policemen." This is because for them, the laws, customs, taboos and other codes of ethics in traditional Akan societies have divine backing; they are believed to have been sanctioned by the gods and ancestors who invoke sanctions on anyone who disobeys them. There is compliance even when one is in solitude due to this firm belief of the people.[43] However, it is difficult to deny the fact that African Traditional Religion has influenced the moral life of the African people today. One major means by which social harmony and morality is be achieved, thus ensuring development in traditional Akan society, is through the application and enforcement of taboos, which are inextricable attributes of African religion.

It is interesting to note that there is occasional "misuse" of some African indigenous practices by some people with mischievous intent. The practice of *Trokosi* is a classic example of religious belief practiced by the Ewe people of Ghana.[44]

Similar rites called "voodoosi" are also practiced in parts of Benin and Togo in West Africa. Young girls are sent to fetish priests at their shrines. The fetish priests keep many other girls and women as slaves. Forms of it are practiced in parts of Benin and Togo where the *practice* is called 'voodoosi'.[45]

This is a form of atonement due to an elder relative's wrongdoings. Another example is also reported in Liberia where girls are put through forced marriages and health issues because of Female Genital Mutilations (FGM), which keep them out of school. It is also reported that young girls are often taken out of or abducted from school for initiation and may remain in the Sande grove for several weeks or months. In addition, the phenomenon of ritual murder has been part of the Ghanaian and South African system of cultural beliefs. There was also an Akan belief that a messenger must accompany a dead chief on his last journey to the land of his ancestors. Young girls are often taken out of or abducted from, school for initiation and may remain in the Sande grove for several weeks or months. In addition, the phenomenon of ritual murder has been part of the Ghanaian and South African system of cultural beliefs. There was also an Akan belief that a messenger must accompany a dead chief on his last journey to the land of his ancestors.[46]

Another belief system relates to socio-political involving human rights abuse on the acquisition of power and wealth by the use of juju or through ritual killing. This involves rituals performed with human blood or body parts. Another case in point is West Africa and present-day South Africa[47] where in certain parts of the country, witchcraft accusations have become so frequent that national governments had to set up various groups to try to tackle what has become a grave social problem that has led in recent years to the violent deaths of hundreds of people.

Witchcraft accusations, including accusations against children, trial by ordeal and its attendant deaths; cases of boys and men being abducted for forcible initiation into poor society and Female Genital Mutilation are examples of human rights abuses emanating from cultural and traditional practices that put African religious practices in the negative limelight.

All over the world, education is said to be the panacea for "backward" religious beliefs and practices.[48] It is against this background that we suggest a collaborative effort by the state, people, non-government organizations, politicians, the Church and administrators to address the issues of Trokosi, Female Genital Mutilation and juju. Organizing workshops, political rallies and media can initiate programs to address these situations. The Church, traditional leaders, politicians and governments can play their part and contribute to the improvement of the standard of living of its citizens. Global actions are also needed to complement national and local initiatives to achieve maximum benefit for poor people throughout African communities.

Conclusion

The term "African Traditional Religion" is used in two complementary senses. Gerrie ter Haar describes traditional religions of Africa as religions with a long and dynamic history that have crossed boundaries and have entered new territory. With the advent of Westernization, education, urbanization and Christianity one would have expected traditional African religions to be weaker and decline in importance. Interestingly, these religions have emerged strong and vital from the confrontation with the so-called world religions. Based on the revitalization processes highlighted by Hackett, it is not anticipated that African Traditional Religion will continue with us forever. On the contrary, it will be worthwhile to see what type of interactions may occur between these modern "traditional" religions, on the one hand, which are taking their place among the religions of the world, and the traditional "world religions," which have associated themselves increasingly with particular communities, on the other. In any case, the study of African Traditional Religion will continue to demand our serious attention.[49]

Notes

1. Mugambi, Jesse Religion and Social Construction of Reality (Nairobi University Press, 1996).
2. Awolalu, J. O. "Sin and its Removal in African Traditional Religion," Journal of the American Academy Religion vol. 44, no. 2 (1976).
3. Gathogo, J. M., The Relevance and Influence of African Religion in Post-Apartheid South Africa and Beyond (Churchman, Summer, 2007). (https://biblicalstudies.org.uk/pdf/churchman/121-02_163.pdf).
4. Mbiti, J. S., African Traditional Religon 1968. Nairobi: East African Education Publishers Shaw Rosaling. The Invention of African Traditional Religion (1990) 20, 339–352.
5. Olupona, J. African Religions: A Very Short Introduction (Oxford University Press, 2014).
6. Gathogo, J. M., The Relevance and Influence of African Religion in Post-Apartheid South Africa and Beyond (Churchman, Summer, 2007). (https://biblicalstudies.org.uk/pdf/churchman/121-02_163.pdf).
7. Ibid.
8. Olupona, J., African Religions: A Very Short Introduction (Oxford University Press, 2014). https://blog.oup.com/2014/05/15-facts-on-african-religions/.
9. Magesa, J., African Religion, The Moral Traditions of Abundant Life (Maryknoll, NY: Orbis Books, 2002).
10. Mbiti, J. S., African Religions and Philosophy. Second edition (Oxford: Heinemann Educational Publishers, 1999).
11. Krüger, J. S., Lubbe, G. J. A. and Steyn, H. C. The Human Search for Meaning: A Multi-Religion Introduction to the Religions of Humankind (Pretoria: Van Schaaik Publishers, 2009).
12. Magesa, African Religion, The Moral Traditions of Abundant Life, 2002.

13. Turaki, Y., Christianity and African Gods: A Method in Theology (Potchefstroomse Universiteit vir Christelike Hoër Onderwys, Potchefstroom, 2009).
14. Krüger, J. S. G., Lubbe, G. J., & . Steyn, H. C., The Human Search for Meaning: A Multi-Religion Introduction to the Religions of Humankind (Pretoria: Van Schaaik Publishers, 2009).
15. Mndende, N. "Ancestors and Healing in African Religion: A South African Context" in Ingo Wulfhorst (ed.), Ancestors, Spirits and Healing in Africa and Asia: A challenge to the church (Geneva: The Lutheran World Federation), 2005, p. 13.
16. John S. Mbiti, African Religions and Philosophy. Second edition (Oxford: Heinemann Educational Publishers, 1999).
17. Gathogo, J. M., The Relevance and Influence of African Religion in Post-Apartheid South Africa and Beyond (Churchman, Summer, 2007). (https://biblicalstudies.org.uk/pdf/churchman/121-02_163.pdf).
18. Mndende, N., "Ancestors and Healing in African Religion: A South African Context" in Ingo Wulfhorst (ed.), Ancestors, Spirits and Healing in Africa and Asia: A challenge to the church (Geneva: The Lutheran World Federation), 2005, p. 13.
19. Bolaji Idowu, E, African Traditional Religion: A Definition (London: SCM Press, 1973).
20. Ibid.
21. John S. Mbiti, African Religions and Philosophy. Second edition (Oxford: Heinemann Educational Publishers, 1999.
22. Gathogo, J. M., The Relevance and Influence of African Religion in Post-Apartheid South Africa and Beyond (Churchman, Summer, 2007). (https://biblicalstudies.org.uk/pdf/churchman/121-02_163.pdf).
23. Olupona, J., African Religions: A Very Short Introduction (Oxford University Press, 2014). https://blog.oup.com/2014/05/15-facts-on-african-religions.
24. Hackett, R., "Revitalization in African Traditional Religion." In: African Traditional Religions in Contemporary Society, ed. J. K. Olupona (New York: Paragon House), pp. 135–148.
25. Horton, Robin. "On The Rationality Of Conversion Part I." Religious Conversion: An African Perspective, edited by Brendan Carmody, Gadsden Publishers, Lusaka, Zambia, 2015, pp. 73–92. JSTOR, www.jstor.org/stable/j.ctvh8qzmc.9. Accessed 23 Feb. 2021.
26. https://neearth.org.
27. https://thisisafrica.me/african-identities/relevance-african-indigenous-religions-21st-centur.y.
28. Hackett, R.L., 'Revitalization in African Traditional Religion', in Olupona 1991: 135–149.
29. Ibid.
30. https://teol.ku.dk/cas/publications/publications/occ._papers/terhaar2000.pdf.
31. Ibid.
32. Gerrie ter Haar ibid.
33. Magesa, African Religion, The Moral Traditions of Abundant Life, 2002.
34. Dopamu, D., Health and Healing within the Traditional African Context. In: Orita, Ibadan Journal of Religious studies XV11/2 December, 1985.
35. teol.ku.dk›cas›publications›publications›occ._papers›terhaar2000.pd.

36. Hackett, R.L.J., 'Revitalization in African Traditional Religion', in Olupona 1991: 135–149.
37. cypressgh.blogspot.com›2018›12›women-are-not-meant-to-be-in-her.html.
38. https://irwellesreport.wordpress.com/2012/03/29/trokosi-tod.
39. https://www.ohchr.org/Documents/Countries/LR/HarmfulTraditionalPracticesLiberia.doc.
40. Awuah-Nyamekye, "Salvaging Nature: The Akan Religio-Cultural Perspective. Worldview: Global Religions, Culture and Ecology, vol. 13, no. 3 (2009) 251–282.
41. Awuah-Nyamekye, "Teaching Sustainable Development from the Perspective of Indigenous Spiritualities of Ghana," In Religion and Sustainable Development Opportunities and Challenges for Higher Education (pp. 25–39), edited by Cathrien de Pater and Irene Dankelman (Berlin: Lit Verlag, 2009).
42. Ibid.
43. https://www.researchgate.net/publication/234093093_Religion_and_Development_African_Traditional_Religion's_Perspective.
44. https://irwellesreport.wordpress.com/2012/03/29/trokosi-todays-slavery.
45. https://www.ohchr.org/Documents/Countries/LR/HarmfulTraditionalPracticesLiberia.doc.
46. www.liberiapastandpresent.org›ArchiveNewspapers›GhanaHistoricalOverviewAndBackgroundRitualKillings.htm.
47. Gerrie ter Haar 'Rats, cockroaches, and people like us': in Human Rights and Responsibilities in the World Religions ED. Joseph Runzo, J., Martin, M., & Arvind Sharma, A., 2003.
48. Dewey, John. "The Democratic Faith and Education." The Antioch Review, vol. 4, no. 2, 1944, pp. 274–283. JSTOR, www.jstor.org/stable/4609010. Accessed 22 Feb. 2021. Dewey, John. "The Democratic Faith and Education." The Antioch Review 4, no. 2 (1944): 274–83. Accessed February 22, 2021. https://doi.org/10.2307/4609010.
49. https://teol.ku.dk/cas/publications/publications/occ._papers/ter-haar2000.pdf.

CHAPTER 34

African Traditional Religion and Sustainability: The New Indigenous Religious Movements

Danoye Oguntola-Laguda

INTRODUCTION

The sustainability of African Traditional Religion (ATR) has been a major cause of concern for both scholars and adherents of the religion. Scholars of African Traditional Religion—E. Bolaji Idowu, John O. Awolalu, P. Adelumo Dopamu, J. O. Kayode, and Ibigbolade S. Aderibigbe—posit a future for the religion but not with clear conviction.[1] This may be based on lack of scriptures, literature, historical figures (that can point to the origin of the religion), and the secret nature of the religion. There is also the problem of methodologies, as well as insider and outsider issues for the study of the religion. The pressure from Islam and Christianity is also a serious concern to the practitioners in Africa. However, the emergence of New Religious Movements (NRM) with flare for African Traditional Religion has brought hope for its sustainability. This is apart from the fact that scholarship has increased in recent times on the social, economic, political, cultural, and ethical values of ATR. Scholars such as Jacob K. Olupona, A. Adogame, Oyeronke, and Grillo have been on the front burner of African Studies into the doctrines, liturgies, sociology, and cultural values of ATR. These "new breeds" have often refused to be drawn into the problem of sustainability or extinction of ATR.[2]

This chapter interrogates the problem of sustainability of African Traditional Religion using New Religious Movements as a response to the growing

D. Oguntola-Laguda (✉)
Lagos State University, Lagos, Nigeria
e-mail: danoye.oguntolalaguda@lasu.edu.ng

© The Author(s), under exclusive license to Springer Nature Switzerland AG 2022
I. S. Aderibigbe, T. Falola (eds.), *The Palgrave Handbook of African Traditional Religion*, https://doi.org/10.1007/978-3-030-89500-6_34

concerns among scholars and adherents of ATR on its future and value not only as an epistemological and theological conception but as a religion with adequate social and moral values that is deep enough to address the tripartite problems of ignorance, diseases, and poverty in Africa. To achieve these objectives, I shall attempt a definition of ATR and explain its features and characteristics. Further, the place of ATR in modern scholarship shall be discussed. This chapter shall enumerate the features of NRM and determine how such groups can be a point of reference in the sustenance of ATR debates. These issues are examined using the example of Ijo Orunmila Adulawo, a neo-Pentecostal group, which combines the liturgy of ATR with Christianity to promote "pristine" African Religion in Lagos, Southwest Nigeria.

Religions in Nigeria

The historiography of Nigeria's religions is as complex as its social and cultural mix. The Nigerian nation has over 250 ethnic groups with over 400 languages in use. These diversities have made the nation a multi-religious environment where African Traditional Religion, Islam, Christianity, and civil religions hold sway.[3] This is not counting the newer spiritual science movements.[4] Although accurate statistics as to the distribution of the populace along religious traditions are not readily available, it is common to hear that Islam and Christianity are dominant. These two traditions have been greatly influenced by African religious traditions, including Nigerian Christianity and Nigerian Islam. This indicates that African Traditional Religion has now been taken into the rituals and social space(s) of Islam and Christianity. In these ways, ATR seems to have lost its pristine forms as it has now become part and parcel of these two dominant religions not only in Nigeria but in Africa as a continent. One glaring feature of the appropriation of the tenets and doctrines is syncretism.[5] It should be noted that pristine forms of ATR are still been maintained by a few practitioners and groups. The politics of religion in Nigerian polity has become more controversial, leading to debates about the secularity of the State.[6]

Despite this situation, African Religion has continued to interrogate national policies and determine events in the country. This is evident in all strata of the Nigerian nation, suggesting that the multiple religious environments are not a hindrance to nation-building and development like some social scientists that belong to the Marxist school want us to believe. This is not to deny the fact that religious practices in Nigeria have engendered conflict, violence, and sometimes "war" as witnessed in the Sagamu riot (1999), Jos conflicts (2000, 2003, 2007, and 2010), Maiduguri (2010), and Kano riot (2010). To gauge the importance of African Traditional Religion in modern Nigeria, we shall undertake a concise periodization of the practice of ATR within the Nigerian religious space in order to locate the relevance and importance of the tradition in the political development, economic realities, and psyche of the Nigerian people. We shall further examine its interrogation and negotiation with other religions (Christianity and Islam) in the Nigerian religious landscape. Further, the response of ATR to the spiritual and religious yearning of the people shall be evaluated to gauge the response of ATR to the imported religious traditions.

Anatomy of Traditional Religion in Nigeria's Multi-religious Heritage

Traditional religion, popularly known as African Traditional Religion (ATR), is the oldest genre of religion in Nigeria. It is tribal and ethnic-based. This perhaps will explain why the religion is delineated by the name of the respective linguistic, cultural, and tribal groupings. These include, but are not limited to, the Yoruba, Igbo, Kalabari, Hausa, and Tiv traditional religions. This categorization does not presuppose uniformity of beliefs and rituals.[7] E. Bolaji Idowu argued that the differences observable in these local forms of ATR are not enough to suggest a plural form of the religion.[8] However, the point by A. Adogame becomes apposite here: "Indigenous religions are more or less localized. Some beliefs may be more widespread while others may vary from one ethnic group to another. What the categorization suggests is an aggregation of shared, similar and related but sometime quite different beliefs and ritual system often shaped by particular ethnic and social groups, power structures and even the characteristics of natural phenomenon in each locality."[9]

African Traditional Religion does not lay claim to any historical origin(s). Nevertheless, the practitioners are convinced that the religion has a divine origin and is transmitted cross-generationally through oral literatures such as myths, songs, legends, sagas, and oracles. Other sources of transmission include names, proverbs, and prayers.[10] These sources vary from one ethnic or tribal grouping to another. Despite its variety of sources, traditional religions in Nigerian societies share common affinities in their ideals, rituals, and cosmologies. Based on this premise, we can argue for a formed pattern of traditional religious thoughts and rituals.

African Tradition Religion, in whatever form, has major and minor beliefs. The former gives meaning and value to the latter. The former include beliefs in the Supreme Being, divinities, ancestors, spirits, magic, and medicine. The Supreme Being is believed to be the Creator of heaven, earth, and all beings. He is the controller of human beings' destinies. The conception and worship of a Supreme Being have raised suspicion in the mind of non-Africans that have interrogated (investigated) the religion. Therefore, the practitioners have been accused of engaging in polytheism (because the Supreme Being is known with many names and sometimes conceived differently), pantheism, and idolatry.[11] The people also express a firm belief in other celestial beings, known as lieutenants of the Supreme Being that act as divinities and ancestors, and assist in the theocratic governance of the world, while the latter are living but dead ancestors. The spirits are incorporeal beings often patronized for their magic powers. The belief of the people in traditional medicine as a cure for ailments that are physical as well as metaphysical is firm and total. There are various minor beliefs. These include beliefs in morality, judgment day, hard work, good neighborliness, worship, and life after death.[12]

African Traditional Religion is a genre of religion that has some unique features. It has no founder that can easily be alluded to for a study of its liturgy and rituals. Rather, we rely on cultural and ethnical practices of the people to develop a theology for the genre. To my mind, ATR has developed over time from the culture of the people. Therefore, the culture gives meaning and value to its theology. The religion has no scripture (written) but has what has been described as oral literatures. It is also non-evangelical as conversion to its rituals is based on experience, observation, and conviction.[13]

In pre-colonial Nigeria, ATR was the sole religion in the Nigerian religious space. However, navigation of the country by Arabian traders through the Saharan trade and the Western explorers on their discovery brought Islam and Christianity into contact with ATR. Consequently, the colonial era in Nigerian history witnessed the growth and development of a multi-religious society with different denominations and forms of these three distinct traditions—African Traditional Religion, Islam, and Christianity. Therefore, the African people "encountered other religious forms and responded by revitalizing themselves through synthesis, reinvention, and change."[14] This change led to the formation of a neo-traditional religious movement, such as the Ijo Orunmila (Adulawo), a movement founded in the 1930s by Yoruba Christians of Anglican denomination seeking to reestablish links with their traditional religious heritage. Adogame informs us that during this period, "[t]he Bori cult a neo-traditional movement prominent among Hausa women, draws partly on Islamic beliefs and practices."[15] However, despite the efforts of ATR, Islam and Christianity became predominant in the Nigerian religious space, and the colonial masters used these traditions as points of contact, negotiation, and intervention in the traditional politics, ethics, and economy of the Nigerian people.

In post-colonial Nigeria, there are efforts by the patrons of ATR to continue the links earlier mentioned. This was evident in the fusion (merger) among the pre-colonial Arousa Church, the Bini indigenous religion, and the National Church of Nigeria to form what is now known as "Godianism." This merger is a product of the social value then attached to the practice of ATR. The practitioners are perceived as "pagans" and unbelievers. Consequently, new traditional movements emerged on the scene. These include the Reformed Ogboni Fraternity (ROF), which was formed based on the fusion of the rituals and beliefs of ATR and Christianity. However, the religion continues to persist due to the peoples' resilient belief in supernatural forces and its various transformations of the Nigerian-derived religions in the Diaspora, including *Santeria* (USA), *Candomble* (Brazil), and the numerous *Orisa*- and *Ifa*-derived religiosities.[16]

Transformation of Traditional Religion in Nigerian Religious Space

From our discussions so far, we observe that African Traditional Religion has witnessed many transformations that have now reshaped the African peoples' rituals, liturgies, and values. One of the most outstanding changes that have reshaped the religion is the formation of New Religious Movement groups. These groups emerged in response to the pressure brought to bear on ATR by Islam and Christianity. Consequently, we have sociological groups, such as the Eyo, Egungun, Agemo, and Reformed Ogboni Fraternity (ROF), the political groups (Osugbo), the neo-Pentecostal groups, and the pristine groups. These groups are not particularly exclusive as their workings (rituals and liturgies) are interwoven and similar. They now occupy the Nigerian religious space presenting ATR with the garb of modernity. The practitioners appropriate the media to advance the cause of their faith. Their romance with the media is very noticeable in the advertisements and sales of various medicaments. These medicines have come to be popular among Nigerians and have become alternative(s) to Western orthodox medicine. Although the claims of the *producers* of these medicaments cannot be readily ascertained, the effectiveness of the medicines, as attested to by the users, cannot be denied. Perhaps the derogative terms used in describing ATR may have necessitated the modernization of its rituals and liturgies. This is apparent in the case of "Godianism," as mentioned above.

In Lagos, Southwest Nigeria, the Ijo, Orunmila Adulawo, and Ato provide a good example. They have an edifice (place of worship) comparable to a Christian Church with standing choirs, catechism, hymn books, and priests. Their sermons are drawn from Yoruba oral scripture *Ifa*.[17] ATR has been repackaged to respond to the social, political, cultural, and economic needs of its patrons. It has become a tool of political negotiations and interactions, social engineering and networking, not only among the adherents but also among scholars of the religion.

The struggle for political power in Nigeria's history has occurred within the framework of religion in ways that magnify ethnic and regional antagonisms and exacerbate misunderstanding in the political and religious space.[18] Although Adogame argues that these antagonisms are between patrons of Islam and Christianity, it has extended to *faithfuls* of ATR who now jostle for space. Sharing of political office has taken a religious dimension. Consequently, political aspirations are taken to the religious space leading to the manipulation of religion as a tool to secure political office and the "established convention of allocating important political and administrative positions on the basis of religious persuasions."[19] Nigerian politicians now patronize ATR to provide magic charms that will assist in their political ambitions. During the 1993 election campaigns, the Social Democratic Party (SDP), in its audited account, posited that it spent ten million naira to prevent rain from disrupting their convention in Jos.

The role of government in religious practices is another area where ATR has evolved. In the past independent era, in fact, during the first republic and even up to the second republic, Islam and Christianity dominated the government's budget as it spent huge sums of money in sponsoring pilgrimages to Mecca and Jerusalem. Although there are still no pilgrimage sponsorships for patrons of ATR, the government now sponsors traditional religion through its festivals. For example, between 1996 and 2009, the Lagos State Government spent over 100 million naira on four Eyo festivals.[20] The Osun State Government has continuously sponsored the Osun-Osogbo festival since 1999 with huge investments. In the north, the Agungun festival is ever endorsed by the Kebbi State Government.

The intervention of government in religion has generated controversy, which has also led to conflicts and in some cases violence. These conflicts are a product of competitions, especially between Islam and Christianity. As observed by Adogame, the pre-colonial era was the most peaceful as there was no competition. During this period, indigenous religion co-existed and interacted most peacefully with Islam and Christianity.[21] African Traditional Religion has been the least aggressive religious genre in Nigeria since its independence.

However, in the last two decades, the situation seems to have changed. Many religious conflicts and violence involving the patrons of ATR have been recorded—the Sagamu riot of 1999 between the Oro group (ATR) and Muslims in the Sabo area of Sagamu town. The Epe religious violence in 2001 was also between Muslims and patrons of ATR. These conflicts are derived from intolerances and boundary-making negotiations among practices of religions in Nigeria.

In Nigeria today, it is unusual for anyone to discuss religion and spirituality in public spaces without a reference to African Traditional Religion. Its acceptance by adherents of Islam and Christianity as well as the State may not be based on conviction or its soteriological contents, but more because it has become a genre of religion in Nigeria that cannot be ignored. This is perhaps due to the efforts of pioneers in African Religion Studies who have studiously researched the traditions. The results of these researchers' findings form the basis of information and enlightenment to all and sundry. It is also a response to the unfortunate submissions of foreign scholars that the African people have no defined religion or if they do, it is devoid of a concept of God.[22]

A byproduct of the scholarship of these African Scholars is the study of African Traditional Religion in Nigeria tertiary institutions today. Bolaji Idowu, John Mbiti, John Awolalu, Dopamu, and Adelumo are prime examples of this genre that interrogates, interacts, and negotiates its continued relevance in the Nigerian religious space in order to create and sustain its pristine identity in modern-day Africa.

New Religious Movements: Ijo Orunmila Adulawo

There are many New Religious Movements (NRM) in the world today. This term refers to those groups which within a cultural and societal context are known as new faiths. They are often referred to as cults. According to the *Encyclopedia Britannica*, "The term has been applied to all new faiths that have arisen worldwide over the past several centuries."[23] These groups have peculiar characteristics and features. Some of these features are as follows:

- They offer innovative religious responses to the situations of their society even though they lay claim to esoteric origin(s).
- They are often regarded as "alternatives" to popular religions in their immediate environment.
- New Religious Movements could be pluralistic, eclectic, and syncretic as they often combine doctrines and practices from diverse sources within their belief system.[24]
- The NRM always come with a leader who may have charismatic traits. Such leaders often laid claim to mysterious and esoteric power that they use in their leadership styles.
- They often arise as a response to some social and cultural challenges facing the society as well as individuals which popular religions cannot satisfy.

According to Leonard G. Goss, "New Religion 'or' alternative religions are breakaways from larger, more traditional religions. They break down into self-improvement groups, Eastern religions or thought systems, unification groups, and Christian deviation sects. Many of these new religions had Christian roots but have departed from historic biblical Christianity and discarded one or more of Christianity's basic beliefs."[25]

- NRM often rely on new scriptures or what Goss called "new authority" apart from the scripture of the group from which they broke out.
- The groups often laid claim to "divine calling" or "anointing" into religious leadership.
- NRM may be secretive. Members who are not part of the "inner circle" may not be open to the spiritualities of the group.
- David G. Bromley argues that NRM always emerged "at points of tension/crisis"[26] in the society. They also develop and operate "new" mystic systems that challenge established institutional logic. They also create rituals that shows that the truth of their mystic system. They also create new types of organizations.[27]

From the above, we can argue that New Religious Movements are formidable religious groups, which often provided alternatives to the popular religions that may have failed in their response to the basic social, economic, and cultural challenges facing their immediate environment. In Nigeria, as it is in some African countries, the NRM are prevalent and their popularity is becoming a point of reference to religiosity and spirituality of people on the continent. In the next section, we shall consider the history, liturgy, and doctrines of Ijo Orunmila (Adulawo) in Lagos, Southwest Nigeria, to support our thesis that African Traditional Religious Movements (ATRM) have emerged with doctrines, liturgies, and spiritualities supporting its sustainability not only in Africa but also in the African Diaspora.

In Lagos, a cosmopolitan environment, where Christian Pentecostals and Islamic Pentecostals dominate the spiritual landscape, the continued existence and survival of African Traditional Religious Movements (ATRM) appears to be unsustainable. However, the ATRM have reorganized in response to the threat posed by the Christian and Islamic Pentecostals.[28] Apart from our case study, other groups, such as the Reformed Ogboni Fraternity, Atinga, and Chrislamherb, have emerged "with new liturgies and doctrines robed in modernity, sophistication … and shed the garb of primitiveness, archaism and secrecy which hitherto are seen as basic characteristics of African Traditional Religion."[29]

In a study conducted between 2010 and 2014, I observed that the ATRM adopted new media (electronic media) to make their doctrines, rituals, and liturgies relevant to the realities of the people and society, including modernity and sophistication that now permeate African religious spaces. Further, the ATRM reorganized to align with the modernity and sophistication expected of religion in the twenty-first century while still retaining some, if not all, of its pristine features.[30] In my study, I created five categories of ATRM (NRM)—cultic groups, healing groups, sociological groups, socio-cultural groups, and evangelical groups. These categories were created as a response to studies by Allan Anderson,[31] Harvey Gallagher Cox,[32] and Ogbu Kalu.[33] I observed that broad categories of traditional worshippers now identify as Christians and Muslims and profess these faiths but still retain their ATR affiliations and practices. Anderson identified the Zion Christian Church in South Africa as an example of Africans in this category. In this regard, members of this church offer sacrifices (chickens) to ancestors in the church.[34] Cox observes, "On a continent plagued by the loss of woodlands and arable land, a religiously based ecological ethics is appearing. This ethics is based on the spirituality that mixes ancient African religious sensibilities with modern environmental awareness, and it is taking place within a movement that has arisen as Christian Pentecostal impulses have interacted with a throbbing universe of African primal religion."[35]

From the submission of Anderson (1993), Kalu (1990), Cox (1994), and my 2010 study on "Pentecostalism and African Religious Movements," it is obvious that we now have New Religious Movements in Africa with defined characteristics and features of NRM as earlier identified. All these groups have iconic leaders with claims to mystic and esoteric knowledge and a "call" to spiritual leadership. Further, these groups are regarded as cults by non-members as they hold dearly to the secrets of their initiation and doctrine. Nevertheless, some groups in the cultic category "are still ancient in all ramifications, seeking spiritual powers and knowledge of the metaphysical world."[36] However, the social, economic, and political relevance of the ATRM cannot be overemphasized. The healing groups are the most popular as they use traditional medical therapies as a response to the challenge of ailments and diseases on the continent. The socio-political groups are still performing their traditional duties of kingmakers in traditional politics of the people. Consequent upon these ethnographical evidences, it is obvious that the African Traditional Religious Movements (ATRM) are abounding not only in Lagos, Nigeria but also in other parts of Africa. These ATRM could be regarded as NRM. We shall now examine Ijo Orunmila Ato as one example of the new ATRM.

Ijo Orunmila (Ato)

This group (ATRM) is registered with the Nigerian Government, through the Corporate Affairs Commission (CAC), as the indigenous faith of Africa (IFA). However, it is popularly known in Lagos as Ijo Orunmila, Ato. It should be noted that another group known as Ijo Orunmila (Adulawo) is also abound in Lagos with similar doctrines, liturgies, and ethics but with different leaders.[37] Ijo Orunmila, Ato was founded in 1920 by Pa Olorunfumi Oshiga. According to the account of his followers, he had a vision in which he was instructed to form a group of traditional religious worshippers, based on the Ifa corpus, by one of the deities in the crowded Yoruba pantheon (the name of the divinity could not be given). Before 1920, Pa Olorunfumi was of the Anglican Communion. He was worshiping at St. Jude's Anglican Church, Ebute-Metta (not too far from the location of the "church" of Ijo Orunmila). After 12 years of receiving "divine instruction" to form the group, Pa Olorunfumi mobilized a reasonable number of Yoruba people in his immediate environment to build a temple where they held their first formal worship at Freeman Street, Ebute-Metta, where the group still worships.[38] The group was to be known as Ijo Akoda (the first church) but the colonial masters rejected the name and advised that the group's name should reflect their belief in *Ifa*. This is why they settled for indigenous faith of Africa (IFA).[39]

The group's worship system is formulated along the line of the Anglican Communion in Nigeria. They have their own creed and hymn book for worship. The worship service is held regularly on Saturday at the temple. This day was chosen to allow members to retain their dual religious identities to worship as Christians. On my last visit to the temple in Lagos, about 165 members attended the worship service.[40] Further, it is to appropriate Saturday, which is "free" on the liturgical days of both Christians and Muslims. I observed that a good percentage of their members still retain their Christian and Muslim names, even when they have added names derived from the Ifa corpus. Such names include Ifabunmi, Ifajimi, Ifagbemi, and Ifatola, among others.

During worship on a Saturday in 2015, I observed the following where the Ifa corpus played a prominent role. The first and second lessons were taken from the Ifa corpus. Moral lessons and prayers were drawn from chapters of Ifa used for the service.[41] The group has its choir, which is always on hand to lead the songs during worship service. Modern musical instruments were also appropriated for the worship. They have a choir master and drummers that bring danceable percussions into the worship service. The High Priest (Oluwo) is assisted by other leaders of the group. These include the Akoda Awo (second in command), Aseda Awo (third in the command chain), and the Abese Awo (who acts as a warden). The leadership hierarchy is based on experience and knowledge of the Ifa corpus. The worship service starts with a procession hymn followed by opening prayers and recitation of the creed by all members. The second and third hymns are followed by the first and second lessons from the Odu Ifa (Ifa corpus). Then, the sermon for the day is delivered by one of the leaders. Toward the end of the service, the *Ifa* oracle is brought out for divination for all members who will approach the *Babalawo* for divination with kola nuts and money offerings. All worshippers present take their turn for the divination while the choir entertains with choruses and lyrics adopted from popular Christian songs. There is also time set aside for peoples' testimonies to the intervention of *Olodumare* and divinities in the lives of the worshippers. The worship service is often rounded up with closing prayers and a recessional hymn.

My observation during the worship of the group (since 2005 till date) suggests that Ijo Orunmila (Ato) is an ATRM founded on the structure and principles of African Traditional Religion (Yoruba version). They believe in the five major beliefs of ATR: belief in God (*Olodumare*), belief in Divinities (*Orisa*), belief in Ancestors (*Iya nla ati Baba nla*), living but dead ancestors,[42] belief in Spirits (*Anjonu*), and belief in Magic and Medicine (*Epe ati Ase*).[43] Based on this belief system, I posit that "their worship is similar to what is obtainable at the Anglican and African (indigenous) churches in Nigeria."[44] However, they rely on *Orunmila* and *Ela* (two of the divinities in the Yoruba pantheon). *Ela* is conceived as the son of *Olodumare*, comparable to Jesus of the Christian faith.[45] It was also observed that the members are often syncretic and have more than one religious identity or affiliation. The social, moral, economic, and spiritual values of the group were not in doubt and members attested to their achievements socially and spiritually.

The group engages in crusades and evangelism (Iwode). The focus of their sermons is always on the values of African Traditional Religion as a guide to morality, wealth, and life after death. Prayer sessions are held daily and night vigils form part of their liturgies. At the inner sanctuary of the temple, altars dedicated to various Yoruba divinities are visible and readily available for propitiation and sacrifices. The divinities and ancestors are approached with gifts and ritual sacrifices of cows, goats, or chickens. They also offer food such as porridge, corn food, and rice, among others.[46]

Ijo Orunmila (Adulawo) engages in all doctrines and liturgies of pristine African Traditional Religion before they appropriate the Christian's liturgies and worship models as an addition. The group socializes and interacts with people in the community of their temple. They attempt to remove the garb of secrecy from the practice of ATR. The syncretic character of the group is not in doubt. This is obvious in their worship where Christian (Anglican) methods of processional hymns, a call to worship, opening prayer, first lesson, second lesson, hymns, sermons, and exhortations form a large part of their liturgies. Although the origin of the group was traced to Pa Olorunfumi Oshiga (a Yoruba man) from Southwest, Nigeria, the group's membership has become cosmopolitan, perhaps due to the nature of their immediate environment at the Freeman Street, Ebute-Metta, where Igbo and Hausa people (from Eastern and Northern Nigeria) are also domicile with their economic activities. These people form part of the membership of Ijo Orunmila (Ato). The creed of the group is as follows:

> *Mo gba Olorun Eledumare gbo*
> *Eniti o da orun ati aye*
> *Mo gba Orunmila gbo*
> *Eniti nse iwoli Olodumare akoko*
> I believe in God, the Almighty
> Maker of heaven and earth
> I believe in Orunmila
> The first prophet of Olodumare

This creed expresses the beliefs and convictions of the group in God, the Creator, and *Orunmila*, the first prophet of God. While other Yoruba divinities were not mentioned in the creed, they form part of the group's beliefs and metaphysical interactions. Apart from the promotion of morality and soteriology that they preach, they hold in high esteem Yoruba social and cultural institutions such as marriage and the family. *Ela*, a divinity in the Yoruba pantheon, is seen as the child of God (*omo Olodumare*).

Based on the above, I wish to argue that the indigenous faith of Africa—Ijo Orunmila (Ato)—is a form of New Religious Movement in Yorubaland, which can be categorized as part of African Traditional Religious Movements (ATRM). The group offers innovative responses to the problems of contemporary Yoruba societies. They combine the doctrines, liturgies, and traditions of Christianity and African Traditional Religion. Unlike the pristine ATR, which has no founder, as an NRM, the group has a founder in Pa Olorunfumi Oshiga. They allow and respect their members who wish to remain Christians or Muslims to still partake in the group's rituals. The African Traditional Religious Movements, as identified by Leonard G. Goss, "are breakaway from larger, more traditional religions,"[47] in this case, Christianity. I have argued elsewhere that Ijo Orunmila (Ato) made appropriate use of new social media as well as popular media in the promotion of their liturgies and doctrines.[48] The spirituality and ethical principles of the group are very high. Therefore, I posit that while we may not categorically refer to the group as Pentecostal, it will not be out of place to categorize them as neo-Pentecostals.

Ijo Orunmila and Sustainability of ATR

Many arguments abound from scholars of religion, anthropologists, sociologists, and historians that due to the pressure brought to bear on African Traditional Religion, it will soon fade into irrelevance and oblivion especially because they are considered as idol worshippers, pantheists, and polytheists.[49] However, Idowu,[50] Kayode,[51] and Mbiti[52] have argued that these terms are not only derogatory, but not a good description of the African people who are adherents of ATR and their religions. Thus, Africa's religious space will not be complete without ATR. As noted by Adogame, ATR "encountered other religious forms and responded by revitalizing themselves through synthesis reinvention and change."[53] It is this change and the attempt to sustain ATR that led to the formation of a neo-traditional and Pentecostal religious movement, Ijo Orunmila, seeking to reestablish links with their traditional religious heritage within the parameters of Christian beliefs and worship. My thesis here is that African Traditional Religion is a religious practice by living people with so much vigor not only on the continent but also in the African Diasporas. With this background, I wish to submit that ATR is sustainable and shall be a driving force for the religiosity of the world within the next century and Africans and their religions (ATR, African Christianity, African Islam, etc.) will continue to spread to all parts of the world.

Conclusion

In this chapter, I argued that the future of African Traditional Religion, as a living religion, is guaranteed against the advocacy of some practitioners of other religions in Africa that ATR is a dead religion and its sustainability is suspect in the face of various challenges confronting its practices. Such challenges include secrecy, lack of literature, lack of written Scripture, multiple conceptions of the religion on the continent, and pressure from Christianity and Islam. A majority of these obstacles are being tackled and the results are in favor of the guaranteed future for ATR. Although the secrecy of the religion persists like those of other religions on the continent, students and scholars of the religion can now research into the history, theology, and doctrines of ATR without necessarily becoming initiated.

Results of such scholastic efforts have been responding to the issue of lack of literature in the study of African Traditional Religion. Pioneer efforts of E. Bolaji Idowu, John S. Mbiti, John O. Awolalu, P. Adelumo Dopamu, and Ibigbolade S. Aderibigbe, among others, in the African Religion Studies cannot be over-emphasized. Recently, scholarships by Sophie Oluwole, Jacob Olupona, Afe Adogame, and Laura Grillo, among others, are reference point for studies in ATR.

I must admit the difficulty with regard to a single scripture for the religion for the whole of Africa, but such texts are now developing even in the African Diaspora, especially in oral forms. We have the Ifa corpus among the Yoruba,

Denta among the Akans of Ghana, and Igbo of Nigeria. The religion in reality has multiple conceptions all over the continent; however, the core theology of ATR is the same where ever it is being practiced. These major beliefs are belief in God, the Supreme Being, divinities, ancestors, spirits, magic, and medicine. From these beliefs emerge other conceptions and ethics like the belief in morality, social interactions, respect for elders and authorities (spiritual and temporal), life after death, and salvation. Of all these responses and markers that are indicative of the sustainability of ATR, the formation of New Religious Movements has been the most formidable not only in Africa but in its Diasporas. In this chapter, the example of Ijo Orunmila (ATO) was used to interrogate the questions of the future of ATR. My observations and findings show an assured future for ATR with critical examination of its theology, doctrines, and ethics. Although the groups can be seen as syncretic, this is a common feature of some forms of Islam and Christianity in Africa and its Diaspora.

NOTES

1. Bolaji Idowu, *African Traditional Religion: A Definition* (London: SCM Press, 1970); J. O. Awolalu and P. A. Dopamu, *West African Traditional Religion* (Lagos: Macmillan Publishers, 1976); J. O. Kayode, Understanding African Traditional Religion (University of Ife Press, 1984); Ibigbolade. S. Aderibigbe, "Religions in Africa," In Ibigbolade S. Aderibigbe and Akinloyè A. Òjó (eds.), *Continental Complexities: A Multidisciplinary Introduction to Africa* (pp. 61–84). San Diego, CA: Cognella Publishing, 2012.
2. Jacob K. Olupona, "African Religion in Global Religions: An Introduction," In Mark Juergensmeyer, *The Oxford Handbook of Global Religions* (pp. 78–86) (New York: Oxford University Press, 2003); Afe Adogame, "How God Became a Nigerian: Religious Impulse and the Unfolding of a Nation," *Journal of Contemporary African Studies*, vol. 28, no. 4 (2010): 479–498; Oyeronke, 2015, Laura Grillo, 2018.
3. Olupona, "African Religion in Global Religions," 78–86.
4. Adogame, "How God Became a Nigerian," 479–498.
5. Oye-Laguda O., "African Religious Movements and Pentecostalism: The Model of Ijo-Orunmila, Ato," In I. S. Aderibigbe and C. M. J. Medine (eds), *Contemporary Perspectives on Religions in Africa and the African Diaspora* (New York: Palgrave Macmillan, 2015). https://doi.org/10.1057/9781137498052_5.
6. Section 10 of the Nigerian Constitution as amended, 1999.
7. Adogame, "How God Became a Nigerian," 479–498.
8. E. Bolaji Idowu, *Olodumare: God in Yoruba Belief* (London, SCM Press, 1996).
9. Adogame, "How God Became a Nigerian," 479–498.
10. Idowu, 1971.
11. Idowu, *Olodumare: God in Yoruba Belief*, 1996; Awolalu and Dopamu, *West African Traditional Religion*, 1976.
12. Oye-Laguda, "African Religious Movements and Pentecostalism," 2015.
13. Aderibigbe, "Religions in Africa," 61–84.
14. Adogame, "How God Became a Nigerian," 479–498.
15. Ibid.

16. Adogame, "How God Became a Nigerian," 479–498; Olupona, "African Religion in Global Religions," 78–86; Rosalind Hackett, *New Religious Movements in Nigeria* (Lewiston, Queenston and New York: Edwin Mellen, 1987; Clarke, 2004.
17. Oye-Laguda, "African Religious Movements and Pentecostalism," 2015.
18. Adogame, "How God Became a Nigerian," 479–498.
19. Ibid.
20. Oye-Laguda, "African Religious Movements and Pentecostalism," 2015.
21. Afe Adogame, "Fighting for God or Fighting in God's Name: The Politics of Religious Violence in Contemporary Nigeria," *Religions: A Scholarly Journal*, vol. 13 (2009).
22. Idowu, *Olodumare: God in Yoruba Belief*, 1996.
23. Leonard G. Goss, "New Religious Movements" in *Encyclopedia Britannica*, 2018 (accessed August 7, 2019), www.britannica.com.
24. Ibid.
25. Ibid.
26. David G. Bromley, "Characteristics of New Religious Movements," Virginia Commonwealth University, www.people.vcu.edu (accessed August 7, 2019).
27. Ibid.
28. Danoye Oguntola-Laguda, "African Religious Movements and Pentecostalism: The Model of Ijo Orunmila, ATO," In Ibigbolade S. Aderibigbe and Carolyn M. Jones Medine (eds.), *Contemporary Perspectives on Religion in Africa and the African Diaspora* (pp. 49–60), New York: Palgrave Macmillan, 2015.
29. Ibid.
30. Danoye Oguntola-Laguda, "Pentecostalism and African Religious Movements in the 21st Century: A Case Study of Indigenous Faith of Africa, Ijo Orunmila," *Journal of Oriental and Africa Studies (JOAS)*, University of Patras, Athens-Greece, vol. 19 (2010): 191–205.
31. Allan Anderson, "African Pentecostalism and the Ancestors: Confronting or Compromising," *Missionalia*, vol. 21, no. 2 (1993): 3.
32. Harvey Gallagher Cox, "Healers and Ecologists: Pentecostalism in Africa," *The Christian Century*, vol. 111, no. 32 (1994): 7.
33. Ogbu U. Kalu, *Testing the Spirit: A Typology of Christianity in Igboland, Revisited 1890–1990* (London: International Institute of African Studies, 1990).
34. Anderson, "African Pentecostalism and the Ancestors," 3.
35. Cox, "Healers and Ecologists," 7.
36. Oguntola-Laguda, "African Religious Movements and Pentecostalism," 49–60.
37. Ibid.
38. Ibid.
39. Ibid.
40. POM, 2019.
41. Oguntola-Laguda, "African Religious Movements and Pentecostalism," 49–60.
42. John S. Mbiti, *African Religions and Philosophy* (London: Heinemann, 1969).
43. Idowu, *African Traditional Religion: A Definition*, 1971.
44. Oguntola-Laguda, "African Religious Movements and Pentecostalism," 49–60.
45. Ibid.
46. Ibid.
47. Goss, "New Religious Movements" in *Encyclopedia Britannica*, 2018.

48. Oguntola-Laguda, "Pentecostalism and African Religious Movements in the 21st Century," 191–205; and Oguntola-Laguda, "African Religious Movements and Pentecostalism," 49–60.
49. Idowu, *Olodumare: God in Yoruba Belief*, 1996; Awolalu and Dopamu, *West African Traditional Religion*, 2005, 2001.
50. Idowu, *Olodumare: God in Yoruba Belief*, 1996.
51. Kayode, *Understanding African Traditional Religion*, 1984.
52. Mbiti, *African Religions and Philosophy*, 1969.
53. Adogame, "How God Became a Nigerian," 479–498.

CHAPTER 35

African Traditional Religion and Christianity in Contemporary Global Religious Space

Rotimi Williams Omotoye

Introduction

Religion is an institution found in every human society. It is not determined by skin color, race, or developed or developing nation. There are many recognized religions being practiced in different nations, countries, and continents of the world. In Nigeria, for example, there are three major recognized religions—African Traditional Religion, Islam, and Christianity.[1] However, in this chapter, we shall focus primarily on African Traditional Religion and Christianity as requested by the editors of the book.

Talking about the Yoruba people, E. Bolaji Idowu said, "[T]he keynote of their life is their religion. In all things they are religious."[2] Therefore, wherever a man is found, there is always the urge and expression of God, even though it may be expressed in different ways and forms. This study assesses the global space occupied by African Traditional Religion and Christianity in the twenty-first century. History is not stagnant; there is always a new approach and new ideas about an event or institution within space and time. The history and place of the two religions, some centuries ago, are not the same today because there has been a paradigm shift in the course of history.

We shall be focusing on Yorubaland, South-Western Nigeria, and the United States as our case study. The former would represent Africa, while the latter would represent the Western world. This will be done in order to avert a generalization of ideas and manage time and space. A question may be asked: Why

R. W. Omotoye (✉)
University of Ilorin, Ilorin, Nigeria

© The Author(s), under exclusive license to Springer Nature Switzerland AG 2022
I. S. Aderibigbe, T. Falola (eds.), *The Palgrave Handbook of African Traditional Religion*, https://doi.org/10.1007/978-3-030-89500-6_35

the choice of Yoruba and the United States? African Traditional Religion and Christianity are thriving and held with adequate tenacity and great commitment in Yorubaland, while Christian ideals and principles played prominent roles in the founding of America as a nation. Even though African religion was not indigenous in America, it got there early, especially in South America through the migration of slaves. The slaves were of African descent, particularly from Yorubaland during the Atlantic Slave Trade between the sixteenth and eighteenth centuries.[3]

In the Yoruba traditional worship, there are three recognized classifications. The first was the Supreme Being called *Olorun* or *Olodumare*.[4] He was the Creator of both heaven and earth; therefore, he was referred to as *Eleda*. He created both Black and White people; therefore, no race can claim His monopoly or superiority of a race over the other. The Divinities and Spirits occupied the second category of worship.

The divinities are regarded as intermediaries between the Supreme Being and human beings. Different scholars have expressed divergent opinions on the number of divinities in Yorubaland. According to Kehinde Olupona, there are 201 gods in Yorubaland alone. John S. Mbiti noted that "the Yoruba have one thousand and seven hundred divinities (*orisa*),[5] this being obviously the largest collection of divinities in a single African people."[6] Ibigbolade S. Aderibigbe noted that "their number ranges between 201 and 1700 in various Yoruba localities."[7] John Awolalu opined that "the actual number of the divinities is not easily determinable; it has variously been estimated to be 200, 201, 400, 401, 460, 600, 601, 1700 or even more." E. Bolaji Idowu noted that "the number of the divinities in the pantheons is not easy to assess. For example, Yoruba oral traditions put them variously at 201, 401, 600, or 1700." Awolalu and Dopamu also noted that "the divinities are many, and their number varies from locality to locality. Among the Yoruba, for example, the number varies between 201, 401, 600, and 1700."[8]

This brings about a reasonable question: why are there so many? Bolaji Idowu provided an answer to this question thus "we will have to face the question whether the Yoruba pantheon has always been as crowded as it now appears to be. Our answer is that, in earlier times, the divinities were much fewer. Yoruba theogony shows that, to begin with, there were only a few of them. Therefore, their present number must be due to certain processes that later set in and caused them to increase and multiply.

In our opinion, migration is a major factor in the multiplicity of gods within and outside the region. Therefore, there is a nexus between the divinities being worshiped in Yorubaland and the United States. So also, the migration of the Christian missionaries and ex-slaves from the Western world played some significant role in Christianizing Africa in general and Yorubaland in particular. That is why there are divinities with similar names in Yorubaland and America. Similarly, there are Christian denominations with similar names in America and Yorubaland.

The Yoruba people of South-Western Nigeria have been well researched with no less than 3500 works. They are found in the present states of Oyo, Ogun, Osun, Ondo, Lagos, and some parts of Kwara and Kogi States. The sub-ethnic groups found in Yorubaland are Ijebu, Oyo, Ife, Ijesa, Ondo, Akoko, Ekiti, Ikale, Egbado, Okun, Oyun, and Igbomina.[9] The other geographical scope of the study is the United States. According to Aderibigbe (2016), African religion succeeded with the introduction of "three selected syncretic religions—Santeria, Candomblé, and Vodou in parts of Southern America and a brand of Christianity in North America." He went further to say that "the most predominantly practiced and of interest to us in different parts of Caribbean and Latin America are:

1. Santeria (Cuba, Dominican Republic, Puerto Rico, and North America)
2. Candomblé (Brazil)
3. Voodoo (Haiti, North America)"[10]

African Traditional Religion succeeded in the United States, Cuba, and Brazil because of the migration of slaves from Africa and Yorubaland to the Western world.

Owusu quoted Harry Lefever thus "that it was the enslaved Africans brought to Cuba in the nineteenth century from Southwestern Nigeria and the Bantu of Congo, rather than the earlier ones of the sixteenth from Haiti, who were the major carriers of the religious beliefs and practices that contributed to the development of the Santeria religion." He went further to say that "[t]hese Yoruba people brought with them their African religion, the worship of Olodumare—the Supreme, High God—manifested in lesser gods or spirits called orishas."[11]

This is a resemblance of divinities in Yorubaland. The religion became attractive to and popular among the non-Yoruba-enslaved people of Cuba. The religion emerged as a new form of religious tradition due to the encounter between the Yoruba religion of Orisha, Roman Catholicism, and French spiritism. Some of those that saw the religion as theirs were Walter King who founded the Order of Damballah Hwedo Ancestor Priest of Harlem. He became a Priest of Santeria in 1969. He founded the Shango (fire) Temple in Harlem and later changed the name to Yoruba Temple. In 1970, he founded the Yoruba Village of Oyotunji at Sheldon in South Carolina, where he and his dwindled followers lived until he died in 2005. The religion was also appealing to the Afro-Americans too.[12]

Today, the worship of traditional Yoruba gods is given prominence and recognition in some cities and being taught in some tertiary institutions in the United States. For example, the University of Georgia, Athens, and Harvard University have a prominent focus on African Religion Studies. Incidentally, two Nigerian professors are employed to teach African Religion Studies at these two universities, namely Professor Ibigbolade S. Aderibigbe and Professor Kehinde Olupona, respectively. The teaching of African Traditional Religion is also given prominent focus in Nigerian universities. Similarly, Christian Studies are offered in many American and Nigerian universities. Therefore, the two religions are taught and practiced globally. However, it is unfortunate that religion, as an academic discipline, is not being offered in some newly established federal, state, and private universities in Nigeria. The National Association for the Study of Religions should address this situation with the proprietors of such Nigerian universities.

The term "African Traditional Religion" has been defined by Awolalu and Dopamu as: "When we speak of African traditional religion, we mean the indigenous religion of the Africans. It is the religion that has been handed down from generation to generation by the forebears of the present generation of Africans."[13] Therefore, it is not a dying religion. In fact, many converts from the religion do claim to be practicing other religions; they are inadvertently found celebrating it consciously or unconsciously. Thus, African Christians in the Diaspora are found practicing it despite being called Christians.

Aderibigbe opines that "the name was not coined in order to brandish the religion as primitive, local, or unprogressive—rather, it is employed to reflect its location in geographical space and to underscore its evolution from the African personal experience."[14] Therefore, it is a living religion in contemporary society.

Christianity, as a religion, was introduced to the geographical sphere called Nigeria at different phases. However, if we are to uphold Tuesday Adamo's historiography, in a beautiful academic presentation titled "What Is African Biblical Studies?," we would be tempted to agree that Christianity started in Africa before Europe.[15] However, eminent Church historians such as Ogbu Kalu, Joseph Akin Omoyajowo, Deji Ayegboyin, and Rotimi Omotoye accepted the fact that Christianity was introduced to the shores of Africa by the Europeans. We would agree with the position of the eminent Church historians.

The first phase of Christianity was introduced "from 1450–1750, some fairly remarkable Portuguese missionary activities took place in Africa, but without much enduring success."[16] Nigerian Church historians believed that Benin and Warri benefitted from the Catholic missionary enterprises in the fifteenth century. Omotoye opines, "The first attempt to introduce Christianity to Benin/Warri areas of Niger Delta in the fifteenth century was carried out by the Catholic Portuguese Missionaries. However, the attempt was a failure because of some factors already clearly stated by some eminent scholars like Ryder, Ade Ajayi, Erivwo, Lamin Sanneh and Peter Clarke."[17]

Hickey noted that the Portuguese missionaries' endeavor had no permanent result because of "the difficulty in communication which made sustained efforts impossible; the lack of quinine and of medication for the coastal fevers; the scourge of the slave trade which seemed to dominate all dealings between Europe and West Africa: and the rivalry between the Portuguese and other European missionaries."[18]

It is generally believed in the submissions of the eminent scholars that the Portuguese mission of the fifteenth century failed in Benin and Warri. However,

Omotoye held the view that the enterprise should be seen as a foundation of the introduction of Christianity in Nigeria. According to him, the European missionaries that came in the nineteenth century were able to learn some lessons from the mistakes and errors of the past. There is a saying in Yorubaland that *"eniti o jin si koto, yio ko awon to ku logbon"* (he who falls into a ditch will teach others some lessons).[19]

The Atlantic Slave Trade occupied almost 300 years from the fifteenth through eighteenth centuries whereby Africans were taken to Europe, America, and Britain to work on their master's plantations. Omotoye has argued consistently that the factors that necessitated the abolition of the Atlantic Slave Trade were in the interest of the European countries. These were technological developments, religious revival, activities of the humanitarians, the independence of America, and Lord Mansfield's judgment of 1792, all of which contributed to the abolition of slavery.[20] Omotoye is of the opinion that slavery became an unprofitable venture because of the new age of science and technology, and other factors mentioned above made its abolition inevitable. Therefore, the migration theory contributed to the introduction of African religion to America, especially Southern America. Thus, the "unwanted slaves" were re-settled in some parts of West Africa. According to Abioje, "Of particular interest are the three countries that became the havens for many freed slaves, namely, Liberia—'land of the free,' which was established by America in 1822; Sierra Leone, whose capital, Freetown, was established by the English in 1787; and Gabon, which was established by the French in 1849, with the capital Libreville, which also means Freetown in French language."[21]

Different Christian bodies were interested in following the ex-slaves to the re-settled locations in complying with the "Great Command" of Jesus Christ. "Go ye therefore, and teach all nations." It should be noted that, in practice, motives were more complex and goals were enunciated differently. Some of the Christian bodies were the Church Missionary Society, the Roman Catholic Church, American Congregationalist Board, the non-denominational London Missionary Society, Sudan United Mission, and the Dutch Reformed Churches. Richard Gray opined that "[t]he first English society, the Society for the Propagation of the Gospel (here-after SPG) founded in 1701, sought to assist 'our loving subjects' in foreign parts who were in danger of falling into 'atheism, infidelity, popish superstition and idolatry.'"[22] The different religious bodies accompanied the ex-slaves and assisted in financing and providing missionary assistance to them. The ex-slaves from the region of Yorubaland were called the *LUCUMI* or *AKU* in Sierra Leone[23] because of their mode of greetings in the morning, afternoon, and evening (*E ku aaro; E ku oson; E ku ale*). It was from there that they came to Yorubaland.

The first place of call was Badagry in 1842. Some of the ex-slaves who were traders went there to trade and met some of their relations from the hinterland. In order to maintain their relationship with the Christian missionaries, they invited the missionaries to continue ministering and propagating Christianity in Badagry. The Methodist mission was the first to arrive under the leadership of Thomas Birch Freeman. He arrived in Badagry in September 1842, while the Church Missionary Society was led by Henry Townsend in December 1842. The gospel missionary work began in earnest with a joint Christmas Eve celebration by the two missionaries. It was held under the *Ajia* tree in Badagry. That was the beginning of ecumenical efforts between the two mission churches in Yorubaland.[24]

It is necessary to mention that the missionaries in the nineteenth century adopted some strategies in converting the traditionalists to Christianity. The introduction of Western education or formal education was used as "bait" by the Christian missionaries to win converts to their religion through their Western style of teaching. Apart from the establishment of schools, medical institutions were established to heal the sick. Employment was provided for the children of those that were converted as clerks and teachers. All efforts were made by the missionaries to discourage the Yoruba people, like other Africans, from practicing African Traditional Religion. Some obnoxious and unacceptable terminologies were used to describe the religion, such as juju, primitive, savage, native, tribe, paganism, heathenism, idolatry, fetishism, and animism.[25]

Apart from the above uncomplimentary remarks about African people and religion, Emil Ludwig was quoted to have said, "How can the untutored African conceive of God? How can this be? Deity is a philosophical concept which savage are incapable of framing."[26] The writer was not objective and fair in his assessment of African religion.

Leo Frobenius opined, "Before the introduction of a genuine faith and a higher standard of culture by the Arabs, the Arabs, the natives had no political organization, nor, strictly speaking, any religion. ... Therefore, it is necessary in examining the pre-Muhammedan conditions of the Negro races, to confine ourselves to the description of their crude fetishism, their vulgar and repulsive idols. None but the most primitive instinct determines the lives and conduct of the negroes, who lack every kind of ethical inspiration."[27] Banding, a French scholar in 1884, wrote, "At the same time, they think that God, after beginning the organisation of the world charged Obatala to finish it and govern it, even withdrew and went into an eternal rest to look after his own happiness."[28]

In the Yoruba concept of creation of the world, *Olodumare* was in charge of creation. *Orisa-nla* was brought into the creation to assist *Olodumare*. Worshipers believe that Olodumare has the ability to make his followers great as well as aid in their prosperity by increasing their populations and blessing them with material goods. The divinity is noted for his purity, and worshippers are expected to be clean and upright in their daily affairs. Despite the roles and functions assigned to him by *Olodumare*, he is still a divinity, a minister, and an intermediary between man and *Olodumare*. Therefore, he cannot take the position of *Olodumare*. It is, therefore, wrong and unacceptable to regard African people and their religion as polytheism. However, some renowned African scholars, such as Mbiti, Parrinder, Idowu, Awolalu, Dopamu, and

Aderibigbe, were able to reject and oppose these unacceptable and obnoxious terminologies.

It may be of interest to mention that for a very long time, Western scholars prevented African religion scholars from attending international conferences on religion. Awolalu Omosade observed that "papers in African religion were first accepted for presentation in the XIIIth Congress of the Association held in Lancaster in 1975."[29] In other words, efforts of earlier pioneers of African religion scholars in Nigeria were frustrated and unrecognized.

The Christian missionaries left Badagry in frustration because the indigenes did not accept the religion as expected of them. In fact, they were demanding some personal items and gifts before conversion to Christianity. The frustrating and unfriendly attitude of the people made Henry Townsend go to Abeokuta. He was well received by Oba Sodeke because of political and religious reasons. It was said that it was a time the Dahomeans were fighting Abeokuta people and, therefore, they needed foreign powers and support. It was also said that *Ifa* divination had predicted the coming of the White missionaries to the community. This was a sign of accommodation and acceptability of Christianity by the African people. The city became the "Sunrise within the tropics." Other Christian denominations such as the Methodist and Baptist made Abeokuta the center of their missions with the exemption of the Catholic Church that made Lagos its center. David Hinderer, a Priest in the C.M.S., was sent to Ibadan in 1851 and Charles Phillips was in Ondo in 1877. Agbebi was sent to Ilesa, and Williams was in Ilesa in 1856. The Baptists focused more on the northeastern part of Yorubaland. Christianity was in Ekitiland after the Internecine War of 1893. It was championed by some ex-slaves, such as Isaac Babamuboni, Helena Doherty, and Mary Oja Ode.[30] Therefore, Christianity gradually became a global and cross-fertilized religion.

African Traditional Religion and Christianity are currently being practiced and have adequate adherents and practitioners in Yorubaland. However, Christians erroneously believed that Christianity was a religion of the elite, enlightened, and civilized people. There is no doubt that Christianity enjoyed the support of the colonial government to succeed. There was collaboration to subvert and suppress the power of traditional institutions of any community seen as opposing the government and Christian missionaries. For example, Ijebu Ode was conquered in 1891 by the British colonial power in collaboration with the Christian missionaries.[31]

Traditional festivals and institutions were disrupted, condemned, and jettisoned in some places. The mode of dressing of the Yoruba people was replaced with European clothing. Traditional names of the converts and their children that enrolled in missionary schools were changed to Christian names. Employment was given to children-bearing Christian names. The vantage position actually assisted in the growth and expansion of Christianity.

In the contemporary era, when there is religious intolerance, unhealthy rivalries, killings, and maiming regarding religious matters in Nigeria, there are minimal incidences of such in Yorubaland. However, it is observed that adherents of Christianity and traditional religion in Yorubaland are interacting more than in any other geo-political region in Nigeria. In some families, the three recognized religions exist harmoniously, and inter-marriages are not totally forbidden. Omotoye, in an earlier study titled "Inter-Religious Dialogue as a Panacea for National Development in Nigeria,"[32] submitted that religious harmony and understanding in Yorubaland should be recommended as a model for other regions in Nigeria. Religious matters are seen as an act of "live and let live." Africa Traditional Religion, too, has become an international religion being practiced and taught in many tertiary institutions. In Yorubaland, many festivals have become global and internationally celebrated.

Osun Osogbo Festival

It is necessary to note that Osun Osogbo has become an annual global festival. Many worshippers of the *Osun* deity come from different nations and continents of the world. It is observed that the celebration of the Osun Osogbo Festival is gradually losing its religious values due to socio-economic advantages attached to it. Many business men and women are becoming interested in the hospitality to be provided to the tourists and gains to be made. Many companies without any religious values are interested in promoting the activities of the festival because of the interest of their products. In fact, some companies that produce alcoholic drinks are seen on stand promoting the festival. We believe that this act is antithetical to the religious values of the festival. In view of the importance attached to the festival, the United Nations Educational, Scientific and Cultural Organization (UNESCO) has accepted it as an international festival.

Oyeronke Olajubu opines that "Osun is perceived as the creative spirit and the spiritual dimension to pregnancy and childbirth because the human body is mainly constituted of water. Moreover, *Osun's* fertility qualities guarantee people their only hope of immortality. The importance of this singular quality cannot be over-emphasised in a culture such as the Yoruba, where the utmost significance is accorded to procreation."[33] It is no wonder that people come from far and near to partake in the annual celebrations of the festival.

The festival was promoted globally by the late Susan Wenger, also known as Adunni Olorisha. She was an Austrian artist who devoted her life to the Osun traditional festival before her death. The festival is celebrated annually during the month of August. The Festival was not celebrated in the year 2020 because of the coronavirus (COVID-19) pandemic lockdown. It may be difficult to keep the government policy of social distancing because of the crowds that normally attend the festival annually.

Olojo Festival in Ile-Ife

This is a cultural festival that was highly promoted by the late Oni Olubuse Sijuwade to an international level during his tenure. It is celebrated with pomp and pageantry annually. The 2019 celebration was led by the Oni Oba Ogunwusi Enitan Adeyeye. It is the celebration of the remembrance of *Ogun* (god of iron), who is believed to be the first son of *Oduduwa*, the progenitor of the Yoruba people. It has become an international festival that cannot be ignored by traditional worshippers, Christians, and Muslims in the community. In fact, its socio-economic importance cannot be ignored or forsaken. Many tourists from the United States, Britain, and European countries are seen at such celebrations annually.

Ojude Oba in Ijebu Ode

Another festival that cannot be ignored in Yorubaland because of its religious and socio-economic values and global involvement is the Ojude Oba Festival in Ijebu Ode. It is an annual festival that has been modernized to accommodate people of other faiths, such as Christians and Muslims. There used to be many attractions during the celebrations. Many people in the community usually file out to pay homage to the *Kabiyesi*, the Awujale of Ijebu Ode. The festival is held annually on the third day after *Eid al-Kabir*. It promotes unity and oneness among the sons and daughters of the community. The significance of this festival is to celebrate the rich culture, heritage, traditional, religious, social, and military life of the people.

Eyo Festival

The Eyo Festival is celebrated in Lagos annually. It is also known as *Adamu Orisha*. The people residing on Lagos Island are the gatekeepers of the festival. These are people of *Isale Eko* that are believed to be indigenes of Lagos. Traditionally, it was celebrated to aid in the departure of the soul of a deceased Lagos king or chief and to welcome a new king. It is observed nowadays that people are more interested in the socio-economic attractions of the festival. It brings out the culture of Lagos people. Tourists from different parts of the world are seen celebrating at the festival.

The Federal Government of Nigeria is encouraging and placing much value on cultural revival. Many towns and villages place much value on traditional festivals in their domain. These include the Iwude Festival in Ilesa, Agbeleku in Erin Ijesa/Erin Oke, Iro Traditional Festival in Erin Ijesa, Opa in Ipetu Ijesa, Ijakadi in Offa, Oke-Ibadan in Ibadan, Eyo Festival, and Ogun Festival in Ondo. Some of these cultural festivals have become international festivals because they are globally acceptable.

Christian missionary activities in Yorubaland between 1842 and 1900 were dominated by the mission or historical churches, such as the Methodist, Church

Missionary Society now known as the Anglican Church, Baptist, and Catholic. The African Church was established in 1901 as a result of disagreement of the educated elite with the established authorities of the Church Missionary Society. The educated elite felt neglected, suppressed, and not properly recognized in the church. This caused the African Christians to establish an African Church where their values and voices would be heard and respected. For example, in Offa, a town in Kwara State, the "movers and shakers" of the community who were pioneers of Christianity decided to establish the African Church. This was due to an episode that was viewed as an insult at Saint Mark's Anglican Church. A young priest in the church refused to give Holy Communion to those who were polygamists in the church. The young man's action was condemned by the polygamists.

The next phase of Christianity was the emergence of African Independent Churches in Yorubaland in the second decade of the twentieth century. The four popular Aladura Churches in Nigeria were founded in Yorubaland and led by Yoruba people. The Cherubim and Seraphim Church was founded by Apostle Moses Orimolade, while the Christ Apostolic Church emerged from the Apostolic Church. One of its recognized leaders and General Evangelist was the late Pastor Ayo Babalola.

Samuel Bileowu Oshoffa founded the Celestial Church of Christ in Port Novo in 1948 before its expansion to Nigeria in 1951. The Church of the Lord (Aladura) was founded by Josiah Oshitelu in 1930.[34] He was an indigene of Ogere, Ogun State. These African Independent Churches brought about Cultural Revolution and recognition of the African culture of dancing, vision, polygamy, and healing into their worship services. The features introduced to Christianity exploded the ideals and richness of African culture and practices globally.

Another phase of Christianity emerged during the 1970s in Nigeria and Yorubaland. The churches in this category are called the Pentecostal Churches. They are many and numerous to mention and count in numbers. However, some of them are the Deeper Life Christian Church, Living Faith Christian Church, Mountain of Fire and Miracles, and the Redeemed Christian Church of God.[35] It is interesting that the founders of these churches were founded in Yorubaland and by Yoruba Pastors or Clergymen, indigenes of Yorubaland. However the churches have now spread globally.

These Pastors and their churches are viewed as charismatic and more embraced by youths and younger generations of Nigerians and African people residing in other countries. As they leave the shores of Nigeria for the developed countries, many of them migrate with their newly acquired and embraced denominations.

My personal experience at the Redeemed Christian Church of God, Amazing Grace Parish at the University of Georgia in Athens, indicated that the worshippers are predominantly immigrants from Nigeria and people from other African countries. In fact, the Pastor of the church is Mrs. Moradeke Abimbola

Aderibigbe, a Nigerian woman married to Ibigbolade S. Aderibigbe, a professor in the Department of Religion at the University of Georgia.[36]

Our observation about the Pentecostal Churches in America and elsewhere was that almost all the members were immigrants from some African countries. The question is: Why are White Americans and even Afro-Americans not found in these churches? A major reason was racism and discrimination between the White Americans and the immigrants. Unfortunately, the Afro-Americans, too, have hatred and discriminatory tendencies against the African Immigrants.

The recent untimely death of George Floyd on May 25, 2020, was a clear act of wickedness and show of racism while in the custody of White American policemen. During his arrest for allegedly using a counterfeit bill, a White police officer knelt on Floyd's neck for about nine and a half minutes after he was already handcuffed and lying face down. His brutal murder in Minneapolis, Minnesota (USA), led to massive protests in the United States and around the world. A funeral service was held in his honor at the Fountain of Praise Church in Houston, Texas. He was laid to rest at a cemetery in Pearland, south of Houston, Texas, on Tuesday, June 9, 2020. Mr. Joe Biden, the Democratic presidential candidate for the November 2020 Election, said at a private visit to the family of the deceased that the death of Mr. Floyd was "one of the great inflection points in American history."[37] President Donald J. Trump's administration was condemned for his failure to acknowledge police brutality and condemn the brutal killing of the African American man.

However, it is important to note that the activities of the Pentecostal Churches are redefining and bringing more values to Christianity in the developed countries of Europe, America, and Britain. We attended an International Conference in Padova, Italy, in 2014. The focus of the conference was on Pentecostalism. Many young African Pastors and their wives were in attendance as observers. They were able to relate their experiences in the Catholic Church based on the environment. According to some of them, their visit to the city of Padova was a blessing for evangelization in the area. Therefore, the arrival of African Charismatic Pastors was an opportunity to preach the gospel to those that brought Christianity to Africa some centuries ago!

It may be of interest to mention the missionary efforts of Pastor Matthew Ashimolowo, a Nigerian based in London. The name of his church is Kingsway International Christian Centre. He is dynamic and a prosperity preacher. He has succeeded in proclaiming the gospel and has established the Kings University in his hometown of Ode Omu, Osun State. In a nutshell, the activities of the Immigrant Churches in America may be styled "Reversed Mission."

Aderibigbe, in his well-researched study titled "African Initiated Churches and African Immigrants in the United States: A Model in the Redeemed Christian Church of God, North America (RCCGNA)," highlighted a comprehensive study of the introduction of the church and personalities involved in making the church a global and acceptable denomination. According to him, "when the RCCG was to be established in North America, the lot fell upon a student James Fadele." He was a medical student at Western Michigan

University at that point in time. "The humble beginning described by Fadele has today become a formidable transnational mission outreach of the RCCG with about 400,320 in North America, Canada and the Caribbean, known as the RCCGNA."[38] The Reversed Mission has been a successful missionary work in America, Britain, and other European countries.

Some other RCCG churches led mostly by Yoruba people and Nigerians in the state of Texas are Salvation Centre, Anderson Square in Austin, led by Pastor Wale Odufuye; House of Glory, Broadway Street, Pearland, led by Pastor Victor Akindana; New Life Chapel in Town Park, Houston, being manned by Pastor Obi Agada; Tower of Refuge, Southwest Freeway, Houston, led by Pastor Benson Akintunji; Dominion Chapel, 1203 Craven Road in Stafford, being directed by Pastor Bayo Fadugba; Restoration Chapel, 107 South Alta Vista Street in Beeville, under the leadership of Pastor Christian Okpalo; Abundant Grace Bellaire Blvd. in Houston led by Pastor Peter Oloso; and Dayspring Chapel, Sabo Road in Houston, led by Pastor Joel Uzoma. Others are Christ Chapel, Western Drive, in Houston led by Pastor Oretayo Salau, and Pavilion of Redemption in Sugarland under the leadership of Pastor Ade Okonrende.[39] Of course, there are many more.

A clear observation indicates that the majority of the Pastors are from the south-western part of Nigeria and they are young immigrants in the United States. It is also germane to note that the institution provides jobs for the Pastors and other workers in the church. The church is also a place of refuge for immigrants that newly arrived in the United States. Some of them are accommodated and trained on how to live their lives in the new environment. However, many of the Pastors are not full-time because they have private businesses or are engaged in government establishments. The government is also concerned and ensuring that churches are not harboring criminals and illegal immigrants. We were informed in Padova, Italy, that Government Security Agents do occasionally come to the churches to arrest perceived illegal immigrants within the vicinity of the churches. The global acceptance of African Traditional Religion and Christianity has shown that the two religions are widely accepted and practiced globally.

Conclusion

African Traditional Religion, which began as an indigenous religion of the African people, is a living religion. The erroneous and unprintable terminologies used by the European scholars and missionaries have been rejected by modern African religion scholars. Today, religion is practiced globally. Christianity, which was introduced to Africa by European missionaries, was accepted in the nineteenth century. Some strategies were introduced to convert the African people. In Yorubaland, Christianity and African religion are being practiced by the people. Initially, African religion was introduced to America, Britain, and European countries during the Atlantic Slave Trade. Religion became acceptable in Southern America. It is interesting to note that the African Independent Churches and Pentecostal Churches are championing evangelism in the developed nations in the twentieth century.

Notes

1. O. E. Alana, "The Relationship Between Christians, Muslims and Afrelists in History with Particular Reference to Nigeria," in R. D. Abubakre et al. (eds.), *Studies in Religious Understanding in Nigeria* (Ilorin: National Association for the Study of Religions, 1993) 206.
2. E. B. Idowu, *Olodumare God in Yoruba Belief* (London: Longman, 1962), 5.
3. Rotimi Omotoye, "A Re-interpretation of the Abolition of the Atlantic Slave Trade in Europe in the 18th century and New Trends in Nigeria," in Ibigbolade S. Aderibigbe, Alloy Ihuah, and Felisters Jepchinchir Kiprono (eds.), *Contextualizing Indigenous Knowledge in Africa and its Diaspora* (Cambridge: Newcastle, 2015), 95.
4. John O. Awolalu, *Yoruba Beliefs and Sacrificial Rites* (Essex: Longman, 1979), 20–51.
5. John S. Mbiti, *African Religion and Philosophy* (London: Heinemann, 1969), 76.
6. Rotimi Omotoye, "The Concept of God and Its Understanding by the Christian Missionaries in Yorubaland," in E. A. Odumuyiwa et al. (eds.), *God: The Contemporary Discussion* (Ilorin: National Association for the Study of Religions, 2005), 101.
7. Ibigbolade S. Aderibigbe, *Contextualizing Religion Study and Practice* (Ilorin: University of Ilorin Press, 2016), 197.
8. J. O. Awolalu and P. A. Dopamu, *West African Traditional Religion* (Ibadan: Macmillan Nigeria Publishers Limited, 1979), 75.
9. Omotoye, "The Concept of God and Its Understanding," 101.
10. Ibigbolade S. Aderibigbe, "The Seventeenth-Century African Slaves and Descendants Identity Empowerment through Religious Rituals: The Americas Experience," in Ibigbolade S. Aderibigbe, Rotimi Williams Omotoye, and Lydia Bosede Akande (eds.), *Contextualizing Africans and Globalization Expressions in Sociopolitical and Religious Contents and Discontents* (London: Lexington Books, 2016), 66.
11. R. Y. Owusu, "Socioreligious Agencies of Santeria Religion in the United States of America," in Ibigbolade S. Aderibigbe and Carolyn M. Jones Medine (eds.), *Contemporary Perspectives on Religions in Africa and the African Diaspora* (New York: Palgrave Macmillan, 2015), 202.
12. Ibid.
13. J. O. Awolalu and P. A. Dopamu, *West African Traditional Religion* (Lagos: Macmillan, 1979), 26.
14. Aderibigbe, *Contextualizing Religion Study and Practice*, 192.
15. D. T. Adamo, "What is African Biblical Studies?" in S. O. Abogunrin et al. (eds.), *Decolonization of Biblical Interpretation in Africa* (Ibadan: Nigerian Association for Biblical Studies (NABIS), 2005), 17–31.
16. P. O. Abioje, "Christianity in Contemporary African Religious Space," in Ibigbolade S. Aderibigbe and Carolyn M. Jones Medine (eds.), *Contemporary Perspectives on Religions in Africa and the African Diaspora* (New York: Palgrave Macmillan, 2015), 81.

17. Rotimi Omotoye, "Communication and the Universality of the Gospel in Yorubaland," in Ade P. Dopamu et al. (eds.), *Science and Religion in the Service of Humanity* (Ilorin: Local Society Initiative (LSI) and The Nigerian Association for the Study and Teaching of Religion and Natural Sciences (NASTRENS), 38.
18. Abioje, "Christianity in Contemporary African Religious Space," 81.
19. Rotimi Williams Omotoye, "Christianity as a Catalyst for Socio-economic and Political Change in Yorubaland and Nigeria: An Account of a Church Historian," The One Hundred and Fifty-Ninth (159th) Inaugural Lecture, University of Ilorin, Ilorin, delivered on Thursday, 25th June, 2015, 6.
20. Rotimi Omotoye, "A Re-interpretation of the Abolition of the Atlantic Slave Trade," 96–100.
21. Abioje, "Christianity in Contemporary African Religious Space," 83.
22. Richard Gray, "The Origins and Organisation of the Nineteenth-Century Missionary Movement," in O. U. Kalu (ed.), *The History of Christianity in West Africa* (Essex: Longman, 1980), 16.
23. O. U. Kalu (ed.), *Christianity in West Africa The Nigerian Story* (Ibadan: Daystar Press, 1978), 244.
24. Rotimi Omotoye, "The Challenges of Survival of a Mission: An Examination of the Anglican Diocese of Badagry," Orita Ibadan Journal of Religious Studies, vol. XLI, no. 1 (June 2009), 233.
25. Awolalu and Dopamu, *West African Traditional Society*, 20–26.
26. Rotimi Omotoye, "The Concept of God and its Understanding," 103–105.
27. Ibid.
28. Ibid.
29. Rotimi Williams Omotoye, "The Study of African Traditional Religion and its Challenges in Contemporary Times," *Ilorin Journal of Religious Studies* (IJOURELS), vol. 1, no. 2 (December 2011), 19.
30. Rotimi Omotoye, "Religion and Service to Humanity," in S. O. Oloruntoba (ed.), *Africa and Its Diaspora History, Identities and Economy* (Austin: Pan-African University Press, 2017), 229–239.
31. Rotimi Omotoye, "Historical Perspective of the Decolonization of the Church in Yorubaland (1842–1960)," in S. O. Abogunrin et al. (eds.), *Decolonization of Biblical Interpretation in Africa* (Ibadan: Nigerian Association for Biblical Studies, 2005), 398.
32. Rotimi Omotoye, "Inter-Religious Dialogue as a Panacea for National Development in Nigeria," *Centrepoint Journal Humanities Edition, University of Ilorin*, vol. 15, no. 1 (June 2012): 57–76.
33. Oyeronke Olajubu, *Women in the Yoruba Religious Sphere* (New York: New York Press, 2003), 78–79.
34. Deji Ayegboyin and S. Ademola Ishola, *African Indigenous Churches: An Historical Perspective* (Lagos: Greater Heights Publications, 1999).
35. Rotimi Williams Omotoye, "An Overview of the Missionary Activities of the Deeper Life Bible Church in Nigeria," in Y.O. Imam, R. I. Adebayo, and A. I. Ali-Agan (eds.), Dynamics of Revealed Knowledge and Human Sciences Essays in Honour of Professor Is-haq Olanrewaju Oloyede (Lagos: Spectrum Books Limited, 2016), 109–133. Read also "Pentecostalism and the Yoruba World View: The Case of Mountain of Fire and Miracles, Nigeria," The International Journal of Religion and Spirituality in Society, vol. 1, no. 2, 181–194, www.religionsociety.com. Read also "The Church and National

Development: The Case of the Redeemed Christian Church of God," *International Journal of Current Research in the Humanities* no 12, 25–49, Ghana, University of Cape Coast.
36. The writer had the opportunity of attending at least five Sunday services at the Amazing Grace Parish of the Redeemed Christian Church of God, University of Georgia, Athens, United States of America.
37. "George Floyd," *Nigeria Tribune*, 3rd June 2020, 3.
38. Ibigbolade S. Aderibigbe, "African Initiated Churches and African Immigrants in the United States: A Model in the Redeemed Christian Church of God, North America (RCCGNA)," 248–251.
39. An Interview with Pastor Samuel Tunde Oladeru, RCCG based in New York. We met at Erin Ijesa in Osun State between January 10 and 12, 2020.

CHAPTER 36

African Religion and Islam in Contemporary Religious Space

Yushau Sodiq

In looking at the relationship between African Traditional Religion (ATR) and globalization, we should not assume that globalization is an inevitable force that will one day replace all traditional values within the world with one common consumerist mass culture. In Africa, globalization has had a significant impact on traditions and cultural values. Still, at the same time, African traditionalism retains resiliency and adaptability that enable it to maintain cohesion both in non-Western environments and in the context of faiths such as Christianity and Islam. African religions are adaptable. Instead of offering inflexible dogmatic beliefs, often, they provide frameworks for viewing and processing information. If a new piece of information does not fit an existing framework, it can modify but not necessarily reject the framework. For example, a form of taboo observed by the African people can be maintained until the old frameworks adapt, and it changes.[1]

African religions and Islam are indigenous traditions in Africa. Islam, since its inception, has roots in Africa and maintains strong relationships with African traditions. Muslims and practitioners of African religions are always neighbors but occasional enemies when each group (consciously or unconsciously) stepped on the toes of another. Nevertheless, they have lived together peacefully. African Traditional Religions (ATRs) are the beliefs and ways of life of the African people, who are neither Muslims nor Christians. ATRs are the beliefs of the indigenous Africans prior to the intrusion of Islam and Christianity.

Y. Sodiq (✉)
Texas Christian University, Fort Worth, TX, USA
e-mail: y.sodiq@tcu.edu

© The Author(s), under exclusive license to Springer Nature Switzerland AG 2022
I. S. Aderibigbe, T. Falola (eds.), *The Palgrave Handbook of African Traditional Religion*, https://doi.org/10.1007/978-3-030-89500-6_36

Today, most of the people of North Africa are Muslims, and most of the people of South Africa are Christians. The majority of those who practice ATR today live in West Africa and part of East Africa. This is not to say that there are no practitioners of ATR at all in South and North Africa, but they are minimal in number.

African Traditional Religions

Applying "African Traditional Religions" for the beliefs and cultures of the African people remains controversial. The authors of the "Concise Oxford Dictionary of World Religion"[2] argue that "there is no such thing as *African Religion* because no single religion corresponds to the term—*African Religion*." However, they assert that there are some characteristics of religious practices, which could be attributed to African religions, such as the belief in a Supreme God and many lesser gods, the importance of ancestors to the living individuals, and the significance of maintaining social and cosmic orders among those people who share the same beliefs. On the other hand, contemporary African scholars, such as John Mbiti, Bolaji Idowu, and Jacob Olupona, argue strongly that there are African religions. These religions have their uniqueness and significance.[3] These scholars opine that there are African traditions even though the term referring to them may be of recent connotation. They insist that African communities continue to immerse themselves into different religious activities like belief in God, offering prayers, and making sacrifices to their deities from time immemorial.

MacGaffey (2012) explains that the term *African Religion* refers to two essential things:

1. That which encompasses all African beliefs and practices that are perceived as religious but are neither Islam nor Christianity.
2. Practices and beliefs that are compatible and comparable to both Christianity and Islam like the belief in one God and the importance of moral values.

In this latter sense, it assumes that African religion offers its adherents the same assurances and teachings that Islam and Christianity offer their followers in terms of guidance and spiritual development. MacGaffey points out the controversy over how some scholars study African religions only from theological and social perspectives and draw a line between the two. He argues that there must be a marriage between the two approaches, as well as a need for critical analysis of both methods. Indeed African Traditional Religions have their unique worldviews, which could be derived from the practices of these traditions.[4]

Some leading scholars on African Traditional Religions elaborate on several unique aspects, which characterize ATR. Olupona in his work *African Religions:*

A Very Short Introduction elucidates some points which bring to light these unique features of ATR. Among them, he states[5]:

1. ATR are faith traditions with less emphasis on doctrines; they are lived traditions, which people practice on a daily basis, no special Fridays or Sundays for the adherents of ATR. They worship and communicate with God daily. God is accessible at any place and at any time.
2. ATR are concerned with the health, wealth, and well-beings of the individuals. Thus, believers perceive all aspects of life as religious. No separation exists between what is considered mundane or sacred. Both are one unit like two wings of a bird. Without both wings, a bird cannot fly. ATR focus primarily on this present life rather than concentrating on the next life as held by both Christianity and Islam. Therefore, according to Olupona, ATR develop diverse institutions for healing, for commerce, and for the general well-being of the individuals. In addition, the healing approach in ATR is holistic in nature in that it addresses all that can bring happiness and protection to the believers.
3. Another uniqueness of ATR is its being an oral tradition. Its orality enables it to be flexible and adaptable. Each community adapts it to its needs and, as such, makes it a vibrant and a living religion. Since its adherents find it adaptable, stagnation does not apply to it. People can practice it the way they want as long as they keep its spirit in mind.

INTERACTION OF ISLAM WITH AFRICAN TRADITIONAL RELIGIONS

Islam is an indigenous religion in Africa. When Muhammad (the prophet of Islam) started preaching Islam in Mecca in 610 C.E., his tribe, the Quraysh, rejected him and his message. Thus, in the sixth year after his declaration of his prophethood, he sought refuge with a Christian King of Ethiopia, King Negus. The king accorded warm reception to the migrated Muslims from Mecca to Ethiopia and allowed them to stay, practice their beliefs, and spread them. That was the first interaction of Islam with the people of Africa, and since then, Islam had taken root in Africa.[6] In 645 C.E., Muslims conquered Egypt, and by the end of the eighth century, Islam had reached West Africa through the North African Muslims from Morocco and Tunisia. Islam took root gradually among the Black Africans.

Initially, the only literate people among the Black Africans were the Muslims. They had scholars who could read and write. Eventually, they became secretaries and advisors to the local kings who employed them for their interests. As Islam began to spread, and the number of Muslim converts increased, tension grew between the Muslims and their neighbors. Muslim leaders embarked on condemning the teachings and worship of the people of Africa, especially those that worshiped the idols and the sacrifices they made to them. The orthodox Muslim scholars requested that the people commit to total submission to one God, Allah. The Africans, even though they believed in one God, also recognized many other lesser gods who were the intermediaries to the Supreme God. This tension between the Muslims and followers of ATR occasionally led to tribal wars. Generally, Muslims and indigenous people lived relatively in harmony because they shared many moral values. However, Muslims embarked on intensive proselytizing and tried to convert Africans into Islam. Yet, practitioners of ATR held on to their beliefs while some converted. Today, they live together peacefully, and each group is proud of its religious identity and values its religious co-existence.

African Muslims in the Contemporary Space

The majority of the people in West Africa embraced Islam beginning in the eighth century, and some scholars said from the eleventh century. In fulfillment of one of their religious duties to Islam, the wealthy among the African Muslims embarked on a journey to Mecca for pilgrimage—the *Hajj*. West African Muslims partook in an international gathering at Mecca. They also engaged with the global communities where they met Muslims from all over the world. Pilgrimage to Mecca gave them a chance to travel out of their own countries. In the olden days, they traveled on foot. They went across the Sahara from Senegal to Ghana, Ghana to Nigeria, Nigeria to Sudan or Egypt, and finally reaching Mecca. As they traveled, they met different people and interacted with diverse cultures. While in Sudan or Egypt, some found themselves stranded due to lack of money and food; however, they stayed and worked until they had enough money to continue their journey to Mecca. Occasionally, Muslims from West Africa remained permanently in Sudan, Egypt, and Mecca and became permanent citizens. In those days, there was no passport needed to reside in any area in Africa. Their residency in other countries exposed them to the international and global community. When the means of transportation improved, primarily through airplanes, multitudes of West African Muslims journeyed to Mecca annually from 1950 until the present.

West African Muslims in America

In the sixteenth and seventeenth centuries, the slave trade began between West Africans and Europeans. The slave traders captured many African people and sold them into slavery. They were shipped to European countries and the Americas. Historians have asserted that about 10–20 percent of those slaves who arrived in the new world (Americas) were Muslims.[7] Some of them were scholars in the Islamic religion; they were literate in the Arabic language.[8] Many other slaves were illiterate and followers of African Traditional Religions, particularly the Yoruba religion of Orisha (òrìṣà). The arrival of these slaves into America was another unexpected opportunity for these Africans to spread their beliefs. They brought their religions to the global world. A few slaves among the Muslims insisted on practicing Islam despite all the odds and severe punishment they received from their slave owners for upholding their religion.

Among these Muslim slave pioneers were Ayoub bin Solomon, Mahmet Yaro, and Omar bin Abdu Rahman. They were proud of their religion and practiced it as much as they could. They refused to drink alcohol or eat pork; they fasted in the month of Ramadan.[9] Ayoub bin Solomon eventually won his freedom from slavery due to his scholarship on Islam and his insistence to practice his religion. He went back to Africa.

While Muslim slaves retained their religion, other African slaves began to practice their Yoruba religion privately. As time went on, they went public. Eventually, their practice gave birth to *Santeria*, a Yoruba Orisha religion, which was still in operation in America. Many African Americans and West African scholars documented how Yoruba Orisha religion became a global religion in the Americas. I do not want to dwell on this area here because other colleagues are doing extensive studies on it, but I would like to shed light on how the legacy left by African Muslim slaves became the foundation for the establishment of Islam in the Americas through the Nation of Islam (N.O.I.) at the beginning of the twentieth century.

The Muslim slaves who came from West Africa had no contact with Christians before they arrived in the Americas.[10] Perhaps scholars among them learned about Christians and Jewish people in their holy book, Qur'an, but it was in America that they met face-to-face with Christians. They were shocked by the moral deficiency of the Christian slaveholders they met. They wondered how they claimed to be followers and admirers of Jesus and yet treated other human beings worse than their animals. However, a few of them who practiced Islam brought Islam to the attention of the public wherever they resided. Eventually, a few Christians began to learn and research Islam. Unfortunately, the descendants of the Muslim slaves could not practice Islam because the slaveholders separated them away from their parents by selling them to other White slaveholders. By the end of the nineteenth century, only a few African Americans remained Muslims. Yet those Muslims knew little about true Islam. At the beginning of the twentieth century, a few African American Muslims interacted with other Muslims abroad (during World War I). On their return to America, they began to re-introduce Islam, as they understood it, to their fellow African Americans. Among those new pioneers of Islam in the early twentieth century were Noble Drew Ali (d. 1930), Malcolm X (d. 1965), and honorable Elijah Muhammad (d. 1975).[11] It was mainly[12] through these leaders that many Americans became aware of Islam as a monotheistic religion and became a rival religion to Christianity in America.

The Nation of Islam

It is important to note that Mr. Wallace Fard was the original founder of what is known today as the Nation of Islam. When Wallace Fard founded his movement, he called it *"The Lost-Found Nation of Islam in the Wilderness."* Many Africans joined the movement under the leadership of Wallace Fard. Honorable Elijah Muhammad joined the N.O.I. around 1930 and was impressed with the knowledge and charismatic quality of Wallace Fard. Elijah Muhammad became the best and most trustworthy follower of Wallace Fard and was ultimately chosen as the successor and leader of the N.O.I. when Wallace Fard disappeared in 1934. Elijah Muhammad assumed the leadership of the N.O.I. and denied the White people membership in the movement even though Wallace Fard himself was a White person who loved to promote Islam among all Americans. He knew the religion very well and had no serious issue, neither with the White people nor with the Black people. Of course, he held some ideological issues against the White Americans on racism.

Honorable Elijah Muhammad, the N.O.I., and the Globalization of Islam in America

When Honorable Elijah Muhammad took over the leadership of the Nation of Islam in 1934, he restructured it and made a space for it in America. He moved the headquarters from Michigan to Chicago. In Chicago, he surrounded himself with able and committed disciples through whom he advanced the racial ideology of the N.O.I. He did everything in the name of Islam even though he and his followers practiced little of it. He turned the N.O.I. into a racist organization whereby only the Black people could join. Thus, Eric Lincoln called the N.O.I. "*Black Muslims.*" Elijah Muhammad mixed Islam and racism, and through it, he brought the attention of the American public to the N.O.I.[13] The Federal Bureau of Investigations, the professors, and the journalists started looking at Islam as a new and racist religion. The exposure of Islam by the N.O.I. to the American community made Islam what it is today. Elijah Muhammad proclaimed Islam, as understood by the N.O.I., a global religion and a rival tradition to Christianity. Hence, his followers established temples in many states in America, Canada, and the Caribbean. The N.O.I. maintained its authority on what constitutes Islam in America from 1930 to the 1980s.

It was after the death of Elijah Muhammad in 1975 and the exposure of his misunderstanding of Islam by his son Imam Warithu Deen Mohammad that other voices of Islam began to resonate in America. The immigrants from Asia and Arabia began challenging the portrayal that Elijah Muhammad depicted of Islam as a racist religion or black religion. With diligence and patience, his son Imam Warithu Deen Mohammad won many members of the Nation of Islam back to mainstream Islam, as expressed in the Qur'an and Sunna of Prophet Muhammad. However, despite all the present advancements that the immigrant Muslims made to Islam in America, without the relentless efforts and dedication of the members of the N.O.I., Islam would have no place in the American public space today. Currently, there are many faces of Islam: the orthodox, the fundamental, the liberal, the reformist, and the LGBTQ Muslims in America. They all live together as Americans. Indeed, credit should be given to the African American Muslim early pioneers who made incredible sacrifices to establish Islam in America.

Globally, Islam has spread to all corners of the world. People from diverse cultures and nations embrace it and make it their own. Islam is no more the religion of the Blacks or the Arabs as misinformed citizens may believe or as portrayed in the media.

African Traditional Religions Go Global

When Islam came to West Africa, some Africans embraced it. Indigenous Africans forged a peaceful relationship with Islam and Muslims. As they interacted, the Muslim scholars introduced African Traditional Religions into the global community by writing about them in their books. Ibn Battuta, the Moroccan geographer, traveled and wrote extensively on African religions in his work about his journey in West Africa in the middle of the fourteenth century. He visited Mali, Gao, and Ghana.[14] Through his works, the Arabs became aware of the nature of African Traditional Religions. Of course, there were interactions between the Africans and the Arabs before the emergence of Islam. While in West Africa, Ibn Battuta attended African religious ritual ceremonies, visited African kings, and joined the Muslims in prayers in the above countries during their festivals. All these happened before the arrival of Christianity into West Africa in the sixteenth century through the Portuguese and the Europeans, the British, and French in the nineteenth century. The slaves, who were sold to Arab merchants and brought to Arabia countries in the nineteenth and early twentieth centuries from Ethiopia, served as domestic servants and agricultural farmers in the Middle East. Many of them were adherents to African Traditional Religions. We do not have any concrete evidence that those slaves were allowed to practice their African religions in their Diaspora in Arabia. Slave trade between the Arabs and Africans began a long time before the advent of Islam in the seventh century. Many of them eventually became Muslims. However, African rulers also enslaved Arabs, especially women, as reported by Ibn Battuta during his visit to Mali in 1353.[15] He reported that he was given a slave boy as a token of hospitality when he was in Mali. This shows that slavery was a common practice in West Africa, Arabia, and Europe. As the Arabs enslaved the Black people, the Black leaders also enslaved the Arabs, as reported by Ibn Battuta. Arab and Turkish leaders enslaved the Europeans during the Ottoman Empire even though little is written about this.[16]

African Traditional Religions in the Contemporary New World

In the seventeenth century, Africans were brought to the new world through the Atlantic Slave Trade. Most of those slaves were followers of African Traditional Religions. Their slaveholders prevented them from practicing their native religions because they thought they had no religion or that their beliefs were primitive. The slaves kept practicing their beliefs secretly. However, wherever they got the opportunity, they offered their prayers publicly. At the same time, the slaveholders did not teach Christianity to their slaves for many years for the fear that it might incite them to ask for their freedom and equitable treatment. Regardless of the maltreatment that the slaves received from their holders, they did not abandon their beliefs; they practiced them even though they did not possess a written text to guide them. Their creed was in their hearts; they practiced their religions wherever they resided.

Later, Christianity was introduced to them. They (some) embraced it for utilitarian purposes. When they had the chance to form their own churches, they integrated their African beliefs into Christianity. Thus, the birth of syncretism between African Traditional Religion and Christianity emerged. The followers of the ATR created religious space for themselves in America. They introduced African dance and native songs into their Christian services and insisted that women must be full participants in the church. They filled the church services with spiritual emotion as an expression of communication with God. The Africans in the Diaspora continued to infuse ATR into their services. This transformed the African American churches into a unique mode of service even until today. Such an encounter with Christianity in the Americas brought ATR into the global stage whereby some Americans are exposed to ATR, and a few started practicing it. Through it, they learn African cultures, ethics, and spirituality. They recognized that African spirituality has a holistic nature by connecting the individuals with the divine in different forms. Such connection keeps an individual at peace with him/herself and with other human beings and generates tranquility at heart. *It enables the practitioners to respect the otherness of others.* They believe that a Supreme God created them all. This God loves and cares for them. Based on this notion of equality before God, ATR accommodates all religions and recognizes that all human beings can co-exist in peace and live in harmony.

Also, African Traditional Religion has this unique quality of tolerance, which other world religions like Islam and Christianity can borrow. It assumes that every human being has his/her belief, and therefore no religion should insist on converting others to their religion or condemning other traditions to eternal hell-fire merely because one does not share or agree to its belief or a person happens to be born in other countries. The ATR's gift of tolerance to the world should be recognized because it has worked successfully in West Africa. It can also greatly impact other traditions if they embrace it. The exclusive concept of religion that only one tradition solely possesses the truth is challenged by this African sense of tolerance and recognition of pluralism.

THE RELATIONSHIP BETWEEN ISLAM IN AMERICA AND AFRICAN TRADITIONAL RELIGIONS

One of the by-products of African slavery in America was that African Muslim slaves in America inspired the Nation of Islam's establishment among the Black people. The Nation of Islam (N.O.I.) reintroduced Islam to the Blacks in the 1930s and brought Islam to the global community with its distinctive African culture infused into the culture of the African American Muslims. The N.O.I. introduced African dress style into their community, especially the women's long dress. They introduced the wearing of hats (*Kufi*) for men in their places of worship. Hence, men and women put something on their heads. This is uncommon among the African Christians in America whose men do not put on hats in the church but dress in Western attire. However, the idea of believing in ancestors as an intermediary to God has influenced African American Muslims' beliefs in America. Members of the N.O.I., under the leadership of Elijah Muhammad, believed strongly that Elijah was the messenger of Allah instead of the Prophet Muhammad of Mecca. They thought that Elijah was an intermediary for them to God, similar to the beliefs of the practitioners of ATR that the ancestors were their links to the Supreme God.

In addition, while Islam requested their followers to offer annual charity to the poor through *Zakat* (almsgiving to the poor), the African American Muslims offered their *Zakat* to Elijah Muhammad hoping that he would distribute it to the poor. Hence, every member was required to donate at least $1 per week to Elijah Muhammad from the 1950s to the 1970s. This idea might have been borrowed from the African religion of making sacrifices and offerings to their leaders/medicine men or ancestors rather than to the Supreme God directly. The members of the N.O.I., in the 1970s, did not perform pilgrimage to Mecca but Chicago in what the N.O.I. called *Saviour's Day* on February 26th each year to mark the birthday of Wallace Fard and to forge unity among Muslims all across America.[17] Charity begins at home, claimed Elijah Muhammad. Therefore, African American Muslims in America must gather once annually in Chicago to recognize one another and work together for the betterment of their lives.[18]

However, when his son Imam Warithu Deen Mohammed took over the leadership of the N.O.I. in 1975, he condemned and changed the pilgrimage to Chicago and insisted that all true Muslims among the N.O.I. should make a pilgrimage to Mecca to fulfill the fifth pillar of Islam as required by the Qur'an (ch 3: 97), the Muslim Holy Scripture. Such an appeal to upholding mainstream Islam inspired Malcolm X, one of the greatest charismatic leaders of the N.O.I. to make *Hajj* to Mecca in 1964. That pilgrimage exposed him to global Islam and changed his life completely. Upon his return from Mecca, he was still ex-communicated. He then established the Muslim Cooperation in New York. He publicly declared in 1964 that Islam was not a Black religion but a religion for all peoples.[19] He admitted his wrong perception of Islam when he was with the N.O.I. To that end, African American Muslims, who followed Imam

Warithu Deen Mohammed and Malcolm X, took their position in the global religious world and became recognized members of the global Muslim community, the Sunnis. They also became aware that Africans, whether they are Christians, Muslims, or followers of ATR, do live together peacefully. The experiences of Malcolm X's visit to different African countries in 1964 after his pilgrimage to Mecca exposed him to how Africans live together harmoniously regardless of their faith. Hence, on his return from Africa, he advocated unity among all Africans.

Conclusion

Every religion has begun small and localized. What makes any religion global and contemporary is the attitude of its followers and commitment toward that religion. If its ethos and doctrines appeal to many human beings, then it becomes global. Religion remains contemporary when its members travel from one country to another, settle in new places, and practice their faith. That is what happened to African slaves from West Africa. When they were forcibly transported from their homeland into the Americas, they carried their beliefs/religions with them. Gradually, they began to practice them; eventually, a few people joined them, and today they have spread into Cuba, Haiti, Brazil, South, and North America. Even though Africans thought of their religions as local beliefs, as they traveled abroad, their religions took their place in the global world due to their adaptability to the modern age. The relevance of ATR to the needs of the modern man enables it to be contemporary because it meets the spiritual needs of its adherents.

What African Traditional Religion has given to the global community in the contemporary age and kept it relevant today are:

1. That ATR concentrates not on the next life, as preached by Christianity, but on the present life simultaneously.
2. That true religion is that which assists its followers in meeting their needs in life and offers great hope for the future.
3. ATR emphasizes tolerance in that every person is assumed to be potentially religious, and therefore all should live with one another peacefully without forcing one religion upon another.
4. That ATR recognizes that no one specific religion has a monopoly on truth. As Africans believe that their religion is true, they do not deny that other religions may be true also. To each its own belief.
5. By holding its space in the global world, ATR does learn from other traditions as others learn from it the importance of tolerance and peaceful co-existence.

Based on the above analysis, the conclusion which Professor Jacob Olupona, one of the pioneers of African Traditional Religions scholarship, made that "the globalization of African religion, therefore, entails not only the *death of*

African traditional values but also in many cases their expansion and protection"[20] has to be revisited. The author is ambivalent about the purport of the first part of this statement. Seeing African Traditional Religion taking its space in the world poses no detriment to African values, in our opinion, rather it gives life to it. The profound uniqueness of these values is cherished more today than before. Followers of Islam and Christianity borrowed some values from ATR, incorporated them into their sermons, and used them when rendering counseling to their adherents. Of course, both Muslim and Christian clergy may deny their borrowing from African values. Still, anyone familiar with African traditions and Islam or Christianity in Africa would recognize that they are drawing on some African religious values. Thus, globalization brings recognition and respect to these African traditions, consciously or unconsciously. African Traditional Religion has taken its due space in the contemporary age. It is here to stay regardless of the relentless encroachment by both Islam and Christianity to eradicate it.

Notes

1. Jacob Olupona, "Thinking Globally About African Religion," In *Thinking Globally: A Global Studies Reader*, edited by Mark Juergensmeyer. (University of California Press, 2013), 241–244.
2. The Concise Oxford Dictionary of World Religions, (Oxford University Press, 1997).
3. Wyatt MacGaffey in his article on "African Traditional Religions," In *Oxford Bibliographies*, 2012. oxfordindex.oup.com/view/10.1093/obo/9780199846733-0064 (accessed November 5, 2020). MacGaffey has written many books on religion in Africa especially in Congo and Ghana.
4. For more information on the worldviews of ATR, *see* Sulayman Nyang's *Islam, Christianity and African Identity*. (Vermont, Brattleboro: Amana Books, 1990), 11–23.
5. Jacob Olupona's introduction in *African Religions: A Very Short Introduction*. (Oxford University Press, 2014), 1–4.
6. Yushau Sodiq, "Islam in Africa," In *The Wiley-Blackwell Companion to African Religions*. Edited by Elias Kifon Bongmba. (U.K.: Wiley-Blackwell Publications, 2012), 323–337.
7. For more information on this topic, *see* Jane I. Smith, *Islam in America*, (Columbia University Press, 1999), Edward E. Curtis IV, *Islam in Black America*, (State University of New York Press, 2002), and Richard Brent Turner, *Islam in the African American Experience*, (Indiana University Press, 1997).
8. *See* Alan Austin, *African Muslims in the Antebellum America: A Source Book*. (New York: Garland Publishing Company, 1995).
9. Alan Austin gave many examples of these African Muslim pioneers in his above-cited work.
10. There was no official practice of Christianity then in West Africa. The Portuguese who came to Africa toward the end of the sixteenth century did not invite the natives to Christianity and thus the majority of West African peoples did not

know about Christianity until the missionaries began to arrive in the nineteenth century to Liberia and then to Nigeria.
11. *See* Edward E. Curtis VI, *Muslims in America: A Short History*. (New York: Oxford University Press, 2009), 25–44 on the "First American Converts to Islam."
12. There were a few White Caucasian Muslims who encountered Islam abroad, embraced it, and preached it to their American fellows on their return to America like Alexander Russell Webb in the early 1900s.
13. For more information on the role of the Nation of Islam in the American public in the 1950s and 1960s, *see* Alex Haley, *The Autobiography of Malcolm X*. (New York: Ballantine Books, 1979), especially Chapters 13 and 14 on Minister Malcolm X and Black Muslims.
14. Ibn Battuta, *The Travels of Ibn Battuta: In the Near East, Asia and Africa 1325–1354*. Translated by Rev. Samuel Lee. (New York: Dover Publications, Inc., 2004).
15. *See* Ibn Battuta's *The Travels of Ibn Battuta* on traveling in West Africa. *See also* Islam and slavery in West Africa in Wikipedia. https://en.wikipedia.org/wiki/slavery_in_the_Ottoman_empire#Ottoman_slavery_in_central_and_Eastern_Europe (accessed on June 21, 2019).
16. For more information on how the leaders of the Ottoman Empire enslaved some Europeans, *see* John A. Hostetler, *Hutterite Society*. (Johns Hopkins University Press, 1974), 63.
17. The Saviour's Day was established by Elijah Muhammad in commemoration of Fard's birthday, February 26, 1877. Imam Warithu Deen Mohammed changed the occasion to "*The Survival Day*" in 1976 to celebrate the achievements of the N.O.I. and made it a week-long ceremony until 1980 when he discontinued it. However, Minister Louis Farrakhan, the current leader of the N.O.I., renewed it in 1981 and it continues to the present day.
18. Minister Louis Farrakhan continues this tradition. The N.O.I. meets every year of the Saviour's Day in Chicago on the third Sunday in February. It is a day of reconnecting with one another and celebration of their achievement.
19. For more information on the Nation of Islam and Malcolm X's conversion to mainstream Islam, *see* Alex Haley. *The Autobiography of Malcolm X*. (New York: Ballantine Books, 1999).
20. Olupona, "Thinking Globally About African Religion," 244.

PART III

On Pedagogy, Research, and Foundation Scholars

CHAPTER 37

'Outsider' and 'Insider' Study of African Traditional Religion

Raymond Ogunade and Grillo Oluwaseun

INTRODUCTION

African indigenous religions are timeless, beginning with the origin of human civilization on the continent, perhaps as early as 200,000 B.C.E., when the *Homo sapiens* is believed to have emerged. Because they date back to prehistoric times, little has been written about their history. These religions have evolved and spread slowly for millennia; stories about gods, spirits, and ancestors have passed from one generation to another in oral mythology.[1] Without equivocation, African Traditional Religions showcased true evolution, especially when one takes into cognizance the age of the world. The world has been claimed to run into billion years of existence, and there are no specifics on the origin of human life. On the list of the claims that address themselves to the origin of human life is the *Homo habilis* and *homo erectus*, and as stated by Olupona (1996), that is when the species of *Homo sapiens* are believed to have emerged.

Prior to the emergence of the *Homo sapiens*, the existence of religion was not on record. Even the existence of human beings was imagined in the realm of animals whose major notable and observable concerns do not include stories about gods, spirits, and ancestors. This left us with the question that queries the emergence of the notion of God to man. It also queries which comes first: religion or the conception of God. This also places side by side whether the conception of God pre-dated the existence of God. What is apparent from the

R. Ogunade (✉) • G. Oluwaseun
University of Ilorin, Ilorin, Nigeria
e-mail: raymond@unilorn.edu.ng

© The Author(s), under exclusive license to Springer Nature Switzerland AG 2022
I. S. Aderibigbe, T. Falola (eds.), *The Palgrave Handbook of African Traditional Religion*, https://doi.org/10.1007/978-3-030-89500-6_37

foregoing is that a time in human experience between the *homo habilis* and *homo erectus* had existed when human beings' concerns were not metaphysical; in other words, everything about human beings was material and now. This may sound primitive; little or no wonder then that foreign scholars or outsiders to African Traditional Religion sometimes described it as primitive, as exemplified in the works of Edward Burnett Tylor (see Larson, 2012).

However, one of the opposites of the word 'primitive' is sophisticated. Religions that qualify to be described as sophisticated do not portray emergence at the inception of human life. In fact, it depicts more of the convolution of thought than any natural form of human behavioral pattern. Such a challenge is found in the Biblical record where Cain went to the Land of Nod, which creation narrative was not mentioned in the Biblical account of creation, and so married a wife that to date remains an unidentified person in Genesis 4:16–17. In a nutshell, what is expected to constitute African Traditional Religion as a weakness is actually one of its strongest points that it develops alongside human history, not just sprouting abruptly.

'OUTSIDER' AND 'INSIDER' DICHOTOMY

Numerous scholars in diverse fields of interest carry out studies of African religions. Major scholarly research about African Traditional Religions had a late start. In the fourteenth century, 'outsiders' began to inquire into the nature of African cultures and religions. Muslim and European colonial traders, travelers, slavers, missionaries, military personnel, mercenaries, and administrators frequently recorded naïve accounts of African cultural customs, traditions, and religions. Although their inquiries were fraught with bias, some outsiders were more reliable than others.[2]

In their work, *Perspectives on the Study of Religions in Sub-Saharan Africa*, Jan Platvoet and Jacob Olupona alluded to the 'marked new partnership between African and non-African Scholars, the so-called "insiders" and "outsiders", in the study of the religions of Africa'.[3] Platvoet pointed to the challenge one faces on the distinction between outsider and insider, referring to the work of Bourdillon, which include categorizing missionaries as outsiders though they more often than not were longtime residents in an African colony or station, so much so that they speak the language and are equally versed in the culture of the indigene and are in some respects highly indigenized. On the other hand, it is categorizing as an insider the African scholars who have been posted in a university but are so westernized[4] (more Catholic than the Pope).

While placing in focus the categorization of the scholars of African Traditional Religion into outsider and insider, one of the facts that persistently come to the fore, according to Platvoet, is that:

> The study of the religions of Africa by outsiders began in retrospect, in very defective and biased ways, in the report by traders, slavers, travelers, missionaries, military men, colonial administrators, etc. about the customs and the traditions

of the African societies which they happened to visit, or to live in for a period of time. These visitors hailed from both the Muslim world (including Muslim Africa) and Europe. Their descriptions of African societies were always very partial—in both senses of this adjective, particularly in respect of religions of Africa societies. Yet, despite glaring faults, they are, if submitted to proper source criticism, often of great value for our historical knowledge of African societies and religions because they unwittingly reported many valuable details which would otherwise have been irretrievably lost. Some of these amateur ethnographers proved more trustworthy than others.[5]

Three crucial aspects of outsiders studying African Traditional Religion were also treated in same work which are: one, giving examples of such outsiders like Ibn Battuta whose records spanned from 1352 to 1354, Willem Bosman's record was from 1688 to 1702, and Bowditch, Dupuis, and Christaller, all in the nineteenth-century Akan region of Ghana.

The second aspect that was treated includes the images created by Western biases that depicted African religions as primitive superstition, riddle with bloody sacrifice, human sacrifice, evil witchcraft, black magic, voodoo, and cannibalism from the fifteenth century once they ventured into sub-Saharan Africa on their ideological, political, commercial, and psychological function for Western colonial and missionary expansion and their baneful influence on the scholarly research of African religion.

The third, which by no means is less crucial, is the expression of the study of African religions and the introduction of concepts like Monotheism, Polytheism, Pantheism, and Atheism by extension, which sits very poorly with African Traditional Religion. In the struggle for the insiders, the indigenous African scholars of African Traditional Religion, in a bid to straighten the imposition of these foreign labels of expressions, have coined some irreconcilable foibles like liberal monotheism, inclusive monotheism, E. Bolaji Idowu's 'diffusive monotheism', Evans-Pritchard's 'refraction' of God into the lower spirits, and the view that ancestors are merely, or primarily, intermediaries between the traditional believers and God.[6]

The dynamics continue to stand for the reason of the gods, the ancestors, and the charms which are observed as independent and final agents in their relationships with humankind. The submission of Platvoet remains pivot in the dichotomy that more often than not ensued in the 'outsider insider' distinction on the study of African Traditional Religion. Through mentioning the Akan God, we extend to God in African Traditional Religion. Even if this poses a crossroad or a similitude of confusion, we argue herein that such elements are not out of place as they feature in almost every religion particularly when one attempts to explain the trinity, for example, or, by extension, transubstantiation during the Mass and Eucharis. Any attempt to explain trinity or transubstantiation will generate as many convoluted thoughts if not more than the language used to designate the relations in the African Traditional Religion of man, God, gods, spirits, ancestors, charms, magic, witchcraft, and the so-called idolatry.

When we examined the works of 'outsiders and insiders', we encountered an interface or a cross-pollination that made us feel strong on the parameters to describe a scholar as an 'outsider' or an 'insider' due to the disposition of their work. One major observation of the works of the Europeans and Islamic scholars of African Traditional Religion is that before having contact with African Traditional Religions, they carried with them a template of what they expected religion to be; thus, if any element must be accepted as a religion, it must be brought to bear under this template. This establishes justifications for studying African Traditional Religions with an unbefitting template, unifying model, and homogenizing the religion. This is a problem, but it is on the one hand.

On the other hand are the 'Insiders' whose work portrays a modicum of inaccurate representations of African Traditional Religion in spite of the fact that they are biologically insiders to Africa, its cultural practices, and obviously religion by some token of missionary conquest or sympathy with the religions of the colonial masters, or what is trendy or a feeling of inadequacy or inferiority complex, indoctrination, brainwashing through the colonial education or the direct theological background some of them had presented works on African Traditional Religion as Europeanized religion. They empolyed hyper diffusion and theological gymnastics in shaping African Traditional Religion after the Judeo-Christian template.

We do not aim to discredit others' intentions, which may be nationalistic to present to the world that we have something similar to a European worldview or something reactionary to showcase to a people who claim that we are incapable because we are indeed capable of presenting African indigenous theology. It is sufficient to identify that some insiders gave African Traditional Religion away through what they deemed a study of African Traditional Religion, which turned out to be an outright misrepresentation of its study. Platvoet analyzed and classified the works of Danquah, Lucas, to some extent, Busia, Mbiti, Evans-Pritchard, Opoku, and Idowu to this category. He further praised the works of Kenyatta and Okot p'Bitek, to some degree.

The scholars and researchers that really brought a robust academic and intellectual discourse to the fore from the preceding are the African Christian Theologians. They more often than not inherited the faculty or Department of Religion from their European predecessors and continued the Eurocentric template to studying African Traditional Religions. Where do they belong, 'Outsiders' or 'Insiders'? This class achieved two feats, both causing serious clogs in the wheels of the growth and development of the study of African Traditional Religions. The first of the two is sustaining or improving on the Judeo-Christian paradigmatic template and an established static and unitary African Traditional Religion. The second is securing this approach for study and of teaching African Traditional Religion in the departments.

African Traditional Religion: From an Object to a Subject

Since the metamorphosis of African Traditional Religion from an object to a subject, the 'Insiders' constitute the vast majority of its scholars. That is why we shall reflect on only one work of a contemporary 'Outsider' before we reflect on works of some 'Insiders' as well. Stephen Prothero is an American professor of History and Comparative Religion at Boston University in the United States. Prothero dedicated forty pages of one of his books written in 2010 with the title *God Is Not One: Eight Rival Religions That Run the World—and Why Their Differences Matter*. The chapter title is 'The Way of Connection'. In an interview on the book, he stated:

> I wanted to make room for Yoruba religion because it's one example of religions that other writers tend to dismiss or to lump together with phrases like primitive religions. In planning this book, I asked the question: What are the leading religions of the world right now? I decided to write on Yoruba Tradition because it has close to 100 million adherents. And it has a real presence in the United States in groups like Santeria. It also has public power there, because of the most important U.S. Supreme Court cases in the last century was the Santeria case in Dade County where there was an effort to outlaw sacrifice of animals.[7]

Prothero's response to another question is also essential to our study here:

> Yes, we are aware of vodou through pop culture. People have seen images and references to this tradition, so I thought readers could use this opportunity to learn about this as a true world religion. I also had a very specific push in doing this. I gave a talk about two years ago in Louisville in an interface gathering and this African-American woman stood up and said I'm sick and tired of hearing about these white religions all the time. When are you to going to write about religions of people of colour—about Africa religion?" Also, I have worked with Wande Abimbola, an important Nigerian Scholar. This is a religion that is ancient and also is urban, and it has flourished in Nigeria and other parts of West Africa. It crossed the Atlantic with the slave trade to Central and North America, and it's famous for merging in some ways with Catholicism to form movements over here. I find it fascinating because of a few concept in Yoruba religion. One is the concept of *àshe*, which can be translated as the power to make things happen. This power takes many forms in the world- in people and in plants and animals, too. And a huge effort in the religion is to tap into *àshe* and create power for yourself. It is a tradition that put the notion of power front and centre and also put the problem of disconnection and the goal of connection front and centre. ... This is a religion that thought for centuries about how to connect humans to one another and to the cosmos and to the gods and to the natural world—and to connect us to our own true selves.[8]

Prothero is basically an 'Outsider', yet as one reads his testimonies, what comes to mind is a revelation of a professional approach to studying religions. As

Prothero's work is viewed under an 'Outsider', E. Bolaji Idowu's work may have to stand in between the two divides, for we adjudged the two works under our review herein as heavily dosed in theological convolutions. The full detail of the critique of *African Traditional Religion: A Definition* (1973) is contained in a Platvoet study.⁹

The high points include the presentation of African Traditional Religion as a historical reality on two grounds: the Pan-Africanist ideology of 'a common Africanness' and the religious postulate, derived from Abrahamic monotheism, that 'the concept of [...] is a common thread [running] throughout the continent', 'is the real cohesive factor', and is 'the ground [on which] we can speak of the religion of Africa in the singular'.¹⁰

The reality that is supposedly derived from Abrahamic monotheism comes to the fore as an articulation area for our interest in this discourse. Abrahamic monotheism by the farthest stretch of the imagination could not go beyond claims without any attempt at reconstructions. Biblical records only presented Abrahamic Henotheism, in particular Judaism and Christianity, in their holy scriptures showcased Henotheism, the idea of a God who is above other Gods as in Exodus 20:3, 'Thou shall have no other gods before me', and sometimes as a God of a nation as in Isaiah 43:3, 'For I am the Lord thy God, the Holy One of Israel, thy Saviour: I gave Egypt for thy ransom and Ethiopia and Seba for thee'. As we earlier stated that problems like monotheism, polytheism, pantheism, and others in the categories of theology are only foisting on African Traditional Religion because they require their own expressions and descriptions, which are very different from theological registers in their study. Therefore, this is one reason it is practically inconsistent to view Idowu's work from the angle of an 'Insider' to the study of African Traditional Religion.

After reconstructing the Yoruba *Orisa* to the pattern of Deity versus divinities in such arrangement parallel to God and His holy angels in the Judeo-Christian order, he needed to further conform to the template. He, therefore, needed a dualistic worldview, in which case the good God will be fighting a dissident group led by an angel-like creature. The absence of this and the unwillingness of *Èsú* to fill this vacuum led the witches to be used as the next available option to perfect the dualistic religious worldview imposed on the study of African Traditional Religion. Witches and witchcrafts, Idosu said, are 'very painful', 'very disastrous', 'urgent reality', 'out and out diabolic'; their disembodied souls flew out at night 'in the form of a particular bird' to extract the ethereal bodies of their victims and devour them in their covens.¹¹ This is how *àwon Ìyàmi òpàkí òlàkí alágogo ide, arógba aso mábalè àwon afínjú eye tí njí jeun tí njí jè lóru* (My mothers who must be respected either they kill or they preserve life, ones in possession of the bell made of bronze, ones who ties 200 wrappers so fitted none drags on the street the elegant birds that wake to dine and roam at night) lose their life-saving grace, as heavy concentration is placed on their evil. However, the balance between evil and good is depicted in the discourse that surrounds them. Such balance is akin to the Biblical record in Isaiah 45:7, where God is quoted as saying, 'I formed light and created darkness, I made peace and also created evil, I the Lord do all of these things'.

Another work of Idowu is *Olodumare: God in Yoruba Belief*. Jacob Olupona described it as 'perhaps the most weighty work on Yoruba religion accessible to us today'.[12] Almost all classic books on Yoruba and Igbo religions draw inspiration from it. However, aside from the Okot p'Bitek criticism for its interpretations as noted by Olupona,[13] we may only add a few questions here that we hope to contribute to a robust intellectual discourse and development of the study of African Traditional Religion. The first question is, if the Yoruba religion addresses itself to the *Òrìṣà*, will *Olodumare* be seen as an *Òrìṣà*? If our response is 'yes', then the dichotomy created between the Deity and the Divinity will not sail for consistency. If it is 'no', *Olodumare* is then wholly other. If *Olodumare* is wholly different as the second answer presumed, would His capital letter 'G' God accord Him the status of *Yahweh*, or would it be a matter of name? Considering that Zipporah had some deeper knowledge of *Yahweh* than Moses and even had to save him from *Yahweh* at this time, Moses was yet to have a relationship with *Yahweh* in the Exodus 4:24–26 narrative. The syncretic approach to the study of African Traditional Religion might have contributed to the first line of the Nicaean creed in Yoruba as it reads in Yoruba: *Mo gba Olórun Baba Olódùmarè gbó*—I believe in God the Father *Olódùmarè* instead of I believe in the father Almighty.[14]

We may leave the works of 'Insiders' who employ a Western theistic category and see 'insiders' who use some phenomenological and sociological approach, such as Y. A. Quadri, in analyzing the impact of African Traditional Religion on many Muslims in Yorubaland, noted justifications erring Yoruba Muslims put forward from a popular Yoruba expression: *bo ti wu ni la nse imale eni*, 'there is no orthopraxis for the Yoruba', or more precisely, 'one practices one Islam as it pleases one'. Quadri pointed at divination as a part of the Yoruba life which includes: patronizes *Ifá* priest before embarking on a project, direction against wrong spouse, travel on an auspicious day if such trades, general success in life endeavors.[15]

At the arrival of Islam in Yorubaland, some Muslims whose *iman* is high would never consult any diviner. However, some Muslims whose *iman* is low would go to a Muslim cleric (*Alufa*) for consultation, and they demand from them the same service from an *Ifá* priest. The *Alufa* would not want them to go back to the *Ifá* priest while their clients were not prepared to accept any consequence as the wish of Allah. Some of the *Alufa* had to devise means of divination, including *Hattu*, which is almost the same thing as *Ifá*. The *Alufa* press certain signs on sand poured in a tray, recite some Quranic verses, and pretend to be foretelling the future. Instead of asking the clients to sacrifice certain things to be placed at a road junction, they ask their clients to offer *sadaqah* to the poor, the blind, the needy, and so on. The *Alufa* may even ask their clients to bring the *sadaqah* to their houses. There is no provision for all these in Islam; what Islam recommends to whoever wants to be guided in his/her endeavor is *Istikharah*.[16]

The *Alufa* also functions in other related areas; this is the preparation of talisman known as *tirah*, which may be hung on the individual houses or carried about or placed under the pillow to ward off evil or attract blessings. In preparing *tirah*, an *Alufa* writes some Quranic verses, including the name of the prophet Muhammed (S.A.W.), some angels, or jinns. He may add some herbal preparations or some other ingredients called *gari tira* and then tie them with thread. He may ask his client to bury it in a grave or place it under a burning fire, depending on the purpose of making the talisman. However, talisman has no place in Islam. The Prophet did not use it as he condemned those who did it and those who patronized them.[17]

Quadri mentions the Yoruba burial rites, which involved merriment on the third day, the seventh day, and the fortieth day, respectively. While these rites are unacceptable in Islam, the Yoruba Muslims find a way around it under the guise of giving *sadaqah*, which involves feeding the poor. Quadri noted that within the sphere of their conscience, they know they are in adaption mode, not engaging in *sadaqah* but in disguise, obeying indigenous cultural dictate of African Traditional Religion. He mentioned the inheritance method, too, where indigenous dictate plays out. Worthy of mention is the inheriting wives of the deceased.[18]

Regarding the above-presented Yoruba in the Islamo-Arabic worldview, our comment is that the ontology of the doings of the people is the same when they do it with *Ifá*. Our observation is that whatever happens in the transaction with the *Alufa* is merely a change in the content's nomenclature. The work of Y. A. Quadri is of an 'Insider' with Islamo-Arabic apologetics on African Traditional Religion. Works of Wándé Abímbólá,[19] Yemí Élébùìbon,[20] and Chief Miss Fárounbí Àiná Mosúnmólá Adéwálé Samadhi[21] are devoid of foreign elements; they are true to phenomenological representation of the Yoruba Traditional Religion. Then, we ask, 'Are these purest, the "Insiders" of our imaginations?' 'What about the faithful "Insiders" of academics that stand to hold the flag flying high for *Orisa* devotion through rigourous academic research, or a profession as in the case of Wole Soyinka who adopted *Ogun* as his companion God, those whose writings are not only articulating but vociferous like Ibigbolade S. Aderibigbe, Toyin Falola, Jacob Kehinde Olupona and scholars of their academic domains?'

Concluding Remarks

We are under an undying compulsion to add a dimension to this discourse so that the conclusion we draw from this study shall contribute to the ongoing discourse on the 'Insider' 'Outsider' dichotomy on the study of African Traditional Religion. May we then take the way of a question, 'Where would one classify Susanne Wenger?' The title *A Life with the Gods in Their Yoruba Homeland* speaks volumes.[22] The freedom to place Susanne Wenger will be given to our readers.

However, our conclusion on the 'Insider' and 'Outsider' contributions to the study of African Traditional Religion shall expunge biological or racial attachment because of our collective humanities, which is capable of expressing itself in sympathy and emotional attachments. The effect of training and other possible subtle psychological manipulations of human minds or outright and open declaration of loyalty to another race other than the ones in which all physical traits bore an accident of birth in a geographical location. To make our point clear, Susanne Wenger would be, for us, classified as an 'Insider', for instance. If we accept that we have the people who studied African Traditional Religion as an object, they may be acceptable as 'Outsiders' regardless of their biology or genetics since there are 'Insiders' who study the religion like 'Outsiders'. We propose to investigate other parameters soon to erase the biases of fundamental human rights of birth and geography embedded in the 'Insider' and 'Outsider' parameters. These may include, among other parameters, a theological approach, descriptive approach, phenomenological approach, and literary approach.

Notes

1. "African Traditional Religions." Worldmark Encyclopedia of Religious Practices. *Encyclopedia.com*. 25 Jul. 2019 https://www.encyclopedia.com.
2. Ibid.
3. Jan Platvoet, and Jacob K. Olupona, "Perspective on the Study of Religions in Sub-Saharan Africa," In Platvoet, J., Cox, J. and Olupona, J., (eds.), *The Study of Religions in Africa Past, Present and Prospects*. (Cambridge: Roots and Branches, 1996), 7.
4. Jan Platvoet, "From Object to Subject: A History of the Religions of Africa," In Platvoet, J., Cox, J. and Olupona, J., (eds.), *The Study of Religions in Africa Past, Present and Prospects*. (Cambridge: Roots and Branches, 1996), 10.
5. Ibid., 106.
6. Ibid., 107.
7. Stephen Prothero. "The Way of Connection," In *God Is Not One: Eight Rival Religions That Run the World—and Why Their Differences Matter* (Harper Academic, 2010). http://stephenprothero.com/books/god-is-not-one/.
8. Ibid.
9. Platvoet, "From Object to Subject, 124.
10. E. Bolaji Idowu, *African Traditional Religion: A Definition*, (London: SCM Press, 1973), 103–104.
11. Ibid., 168.
12. Jacob Olupona, "The Study of Religions in Nigeria," In Platvoet, J., Cox, J. and Olupona, J., (eds.), *The Study of Religions in Africa Past, Present and Prospects*. (Cambridge: Roots and Branches, 1996), 199.
13. Ibid.
14. https://en.m.wikipedia.org.>wiki.
15. Y. A. Quadri, "The Yoruba Muslim of Nigeria and the Problem of Cultural Identity," In P. Ade-Dopamu and E. A. Odumuyiwa, (eds.), *Religion, Science*

and Culture, (Ikenne-Remo: Nigeria Association for the Study of Religion, 2003), 240–249.
16. Ibid.
17. Ibid.
18. Ibid.
19. Wándé Abímbólá, *Ifa Will Mend Our Broken World*, (Boston, MA: Aims Book, 1997).
20. Yemí Elébùìbon, *The Healing Power of Sacrifice*, (New York: Publishing in the Name of Orunmila, 2000).
21. Fáróunbí Àìná Mosúnmólá Adéwálé Samadhi, *Fundamentals of the Yoruba Religion (Orisha Worship)*. (San Bernardino, CA: Ilé Òrúnmìlà Communications, 1993).
22. Susanne Wenger and Gert Chesi. *A Life with the Gods in Their Yoruba Homeland* (Austria: Perlinger, 1983).

CHAPTER 38

Codification, Documentation, and Transmission of Knowledge in African Traditional Religion

Toyin Falola

INTRODUCTION

This chapter examines the nature and forms of knowledge in African Traditional Religion (ATR) through the diverse beliefs, practices, philosophies, customs, and traditions of the African people. This knowledge is considered indigenous and traditional, as it presents a different notion from that of Western knowledge subject to empirical studies. The nature of this knowledge is holistic as it embraces and straddles every aspect of the African people: their culture, education, health, family, beliefs, philosophy, traditions, and so on. Some of the forms of knowledge are the beliefs in reincarnation, Ifa divination system, the knowledge of the African God, and so on. This chapter is an attempt to scratch the surface of knowledge in ATR as the scope of the research is limited in dealing with every aspect of knowledge because of the diversity of the forms of knowledge and the spatial entity of Africa. Rather than engage in multiple generalizations, the chapter uses the Yoruba of Nigeria as its example. This chapter then discusses different forms of knowledge in ATR, especially among the Yoruba. Furthermore, the chapter discusses the codification and documentation of knowledge in ATR through the publication of works and essays on the subject. Historical review of attempts at documenting knowledge in ATR is briefly explored. Challenges facing the attempts at codifying and documenting forms of knowledge in ATR are also discussed in the chapter. These

T. Falola (✉)
Department of History, University of Texas at Austin, Austin, TX, USA
e-mail: toyinfalola@austin.utexas.edu

© The Author(s), under exclusive license to Springer Nature Switzerland AG 2022
I. S. Aderibigbe, T. Falola (eds.), *The Palgrave Handbook of African Traditional Religion*, https://doi.org/10.1007/978-3-030-89500-6_38

challenges of codification and documentation of knowledge in ATR are explored to reveal and discuss different factors such as the nature of knowledge as esoteric, unwilling custodians, and language barriers, amongst others.

The work explores the various media of transmission of knowledge in ATR: written formats, video, and audio recordings are some of the media of knowledge dissemination. The transition from the oral tradition to the written tradition is explored to reveal the processes and efforts by scholars to reduce these knowledge forms to writing. The advent of digital media has also contributed to the dissemination of knowledge in ATR.

Codifying knowledge requires the use of "cognitive" and technical means to make the knowledge available and accessible to individuals and communities at anytime and anywhere.[1] Much of the African traditional religious knowledge is oral-based and has remained so for centuries before the invention of technological tools for capturing, recording, and codifying them. Toukam and Wamba observe that knowledge codification involves both codified and tacit forms of knowledge, thus complicating the codification process, together with the codification language.[2] Complexities in codifying African traditional religious knowledge arise from the fact that some aspects of the knowledge are considered esoteric and accessible to only a few members of the cult or initiates. As Charles Awe Masango says:

> The secret element of Africa's traditional medicine may not be codified because it is not revealed to non-practitioners for fear that it will be stolen and exploited without the consent of the possessors of the resources and knowledge.[3]

One of the reasons advanced for the non-codification of traditional religious knowledge in medicine is the absence of guidelines for policy standardization, formulation, regulation, promotion, and development of traditional medicine.[4] This factor becomes a problem in the advancement of knowledge inherent in ATR as it lacks the ability to stand at par with Western medicine. Masango further contends that the non-integration of traditional and orthodox medical practices may be a reason for the non-codification of the esoteric elements of traditional medicine. While Masango's argument for the esoteric traditional medical knowledge is true, the same can be stated for the non-esoteric aspect of traditional medicine in Africa.

Codification of African traditional religious knowledge is characterized by some difficulties arising from the nature of the knowledge in various aspects of the religion. There are peculiar differences, as is expected of different belief systems and religious orientations in African societies. Some of the areas of departure among these religious expressions include mode of veneration, guidelines for proper conduct, taboos, and resources for sacrifice. However, these differences make a unique reason for the codification of ATR knowledge, as it will prove the diversified knowledge production in the African milieu. The fact that traditional medicine is the main source of health care for many Africans is a positive reason for its codification. The sole dependence on this healthcare system for diagnoses, treatment, or cure of common health issues makes it a fundamental aspect of ATR knowledge ripe for codification. The accessibility of ATR knowledge to both literate and illiterate members of the community adds to the reason for its codification. Both poor and rich people can afford the services of healers and medical practitioners. The ease of getting adequate care and materials for treatment, unlike its Western counterpart, attests to the need for codification.

Another salient reason for codification is premised on the basis of alignment with the African people's orientation and personal beliefs. Prior to the introduction of foreign religions such as Christianity and Islam (and even thereafter), the people believe in the efficacy of the knowledge in ATR to be sufficient for their needs. Many Africans believe that the cause of their illnesses might be traced to an infringement of sacred laws, rules, and taboos placed by their progenitors and divinities attached to their lineage, family, and community. This necessarily necessitates the consultation of trusted traditional religious heads that can readily provide knowledge about the person's cause of predicament. Suffice to say that they believe that any problem they experience is linked to a supernatural force which may be manipulating the elements against them.

The diversity of knowledge available in ATR and its ecological heritage, which the people have depended upon and drawn from to solve their myriad socio-cultural, socio-political, and economic problems from time immemorial, is yet another basis for the codification of ATR knowledge. The dependence on the knowledge and thought systems in ATR to provide answers to various life problems and issues for the people makes its codification necessary and important. For instance, among the Yoruba, the knowledge from Ifa divination—one of the praise poetry for venerating Ifa—is "Ifa as'oro d'ayo," which means "Ifa the ocean of joyful solutions and answers." The body of knowledge in ATR is very vast that the scope of this chapter will be too constricted to accommodate it all. The ecological knowledge in ATR is used to interpret the weather and metrological omens for events in the society as well as for personal uses. The knowledge of ecology in ATR stimulates the response of farmers and indigenous business merchants to plan and strategize for good harvests or to prepare themselves for the impending drought of resources. The knowledge of ecological studies of the African people needs to be codified for further study and application in various parts of the continent. The system of knowledge application in ATR and how it is applied to real life cases needs to be codified and documented for empirical investigation and knowledge production in Africa.

Comparison between ATR knowledge and Western knowledge to ascertain areas of similarity and departure is one of the reasons for the codification of this type of knowledge. Oftentimes, indigenous knowledge has been sidelined and ridiculed by both Eurocentric writers and Africans for not representing the same ideas and thought systems of the Europeans. The codification of the thought system in ATR will either prove or debunk the general negative notion that ATR knowledge is inferior to its Western counterpart. ATR knowledge is neither inferior nor subordinate to the Western system, as it has been proven to be scientifically stable, marketable, and durable for public and private consumption. Following this line of argument, ATR knowledge needs extensive codification for worldwide recognition and documentation.[5]

The reasons provided for the lack of codification of ATR knowledge include the literacy level of the custodians of ATR knowledge. Research shows that many of these knowledge custodians do not possess adequate skills or knowledge for the codification. These indigenous scholars of ATR knowledge may not possess skills of writing, and if they do, the language of codification would still prove an impediment to the process. This problem of literacy can be solved if the language of codification is the indigenous one, and materials are subsequently translated to other languages like English for wider dissemination. Also, the continuous advocacy for ATR inclusion in the educational system and syllabi will also enhance its codification and engagements with custodians of ATR knowledge.

Again, ATR knowledge codification may be unsuccessful due to biased and negative labeling of ATR as primitive by governments, institutions, and educational organizations in Africa. The underfunding activities and inadequate recognition of ATR knowledge by the African government have contributed to the limited codification of ATR knowledge. The pejorative labeling of ATR as primitive, barbaric, and backward has increasingly influenced governments' decision to defund institutions and private custodians of ATR knowledge codification.

It is pertinent to note that the promotion, recognition, and support of ATR knowledge by government bodies and institutions are essential to the codification of ATR knowledge. The exclusion and neglect of ATR institutions such as the traditional healthcare system, centers, and programs also contribute to the lack of ATR knowledge codification. African governments must ensure policies and programs that will enhance ATR codification, transmission, and dissemination. Furthermore, the provision of a body for ATR knowledge standardization is pertinent to the codification of ATR knowledge. For example, the standardization of traditional medical practice, preparation process, and certification of products will also enhance its codification. The establishment of an oversight institution for the regulation, production, and control of ATR knowledge in areas such as medicine is also necessary.

The protection of the intellectual property of ATR knowledge producers will also secure the future of the knowledge and situate it in Africa. Patent protection of ATR knowledge will enhance knowledge exchange and economic development across the continent.

Historical Review of Forms of ATR Knowledge Documentation

ATR knowledge in the precolonial period was passed orally from one generation or custodian to another generation and/or custodian. Knowledge was an essential commodity in the society, useful for reproduction and recreation for the younger generation to use and transfer to the next one. Knowledge could be a product of people's religion, activities, culture, and observations of ceremonies from the primordial period to the present.

African traditional religion possesses myriads of knowledge which are useful for the preservation of the people's faith and practices. These knowledge materials are necessary ingredients for the stabilization of a community or society's history and promotion of their identity as people of a specific culture and period. There has been an explosion of discourses on the preservation of indigenous knowledge and resources which are gradually being eroded by the advent of Western ideas and knowledge. The emphasis to document and codify these indigenous knowledge resources arises from the paucity of materials on them. Bello et al. enumerate the benefits of documenting and preserving African indigenous knowledge, which include making Africa a center for knowledge production instead of an overly active consumer; promoting collaboration of knowledge between continents, that is, Africa and other continents; and promoting economic development and so on.[6] The necessity of codifying, documenting, and transferring traditional knowledge cannot be overemphasized.

Codification and Documentation by Mythologies

Myths present a digestible medium for ATR knowledge which were codified as sacred historical resources from the preliterate era. The salutary importance of mythical narratives in the African milieu is the validation of religious knowledge in edicts and injunctions given by the ancestors or forebears. Myths are anthropological resources that provide theoretical background to religious knowledge in Africa. Myths are both knowledge and a medium of ATR. Myths are forms of knowledge of the religion extracted from principles, philosophies, and beliefs encoded as narratives to be transmitted to the younger generation. Etiological myths in African societies express the notion of the transience of life, physical and spiritual spaces, and beliefs in reincarnation, death, and afterlife. Myths and mythology engage spiritual and cultural aspects of the indigenous people. Among the Yoruba, myths about the Supreme Being (Olodumare), deities (e.g., Obatala, Ogun, and Sango), and goddesses (e.g., Oya, Osun, and Oke'Badan) do exist. Myths and myth creation understandably involve the process of, or attempts by, the people to explain the "inexplicable." Myths were presumably generated by pioneer settlers of a community and passed on from one generation to another.[7] Ademola Dasylva further enunciates that myths are products of belief systems that in turn define the indigenous Yoruba universe, their religious worship, and ritual practices that best classify them as believers.[8]

Myths, as expressed here, embody a diverse body of knowledge. It is the medium for translating oral African religious texts and narratives which take the form of stories, legends, myths, and history.

Myths as folkloric elements were originally transmitted by word of mouth. Now, in the contemporary Yoruba society in response to the characteristic dynamic nature of culture, some myths have migrated by means of printing technology into written creative works.[9] The transition and transposition of folklore as sites of ATR knowledge have been manipulated through the invention of the printing press. Knowledge of this form cannot remain oral because of the cultural and religious wisdom that can be extracted and imported to other fields of African knowledge.

Dasylva further observes the exports of this religious knowledge into literature by writers such as Daniel O. Fagunwa, Amos Tutuola, Adebayo Faleti, Akinwumi Isola, Niyi Osundare, and Ademola Dasylva. He also notes that some of these folkloric forms have metamorphosed beyond print to television series like Jimoh Aliu's *Arelu* films and Hubert Ogunde's *Aiye* and Nollywood home-videos films.[10] Adaptations of knowledge in the forms of legends have also been carried out based on ATR.

Documentation of Proverbs in ATR

Proverbs are part of African knowledge as they are widely held truths studied by sages over a period of time and considered to be truthful. Proverbs are short statements that generally address the physical, spiritual, material, and psychological aspects of human activities. Proverbs have often been credited with a place of pride in speeches and discussions in African communities. Proverbs cut across every aspect of human relationships and human facets of relationships with nature and the environment. They are part of ancestral heritage and spiritual codes from the practice of African religions. Proverbs are the combined knowledge of the progenitors and deified ancestors that help to guide human communication and interaction with their spaces. The knowledge in proverbs has been collected truths, wisdom, philosophies, and moral reflections of spiritual heads, leaders, and ancestors. Omofoyewa opines that proverbs are the main ingredients needed to drive home elders' wise counsel or rebuke forcefully and beautifully.[11] Drawing from the Nigerian example, Omofoyewa speaks to the extensive use of proverbs in the modern era:

> Some television stations and cable outlets, such as Nigerian Television Authority (NTA), Osun State Broadcasting Corporation (OSBC), Ogun State Television (OGTV), Lagos State Television (LTV), Orisun Television, African Magic, etc., often do virtual broadcasts of African proverbs, particularly Yoruba proverbs, at intervals, all in a bid to further propagate their use and understanding. Furthermore, the internet also provides a new ground for the study of proverbs. There are many as possible online applications of Yoruba proverbs (Owe Yoruba), downloadable on Play Store, Galaxy Apps., mobogenie etc. Some other sites even

pave the way for online participation and thereby allow individuals to add more proverbs to the links.[12]

Proverbs have been transmitted and documented in various formats, as eloquently explored above. Proverbs are wisdom nuggets in ATR targeted at correction of ills in the society, family, and nation. It is why Omofoyewa states that while the Yoruba acknowledge the value of proverbs in speech as terse, memorable enchanting expressions and wise philosophical sayings that can beautify communication, they still hold that only the wise among them can use proverbs appropriately or understand their meanings properly.[13] The knowledge gained from proverbs is applied to different issues and problems in the society because they have been statements of truths studied over time. Knowledge in African traditional religion permeates the production of proverbs and wise sayings in African societies.

Knowledge in Egungun Poetry (*IWI*)

Egungun is another deity of the Yoruba people that is synonymous with the reincarnated spirit of the ancestors. In the Yoruba religion, Egungun is the ancestral spirit who reincarnates in human form to mediate between humans and Olodumare, the Yoruba Supreme Being.[14] The Egungun worship is yet another site of knowledge rife with literary, secular, and spiritual resources. The Yoruba deities and ancestors are part of the *orisa*, and Egungun is central to them. These orisa are emissaries from the Supreme Being who act as links between humans and the unseen world. Egungun may be a family, community, and group practice where the people or groups are mandated to participate in the various festivities, activities, rituals, and ceremonies organized as part of the religious activities of the religion. In Egungun, sites of knowledge include the panegyric poetry chant known as "ewi egungun." The employment of different traditional and cultural resources elucidates the literary and linguistic materials producing knowledge inherent in the system.

In *egungun*, knowledge is excavated in the system of veneration. Bello et al. observe that the invocation of the ancestor is performed when the adherents dance, drum, and are possessed by ancestral spirits.[15] There are equivalents of the Egungun festival performed in different African societies, with variants and slight differences but with the same goal of documentation and codification.

Songs as Documentation of Knowledge

Knowledge in ATR is rendered in lyrical forms, as songs encompass every activity and practice of the people. As in all human societies, they pass on knowledge, wisdom, and manners from one generation to the next by word of mouth.[16] During rites and ritual activities, songs are performed to create the right mood and ambience for the religious ceremony. Songs are used to celebrate all kinds of events, whether religious or secular, since they contain beliefs, philosophies, and worldviews. Songs about religious practices are also composed to keep the people aware of the significance of the beliefs and knowledge inherent therein. There are different types of songs as they have different functions and significance in the worship of the divinities attached to these religions. Hamzat concedes with this claim as she states that singing is described by a function to which it is associated. This means we have songs that are associated with religious, ritual, or spiritual worship or festivals (orin esin). They are strictly used in the worship of the deities. Some of the songs are restricted to specific locations.[17] Hamzat claims that some of the restricted songs such as *arungbe* (songs used by Oro worshippers in Egbaland); *orin Oke'badan* is peculiar to Ibadan; and *orin agemo* is localized in Ijebu Remo. *Dadakuada* is associated with Ilorin, while *waka* and *apala* are common in Ibadan.[18] These songs may contain lewd contents and lyrics as a psychotherapeutic release of repressed emotions and urges, but it is a safe medium of expelling these desires. This is evident in the *orin Oke'badan* that is sung by the adherents of the deity during the Oke'badan festival. Some of these songs are also peculiar to some groups of people such as twins, and guild's cults like the hunters' song and the special song for specific rites like the Iremoje used in the initiation of passage rites of a dead hunter.[19]

Songs that describe religious beliefs about the inevitability of death, reincarnation, God's supremacy and power, and the power and prowess of deities such as Sango and Ogun are composed as musical renditions of knowledge in ATR. Songs engender knowledge on beliefs and practices such that when they are sung they invoke the deity to action. Songs express philosophical knowledge in ATR through composition; musical knowledge is being transposed into notes and rhymes for the education and entertainment of the people. It also presents one of the easiest ways of teaching children about their heritage and customs. The *orin ibeji* (twins' song) is a socio-religious song composed to espouse the sacredness of these sets of children who are also known as deities in the Yoruba religion. The song performs several functions like calming the twins when they are agitated, lulling them to sleep, and pacifying them as deities.

Religion Knowledge in Festivals

Festivals and ceremonies are socio-religious aspects of ATR knowledge. These festivals, events, and ceremonies are enactments of indigenous knowledge. The Osun-Osogbo is a festival of the existence of the Osun deity and the socio-spiritual significance of the veneration of this divinity in the southwestern part of Nigeria. The myth behind Osun states that the deity was a woman married to Sango, the god of thunder, before she turned into a river. The Ifa festival is yet another religious event observed among the Yoruba and other devotees scattered across the world.[20] As explained by Abigail Odozi Ogwezzy-Ndisika and Babatunde Adeshina Faustino:

The festival takes a whole week and on each day, the priests consult the oracle about the progress of their faithful. On the 5th day, a special ceremony is held for every family in the town or village who wants to know what is in store for them in the year. This ceremony is called "ibo" and those who consult the Ifa oracle are told what is in store for them now and in the future. Those who are concerned about their future are told of rituals to be done that will avert the negative events.[21]

Festivals in African societies are social and religious events that bundle up different units of knowledge and present them in both sacred and secular modes, while also creating an atmosphere of entertainment for the people. Festivals ensure the continuation of religious events, beliefs, practices, and systems of knowledge in African communities.

To take yet another example, there is the Eyo festival, also known as the Adamu Orisa play. It is a festival that takes place in the Lagos Island Local Government Area of Lagos State, described as:

The eyo festival is performed as a rite of passage for a dead Oba or chief or an important personality in the country. It is also used to welcome important and highly influential personalities into the country. The (Adamu Orisa) Eyo makes use of 'aga' (hat) made of plywood and cloth, 'opa-n-bata' (the staff) made of palm tree with designs on it, 'iboju eyo' (cloth) used for covering the face, 'aropale' (the white robe).[22]

The origin, subjects, and themes of these festivals are rooted in ATR. Orunmila is the subject of the Ifa festival and Osun is the subject of the Osun-Osogbo festival, believed to be the deity of fertility and children. These festivals commemorate the knowledge in the practice of various religious activities. Festivals encode various forms of African knowledge such as divination, ritual, rites, sacrifices, and invocation.

LITERARY KNOWLEDGE OF ATR

In the literary aspect of ATR knowledge, Africans produce knowledge through their study and relationship with the Supreme Being and the divinities. Such observations and relationships inspire them to compose narratives about the existence of God and the plethora of deities. An example of literary knowledge in ATR is the composition of poetry. African people are deep thinkers and poetic; their veneration of deities explodes into creative poetic renditions of their knowledge of God and deities. One of such genres of literature is the panegyric poetry. In the performance of rituals, rites, and ceremonies, the African people compose poems to express their faith, belief, and idea of God. Many of these African deities have special poems for their veneration; the poems explore the theme of power, strength, valor, and sovereignty of the deity as the progenitor of the religion. For reference, the *Iwi Egungun* is the panegyric poetry attached to the deified masquerade ancestor Egungun.

Specifically, the Yoruba employ literary skills to produce knowledge in Egungun as a type of African religion. *Iwi* are poems linked to the Egungun masquerade and are used to extol the virtue and values of the particular Egungun and the related ancestors.[23]

Through Egungun, the ancestor spirit manifests under a specially created costume, called *ago* or *eku*, that is worn to cover the head and the whole body of the masked performer.[24] Famule further states that the primary purpose of the *ago* or *eku* (the masking costume of *Egungun*) is to obliterate the masker's human identity, in order to conceal the power that gave form to the ancestor spirit through the masker, the energizer of the *ago* or *eku*.[25]

Documentation of ATR knowledge is the procedure in which knowledge is collected, gathered, arranged, registered, and recorded in a certain way as a means of preserving, managing, disseminating, and safeguarding or preventing it from extinction and loss. The importance of the codification and documentation of knowledge in ATR cannot be overemphasized as it is generally classified under traditional knowledge as a form. The systematic codification and documentation of knowledge in ATR is necessary as this knowledge is capable of generating foreign exchange and monetary benefits. Foremost of the reasons for codification and documentation of ATR knowledge is the systematized protection, preservation, and storage of this traditional knowledge for future use by generations of African people. Again, codifying and documenting ATR knowledge is necessary for collaborative research purposes between and among different groups and actors for the production of knowledge. The process of codification and documentation of knowledge in ATR will necessitate the identification and recognition of indigenous groups and communities responsible for the production of such traditional knowledge. When the identification of communities responsible for this knowledge is acknowledged, it prevents the stealing of this form of knowledge peculiar to their religion as benefits of codification and documentation of knowledge in ATR.

While there are salutary reasons for the codification and documentation of knowledge in ATR, there are also some disadvantages recognized in the efforts to document this knowledge type. One of the demerits of documentation is the misappropriation of this knowledge, especially the esoteric form. Indeed, deep research needs to be undertaken to ascertain the contexts where this knowledge may be deployed and the imminent harm that it can generate before codifying and documenting this knowledge form. Another demerit of documentation of ATR knowledge is the uncensored proliferation of secret ATR knowledge for public consumption and the loss of control by the communities of this traditional knowledge. Documentation of knowledge in ATR does not automatically guarantee protection of rights and ownership of this form of knowledge. A well-planned codification and documentation must ensure that ATR knowledge is properly protected legally and the risk of unlawful use and production is eliminated.

Documentation of knowledge in ATR may be in the form of a register. A registry has been defined as "an ordered collection or repository of information," with "the connotation of a repository or list of information that has an official status."[26] The codification and documentation of knowledge in ATR can take various forms depending on the type of knowledge. Documentation can be through written, video, audio, pictures, and image format. The language of documentation is also important for efficient knowledge preservation and storage. The language of documentation may be in the original indigenous dialects, languages, or other languages. The documentation may also follow modern technological patterns or conventional process or the combination of both systems. Documentation of ATR medicinal knowledge can be written, especially as it is orally transmitted from the custodians of this form of knowledge. This written knowledge may be digitized and stored electronically. Furthermore, knowledge in ATR in the form of arts or still life can be photographed and preserved electronically. Videotaping ATR knowledge such as divination processes, ceremonies, festivals, and rituals and rites can help with documentation. In cases whereby images of participants of ritual practices or events are prohibited, audio voice-recordings can be used to record the ATR knowledge. In some cases, multimedia documentation can be achieved through note-taking, recordings, photography, and videotaping.

CHALLENGES FACING DOCUMENTATION OF KNOWLEDGE IN ATR

Documentation and codification of ATR knowledge in the contemporary age of multimodal formats has some challenges. A few of the issues influencing the documentation and codification of knowledge in ATR are discussed below.

Process of Documentation

According to the World International Property Organization:

> As a general rule, research institutions, NGOs, or other third parties undertaking documentation need to ensure that customary laws and practices are fully respected at all stages of the TK documentation project. Whether expressed in written guidelines, codes of conduct, community protocols, formal agreements (written or oral) or even simple instructions given by TK custodians, communities or their representatives, efforts should be made to ensure such requirements are met.[27]

The lack of adequate information on rules and regulations of engagement with custodians of knowledge in ATR may yet halt or diminish the prospect of documentation. As the World International Property Organization advises:

> Customary laws and practices need to be considered before documentation takes place, but may also arise during the documentation process. Indeed, when documentation of knowledge in ATR activities begin, this may bring to light conflicts with customary laws and practices not envisaged at the date and agreement for documentation was made.[28]

These unforeseen and unplanned caveats may affect the documentation project, as conflict may arise between documenters and custodians of ATR knowledge about rules of coverage and documentation. The rules affect the documentation format, processes, and output when issues of customary regulations arise during documentation of knowledge in ATR.

One of the foremost challenges of codification and documentation of different knowledge forms of ATR in contemporary documentation formats is how and what knowledge can be collected and which format is the best for what form of ATR knowledge. Knowledge in ATR in African societies may require different processes of collection and different documentation formats, which may prove difficult to transform into other formats. This challenge also includes how the knowledge can be documented and who is to perform such an action. Knowledge considered secret or esoteric may be impossible to document by a non-initiate or member of the cult or group. In this case, written formats may not be the right choice of format as the physical presence of an observer or researcher is prohibited. The option of audio recording may prove effective as the presence of the researcher is not necessary if a member of the cult or the custodian of the knowledge is taught how to make recordings. In this situation, videotaping of knowledge in ritual practices of ATR may be difficult if not impossible to document because of the secrecy of the knowledge or the wishes of the custodian(s) to remain anonymous. Different forms of knowledge in ATR require suitable formats of documentation based on the nature, mode of collection, custodian's wishes, religious laws, and instructions of the knowledge form.

Language as a Barrier to Documentation

Language of knowledge in ATR may yet present another challenge to the codification and documentation process, which also influences access to the knowledge and the format of documentation. The decision whether to document knowledge in the original indigenous language(s) or foreign ones for international intelligibility may also halt or pose a threat to the documentation of ATR knowledge in African communities where the language of the knowledge is underdeveloped for such a multifaceted documentation format. The choice of language may also determine the format of documentation. In other words, there are barriers of language and format in codifying and documenting knowledge in ATR because the choice of language with limited international acceptability may cause serious risk for piracy and offices responsible for patents in other places where the knowledge may be used.

Ownership Dispute/Claim

One of the challenges of codification and documentation is the nature of the knowledge which is communally owned. The right to document and codify knowledge in ATR in a multimodal format may be impossible to document due to conflict of interests among groups and communities where the knowledge originates from. The writing, recording, videotaping, and digitizing of ATR knowledge from some indigenous groups of people or communities may generate conflict about what benefits will be gained and how it will be equally distributed among members of the community:

> Where rights over TK (Traditional Knowledge) are recognized, communities or individual community members may still wish to ensure that they retain ownership when granting permission to third parties to collect TK or access it via a database or a register.[29]

The copyright laws in the country regarding the ownership of knowledge in ATR will also determine how documentation of such forms of knowledge will be carried out. The recognition of traditional knowledge in the law determines documentation procedures and compliance with the regulations before documentation projects are permitted. The red-tape involved in collecting and documenting this form of ATR may be rigorous and tedious and possibly discourage individual researchers or groups planning to undertake such a project. As Begona Venero Aguirre and others conclude:

> If national law does not recognize or establish clear rights of indigenous peoples and local communities over their TK, special consideration must be given to the potential benefits and drawbacks of documentation. This will require an analysis of the legal options available to ensure that TK is not appropriated by third parties.[30]

The control and right to forms of knowledge in ATR may make documentation a difficult exercise and perhaps a fruitless project when in the future legal issues about the form of knowledge and acquisition arise. Independent researchers and organizations may be discouraged from documentation of knowledge in ATR when they examine possible legal conflicts that may result from the project.

Media of Knowledge Transmission

Knowledge in ATR has been transmitted in the precolonial era through oral recitation and transmission through the word of mouth from the custodians such as progenitors, priests, priestesses, healers, herbalists, surgeons, midwives, devotees, and practitioners to adherents, initiates, apprentices, and descendants. Oral traditions are one of the forms of ATR knowledge and its mode of transmission. Prior to the advent of writing and the printing press, knowledge of ATR was generally transferred through traditional institutions such as cults, guilds, vocation cults, and informal gatherings. "Orality" in the precolonial African societies was the natural form of knowledge in African traditional religion, as with many other forms of knowledge. Oral literature developed from the auspices of oral traditions into a vast area of African epistemology. As Timothy Ajani opines:

> Long before the written tradition, Yoruba oral literature existed for centuries. Professional griots in the society, particularly in the courts of the obas (kings), dutifully transmitted the lore of the people from one generation to the next under the bright moonlit African night. Parents and community leaders likewise considered it an important part of their societal responsibility to educate and entertain the younger generation about their common ancestry, societal values, beliefs, collective thought, histories, and worldview through alo (riddle) and itan (story, history).[31]

Knowledge in ATR in oral forms gradually gave way to the written format through the advent of colonialism and the introduction of writing by missionaries in several parts of Africa. The efforts of African missionaries in developing a standard orthography for different African languages laid a foundation for the transmission of knowledge in ATR. The attempts to reduce African languages into writing and the works of linguists in developing a standard orthography culminated into the publication of books on grammar, dictionary, vocabulary, literature, and so on. One of such efforts was that of Bishop Samuel Ajayi Crowther, the Fourah Bay-educated Yoruba linguist and priest who played a pivotal role in the standardization of the Yoruba language through the publication of works on Yoruba grammar, a Yoruba dictionary, and the Yoruba version of the Bible, among others.[32] The efforts of this priest and many others like him across Africa have influenced the transmission of oral knowledge in African traditional religion into the written form. Ajani opines that with the advent of written language, there was a smooth transition of platforms from the oral to the written code.[33]

It is very enlightening to note that the first sets of works to be written and published by Africans borrowed and relied on oral tradition. Some of these works used knowledge from the beliefs, practices, philosophies, and thoughts in African traditional religion as the themes, subjects, and titles of their works. Ajani further reiterates that the written tradition was built on the solid foundation provided by the former oral tradition, a foundation built and solidified over many centuries and millennia, bringing the past into the present, as it were.[34] ATR knowledge has been transformed from its oral form to written version, as former storytellers and griots were the mediums through which oral traditions were disseminated, the newer tradition—written literature—was, and continues to be, propagated through multiple platforms: the tried-and-tested pen and paper, then the printing press, and more recently the computer and the World Wide Web. The latter is the platform of the new media: websites, blogs, digital media (such as electronic books), and social media outlets (such as blogs, social networks, and forums).[35]

Formats: Oral and Written

The introduction of written language has transformed the oral knowledge in ATR into the efforts and works of writers like Amos Tutuola whose work *The Palm-Drinkard and His Dead Palm-Wine Tapster in the Deads' Town* (1952),[36] written in English, explores the belief in magic, charm, and the extraterrestrial world of the ATR of the Yoruba people. The quest of the palm-wine drunkard was made possible through the knowledge of powerful charms and incantations in ATR. Tutuola's work has transmitted this oral knowledge of ATR to a written text for international consumption. The work validates the existence of knowledge in ATR. Another writer, D. O. Fagunwa, produced many works that, although are written in Yoruba, also explore themes and knowledge of ATR. Ajani states that Fagunwa's seminal work, *Ogboju Ode Ninu Igbo Irunmole (The Forest of a Thousand Daemons)*, was published in 1938 and bore the entire hallmark of the oral tales of old: monsters, magic, spirits, deities, and so on. It had the distinction of being the first full-length literary work to be produced in the Yoruba language and continues to be the most widely read novel in the Yoruba language.[37]

From expressions of knowledge in literary works such as novels, plays, and poetry, ATR continues to be one of the sources of materials from which images, themes, subjects, and so on are borrowed. The works of dramatists like Wole Soyinka draw heavily from Yoruba religious beliefs and mythology, mixed with contemporary issues.[38] His works are littered with references to his patron deity, Ogun.[39] The play, *Death and the King's Horseman* (1975), borrows from the religious practice of the Yoruba whereby the king has a forerunner who must be buried with him when the king dies. Many other writers have also borrowed beliefs and philosophies from ATR to be used in poetry, movies, essays, books, and research discourses. The oral and written forms of knowledge in ATR have both presented several merits. The advent of digital media has also influenced the transmission of knowledge in ATR such that there are spoken words in digital forms, digital books, social media platforms, websites, blogs, and multimedia.

Advantages/Disadvantages of Oral Form of Knowledge in ATR

Oral forms of knowledge of ATR have presented data in its older state, with modifications that suit new eras. This is one of the advantages of the oral form of knowledge in ATR. It affords the listeners, receivers, and adherents a close feel of knowledge in a digestible form. Oral forms, as in the case of Ifa poetry, present knowledge in the Ifa corpus in a complex yet meaningful way. Africans can easily assimilate this knowledge as they are being transmitted from the custodians. The oral form also presents an easy access to knowledge and its transmission from one generation to the next. The knowledge is available to all, whether educated or uneducated, as long as they are eligible to acquire such knowledge in ATR. The oral form of knowledge in the advancement of ATR knowledge is easily transmitted to both young and old. However, the oral forms have limited reach of audiences compared to the written forms, with the tendency to reach wider audiences, both locally and internationally. While the written forms of knowledge present wider audiences, they also have the demerit of losing vital oral parts of the knowledge that may not be easily translated into writing. The language of writing may also present problems because while knowledge in indigenous languages is pristine in its oral form, writing it may present issues of inaccuracy.

Written forms of knowledge aid in the promotion of African knowledge and religion through scholarly research and publication on different aspects of African traditional religion. In contrast to oral forms, written forms of knowledge are preserved for years without the reliance on human memory which may fail due to old age, thereby causing the loss of valuable knowledge. The written forms in books on Ifa poetry, Egungun poetry, court poetry, myths, legends, proverbs, beliefs, and philosophical writings, among others, preserve this knowledge for use in schools and higher institutions of learning. It also keeps records that can be consulted for future research in the area which would contribute to the advancement of research on such ATR knowledge. However, oral forms may be the only viable form of transmission of some sacred or esoteric forms of knowledge. The custodians of some esoteric forms of knowledge in ATR may be unwilling to divulge this sacred knowledge to non-initiates, much less allow for its documentation. One of the demerits of this oral form is the gradual dearth and loss of sacred knowledge as they are confined to human memory and retention, which has its limits. The written format provides a suitable and dependable means of transmission of knowledge in ATR.

Written forms of knowledge present diverse opportunities for the advancement of this knowledge system and also for the African continent. The written forms may be developed to digital forms such as blogs, social media, audiobooks, digital books, and websites, especially in the age of technological advancement. Oral forms of knowledge rely heavily on a single mode of transmission, and this may likely not appeal to generations of young Africans who require exciting media of knowledge to stimulate their interests. However, the written forms also lack the potential to present oral codes and gesticulations, body movements, rhythm, and mnemonic devices employed during oral performance and transmission of knowledge in ATR. Forms of knowledge in drumming, dances, images, and art may prove difficult or impossible to be transformed as written forms. Both oral and written forms of knowledge in African traditional religion present both potentials and difficulties for the advancement of knowledge. However, with careful innovation and technology, both media of knowledge can be maximized to produce optimum advantages for the advancement of knowledge in ATR.

In conclusion, knowledge in African traditional religion possesses massive potential for engaging the issues in the African continents if concerted efforts are made to develop, theorize, document, and disseminate this knowledge.

Notes

1. Dieudonne Toukam and Samuel Fosso Wamba, "Contribution and Limits of IT-enabled Codification and Dissemination of Traditional Knowledge: Case of Bamileke People," *HICSS* 12 (2012): 1.
2. Ibid., 2.
3. Charles Akewe Masango, "Indigenous Knowledge Codification of African Traditional Medicine: Inhibited by Status Quo Based on Secrecy?" *Information Development* XX (2019): 1–12.
4. Ibid., 7.
5. Masango, "Indigenous Knowledge."
6. L. A. Bello, J. O. Kayode, Y.O., Ahmed, A.O., Adeyemi, and T. I. Yusuf, "The Management, Dissemination of Ifa Oracle and Egungun Festival for Knowledge Preservation and Promotion of African Cultural Heritage in Osun State," *Nigerian Journal of Philosophy, Culture and Religion* 43 (2019): 7–12.
7. Ademola O. Dasylva, "Folklore, Oral Traditions, and Oral Literature," in *Culture and Customs of the Yoruba*, eds. Toyin Falola and Akintunde Akinyemi (Austin, Texas: Pan-African University Press, 2017), 141.
8. Ibid.
9. Ibid., 142.
10. Ibid.
11. Kazeem Adebayo Omofoyewa, "Idioms, Proverbs, and Dictums," in *Culture and Customs of the Yoruba*, eds. Toyin Falola and Akintunde Akinyemi (Austin, Texas: Pan-African University Press, 2017), 102.
12. Ibid., 104.
13. Ibid., 102.
14. Ibid.
15. Bello et al., "The Management, Dissemination of Ifa Oracle and Egungun Festival," 8.
16. Saudat Adebisi O. Hamzat, "Songs," in *Culture and Customs of the Yoruba*, eds. Toyin Falola and Akintunde Akinyemi (Austin, Texas: Pan-African University Press), 159.
17. Ibid., 162.
18. Ibid.
19. Ibid.
20. Abigail Odozi Ogwezzy-Ndisika and Babatunde Adeshina Faustino, "Extra-Mundane Communication: Insights from Festivals and Carnivals," in *Culture and Customs of the Yoruba*, eds. Toyin Falola and Akintunde Akinyemi (Austin, Texas: Pan-African University Press), 339–354.
21. Ibid.
22. Ibid., 346.
23. Sola Adeyemi, "Performing Arts," in *Culture and Customs of the Yoruba*, eds. Toyin Falola and Akintunde Akinyemi (Austin, Texas: Pan-African University Press), 249.
24. Olawole Famule, "Masks, Masque, and Masquerades," in *Culture and Customs of the Yoruba*, eds. Toyin Falola and Akintunde Akinyemi (Austin, Texas: Pan-African University Press), 393.
25. Ibid.

26. World International Property Organization, "Documenting Traditional Knowledge – A Toolkit," WIPO, Geneva, 2017, 11.
27. Ibid., 10.
28. Ibid.
29. Begona Venero Aguirre, Wend Wendland, Fei Jiao, Kiri Toki and Shakeel Bhatti, "Documenting Traditional Knowledge – A Toolkit," in *World Intellectual Property Organization (WIPO)*, ed. Toby Boyd (Geneva, 2017), 10.
30. WIPO, 2017, 10.
31. Timothy T. Ajani, "Writing System and Literature," in *Yoruba Culture and Customs*, eds. Toyin Falola and Akintunde Akinyemi (Austin, Texas: Pan-African University Press), 977.
32. Ibid., 975.
33. Ibid., 977.
34. Ibid.
35. Ibid.
36. Ibid., 978.
37. Ibid., 979.
38. Ibid., 980.
39. Ibid.

CHAPTER 39

African Traditional Religion and Indigenous Knowledge System

Toyin Falola

INTRODUCTION

African traditional religious knowledge refers to the philosophies, beliefs, songs, dance, traditions, customs and activities that possess eruptions of understanding, discourses and wisdom that are used for the continuation of the religious ways of knowing. African traditional religion (ATR) encompasses scientific, local and indigenous wisdom embedded in the plethora of religious practices and beliefs scattered and encoded in the socio-political, religious, secular, spiritual and traditional engagements of the African people. The aim of this chapter is to explore ATR.

The notion of African traditional religious knowledge entails philosophical deposits gleaned from the study of religious practices and beliefs that the indigenous depends on for the continuance of its past to maintain its society. These philosophies are enshrined in religious and spiritual edicts, beliefs and activities that have been observed to be sacred and essential to the adherence to the religions' ethics. The knowledge in ATR enlightens the people of how and in what way they are to lead a good life. These philosophies are drawn from the historical, etiological and material resources of these traditional religions. The origin of the transmission of this knowledge from the ancient period is through oral and aural carriage from one generation to the next one. Orality in the primordial age was the major system of knowledge transmission as the

T. Falola (✉)
Department of History, University of Texas at Austin, Austin, TX, USA
e-mail: toyinfalola@austin.utexas.edu

© The Author(s), under exclusive license to Springer Nature Switzerland AG 2022
I. S. Aderibigbe, T. Falola (eds.), *The Palgrave Handbook of African Traditional Religion*, https://doi.org/10.1007/978-3-030-89500-6_39

515

introduction of the modern system of documentation was not yet known to the indigenous African people. The priests and priestesses were the custodians of African traditional religious knowledge: they received, transcribed and interpreted the codes that were unknown to the non-initiates. ATR may be conceived as both veiled and open codes of thoughts, wisdom and philosophies for the aesthetic and spiritual edification of the people.

ATR covers those aspects that may be described as indigenous religious beliefs and practices.[1] Mbiti defines the religion to include "attitudes of mind and belief that have evolved in many societies of Africa and affect the way of life of most African people."[2] Knowledge in ATR is known as traditional or indigenous wisdom, part of a category of knowledge known as Traditional Knowledge (TK) or indigenous knowledge (IK). The type of wisdom found in indigenous settings is known by different labels and meanings as it largely determines the meaning that will be derived from its conceptualization.[3]

Indigenous knowledge is transmitted orally and contains elements of what is called "culture" and experience gathered by observing the environment.[4] This notion of culture projects a more comprehensive outlook of what constitutes knowledge in African societies,[5] which includes songs, languages, music and other creative aspects of life.[6] This notion of traditional knowledge also indicates a holistic conceptualization of knowledge in ATR as religion permeates every aspect and facet of African lives and societies. Most importantly, these notions of traditional knowledge have presented a heterogeneous view of knowledge. It is a holistic and inclusive form of knowledge in that it encompasses the mental, intellectual, spiritual and physical development of the individual self and the interconnections between people and the environment.[7] This knowledge has been treated as expansive.[8] An elaborate definition puts the knowledge system as:

> Traditional Knowledge is cumulative and dynamic. It builds upon the historic experiences of a people and adapts to social, economic, environmental, spiritual and political change. The quantity and quality of Traditional Knowledge differs among community members according to their gender, age, social standing, profession and intellectual capabilities. While those concerned about biological diversity will be most interested in knowledge about the environment, this information must be understood in a manner which encompasses knowledge about the cultural, economic, political and spiritual relationships with the land.[9]

From the notions of traditional knowledge expressed above, knowledge in ATR encompasses aspects of ecology, philosophy, anthropology, psychology, medicine, agriculture, education, arts and crafts, music and literature of the communities. Mbiti also agrees by conceding that because traditional religion permeates all the departments of life, there is no formal distinction between the spiritual and the secular, between the religious and non-religious, between the spiritual and the material areas of life.[10] These bodies and forms of knowledge are unique and diverse, distinguishing the African people as distinct people producing knowledge and utilizing them in all phases and aspects of their lives.

Knowledge in ATR has several characteristics that make it indigenous. Some of the characteristics are as follows.

COMMUNAL OWNERSHIP

Knowledge in ATR belongs to a group or collective community where individual claims may not be clear. This type of knowledge is a heritage passed from one generation to the next through practices in the religion. Knowledge in ATR is communally owned as it is generated through several traditional institutions.

Holistic

Knowledge in ATR is encompassing of all the peoples' lives and it penetrates their culture, economy, beliefs, philosophy, education, fashion, arts and crafts and so on. This knowledge is not isolated nor removed from the comprehension of the African people's existence. Knowledge in African traditional religion saturates their system of governance, politics, organization of cults, societies and groups, among others.

Oral Form

Knowledge in ATR is transmitted through the word of mouth from the progenitors to their descendants from generations to generations. This is usually known as oral traditions, which is a form of knowledge in precolonial African societies. Children, youths and adults have cultivated this mode as the medium of knowledge dissemination. Stories, songs, poetry, beliefs, philosophy, proverbs, riddles and so on have largely been in this oral form for centuries before the advent of the written tradition and print press.

Some of the forms and types of knowledge are expressed in beliefs, philosophy, literary, musical and artistic expressions. These practices exude notions of knowledge in the system of veneration, ritual activities, ideology and philosophies:

> Many initiatives are being pursued all over the world to record, register and digitize intangible cultural heritage: individuals (such as ethnologists, folklorists and anthropologists), institutions (such as museums and archives) and governments (especially ministries of culture) have for decades recorded and disseminated expressions of our planet's rich cultural diversity.[11]

The Belief in Ancestral Reincarnation

One of the forms of knowledge in ATR is the common belief in spirit reincarnation that permeates the worship of deities and veneration of ancestors. This knowledge among worshippers of ATR is also grounded in the idea of the masquerade (known as the Egungun among the Yoruba) with different variants in other African communities. Reincarnation is one of the systems of reconnection and validation of the existence of another world where ancestors go to and thereby replicate themselves in the present or future generation in the physical world of the living. Africans believe their ancestors come back and reincarnate themselves in the form of their children as some of them carry resemblances of the previous ancestors. Reincarnation is presented in Egungun worship as the deity is believed to have reincarnated in the present spiritual head or leader. Spirit possession is also a form of reincarnation whereby humans are possessed by the spirits of their ancestors. The Egungun is known in Yoruba divinity as "Ara Orun" literally meaning "indigene of heaven," which is invoked by the Alapinni or the head/leadership of the cult after other rituals must have been observed for the ancestral spirit to possess the acolyte.[12]

The one possessed takes the demeanor and attitude of the ancestral spirit; the reincarnated persona speaks through the votary as other adherents pay homage and listen to him. Famule notes that as the ancestor reincarnation pertains to Egungun, upon the invocation of the spirits of the dead, especially through Odun Egungun (the ritual festival for Egungun), the ancestor(s) of the family lineage do manifest physically in the appearance of Egungun. Thus, not only is Odun Egungun an important form of ancestor veneration, it is also one of the many ritual devices that the Yoruba explore in order to provide a form (or tangibility) to their abstract, metaphysical or ontological concepts and ideas.[13] This belief in reincarnation is substantiated in the system of names and naming children from such families who practice this ATR: names like Babatunde (father has come again), Yetunde (mother is here again), Ojetunde (Oje is here again), Awotunde (Awo is here again), Awojide (Awo is awake again), Ifatomiwa (Ifa has come to me again) and Olojede (an Oje has come/returned).[14]

The belief in reincarnation of ancestral spirit also pervades other religious expressions of ATR in the Yoruba world. Some of these names may carry "baba" (father) and "yeye" (mother) prefixes added to the names such as Babajide (father is awake) and Yewande (mother has come back to me). Other professions like hunting also reflect the belief in reincarnation in their names, like Odewale (hunter has come home) and Odetunde (hunter has come again) Adherents of other deities like Ogun also belief in reincarnation and this is reflected in names like Ogunbiyi (Ogun birthed this) and Ogunwale (Ogun has come home). All these names reflect the significance of ancestral reincarnation in ATR and the knowledge of self-prefiguration in the next generation. The replication and continuation of ancestral legacy and spirit in the generations after them is also one of the knowledge inherent in this belief promoted by ATR.

Knowledge and Veneration of a Transcendental Being

Many of the African traditional religions possess and propagate the belief in the transcendental spirit at the center of the religion. This Supreme Being is the highest authority that the people believe in to assist them in both physical and spiritual matters. The belief that there is someone supreme who controls the affairs of the world is central to ATR. Myths are created to elaborate on the knowledge of the existence of the Supreme Being, who is the creator of the world. For instance, Yoruba myths about the creation story testify to the existence of Olodumare and his messengers (*orisa*) whom he sent to form the earth. These deities or divinities act as God's connection/link to humans. The divinities are representatives of God on earth through which the people can approach him. ATR is pluralistic in nature and so the different deities represent the many ways the Supreme God can be venerated.

Africans believe in the existence of a Supreme Being known by different names in different communities. This Supreme Being is the creator of all living things and phenomena and through which life force flows to humans.[15] African religious adherents espouse the belief in a supernatural being whose existence is divisible in the multiple dimensions of veneration in divinities and deified ancestors. There may not be a documentary script for African traditional religions; however, the core of their worship explores and expresses the sovereignty of a transcendental almighty God which is foregrounded in their ritual, rites, songs, ceremonies, festivals, proverbs and oral narratives and prayers. In their prayers, for instance, the supremacy of this almighty God is proclaimed and affirmed by adherents. They even compose songs, poetry, anecdotes and idioms to validate the existence of the Supreme God. The descriptions sometimes show that He is limitless and bigger than mortal comprehension. It is the reason there are several names and appellations to represent the image and essence of his greatness.

Ekeke and Ekeopara agree with this claim when they state that for a complete comprehension of the concept of God, the Supreme Being in Africa, the careful study of the entirety of the people's culture is important. The Supreme God in the African traditional religion is expressed not in the monistic frame but in the heterogeneous mediums of worship.[16] Ekeke and Ekeopara traced the origin of the belief in God and religion in Africa to the reflection of the universe—its formation and its creation by the Supreme God. The vastness of the world and its components remain a graphic confirmation of a powerful Supreme Being who is capable of establishing such a world and keeping it stabilized.[17] The reasons Ekeke and Ekeopara state that the recognition of God in Africa can be replicated for many African communities and for almost every human engagement with the idea of a supernatural force as the creator. However, the need for humans to account for their existence and nature may have informed the concept of God in Africans as with other people of the world. The absence of African traditional religious documents to support many of the claims makes this knowledge of a Supreme Being particularly African-centered.

Regarding the idea of God, a view has summarized it thus:

> Africans do not perceive of God as an abstract entity whose existence is in the mind. He is seen and perceived as a real personal entity whose help is sought in times of trouble and who is believed to be the protector of the people. The various names given to God in African attest to this. The fact that God is real to Africans is enshrined in the meaning of the name they call him. The Yoruba of Nigeria call God Olodumare or Edumere meaning "The King or Chief unique who holds the sceptre, wields authority and has the quality which is superlative in worth, and he is at the same time permanent, unchanging and reliable." Another Yoruba name for God is Olorun meaning "the owner of heaven" or "the Lord of heaven" showing God as the author of all things both visible and invisible.[18]

The argument put forward by Ekeke and Ekeopara that God is felt as a real personal entity by Africans is overstretched; what they may be trying to affirm is that Africans personalize the existence of God with things around and within them, which is more apt and reasonable than asserting that the African perspective of God is more real than that of any other religion. The names given to God by different groups and ethnic categories in Africa simply validates that God in Africa is personified with the reflective observation of their cosmology. Mbiti also concedes by stating that God comes into the picture as an explanation of man's contact with time. God is not pictured in an ethical relationship with man.[19]

The Belief in a Guardian Spirit

Another concept of knowledge prevalent in African traditional religion is the belief in a guardian—spirit or man's double.[20] The belief in a spirit or deity that assists humans in choosing the right direction and acts on the person's behalf is a knowledge that African people possess through their beliefs in ATR. Ekeke and Ekeopara further affirm:

> This spirit is known by many names in Africa. Yoruba people call it ori, Igbo people call it chi, while the Edo people call it ehi. It guards one's steps leading the one to his/her destiny in life. In most cases, it is this spirit that helps to wade off evil spirits that may want to derail the individual from achieving his ultimate in life. This is why most Africans will make sure they sacrifice and appease their

guardian—spirit whenever they want to take any important decision or they want to go on a journey.[21]

This thought system in African traditional religion is premised on the worship of this spirit-head and also recognizes the importance of this deity to the fate of the African people. For reference, take the Yoruba proverb, "Ori la ba bo, a ba fi orisa si le," meaning "the head-deity should be venerated instead of the divinities." This statement shows the pivotal knowledge and significance of the spirit in African traditional religion. This knowledge is applied to the circumstances the African people may experience in life; they take whatever circumstances that may happen to them as what their deity has chosen for them. This knowledge of the powerfulness of the deity permeates the actions, activities and expectations of the African people. The head-deity charts the course of the African people's lives and may be manipulated by malevolent forces if the individual's deity is weak and vulnerable. The spirit also defends the individual from imminent harm and danger posed to the deity's owner. This is why Africans sometimes invoke and pray to the head-deity to be vigilant and fend off attacks from malevolent forces like the witches.

Knowledge in Abiku

The question is not whether abiku is a myth but whether there is a mythical narrative supporting the existence of these beings and their significance in African traditional religion. In the Yoruba society, the belief in the supernatural power of an abiku child is generated from the knowledge that there are certain children born with mystic abilities of dying and being reborn by the same mother several times till they have been permanently confined to their spiritual abode never to plague the mother or they have been secured to the physical world of the living where they lead normal lives. There have been a lot of creative outputs on this particular mythical narrative. J.P. Clark, Wole Soyinka, Ben Okri and scores of other literary writers have produced works establishing the mythical and mystic displays of an abiku. The socio-cultural and religious knowledge that the myth of abiku has produced cannot be confined to a single page because of its literary and philosophical-cum religious characteristics.

KNOWLEDGE IN IFA LITERARY CORPUS

Ifa represents a body of knowledge which is premised on the wisdom inherent in the system of geomancy. In West Africa and among the Yoruba in particular, Ifa divination as a significant knowledge system and medium through which Orunmila communicates with the people is a familiar setting; so are divination stories.[22] Ifa is one of the plethora of African traditional religion among the Yoruba people of Southwest Nigeria. Ifa contains the literary corpus as well as the religious aspects which are interwoven. The Ifa literary corpus is known as the Odu Ifa which is about 256 in number, with innumerable sub-divisions of poetry verses named Ese Ifa. The Ifa literary corpus and the system of geomancy are knowledge which the people believe in for several pivotal reasons. The Ifa divination system is one of the oldest systems of knowledge of the Yoruba people which validates their history, beliefs, customs and tradition, culture, religion, ancestry and cosmology. Ifa divination system embodies knowledge of the Yoruba cosmic beliefs and thoughts system. Ifa is a system of geomancy, one of the divinatory techniques used by the Yoruba to gain knowledge of their complex cosmos and understand the intellectual configuration of the human universe. It is usually regarded as a process of pursuit of knowledge about the course of life and is consulted at successive stages in a person's life.[23] This system is believed to be a reliable method of enquiry and knowledge seeking way established on the foundation of truth and wisdom of the Yoruba people. Orunmila, also known as Ifa, is the originator of the Ifa divination system which is employed to gather knowledge about the metaphysical world.[24] The amount of knowledge resident in Ifa religion is very vast as it encompasses the field of medicine, philosophy, marriage, anthropology, ecology, economy, governance and leadership, among others. Ifa divination is an instrument in keeping the energy in balance and guiding the soul's successful movement through both realms of the sphere.[25] It is a compass for the Yoruba to channel their lives and journeys through the course of their earthly activities. Ifa divination is a site for African knowledge, through its intermediary medium of wisdom production to the Yoruba. These sources of knowledge in Ifa divination include akosejaiye, marriage enquiry, naming of child, coronation knowledge and so on. As it is a practice among the Yoruba to consult Ifa divination at the birth of a child, during the akosejaiye (or on stepping into the world) rite, the odu Ifa that emerges at such occasions are also taken as special symbols of such individuals.[26]

Akosejaiye refers to the ritual and ceremony performed during the birth of a child into a Yoruba family. This akosejaiye requires the babalawo/Ifa priest to divine, using the divination bead/chain, to inquire the child's destiny and what occupation or job s/he is to take up when s/he is older to be successful. In this process, the Ifa priest performs some rituals such as touching the baby's feet to the divination tray and consulting Ifa for advice or message on behalf of the child's parents. The transmission of Ifa knowledge such as the Ifa poetry (ese Ifa) is done orally from the Ifa priests, who is the trainer or custodian of knowledge, to the Ifa apprentice who also digests this oral material and commits it to memory until he becomes proficient enough to pass it down to the next initiate or trainee. Bello et al. also claim that this knowledge is usually transmitted from one generation to the next through traditional socialization processes by elders of indigenous communities.[27] While the observation of African knowledge transmission may be appropriate for some, it is, however, different for some ATR that are considered sacred and closed to the general public. Only initiates and male adherents may be allowed to receive instruction/training from the cult. In the case of Ifa, both men and women are allowed to perform and receive training from an older priest as there are babalawo and iyanifa or mamalawo, literally interpreted as "father of secret" for the male priest and "mother of secret" for the female custodian of Ifa. Unlike the inclusion of women as priestesses and custodians of the Ifa religion, Egungun leadership is taken up only by the male ordained elder in the family, group or community. Although women freely participate in other aspects of the religious activities in Egungun religion, like dancing, chanting and singing during the street tour and performance, they cannot claim a religious position in the cult.

The oral medium of transmitting Ifa poetry was the primary method of knowledge dissemination in the precolonial period; however, there is a gradual but slow progression from the oral transmission method to the digital format, which may include audio recording, videotaping, writing and the combination of all these forms as multimedia. Bello et al. argue that the dependence on the oral mode of African knowledge transmission, as in the case of Ifa and many others like it, is becoming obsolete, unreliable and unproductive in the sense that this knowledge becomes inconsistent due to human memory and comprehension, and also the inadequate capacity to transmit to many people and at a faster rate. The transmission medium for African traditional religion such as Ifa knowledge is imitation, observation, collaboration and recitation.

Taboos as Knowledge

African people believe in sacred laws and rules that regulate their relationship with other humans and deities. Taboos are systems of regulations which stabilize the activities of humans and their relationship with other fellow humans and also to their ancestors.[28] Taboos in African traditional religion are forms of knowledge and principles for containing human actions and frailties. As Omolewu explains:

> When one lacked an intellectual ability to impart the importance of some moral principles, taboos were a useful way of transmitting the same value from a different perspective. Those values, worded as taboos, were expressed at various occasions such as circumcision, marriage negotiations and funeral rites. It was an effective system of preventing and transmitting moral values, keeping in mind that traditional African culture was an oral one. Not only this, but taboos were also a means of social control and without them there would be chaos. The motivations for abiding by the normative principles are provided and reinforced by the religious sanctions from the gods and the ancestors or directly from the Supreme Being.[29]

Taboo is a knowledge system sustained by African traditional religion as a structure for keeping the society regulated. Unlike in the modern period where there are constitutions, rule of law, courts, justice system and law enforcement agencies, taboos represent the rule of law, constitution and justice system of the African people in the past. There are social-cultural taboos, religious taboos, health/sanitation taboos and socio-political taboos. All these types of taboos present the ingenuity and knowledge of the African people to generate rules that regulate human behavior and also appoint justice when they are contravened. These taboos are derived from the knowledge of sacred rules, religious edicts and principles of morality in African traditional religion.

Vocations as Sites of Knowledge

In African communities there are vocations and crafts that explore knowledge in ATR. In Yoruba traditional culture, as in other cultures of the world, the organization of religion and some professional guilds are cult-based. Each traditionally organized vocation has one *orisa* (god and goddesses) as patron. Ogun, the god of iron, is the patron of all those who make use of iron utensils. Diviners, especially babalawo (Ifa priests), worship Orunmila as their patron. Egungun is the deity patron of the eegun alare (masque dramatists) and Ayangalu is that of the drummers.[30] Occupations present a unique site of ATR knowledge where the belief in spiritual and ancestral worship can be explored in many African societies. The practice of pouring libation before the start of a craft at the place of work shows these crafts men and women's belief in paying homage to the divinities of their professions. Ogundeji avers that Ogun is primarily worshiped by the ode (hunters), ologun (warriors), alagbede (blacksmiths), oloola (human body artist/one who circumcises), gbenagbena (sculptors) and onisona (leather artist), including automobile mechanics and drivers in modern times.[31] The symbol of the deities is also placed in a strategic place in the workshop of the crafts men and women. For Ogun, a stump of iron is located in the crafts man house or workshop, symbolizing the continual worship of the deities at the center of their profession and to seek more favor for their business. These symbols and other iron instruments, taken also as Ogun's emblems, are employed in oath-taking, not only by members of the vocational guild but also by the Yoruba in general. For everyone under the suzerainty of Ogun, inasmuch as they use one type of iron implement or the other, even domestically, taking an oath or swearing using any of the emblems or iron instruments is considered swearing with or before Ogun, and it is believed that Ogun usually deals catastrophically with perjurers.[32] Other professions in African communities exhibit knowledge in ATR through the practice of their crafts and the carrying out of diverse rituals and rites to their patrons.

Knowledge in Medicine

African medical knowledge has been defined to "include varied health practices, approaches, knowledge and beliefs incorporating plant, animal and/or mineral based medicines, spiritual therapies, manual techniques and exercises applied singularly or in combination to maintain well-being, as well as to treat, diagnose or prevent illnesses."[33] There is traditional medical knowledge acquired from religion which is combined with herbs for treatment and diagnoses. Knowledge of traditional medicine may be esoteric as well as non-esoteric for the treatment of common and strange diseases and ailments. African traditional medicine is the practice, technique, tools and resources used for healing known and common ailments. The knowledge is usually transmitted orally and handled by African traditional religious heads, healers, pharmacists and herbalists, who may have been trained in both physical and spiritual aspects of indigenous medicine. These religious custodians of African knowledge apply their skills when they observe that their patients or clients suffer from a medical malady that can be treated through the use of herbs, concoctions, roots and drinks specially prepared for such ailment.[34]

The use of roots, herbs, plants, barks, stems, leaves and so on for the treatment of illnesses is also found in the knowledge about Ifa divination. When the Ifa priest is consulted by a client to decipher the cause of an ailment such as infertility, impotency, miscarriage or even stillbirth, the babalawo uses the divination bead to inquire the cause, reason and solution to the problem. The babalawo has combined the knowledge in religion with medicine to proffer a suitable remedy to the medical issue of the client. Again, this knowledge in religion may require the performance of sacrifice to a specific deity or divinity who may have inflicted diseases like smallpox, chicken pox, measles, epilepsy, migraine or even a simple ailment such as headache, diarrhea and fever. The solution may be split into two, the offering of sacrifice to the deity and the use of herbal medicine. There are healing practices that are culled from African knowledge and systematically used to cure diseases and illnesses. These practices are used by healers who may or may not be religious heads but they however need to ascertain if there is any malevolent force behind the sickness:

> One can argue that the non-esoteric aspect of African traditional medicine can be codified as it embodies no secret, while the esoteric aspect may not be codified as it is considered to be secret for a select few traditional healers.[35]

This argument seeks to state that there are aspects of knowledge of the traditional medicine which are open and can easily be codified while some are shrouded with the veil of secrecy of the cult, only open and accessible to initiates and may prove difficult for codification and dissemination. Masango states that the esoteric aspect of African medicine is exploited by traditional healers for livelihood as it is a specialty within their profession.[36] Traditional medical practices rely on African knowledge for their appropriation to certain ailments that physical treatment may be impossible to diagnose and treat. There is a relationship between the physical and spiritual realm in African knowledge reflected in indigenous medicine.

Invocation of spiritual forces and incantatory narratives are sometimes needed to perform religious and medical treatment for some unscientific issues.

The invocation becomes a spiritual medium for employing religious knowledge. The divinity or religious entity is summoned to provide a solution to the issue at hand. The invoked deity may require strings of offerings or ritual to be carried out for the problem to be resolved. The pouring of libation on the figure represents a totemic approach which is done prior to the call for help from the ancestral figure.

Modern medicine, as observed, has its base in African knowledge through the use of various plants and herbs such as gum Arabia famous for treating bronchitis, diarrhea, leprosy, typhoid fever and respiratory infection.[37] The presence of rich resources in plants and herbs of traditional African medicine is gradually being used in modern medicine to cure different types of ailments. There are herbal and non-herbal components in traditional African medicine which may be available to the public. Traditional medicine covers a range of different practices, resources, experiences, materials and wisdom which makes it a unique area of African traditional religious knowledge. The consultation of the divinity, as in Ifa divination, is a mystical knowledge which may not be subjected to empirical studies like Western medicine. Both the deployment of divination knowledge and the use of incantations as sources of ATR knowledge for the treatment of both physical and spiritual maladies are often common in African traditional medicine.

ATR Knowledge in Surgery

Surgery is another aspect of traditional medicine that is situated in African knowledge. Traditional healers include bonesetters, midwives, surgeons, herb sellers and herbalists. Traditional surgeons handle minor ailments that need surgery. These ailments may include boils, broken bones, circumcision for male children, facial and body markings. These traditional surgeons use different indigenous instruments to carry out medical issues that require their skills and knowledge. They also consult deities to ascertain the cause and treatment of the ailments and then perform the necessary actions. Circumcision of children in the precolonial age in many African communities required the services of these trained surgeons, and the performance of rituals and rites was paramount to the success of the circumcision. Mostly, this circumcision was carried out as a sign of the rites of passage in some African communities. Whether it was for social or spiritual purpose, traditional surgeons used their understanding and beliefs in African traditional religion when performing their services so as not to cause deaths or further injuries.

Knowledge in Incantations

Incantations are employment of cosmological knowledge, physical and metaphysical understanding of the world diffused through oral poetic narratives. African people know the value of words and the manipulation of the cosmology through incantatory poems derived from their practice and belief in its potency. The wisdom of diverse ecological, metaphysical, physical and extraterrestrial phenomena is combined in the making of incantations. Incantations present the hidden knowledge into focus while invoking the power in that knowledge to work for them. Incantations are oral texts exploring the sacred science of the African people in calling things into existence. African religious knowledge is diffused in bits in incantations; the knowledge of using words to create energies from oral codes to unlock and bring the cosmology to produce required results or effects for the performer. Incantations are like African science formulas for bringing sound wisdom of the spiritual forces subject to the performer's command and manipulation. It is in this regard that Soetan opines that there is a belief that every object has a secret name given by God before humans arbitrarily named things. Therefore, if one can decode the secret names of objects, he or she can command entities to do his or her bidding.[38] The use of incantations can perform actions such as disappearing acts, changing form from human to animal and vice versa, giving extraordinary strength and so on. In the example given below, the performer of this incantation binds the elements and nature of the animals to be transferred to him:

> A kii binu agbe t'oun t'aro,
> A kii binu aluko t'oun t'osun,
> A kii binu odidere t'oun t'ikoode,
> Araye, e ma binu mi o.
>
> No one hates the blue turaco in its blue hue,
> No one abhors the cuckoo bird with its beauty,
> No one dislikes the parrot with its colorful tail,
> May people never hate me.[39]

The performer of this incantation distills the knowledge that these animals are loved for their unique nature and so has commanded the unquestionable and unbiased affection given to these subjects be transferred unto him/her. This is one knowledge that can be learned from the belief in the potency of incantations as powerful vessels brewed from African traditional religion. The utilization of incantations is the drawing of knowledge from supernatural and physical resources in African religions. It is why Soetan avers that it is a thought process that shows a complete understanding of how elements function in the cosmos. It embodies scientific knowledge that is construed differently from modern-day chemistry and other orthodox wisdom.[40]

Charms as Powerful Knowledge

Knowledge from ATR is transposed into charms and amulets as sources of power and spiritual knowledge. Charms and amulets are some of the tools of African traditional knowledge evoked for various reasons. Charms represent technological knowledge and invention that distinguish Africans and their religions from Western wisdom. Serving utilitarian purposes, a charm is not in any way a satanic or demonic practice; instead, it is a symbolic code that speaks to both the terrestrial and the extraterrestrial forces.[41] This knowledge in African traditional religion is used in engineering actions such as protection from malevolent forces, dispelling bad fortunes and creating a better world for them. Charms are on their own knowledge because they can subvert the world order; they can manipulate, rearrange and create an alternate reality for the performer or user. A charm juxtaposes knowledge of the cosmos, a permutation of the elements to yield desired results, which may be sometimes represented through the use of amulets.[42]

> Charms are a byproduct of religion, and they allude to theological assumptions that connect other sacrificial rites. Their nuclei are composed of pantheon worship, notably Ifa divination. The ifa corpus contains the chronicles of the deities, people, and objects in anthropomorphic relationship. What charms do, in most cases, is allude to these anthropomorphic events. By doing so, charm ingredients transmogrify to bring about efficacy by animating the objects. It is this profound believe in primordial life that sustains the efficacy of charms and amulets in the culture.[43]

Charms are "technology" and wisdom used by the indigenous people for their civilization, security network, development, growth and production. Soetan states examples such as wealth portion (*oogun aje*), invisibility charm (*afeeri*), disappearance formula (*egbe*), bulletproof charms (*ayeta*) and coital bolt (*magun*). Others include antidotes (*aporo*), favor-induced charm (*eyonu*) and curative charms (*oogun ori fifo, inu rirun*).[44] This knowledge may be used during wars by warriors, used on farmlands and properties to prevent thieves or used by hunters for protection when in danger. Adejumo states that the use of charms is another form of security and protection in both traditional and contemporary Yoruba societies.[45] She further states that this kind of knowledge and technology as security is precipitated on the belief in the power of God.[46]

RITUAL AS KNOWLEDGE

Ritual is one of the demonstrative media of ATR knowledge in societies where the practices of ritual and rites are carried out for the propitiation of divinities. Rituals convey messages from humans to their deities as token of their devotion. Rituals are religious ceremonies and activities performed at the shrine or designated location of the divinity that is being invoked for a specific reason. Aderibigbe notes that, essentially, rituals constitute a major form of spirituality by which a person or community negotiates responsible relationships with other members of the community, other communities, their ancestors, the spiritual forces of nature, divinities and, ultimately, the Supreme Being.[47] In many African religions, ritual is an essential part of worship because it is the communication between different entities and forces. Ritual encodes the knowledge that humans can approach their deities and ancestors with offerings for the sustenance of a harmonious relationship. Balance between the physical, supernatural and metaphysical worlds is maintained through ritual practices. Rituals are performed for different reasons, one of which is the seeking for justice. Africans believe in the power of invoking their deities through ritual and sacrifices to seek justice against an offender. For example, Sango, the god of thunder, may be invoked through rituals and sacrifice to avenge a devotee who has been wrongfully cheated. This ritual may involve offering the taboo of the deity on behalf of the person the adherent is seeking justice. Sango who is known for his fiery temper and demeanor responds with thunder against the offender as justice until the offender makes restitution. This judicial knowledge invoked through ritual is one of the knowledge in ATR. Ritual becomes a medium for judicial appropriation in many African traditional religion system and societies.[48] Ritual as knowledge in ATR is a leveler of spaces between the deity and the performer of rituals.

THE BELIEF IN SACRIFICES AS A LINK TO THE DEITIES

The African people believe in the efficacy of ritual offerings and sacrifices to the deities and their God. These sacrifices and offerings are meant to invoke the deities for different reasons which include pacification of an aggrieved deity, invocation for blessings, economic gains and general enquiries. Sacrifices in the African setting and in ATR are essential as a mode of veneration just as the Western Christian religion has its own system of worship for the adherents. While there are different systems of worship in ATR, the belief in sacrifice as a link to invoke the deities is central to all types of African religions. Sacrifices may also be offered to other sub-categories of spirits and beings in the extraterrestrial world that possess power and may manipulate humans. Witches as powerful humans with metaphysical abilities are also appeased with sacrifices.

Sacrifice in African traditional religion is a practice that presents the knowledge of dual partnership between divinities and their human subjects. Sacrifices symbolize the expression of total dependence of humans on the supernatural.[49] Sacrifices include the offering of food substances, animals and other edibles such as kolanuts, palm oil, solid pap, snail, honey and alligator pepper; when it comes to the issue of death among the Ewes and some tribes in the northern region of Ghana, dogs or cats are sometimes buried alive at midnight to save the soul of the one at the point of death.[50] Aderibigbe also agrees to this claim as he states that the shedding of blood in ritual sacrifice precedes most ceremonies in which blessings are sought from the ancestors or divinities.[51] The significance of blood spilling, especially of the animal type, symbolizes the exchange of human life with that of the animal. The blood of animals killed during sacrifices may be sprinkled on the client or person for whom the ritual is being performed. The knowledge in sacrifices is the cleansing that the African people believe it possesses through the substitution of animal blood and lives for that of humans.

ATR Knowledge in Traditions and Customs

Traditions and customs of the African people contain moral and ethical codes for the veneration of the divinities through different systems of worship. There are aspects of African traditional religion that are encoded into the customs of the people to enhance a moral and stable society. For instance, taboos and superstitions are extracts from African traditional religion meant to prevent the community from harm, criminal activities and incurring harm or consequences from the deities. The African divinities are regarded as the conscience of the society as they regulate the norms, mores and activities in the society through edicts, warnings, messages and so on which are bound up by the communal rules of propriety. Some of the traditions of the people that contain ATR knowledge are rites of passage, marriage rites, burial/funeral rites and naming ceremony rites. Rites are pivotal practices in ATR which entail knowledge that are codified and transmitted to the next sets of generation through recreation.

Marriage rites and customs are aspects of ATR which are encoded for the progress and union of the couple. The rituals and ceremonies that are performed are religious and are meant to certify that the two people who are to be married are qualified and suitable for this stage. Initiation rites are also systems of knowledge established to pass on beliefs, practices and philosophy about life to the next generations of youths. Other forms of knowledge in ATR are burial rites and rites of passage carried out to propagate the belief in the afterlife, death as the ultimate leveler, transience of life, inevitability of death and so on.

Philosophies as Knowledge

> In philosophy, Western or African, logic and epistemology are very fundamental. They constitute the major branches of philosophy. They are concerned with the object and method of human knowledge. Remove knowledge, human life would be meaningless; any neglect on logic makes a particular claim to knowledge questionable and difficult for general acceptance. One thing to note is that without logic in epistemology, true or valid knowledge may not be attained.[52]

Philosophical sayings and views of the African people connote their knowledge and thought system gathered from their interaction with their divinities, their fellow human beings, their environments and space. Afolayan states also that a worldview is a philosophical attempt to grapple with the complexities of existence in a strange universe. Worldviews derive from many years and many experiences of pre-conceptually or pre-theoretically coming to terms with a mysterious universe and vicissitudes.[53] Africans have a very huge pile of epistemology sustained by African traditional religion.

The art of sound, correct and critical reasoning is in the domain of logic. Logic concerns itself with the proper method of reasoning. It distinguishes correct reasoning from incorrect reasoning; removes ambiguities and obscurities from human discourse. Logic brings out truth from falsity, consistency from inconsistency, orderliness from disorder, valid argument from invalid argument. Logic dissipates confusion that usually arises in our everyday discourse. It is logic that differentiates rational beings from irrational beings. The proper application of logic is what separates human beings from the lower animals.[54]

In African societies logic is at the core of their beliefs, thought system, views and actions, as the structure of their thoughts and epistemology are distinct, clear and coherent. The ability to process thoughts, test them and make logical conclusions has been expressly explored in African philosophy. Philosophies in African communities address issues of African epistemology such as critical reasoning of African worldviews, beliefs and thoughts.[55] All of these forms of knowledge are infused into the African philosophy which will be discussed below. From the careful evaluation and study of phenomena around them Africans make inferential conclusions and then philosophize based on this. One of this knowledge is expressed in the statement, "Igba o lo bi orere, aye o lo bi opa ibon," literally meaning "time is in cycles, and a lifetime is hardly a straight trail like the barrel of a gun." This philosophy has been a careful observation of time and year rotation. As Adeshina Afolayan points out:

> Yoruba philosophy, therefore, refers to the philosophical discourse—traditional and contemporary—on the aggregates of assumptions, principles, worldviews, and attitudes that have been deployed, interrogated, and refined over millennia of philosophical activities generated by the Yoruba confrontation with the universe, as well as their culture and existential predicament. In its traditional form, Yoruba philosophy represents the cumulative attempts by the Yoruba people to come to terms with the universe and their very existence with the cosmos. It refers to the vast array of ideas and beliefs—on person and personhood, morality, destiny, God, action, justice, equity and equality, knowledge, health, ultimate reality, the cosmos, and so on—by which the Yoruba have ordered their existence and understanding of life and the universe before the advent of colonialism.[56]

The metaphysics branch of philosophy of the Yoruba is situated in the ontology of predestination, which Afolayan states that it has three possibilities: *akunleyan* (the destiny chosen while kneeling down), *akunlegba* (the destiny received while kneeling down) and *ayanmo* (which combines the idea of choice and affixation).[57] The philosophy of the Yoruba about destiny states *ori* as the spirit who chooses the trajectory of a person's fate. However, this philosophy about destiny and the spirit *ori* presents *ori* as a personal deity. Afolayan notes that once *eniyan* (human) successfully transmits from a prenatal to a postnatal existence, the destiny is inaugurated and the individual is expected to navigate the human society while contending with the specific vicissitudes of the particular destiny chosen.[58] This philosophy about the ontology of destiny is drawn from the ATR about creation and its impact on human life. This philosophy is visible in this statement, *ori la ba bo, a ba f'orisa si le* (Ori ought to be venerated instead of the divinities), as it chooses the human's destiny and its trajectory.

Again, African people philosophize about morality through their understanding of African traditional religion. Character, for the Yoruba, is *iwa*. Character is placed by the Yoruba within ontological and aesthetic contexts. It is this root word that immediately ties *iwa* to *ewa* (beauty). *Iwa* and *ewa* could, in this sense, therefore, refer to "a mode of being."[59] "Iwa l'ewa omo eniyan" is a philosophical statement of the Yoruba that means "a good character is the beauty of a person." Afolayan concedes that a good character is akin to aesthetic reconfiguration of human sociation and upholds the cosmological equilibrium under Esu's charge.[60] The knowledge of a good character is a philosophical rendition of the principles of good behavior and morality in African traditional religion. This knowledge is circulated by every aspect of the African religions and passed onto the people by various beliefs and practices.

Notes

1. Nana Osei Bonsu, "African Traditional Religion: An Examination of Terminologies used for Describing the Indigenous Faith of African People, Using an Afrocentric aradigm," *The Journal of Pan African Studies*, Vol. 9, No. 9 (2016): 109.
2. John S. Mbiti, *African Religion and Philosophy* (London: Heinemann Educational Publishers, 1969).
3. TKdefs-FH19, Definitions of Traditional Knowledge-National Aboriginal forestry.org. http://nafaforestry.org/forest_home/documents/TKdefs-FH-19, 1.
4. Ibid., 2.
5. Ibid.
6. Ibid.
7. George J.S. Dei, "Indigenous African Knowledge Systems: Local Traditions of Sustainable Forestry," *Singapore Journal of Tropical Geography*, Vol. 14, No. 1 (1993): 28–41, 128.
8. D. Heibert and K. Van Rees, "Traditional Knowledge on Forestry Issues within the Prince Albert Grand Council," Draft. Prince Albert, SK: Prince Albert Model Forest, 1998, quoted in TKdefs-FH19, Definitions of Traditional Knowledge- National Aboriginal forestry.org. http://nafaforestry.org/forest_home/documents/TKdefs-FH-19, 3.
9. A. Brockman, B. Masuzumi and S. Augustine, When All Peoples Have the Same Story, Humans Will Cease to Exist. Protecting and Conserving Traditional Knowledge: A Report to the Biodiversity Convention Office. September 1997. Dene Cultural Institute. Quoted in "Definitions of Traditional Knowledge-National Aboriginal forestry.org, 1997. http://nafaforestry.org/forest_home/documents/TKdefs-FH-19", 3.
10. Mbiti, *African Religion and Philosophy*, 2.

11. World Intellectual Property Organization, Documenting Traditional Knowledge – A Toolkit, edited by Toby Boyd, 2017, 27. http://www.wipo.int/about-wipo/en/offices.
12. Olawole Famule, "Masks, Masque, and Masquerades," in *Culture and Customs of the Yoruba*, edited by Toyin Falola and Akintunde Akinyemi, (Austin, TX: Pan-African University Press), 2017, 394.
13. Ibid., 395.
14. Ibid.
15. Emeka C. Ekeke and Chike A. Ekeopara, "God, Divinities and Spirits in African Traditional Religious Ontology," *American Journal of Social and Management Sciences*, Vol. 1, No. 2 (2010): 209–218.
16. Ibid., 210.
17. Ibid., 210–211.
18. Ibid. 211.
19. Mbiti, *African Religion and Philosophy*, 4.
20. Ekeke and Ekeopara, "God, Divinities and Spirits in African Traditional Religious Ontology," 217.
21. Ibid.
22. Ademola O. Dasylva, "Folklore, Oral Traditions, and Oral Literature" in Falola and Akinyemi, eds., *Culture and Customs of the Yoruba*, 153.
23. Omotade Adegbindin, "Divinatory Systems" in Falola and Akinyemi, eds. *Culture and Customs of the Yoruba* (Austin, TX: Pan-African University Press), 2017, 364.
24. L. A. Bello, J. O. Kayode, Y. O. Ahmed, A. O. Adeyemo, and T. I. Yusuf, "The Management, Dissemination of Ifa Oracle and Egungun Festival for Knowledge Preservation and Promotion of African Cultural Heritage in Osun State, Nigeria," *Journal of Philosophy, Culture and Religion*, Vol. 43 (2019): 7–12.
25. Ibid., 8.
26. Ogundeji, "Signs, Symbols, and Symbolism," in Falola and Akinyemi, eds., *Culture and Customs of the Yoruba*, 272–273.
27. Bello et al., "The Management, Dissemination of Ifa Oracle and Egungun Festival for Knowledge Preservation and Promotion of African Cultural Heritage in Osun State, Nigeria," 8–9.
28. Ibid.
29. Olatubosun Christopher Omolewu, "Taboo" in Falola and Akinyemi, eds., *Culture and Customs of the Yoruba*, 448.
30. Ogundeji, "Signs, Symbols, and Symbolism," 270.
31. Ibid.
32. Ibid.
33. Charles Akwe Masango, "Indigenous Knowledge Codification of African Traditional Medicine: Inhibited by Status Quo Based on Secrecy?" 2019, Information Development (2019): 1–12, DOI: 10.1177/0266666919853007 journals.sagepub.com/home/idv.
34. Peter White, "The Concept of Diseases and Health Care in African Traditional Religion in Ghana," HTS Teologiese Studies/Theological Studies Vol. 71, No. 3 (2015): Art, 2.
35. Masango, "Indigenous Knowledge Codification of African Traditional Medicine," 2.
36. Ibid.

37. Fawzi M. Mahomoodally, "Traditional Medicines in Africa: An Appraisal of Ten Potent African Medicinal Plants," *Evidence-Based Complementary and Alternative Medicine* (2013): 1–14.
38. Segun Soetan, "Charms and Amulets," in Falola and Akinyemi, eds., *Culture and Customs of the Yoruba*, 227–235.
39. Ibid., 230.
40. Ibid, 235.
41. Soetan, "Charms and Amulets," 228.
42. Ibid.
43. Ibid., 229.
44. Ibid., 232.
45. Arinpe G. Adejumo, "Security and Protection," in Falola and Akinyemi, eds., *Culture and Customs of the Yoruba*, 865–876.
46. Ibid.
47. Aderibigbe, "Ritual and Sacrifice," in Falola and Akinyemi, eds., *Culture and Customs of the Yoruba*, 327.
48. Peter White, "The Concept of Diseases and Health Care in African Traditional Religion in Ghana," *HTS Teologiese Studies/Theological Studies*, Vol. 71, No. 3 (2015): Art. #2762, 1–7.
49. Ibid., 329.
50. White, "The Concept of Diseases and Health Care in African Traditional Religion in Ghana," 3.
51. Ibigbolade, 329.
52. Ejikemeuwa J.O. Ndunuisi, "Nature and Function of Logic in African Epistemology," *Journal of Humanities and Social Science* (IOSR-JHSS) Vol. 19, No. 11 (2014): 32.
53. Adeshina Afolayan, "From the Cosmos to the Society: Worldview as/and Philosophy" in Falola and Akinyemi, eds., *Culture and Customs of the Yoruba*, 877.
54. Ndubuisi, "Nature and Function of Logic in African Epistemology," 32.
55. Ibid., 33.
56. Afolayan, "From the Cosmos to the Society," 879.
57. Ibid., 883.
58. Ibid.
59. Ibid., 886.
60. Ibid.

CHAPTER 40

Gnostic and Epistemological Themes in African Traditional Religion

Marcus L. Harvey

INTRODUCTION

By the late 1970s, the category "African Traditional Religion" had gained steam in a discursive environment whose growth was fomented by eighteenth- and nineteenth-century Eurocentric beliefs about African "primitives" held by eminent European intellectuals. A common axiom tying these beliefs together was that "there is nothing to be learned from 'them' [Africans] unless it is already 'ours' ['Europeans'] or comes from 'us.'"[1] This form of reasoning undergirded, for example, conservative British statesman and former Prime Minister Arthur James Balfour's imperialist attitude toward "oriental" Egypt in a controversial 1910 parliamentary lecture, an attitude reflected in the belief that "British knowledge of Egypt *is* Egypt."[2] It may come as no surprise then that, 60 years later, Ugandan social critic Okot P'Bitek concluded that "Western scholars have never been genuinely interested in African religions *per se*. Their works have all been part and parcel of some controversy or debate in the Western world."[3]

Whether we agree with P'Bitek or not, the study of African Traditional Religion from a gnostic or epistemological perspective is a fraught enterprise. It resists Hume's and Kant's shared insistence upon useful, morally grounded African knowledge being an impossibility, stubbornly forcing the question of what knowledge *is*—or what it means to *know*—from within an African

M. L. Harvey (✉)
University of North Carolina, Asheville, NC, USA
e-mail: mharvey1@unca.edu

© The Author(s), under exclusive license to Springer Nature Switzerland AG 2022
I. S. Aderibigbe, T. Falola (eds.), *The Palgrave Handbook of African Traditional Religion*, https://doi.org/10.1007/978-3-030-89500-6_40

religious frame of reference embedded both in the ancestral African past and in the so-called modern, contemporary present.[4] So if, as Foucault suggests, distinct sociocultural conditions make possible the creation of diverse ideas, knowledges, theories, and philosophies, what, then, are the conditions that enable traditional (or indigenous) African religious *gnosis*, or *knowing*? How is *knowing* understood from a traditional African religious perspective? What is the relationship of such *knowing* to contemporary modernity?[5] It seems reasonable to ask the latter question when we consider Latour's theorization of modernity as a complex state of affairs that "comes in as many versions as there are thinkers or journalists" while simultaneously pointing to "the passage of time," a "new regime," and a contentious, "revolutionary rupture in time" where there are "modern winners" and "ancient losers."[6] Engagement of this question is buttressed as well by a growing interest among scholars across disciplines in African, transcultural, and global modernities.[7] This question, along with the others just posed, represents the basic concerns of this chapter.

I should also note that the ensuing analysis takes its cue from the phenomenology of religion and places a heavy emphasis on epistemology. Thus, my approach to African traditional religious knowing bears interpretive proximity to studies like Opoku's *West African Traditional Religion* and Bockie's *Death and the Invisible Powers*. As signaled in Mudimbe's *The Invention of Africa*, a landmark work that raises epistemological questions regarding our understanding of African people groups, traditions, and thought-worlds, the language of *gnosis*, from the Greek *gnosko* ("to know"), can be useful to discussions of African epistemology given its association with "seeking to know, inquiry, methods of knowing, investigation, and … acquaintance with someone."[8] Even more important, terms found in the Akan (southern Ghana), Yorùbá (southwestern Nigeria), and Dagara (southwestern Burkina Faso) lexicons such as *ebisadze* ("to ascertain or inquire" through divination, a "mystical"—or "gnostic"—technology utilized by trained priests [*akomfo*] to establish materially effective communication with the spiritual world), *Ifá* (a name assigned to the divinity of knowledge and wisdom in the Yorùbá tradition, to a vast body of knowledge concentrated in the Ifá literary corpus [*Odù Ifá*], the sacred oral text of Yorùbá religion, and to a core divination system known as *Ifá dídá*), and *yielbongura* ("the thing that *knowledge* cannot eat") invite scholarly attention to African Traditional Religion at the level of knowledge.[9]

And yet the scope of this chapter is guided by Opoku's admonition that the "central reality" of African Traditional Religion cannot be presented in any text, for "the reality of this religion … defies adequate objectification, and remains a mystery."[10] My argument, then, is that a contemporary *sense* of what it means to *know* within a traditional African religious environment can be established through attention to two themes that emerge upon a general consideration of cosmological details shared across a variety of African people groups followed by a more focused examination of oral religious discourse, primarily Akan proverbs with spiritual implications or references. Two themes are highlighted in the proverbs: 1) knowing as an elusive yet adaptable relationship with spirit requiring constant interplay between the ancestral African past and the immediate present; 2) knowing as a moral crucible. We shall begin our elucidation of these themes by first making several broad observations about traditional African religious cosmologies.

Traditional African Religious Cosmologies

Cosmologies encompass interwoven narratives, ideas, and practices that organize peoples' understanding of "the universe in space and time and the place of human beings in it."[11] Such accounts—or theories—of reality are found in abundance among the several thousand people groups that comprise the nearly 12-million-square-mile African continent. In virtually every case, one encounters a theory taking one form or another that understands the physical world via the spiritual world in ways that have bearing on the two themes that frame my epistemological analysis. However, we must be vigilant to avoid characterizing the African cosmologies as homogeneous in nature. They are each in their own complex way distinct, often with ample room for regional and internal variation, disagreement, and debate.

For instance, while ancestral spirits play a key role in the religious cosmologies of many African societies, it would be misleading to suggest that this importance is always the same in degree. The cosmologies associated with the Akan, Yorùbá, and Mende societies accord profound importance to the ancestors—physically deceased persons who once lived in the corporeal world but now inhabit the spiritual realm in a custodial capacity, having met—as adults—certain ethical standards instituted by tradition. From an African point of view, the ethical life is defined by successful ritual passage into adulthood, the honoring of all ritual and family obligations, fidelity to the "social responsibilities of protecting and preserving societal secrets" and taboos, productivity, and overall good character, to name only a few criteria.[12] Within these societies, ancestors can be interpreted as wise, demanding spiritual presences who wield great power in the interest of protecting the aforementioned ethical standards and the traditions that support them, even if doing so requires the punishment of wayward living descendants. The same is true for the Ndembu of Zambia and many other groups.[13]

In contrast, the Zande of the Democratic Republic of the Congo (DRC) regard ancestral spirits as far less useful, placing more emphasis on a sharp distinction between "internal and external powers."[14] If we think of ancestral spirits as mediators, by which I mean that their activity impacts the bi-directional relationship between the corporeal and incorporeal worlds, then what surfaces in our discussion of the status of these spirits in Akan, Yorùbá, Mende, and Ndembu cosmology as compared to their status in Zande cosmology is an incongruence. To cite one more example, although the cosmology of the Zulus of KwaZulu-Natal Province in South Africa shares much in common with that of the Yansi of Kinshasa in the DRC, Zulu cosmology nonetheless involves different mediational spirits that coincide with the Southern Bantu social system.[15] As indicated by this example and the work of researchers like Augé, African cosmologies interact with and adapt to "historical change, diffusion, and local variations."[16] Far from being abstract, ahistorical inventions with no significant connection to social life, African cosmologies provide traditional yet malleable anchors that ground African communities in an orienting sense of identity and spiritual affiliation as they negotiate contemporary modernities.

Keeping in mind the adaptable heterogeneity, nuance, and meaning-making function of African cosmologies, it is also helpful to recognize two generally shared theoretical characteristics before treating the two central themes that afford a glimpse into the thought-worlds of African Traditional Religion. To be sure, more than two characteristics could be identified herein.[17] However, the selected characteristics discussed below, though not intended to yield a comprehensive understanding, nevertheless acquaint us with some of the key fundaments of African cosmology while remaining sensitive to space constraints.

One theoretical characteristic typifying African cosmology has to do with a particular ontological understanding of the corporeal and incorporeal worlds. According to this understanding, the incorporeal world is the matrix of the corporeal world, meaning that spirit, or rather the powerful, vivifying agency of spiritual beings, is the source from which all matter and life spring. In an African frame of reference, spiritual agency is the precondition not only for the very existence of matter itself, but also for the imagination thereof.[18] The spiritual and material worlds, therefore, exist together in an inextricable relationship wherein each side facilitates varying degrees of intelligibility for the other. Notwithstanding these degrees of intelligibility, the relationship that makes them possible is not necessarily perceptible to the average person who lacks the requisite initiation and training. For both the initiated and the uninitiated, African cosmologies enjoin disciplined engagement of the spiritual world as a means of addressing immediate issues (illness, familial ruptures, obstacles to success, wider social conflict and upheaval, etc.) *now*.[19] As Opoku's earlier-cited statement suggests, the formless goal of intellectually mastering spiritual reality, an evanescent, fluid reality that escapes the full human grasp, does not at all factor into the epistemological calculus of the traditional African religious imagination.[20] Thus, initiation and training are not guarantors that the deeper mysteries of spiritual engagement will someday be *fully* unraveled.

In the Yorùbá tradition, where, like in many other African religious traditions, we find mythic origin narratives explaining how the earth, humans, and the natural world came into existence, we also find within the same narratives an awareness of the limits of what can be known about the relationship between the corporeal and incorporeal domains, even by the *òrìṣà* (deities) themselves. Connected to one narrative detailing how *Olódùmarè* (the chief Yorùbá deity and "sole giver of life") attempted to effect the creation of the earth through the agency of *Ọbàtálá* (the eldest òrìṣà who, due to drunkenness, has this prestigious responsibility taken from him by his opportunistic brother *Odùduwà*), a five-toed hen, and a pigeon is a story about Ọbàtálá later growing envious of the knowledge Olódùmarè possesses as the giver of life. Ọbàtálá, therefore, hatches a scheme to spy on Olódùmarè in order to learn the secret of bestowing human life to lifeless forms. However, not to be outmaneuvered, Olódùmarè knows of Ọbàtálá's shifty scheme (by this point Olódùmarè had recommissioned Ọbàtálá as the molder of human forms into which Olódùmarè would infuse quickening breath [èmí]) and foils it by causing him to fall asleep just before witnessing the spiritual mechanics involved in the bestowal of human life.[21] A moral epistemological principle we might glean from this story is that *complete* knowledge of the relationship between corporeality and incorporeality belongs to no one. In the story, Ọbàtálá seeks a level of knowledge higher than the level allotted him by Olódùmarè and in so doing violates this principle. Ọbàtálá's epistemological humility is sternly tested by a selfish desire to possess, or master, knowledge never intended for him. He fails this crucible, and as a result is directed through forced slumber to realize the importance of holding his desire at bay by exercising moral discipline.

A second theoretical characteristic of African cosmologies lies at the heart of the first, namely, the belief that the incorporeal realm is populated by a diverse community of potent spirits. Often associated with natural objects such as the earth, large rocks, trees, forests, rivers, and oceans, protective spirits are usually communally "owned," while spirits whose power can be used to heal or harm tend to be individually "owned," sometimes in the form of "medicine."[22] The categorical names of protective spirits, including ancestors, vary among cosmologies and people groups. The Akan speak of the *tete abosom*, the Yorùbá of the *òrìṣà*, and the Dagara of the *kontombili*, whereas the Ewe of Ghana and Togo use the term *togbuitrowo*.[23] Furthermore, the Akan use the title *nsamanfo* for the ancestors, the Yorùbá use *egún*, and the Ewe use *togbui*.[24] Harmful spirits are known by the Akan as *bosom brafoɔ*, by the Yorùbá as *ajogun ibi*, by the Ewe as *dzositrowo*, and by the Manianga of Lower DRC as *mpeve zambi*.[25]

Most African cosmologies hold that human beings should cultivate strong, durable relationships on a communal and individual basis with specific spirits. But why, and to what purpose? African cosmologies acknowledge, whether plainly or tacitly, that the universe human beings inhabit is essentially entropic and hence volatile and unpredictable. In other words, the very context that makes human life possible is defined at the most elemental level by unremitting danger, not safety, nor certainty. This understanding informs, for example, the Dagara society's perspective on the indispensable role of exposure to potentially lethal physical and spiritual danger during Baor, a transformative initiatory rite undertaken by adolescent Dagara boys in order to become adult men. An explanation given by Malidoma Somé's father in response to his son's desire to know more about Baor prior to experiencing it is illustrative of the above perspective: "Knowing Baor will not protect you ... You cannot want Baor and protection at the same time. ... Protection is toxic to the person being safeguarded. ... When you protect something, the thing you are keeping safe decays. People come into this life with a purpose that enables them to protect themselves."[26]

Importantly, from an African purview, the main purpose of spiritual relationship is not solely protection. Rather, the aim is to provide human beings with the ancestral self-knowledge, wisdom, and power needed to effectively—but not always safely—pursue a meaningful life and thereby gain the "three blessings of a good life—*ìre owó*, *ìre ọmọ*, and *ìre àláàfíà* (wealth, children, and long life)."[27] Governed to a significant extent by the felt agency of incorporeal beings and ancestral presences, the spiritual world (*òrun*) is a dynamic reservoir of insight and power that, through disciplined relationship, can be accessed and "worked" toward the goals of survival and human flourishing.[28] The technical divinatory process of tapping into this dynamic reservoir involves a dialectical interplay between, on one hand, the spiritual realm attested by past ancestral belief (*ìgbàgbọ́*) and custom (*àṣà*, which, interestingly, can connote both the "traditional" and the "modern"), and, on the other hand, the perilous vicissitudes of the present.[29] This brings us to the next phase of our analysis, where we shall explore several examples of oral religious discourse in view of our thematic focus.

Oral Religious Discourse and African Epistemology

This phase of analysis treats Akan aphorismal statements as religiously pitched oral discourse. Moreover, the analysis rests upon the assumption that such statements embed epistemological reflection. Proverbs thus emerge for our purposes as data points that allow a look at the apparatus of thought underpinning African Traditional Religion.

In our previous discussion of Yorùbá creation myths, we were acquainted with the story of Ọbàtálá, who, despite the powerful status afforded by his senior rank among the òrìṣà, sought knowledge to which his rank did not entitle him. The knowledge Ọbàtálá wanted was the exclusive domain of Olódùmarè and, as such, was unavailable to him. It slipped Ọbàtálá's grasp even though his trickery was designed to ensnare it for his benefit. This outcome may be unexpected given the scope of Ọbàtálá's guile. However, there is a proverb in the Yorùbá tradition that may render the failure of Ọbàtálá's stratagem inevitable. It states, *Ìsé Olódùmarè, àwámárídí* ("Olódùmarè's action is unfathomable").[30] If Olódùmarè's actions are "unfathomable," then they are not—indeed cannot be—objects of knowledge. This is to say that Olódùmarè's actions are not available for mastery by any intellect, regardless of whether the intellect belongs to a human being or an òrìṣà. "Ìsé Olódùmarè, àwámárídí" suggests that, for the Yorùbá, knowing at its highest level is arcane, opaque, and achievable only by Olódùmarè himself. To put the matter in metaphorical terms, the taller the vine of knowing grows—the existence of which is made possible by vital relationships with Olódùmarè (think of the limits placed on Ọbàtálá's knowing capacity through his relationship to Olódùmarè's authority) as well as among the òrìṣà and their human devotees—the more the attainability of knowledge recedes from view. Knowing, and therefore knowledge itself, is ultimately elusive.

A degree of epistemological continuity along this line can also be found in the Akan tradition. The following proverbs are important to consider here: *Obi nnim a, ɛyɛ nyansakyerɛ* ("'No one knows,' is to profess wisdom"); *Obi nnim adekyeɛ mu asɛm* ("No one knows what the morning will provide"); *Onipa adwene nyɛ Onyame adwene* ("A person's mind is not the mind of Onyame" [*Onyame* being the principal Akan deity]); *Ɔbosom na ɛkyerɛ ɔkomfoɔ ntwaho* ("It is the spirit that teaches the priest to whirl around"); and *Ɔbosomfoɔ anom asɛm nsa da* ("A priest's advice is never exhausted").[31]

What can be made of the phrase *Obi nnim* ("No one knows") in the first two proverbs? If we think of "knowing" as a relative ontological condition, then the phrase takes knowing out of the hands of any single individual ("No *one* knows"). Implicit in this phrase is the idea that knowing exists in the human world only as a shared, relational condition. Conversely, the inability to reduce knowing to any single subjectivity is also common to the human condition. Hence, knowing in both of these senses is a kind of thread that tethers human beings together.

And, according to the first proverb, from an awareness of the insurmountable riddle of "knowing" comes wisdom, an experience-forged keenness of judgment that transcends knowing. So when the Akan utter the second proverb, *Obi nnim adekyeɛ mu asɛm* ("No one knows what the morning will provide"), what is being conveyed is not so much an expression of ignorance as it is a wise acceptance of the limitations of human beings' knowing and of the fact that the operation of the world around us is not entirely within our control. "The morning" will provide *something*, but humans do not always know nor determine what that something is. Why is this the case? Much like the Yorùbá, the Akan understand the spiritual realm (*asamando*) to be the primary fulcrum that turns the machinery of our present reality, not natural law or human agency alone.[32] As the fulcrum of reality in its current iteration, the spiritual realm does not divulge its mysteries to satisfy the curiosity of the intellect. While the spiritual realm may stand at a proximal epistemological distance from the reach of the human mind, it stands at a distance nonetheless. This is why the Akan aver that the human mind is not that of Onyame.

Still, it must be understood as well that the spiritual domain over which Onyame presides does not exist merely to delimit human beings' knowing and agency. It also serves as a vital fund of knowledge needed for the guidance of human life. Comprehending this, many Akan priests (*akɔmfo*) undergo extensive training in the practice of mediumship (*akom*), wherein a deity will temporarily manifest through or "alight" (*nsie-yee*) on a priest's body in order to deliver important messages to the wider community.[33] Such is the context for the proverb, *Ɔbosom na ɛkyerɛ ɔkomfoɔ ntwaho* ("It is the spirit that *teaches [emphasis added]* the priest to whirl around"). A paradox presents itself upon interpreting this proverb: spirit at once eludes *and* teaches. Put otherwise, although mysterious, the centuries-old spiritual reality of the ancestors nevertheless teaches the priest to be a vessel of spiritual knowledge, but not just any vessel. The Akan insist that "[a] priest's advice is never exhausted" (*Ɔbosomfoɔ anom asɛm nsa da*). If priestly advice is inexhaustible, then the priest must be a *relevant, adaptable* vessel of spiritual knowledge who can speak to the changing demands of the times in ways that effectively direct human action. Ergo, for the Akan, spiritual knowing, or religious *gnosis*, is not imprisoned in the past. To the contrary, it perforce keeps pace with the rhythms of time via divinatory rituals, the fecund nexus point enabling ongoing interplay between the past and the present. Along with the weighty responsibility of *akom*, Akan priests, as gnostic vessels, also shoulder a moral burden articulated in the second and final theme to be considered—knowing as a moral crucible.

The next few proverbs invite reflection on the morality of "religious knowing" in Akan society. They include *Adeɛ yɛ yie bebrebe a, na ato ne sɛɛ* ("If something flourishes too much, it begins to spoil"); *Tumi dodoɔ yɛ gyimi* ("Too much power leads to stupidity"); *Wopɛ sɛ wohunu nneɛma nyinaa a, w'ani fura* ("If you want to see everything, you become blind"); and *Ɔbosom a ɔnkasa na yɛto no aboɔ* ("It is the spirit that does not talk that we throw stones at").[34]

Most things are capable of flourishing in some way. Religious gnosis is no different in this respect. In fact, as discussed earlier, religious gnosis is linked to the blessings of wealth, children, and long life, three goals toward which African Traditional Religion strives. Why, then, do the Akan warn that "[i]f something flourishes too much, it begins to spoil" (*Adeɛ yɛ yie bebrebe a, na ato ne sɛɛ*)? Concerning religious gnosis, I would posit that this admonition is motivated by an acute awareness that religious gnosis is a potentially volatile form of power whose use must be governed by a firm discipline grounded in the moral values of the community. To imagine one example, a priest's demonstrated proclivity for selfish excess in his use of spiritual knowledge would be regarded as an *immoral* proclivity indicative of a lack of proper discipline and as a grave threat to the well-being of the community. The priest in this example would be seen as having failed the moral crucible of responsibly carrying the burden placed upon him by religious gnosis. His standing as a trustworthy epistemological vessel in the community would be diminished, if not annulled.

Lastly, another related dimension of the moral responsibility accompanying religious gnosis involves sharing. The knowledge given to human communities by spiritual beings through the body of a priest is not intended to be privately hoarded, but rather distributed for human benefit. Spiritual knowledge usually extends itself as needed, often withdrawing only in the absence of a proper vessel for transmission. The Akan priest is thus expected to openly communicate on behalf of a spirit; indeed, she has a moral obligation to do so. This is why the Akan say, "It is the spirit that does not talk that we throw stones at" (*Ɔbosom a ɔnkasa na yɛto no aboɔ*). While the priest is a mouthpiece (*ɔkyeame*) through which religious gnosis flows, the gnosis itself remains an invaluable *community* asset.[35] A pressing question the Akan priest never escapes is, "Can you communicate ancestral religious gnosis in a manner relevant to and useful for the present moment?" It is toward this moral epistemological goal that she must daily struggle.

Conclusion

At its most basic level, the analysis developed herein puts forward African *thought* as a channel of insight into the phenomenon dubbed "African Traditional Religion." Furthermore, both African thought and African Traditional Religion are seen as being in conversation with late modernity rather than in opposition to it. Even so, we must avoid the notion that African societies have not created ideas and religio-philosophical traditions that perdure over time in stable patterns that are distinguishable from those of modern Euro-Western epistemes. African Traditional Religion presents us with an opportunity to fundamentally reimagine our understanding of what it means to "know." What is at stake in mustering the courage to embrace this opportunity is an epistemological future inclusive of, and consequently deepened by, African religious gnosis.

Notes

1. V. Y. Mudimbe, *The Invention of Africa: Gnosis, Philosophy, and the Order of Knowledge* (Bloomington: Indiana University Press, 1988), 15.
2. Edward W. Said, *Orientalism* (New York: Vintage Books, 1979), 32.
3. Okot P'Bitek, *Decolonizing African Religions: A Short History of African Religions in Western Scholarship*, rev. ed. (New York: Diasporic Africa Press, 2011), 1.
4. See, for instance, David Hume, "Of National Characters," in *Essays: Moral, Political, Literary*, eds. T. H. Green and T. H. Grose, vol. 1 (London: Longmans, Green, and Co., 1875), 244–257; Immanuel Kant, *Observations on the Feeling of the Beautiful and Sublime*, trans. John T. Goldthwait (Berkeley: University of California Press, 1960), 97–116.
5. Michel Foucault, *The Order of Things: An Archaeology of the Human Sciences* (New York: Vintage Books, 1994), xxi–xxii.
6. Bruno Latour, *We Have Never Been Modern*, trans. Catherine Porter (Cambridge: Harvard University Press, 1993), 10.
7. Some examples include P. Mungwini, "'Surveillance and Cultural Panopticism': Situating Foucault in African Modernities," *South African Journal of Philosophy* vol. 31, no. 2 (2012): 340–353; Elisabeth Bekers, Sissy Helff, and Daniela Merolla, eds., *Transcultural Modernities: Narrating Africa in Europe* (Amsterdam: Rodopi, 2009); Mike Featherstone, Scott Lash, and Roland Robertson, *Global Modernities* (London: SAGE Publications, 1995).
8. Mudimbe, *The Invention of Africa*, ix.
9. Anthony Ephirim-Donkor, "Akom: The Ultimate Mediumship Experience among the Akan," *Journal of the American Academy of Religion* vol. 76, no. 1 (2008): 60, 71; Kọ́lá Abímbọ́lá, *Yorùbá Culture: A Philosophical Account* (Birmingham, UK: Iroko Academic Publishers, 2006), 47; Malidoma Somé, *Of Water and the Spirit: Ritual, Magic, and Initiation in the Life of an African Shaman* (New York: Penguin Books, 1994), 8. My conceptualization of African divination practices as "mystical technologies" stems from Dianne Stewart's original use of the term several years ago during a phone conversation. For one

of the most comprehensive studies on an African divination system, see William R. Bascom, *Ifá Divination: Communication Between Gods and Men in West Africa* (Bloomington: Indiana University Press, 1991).

10. Kofi Asare Opoku, *West African Traditional Religion* (Accra: FEP International Private Limited, 1978), preface.
11. Wyatt MacGaffey, "The Cultural Tradition of the African Forests," in *Insight and Artistry in African Divination*, ed. John Pemberton III (Washington, D.C.: Smithsonian Institution Press, 2000), 17.
12. Anthony Ephirim-Donkor, *African Spirituality: On Becoming Ancestors*, rev. ed. (Lanham, MD: University Press of America, 2011), 115; For the Yorùbá, good character is a "conglomeration of principles of moral conduct." See Abímbọ́lá, *Yorùbá Culture*, 84–86.
13. MacGaffey, "The Cultural Tradition of the African Forests," 19.
14. Ibid.
15. Ibid.
16. Ibid. See Marc Augé, *Théorie des Pouvoirs et Idéologie: Étude de Cas en Côte d'Ivoire* (Paris: Hermann, 1975).
17. Dianne Stewart lists six "foundational characteristics of continental African religions" that are relevant to my analysis: "(1) a communotheistic (as opposed to a monotheistic or polytheistic) understanding of the Divine, which corresponds with a community of venerated deities and invisible beings; (2) ancestral veneration; (3) possession trance and mediumship; (4) food offerings and animal sacrifice; (5) divination and herbalism; and (6) an entrenched belief in neutral mystical power." Dianne M. Stewart, *Three Eyes for the Journey: African Dimensions of the Jamaican Religious Experience* (New York: Oxford University Press, 2005), 24.
18. Although much broader in scope with a focus on the violence and creativity of diasporic Atlanticization, the work of James Noel comes to mind. See James Noel, *Black Religion and the Imagination of Matter in the Atlantic World* (New York: Palgrave Macmillan, 2009).
19. For an excellent study showcasing the centrality of healing in the practical repertoires of continental and diasporic African spiritual systems, see Kyrah Malika Daniels, "The Undressing of Two Sacred Healing Bundles: Curative Arts of the Black Atlantic in Haiti and Ancient Kongo," *Journal of Africana Religions* vol. 1, no. 3 (2013): 416–429.
20. Somé fittingly uses the word "liquid" to describe the knowledge accessed during the Dagara initiatory rite of Baor. See Somé, *Of Water and the Spirit*, 203–204.
21. Abímbọ́lá, *Yorùbá Culture: A Philosophical Account*, 80; E. Bọ́lájí Idòwú, *Olódùmarè: God in Yorùbá Belief* (London: Longmans, 1962), 18–32.
22. Opoku, *West African Traditional Religion*, 55–65.
23. Ibid., 55; Somé, *Of Water and the Spirit*, 15.
24. Kwame Gyekye, *An Essay on African Philosophical Thought: The Akan Conceptual Scheme*, rev. ed. (Philadelphia, PA: Temple University Press, 1995), 68; Jacob Olúpọ̀nà's discussion of the Odùduwà Festival—Odùduwà being the first god-king and founder of the sacred Yorùbá city of Ilé-Ifẹ̀ and the progenitor of the Yorùbá people—and *Egúngún*, the Yorùbá ancestral lineage masquerades, is instructive. See Jacob K. Olúpọ̀nà, *City of 201 Gods: Ilé-Ifẹ̀ in Time, Space, and the Imagination* (Berkeley: University of California Press, 2011), 229–248.

25. Opoku, *West African Traditional Religion*, 56; Abímbọ́lá, *Yorùbá Culture: A Philosophical Account*, 49; Simon Bockie, *Death and the Invisible Powers: The World of Kongo Belief* (Bloomington: Indiana University Press, 1993), 64.
26. Somé, *Of Water and the Spirit*, 180. For more on Baor, see Chapters 14–25.
27. Olúpọ̀nà, *City of 201 Gods*, 87.
28. The Yorùbá word *ọ̀run* subdivides the spiritual world into three "regions": *ọ̀run-òkè* ("heaven"-above), *ọ̀run-odò* ("heaven"-below), and *ọ̀run-àpáàdì* ("'heaven-of-broken-pots'—i.e., the region of the supernatural world into which 'souls' that committed egregious immoral acts are banished"). Abímbọ́lá, *Yorùbá Culture: A Philosophical Account*, 131. I am also reminded here of Joseph Murphy's use of the concept of "working the spirit" in his analysis of African-derived and Black Atlantic religious traditions. See Joseph M. Murphy, *Working the Spirit: Ceremonies of the African Diaspora* (Boston, MA: Beacon Press, 1994).
29. Olúpọ̀nà, *City of 201 Gods*, 87; Olabiyi Babalola Yai, "In Praise of Metonymy: The Concepts of 'Tradition' and 'Creativity'" in the *Transmission of Yorùbá Artistry over Time and Space, Research in African Literatures* vol. 24, no. 4 (1993): 36.
30. Babatunde Lawal, "Èjìwàpò: The Dialectics of Twoness in Yorùbá Art and Culture," *African Arts* vol. 41, no. 1 (2008): 38.
31. Peggy Appiah, Kwame Anthony Appiah, and Ivor Agyeman-Duah, *Bu Me Bɛ: Proverbs of the Akans* (Banbury: Ayebia Clarke Limited, 2007), 39, 62–63, 201.
32. Gyekye, *An Essay on African Philosophical Thought*, 86.
33. Ephirim-Donkor, "Akom: The Ultimate Mediumship Experience among the Akan," 65.
34. Appiah, Appiah, and Agyeman-Duah, *Bu Me Bɛ*, 88, 283, 225, 61.
35. John Pobee, "Aspects of African Traditional Religion," *Sociological Analysis* 37, no. 1 (1976): 11.

CHAPTER 41

African Traditional Religion in African and African Diaspora Scholarship

Raymond Ogunade and Olorunfemi Dada

INTRODUCTION

This chapter examines the works of some African scholars on some issues such as no written scripture, the right name for the indigenous African belief system, appropriate methods for the study of the religion, and the evolutionary stages of African Traditional Religion (ATR). The second sub-heading discusses some peculiar issues in the African Diaspora scholarship of ATR. The chapter uses more instances from the Yorùbá belief system than other cultures. It is germane to state that the African scholars of ATR in Africa and the Diaspora have contributed to the resuscitation and globalization of ATR through research publications, meaning that religion is not a subject of study for only the Europeans. Hence, this chapter considers some of these publications as they pertain to the issues cited earlier.

AFRICAN TRADITIONAL RELIGION IN AFRICAN SCHOLARSHIP

Sacred scripture is a crucial source of reference for religious knowledge and the study of religion, but ATR has no written sacred scripture. Mbiti[1] identifies this as one of the challenges that make the study of ATR difficult. The lack of any written scripture makes it worthwhile for scholars to study ATR epistemologically through existing literature and ontologically through fieldwork because, in the first place, all human history started from oral traditions. Hence, oral traditions are "the only means of knowing anything at all of the peoples'

R. Ogunade (✉) • O. Dada
University of Ilorin, Ilorin, Nigeria

© The Author(s), under exclusive license to Springer Nature Switzerland AG 2022
I. S. Aderibigbe, T. Falola (eds.), *The Palgrave Handbook of African Traditional Religion*, https://doi.org/10.1007/978-3-030-89500-6_41

interpretation of the universe and the supersensible world, and what they think and believe about the relationship between the two."[2] In turn, it means that religion should be studied by studying the adherents of the religion. African Traditional Religion, according to Jonathan Draper and Kenneth Mtata,[3] "is not only oral in its orientation; it is essentially performative and communal." The written scripture depends on human beings to perform what is written through communal existence and ritual expressions in society.

The peoples' performance or expression exists in dance, songs, the sound of drums, hunting, farming, trading, and traditional leadership patterns, expressions of myths, proverbs, eulogies, adages, arts and crafts, riddles, wise sayings, symbols and emblems in sacred spots, paintings, moldings, carvings, sculptures, and indigenous names of people. These are the sources of information on or means to study ATR. The performative styles of the oral traditions are passed from one generation to another to ensure their continuity, but by implication, the oration of ATR points to the fluidity and non-static nature of the religion. Nevertheless, the unavailability of sacred scripture is still an issue in the study of ATR. It is commendable that African scholars of ATR acknowledge that the religion has no written sacred scripture, and they have supplied ways of knowing the religion. Still, mainly, they are yet to state why there is no written scripture for the religion which people can easily consult. Critical minds would like to know, perhaps, the fact that the religion has no written scripture is premised on the reality that the religion has no founder. Or, is it because of the religious varieties, the existence of many languages, traditions, and cultures? Is it a command from God that there should not be any written scripture or Africans depend solely on oration, or they are not lettered, even in their indigenous language, or they do not see the need for it?

The varieties of indigenous religious forms, languages, and traditions in Africa may make the writing of a single sacred scripture difficult. This can be overcome by applying the cultural area style postulated by Friday Mbon[4] as a viable method to approach the study of ATR. This approach requires each African scholar of ATR to concentrate or study a particular locality due to the vastness of the African society and to avoid over-generalization. The aspect of methodology as discussed by African scholars will be highlighted later, but with regard to the questions above, it appears to us that many localities in Africa do not see the need for any written document before now, and this makes African traditions to be easily eroded by Westernization and foreign religions. For instance, we had interactions with Wande Abimbola on December 17, 2019, in Oyo. Among other things he said, it was a big surprise to us that in the year 2000, United Nations Educational, Scientific and Cultural Organization (UNESCO) asked nations to present their oral and intangible heritage for assessment, but the Nigerian Government said there was nothing to present for such purpose. This implies that many Africans, just as many African scholars agree, only remember and patronize ATR for a solution when the solution is not forthcoming through their foreign religions.

The point is that the unavailability of the written document of the religion is a straight path for the religion to go into extinction.[5] Therefore, some African and non-African scholars and practitioners such as Wande Abimbola recognize and address this issue thus:

> Many widely known scholars, including Professors William Bascom and Wande Abimbola, among others, have documented sections of Ifa corpus from the early 40's. Professor Wande Abimbola initially documented some Ifa chapters in the Yorùbá language, but after some years, he also wrote some Ifa chapters in the English language. His writings aided the mobility of Ifa messages across cultures and provided the tool for an academic consideration of Ifa as a body of scientific knowledge and philosophy. Since the efforts of Professor Wande Abimbola, other scholars and practitioners of Ifa have documented different aspects of Ifa corpus. A current effort worth mentioning is the ongoing work on the *Iwe Odu Ifa* (Book on the chapters of Ifa) by the International Association of Ifa Practitioners. Their efforts at the documentation of Ifa have aided the spread of Yorùbá religion in an unprecedented dimension. One of the consequences of the documentation of Ifa is the conversion of non-Africans in the Diaspora into Yorùbá religion. This contact of Ifa with non-Yorùbá adherents produced significant developments, which include the adoption of Ifa as an intangible heritage of UNESCO on 25th of November 2005 and the contact between Ifa and the internet.[6]

In addition to the above, this led to the establishment of the Ifá Heritage Institute, Oyo, in 2008 by Wande Abimbola through the partial support of UNESCO. This is a good step since Ifá is the foundation of every Yorùbá traditional practice.[7] Furthermore, Ojebode and Awonusi[8] showcase how Christian practices were indigenized into Ifá worship in Sagamu and Ogere, Ogun State, by making use of a pulpit in the temple for officiating ministers, a lectern where the Book of Holy Corpus is placed and read, ministers and choirs wear robes, and worshippers sing hymns for the procession into the temple with an altar boy; they use local and foreign musical instruments such as keyboards, guitars, drum sets, gongs, and traditional drums. They collect offerings and conduct Sunday services, among other practices. These efforts are done to modernize the traditional religion to encourage youths. However, it should be noted that the documentation of Ifá corpus cannot serve and represent other religious traditions in Africa. In this case, it may be more convenient to apply regionalism in naming the religion based on the individual culture area. This will definitely place a question mark on whether the name of the religion should be African Traditional Religion and to know the origin of the term "religion" in Africa.

Currently, there exist disputes regarding the appropriate name for the religion. However, it is worthy of mentioning that the term "religion" is foreign to Africans and its adoption as a term for African traditions is a colonial production[9] through the effort of the academic anthropologists which the colonial masters appointed right from 1908 to supply information on African societies.[10] According to Jacob Olupona,[11] "the word religion is problematic for many Africans, because it suggests that religion is separate from the other aspects of one's culture, society, or environment. But for many Africans, religion can never be separated from all these. It is a way of life, and it can never be separated from the public sphere. Religion informs everything in Traditional African Society, including political art, marriage, health, diet, dress, economics, and death." Consequently, Idowu[12] recognized the fact that the term "African Traditional Religion" can only be used tentatively in the study of the African belief system. This opens room for different scholars to use different names depending on their personal interests and perspectives. The names include African indigenous religion (AIR), African Religion (AR), African Religions (ARs), African Traditional Religion (ATR), African Traditional Religions (ATRs), African System of Thought, and Primal Heritage, among others. Dopamu[13] reports that Parrinder and Mbiti make use of both African Traditional Religion and African Religion, while he (Dopamu) uses the term African Religion (*Afrel* and the adherents are the Afrelists). Mbon[14] holds that African beliefs and practices should be tagged African Traditional Religions due to the many tribes, languages, and traditions in Africa and to acknowledge these, rather than the title African Traditional Religion which will not show the varieties in the religion. The common trend among scholars of ATR is the use of ATR, ATRs, or *Afrel*, and to state the scope of the study in the body of the research work. In some cases, some scholars prefer to specify the culture area at the title stage with the term religion, for instance, Yorùbá Religion, with the acronym *Yorel* and *Yorelian* for the adherent,[15] Edo Religion, Akan Religion, and Igbo Religion, among others.

It is clear that the title African Traditional Religion or *Afrel* is mostly used by some scholars to connect all adherents of the traditional beliefs and practices in Africa, regardless of their cultural areas, just as the terms "Christianity" and "Islam" serve the same purpose and put ATR on the same rank with these foreign religions with a single name. But other scholars believe that the use of the term ATR will lead to over-generalization. In all cases, whether it is African Traditional Religion or African Traditional Religions, African Religion, or African Religions, the validity of any study on African beliefs and practices is a matter of approach or methodology adopted for that particular study. Methodology or approach, as avers by Mbon,[16] is "the most contentious and thorny sets of issues in contemporary academic debate in the study of religion." The question of what should be the appropriate methodology for the study of ATR still lingers to date among the African scholars of ATR, and a meaningful study of ATR is impossible without an appropriate methodology, which can enable scholars to treat ATR as holistic as it is. The efforts of the early African scholars of ATR were geared toward seeking ways to make ATR be religiously conformed to other World Religions. They sought to correct the wrong nomenclatures, ATR as fetishism, polytheism, juju, ancestral worship, the high God, the withdrawn God, paganism, heathenism, and animism, among others, attached to ATR by some foreign scholars who examined ATR as an object rather than as a subject and make the religion comparable to other religions, but this makes them less concerned about the issue of the methodology of the study of ATR. According to Danfulani and Danfulani,[17] this anxious act leads to "oversimplification of the nature and structure of rituals, symbols and practices of African Traditional Religion, thus glossing over their diversities and complexities." The early African scholars made a Western interpretation of ATR since many of them are African Christian theologians, African Nationalists writers, and pre-independent writers, and many of them were trained by the colonials.[18]

Early African scholars such as Bolaji Idowu and John Mbiti were criticized by Okot p'Bitek for attempting to Hellenize the African belief in God by qualifying Him with the Judeo-Christian concept of God as being omnipresent, eternal, omniscience, and omnipotent, among others.[19] Danfulani and Danfulani further note that these scholars used "African deities as mercenaries in foreign battles"[20] to show that the Africans knew God or had the concept of God before the coming of the missionaries to preach Christianity. These scholars had good intentions, but their approach may be questionable to Okot p'Bitek. It is certain that they were motivated by seeing the need to protect African traditions and adopt existing Western concepts as a template since ATR studies were at the infancy stage then. They will be right in making use of the deities to argue the religiosity of the African people since the deities are the key objective phenomena or representatives of God in ATR. But as Cox[21] reports on the critique by Okot p'Bitek, it will be wrong to accord the attributes of being omnipotent, eternal, omniscience, and omnipresent to the deities, which they have not done. However, contemporary African scholars of ATR such as Wotogbe-Weneka Wellington, Olademo Oyeronke, Orimoogunje Oladele, Laguda Danoye-Oguntola, Ogungile David, Aderibigbe Ibigbolade, and Kalu Ogbu, among others, stand to correct this.[22] In other words, two religions, for example, Hinduism and Sikhism, Islam and Sikhism, Judaism and Christianity, may appear similar, but each still retains its distinction/identity and should be studied distinctively with appropriate methodology.

Attempts at Appropriate Methodology for the Study of ATR

What then is the appropriate method for the study of African Traditional Religion? Danfulani and Danfulani[23] recommend a multi-disciplinary, poly-methodological, or multi-dimensional approach which employs the historical, anthropological, and phenomenological methods and is a more practical approach to the study of African Traditional Religion. This seems to be different from Droogers' interpretative approach, rather than the observable one. This approach should involve discursive and critical narratives that are embedded in sharper and historical consciousness.

It is however important to point out that whichever approaches are adopted, the rationale for them must be based on concrete fieldwork. This should provide the right foundation for embarking on the study in the first place. Thus, the application of the above methods and approach will enhance the scientific study of ATR. In addition to that, since African spirituality is holistic, ATR "must be sought in the everyday, not in some category of special or bounded activities"[24] because the religion involves every day and every experience, social object and institution, and practice. It is appealing to close our discussion on the appropriate methodology for the study of ATR with the three divisions of ATR in African scholarship by Onunwa.[25] The first is the African Nationalists writers, the second is pre-independent writers, and the third is the African Christian scholars. We need to add a fourth division: the African religious adherents-scholars (they write on ATR and practice the religion), where people like Wande Abimbola, Tony Menelik Van Der Meer, and Ifayemi Elebuibon, among others, with practical information on ATR should be placed. The scholarship of these scholars at different periods, coupled with the activities of some early foreign scholars, means that ATR had passed through stages. There are six stages; the first three were identified by Idowu, and the last three by Dopamu, which are identified briefly below.

The first period is the era of ignorance and false certainty or stories about Africans and their religion. The second dispensation is the time of doubt and resisted illumination when the assumption of the stay-at-home investigators was debunked by some scholars. The third stage is the period of an intellectual dilemma on whether to accept that the Africans have a conception of God.[26] Fourth, this is the period of spiritual edification when African Christian scholars or theologians started to study ATR. The next period is a time of hypocrisy when some Christians and Muslims patronized ATR religious specialists, diviners, and herbalists secretly but condemned the religion publicly. Africans are proud of their traditions in the last period, tagged as a period of cultural pride and reformation.[27] These periods are relevant to the study of ATR, but ATR is currently in the period of modernization and impact. The scholars of ATR, at this contemporary time, treat and advance ATR as a model for other religions. For example, Edward,[28] in his work titled "Indigenous African Traditions as Models for Theorizing Religion," makes use of the ethical and moral requirements that a diviner in African societies must possess and the social order or communal life in Africa as a model for theorizing religions. We remember that Soyinka[29] also showcases the tolerance and cooperation among Yorùbá divinities as a model for other religions in Nigeria. Tolerance and cooperation also exist among the devotees of different divinities in the sense that they celebrate festivals together. The devotees of Sango, for instance, never see the devotees of other divinities as inferior or fight or have mistrust toward one another due to the diversity in their traditional religion. This period is a season when scholars of ATR often present the impact of the religion on national development through its moral, ethical, social, and spiritual values and teachings. This is seen in many African scholars' works such as Mbon's[30] "African Traditional Socio-Religious Ethics and National Development," Alamu's[31] "Traditional Religion, Sacred Places and Sustainability in Africa: The Role and Contribution of Sacred

Places in Nigeria," and Dada's[32] "Harnessing Traditional Yorùbá Communal Values and Ideas for Self-Reliance and Development."

In another sense, the period of modernization and impact is marked by the use of technological devices to preserve and propagate ATR. This includes the digitalization of Ifá, as reported by Olajubu,[33] uploading of African Traditional Religious festivals, rituals, songs, and dances among others on the internet, YouTube, Nairaland, and Facebook, among others, in Africa and Diaspora. For instance, Brandon[34] notes that Africans in the Diaspora have approximately 160 Internet websites dedicated to different aspects of Yorùbá Religion in the United States. Olajubu[35] highlights some websites which are devoted to the Yorùbá Religion—www.theancestralcall.com, www.orisa.org, www.ifainc.org, www.yorubareligion.org, www.ifacollege.com, www.ifafoundation.org, www.orisareligion.com, www.ileorunmila.com, and www.ifaspiritualmarrket.com. This current development shows that ATR has moved from local to global and from global to virtual through the internet.[36] Therefore, consultations, interactions, and trading of spiritual items can be done through non-physical means.

Further, the formalizing of *Ifá* education is visible in this period when students of the *Ifá* Heritage Institute, Oyo in Oyo State, Nigeria, undergo courses in *Ifá* studies, languages such as Yorùbá, French, Portuguese, and Spanish, traditional medicine and technology, and performing arts. The modernization also occurs in this period through individuals and governments' recognition that African sacred spots such as rivers, mountains, hills, forests, and lakes can also be used for tourism for the social and economic development of the society. The era of modernization of ATR has its positive and negative sides, which has not been considerably studied by African scholars; hence, it should be a central focus in contemporary academic discourse.

African Traditional Religion in African Diaspora Scholarship

The issues discussed so far are related to, and obtainable in, the African Diaspora coupled with some peculiar issues in the Diaspora. The peculiar issues, as addressed in some African Diaspora scholarship, will be examined in this section. The existence of ATR in the Diaspora is the result of the Atlantic Slave Trade in which from "1616 to 1863, about two million Africans were taken into slavery to Americas from the Bight of Benin, with about 600,000 to Brazil, 200,000 to St. Dominque while Cuba had 111,000 and Jamaica 75,000, out of which many were of Yorùbá origin."[37] The fact that the majority of these slaves had a Yorùbá origin makes it easy for ATR to exist under a common name, generally as *Orisha* religion in the Diaspora and specifically as *Santeria* in Cuba, *Voodoo* in Haiti, *Hoodoo* in the United States, and *Candomblé* in Brazil.

The religion was established in the new world by the slaves pretending to have been converted to Catholicism and then combining their African religious experience with the host community's Christian religious expression to form a new identity in a multi-racial context society.[38] They feigned their conversion by equating Catholic saints to African divinities, and thereby, the day of veneration for each saint would be the day of worship of the divinity. For instance, *Sango* was venerated as St. John; *Sopona/Shakpana* as St. Jerome or St. Francis; *Orisala/Orishala* as St. Benedict; *Oya* as St. Catherine; and *Amanja/Omanja* (*Yemaja*) as St. Anne in Trinidad.[39] In the course of this event, Orisha traditions went through denigration and discrimination from the host countries. But they lived in the imagination of the experience of the homeland without fear of discrimination and suppression.[40] Further, the expression of this imaged identity through African culture and spirituality, and Christianism is a method employed by Africans in the Diaspora to resist the suppression from the host communities.[41] The Orisha (divinity) religion, in the processes of time and space, is a global religious practice in Cuba, Brazil, the United States, Trinidad, and other countries.[42] It is apparent that ATR in the Diaspora is a blend of African traditions and Western culture.

The contact between African and Western cultures, according to Murphy,[43] may have had a negative influence on the African peoples' value for communal life and changed it to individualism. The spirit and community interaction is prominent in African invisible-visible relationships, but in the Western religious space, the interaction is between spirit and individual; it is a matter of personal experience which is encouraged by the use of the internet in modern times. Technology makes it possible for an individual to be in isolation and have consultations on the net and via telephone and fax messages. Hence, the individual may choose to interact with only one person or a few people. Although interaction can take place on the internet and reduces the stress and expenses of traveling a thousand miles, this activity will limit the religious exposure of the individual since ATR is performative and communal in nature. Also, people who wish to patronize *Ifá* priests and buy religious items on the internet are liable to be scammed because many traditional religious sites are porously monitored.[44] The issue of scams in ATR also exists in physical consultations, and this is why a functioning regulatory body should be put in place to regulate the activities of traditional religious specialists in Africa and the Diaspora.

Other peculiar issues are identified by Van Der Meer under three sub-headings: dilemmas, controversies, and challenges facing the practitioners of ATR in the Diaspora. These three sub-headings will be put together as peculiar issues facing ATR devotees in the Diaspora. The first issue concerns the unavailability of a conducive environment or sacred spaces such as rocks, rivers, forests, hills, and mountains for the performance of rituals and sacrifices in the United States.[45] Second, Van Der Meer reports that some *Ifá* priests in the United States do recite *Ifá* verses from an *Ifá* book or the internet during consultations, which is against Yorùbá's *Ifá* priest oration.[46] Again, there is a quandary on whether the verses should be basically recited in the Yorùbá language or the English language. He holds that the Yorùbá language is essential to *Ifá* practice and rituals to ensure and sustain its efficacy, and well knowledgeable Yorùbá *Ifá* priests who still understand English are necessary to solve this problem.[47] However, the paucity of these priests is another problem. Lastly, the remaining issues are the huge amount of money charged for *Ifá* initiation in the United States, which makes *Ifá* initiation out of reach for the poor, and controversies over women's and Europeans' involvement in *Ifá* cults as specialists, and some Europeans as scholars of the religion.[48] The resistance to the initiation and exposure of the traditional religious knowledge to the White population are premised on African slavery and racial experience in the foreign land. However, Van Der Meer supports the participation of women and White people in *Ifá* cult and scholarship and that the Orisha religious practice should be made open to people.[49] These issues point to the fact that African Traditional Religion is dynamic and should be studied at regular intervals. Consequently, journals of ATR or association of the study or scholars of ATR should be created for research visibility and interconnectivity or networking in Africa and the Diaspora.

Notes

1. John S. Mbiti, *African Religion and Philosophy* (London: Heinemann Educational Books Inc., 1969), 4.
2. J. O. Awolalu and P. A. Dopamu. *West African Traditional Religion* (Lagos: Macmillan, 2005), 30.
3. Jonathan A. Draper and Kenneth Mtata, "Orality, Literature, and African Religions." In Bongmba, E. K., ed., *The Wiley-Blackwell Companion to African Religions* (Chichester: John Wiley and Sons Publication, 2012), 98.
4. Friday Mbon. "Some Methodological Issues in the Academic Study of West African Traditional Religions." In Platvoet, J., Cox, J., and Olupona, J., eds., *The Study of Religions in Africa: Past, Present and Prospects* (Cambridge: Roots and Branches, 1996), 176.
5. Lere Adeyemi. "Traditional Religious Festivals and Modernity in Mobaland, Ekiti State, Nigeria." In Y. O. Imam et al., eds., *Religion and Human Capital Development: Essays in Honour of Prof. Yasir Anjola Quadri* (Ilorin: Department of Religions, 2017), 297.
6. Oyeronke Olajubu, "The Documentation and Propagation of the Corpus and the Challenge of Modern Information Technology: The Internet as a Focus." *Orita: Ibadan Journal of Religious Studies* vol. XXXVIII, no. 1 & 2 (June and December 2006): 156.
7. Yekeen Ajíbádé Àjàyí, *Yorùbá Cosmology and Aesthetics: The Culture Confluence of Divination, Incantation and Drum-Talking, The Ninetieth Inaugural Lecture* (Ilorin: University of Ilorin Press, 2009), 8.
8. Ojebode, A., and Awonusi, F., "Modernization of Extra-Mundane Communication among Ifa Worshippers: A Rebuttal of the Neo-Secularization Thesis?" *African Notes* vol. 40, no. 1 & 2, (2016): 68–79.
9. Edward P. Antonio. "Indigenous African Traditions as Models for Theorizing Religion." In Richard, K., *Religion, Theory, Critique, Classic and Contemporary Approaches and Methodologies* (New York: Columbia University Press, 2017), 148.

10. Jan G. Platvoet. "From Object to Subject: A History of the Study of the Religions of Africa." In Platvoet, J., Cox, J., and Olupona, J., eds., *The Study of Religions in Africa: Past, Present and Prospects* (Cambridge: Roots and Branches, 1996), 109.
11. Jacob Olupona, "The Spirituality of Africa," The Harvard Gazette, October 6, 2015. https://news.harvard.edu/gazette/story/2015/10/the-spirituality-of-africa/ (accessed November 6, 2020).
12. Platvoet, "From Object to Subject," 124.
13. Dopamu, P. A., "African Religion in Nigerian Society: Past, Present and Future." In Abubakre et al., eds., *Studies in Religious Understanding in Nigeria* (Ilorin: Christy-David Printer, 1993), 239.
14. Mbon, "Some Methodological Issues in the Academic Study of West African Traditional Religions," 176.
15. R. O. Ogunade, "The Resilience and Challenges of Yorùbá Religious Worship in Modern Context," in Munyaradzi, M., et al., eds., *The African Conundrum: Rethinking the Trajectories of Historical, Cultural, Philosophical and Development Experiences of Africa* (Mankon: Langaa Research and Publishing CIG, 2017), 97.
16. Mbon, "Some Methodological Issues in the Academic Study of West African Traditional Religions," 172.
17. C. Danfulani, and Umar Habila Dadem Danfulani, "Methodology of and Problems Encountered in the Study of African Traditional Religion," *Journal of Religion and Culture* vol. 19 no. 1 (2019): 1.
18. James L. Cox, "Methodological Views on African Religions." In Elias Kifon Bongmba, ed., *The Wiley-Blackwell Companion to African Religions* (Chichester: John Wiley and Sons Publication, 2012), 35.
19. Danfulani and Danfulani, "Methodology of and Problems...," 4.
20. Ibid.
21. Cox, "Methodological Views on African Religions," 34.
22. Ibid., 38.
23. Danfulani and Danfulani, "Methodology of and Problems...," 10.
24. Antonio, "Indigenous African Traditions as Models for Theorizing Religion," 150.
25. U. R. Onunwa, "African Traditional Religion in African Scholarship." In E. M. Uka, ed., *Readings in African Traditional Religion: Structure, Meaning, Relevance, Future* (Frankfurt am Main: Peter Lang, 1991), 110–115.
26. E. Bolaji Idowu. *African Traditional Religion* (London: SCM Press, 1973), 89–92.
27. Dopamu, "African Religion in Nigerian Society," 241–245.
28. Antonio, "Indigenous African Traditions as Models for Theorizing Religion," 147–153.
29. Wole Soyinka. "The Tolerant Gods." In Jacob K. Olupona and Terry Rey, eds., *Òrìsà Devotion as World Religion: The Globalization of Yorùbá Religions Culture* (Madison, WI: University of Wisconsin Press, 2008), 31–50.
30. Friday M. Mbon, "African Traditional Socio-Religious Ethics and National Development." In Jacob K. Olupona, ed., *African Traditional Religions in Contemporary Society* (Minnesota: Paragon House, 1991), 101–108.
31. A. G. Alamu, "Traditional Religion, Sacred Places and Sustainability in Africa: The Role and Contribution of Sacred Places in Nigeria." In Munyaradzi Mawere and Samuel Awuah-Nyamkye, eds., *Harnessing Cultural Capital for*

Sustainability: A Pan Africanist Perspective (Mankon: Langaa Research and Publishing CIG, 2015), 174–175.

32. A. O. Dada, "Harnessing Traditional Yorùbá Communal Values and Ideas for Self-Reliance and Development." *Orita: Ibadan Journal of Religious Studies* vol. XLI no. 2 (December 2009): 34–45.
33. Olajubu, "The Documentation and Propagation of the Corpus and the Challenge of Modern Information Technology," 153–166.
34. George E. Brandon, "From Oral to Digital: Rethinking the Transmission of Tradition in Yorùbá Religion," In Jacob K. Olupona and Terry Rey, eds., *Òrìsà Devotion as World Religion: The Globalization of Yorùbá Religions Culture* (Madison, WI: University of Wisconsin Press, 2008), 463–464.
35. Olajubu, "The Documentation and Propagation of the Corpus...," 155.
36. Joseph M. Murphy, "Òrìsà Traditions and the Internet Diaspora," In Jacob K. Olupona and Terry Rey, eds., *Òrìsà Devotion as World Religion: The Globalization of Yorùbá Religions Culture* (Madison, WI: University of Wisconsin Press, 2008), 471.
37. A. Salawu, "Yorùbá Gods in Exile: Implication for Translation," *Orita: Ibadan Journal of Religious Studies* vol. XLVII, no. 1 & 2 (June and December 2015): 158.
38. Dianne Marie Stewart Diakete, "Orisha Traditions in the West," In David O. Ogungbile, ed., *African Indigenous Religious Traditions in Local and Global Contexts: Perspectives on Nigeria.* (Lagos: Malthouse Press, 2015), 340; Salawu, "Yorùbá Gods in Exile," 173.
39. Salawu, "Yorùbá Gods in Exile," 173.
40. David O. Ogungbile, "Borderless Homeland: Memory, Identity and the Spiritual Experience of an African Diaspora Community," In David O. Ogungbile, ed., *African Indigenous Religious Traditions in Local and Global Contexts: Perspectives on Nigeria* (Lagos: Malthouse Press, 2015), 410.
41. Diakete, "Orisha Traditions in the West," 339.
42. Jacob K. Olupona and Terry Rey, "Introduction," In Jacob K. Olupona and Terry Rey, eds., *Òrìsà Devotion as World Religion: The Globalization of Yorùbá Religious Culture* (Madison, WI: University of Wisconsin Press, 2008), 3–8. Also see Olabiyi Babalola Yai, "Yorùbá Religion and Globalization: Some Reflections," In Olupona, J. K., and Rey, T. eds. *Òrìsà Devotion as World Religion: The Globalization of Yorùbá Religious Culture* (Madison, WI: University of Wisconsin Press, 2008), 233–246.
43. Murphy, "Òrìsà Traditions and the Internet Diaspora," 479.
44. Olajubu, O., "The Documentation and Propagation of the Corpus...," 159.
45. Tony Van Der Meer, "Dilemmas, Controversies and Challenges of African Descendant Ifa Priest and Practitioners in the United States: Some Reflections," In David O. Ogungbile, ed., *African Indigenous Religious Traditions in Local and Global Contexts: Perspectives on Nigeria* (Lagos: Malthouse Press, 2015), 357.
46. Van Der Meer, T. M. "Dilemmas, Controversies and Challenges," 358.
47. Ibid.
48. Ibid., 358–360.
49. Ibid.

CHAPTER 42

African Traditional Religion in Global Scholarship

Toyin Falola

The predominant challenges encountered in the global scholarship of African religion bother on the ethical and methodological approaches employed in the process. Ethical questions around every research address the moral values exhibited by the researchers themselves—why the methodologies that are used speak to the formula and models of gathering data. Basically, the ethical foundation of research begins from the mindset of the researchers to the object of research, which may or may not be very healthy toward the phenomenon. African religion has suffered denigration that hovers around all aspects of African lives and this, therefore, explains why objective evaluation of the religion was improbable from time immemorial. This creates a foundational problem for eventual research. In fact, it created the unreceptive mindsets that the practitioners of African religion have toward any research, genuine or otherwise. Subsequent upon an understanding that the West is not particularly interested in the objective observation of their religion, they became resistant to even objective research studies and questions of inquiry.

Obviously, the perception of God from the two divides differs considerably. While the West and the Arabs perceive God as a being capable of sharing a personal relationship with humans, such belief does not exist in that mode in many parts of Africa. The existential philosophy in Abrahamic religions that God is an entity to be loved or feared does not have a place in Africa, where God is considered separately distinct and unaffected by the emotions of the

---

T. Falola (✉)
Department of History, University of Texas at Austin, Austin, TX, USA
e-mail: toyinfalola@austin.utexas.edu

© The Author(s), under exclusive license to Springer Nature Switzerland AG 2022
I. S. Aderibigbe, T. Falola (eds.), *The Palgrave Handbook of African Traditional Religion*, https://doi.org/10.1007/978-3-030-89500-6_42

creatures because of its unsubstituted greatness. In fact, the idea that God must or can be loved or feared remains alien among some African groups. This is captured by the question posed by Molefi Asante and Ama Mazama, while explaining Africa and their perception of God in the *Encyclopedia of African Religion*, "Why should an Akan person fear Almighty God Nyankopon or the Yoruba people become frightened of Olorun or the Herero be scared of Omukuru?"[1] However, the West and Arabic perception of God is obviously different. Without understanding the epistemological background for the African understanding of the universe, Western scholars made unsubstantiated assertions about African religion. For example, Leo Frobenius has this to say about African religion:

> *Before the introduction of a genuine faith and a higher standard of culture by the Arabs, the natives had no political organization, nor, strictly speaking, any religion.... Therefore, it is necessary in examining the pre-Muhammedan conditions of the Negro races, to confine ourselves to the description of their crude fetishism, their vulgar and repulsive idols. None but the most primitive instinct determines the lives and conduct of the Negros who lack every kind of ethical inspiration.*[2]

Apparently, such a conclusion above—apart from dispiriting the custodians of the religion, provided they have access to the unguarded comment of Frobenius above—would influence the mindset of Western scholars who seek to embark on research on African religion for scholarship. This is a question of ethics in researching African religion because the researcher is beforehand influenced by a parochial mindset of denying the essentiality of the religion, and this would become an impediment to reliable information gathering and sharing. Since objective research places value on the safety of the interviewees, even if their physical safety is guaranteed in the data gathering process, their mental, social, career, and religious well-being are under severe threats given this erroneous assumption. In essence, a fair mindset devoid of premeditated bias is instrumental to the advancement of scholarship, and African religion is not in any way different from this reality if it is the subject of research.

Another challenge inherent in African religion and global scholarship, which centers on the person carrying out the research is around applied methodology. In every research, the question of method used in the process of gathering information is equally important. Generally, there are qualitative and quantitative methods used in the process of data gathering. Qualitative data gathering styles involve the collection of data in the natural environment with a view to gaining a reliable, testable, and appropriate insight that can drive objective evaluation. This style requires maximum time as opposed to momentary dedication of time and attention to the phenomenon of research, in this case African religion. On the other hand, however, quantitative research centers on gathering of information in figures or numbers. In this type of information gathering, structured interviews are only entertained. If these sources are flawed, it tears down the integrity of research generally. It is instructive that the two methods above have their positive and negative sides in research. While the quantitative method provides objective analysis, it also hinders more details from interviewees. Again, when qualitative data gathering gives an opportunity for first-hand and reliable information, it consumes time.

Now, considering the fact that African religion is usually the victim of sweeping generalizations, as already identified, it is almost impossible for it to attract the category of scholars who would dedicate their time to infiltrate the religion for closer observations and reflections. Therefore, the armchair and instant researchers would provide mostly unreliable information about African religion, impeding true evaluation or perception of people about it because of the brief nature of their research. This is not including the reality that Africans are diverse in ethnic identity, although with philosophically identical religion. Therefore, it would be readily difficult to infiltrate the almost 100 religious denominations in Africa.[3] To do this is not impossible; it is only tasking and requires undiluted commitment and dedication. The reasons for this are obvious. One, Africans would have to test the genuineness of research agents to understand their motives. Since the politics of ridiculing African religion has become normalized in general scholarship, adherents have automatically become very sensitive in relating with people who are initially skeptical about their religion and practices, and have made unguarded comments denigrating it in the process. This is necessary because it would enable them to protect their dignity and honor in the process of sharing information about their religion, especially with people they already suspect. The fact that successful researches about African religion can only be conducted with the cooperation of practitioners attests to this submission.

Again, for those employing quantitative approaches to the generation of data about African religion, the result may not reflect the actual phenomenon of research, especially as it concerns African religion in this context. This is hinged on two different reasons: data interpretation and respondent's reactions. Unless the researcher is eminently honorable and is able to keep a level of ethics in their research interpretation, there are possibilities of interjecting bias into the interpretation of the gathered data. African religion is not like market prices of products over which straightforward response is expected from the interviewees. What respondents of the same religion provide can be different even on the same questions. Therefore, it requires the unbiased mindset of the researchers to appropriately interpret such data. In some other cases, certain conditions may determine the reaction of respondents to the questionnaires. For example, in situations where a body of researchers make unrequited vows to satisfy certain preconditions and fail eventually, even if they carry out a smooth research in that dispensation, the effects will be felt by subsequent information hunters as the relationship kept with them would automatically impede the objective research process. This is another challenge facing global scholarship of African religion. A number of African respondents on religion-related inquiries have suffered character assassination and unfulfilled promises, which have changed their views of researchers.

Having discovered that the challenges above are associated with the researchers themselves, it is important to introduce the challenges that are specifically stretched on the religion and those practicing it as well. For a start, the dynamism of African religion in being multi-cultural and multi-lingual, and also the almost interminable varieties of the religion, constitutes another ground for the challenges facing African religion in global scholarship. Religion in Africa is linked to the people's ethnic and linguistic identity where homogeneity in these factors is transposed on their religious beliefs. Even though there are general assumptions that the character of African religion is conventionally unique, as common understandings of God depict that He exists almost in an elevated, exalted, and distant form in His celestial organicity, the attitude of devotion and worship is quite different. It is common knowledge that among many groups, God is not worshiped. Where He is, the cult of God worship is not widespread, as, for example, among the Yoruba people and Olodumare, He is considered too magnificent to be represented in indexical or semiotic image. However, these people worship the gods who are believed to represent, mediate, and deliver the messages of Olodumare, the Supreme Deity, to humankind. A very fast journey into the Igbo culture, however, would reveal that they equally have a unique celestial body that they revere in Chineke, while they have gods too through which they reach the Supreme One.

It would, therefore, be readily cumbersome to gather information about how Yoruba people have been conducting their religious institutions; how the Burundi organize theirs; how the Bulu practices theirs; and how the Akamba people of Kenya do their own, for example. As such, the variations of these religious practices have been the constant challenge that stands in the way of objective research of African belief systems. Apart from the fact that this problem is ubiquitous, there is the challenge of having to conduct researches among people whose loyalty to their creed is stronger than their interest to allow objective research. For one thing, they are not morally bound to the research process as the researcher is, and this would always affect their reactions to the questions placed before them in a data gathering situation. Many adherents of African religion consider it very sacred because that belief was handed to them from generation to generation. In some African religious practices, it is established that certain aspects of the religion are restricted from women to overtake. Likewise, there are others that are specifically meant for females as well, such as Osun among the Yoruba people. In situations where female researchers seek to conduct findings in the area where their gender is forbidden to reach, they would most predictably generate falsified data, if they are even capable of getting them at all, unless they approach it through a secondary source. This is the same thing when research agents who are considered as outsiders embark on findings such as the one forbidden to outsiders. Sacredness, as such, remains one of the challenges confronting global research in African religion.

The dynamics of multi-lingualism becomes another impediment to research on African religion, particularly in relation to global research, because the problem of interpretation becomes compounded with a multiplicity of languages. If the concentration of a researcher, for example, is a country, it would definitely be difficult to conduct reliable information gathering because of different circumstances that are readily militating against such. For example, we have identified that infiltrating these practices is one of the most reliable ways to gather the untainted information, as that would hand the person first-hand experience. Considering the time that it requires, therefore, dedicating the time to finding this would be predictably difficult. Apart from the inherent challenges of coping with the cultural differences found from one culture to another, adapting with the linguistic identity of places can be somewhat uneasy. If a researcher decides to consider the African religion domiciled in a country like Nigeria, for example, getting a thorough examination of events—especially when they decide to join different cultural groups to understand their practices—would be hard. The hazards involved in it are overwhelming or generally consuming. Extraneous circumstances such as internal unrest or violent activities could also impede such an embarkation. In other words, multiculturalism and variation in linguistic identity, including the creed of secrecy, can affect objective research.

Obviously, another enduring problem readily confronting the research of African religion is the problem of documentation. African religion principles and philosophies have been etched into the memory of the people from time immemorial. That was the popular method of preserving history generally in Africa before the invasion of the continent by the European expansionists. Although the style varies from one custodian of the religion to another, the fact that lack of written documentation prevents objective insight into them cannot be downplayed. When the philosophies and system of practicing a religion are committed to human memory, the reliability of what is to be gathered from them cannot be ascertained. This is because of the tendency of human memory to fail the owner. The challenges of hazy memory however cannot be as problematic as the insincerity of the respondents. For example, moral uprightness and ethical concerns are bound to collide with each other in situations where the respondents forget some salient things about their practices. In many cases, they resolve to improvisation, which in some situations may betray the conventional processes to be followed. As such, the insincerity of respondents to declare their ignorance of some events when questioned could be a potential danger to the conduct of objective research.

Instead of admitting their own shortcomings, many would decide to continue in interview, assured of the ignorance of the researchers and banking on their own seemingly unquestionable status in the domain of knowledge to be shared. The lack of documentation, therefore, has the potential to force researchers to gather untrue information, and the fact that they would evaluate and generate laws based on these untrue data further complicates the understanding of African religion. One general way to discover the fraudulence in gathering data from undocumented sources is that the same source has the potential to provide contradicting information, especially if the researchers deliberately disguise to come back for the former issue of inquiry. Usually, many of the adherents of the religion are disposed to giving wrong information generally. This is usually possible because many African religious practitioners are not actually ordained by known regulatory groups. Therefore, the idea of identifying the ones that are reliable or not can be very demanding for an outside researcher. If this in the end becomes the case, it would be inconsequential to relax our knowledge of African religion on information provided by incredible sources. In fact, African religion continues to have problems of misconception because the data gathered by many scholars are questionable.

During the early period of European missionaries in the continent, a majority of them gathered their information from unreliable sources, and that was the reason for vehemently condemning African systems of spirituality. It was not until T. J. Bowen moved very closely with the Yoruba people who practice African religion that he changed his perception about them. Being a missionary, Bowen conceded eventually, "In Yoruba, many of the notions which the people entertain of God are remarkably correct. They make him the efficient, though not always the instrumental Creator."[4] In the occasion that researchers such as Bowen have not observed the practices from a very close proximity, the conclusion would have been identical to the popular ones made already in relation to African religion by Western absolutists. Therefore, the challenge associated with the absence of documentation of these practices would always impede the way to true scholarship of the phenomenon of African religion, especially in the global context. The non-availability of uniform material that would direct researchers toward improved processes of inquiry and objective evaluation or findings has continued to constitute greater challenges for the study of African religion. Although, this is not to destroy the integrity of the practitioners, because there are instances where their information is always accurate, not minding the different places where research is carried out. With the Yoruba religion, for example, what the practitioners in Ondo would tell researchers about *Eji Ogbe* (one of the Ifa corpora) is the same as what the practitioner in Iseyin, Oyo State, would give.

It is important to state that colonization and its destructive escapades are equally responsible for the challenges faced in the course of research into African religion. African religion thrives on the reliance of the people on imagistic representations. In other words, many adherents carve various images which have proven potency when seen physically and are venerated routinely. There are images whose invocation commands essentially powerful activities that can be immediately felt and sometimes seen. What this is saying is that these images have been conjured to create a spiritual symphony that the adherents can easily identify with during the process of veneration, invocation, or praising. These images, however, were the first target of missionary activities, consolidated by the overzealous African converts who were exceedingly interested in impressing their new religious friends and denominations. As such, a majority of these images were either destroyed by the missionaries or carted away by them. While they were doing these dangerous activities on African religion models, their accomplices at home were either facilitating more destructions of these items or engaging excessively in intimidating the custodians of these practices. Out of exhaustion from defending these customs, the practitioners withdrew to themselves or were forced to abandon their antiques in search of physical and mental safety.

The challenge begins when conducting researches about the efficacy of these gods whose images are already in the Western abode. Two problems immediately are bound to occur from this. One, the expected results would have been obstructed by the absence of the corresponding antiquity whose images would corroborate the rendition of some verbal rituals to provoke their instant results. In some cases, the spiritual force can be transferred to another image, while in some other cases the force is lost. Two, the result could be undesirable as it may be characterized by anger, deceit, or indifference. As such, the researcher whose research work will determine their own formulation of hypothesis or general comments about the religion would be affected by the results got from the current experimentation. In fact, the diplomatic researcher would provide a less damaging comment about the religion in order to ensure a smooth research process. Those who are unconcerned about how the practitioners feel will further make comments that would denigrate the African religion more. Therefore, the challenges of conducting researches on African religion would remain a very intransigent one, especially when factors like this are continuously raising their heads. The level at which Abrahamic religious converts negate the epistemological essence and the ontological property of African religion stands in the way of objective inquiry into African religion.

The act of encroachment done over the images of African religion during slavery and other periods of encounter between the African people and the European world constitutes a very big factor against the objective examination of African religion. This is where the problem gets tricky. The European encroachers who are keeping these images in their custody refuse stubbornly to return them to the rightful owners. Many of the Benin antiquities are still in European museums, serving no true purpose for the West other than the economic values they are adding to them, and, very regrettably, are not fulfilling their spiritual essence to the Africans who own them. Given the long years that have passed between colonization and now, even if the Europeans resort to returning these materials back to their rightful owners, the current generation who are ignorant of the spiritual essence of these antiques may not make appropriate use of them. In essence, they are most likely going to mismanage them or mis-appreciate them generally. Except when they are kept within the confines of those who understand their social and spiritual usefulness, they would make very little difference in the lives of African believers in the religion. As such, the process of having an understanding of these images and how they work has been impeded and trashed.

Another existential challenge facing African religion in global scholarship is politics in knowledge essentialism. Gathering knowledge worldwide follows certain processes ranging from observation and experience to inspiration. Different people, however, have their methods of application of these typologies to arrive at their own knowledge. While this seems to be the basic processes needed to be satisfied before validating the knowledge got from such end, humans have introduced the politics of categorization to sequester some epistemic identity of some people. At the peak of the pyramidal structure of this attitude are the Europeans whose method of arriving at knowledge was imposed as the conventional methods, sweeping every other means of knowledge generation under the carpet. This imposed frame, however superficial it appears, becomes the standard with which global knowledge production is evaluated and judged on, and it also helps decide which knowledge should be considered genuine or otherwise. With Western standards set as the defining structures of knowledge generation, the knowledge coming from Africa especially became severely crushed, and determined as below others in the values it espouses and the philosophy that it demonstrates. Without logical background, the empiricism of African knowledge base was bashed. Subsequently, every expression of African knowledge, either on spiritual or empirical aspects, was derided as incapable of matching Western ones.

This became the foundation for the challenge that African religion was to eventually face. The normal intellectual attraction deserved by African religion was denied over the attitudes that have dominated the Western-induced scholarship. African religion is understood to flourish on a number of different components that generate knowledge to address human challenges. African religion is all-encompassing, as it is through the religion that the medical system of the people is founded. In other words, the health-related welfare of the people is an offshoot of African religion. Therefore, it is not uncommon to see African religion diviners who serve the combined duty of healers (doctors in the Western sense) and mediators between the people and their gods. In fact, in some situations, they are relied on to communicate with the spirit on the guidelines to make some social philosophy with which the society would be run. The healing component of African religion is therefore considered contextually fitting for our understanding of why African religion generally is faced with great challenges in global scholarship. The justification for this is simple. Among the Yoruba people, for example, it is believed that one of the gods is in charge of providing knowledge on the herbal matrix for the production of the materials needed for medical impact. This reverberates in all their engagements, as the belief is widespread.

However, this contradicts the systematic approach of the West to knowledge, which invariably makes them condemn any knowledge generation that foils their own conventional process. The idea, therefore, becomes that true knowledge should be able to satisfy the empirically evaluative processes of the Western episteme, regardless of variations in approaches. Thus, the Western scholarly community was enthroning a culture of universalism which recognized only the Western approach to knowledge and the knowledge they profess. To the African people, however, knowledge can be deducted through reasoning, logic, and even inspiration sometimes. Western knowledge economy is thus dominated by Aristotelian logic that allows for the logical and reasoning method in determining knowledge essentialism. While the Western knowledge domain is dominated by this orientation, African knowledge economy is trashed for its "non-scientific" approach. It is however factual that there are knowledge expressions that are deducted through inspiration even in various academic domains, especially in astrophysics, among other areas. When one considers the fact that Yoruba knowledge economy has survived for thousands of years before the emancipation of Western knowledge episteme, one would understand why their knowledge of proper and improper consumables, climate, astrology, and metaphysics was not only deducted from reasoning, but also from inspiration.

What this point emphasizes is that the unyielding reliance of the global scholarship on methodologies employed by the African researchers would always stand in their way of making sense of African religion. Despite the fact that a majority of these scholars or skeptics continuously condemn the ontological essence of African religion and knowledge economy, there are a number of Western researchers who familiarize themselves with some of these religious practices and have added to their knowledge and confirmed the genuineness of the religion. The popular attitude directed to those who practice the African religion will always deny true inquiry, as already indicated. The ones who are convinced of the religion and the potency of its claims in its different components, just as identified in the case of the medical system generated through their method of deduction, would have their reasons for supporting and practicing their beliefs and convictions. When the people are continuously stereotyped, their disposition to impartial investigators would be hostile and maybe sometimes deceptive. This would hinder true knowledge generation.

Two things have to be delineated to understand the complexity that surrounds the scholarship of African religion—local and international scholarship: one, the fact that scholars of African religion necessarily are not the practitioners of the religion and, two, that unlike the Abrahamic religions, African religion does not seek to subjugate other religious inclinations for its survival. The philosophy that birthed the African religion did not establish any ground for contention or validation. In fact, this explains why many of the African people could conduct their spirituality the very way they consider appropriate, logical, and satisfactory. Their understanding of religion and spirituality explains why they are pleased with whatever ways people choose to organize their religious beliefs and engagement methods. Given this reality, therefore, a majority of African religion practitioners do not share the urgency of documenting their religious philosophies and thoughts for scholarly engagements as researchers seek in their minds. This thus creates the mental distance between the two groups. When one is pulling in to enhance closeness, the other is dragging it further, because they usually do not have a common conviction or the full grasp behind the motive of the researchers. Trust is a very costly commodity that African religion practitioners do not accede to very easily when disclosing their religious philosophies.

It is this disinterest in taking over the world's religious climate that perhaps discouraged African religion practitioners from having a unifying constitution that would have had a continental persuasion to crusade for adherents globally. As such, the people who practice African religion are those who personally are convinced by its fecundity and potency, especially when the practitioners do not have familiar ties with the religion. For example, the growth of African religion in some parts of South America is tied to their level of conviction and not propagation. This automatically creates a complicated atmosphere for research work because practitioners do not share the conviction of the researcher that the religion must be documented for global study. When the scholars are not practitioners, their level of understanding of these religions would be measurably minimal, unless they infiltrate groups of these practitioners to study the religion from a closer angle. However, being a practitioner gives the researcher an edge in their scholarship. An example can be seen in Wande Abimbola, who is both a practitioner of Yoruba religion and an African religion scholar. The problem of form of research, that is the approach, is one that arises from this dichotomy.

This is more compounded by the reality of secrecy that is inherent in the majority of African religious practices, as members believe that the knowledge of it should be determined by one's relationship with the religion. Even among Africans who are not members of the religion, hardly anything is known by them about the religion. This becomes a problem for research because respondents are convinced that the research does not affect them as it affects the researcher, who, perhaps, they believe is pursuing a career growth. In fact, this problem would be difficult to surmount in the understanding that respondents' interest cannot be guaranteed outright. And in the case that they are remunerated or induced to enhance their concentration or interest in the research, the quality of their response would be subject to debate. Therefore, the road to getting enough materials on African religion is arduous and demands patience. The reasons for this have been stated. It is bound to experience a change when there are more practitioners of African religion who are convinced of Western scholarship and are inclined to showcasing their beliefs to the world. The case of Abimbola and others comes readily to mind.

As a corollary of the above, African religion continues to prove difficult for research because the membership into it is not appropriately regulated. This is actually a structural problem that affects even the distant observers of the religion. When information is obtained from unreliable sources, there is little opportunity to confirm the authenticity of the results got from such a research exercise. It will undoubtedly have an impact on the analysis of the content and the results generated. Despite the fact that there were many practitioners of the religion within reach, in addition to the bulk of works conducted by various scholars of African religion, their angle of scholarship did not begin to get any serious academic attention until about several decades ago. This is rooted in the understanding that the findings and propositions made by scholars do not rest on solid foundations and cannot withstand critical academic evaluation.

What would have seemed to be the strengths of the discipline in the academic community seem to be used against it. Insider information provided by practitioners of African religion, who at the same time were researchers about it, was conceived as being unreliable over the assumption that it has been colored by personal sentiment. Apart from the reality that there is a dearth of research on the discipline, the problem of not recognizing the little ones that do exist scares the potential scholars away.

Although there are some relatively recent groups created to ensure the installation of regulatory policy on the practice of African religion, for example the society of Orisa worshippers and adherents among the Yoruba people, such societies are still very few in relation to the different African religious groups. The problem faced when there is no regulatory body is that anyone could be swindled to believe any group that parade themselves as custodians of African religious knowledge and, therefore, provide disjointed information about the religion. Violators are open to sanction when there are regulatory bodies, and these bodies can be directly consulted or connected when researching about African religion, instead of approaching anyone who lay claims to the knowledge of African religion. Researching about African religion, even when the research method is quantitative and makes use of structured questionnaires, only requires people that have first-hand experience of the religion, and they are usually dwellers of urban environments. Although it is established that some of them are also victims of migration in the contemporary world, the reality remains that many of them are engrossed in pastoral activities, as that places them closely with nature.

Therefore, outsider researchers who do not understand some basics related to the practice of African religion could fall victims of swindlers who parade themselves as authorities over African religion, who perhaps were attracted by the promised remunerations by the researchers. This identifies the challenges that are associated with the non-registration of members. If the religion has been documented into writing where anyone can perhaps refute, confirm, or accept arguments anytime they are confronted with doubts, discovering people who wrongly lay claims to knowing about the religion would have been relatively easier. Therefore, if some groups of researchers uninformed about the motive of their research visit the Ashanti religion practitioners differently, or Fanti religion separately, they are bound to generate contradictory information—particularly if they are unlucky to have deceptive respondents who they cannot identify or understand. As such, problems relating to the research would persist as long as there are no regulatory bodies.

Subsequent to the challenges identified above, the following observations are necessary and inevitable for the advancement of African religion study in global scholarship. Important in taking African religion to a global height is the need for constant study of the religion. Given the multiplicity of the religious ideologies manifesting in various languages and cultures in Africa, it is incumbent that there is an increased dedication of interest to study each of these typologies for better and informed understanding. One of the very reasons why

ATR still survives the backlog of institutional racism and collaborated criticism is because the religion is dynamic and evolving. One of the things that single the religion out from its Abrahamic counterparts is because it evolves and contracts to accommodate new values and ethos way more than those religious inclinations always seem to be capable of. Perhaps this remains why the solidity of the religion is strengthened beyond calculations. If the religion had been rigid, especially like the religions of the past that are dying out of the steam that sustained others, it would have become the victim of outrageous or deprecatory campaigns of the Abrahamic ones, ever since the latter's inception in Africa. Given its dynamism, it was able to remain solid despite high temperatures it was subjected to.

Doctrinal differences between African religion and every other religion, especially the Abrahamic variants, account for the reasons it remains strong in the contemporary period. African religion emphasizes good human conduct and neighborliness. It reiterates the fact that being good to people has immediate and long-term effects, particularly in the physical world. Unlike Christianity and Islam, African religion does not theorize after-life with physical activities found in what others term heaven or hell. Therefore, emphasis is placed on good character and the need for communal togetherness, as these are considered as the basic rules of advancement as a people. In fact, that explains why Africans are not concerned by the faith professed even by their neighbors, as long as the basic tenets of their mutual philosophy rooted in African religion are satisfied. As such, many practitioners of African religion mingle very easily with adherents of Abrahamic faiths, and even those who are the custodians of Abrahamic religions also alternate with their ancestral worship, represented by African religion, because the latter seems to be all-encompassing. As long as they are not persecuted because of the faith they profess, it is very easy to find African religion practitioners who mingle and harbor no resentment to others of a different faith.

It is therefore worthy of research to consider those attributes of the religion that keep it strong in every trying weather. The characteristics of various African spiritualities should be studied very closely and diligently. To achieve this, there must be continuous research works on African religion, through dedicated inquiry to understand the reasons behind its dynamism. Comparing the belligerence of Abrahamic faith adherents to that of African religion, the former should have lost the steam of relevance way before the contemporary time. In fact, the reality that the study of African religion is attracting more scholarly engagements attests to the understanding that the academic community now values the religion and the philosophy it produces. More research therefore means more understanding and better scholarly information about African religion. The first step to achieving this is making efforts to convince African religion practitioners of the reasons to have their religion documented for global reach and then the generational preservation of the legacy. Just like other aspects of knowledge, updating the general research about the phenomenon of African religion and its vast philosophy would help improve on these areas.

Similar to this is the fact that African religion needs to create a regulatory system that would constitute the required media of research, which would be saddled with the responsibility of disseminating information, and documenting findings across different countries and boundaries. There seems to have been some efforts in this direction, as organizations such as the International Council for IFA Religion have been enthroned by the adherents of Ifa worship. Societies such as this would be responsible for the timely coordination of activities and intervention and have the power to network beyond countries. The organization of symposiums where adherents would converge to share their ideas would be made the primary aim of such groups, to strengthen the validity of the different components of the religion. Basically, aspects of medical research, astrophysics, and even the literary aspects of the religion would be explored for academic and social purposes. Establishing a very solid background on this angle will catapult African religion to another height. Their achievements of it would be the springboard upon which they would elect to take their right position in the scheme of things. As already pinpointed when identifying the weakness of not having a unifying system or body that regulates the activities of adherents, the installation of such a group or groups would enhance peaceful organization of events.

While it is believed that the constitution of a media body would inspire the redefinition of African religion, as this is important to their growth, membership of this group must not be solely dominated by the scholars of African religion. In other words, practitioners of the religion, irrespective of their educational background, deserve slots in the membership forum. The reason is to enhance a robust academic insight and provide the opportunity for an eclectic approach to the understanding or study of the religion. There may arise the problem of reaching consensus on the form of approach that is best suited for finding about African religion, as the academic members may needlessly insist on an approach because of their professional competence in the field of research. However, African religion practitioners at the other end may insist on employing a different approach. This, however, would be resolved over the understanding that they set out to achieve a common goal. It is necessary because the synergy of the two different groups would provide the avenue for them to offer experiential and intuitive knowledge in a bid to consolidate the findings of the research group. Different sub-bodies would be constituted in the group to fulfill certain preconditions.

As it is done in the academic community, journals dedicated to findings would be introduced, as this would facilitate further future research where previous findings would be reinforced, refuted, or consolidated with more reliable information. The group will be responsible for the publication of works that exclusively center on African religion for global visibility, interconnectivity, or networking in Africa and in the diaspora. It is widely accepted that African religion prides itself in the study of nature, and this can only be reinforced by engaging in further research about the phenomenon itself. Nature changes and as such challenges human thinking to equally change and upgrade their knowledge from time to time to keep in line with the dictates of the contemporary world. A group of researchers would be dedicated to continuous academic inquiry about the evolution of African religion. The reason for the wider acceptance of African religion in the present time is not unconnected to the fallout of Abrahamic religions that appear to be more rigid and resistant to changes, over their claim to absolute knowledge of events and are averse to paradigm shifts. When these are appropriately studied, African religion would be more enriched to consider their shortcomings and make necessary improvements to produce an African religion worthy of global scholarship.

We should not foreclose the probability of imposition of disciplinary perspective to the research assignment. Since the inception of the scholarly engagements on African religion, the research has attracted interest from scholars from different fields of study who are bound to relate with the phenomenon of study from the perspective of their discipline. Therefore, anthropologists who are interested in any research on African religion would most likely dwell on areas that suit their profession, as the others would make minimal meaning to them. This is equally applicable to those in the domain of theology; their basis of inquiry about African religion will be conditioned mostly not by the social importance of the religion but by the sacredness of it. Conversely, researchers whose fields differ, like those in anthropology, sociology, and literature, would be unconcerned about the sacredness of the religion. Instead, they would be preoccupied with finding out about the religion with relation to its social functions, moral values, and human engineering potentials. Of course, this would create a wide dichotomy among researchers especially when they belong to varying disciplines, as identified here. This is actually because the interpretation of data would be subject to the bias or persuasion of the scholars conducting the research.

Therefore, with such researches, without the unification of interests or a corresponding meeting point among scholars of diverse disciplines, the result which would be generated from different research studies would vary and conflict with one another on various occasions. The persistence of this challenge would pose a great impediment to scholarship of African religion in the global academic community. For example, when the research is not conducted by those who are theologically inclined, aspects of religion that affect people's participation would be influenced by various sociocultural factors such as their level of economic stability or social necessities. The essence of the religion in relation to the spiritual importance would not be given the appropriate attention. In fact, the people's loyalty to such religion would be determined by the fulfillment of these sociocultural predeterminations. For example, there are those devotees of African religion whose primary driver of interest was the assurance of the attainment of their goals, without which would immediately affect their loyalty or commitment. Given the reality that researching African religion does not rest alone on the elicited responses offered by the custodians of the faith, the interrogation of the outside population who are devotees too will form the basis for getting reliable data.

In another instance, when those who are theologically informed conduct researches on the African religion, for example, what would form the basis of their focus would be primarily different. As mentioned earlier on the ethical questions that surround the researchers when conducting their findings, this also is somewhat binding on the respondents too. For theologically informed researchers, it is comparatively easier to understand some basic information as regard responses generated from either the mediators of African religion or the adherents themselves. Therefore, it is incumbent on these researchers to generate definitions and delineation of values in different responses elicited to them and then proceed to making assertions which could be refuted or accepted by colleagues in the same field. Theories that can be used to further understand African religion should be formed by these scholars for a start. Through their efforts, they would assist to articulate the aspects of the religion that are specifically cultural or secular from the aspect that is basically religious. The work by subsequent researchers would therefore become relatively easier for making boundaries.

One important area where African religion deserves extensive research is the angle of their knowledge got through inspiration. African religion does not seek to interpret nature through deductive or inferential reasoning only; there are several revelations of actual ideas that are discovered by inspiration. In fact, when this condition is accepted in the global scholarship, making progress in understanding the religion would be relatively easy. How do they come about their understanding of the things to avoid or embrace? How did those termed as primitive understand that some herbs are poisonous to human health? How did they come about deposing pointless leadership? Regarding the solutions they employed to curb social decadence or violence, how did they come about them? Answering all these questions and more are fundamental to understanding the interconnectivity of African religion and their ways of life. Africans and their religious inclinations have been in existence for a very long time and thrived in their engagements to be discarded as having baseless foundations. Through the religion, social codes are fabricated, spiritual activities are dictated, and moral behaviors are encouraged. In fact, the primary custodians of African religion are the immediate contacts to be reached or consulted whenever things are going southward in their society.

Among the Yoruba people, for example, Ifa had been their primary source of social, political, and moral philosophy for thousands of years before the incursion of the external invaders. Doubting the potency of the method therefore would perhaps take researchers away from getting to the background of the religion and its social configurations. Like many other divination systems that the continent has, Ifa is predictive of future events and its prescience and clairvoyance solidify the trust of the people in the act. Without having the "scientific" approach that modern systems of knowledge acquisition are capable of, this system is considered a reliable source of projecting information. Rather than being judgmental, for example, the suggested forum for African religion practitioners should be collaborated with, with a view to studying the basis for this knowledge so that it could be replicated, retrieved, and, in some cases, used as an instrument of reconstruction. It is considerably easier to subject their process to testing and observe the results generated in the long run to prescribe methods and approaches to solving existential issues, just like the science researchers do in contemporary times.

Therefore, aspects of knowledge obtained through deduction should be studied. Intuitive knowledge in African knowledge economy should be given higher concentration, while the ones discovered through inspiration need to be well documented. The reason is that it would provide the avenue for researchers to focus their attention on the area of connection between the religion and their knowledge economy generally. The connection between the veneration of gods or ancestors and the physical manifestation of the effects of doing so deserves scholarly engagements. Of course, this would not involve taking the scientific approach of using logic to arrive at an end. Otherwise, the religion would still not be considered as an important source of getting knowledge at the global scenery. Rather than be seen as a contender of the other available means of information acquisition, the African method should be seen as a complementary exercise in the acquisition of knowledge. The rituals and their social significance, the invocation and their psychological or physical effects, and the connection between conflict resolution and the invitation of ancestral presence should all be studied for the advancement of global scholarship on African religion.

Accordingly, getting a worthwhile research exercise about African religion begins with a change of attitude of the researchers themselves. The unfounded misinformation that has inspired the Western observants of African engagement and social dialectics would need to be demystified for the conduct of reliable and objective research. This begins with the deconstruction of the ideas of superiority already acclaimed by the West. This creates an imbalance and a lopsided atmosphere for research because it forces the researcher to see the potential respondents as disposable elements in the post-research experience or as people without appreciable sense of worth, who could be discarded at will. Operating on this amoral philosophy, it would be continuously difficult to extract exact information from the practitioners of African religion. The ethics of research start from the acceptance that respondents who will provide the needed data of research deserve some level of regard because the success of the researcher(s) is dependent on their cooperation. Without accepting the fact that respondents deserve as much regard as the data to be gathered, there could be further challenges in global scholarship of African religion generally. Usually, African respondents are treated with indignation when compared to how researchers conduct their research in other settings, not minding how it is going to affect the research data.

This attitude creates a distance between the researchers and the corresponding respondents. In fact, it is the basis for the mutual suspicion and secrecy that impedes uninterrupted flows between the two individuals at the various ends. Globally, when people are treated with disrespect, they are usually aware of every insubordination no matter how "dumb" they appear. Interestingly, people react differently to what they perceive as indignation. In most cases, their reaction could be noticed in their indifference to the phenomenon of research, and in some other ways, they would elect to provide insincere feedback, the two of which have significant consequences on the reliability of research. In every conceivable way, respondents—regardless of their race and educational exposure—deserve maximum respect, as their response is directly relational to the success of the exercise. The research community understands quite well the outpouring benefits of the success of research and how this would facilitate the career growth of the researchers. Therefore, the respondents would obstruct accurate information whenever they perceive an act of disrespect to their person. When researching about African religion, it is morally necessary that researchers drop every act of indignation that would subvert worthwhile research exercises.

Beyond this, the research community must be encouraged to participate wholeheartedly in giving accurate information or data about the questions and interviews of the researchers. Getting this requires telling the research community about the prospect of return impact that the research study would bring to the people. When assured of the spiritual, economic, and social improvement that comes with their true response in a research process, they would be inclined to participate accordingly in the process. To Africans, especially the custodians of African religion, money is not always the instrument of seduction to attract their participation in some events. In fact, it may induce suspicion. This means that when researchers actively place the people's worth around money, it affects their relationship in the long run, as it may influence how their responses are given. This is because they would already create a business mindset in the atmosphere of inquiry where their response is seen in the form of paying back for the mobilization instigated. For some others, it would scare them away immediately. To forestall this, therefore, researchers must study the context and nature of the respondents to know if what to give is either money or good human conduct to win their participatory interest.

The road to this is actually straightforward but sometimes difficult to follow by researchers. Ethical responsibility of the research determines how they handle cases such as this. For those who do not consider the responding community as worthwhile of dignity and respect, it would be very difficult to operate on such moral philosophy and principles. In research, the right of participants to their privacy and dignity is spelled out. However, many researchers betray and violate these standards, especially in their post-research engagements. The maintenance of respondent value begins from the identification of the essentialism of their belief systems. African religion has been a subject of derision in global scholarship over the stigmatization that is deliberately impressed on it by the universalist scholars. Passing and standing on such judgment affects the research process in very many ways. One, it creates between the respondents and researchers a mental distance that can obstruct true findings. African religion is touted as barbaric and primitive, labeled purely as superstitious and full of magic in a bid to impose the view of Western knowledge episteme on the religion, or use the Western standard to judge the practices.[5] Definitely, it would be difficult to conduct an objective research with such a mindset.

NOTES

1. Asante Molefi and Mazama Ama, *Encyclopedia of African Religion* (Thousand Oaks: SAGE Publications, Inc., 2009), xxiii.
2. Rotimi Omotoye, "The Study of African Traditional Religion and Its Challenges in Contemporary Times," *Ilorin Journal of Religious Studies* Vol. 1, No. 2. (2011): 21–40.
3. Aloysius M. Lugira, *African Traditional Religion*, Third Edition (New York: Chelsea House, 2009), 11.
4. Ibid.
5. J. M. Murphy, "Black Religion and 'Black Magic': Prejudice and Projection in Images of African-Derived Religions," *Religion* 20 (1990): 323–324.

BIBLIOGRAPHY

Asante, Molefi and Ama Mazama. *Encyclopedia of African Religion* Thousand Oaks: SAGE Publications, Inc., 2009.

Lugira, Aloysius M. *African Traditional Religion*. 3rd ed. New York: Chelsea House, 2009.

Murphy, J. M. "Black Religion and 'Black Magic': Prejudice and Projection in Images of African-Derived Religions." *Religion* 20 (1990): 323–337.

Omotoye, Rotimi. "The Study of African Traditional Religion and Its Challenges in Contemporary Times." *Ilorin Journal of Religious Studies* Vol. 1, No. 2 (2011): 21–40.

CHAPTER 43

African Traditional Religion in the Context of World Religions: Challenges to Scholars and Students

Robert Yaw Owusu

INTRODUCTION

African Traditional Region (ATR), together with other indigenous religions, has been given many negative labels, mostly by outsiders and even by some less-informed Africans. These labels do not adequately mirror the cosmological view and religious practices of the followers of these religions. Labels such as "animism," "fetishism," "paganism," "heathenism," "primitive religions," "tribal," "voodoos," "magic," "primal religions,"[1] and many others fail to wholly express African Traditional Religion (ATR). Some scholars regard ATR as a preparatory religion, a primal religious experience whose role was to provide the backdrop for modern religions now termed "World Religions." There have been many good books on world religions that entirely omit African Traditional Religions or just mention it in passing. For instance, in her renowned book, *Living Religions* (8th edition), Mary Pat Fisher allotted only 39 pages to describing and discussing indigenous religions, which includes African Traditional Religion, Native American religions, Australian aborigines' religion, Malaysian traditional religion, and Shamanism, but assigned 110 pages to Hinduism and 58 pages to Judaism. The complex religious system of the Yorùbá culture occupied a few of the 39 pages. John L. Esposito and others, in *World Religions Today* (4th edition), have only 36 pages on indigenous

R. Y. Owusu (✉)
Clark Atlanta University, Atlanta, GA, USA

© The Author(s), under exclusive license to Springer Nature Switzerland AG 2022
I. S. Aderibigbe, T. Falola (eds.), *The Palgrave Handbook of African Traditional Religion*, https://doi.org/10.1007/978-3-030-89500-6_43

religions out of the book's 609 pages. African religion often does not qualify for a separate chapter for a thorough study.

Judaism is one of the smallest religions in terms of adherents but is regarded as a world religion. This is due, it is argued, to Judaic influence on and as the mother of Christianity and Islam, the two leading religions of the world in terms of followers and socio-political impact. With ATR being a religion of influence for thousands of years and with over one billion people in Africa and worldwide, ATR must be acknowledged and studied as a world religion just as they do with Judaism, Hinduism, and others. Studies have identified the tremendous influence of ATR on African Christianity and Islam. A challenge to scholars of religion is that African religion needs to be encountered anew.

Also, I would argue that ATR has the same elements that are used to describe the nature and features of world religions, whether by the seven dimensions by Ninian Smart,[2] the four elements by Bruce Lincoln,[3] or John S. Mbiti's five characteristics.[4] For this reason, ATR qualifies to be regarded as a world religion. Looking at Christianity, for instance, when the Bible became available to Africans, there arose a shift from understanding the Bible from the viewpoint of Euro-Americans to understanding the narrative from the Judaic or first-century Christians' perspective. African Christians see a close affinity between Judaic culture, particularly the Hebrew Bible (Old Testament) and the African culture. Like Judaism, African Traditional Religion is dynamic and active and, therefore, capable of transformation when it is appropriately engaged. Religions that are not active and cannot change eventually die. This religion has been in existence since time unknown and is still active and effective. This alone should tell us that African Traditional Religion demands a new and proper orientation from religious scholars.

WHAT IS A WORLD RELIGION?

The term "world religion" is explained as a religion that has a presence across the continents. Some say it is a religion with a diverse and widespread following. The concept of "world religions," though it has been in use for over a century, is still regarded by many religious scholars as questionable. In my sixteen years of teaching World Religions, I found the term quite ambiguous. It is an unsettled term; hence scholars keep adding to the list. The term sometimes is hyphenated, "world-religions," many times without the hyphen; at times it appears in a possessive form, "The World's Religions," or as "major religions of the world." There have been many books written to explain its origin, and it is claimed that the concept was coined by a famous German Catholic theologian and scholar by the name of Johann Sebastian von Drey.[5]

In her book, *The Invention of World Religions*, Tomoko Masuzawa describes what she calls "the historical fact" concerning the Europeans' quest for systemic domination and so have "had a well-established convention categorizing the peoples of the world into four parts, rather unequal in size and uneven in specificity, namely, Christians, Jews, Mohammedans (as Muslims were called then) and the rest." The "rest," she claims, comprised those variously known as "heathens, pagans, idolaters, or sometimes polytheistic."[6] This classification, termed "binary classification,"[7] prevailed for some time until, in the latter half of the nineteenth century and early twentieth century, a new ordering "suddenly appeared that not only allowed an additional classification of other 'minor' religions but also listed ten to a dozen world religions that replaced the old hierarchy of nations" [i.e., people groups].[8]

The difficulty to include ATR in the study of world religions may stem from the kind of classification that mirrors the Europeans' quest for domination, whether by the binary classification or by another category she calls "the tripartite classification."[9] Both classifications leave no room to include the "other" religions on the world religions platform. According to Masuzawa, the binary classification that classifies the religions as "East" and "West" is "inherently asymmetrical, universally conceived system of classification [that] exude a pretense of symmetry that appears to balance 'East' and 'West.'"[10] The notion of an "East" and "West" category was created by Europeans in their philological quest for racial control or greatness, argues Masuzawa.[11]

The "East-West" classification partitions the religions into Abrahamic religions (for the West) and all others (for the East). Even when the concept specifically mentions Asian religions in place of the "East," the fact that it is in reference to the East immediately excludes the African religions. Africa is not in the East, and therefore the "all others" do not include it. Moreover, the "East" and "West" classification is ambiguous and arbitrary because we are not sure of the criterion used for the demarcation. We all know it was not by longitudinal divide, and therefore we can conclude that it could most likely be racial, the only alternative left.

Also, to claim Judaism, Christianity, and Islam for the "West" raises a serious concern since the history of religions tells of the massive presence and influence of Christianity and Islam in the "East." The split of the Christian church in 1054 CE was between the Western part and the Eastern part of the "holy" Roman Empire. The Western part became the Catholic or the universal church, and the Eastern part became the Orthodox or Byzantine church. That division was the result of prolonged doctrinal and political conflict but not racial. In that division, the Ethiopian church was on the side of the Eastern branch, and whatever was left in North Africa as a church was a part of the Western branch. Islam also had a strong presence in both regions before the emergence of the concept of world religions (the Ottoman Empire was a multinational, multicultural empire dominating most of Southeast Europe, parts of Central Europe, Western Asia, parts of Eastern Europe, and the Caucuses). Regarding the original home of the Abrahamic religion, they were in the Ancient Near East (now the Middle East), not Europe.

The tripartite classification generally appears to be geopolitically based: (1) in Ancient Near East (Judaism, Christianity, Islam); (2) in South Asia (Hinduism, Buddhism, Zoroastrianism, Jainism); (3) and on the Far East (Confucianism, Taoism, Shintoism).[12] If observed closely, one realizes that these demarcations are aligned with ethnic or language differences: Ancient Near East has a Semitic language or "Hamito-Semitic" people group; South Asia has "Aryan or Indo-European people"; and the Far East has "Turanian or Oriental people."[13] This classification also leaves African Traditional Religion and African people out. Masuzawa, therefore, rightly asserts, "This originally philological and later racial demarcation complicates the constitution of the West, while the rest of the world seems to turn into an ever-receding region of the premodern lurking at the edge of world historical stage."[14]

As mentioned in the introduction, the disconcerting names such as "primitive," "pre-literature," "tribal," or "basic religions" used for African Traditional Religions and other indigenous religions even to this present age place a limitation on the role these "little traditions"[15] can play and are, therefore, meant to keep them outside the mainstream scholarly platform in perpetuity. It is an undue state created by Western scholarship, making it difficult to elevate these traditions to the level of the "great traditions" for scholarly purposes. Until recently, African politics and the economy had no footholds of their own, leaning heavily on the strengths of their former colonial rulers. It was when the continent started to show substance in its political framework and formulated its own economic agenda that it began to gain attention in the global political and economic market. Similarly, ATR must exert self-will and be its own self-propelled agency to launch a move for self-elevation onto the world stage of Faith Traditions. This calls for thorough homework, some of which will be discussed in the next section.

How many world religions are there today? In deciding what religion to include in the studies of world religions, it is argued thus, "the tendency is to focus on religions with large numbers of followers [multiculturally] so that by the end of the [course], students will have learned about the beliefs of a large percentage of the world's population."[16] The question is, if this is a compelling motive, then why study endangered species of a small number that is threatened with extinction? As small as the number may be, resources are made accessible and efforts are undertaken to help preserve them. Religion is so meaningful to all peoples that none must be assigned to an irrelevant state or be regarded as not significant enough for study on the world scholarly stage.

Friedrich Max Mueller, known as the father of the modern academic study of religion, has said that "to know one religion is to know none." Ignoring a thorough study of African Tradition Religion as "a major" religion of the world that has shaped African people's worldview and impacted other cultures means less knowledge and minimal understanding toward African people and their way of life. It is a mere tautology to say that our global world is diverse because wherever you turn to, you encounter a culture that is different or almost different from your own. Yet, if critically examined, that different culture may not be significantly different from yours. The differences are significant and relevant, but the compelling similarities should not be disregarded. You cannot ignore this global phenomenon and seek to be relevant in today's world. It is laughable to hear people of other cultures, particularly the older generation of the

Western cultures, still describing African religious culture like that portrayed in the infamous *Tarzan* movies in Africa. One can attribute such an attitude to a lack of exposure to or an appreciation of African religious culture. It is the view of this author that the adjective "major" attached to religions (major religion or religions) must be eliminated because every religion, no matter the number of members, demands to be studied as a religion of the world. After all, they are all of or in the world.

If Mueller's assertion stands, then it is imperative for the academic study of religion to engage ATR that impacts the lives of over one billion people in the same approach we have toward other world religions. African Traditional Religion, like other world religions, has its own narratives and myths, philosophy, ethical values, morality, rituals, practices, ceremonies and festivals, symbols, communities, institutions, priests, prophets, progenitors, and deities. Each of these elements in African Traditional Religion needs to be studied using a comparative approach.

CHALLENGES OF AFRICAN TRADITIONAL RELIGION TO DEAL WITH IN SCHOLARLY INQUIRY

The West's missionizing approach and Western anthropologists' description of Africa and its culture were problematic. The approach undermined and damaged African religion and culture.

Wrong Missionizing Approach

Most Western and later North American missionaries were prejudicial in their relationship to Africans and their way of life. They assumed theirs was a superior culture and that of the African, inferior. This superior-inferior mindset determined the method of engaging the indigenous religion as well as the socio-economic and political cultures. The approach they used was that of *assimilation* and *acculturation* instead of *integration* or *inculturation*. *Assimilation* refers to "the process through which individuals and groups of differing heritages acquire the basic habits, attitudes, and mode of life of an embracing culture" (Merriam-Webster Online Dictionary, 2020). During the Euro-American missionizing era, African Traditional Religion was given no chance to wrestle with and shape the culturally cushioned religious models of Europe and North America. Africans were forced to adapt to or absorb the European religious and cultural models as a civilizing agency. Their assimilation method was a disaster for the people of Africa, causing their African religion and way of life to be significantly suppressed, rendering them non-competitive in the global religious landscape. Today, much of the damage has been reclaimed, though.

A concept similar to assimilation is *acculturation*. This concept is "often tied to political conquest or expansion, and is applied to the process of change in beliefs or traditional practices that occurs when the cultural system of one group displaces that of another" (Merriam-Webster Online Dictionary, 2020). Both assimilation and acculturation do not allow a gradual evolutionary process that occurs when two different cultures or beliefs and practices converge or crash. The African operational systems nose-dived.

Inculturation or *integration*, on the other hand, is another form of collaboration that allows a gradual evolutionary process to take place and bring about something new or something reflective of the inputs—in this case, the ATR and Euro-American Christianity or, in a better way, the ATR and Biblical Christianity. In my view, the two—Euro-American Christianity and Biblical Christianity—are not the same. Euro-American Christianity has Western tones, clothing, images, and shadows, whereas Biblical Christianity refers to Christianity of the Bible ("original" Judean culture). The result of the interaction between the ATR and the Biblical culture would be different from the interaction between the ATR and the Euro-American Christian culture. It was, therefore, not a surprise that when the Bible became available to Africans, there had been a shift from an understanding of the Bible from the Euro-American models to an understanding of the text from the Judaic or first-century Christian's perspective. African Christians have discovered a close affinity between the Judaic culture (the Old Testament) and the African Traditional Religion and culture. If African Traditional Religion had been allowed to be competitive then, there would be no "World Religions" class today but a class on the "religions of the world" or a class on "the world's religions." The term "world religions," it is believed, was simply put in place to discriminate against indigenous religions of certain races or people groups since most of the "other non-major religions" of the tripartite classification like Sikhism, Jainism, and Confucianism are now treated as world religions in many World Religions courses or textbooks.

A Lack of Religious Literacy

First, there is a common notion among many African people that religion is something we do, not something we study, teach, or learn. Until recently, many African religious leaders, prophets, and priests shunned the idea of formal training. I am not referring to the "mainstream" body of Christian clergy—the Catholics, Methodists, Presbyterians, Episcopalians, Baptists, and Anglicans. I am referring to the African-initiated churches in general. Some even consider formal training as unspiritual or a means of draining spiritual enthusiasm. Formal and informal training in ATR is also about "doing" religion. The philosophical and reflection aspects are mostly disregarded. Supplying students with knowledge about religious and philosophical traditions is a universal and essential objective of Interfaith Studies courses.

In addition, a standard understanding of religious traditions and the practical implications of this literacy are considered necessary competencies for interfaith engagement: for example, the importance of a vegetarian diet for many

Hindus, the practices that Jewish people may observe during Shabbat or the Muslims' five pillars, the differences between Mahayana and Theravada Buddhism, or historical occurrences in the Bible. The array of topics discussed is partly informed by the objectives of each individual course. The question here is, how do we determine a course for a religion without a text as a source or resource but only by word of mouth? This is a serious challenge for ATR scholars. Of course, the oral tradition is one of the sources for African Traditional Religion studies, and the many books written about it are all commentaries. By a lack of literacy, I am not referring to merely reading and writing or speaking a foreign language. Rather, it focuses on the critical analytical approach applied to the content—thought and practices—of the tradition and its implication for contemporary society.

Linked to the problem of a lack of literacy in ATR is its insistence on orality instead of written sacred texts as the means of transmission and preservation of the tradition. Sacred texts have a mythical narrative of the world's origins, deities, human beings, and human conditions. Sacred texts have instructional components, songs, dirges, and wise sayings that elucidate practical ways of life of the community. Sacred texts define Faith's boundaries as well as the purpose and end of this tradition. Sacred texts serve as a preserved record of the history of the people and society, including the protagonists known as the elders, sages or ancestors, ancestress, the deity and divinities, significant holidays (festivals), memorials, and celebrations. The lack of sacred texts has negative repercussions on religious literacy.

But will it be possible, even necessary, to have one sacred text? Not really. Considering the complexity of the deities and divinities in ATR and the complex ethno-linguistic cultures and their beliefs and practices, multiple texts similar to the Hindu Vedas will be appropriate. Judaism, with its mono-linguistic and cultural tradition, has both oral and written texts. Without any written records, African Traditional Religion scholars have to deal with oral narratives and varying opinions and interpretations shaped by time and transmission, making the study odious, costly, and unattractive.

The Preparatory Idea

Secondly, it seems to be an accepted position that African Traditional Religion is a preparatory indigenous way of life whose function was to prepare the way for the emergence of modern religions such as Christianity and Islam in their various forms and models in Africa and the Diaspora (i.e., African Christianity, African Islamic Faith, and Black religion and spirituality). Poor and inadequate studies of African Traditional Religion, especially by foreign missionaries, anthropologists, and the indiscreet, tactless African scholars who have bought into the marginalized ideas and misconceptions about African religion and culture have maintained this preparatory notion. Nevertheless, as Rotimi Omotoye and other eminent scholars of African Traditional Religion have said, African

Traditional Religion is not a "fossil religion."[17] It exhibits signs of growth in the twenty-first century alongside other world religions.

As I pointed out earlier, African Traditional Religion directly affects tens of millions of Africans as a way of life and identity and many millions more indirectly. Many followers of Christianity and Islam in Africa may reject the spiritual practices and certain beliefs of African Traditional Religion. The reality is that many social practices, ethics, and metaphors have found their way into Christianity and Islam and will soon do so in Buddhism now on the rise in Africa and the Diaspora. Thus, the Christian churches in Africa today look different from those of the time of the foreign missionaries. African Traditional Religion's worldview is now a shared view with the larger part of the world in view of the presence of African traditional spiritualists and African Diaspora across continents.

One area of ATR that needs reform is its worship centers or shrines. Most of the shrines leave much to be desired and need to be polished to meet the twenty-first-century eye. Actually, they need a new architecture. In countries like Togo and Benin, for example, almost every home has a shrine similar to the puja in Hinduism. It is said that worship in ATR is private and has no designated central place, and so why the call for temples (like church buildings)? There is a public dimension of worship where individuals go to a designated priest, priestess, seer, or diviner to inquire (*abisa* in Akan) and seek help. Usually, that place is where the deity or his image is housed (*abosomfie, ɔsombea*, or *asɔnee* in *Twi*). Worship and rituals such as sacrifice, libation, counseling, mediation, and artistic display of the priest or priestess are performed there. The construction and appearance of these public shrines, as they are now, make the modern person think that ATR is still living in the pre-modern world and has no regard for sanitation and scientific medicine preparation.

Complex Diversity

A third challenge of African Traditional Religion for scholars is the complex diversity of Africa. Africa is not a country, yet foreigners often refer to Africa as if it is one country. Africa has fifty-four countries and thousands of ethnolinguistic communities, making research very complex and challenging to represent the entire people of this vast continent. The term "African Traditional Religion," in reality, is not the name African folks call their religion. Different adherents have various names for their beliefs and practices. Among the Akans in Ghana, for instance, some follow a deity called *Antoa Nyamaa* and are therefore called *Antoa Nyamaa* worshippers. So are those who follow *Tano, Bosom Po, Tegare*, and so on. The difficulty of finding a common name for even these faith traditions in one ethnic group in one of the fifty-four countries of Africa tells of the odious task that scholars face in studying ATR. Perhaps, that is why some African scholars like Jacob K. Olupona of Harvard Divinity School and Theo Sundermeier, a missiologist, use the name African Traditional Religions (plural) or African indigenous religions (AIR).[18] The complexity of naming and describing this religion to the satisfaction of all has led to overgeneralizations, which has also contributed to the misconceptions and wrong conclusions of researchers in ATR.[19] But there could be a way out in the same way that Hindu scholars have been able to bring the complex religions of the Indus Valley people, the Dravidians of ancient civilizations, and the foreign invaders called Aryans under one umbrella now called Hinduism—a term that has no bearing to the original diverse people of this region.[20] That is why this chapter agrees to the use of the name African Traditional Religion (singular) as the umbrella which provides or assumes common concepts, beliefs, and practices and ceremonies for the complex diversities of this African way of life while at the same time distinguishing it from the "foreign" religions. It is like the struggle we encounter in our effort to understand the meaning of "world religions."

Secrecy and Drive

Scholars and students of ATR face the challenge of secrecy on the part of the priesthood, medicine men and women, and the elderly. African Traditional Religion's beliefs and practices are shrouded in secrecy, and when asked for further or detailed disclosure, you are told, "you don't need to know them. Just follow them. *Ɛyɛ amanneɛ; yɛbɛ toeɛ* (they are traditions handed down to us without questioning)." Many men and women endowed with the knowledge and practice of medicine have died without disclosing their abilities to others to benefit society.

Another issue of concern is the motivations of ATR. What is the ultimate agenda of ATR? What drives this religion? What is the one mission that runs through this ancient-cum-modern religio-cultural tradition? And how is it conveyed or "sold" to the rest of the world? Similar to other religions, ATR seeks to respond to questions of ultimate concern—where do we come from? What are we doing here? Where are we going? What happens when we die? ATR is clear and strong in its assertion of how we got here as human beings. It is also very emphatic on the life hereafter, which could be either a reincarnation or a settling down in the realm of the living dead. In my view, however, when it comes to the here and now, ATR becomes quite complicated. Many of the beliefs and practices are centered on fear and are quite disconcerting.

The term "fear" implies "anxiety and usually loss of courage."[21] It involves "panic, trepidation, timidity, trembling, and hesitation."[22] There is a fear of life itself, fear to ask certain questions, fear to answer specific questions, fear of the dead, fear to confront unchartered territories. It is the kind that pushes away momentum. By this, I mean ATR is not open to systematic critical questioning demanded by modern religious studies. The quest for the here and now with minimal regard for tomorrow raises the question about our sense of community as an inclusive of the past generation, the present generation, and the future generation. If ATR is studied as a world religion, these concerns will be confronted vis-à-vis other world religion models, and aspects of African

Traditional Religion's worldview that promote life's ultimate purpose will be dynamically engaged to benefit the world. For instance, ATR is friendly to the earth (nature) and the environment; the fear is that this may all die out with time because the metaphors alluding to this ethic are all dying out as many traditional symbols of expression of African lifeway are also extinguishing. A world religions scholar, Michael Molloy, says, "[I]ndigenous religions are being threatened by, among other things, loss of traditional languages."[23] The loss of languages resulting from a shift in society is a serious matter from a philosophical or an aesthetic point of view.[24] Maarten Mous also argues that loss of language deprives us of data that is crucial for increasing our "insight into the human language capacity" and "limits our possibilities to recover history," thus leading to the disappearance of indigenous knowledge.[25]

In some instances, the use of blood sacrifice has caused the young to frown upon this religion. Whether other religions use it or not, blood sacrifice makes the religion appear horrible and cruel and thus increases the fear factor in ATR. Many religions that used to offer blood sacrifice have, in the course of history, replaced it with other genial elements that serve the same purpose.

Membership

Another area of scholarly concern is membership data. How many are the adherents of ATR? How does one become a member? Is it by birth? By being born by African parents? Can we draw a line between African sociocultural life and religio-cultural life so that we can know the actual members of the religion? If all of life is integrated into African cosmology, can one conclude that every African is a member of ATR because they believe in the concept of lifeway? In Hinduism, one has to believe in the authority of the Vedas (their scriptures) and any of the designated deities in order to be a follower. So they have *astikas* (believers) and *nastikas* (unbelievers like Buddhists who do not believe in the Vedas or their Gods). In Judaism, one has to believe in the Torah as a revelation of *Yahweh*, the One and Only Creator God to be worshiped. African Traditional Religion needs to have a point of entrance—for someone to be counted as a member.

Religion has now entered into today's competitive market not only in its quest to recruit more followers but also to showcase its relevance and power block. Social media networks like Instagram, Twitter, and Facebook weigh their influence, power, and popularity by the number of followers or the number of people and spheres they have reached. This indicates the impact they are making in the world. If African Traditional Religion wrongly assumes that if you are an African, you are most likely an adherent, then ATR would be heading for doom. Along the same vein, ATR needs to expand its drive beyond the Black race. Is this a Herculean task for ATR? The Pew Research Center on Religion and Public Life put the ATR membership figure for sub-Saharan Africa at 27,010,000 in 2010 (i.e., 3.3% of the total population of the region) and projected it to increase to 61,470,000 in 2050 (an increase by 34,460,000 at a 2.1 growth rate and constitutes 3.2% of the region's population).[26]

It is also problematic to assume that it is only ATR that undergirds African spirituality. The dynamic character of African culture makes it possible to adapt and inculturate new forms of spirituality; hence, ATR needs to examine the depth of its influence on contemporary African cultures. Christianity, Islam, and some Asian religions have made, and continue to make, substantial inroads into African religious and social culture.

Conclusion

From our discussion of the narrative underlying the concept of "world religions," I take the position with other scholars that the study of "the religions of the world" or "the world's religions" appear to have the same meaning and therefore can be used interchangeably. These terms, in my view, are preferred to the term "world religions" because the former are inclusive of all religions irrespective of their racial or ethno-linguistic attachment, their geographical locations, or the number and composition of their adherents. This, in my perspective, will help answer the challenges that scholars, researchers, and students of world religions face. Also, African Traditional Religion must preserve its linguistic and aesthetic heritage for a better encounter with the major world religions. Language, self-consciousness, and identity are intertwined. If you give up your language, you lose some aspects of consciousness, affecting your role in the global competition for relevance in today's modern world. If you do not provide the right amount of input into a system, you definitely lose a significant share of the output. When African Traditional Religion is engaged in the study of world religions as a major tradition, its vocabulary will be preserved because the quest for the meaning of the indigenous idioms, metaphors, and other symbolic expressions will be researched and preserved to increase knowledge. And the world will benefit from such knowledge.

Notes

1. Tomoko Masuzawa, *The Invention of World Religions: Or, How European Universalism Was Preserved in the Language of Pluralism* 4/15/05 Edition, (Chicago, IL: University of Chicago Press; edition [May 15, 2005]), 3.
2. Ninian Smart, *The World's Religions, 2nd ed.*, (Cambridge, UK: Cambridge University Press, 1998), 13–21. Smart lists seven dimensions of religion: mythical and narrative, ritual, experiential and emotional, ethical and legal, social and institutional, doctrinal and philosophical, and material (symbols).
3. Bruce Lincoln, *Holy Terror: Thinking About Religion After September 11* (The University of Chicago Press; 2nd edition [June 15, 2006]), 5–7. Lincoln's four domains of religion are discourse, practice, community, and institution: discourse involves something beyond "us"; practices strive to make the world/people better; community forms around acts and beliefs; and institutions hold the truth.

4. John S. Mbiti, *Introduction to African Religion*, 2nd ed., 1991, 1975. (Reissued by Waveland Press, Inc., 2015), 11–12.
5. Benjamin Murphy, "Why Is the African Traditional Religion Not Regarded as the World Religion?" Quora, March 27, 2019.
   https://www.quora.com/Why-is-the-African-traditional-religion-not-regarded-as-the-world-religion (accessed November 6, 2020).
6. Masuzawa, *The Invention of World Religions*, 3.
7. Ibid.
8. Ibid.
9. Ibid.
10. Ibid.
11. Ibid.
12. Ibid.
13. Ibid.
14. Ibid.
15. Ibid.
16. Murphy, "Why Is the African Traditional Religion Not Regarded as the World Religion?" [online].
17. Rotimi Williams Omotoye, "The Study of African Traditional Religion and Its Challenges in Contemporary Times," *Ilorin Journal of Religious Studies, (IJOURELS)* vol. 1, no. 2 (2011): 21–40, 23.
18. See Jacob Olupona's edited work, *African Traditional Religions in Contemporary Society* (1998, 1991), and Theo Sundermeier's *The Individual and Community in African Traditional Religions* (1998).
19. Omotoye, "The Study of African Traditional Religion and its Challenges in Contemporary Times," 22.
20. Robert Yaw Owusu, *Introduction to Religion: A Customized Version of An Exploration of World Religions by Robert Y. Owusu and Richard Bennett, Designed Specifically for Robert Y. Owusu at Kennesaw State University* (Dubuque, IA: Kendall Hunt, 2016), 6.
21. "Fear," *Merriam-Webster Online Dictionary*. https://www.merriam-webster.com/dictionary/fear
22. Ibid.
23. Michael Molloy, *Experiencing the World's Religions: Tradition, Challenge, and Change, 6th Edition*, (New York: McGraw-Hill, 2012), 65.
24. Maarten Mous, "Loss of Linguistic Diversity in Africa," in *Metaphor in Cognitive Linguistics: Selected Papers from the 5th International Cognitive Linguistic Conference, Amsterdam, 1997*, eds. Raymond W. Gibbs, Jr. and Gerald J. Steen (John Benjamins Publishing Co., 1999), 157. Mous lists five shifts that have caused indigenous cultures to lose their languages.
25. Ibid., 161.
26. Pew Research Center, "Size and Projected Growth of Major Religious Groups of Sub-Saharan Africa, 2010-2050." March 30, 2015. https://www.pewforum.org/2015/04/02/sub-saharan-africa/163-3/ (accessed November 6, 2020).

CHAPTER 44

African Traditional Religion Scholarship: E. Bolaji Idowu and John S. Mbiti

Rotimi Williams Omotoye

INTRODUCTION

E. Bolaji Idowu and John S. Mbiti were among the first generation of academic giants in the field of African Traditional Religion in Africa. This chapter examines the contributions of these two scholars to the study of the discipline. The methodology adopted was historical. The texts written by them were significant in the course of this research. Bolaji Idowu, the first to be considered, was a Minister of the Methodist Church Nigeria. Two of his books titled *Olodumare: God in Yoruba Belief* and *African Traditional Religion: A Definition* were well researched and of good quality. The second African religion scholar, John Mbiti, was from Kenya, East Africa. He served at Makerere University as a professor, and director of the Ecumenical Institute in Bossey, Switzerland, among other institutions of note where he served as a scholar. He published a monumental book titled *African Religions and Philosophy*. However, there are others, such as *Concepts of God in Africa* and *Akamba Stories*.

The contributions and challenges of these two scholars were explored in the academic study of religion. They developed an interest in African traditional religion at a time when European scholars and Christian missionaries were hostile to the study of African religion. Even though they were Christians, they devoted much time to the study of African religion, especially the concept of God in Africa. They rejected the obnoxious and unacceptable terminologies used by Western scholars in describing the African religion. This research study

R. W. Omotoye (✉)
University of Ilorin, Ilorin, Nigeria

© The Author(s), under exclusive license to Springer Nature Switzerland AG 2022
I. S. Aderibigbe, T. Falola (eds.), *The Palgrave Handbook of African Traditional Religion*, https://doi.org/10.1007/978-3-030-89500-6_44

highlights the contributions that Idowu and Mbiti made to the study of African religion, creating further opportunities and windows for the study of African religion in Africa.

E. Bolaji Idowu: The Father of Reconstruction and Decolonization of African Traditional Religion

E. Bolaji Idowu (1913–1993) was one of the early African scholars in the field of Religious Studies, particularly the study of African Traditional Religion. His book, *Olodumare: God in Yoruba Belief*, has become monumental and imperishable literature in the study of African religion.[1] Even though a Christian Clergy of the Methodist Church, he was able to defend the African concept of God by reconstructing and decolonizing African religion from the negative approach of Western scholars, missionaries, sociologists, and racist writers. The foreign writers before the nineteenth century did not see anything researchable in the African religion. Therefore, we shall focus on earlier misconceived writings of some European scholars and missionaries, which Idowu was able to reconstruct through his concentration on the African concept of God.

However, having demonstrated nationalism, patriotism, and courage at the risk of his vocation as the Primate of the Methodist Church in Nigeria, some African Christian leaders that had sympathy for Western Christian missionaries criticized him for defending African traditional religion, which was viewed as a "primitive" religion. Some African writers, too, criticized him for using Christian perspectives to write about African religion. What a double jeopardy from two African bodies?

In trying to defend Idowu from local "colonialists," Olupona opines, "My aim is to rescue him from the accusation that he Christianizes African religion, by repositioning his work for the modern age."[2] For all intents and purposes, Idowu's work has remained classical, respected, and relevant within time and space.

Jacob F. Adeniyi Ajayi and Emmanuel Ayandele observed that "African Traditional Religion poses a great challenge to scholars of West African religious history. Still the effective religion of most West Africans, it is the most important religion that needs to be studied and understood if we are to understand West African history in general and religious history in particular. And yet it is the most neglected."[3] The latter part of the above comment must have challenged Bolaji Idowu's academic prowess and other contemporary scholars to the academic study of African traditional religion.

His contemporaries and modern scholars in the field of African scholarship are John S. Mbiti, Geoffrey Parrinder, Jonathan Olumide Lucas, Edmund Christopher Ilogu, Joseph Omosade Awolalu, Peter Adelumo Dopamu, Simon G. A. Onibere, and Michael Y. Nabofa. It should be noted that Ibigbolade S. Aderibigbe and Jacob K. Olupona are based in two prestigious universities in America teaching African religions. The former is at the University of Georgia, Athens, and the latter at Harvard University.

I became more interested in Idowu's work when I attended and presented related papers on the Yorùbá people and Christianity at two different conferences organized by the Nigerian Association for the Study of Religions (NASR) in 2005 and the Nigerian Association for Biblical Studies (NABIS) also in 2005. The theme of the former conference was titled *God: The Contemporary Discussion*, while the latter was *The Decolonization of Biblical Studies in Africa*. The papers presented at the two conferences are relevant to this chapter. The first paper was titled "The Concept of God and Its Understanding by the Christian Missionaries in Yorubaland,"[4] and the second paper was titled "Historical Perspective of the Decolonization of the Church in Yorubaland (1842–1960)."[5] I had to consult Idowu's book *Olodumare: God in Yoruba Belief* in providing adequate background to the two papers.

Who Was Bolaji Idowu?

It is of interest to note that the Department of Religious Studies at the University of Ibadan in Nigeria, where Bolaji Idowu lectured and became a professor, wrote a Festschrift on him titled *Under the Shelter of Olodumare*.[6] This literature has provided a good source of material on his personality. According to Ajayi and Ayandele, "the theological aspect of African Traditional Religion has received attention in greater depth by E. B. Idowu, who became an academic member of the department of Religious Studies at the University of Ibadan in 1958 and rose to become a professor and the first Nigerian head of the department."[7]

As a Clergy of the Methodist Church of Nigeria, he was reputed for not just rising to become the head of the Church in Nigeria, but also for his groundbreaking works on Yorùbá ethnographic and theological studies.

According to Samuel Emeka Kanu Uche, "His grandmother was believed to have predicted that Bolaji Idowu would become a vessel of God in the white man's religion (Christianity). He was sent to school and came under the influence of Rev. A. T. Ola Olude, who led him to Christ. At Wesley College, he was trained for four years, and afterword served as the sub-Pastor and the Headmaster in a Primary school at Ogere."[8] He later returned to Wesley College, where he was trained to become an ordained Minister. He was later posted to Trinity Methodist Church, Tinubu.

Okolugbo opined that "Bolaji Idowu's research into the study of *Olodumare: God in Yoruba Belief* has won international recognition and admiration. Through a thorough study of the names, attributes, and cults of *Olodumare*, Bolaji Idowu proved to the world that 'God is real to Africans and that is why Africans call Him by names which are descriptive both of His nature and of His attributes.'"[9] This position is not only true of the Yorùbá people but represents the African people. His significant publications included:

1. *Olodumare: God in Yoruba Belief*, published in 1962.
2. *Towards an Indigenous Church*, published in 1965.
3. *Biblical Revelation and African Beliefs*, published in 1969.
4. *African Religion and Philosophy* (Second Edition), published in 1969.
5. *Concepts of God in Africa*, published in 1970.
6. *African Traditional Religion: A Definition*, published in 1975.
7. *Introduction to African Religion*, published in 1975.

Interaction and Engagement of Idowu's Book—Olodumare: God in Yoruba Belief

As a student of Religious Studies at the Obafemi Awolowo University, Ile-Ife (1981–1985), we were introduced to the book by Professor S. G. A. Onibere, another prominent scholar of African religion. Since then, it has been literature to be always read. I am a Church historian, but I cannot afford not to make references to the book in the course of writing about the richness of the Yorùbá peoples' religious life.

We often quote one of Idowu's phrases, "However, the real keynote of the life of the Yoruba is neither in their noble ancestry nor in the past deeds of their heroes. The keynote of their life is their religion. In all things, they are religious. Religion forms the foundation and all-governing principle of life for them."[10] This quotation is still relevant and appropriate whenever an evaluation of the religious life of the Yorùbá people is being done to date.

Reinterpretation and Decolonization of Foreign Writers on African Religion

Our focus in this study is to engage Idowu's interaction and comments about some foreign writers' uncomplimentary and unacceptable views about African religion. The expressions were based on ignorance, lack of sympathy in the study of African religion, and racism.

Two of Bolaji Idowu's books, namely *Olodumare: God in Yoruba Belief* and *African Traditional Religion: A Definition*, are useful for this study. As earlier mentioned, our concentration would be on some foreign scholars that did not see African people as having a "concept of God," which was the focus of Idowu. Peter Adelumo Dopamu noted Bolaji Idowu's three periods of history of the African religion. According to him, the first period was that of ignorance and false certainty. This period witnessed false tales and stories about Africa. The second was a period of doubt and resisted illumination. This period was marked by the appearance of genuine researchers who reached a clear conclusion after exhaustive researches that there could be no people anywhere in the world who were devoid of culture and religion. However, these researchers were rejected by Western scholars who were described by Idowu as stay-at-home-investigators. The third period was that of an intellectual dilemma. The predicament in which scholars of this period found themselves was whether or not to accept the convincing evidence that Africans do indeed have a concept of God. "If there is an African concept of God, if Africans know God, what or which God? Their own God or 'the real God'? ... In order to meet this predicament, various evasive means have been adopted." We find examples in the obnoxious titles of "the withdrawn god" and "the high god."[11]

At this juncture, we shall examine some of the foreign writers' submissions that are relevant to this study. Idowu, in his two books, made reference to Leo Frobenius. Idowu opined, "Leo Frobenius appears to have become somewhat sentimental; however, he probably remembered too much of his classical education in his interpretations and so got himself mixed up. In West Africa, with particular reference to Ile-Ife, the Sacred City, and the cradle of the Yoruba, he thought that he discovered 'the Lost Atlantis.'"[12] He was not the only person or scholar guilty of this submission. Many scholars have traced the origin of the Yorùbá civilization to Egypt. In other words, the religion and culture of the people were seen as imported by the people. The Atlantis theory of Leo Frobenius was based on ignorance and lack of proper understanding of the culture, religion, and biased mind.

Idowu also accused the Portuguese explorers and the French writers of "besetting temptation to take appearance for reality without adequate verification."[13] For example, the word "fetich" means "that which is made" to describe the African religion. This was one of the wrong terminologies used to characterize African religions. Another obnoxious and unacceptable terminology was juju. In French, the word *jou-jou* means "toy." In other words, African religion was regarded as an institution to be toyed with. African scholars have also rejected and condemned such an obnoxious term. Idowu noted that Father Schmidt condemned Eric S. Waterhouse for "exporting Christian theological terms for the purpose of describing the concept of the Supreme Being among 'primitive races.'"[14] The stages of development and civilization may not be the same; it is not acceptable to refer to another race as "primitive."

Rotimi Omotoye quoted Emil Ludwig to have said, "How can the untutored African conceive of God? How can this be? Deity is a philosophical concept which savages are incapable of framing." Omotoye submitted that Emil "believed that the White and Black people could not worship the same God."[15] This position was an error of judgment and based on racism.

Peter Adelumo Dopamu also drew our attention to the work of James Frazer titled *The Golden Bough*, where he described three stages of human intellectual development, that is, from magic to religion and from religion to science. Dopamu was able to point out the inadequacy and failure of this theory in Africa. According to him, such a theory is bogus because magic and religion are found in all cultures.[16]

John Samuel Mbiti

The second African religion scholar to be considered in this chapter was John Samuel Mbiti (1931–2019). He was a contemporary of E. Bolaji Idowu in the academic study of African religion. He was born on 30 November 1931 in Mulago, Kitui, Kitui County, Eastern Kenya, and died on 5 October 2019 at a nursing home in Burgdorf, Switzerland.[17] He was brought up in a Christian family. His parents were Samuel Mutuvi Ngaangi and Valesi Mbandi Kiimba. His Christian background influenced his training as a student, and finally, he became an ordained Priest in the Anglican Church of England.

He was a student of the Alliance High School in Nairobi and later went to the University College of Makerere and the University of London, where he graduated in 1953. He obtained his doctorate in 1963 at the University of Cambridge in the United Kingdom. He taught Religion and Theology at Makerere University, Uganda, from 1964 to 1974 and became the director of the prestigious Ecumenical Institute situated at Bogis-Bossey, Switzerland, from 1974 to 1980.[18] Mbiti was a world-renowned scholar; he was an Emeritus Professor at the University of Bern and a Parish Priest at Burgdorf, Switzerland, for 15 years. He was a successful married man with his wife, Verena Mbiti-Siegenthaler, and was blessed with four children.

John Mbiti's Academic Prowess in the African Religion

John Mbiti's interest was in the field of African religion. His primary focus was a defense of African religion, which was relegated by White Christian missionaries, sociologists, historians, and theologians from the West. Even though he was a Clergy in the Church of England, Anglican Communion, he protected the African religion, especially the African concept of God. It was a challenging aspect of his academic career to combine it with church activities. Mbiti's work was more philosophical in understanding than that of Idowu.

John Mbiti's first book, *African Religions and Philosophy*, was published in 1969. This was a monumental book because he was able to defend the African concept of God. He condemned the attitude of the White writers and missionaries that used uncomplimentary and obnoxious terms to describe the African religion. Mbiti opined that "traditional African religions deserve the same respect as Christianity, Islam, Judaism, and Buddhism."[19] His other academic published works included:

(a) *Akamba Stories*, published in 1968.
(b) *Poems of Nature and Faith. Poets of Africa*, published in 1969.
(c) *Concepts of God in Africa*, published in 1970.
(d) *New Testament Eschatology in an African Background*, published in 1971.
(e) *Love and Marriage in Africa*, published in 1973.

(f) *Introduction to African Religion*, published in 1975.
(g) *The Prayers of African Religion*, published in 1975.
(h) *African Proverbs*, published in 1997.

John W. Kinney discusses Mbiti's work under the caption of "The Theology of John Mbiti: His Sources, Norms, and Method." According to Kinney, "Dr. Mbiti has gained international recognition as a scholar through his prolific writings relating to traditional African religions and the development of Christian theology in Africa." He went further to say, "He is respected and appreciated in Africa as a 'pioneer' in the systematic analysis of traditional African religious concepts."[20]

In his book, *African Religions and Philosophy*, Mbiti addressed the nature of God in Chapter 4, emphasizing that God is the creator and sustainer of the World.[21] He succeeded in maintaining the African peoples' position of God as omnipotent, omniscient, transcendent, and immanent. God is seen as the Supreme Being. His supremacy is expressed in proverbs, short statements, songs, prayers, names, myths, stories, and religious ceremonies. He went on to say that God "is no stranger to African peoples, and in traditional life, there are no atheists."[22] He discussed the eternal, intrinsic, and moral attributes of God. The eternal attributes of God clearly show His infinite and immutable power. He is incomprehensible and mysterious. In his moral attributes, God is faithful, just, and righteous.

However, some critics believed that Mbiti could not distinguish between his Christian background and the traditional African interpretation of phenomena. According to Kinney, "Dr. Mbiti suggests that there are four areas which variously have to make their contributions toward the evolution of theology in Africa: (a) the Bible and biblical theology, (b) Christian theology from the major traditions of Christendom, (c) a serious study of African religions and philosophy, (d) the theology of the living church."[23] There is no doubt that Mbiti made use of his Christian background to address some African issues relating, in particular, to the concept of God.

In conclusion, Idowu and Mbiti, no doubt, are viewed as pioneers of African religion scholarship. They encountered many challenges because of the prevailing situation that was dominated by Western scholars of the time. However, they succeeded in providing the necessary tools for a proper and accurate understanding of African religion and the concept of God in their works. However, they were not unaware of some teething hindrances in the study of African religion. The geographical size of Africa as a continent, secrecy among the African people, and lack of written records are issues affecting the proper and adequate study of African Traditional Religion. Despite these predicaments, Idowu and Mbiti were able to make a significant mark in the study of the African concept of God.

Notes

1. E. Bolaji Idowu, *Olodumare: God in Yoruba Belief*, (Lagos: Longman Nigeria Limited, 1962).
2. Jacob K. Olupona, "Reinterpreting Olodumare: God in Yoruba Belief," in S. O. Abogunrin and Deji Ayegboyin, (eds), *Under the Shelter of Olódùmarè: Essays in Memory of Professor E. Bolaji Idowu* (Ibadan: John Archers Publishers, 2014), 18.
3. Jacob F. Adeniyi Ajayi, and Emmanuel A. Ayandele, "Emerging Themes of West African Religious History," in E. A. Ade Adegbola, (ed.), *Traditional Religion in West Africa* (Ibadan: Sefer Books Limited, 1983), 446.
4. Rotimi W. Omotoye, "The Concept of God and Its Understanding by the Christian Missionaries in Yorubaland," in E. Ade Odumuyiwa et al., (eds.), *God: The Contemporary Discussion*, (Ilorin: Nigerian Association for the Study of Religions, 2005).
5. Rotimi W. Omotoye, "Historical Perspective of the Decolonization of the Church in Yorubaland (1842–1960)" in S. O. Abogunrin et al., (eds.), *Decolonization of Biblical Interpretation in Africa* (Ibadan: M. Alofe Publishers, 2005).
6. See Abogunrin and Ayegboyin, *Under the Shelter of Olódùmarè*.
7. Ajayi and Ayandele, "Emerging Themes of West African Religious History," 446.
8. Samuel Emeka Kanu Uche, "Foreword," in S. O. Abogunrin and Deji Ayegboyin, (eds), *Under the Shelter of Olódùmarè: Essays in Memory of Professor E. Bolaji Idowu* (Ibadan: John Archers Publishers, 2014).
9. E. O. Okolugbo, "Emmanuel Bolaji Idowu: A Vocal Spiritual Bridge Between Christianity and African Traditional Religious," in S. O. Abogunrin and Deji Ayegboyin, (eds), *Under the Shelter of Olódùmarè: Essays in Memory of Professor E. Bolaji Idowu* (Ibadan: John Archers Publishers, 2014), 95.
10. Idowu, *Olodumare: God in Yoruba Belief*, 5.
11. Peter Adelumo Dopamu, "African Religion in Nigerian Society: Past, Present and the Future," in R. D. Abubakre et al., (eds.), *Studies in Religious Understanding in Nigeria*, (Ilorin: Nigerian Association for the Study of Religion, 1993), 240.
12. E. Bolaji Idowu, *African Traditional Religion: A Definition*, (London: SCM Press, 1973) 3. See also E. B. Idowu, *Olodumare: God in Yoruba Belief*, 2–4; Ajayi and Ayandele, "Emerging Themes of West African Religious History," 449.
13. Ibid.
14. Ibid.
15. Omotoye, "The Concept of God and Its Understanding by the Christian Missionaries in Yorubaland," 103.
16. Dopamu, "African Religion in Nigerian Society: Past, Present and the Future," 239–247.
17. John Samuel Mbiti, https//en.wikipedia.org/wiki/John-Mbiti (accessed March 20, 2020); See also "John Mbiti, 87, Dies; Punctured Myths About African Religions," The New York Times, https://www.nytimes.com/2019/10/24/world/africa/john-mbiti-dead.html (accessed November 7, 2020).
18. Ibid.

19. John W. Kinney, "The Theology of John Mbiti: His Sources, Norms, and Method," (Richmond: School of Theology of Virginia Union University, 1979), 65.
20. Ibid.
21. John S. Mbiti, African Religions and Philosophy (London: Heinemann Educational Books, 1969), 29.
22. Ibid.
23. Kinney, "The Theology of John Mbiti," 65.

CHAPTER 45

African Traditional Religion and Humanities' Scholarship: The Contributions of Edward Geoffrey Parrinder and Kofi Asare Opoku

Olatunde Oyewole Ogunbiyi and Lydia Bosede Akande

INTRODUCTION

In contemporary academic discussions on African Traditional Religion, there is an emphasis on considering the works of "patriarch" scholars and their attendant influences on the field. These scholars have blazed the trail for future scholars that will either tow or abandon the path they had opened for posterity. It is important to examine the works of these scholars for several reasons, a few of which are highlighted in this study. Many of the scholars themselves are dying out, and their exits are a cause for concern. The legacies they leave behind should be made available for upcoming researchers to act as springboards for future studies. Besides, they were the ones who actually started a serious academic examination of African Traditional Religion. This is a religion that has hitherto been subjected to a series of misinterpretations and consequent misrepresentations. Theirs were apologies of African Traditional Religion in the face of virulent persecutions from Western scholars when prejudice was the order of the day for anything that was not Western. A few of these patriarch scholars of African Traditional Religion were Europeans, while others were Africans.

Among these are the likes of Geoffrey Parrinder, John S. Mbiti, E. Bolaji Idowu, Joseph Omosade Awolalu, Kofi Opoku Asare, and P. Adelumo

---

O. O. Ogunbiyi • L. B. Akande (✉)
University of Ilorin, Ilorin, Nigeria
e-mail: akande.lb@unilorin.edu.ng

© The Author(s), under exclusive license to Springer Nature Switzerland AG 2022
I. S. Aderibigbe, T. Falola (eds.), *The Palgrave Handbook of African Traditional Religion*, https://doi.org/10.1007/978-3-030-89500-6_45

Dopamu. This chapter examines two out of these erudite scholars. They are Edward Geoffrey Parrinder and Kofi Asare Opoku. The reasons for the writers' choice of these enigmatic figures lie in the fact that Edward Parrinder was a European, yet he wrote an unbiased account of his fieldwork in Africa. The other scholar who merits a space in this exercise is Kofi Asare Opoku, who can be described as a second-generation scholar. He was an African and a contributor to the academic studies of African Traditional Religion across universities both in Nigeria and overseas. It is worthy of mention that all the scholars earlier mentioned, including the two to be studied, have made tremendous contributions and sacrifices in the field of academics.

The work is further divided into four major areas and examines African Traditional Religion in its pristine form. This will provide a basis for the earlier scholars' perception of the religion. The third section is devoted to the study of the personality of Parrinder and his academic legacies as it relates only to African Traditional Religion because, as a versatile scholar, he touched every aspect of "World Religions." A similar emphasis is carried out on Opoku in the fourth section of this chapter, while the fifth section is an assessment of their works. The approaches that are used are multi-disciplinary, which include the historical and theological approaches. The historical approach affords the researchers the ability to trace the history of African Traditional Religious scholarship and the profiles of the scholars under review, while the theological approach examines their works in line with the religious consciousness of the Africans.

African Traditional Religion in its Pristine Form

Religion has been one of the most difficult concepts to define. Attempting to capture this fact, Nana Osei Bonsu puts it this way: "Religion, like any other philosophical concept does not have a single universally accepted definition. This is because religion deals with immaterial objects that cannot be empirically verified. It has been defined differently by people of diverse interests, academic and cultural backgrounds."[1]

In most cases, people focus on their expressions or manifestations rather than its essence, which should be a significant area of concern.[2] There exist diverse definitions, as many as there are disciplines. Each of these disciplines attempts to define religion from the spectacles of their own discipline. As of today, there is no acceptable definition of "religion." In an attempt to define the word, Rahner[3] examines the etymological connotation of the word as he traced the root of the word "religion" to the Latin word *religio* with its different verb forms—*relegere*, *religari*, and *reeligere*.

This etymological construct will serve as the premise for the overview of the African Traditional Religion. African Traditional Religion is hitherto referred to as ATR and is the aboriginal religion of the Africans. It is the indigenous beliefs and practices of the African people that have existed before the advent of foreigners on the African land space. ATR is the religion that has been transmitted from one generation to the other through oral transmission. This is the faith that has been practiced from time immemorial to the present time by the African people, some of who even claimed to be Muslims or Christians. The religion is considered "traditional" since it is indigenous to the Africans and the transmission mode from the generations unknown to the present day. In the words of Awolalu, "This is not a 'fossil' religion, a thing of the past or a dead religion. It is a religion that is practiced by living men and women."[4] Interestingly, the religion, like other religions of the world, has undergone several changes in lieu of the technological advancements and globalizing agencies, which makes the term to be one that only speaks of the religion in terms of age and difference from foreign religions that came afterward to Africa.

There have been a lot of debates that later scholars have come to engage themselves in regarding ATR. Some have preferred to see the religion in the singular; others have chosen to see it in the plural. Bolaji Idowu, Awolalu, and Dopamu see the religion in the singular, while Parrinder and Mbiti prefer to view the religion as plural. Hence, some view it as African Traditional Religion, while others view it as African Traditional Religions. Those who see it in the singular postulate a homogenous perception of the peoples' faith, not denying the diversity in languages and ethnicity but focusing on the structural similarities inherent in their faith. Still, others prefer to view it from the linguistic differences of the Africans, the size of the continent, and the apparent dichotomy in number, theologies, and emphasis and conclude that the religion should be seen in the plural. The chapter's authors are of the opinion that the religion of the people is actually one. This is anchored on the similarities in the structure of African Religion, which by far outweigh the dissimilarities, especially in the structure of the religion.

When compared to other world religions, ATR has no scriptures like the Qu'ran or the Bible. It is a religion that is based on oral transmissions, which has existed for centuries, though it must also be emphasized that the religion has its own corpora, some of which are still reduced into writing. In addition to this, the religion differs from others because it does not possess temples like the foreign religion that came after. As far as the Africans are concerned, God can be worshiped anywhere, and he is not localized to a particular place. It must be added here that the religion has sacred places known as grooves, shrines, and oftentimes houses where God is worshiped. The founder of the religion is shrouded in mystery. He is not known, though it must be emphasized that the religion is not the religion of a man but a collective. In light of this, the religion has no revivalists, reformers, or evangelists to propagate it. Nevertheless, ATR devotees have been known to be loyal to their religion.

The Africans construct their cosmos from three-dimensional, distinct but inseparable worlds; these are the human order with their social concepts, the non-human world that is physical and natural, plus the spiritual world where the unseen forces inhabit. These three are mutually interrelated, constituting a unity and depending on one another. Around this worldview hangs their perception of the beings they revere as a people. This consists of recognizing mysterious powers that can be either benevolent or malevolent, the innumerable rituals, and practices that regulate the consciousness of the African people. It is in light of this that, in **African Traditional Religion, it is difficult to determine the boundaries existing between the daily and religious life of the people of Africa. It is not possible to decide on where the physical dovetails into the spiritual or vice versa in the life of the Africans.**

Parrinder's Life and Career

Early Life: 1910–1933

Edward Geoffrey Simos Parrinder (April 10, 1910–June 16, 2005) was a Professor of Comparative Religion at King's College London. He was a Methodist minister and missionary in several parts of Africa and author of over thirty books that he was privileged to have written because of his stay in several parts of the world.[5] For about twenty years, he was a missionary in the Benin Republic and Ivory Coast.

Parrinder was born in New Barnet, Hertfordshire, on April 30, 1910, to William Patrick and Florence Mary.[6] His father was a devout Wesleyan Methodist member who worked in London and eventually had his own business until about 1930 when it went bankrupt. At one time, he considered taking up missionary work to Africa but was persuaded by his own parents. It was Edward who eventually became the missionary. While reviewing his works, Hastings has the following to say about the background:

> In 1919, his parents moved to Leigh-on-Sea in Essex; there, he was educated at the Leigh Hall College. At the age of sixteen, after copleting his secondary school education, she started work as a booking clerk with the railway. While working with the railways, he studied at Richmond College in London between 1929-1932 and became a minister of the Methodist denomination. he also went to Montpellier, a city in France, to study French and further his study of Theology. In 1933, against all attempts to dissuade him, he left London for the Republic of Benin (formerly called Dahomey). Here, he began his carreer as a Missionary and Researcher on the Traditional Religion of the Africans. His souourn in Africa enabled him to have a particular observation enperience with the african people and their culture. Though he was shuttling from Africa to Europe. He spent a total of nineteen years in Africa.[7]

Missionary and Academician 1936–2005

The bedrock of Parrinder's research work was his thirst for soul winning. His mission for living in Europe for Africa is that of spreading the gospel in Africa. This was an unconscious responsibility passed on to him by his father, who wanted to take up missionary activities in Africa but was dissuaded by his parents. He thus became a minister and an academician with a passion for studying world religions. From Benin, he proceeded to the Ivory Coast; these countries are French-speaking West African countries. His sojourn in these places lasted between 1933 and 1946. In 1936, he returned to England to marry Mary, his heartthrob whom he met at a meeting of the Methodists, and also to be ordained as a minister. He was involved in Methodist circuit work both in Redruth, Cornwall (1940–1943), and in Guernsey (1946–1949) as he shuttled from Africa.

An extremely versatile fellow, Parrinder seized the opportunity of his work with the Methodist to advance his study where he had his B.A. and B.D. degrees and then proceeded to obtain his M.A., M.Th., and Ph.D., focusing on the indigenous religious beliefs of West Africans. This led him to join the league of authors as he started publishing books. His first book, *West African Religion* (1949), was followed by more research on religion in Ibadan, published as *Religion in an African City* (1953). Other important publications were *African Psychology* (1951), *African Traditional Religion* (1954), *Witchcraft* (1958), and *The Story of Ketu* (1956).

Between 1949 and 1958, he taught Religious Studies at the University College in Ibadan. In 1949, he was appointed to the highly innovative Department of Religious Studies at the University College, Ibadan in Nigeria, first as a lecturer (1949–1950) and then as a senior lecturer (1950–1958), teaching many African students and making lasting friendships.[8] He was able to influence several African students who later collaborated with him in the further study of African Religion. In 1958, he became a reader in the Comparative Study of Religions at the King's College in London, where the future Archbishop Desmond Tutu was among his students. Parrinder was a founding member of the British Association for the Study of Religions, its honorary Secretary (1960–1972), President (1972–1977), and a life member. Awarded a personal Chair in 1970, he was Dean of the faculty of Theology (1972–1974) and retired in 1977.

King, an avid follower of Parrinder, offers additional information about him in a book he edited in honor of the eminent scholar. He had this to say about him:

> While a Professor in the Comparative Study of Religions at King's College in London, Parrinder was a prolific writer, most notably on African Relgions. His works on Indian Religions. Islam and Comparativee themes that appealed to a broad reading public, and helped promote a better understanding and closer collaboration between members of different faiths and cultures. His textbook, What World Religions Teach Us (1968), became a best seller. He was active in the London Society for the Study of Religion wharee he was President (1980-1982), and the London Society of Jews and Christians, where he was also President (1981-1990) and honorary life President. As a founder member and co-president of the Shap working party, he helped advance the study of religion as a significant subject.[9]

He served on the editorial boards of several journals and gave many prestigious lectures around the world.[10] He was also a visiting professor at the International Christian University in Tokyo (1977–1978) and a visiting lecturer at the University of Surrey (1978–1982). His publishing output was phenomenal, including twenty-nine single-authored and six edited books between 1949 and 1992, as well as numerous shorter works. He continued writing until January 2003, after forty-five years of producing his last report on religion for the *Annual Register of World Events*. He always remained humble and kind, even a little shy. He is survived by his wife and their son and daughter. One son predeceased him.

Contributions to the Study of African Religion

The distinguished scholar Edward Geoffrey Simons Parrinder, who died at the age of ninety-five,[11] advocated for the study of world religions at all levels of education. As a teacher, writer, and member of the World Congress of Faiths and the Shap working party on world religions in education, set up in 1969, he gave much encouragement to those working in schools and colleges in Britain and abroad. The *Oxford Dictionary of National Biography*[12] also listed him as one of the scholars worthy of mention. The work attests to the fact that Parrinder was a widely traveled missionary and teacher, who assisted in the production of researchers who pioneered and continued to contribute to the study of religion of the Africans. His efforts, as seen in his books, show that he was familiar with the religious practices of the African people, especially in West Africa. His extensive sojourn in Ibadan allowed him to understand the practical aspects of Yorùbá culture and general worldview. For a man who had traversed the whole world, it was possible for him to compare and contrast African Religion with such world religions as Christianity, Buddhism, Islam, Hinduism, and a host of other spiritualities.

Books

Geoffrey Parrinder wrote several books, most of which were centered on his research as he labored as a Methodist missionary in different parts of West Africa and Asia. The following is a list of some of his writings, culled from Wikipedia.[13]

- *West African Religion* (1949, 1961)[14]
- *African Psychology* (1951)
- *An African City* (1953)
- *African Traditional Religion*, London: SPCK (1954)
- *The Story of Ketu* (1956)
- *Witchcraft, European and African* (1958), London: Faber & Faber, (1963) (1970) ISBN 0-571-09060-5
- *The Christian Approach to the Animist*
- *The Christian Debate*

- *Worship in the World's Religions* (1961, 1974)
- *Comparative Religion*
- *Asian Religions*
- *The Faiths of Mankind: A Guide to the World's Living Religions*, Crowell (1965)
- *African Mythology*, Hamlyn Publishing Group Ltd. (1967), ISBN 0-600-00042-7
- *What World Religions Teach Us* (1968)
- *Man and His Gods* (1971; US title: *Religions of the World*)
  – Revised edition: *World Religions: From Ancient History to the Present* (1983), Geoffrey Parrinder (editor), Facts on File, ISBN 0-87196-129-6
- *A Dictionary of Non-Christian Religions*, Westminster John Knox Press (1973), ISBN 0-664-20981-5
- *A Book of World Religions*
- *Jesus in the Quran*, Oneworld Publications (1995), ISBN 1-85168-094-2
- *Avatar and Incarnation: A Comparison of Indian & Christian Beliefs*, London: Faber & Faber (1970), Oxford University Press. (1982) ISBN 0-19-520361-5
- *Upanishads, Gita, and Bible: A Comparative Study of Hindu and Christian Scriptures*, Harper & Row (1972), ISBN 0-06-131660-1
- *African Traditional Religion*, Greenwood Pub. Group, 3rd edition (1970), ISBN 0-8371-3401-3
- *The Bhagavad Gita: A Verse Translation*, London: Sheldon Press (1974), ISBN 0-85969-018-0, Dutton Books (1975), ISBN 0-525-47390-4, Oneworld Publications (1996) ISBN 1-85168-117-5
- *The Indestructible Soul*
- *The Wisdom of the Forest: Selections from the Hindu Upanishads*, New York: New Directions, (1976), ISBN 0-8112-0606-8
- *Mysticism in the World's Religions*, London: Sheldon Press (1976), ISBN 0-85969-085-7. Oxford University Press in USA: (1977), ISBN 0-19-502185-1. Oneworld Publications: (1995), ISBN 1-85168-101-9
- *Sex in the World's Religions*, Oxford University Press (1980), ISBN 0-19-520202-3
- *Encountering World Religions: Questions of Religious Truth*, Crossroad Pub. Co. (1987), ISBN 0-8245-0826-2
- *Son of Joseph: The Parentage of Jesus*, T. & T. Clark Publishers, Ltd. (1993), ISBN 0-567-29213-4
- *A Concise Encyclopedia of Christianity*, Oneworld Publications (1998), ISBN 1-85168-174-4
- *Wisdom of Jesus*, Oneworld Publications (2000), ISBN 1-85168-225-2
- *The Routledge Dictionary of Religious and Spiritual Quotations*, New York: Routledge (2001), ISBN 0-415-23393-3
- *West African Psychology: A Comparative Study of Psychological and Religious Thought*, James Clarke Company, (2002), ISBN 0-227-17053-9
- *Sexual Morality in the World Religions*, Oneworld Publications, (2003), ISBN 1-85168-108-6

The books he wrote have helped advance the study of ATR in quite a variety of ways. Aside from the fact that the books were evidence of his research on African soil, they negate the Europeans' perception of the African people and their religion. Being that as it were, the books became points of departure from latter scholars like Dopamu, who were beneficiaries of his works.

Kofi Asare Opoku

Kofi Asare Opoku is a prolific writer who touched virtually every aspect of African Religion from the Ghanaian perspective. His writings, commencing from African Religion, expanded to the capturing of African indigenous Churches and then to comparing the religion with other world religions. His academic career spanned over forty years, which has taken him all over the world. The primary courses he taught included Religion and Culture. He wrote with the passion of one who loves the African Religion though not a practitioner. Also, one is not left in doubt about his knowledge of the people's religion. In several ways, Opoku has influenced and will continue to influence generations of scholars both in Africa and beyond. Opoku rose to the position of Associate Professor of Religion and Ethics in the Institute of African Studies at the University of Ghana located in Legon. He then proceeded to Lafayette College in Pennsylvania, the United States, where he rose to the position of a Professor of Religious Studies. He was once the Chairman of the Kwabena Nketia Centre for Africana Studies. He retired and went back to Ghana, where he is contributing to community development through his farming business. The farm is located at Mampong, Akuapem, in the Eastern Region of Ghana.[15]

Contributions of Kofi Opoku Asare

As a lecturer, Opoku's influence transcends the African continent. He was a widely traveled scholar whose labor was in high demand. He lectured in Ghana, South Africa, and also in the United States. Apart from these, he is known to have traversed the world as a visiting lecturer or as a conference attendee where much of his presentations were on the subject matter of African Religion. It is along this line that he was able to raise the next generation of African Traditional Religious scholars. They today have continued his legacy in African tertiary institutions and outside the shores of Africa. Many of these scholars have become professors in various universities in Ghana and across the world. The academic study of African Religion gained prominence, with students obtaining their doctoral degrees in the discipline. This has led to the commencement of African Religion as a discipline in various universities across Ghana.

By providing the academic footing for African Religion, Opoku Asare was able to bring to the limelight quite a lot of materials that had hitherto not been brought to the fore by earlier writers. In addition to this, he is in line with fellow scholars like Mbiti, Idowu, Awolalu, Dopamu, and Abimbola, to mention only a few who have attempted to defend the religion of their forebears. This they do in their writing apologetic books stating in clear terms the African peoples' understanding of their spiritualties. He not only wrote apologetics. He also, as a result of his being familiar with the nuances of the traditional religion, was able to present an account of the religion of his people. This he did through the writing of several books and article presentations in conferences and publications. His book, *West African Traditional Religion* (1978),[16] captures the essence of the traditional religion of the people of West Africa. In many of his writings, he spoke about the worldview of Africans, especially the Akan people. In one of his articles, he spoke about their concept of God and their cultural beliefs.[17] His view here is further complemented by his exposition of the folk beliefs of the Africans.[18] Closely following this is an examination of the Mami Water phenomenon that is common among the West African coastal ethnic groups. These ethnic groups often believe in the existence of a river divinity called Mami Water. He examined the phenomenon among the Ewe of Ghana. His conclusion is that the riverine divinities are a part of the African spiritual landscape.[19]

Concerning his primary contribution to the academic field of African Religion, his appreciation of African proverbs transcends other contributions. He wrote several books on the topic and made innumerable contributions to the same at conferences, on talk shows, and even in newspapers. Worthy of mention here was his talk show about the fact that Valentine is not strange to Africans as it is in the heart of all Africans to express love to their kith and kin and everyone on the face of the earth.[20] According to him, proverbs are an integral part of the Africans, especially the West Africans, particularly the Ghanaians, that nothing is often said without interjections of appropriate proverbs. These proverbs are a repertoire of the African peoples' philosophy and world view. Out of the several books he published with a view to driving home his emphasis on proverbs include *Speak to the Winds: Proverbs from Africa* (1975)[21] and *Hearing and Keeping: Akan Proverbs* (1975).

His interest in the African indigenous Churches is worthy of mention. Opoku's bent on African Religion made his escapade in indigenous African Churches worthwhile. He was able to present the manner in which the African Christians were able to contextualize the Christianity that was imported into Africa by the Europeans. Opoku was able to study churches like the Musama Christo Disco Church.[22] This is a church that combines Christianity with several Akan religio-cultural practices. In one of his interesting articles, he detailed the deep relationship between the traditional religious consciousness of Ghanaians and their approach to Christianity that was introduced to them.[23] African Church, the dramatic effect of this, according to Opoku, is the general acceptance of this form of Christianity by the Akan populace. He looked at the African indigenous Churches as the confluence of African traditional and

European Christian spiritualities. According to him, the African Churches have done a lot to situate Christianity in Africa.[24]

Opoku's academic interest in African Religion made him not to treat the enigmatic subject in abstract or in isolation. He also situated the religion in the context of other world religions. One of his writings along this line is his work on mysticism, where he made it clear that Africans also have mystics as it is understood in other religions. In this work, he tried to compare African mysticism with that of the East.[25] Furthermore, he considers the independence of the mind as an issue that had always occupied his mind since he was in the Seminary.[26]

A scholar of high repute, he related, interpreted, and intertwined African Religion with several other disciplines. He explored African Religion in the area of the provision of alternative medicine where African medicines have proven to have better efficacious effects than the Western counterparts in several areas.[27] By extension, he related the African as a cultural experience.[28] While investigating religion in Africa during the colonial era,[29] he explored the communal living of the Africans that has made them unique from other ethnic groups the world over.[30]

Appraisal of E. G. Parrinder and K. A. Opoku to the Scholarship of African Religion

The works of the duo of E. G. Parrinder and K. A. Opoku will continue to speak on. Judging by their appearances in the transitional study of the Africans, both contributed abundantly to the study of African Religion in Africa. Parrinder stood at the transition between two poles, the scholars of African Religion. On one side are those who were non-Africans who wished to portray the African Religion as bad. It is in this group that armchair investigators, Christian missionaries, colonial administrators, and explorers belong. The majority of these people were filled with racial prejudice, false reporters, and those who believe that Africans are so weak they cannot conceive of a God. On the other side are the Africans who were contemporary beneficiaries of their forefathers' faith though educated now in the Western style. These ones knew what foreigners said about their religion was incorrect, and they had the true account of the religion of their fathers. Parrinder is in the midst of these two people. He had studied the religions of the continent of Africa up to Asia, and he was convinced that beyond the lies that his fellow foreigners tell the world, the truth cannot be hidden. What makes the contributions of Parrinder valuable is that he gave an unbiased account of the Africans as a European Christian missionary. Besides, he actually visited Africa to study the religious consciousness of the African people and their culture for himself, and he presented his findings in an honest manner in several ways. He was a Christian researcher into the spirituality of the Africans. Both of them were studied at one time or another, African Religion, and at other times comparing African Religion with other world religions. Opoku was also a transitional researcher. While Parrinder stood between his people on one side and the likes of Mbiti, Awolalu, and Idowu on the other side, Opoku stood between these patriarch scholars and the contemporary researchers as they exist today. While the patriarch scholars focus primarily on writing apologies about African Religion, Opoku was able to ride upon their shoulders to dig into deeper recesses of African traditional religious ontology. Having the works of earlier scholars of African Traditional Religion until the patriarch scholars, he was able to advance the epistemology of African Religion beyond the frontiers of these earlier scholars.

Conclusion

Today, the academic study of African Traditional Religion is soaring high in the field of Religious Studies. Thanks to the efforts of virulent scholars like the ones we are just studying. This is evidenced by the quantum of student graduates, graduating up to the doctoral level. Many of those that these erudite scholars have influenced have risen to become Professors of African Religion and Comparative Religious Studies with an emphasis on African Religion. Owing to these scholars' efforts, African Religion is not only taught in African universities but it is also taught in many universities throughout the world. This has led to the conversion of foreigners who have, at various times, visited Africa to see how God is worshiped in this religion. The advances made by these scholars have been interpreted in several academic disciplines leading to the revitalization of African Traditional Religion and its awareness all over the world. It must, however, be said that in spite of the contributions of these fathers of the academic study of African Religion, much is yet to be explored, and the stage is open for new depths into the living traditions of the African people.

Notes

1. Nana Osei Bonsu, "African Traditional Religion: An Examination of Terminologies Used for Describing the Indigenous Faith of African People, Using an Afrocentric Paradigm," *Africology: The Journal of Pan African Studies*, vol. 9, no. 9, November 2016.
2. Ogolla Maurice, "The Challenges Facing Religion in the Contemporary World: The Kenyan Situation," *International Journal of Humanities and Social Science*, vol. 4, no. 3, February 2014.
3. Karl Rahner, "Religion," *Encyclopedia of Theology*, (Crossroad Pub. Co., 1975).
4. J. O. Awolalu, What Is African Traditional Religion? In *Studies in Comparative Religion*, vol. 10, no. 2. (Spring, 1976), 1–10. World Wisdom, Inc. www.studiesincomparativereligion.com
5. https://peoplepill.com/people/geoffrey-parrinder
6. Martin Howard Frank Forward, "An Examination of Geoffrey Parrinder's Contribution to the Study of Religion," Ph.D. Thesis Department of Theology and Religious Studies, (University of Bristol, 1995).

7. Adrian Hastings, Review: Geoffrey Parrinder, Reviewed Works: In the Belly of the Snake: West Africa over Sixty Years Ago by Geoffrey Parrinder; A Bag of Needments: Geoffrey Parrinder and the Study of Religion, in *Journal of Religion in Africa* Vol. 31, 2001, pp. 354–359.
8. H. W. Turner, Geoffrey Parrinder's contributions to studies of religion in Africa, in *Religion*, Volume 10, Issue 2, Autumn 1980, pages 156–164.
9. Ursula King (Ed.), Turning Points in Religious Studies Essay in Honour of Geoffrey Parrinder, Edinburgh: T & T Clark 1990.
10. Martin Howard Frank Forward, "An Examination of Geoffrey Parrinder's Contribution to the Study of Religion," Ph.D. Thesis Department of Theology and Religious Studies, (University of Bristol, 1995).
11. https://www.theguardian.com/news/2005/aug/05/guardianobituaries.religion
12. Ursula King, Geoffrey Parrinder in Lawrence Goldman (ed), *Oxford Dictionary of National Biography, 2005–2008*, (Oxford: OUP, 2013) 882–883.
13. Geoffrey Parrinder, Wikipedia, https://en.wikipedia.org/wiki/Geoffrey_Parrinder
14. Ibid. See books published by Parrinder.
15. "*The Calling*," The Institute for Diasporan and African Culture Newsletter, vol. 1, no. 1, November 2008.
16. Kofi Asare Opoku, *West African Traditional Religion* (Accra: FEP International Private Limited, 1978).
17. Kofi Asare Opoku, "The Worldview of the Akan," *Tarikh* 26 7, no. 2 (Published for the Historical Society of Nigeria, Longman, 1982), 61–73.
18. Kofi Asare Opoku, "Traditional African Religious Society," in Mark Juergensmeyer (ed), *The Oxford Handbook of Global Religions* (Oxford: Oxford University Press, 2006).
19. Kathleen O'Brien Wicker and Kofi Asare Opoku, *Togbi Dawuso Dofe: Mami Water in Ewe Tradition*. (Ghana: Legon-Accra: Sub-Saharan Publishers, 2007).
20. Kofi Asare Opoku, "Valentine is not alien to us" on *Sane Gbaa* a 3 pm Saturday, Eezy FM's weekend show 11 February 2017.
21. Kofi Asare Opoku, *Speak to the Winds: Proverbs from Africa* (New York: Lothrop, Lee and Shepard, 1975).
22. Kofi Asare Opoku, "Changes Within Christianity: The Case of the Musama Disco Christo Church," in *Christianity in Independent Africa*, eds., E. Fashole-Luke et al. (London: Rex Collins, 1978).
23. Kofi Asare Opoku, "Traditional Religious Beliefs and Spiritual Churches in Ghana: A Preliminary Statement," *Research Review*, Legon: University of Ghana, vol. 4, no. 2 (1968): 47–60.
24. Kofi Asare Opoku, "Traditional Religious Beliefs and Spiritual Churches in Ghana: A Preliminary Statement" https://core.ac.uk/download/pdf/43542303.pdf. Assessed 6 March 2020.
25. Kofi Asare Opoku, "African Mysticism," in *Mysticism and Mystical Experience, East and West*, Donald H. Bishop, ed., (Selinsgrove, PA: Susquehanna University Press; London and Toronto: Associated University Presses, 1987).
26. Kofi Asare Opoku, "Independence of the Mind," *Journal of Black Studies*, 1970. https://doi.org/10.1177/002193477000100204 (accessed March 3, 2020).

27. Kofi Asare Opoku, Yong-bok Kim, and Antoinette Clark Wire, *Healing for God's World: Remedies from Three Continents* (New York: Friendship Press, 1991).
28. Kofi Asare Opoku, "Science to the African is a Cultural Experience," in *Amandla*, Wednesday January 30, 2019.
29. Kofi Asare Opoku, "Religion in Africa During the Colonial Era," in *UNESCO General History of Africa Under Colonial Domination 1881–1935* A. A. Boahen (Paris: UNESCO, 1985).
30. Kofi Asare Opoku, "Communalism and Community in the African Heritage," in *Dialogue in Community: Essays in Honour of S. J. Samartha, C. D. Jathanna*, ed. (Mangalore, India: The Karnataka Theological Research Institute, 1982). https://onlinelibrary.wiley.com/doi/abs/10.1111/j.1758-6631.1990.tb02204.x (accessed November 8, 2020).

CHAPTER 46

Scholarship in African Traditional Religion: The Works of Joseph Omosade Awolalu and Peter Ade Dopamu

Danoye Oguntola-Laguda and Joseph Moyinoluwa Talabi

INTRODUCTION

Scholarships in African Traditional Religion (ATR) have gone through a series of evolution processes. These processes could be divided into three historical epochs. In the pre-colonial era, scholarship in ATR was dominated by foreign scholars who were either Christians or Muslims. The focus of the scholars in this category was to report the situation of religion and spirituality of the people in the colonies. Therefore, what they did was to use the paradigm of the popular religions—Islam and Christianity—to determine the reality of religion in Nigeria like other African countries. The conclusions of these scholars suggest that before the arrival of the colonial masters, there was no religion in Africa. Consequently, the religion known to the people was introduced to the continent by the Christian missionaries in Nigeria and Ghana.[1] However, during the colonial era, there was improvement in scholarship in ATR as many Africans who had been sold into slavery returned to the continent and engaged in the propagation of the religion of their slave masters. Those in this category were mostly Christians. The focus of scholarship in ATR during this period was to debunk the indigenous religion(s) of the people in order to "sell" Christianity to the people. It is during this period that derogatory terms were used in describing ATR. Such sociological terms that were given religious

D. Oguntola-Laguda (✉) • J. M. Talabi
Lagos State University, Lagos, Nigeria

© The Author(s), under exclusive license to Springer Nature Switzerland AG 2022
I. S. Aderibigbe, T. Falola (eds.), *The Palgrave Handbook of African Traditional Religion*, https://doi.org/10.1007/978-3-030-89500-6_46

connotations include paganism, tribalism, natives, primitives, and archaic, among others. The efforts of Ajayi Crowther and Samuel Johnson were very conspicuous during this period. In the post-colonial period, serious academic works emerged on the scene, especially in Nigeria and Kenya, with the works of E. Bolaji Idowu[2] and John S. Mbiti[3] being the leading scholars. The latter, in particular, gave mentorship to Joseph Omosade Awolalu, who, in turn, mentored and trained Peter Ade Dopamu. The interactions among these trios began in the Department of Religious Studies at the University of Ibadan. The focus of these scholars in this category, who are mostly Nigerians, was mainly to respond to the obnoxious submissions of the two categories of scholars in ATR earlier mentioned and set the record straight on what should be the content, structure, and theology of ATR. These scholars' methodologies are historical, epistemological, descriptive, and analytical. It is important to note that Peter Ade Dopamu later introduced Comparative Religious Analysis into his work, especially with regard to magic, medicine, and traditional healing. This chapter examines the literature of two great scholars in the post-colonial academic study of African Traditional Religion in Nigeria with an emphasis on some of the themes that dominate their academic engagements. This study attempts to critically engage their submissions and see how these represent what is now prevalent in African Traditional Religion scholarship in the modern and post-modern era.

Joseph Omosade Awolalu

When we speak of African Traditional Religion, we mean the indigenous religion of the African people. It is the religion of the Africans. It is not a fossil religion (a thing of the past) but a religion that the African people made theirs by living it and practicing it. This is a religion that has little or no written scriptural texts, yet it is "written" everywhere for those who care to see and read. It is largely written in peoples' myths and folktales, in their songs and dances, in their liturgies and Shrines, and in their proverbs and pithy sayings. It is a religion whose historical founder is neither known nor worshiped; it's a religion that has no zeal for membership drive, yet it offers persistent fascination for Africans, young and old.[4] As a point of reference, it is worth mentioning here that Awolalu was a product of St. Andrews College, Oyo (SACOBA), a Priest in the Anglican Church of Nigeria, and an Administrator in the said Communion.[5]

Awolalu's contributions to the study of African Traditional Religion are arguably the major highlight of his life as a scholar under the renowned erudite Professor E. Bolaji Idowu. In Nigeria, he was the second indigenous lecturer to have taught in the area at the University of Ibadan. He was proficient and versatile in indigenous religious beliefs and practices. His main focus was on Yoruba beliefs, sacrificial rites, sin and its removal, the future of African Traditional Religion, taboo, God and society, and life cycle, among others. Awolalu's scholarly works covered extensive areas of African Traditional

Religious Studies. Herein is an evaluation of the importance of his scholarship on the academic African Religion Studies. Many scholars have appraised Awolalu's contributions to the study of ATR.[6] His intellectual sagacity and capability to engage his readers on contemporary issues has made his work more interesting to readers. His works are published in many journals and books, and several of his pioneering works have been greatly referenced by many of the modern-day scholars. Some of Awolalu's pioneering works that have influenced modern discourse are reviewed in a concise way.

The Concepts of African Traditional Religions, African Traditional Religion, African Religion, and African Indigenous Religion

One of the problems that early investigators were confronted with was the use of a proper name that could befit the religion practiced in Africa. John S. Mbiti proposed that the religion should be called "African Traditional Religions" because of the multiple tribes in Africa. His major argument is that these tribes practice the religion based on what each believes, because there is no common ground to conclude that there is an obvious relationship in their worship system, which is enough to accept his claim. He posited further that it could be a great mistake to singularize the religion of the people due to their diverse cultures and multiple dialects.[7] Awolalu weighed in on this debate by rejecting Mbiti's nomenclature for African religion. According to him, pluralizing African religion would not be a true representation of the peculiarities of the religion across the continent. According to him, if Mbiti's thesis is accepted, it will further give strength to the attacks from the Western scholars who see nothing good coming from Africa. Therefore, they argued that the religion was paganistic, primitive, and lacked any value. Awolalu was particularly disturbed about the strong arguments that could be used against the religion because the debate came at a time when early scholars in African religion—even by African scholars—were trying to respond to the obnoxious submissions of foreign scholars, such as A. B. Ellis, Emile Ludwig, and Dierich Westermann—that Africans, before the arrival of foreign religions was introduced to the continent, lacked any form of religion or organization. Awolalu's argument was unanimously agreed upon because he noted that if we should, by error or omission mistakenly accept Mbiti's thesis, the religion of Africa would be buried soon because Christianity is not seen in a plural sense and Islam is not pluralized; why then should we pluralize the religion of Africans? This argument is exceptionally valid and it was objectively analyzed. Awolalu, therefore, proposed that the religion be known as African Traditional Religion. This expression is not to be viewed from a geographical perspective but from a cultural understanding that the religion is rooted in a particular space—Africa.

Idowu argued that the religion should be called "African Indigenous Religion" because the word "indigenous" is more appropriate compared to the term "traditional."[8] The word "indigenous," for instance, indigenizes the religion and should be a perfect name for the religion. We appreciate the works of Idowu because it gives us a clearer understanding of the nomenclature that best describes African Traditional Religion. However, scholars have continued to use Awolalu's thesis in the study of the religion. Today, the religion is popularly known as African Traditional Religion not only in Africa but in Global Studies on African religion.

Yorùbá Beliefs and Sacrificial Rites

This is one of the major works by Awolalu.[9] As a matter of fact, the subject matter was the focus of this doctoral work. Awolalu opined that the effective way of communicating with God is through sacrifice, as God sees it as something that makes the world go round. Awolalu believed that any situation a man finds himself in on earth is either a result of man's good relationship with his maker or the other way around. He explained that sacrifice is very central to the practice of ATR more because it is used to maintain a cordial relationship with God.[10] In ATR, especially during the pre-colonial and post-colonial periods, sacrifices were used to maintain relationships in every facet of life and that is why at birth, puberty, marriage, and even death, sacrifices are used to show appreciation and solicit God's support and guidance. For Awolalu, the neglect of sacrifice in Africa and particularly in Yorubaland has not been good for the people. He explained that during the civil wars (in Yorubaland), it was sacrifice that was used to ward off external invasions. He went on to explain that killings and kidnappings that were the order of the day in Yorubaland was a result of the neglect of sacrifice.[11]

Awolalu affirmed that the importance of foundational sacrifice, which was held in high esteem then, had now been neglected. Before anyone embarked on any enterprise, a foundational sacrifice was the first assignment. This was done to appease the gods connected to the particular enterprise, but today, it has been totally neglected. A man who wants to build a house is expected to sacrifice to the god of the earth. The man who desires to engage in a new business is advised to offer a foundational sacrifice. It is thought that if an individual does this, he will have a stress-free enterprise.

The Yorùbá believe that sickness can cut short the life of a man. If sickness surfaces and herbs and other means have been employed and the situation is relapsing, it could lead to death. However, if the man's family believes that he will not die of an illness, a substitutionary sacrifice could be used to elongate his life. Once this is accomplished, the man might not die. This, therefore, indicates the importance of this type of sacrifice. Animals are often used to ward off ailments, whereas an animal will be used to rub the man's body. The implication of this is that once the animal touches the person's body, the sickness would be transferred to it and it would die immediately. By implication, it has taken the death of the man. This is hardly practiced in our contemporary society because the culture is glaringly eroding. There are several types of sacrifices that Awolalu highlighted but are not discussed here due to space limits.

It is of utmost importance to say at this juncture that sacrifice is a ritual in every religion. It is a practice that is cherished by all religions of the world. In Africa, it is believed that sacrifice is so important that, in the pre-colonial system, there was something called human sacrifice. The essence of this was that a man must be sacrificed to ward off the sins of his fellow men. Awolalu explained that modernization and civilization have changed this, and animals are used in place of humans. According to him, sacrifice is an old practice in Yorubaland. The religion of the Yoruba recognizes Esu as the god of sacrifice. Esu is indispensable when sacrifice is mentioned because he is the one assigned to this responsibility by *Olodumare*.[12] It is, therefore, necessary to mention that sacrifice is essential in the religious practice of the Yoruba people and Awolalu was the first scholar to elaborately discuss sacrifice not only among the Yoruba, but his subsequent works explained in detail the African's perception of sacrifice.[13]

Sins and its Removal

Awolalu's work on sin and its removal was a geocentric shift of emotion from what he was known for, and it clearly earned him a name internationally.[14] Awolalu showcased orderliness in the scheme of things in an African cosmological setting with emphasis on sin and how human beings can be restored to their original state before he/she commits sin. Awolalu, in his bid to explain the Africans' worldview, noted that God and man had a strong relationship at the beginning, but sin drew a line of demarcation between them. He postulated that sin could cause disequilibrium between man and God and when this happens, it could affect the entire society. So, when this is noticed, effort is being made to re-strategize on how to re-establish a seamless relationship with God. This society is composed of men and women. In the case of living together, man could err and once this is noticed, it could either affect the man negatively or affect the entire society. That is why Awolalu pointed out that, in Africa, no man lives alone; it is strictly a communal setting. Thus, whatever affects a man can also affect the whole society. Since the African world is not angelic in nature, it is possible that one can go astray in several ways. For instance, a man can unjustly kill his fellow man, and since bloodletting is a taboo in Africa, it could bring catastrophe on the entire society. How then is sin removed in Africa?[15]

The culprit is compelled to confess his sins privately or publicly depending on the nature of the sin committed. Having done this, the oracle will be consulted to know the next thing to do. The dictates of the Oracle must be strictly and carefully followed. When this is done, the priest or priestess will again be consulted to know the next line of action before he will be declared free. This practice, according to Awolalu, is not only a practice among the Yoruba but also practiced among some prominent tribes in Africa.[16] Awolalu's well-documented research about how communal life is maintained in Africa gave a lot of credence to his work and gave a correct picture of the structure of the African society and their religion.

Peter Ade Dopamu

It is an unassailable fact that the late Professor Peter Ade Dopamu's contribution to African Traditional Religion Studies cannot be swept under the carpet. He imbued his writing with a new strength that makes his work compulsively readable. This is because he was widely read. His contributions have galvanized the contemporary scholars into researches in ATR and energized the spirits of many students of Comparative Religion or Religious Studies. Some of this works include *West African Traditional Religion*,[17] *Èsù, the Invisible Foe of Man: A comparative study of Satan in Christianity Islam and Yorùbá Religion*,[18] *Understanding Yorùbá Life and Culture*,[19] *Science in the Perspective of African Religion*,[20] and *Traditional Medicine with Particular Reference to the Yorùbá of Western Nigeria*,[21] among others. It becomes practically impossible to discuss all the highlighted works here. However, we shall attempt a thematic discourse of some of his pioneering works that modern scholars are building upon.

Magic, Medicine, and Religion

No doubt, this is an aspect in African Traditional Religion that will remain forever relevant because it embraces all the features of African traditional religions. However, magic, medicine, and religion in the Yorùbá context was judicially slanted through sit-at-home investigations by armchair scholars. Dopamu assisted in helping us understand, with sufficient explanations, that what the former writers documented about the phenomena were not an adequate representation of the concept of magic, medicine, and religion, especially in relation to the Yorùbá people of Nigeria. He used proper Yorùbá terms to interrogate these phenomena. This, he did by first giving the definitions attributable to the foreign scholars and explaining the proper terms in Yorùbá religion. Dopamu's academic voyage and intellectual versatility had given scholars in the area of Yorùbá Traditional Religion more knowledge to understand that some scholars distinguish magic and medicine in a particular way, while some will treat both as one. For example, according to W.H.R. Rivers (1924), magic means "A group of processes in which man uses rites which depend for their efficacy on his own power, or on powers believed to be inherent in, or the attributes of certain objects and processes which are used in these rites." And medicine to him means "A term for a set of social practices by which man seeks to direct and control a specific group of natural phenomena viz those especially affecting man himself, which so influence his behavior as to unfit him for the normal accomplishment of his physical and social functions phenomena which lower his vitality and tend towards death."[22]

Knowing that these definitions could cause confusion among upcoming scholars, Dopamu immediately refuted it. He noted that the definitions of magic and medicine, as stated by W.H.R. Rivers, are misleading, and taken as a whole they do not work, at least from the Yorùbá perspective. Although in magic, man makes use of some certain objects to obtain his ends, he does not attribute the achievement of this end to his own power but to a power unseen which he believes he could influence.[23] In religion, man believes that certain powers reside in objects and he uses these objects to symbolize the object of his faith. So, also in magic, man makes use of these objects to influence the power therein. If he believes that the efficacy of magic depends on his own power, he will not address the powers by their names as he certainly does in incantations in his attempt to do his will.[24]

Dopamu also responded to the definition of medicine as given by W.H.F. Rivers. According to him, the definition for medicine cannot be taken for its face value. There are certain things that affect man and prevent him from accomplishing his physical and social functions, but which are not controlled by medicine. For instance, a sorcerer, via the use of bad magic, may cause an epidemic in a society or inflict some injuries on his victim. In either case, it is not medicine that is used to nullify the activities of a sorcerer but a strong counter-magic. He agreed that it is true that diseases can also prevent man from fulfilling physical and social functions and that these can be overcome with medicine, but other factors can still work against man in this regard and they may not be controlled by medicine; witchcraft is no exception.[25]

In trying to define "magic," Farrow gave the impression that magic and medicine are one, although he stylishly gave a flimsy distinction in his discussion, which apparently contradicted his thinking.[26] He claimed that the Yorùbá word *òògùn* (magic) is *mana* and can be expressed in English by the word "medicine" but not medicine of a material kind; for instance, drugs, for which the term *egboogi* is generally used, but of that kind which is practiced by a medicine-man, or witch-doctor. He went on to talk of counter charm and sympathetic magic, and then by implication hints that those who practice bad medicine practice witchcraft. This is confusing. No one with a thorough knowledge of the Yorùbá traditions will venture into such a field of generalization or in a pitfall of in-articulation. Although the Yorùbá word for magic and medicine is *oòògùn*, Dopamu emphasized that the Yorùbá still use other terms for them, such as *egboogi*. And because the Yorùbá have various names for magic and medicine, which are almost synonymous, it is unfair to complicate the situation by using these terms in a loose and incorrect sense. It is a socio-scientific method, to be specific, in the use of term for the purpose of clarification.

As if that was not enough, Dopamu was astounded to see how the phenomena were discussed by a Yorùbá man, J. O. Lucas, who was among the early elites. Expectedly, he was meant to correct the damaged image of the phenomena, but he rather joined the European scholars in ensuring that the damage was total. J. O. Lucas followed closely the footsteps of Farrow in his treatment of magic in Yorùbáland, as he postulated that the Yorùbá word *òògùn* (magic) should be understood to mean: "An occult, mysterious or supernatural power by means of which one's end is achieved."[27] Also, he noted that the Yorùbá word *egboogi* could be translated as "medicine," and this should refer primarily to material medicine. Dopamu, in his bid to clarify this, quickly rejected this supposition. As a disciplined and cultured scholar, he knew the prospective damage this could cause in the future since Lucas happened to be a Yorùbá, and he could easily mislead his readers. African magic and medicine are inevitably intermingled. Thus, certain investigators have refrained from distinguishing between them. They have adopted a non-committed attitude of employing one umbrella term to embrace both. That is why Nadal and Field used the term "medicine" to embrace the practice of magic and medicine.

M. J. Field (1937), for example, pointed out that "Anthropologists generally use the word magic where I have used the word medicine, but it is best avoided, as laymen always take it to mean miracle-working." She was even so excited to have added another point to buttress her knowledge of magic and medicine in Africa when she noted that "Magic, as it is often called in West Africa, 'medicine,' always involves concrete apparatus ... and a ritual which this apparatus is handled. There is no activity in life which cannot be assisted by medicine. A hunter can medicine his gun and his bullets to make them unerring and his god to make it fleet, a fisherman can medicine his canoe ad nets and a lorry-driver his lorry."[28]

Nadal even supported the above thesis using the Nupe people of Nigeria as example.[29] He claimed that the Nupe word for "medicine" is ambiguous in that it refers both to skills of an esoteric and miraculous kind and to healing practices which is profane and acquired by ordinary learning. That is why he said that medicine is the literal translation of the vernacular term which is applied not only to magic substances but also to medicinal herbs or drugs of any kind, native as well as Europeans, whose properties are assessed essentially empirically. The term "medicine" has been adopted mainly because it is simple and convenient without distorting too much the meaning of the Nupe word for medicine, *cigbe*.

Dopamu described these two scholars, Nadal and Field, as those who see the facts as they are, but unwilling to adopt the ordinary run-of-the-mill sort of theory, and thus miss the essential in the exercise of circumlocution; they stick to a term. But, they further realize the difficulty in the adoption of this term; hence, they go further to indicate the duality of the term and show us that the term covers two concepts. However, it would have been clearer had they found different terms among the Nupe people to accurately describe the use of magic and medicine in Africa.

Some writers even describe magic as science. This is exactly the position of J. G. Frazer.[30] He therefore describes magic as not just being spurious system but also fallacious and false science. Talbot also agreed with Frazer's thesis that magic is science. However, it is of very primitive kind. It is an attempt to gain knowledge and power over the laws of nature and the underlying entities. It is a method of thought, a way of looking upon nature, which was a common form in the earliest times.[31]

Dopamu corrected this spurious notion by pointing out that there is no justification for regarding magic as science in our modern sense of the word. Frazer and his associates should have taken into account the spiritual nature of magic as well as its reference to a supernatural agency. Magic has to do with unseen power or powers believed to inhabit certain objects, while science is based on observational and experimental knowledge. Dopamu also noted that we can only use the word "science" with reservation when we talk of magic. There are cases when the potency of magic is tested on animals or inanimate objects before such magic is relied upon. In this case, the magician has performed an experiment which is akin to science.[32]

The above has shown that Dopamu's efforts in the study of Yorùbá magic and medicine are versatile. He has succeeded in laying a consistent and structurally harmonious foundation that modern scholars like Obafemi Jegede (Jegede 1), S. K. Olaleye,[33] Styers Randal,[34] T. M. Sawandili,[35] B. Stephen,[36] K. R. Raccette,[37] K. Rojcikoya,[38] S. M. Raji,[39] Joshua Odusola,[40] S. Manguinhos,[41] G. H. Koiening,[42] E. O. Babalola,[43] Abilawon Seun (Abilawon, 23), M. A. Bamgboshe,[44] D. O. Ogungbile,[45] R. German,[46] and others have built upon. The main aim for academically combating the European scholars was to tacitly and implicitly present the issues raised by the sit-at-home scholars, which has left issues and chased tissues. Today, hardly will anyone write about magic and medicine in Yorùbáland or Africa at large without referencing Dopamu. He was a scholar who critically and empirically analyzed Yorùbá's magic and medicine. His work on the topic of discussion has been useful for modern-day scholars. When one reads through his thesis on magic and medicine, one would agree that the work unwinds the pool of his narratives at a masterful, page-turning pace that pulls readers in and keeps them wanting more.

It is Dopamu's work on magic and medicine that seeks to tell it all, bare it all, and "unmask the masquerade" in the study of Yorùbá-Africa magic and medicine. Dopamu and Awolalu's book, *West African Traditional Religion*, is engrossed in spellbinding, entertaining, and compelling narratives. It shows the true meaning of African Traditional Religion and Yorùbá magic and medicine. Nevertheless, Dopamu's work on magic and medicine, which has been highly rated, could be the stick with which critics from other tribes in Nigeria could use to beat him. Since he mentioned that Yorùbá magic and medicine looks the same as that of other tribes in Nigeria, he is expected to create a chapter with some of the other tribes' understanding of magic and medicine and where they are related to that of Yorùbá are discussed. It is not as if he did not mention this, but a whole chapter could have been dedicated to delineate it in a clear chronological order.

The Right Nomenclature for African Traditional Religion

There has been resentment against African Traditional Religion by foreign scholars who claimed that the African people's religion is non-existent in concept and practice. Their initial effort was to determine if the people of Africa had any form of religion, and if they did, then what were its contents, structure, and theology. Although many of their efforts were biased, and to a large extent, lacked objectivity, we cannot but agree that they formed a background upon which subsequent works on African religion are based. These scholars were Christian missionaries who had come to Africa for colonial purposes and the propagation of Christianity. It is not a surprise, therefore, that they engaged in a derogatory study of religion of the forebears of Africans. As a matter of fact, they brought education to the African people so they had the opportunity to write not only about the colonial efforts but also about the culture and religion of the people. Unfortunately, they did not document what they were told by the African people objectively. Further, they attempted to use the structure of Christianity to determine the religion of the colonized people, thereby engaging in comparative religion, which in some cases lack objectivity. They were blindfolded to the facts of ATR given to them by the African people. It is based on these premises that they deny the existence of God in ATR or jumped to the conclusion that God to the people was *deus absconditus*, that is, God that has withdrawn from the affairs of Africans, *dues remotus*, a remote God.

This modification of documentation was meant to deny the religion of Africans. African Traditional Religion has gone through a roller coastal period of surviving attacks, sustained by smear campaigns of persecution and humiliation. Those Africans who did not accept foreign religions were viewed as feisty, argumentative, and antagonistic. When foreign religions finally gained entrance into the shore of Africa through colonialism, they immediately strategized on how to blackmail the indigenous religion, giving it opprobrious names in order to relegate it. A public-spirited person and full democrat character is expected to respect the practices of the people who host him; this was totally and intentionally abandoned by them. They failed to develop any process of identifying, training, or rewarding the indigenous people who were magnanimous in offering information about their religious beliefs and practices. All these constitute major departures from what they said they came to do in Africa. Many of the European adventurers, after the colonial period, later fell in love with ATR because they did not want to be pretentious like the early writers, such as Nadal mentioned above. For instance, if Susan Wenger (an Austrian-born, German researcher) had not seen real potential in ATR or recognized an untapped talent of the African people, she would not have ended up being a Priestess at the Òsun Shrine. The fact that many of them now practice the religion is enough evidence to show that the early investigators only came to promote their religions—Christianity and Islam.

Peter Ade Dopamu was one of the African scholars who rallied around and saved this situation from the pettiness and vindictiveness of the European investigators who were ready to sacrifice ATR on the altar of foreign religions. Dopamu had seen a salacious synthesis of the decadence in what the wrong nomenclature could cause to the study of ATR and the little people who possessed their needs. There was so much blame to share not only among the early writers but those indigenous people who became apologetic to the submissions of the foreign scholars. Some of the opprobrious terms used are as follows: the high-gods of the primitive peoples, the withdrawn god, polytheism, fetishism, idolatry, heathenism, paganism, animism, primitive, *jùjú*, *mana*, and so on.[47] It took the intervention of Idowu,[48] Dopamu, and Awolalu,[49] and some other notable African scholars to demystify these terms. Dopamu and Awolalu made sure that they got to the root meanings of these derogatory terms. They later discovered that 99 percent of such terms used by these investigators are mere sociological terms that had nothing to do with the religion of Africans.[50] Such terms are derogatory, sad, ominous, and dreadful; it is a paradoxical mixture of an anguish soul and a zealous clamor of a dejected and bias scholarship. Such terms include, for example, fetishism that originated from the early Portuguese traders or travelers who came to West Africa and observed the use of objects such as charms, amulets, mascots, and talisman by the natives. They found these objects similar to objects in their own country. In actual fact the word was derived from the Latin word Factitious that means magic.

Another term is heathenism which is originally a sociological term. It is a word of a Germanic root heath meaning waste separated from the town where outlaws, robbers, vagabonds, and people of doubtful character live.[51] This sociological term has curiously been used to describe the religion practiced in Africa. Going by the various meanings attributable to the terms discussed above, it is not appropriate to use those terms to describe the religion of a people of Africa and any continent for that matter.

Dopamu used his critical mind with the help of other African scholars to disabuse the minds of those who have been calling the religion names it should not be called. First, he etymologically analyzed those terms in order to prove that they are not fit to describe African religion. Imagine if he had not collaborated with African scholars such as Awolalu in ATR to debunk these terms created by the Westerners, today, there would be a serious problem. Those who still use fetishism, polytheism, and heathenism to describe African religion are those who have been converted to Christianity and Islam. It is very difficult for someone who genuinely studies or practices African Traditional Religion to call it heathenism or idolatry because they know the implication of this on their religion. It is even startling to note that those who call ATR different names are secretly patronizing the indigenous priests.

Dopamu once told the story of a Catholic Priest who visited his father who happened to be an *Ifá* priest. The Catholic Priest came to see his father to help him find a solution to a long-time ailment he had been battling with. After the father gave him medicine for the ailment, he told the former that if he likes, he should go to the altar on Sunday and tell his laities that they should not collect anything from the "idol worshippers." He said his father warned the man to make use of his conscience.[52] One wonders that despite the egregious term used to describe African religion, the religion still experiences high patronage. Although some business men and women, politicians, and scholars may not want people to know that they practice the religion, hardly will a Babaláwo (Herbalist) wake up on a day without having a client. In his study, Dopamu noted that the religion has been experiencing decline lately and this is mainly due to the fact that some young people are not ready to learn the art from their elders. They prefer businesses, which give them daily income in faster ways, such as riding a commercial motorcycle.[53]

Several reasons could be adduced to Dopamu's versatility in the study of ATR. One, he was more knowledgeable than many scholars because his father was a priest of *Ifa* and *onisegun* (healer), and his mother was a priestess. He was familiar with the correct pronunciation of some vernaculars and he made use of them properly. His contributions to the study of ART served and are still serving as an eye-opener to those that are coming behind him. He knew the correct spellings of many Yorùbá words and was able to chant incantations appropriately. He was fully prepared even before he decided to study African Traditional Religion.[54] When his father was not around, he attended to clients on several occasions. He learned the herbs to use in case there was an urgent need for him to attend to clients, and anytime he decided to put pen to paper, he was respected and appreciated. No wonder, his supervisor, Professor J. O. Awolalu said that he had not had a student as brilliant as the Late P. A. Dopamu. Little wonders, therefore, that they jointly published a Magnus opus, *African Traditional Religion*.[55] The indigenous knowledge that Dopamu had in his possession cannot be quantified. He said in one of his lectures that his supervisor, Professor J. O. Awolalu, once said that "if not for the fact that paper writing calls for objectivity, he (Dopamu) could write every paper without consulting informants." This is to show that he was extraordinarily proficient and had something cherishable upstairs.[56] His contributions toward making ATR known was informed by the indigenous knowledge he gathered from his father and the society plus being a priest himself.

At one point, when some Western scholars started writing and publishing books on women's rejection and relegation in ATR, he immediately ordered a review of the book he co-authored with J. O. Awolalu (*West African Traditional Religion*). He created a space for women's involvement in the religious practice of the Africans. Today, there are several books on feminism referencing this aspect in his book. They have argued that women's involvement in African religion cannot be easily obliterated. Prior to that time, many believed that women had no voice. Some people even believed that women's role in religious rites and rituals was to cook for their husbands during festivals. Apart from this, Dopamu successfully argued that God in the Western religions is the same in Africa Traditional Religion. He gave a convincing explanation that as God does not have any image to them, he also has no image in Africa.[57] He also informed us that, in Christianity, there is belief in praying everywhere so also in Africa, we have what is called ejaculatory prayers.[58] He reiterated that Africans only believe in divinities because there must be agents that should help God in running the affairs of the world, and by implication, the divinities are only a means to an end and not an end by themselves. He likened the roles of the divinities to that of Jesus. Just like the Bible argues that no one can see God except he passes through Jesus Christ. Also, in African religion, no sacrifice is acceptable except it passes through Esu (divinity in charge of sacrifice). In Christianity, we find out the mind of God from the prophets. In ATR, the mind of God is known through the indigenous priests (Babalawo-diviners).

Dopamu writes with grip, streamlined energy, and self-deprecating charm. His book, *West African Traditional Religion*, does not need to coast on the authors' mega popularity. It is a reminder of how the authors' juggernaut began. Every breathing soul knows that the book is thoughtful and has a wide-ranging and thought-provoking influence in African Religion Studies. Scholars find it difficult to study ATR (especially as it concerns the Yoruba) without the book. Not only are his pioneering works still being used as working sticks to beginners in the study of African religion, he was a multifaceted and multidimensional scholar who made all "ingredients" available to cook the subsequent works in African religion. He had the intellectual ability and capability to keep renewing himself in his academic voyage.

Esu

One of the Africans who was converted to Christianity through slavery was Bishop Àjàyí Crowther. He had wittingly described the revered Esu divinity among the Yorùbá people of Western Nigeria as Satan.[59] To even worsen the situation, he described and drew the image of his biblical Esu as one that has two wings. It is true that Esu has both good and bad attributes and he is not in any way different from everything created by God. Esu among the Yorùbá could help a man to reach his goal when he is properly and ceremoniously appeased. Esu is not completely devious as being perceived by the Western religions. Christianity, for instance, has seen Esu as an advocate of unfortunate situations. This is deliberately used to lure adherents of African religion into believing that once they are converted to Christianity, they will have nothing to do with Esu again.

It is clear from the foregoing that the ultimate aim of Christianity and Islam was to take its new adherents a considerable distance from their spiritual roots. Those that could not be converted were condemned in strong terms by Christians and Muslims. They used derogatory terms like kÈfÈrí, (karir, olórìsÀ) (pagan, idol worshipers, ajebo, idols, etc.) to describe the adherents of Yorùbá religion. The most disturbing thing was the description of everything as Esu, Satan the Devil (Dopamu, 34). Although Dopamu argued that the evil attributes of Esu; overshadows his good values, this may not be totally correct. It is agreeable to believe that the bad aspect of Esu could be responsible for the reason ÀjÀyí Crowther called him Satan since Satan is known for evil (in Christianity) but that does not mean that Dopamu should see Esu as totally devious. At the end of his discourse, he pointed out that biblically, Satan is different from Esu and this pioneering work of his has corrected some anomalies of the vilification Esu is surrounded with. For instance, Dopamu's work on Esu caused Catholicism to properly use the word *Satani* (Satten) in their Yorùbá Bible. It is now impossible to find the word Esu in Catholic Yorùbá Bibles. This is because Dopamu laid the foundation.[60]

There is a shift from the initial discourse of Esu in Dopamu's scholarship. In the first instance, he argued that Esu was the invisible foe of man.[61] This suggests that Esu in Yoruba Traditional Religion is evil and as such an enemy of human beings. In another breath, he argued that Esu was the head of the evil world that made existence difficult for people. Those personage and agencies under him are evil. These include Aje (witches), Ajogun (sadistic foes), and Adaunse (wicked charmers). Dopamu also became apologetic to his calling as a Christian, Knight of Saint Christopher (KSC). It should be noted that Esu should be understood from three perspectives, namely Yoruba Christian, Yoruba Muslim, and Yoruba Traditional. The translations of the Yoruba Christians' understanding of the Devil as Esu can be excused if only for epistemological reason. The same could be true of Yoruba Muslims' submission that *Shaytan* is Esu. These are products of translation of the scriptures of these religions to the Yoruba language. To the Traditionalists, Esu is not evil. He is a divinity under the control of *Olodumare*, who created him and gave him responsibilities. If there are evil tendencies in his activities, it must be due to the desire of his creator, *Olodumare*.[62]

God Here and God There: The Relativism of the Concept of God in African and Western Cultures

The essence of some religions including ATR is God as the ultimate Supreme Being, and it is believed that He created heaven and earth. It is also believed that He constructed everything in the world. What is disturbing is that, in Christianity, creation stories from other religions are invalid and must not be accepted. Dopamu's effort in correcting this obnoxious thinking is unprecedented. Dopamu believed that Christianity and Islam were known for imposition and this is not acceptable. His main thesis is that if you are saying that God created heaven and earth and others believe that the creation of heaven and earth was proposed and executed by God, then it should not be an issue. What should be a matter of concern is if a particular people debunk this fact and say that man created God, and since no grope or person has raised this, others' opinion should be respected. Dopamu stressed that

> [t]he Yorùbá have it that in the timeless beginning, or timeless prehistory, there was OlódùmarÈ, the Supreme Deity and with Him in the Sky, heaven lived the numerous divinities. Among them were ÒrìsÀ-ńlá, also called ObÀtálÀ, the arch-divinity and

deputy of OlódùmarÈ in the ordering of things, ÒrúnmìlÀ also called Ìfa, the Deputy of OlódùmarÈ in matters of knowledge, and Èsù, the Inspector of rituals. Far below the sky heave, there was a watery marshy waste and endless stretch of water and wild marshes. Over this vast expanses of water, Olókun, the god of the sea, ruled. But the divinities in the sky heaven usually came down on the wild marshes to perform their hunting activities. They descended on it with the aid of spider's web. However, Olódùmare looked down on the watery marshy waste and pondered over it. He considered what He could do with it. Could it be left permanently as a waste? Could it not be turned into a purposeful spot? Could this great wet monotony not be populated by divinities and other living things? A plan then emerged when OlódùmarÈ decided to form the watery, marshy, wet, monotony into a solid earth. But did He in His almightiness need to go to the sport Himself to do the work? No. and so in doing the work, He summoned ÒrìsÀ-ńlá and commissioned him. He gave ÒrìsÀ-ńlá the material of leaf packet of loose earth (or a snail shell full of sand), and for his tools, he was given a white hen and a pigeon to spread the earth.[63]

Every tribe has its own account of creation, and Yorùbá is not an exception. What is of utmost interest is that every tribe in Africa see God as the Supreme Being. So, in Christianity and Islam, God, in the African school of thought, is unique; no one can compare himself to Him, in fact, no man has ever seen Him. The divinities are never in His caliber because He created and brought them into existence. Dopamu believed that His uniqueness is so special that if He decides to do anything, nobody including the angels is able to query Him. He is wholly other and He does things the way He wants. He has the power to bless and He also has the power to curse.[64] He is King and He rules over the kingdoms of the earthly kings. He is the only King that the earthly kings prostrate to because without Him, the earthly kings cannot operate. In fact, in some African communities, the kings lead their subjects in worshiping God because it is believed that all power belongs to Him. Among the Yorùbá, for instance, it is believed that the Ooni of Ife or AláÀfin of Òyó represents the divinities of Olódùmare. When it is time to worship God, he leads them to the shrine, the divinities take messages from them, and they in turn report to OlódùmarÈ (God). God, in Africa, is omnipresent; He sees every man and takes account of what every man does. In the process, He listens to every man's supplication, approves the ones He wants, and disapproves the ones He does not want. Dopamu, therefore, asked if these set of beliefs was anything different from that of Christians or Islam. Having taken note of this, it could be said that they do not in any way differ from that of Christianity and Islam. Hence, God is everywhere but perceived differently.[65]

Conclusion

In conclusion, Awolalu and Dopamu's names have been written in gold in the study of African Traditional Religion. What we discussed herein is an abbreviated summary of their thoughts and how they have been able to deconstruct the submissions of scholars in the pre-colonial and colonial periods in academic scholarship on ATR. Further, they have been able to shape the thoughts of scholars, such as Jacob Olupona, Afe Adogame, and Ibigbolade S. Aderibigbe, among others, that came after them and used some of their thesis to interrogate the study and practice of ATR not only in Africa but also in African Diasporas (especially the Yoruba communities). Awolalu and Dopamu were able to correct the fabrications and assumptions of the foreign scholars using historical and epistemological approaches as their methodologies. They were able to do all these because they saw things for themselves and were part of the practice before their conversion to Christianity. It should be noted that while these two icons of academic African Traditional Religion Studies were thorough and critical in their research and publications, the influence of their faith, Christianity, cannot be over-emphasized.

Notes

1. Ellis, 2.
2. E. Bolaji Idowu, *African Traditional Religion: A Definition* (London: Longman Press, 1962).
3. John S. Mbiti, *Concepts of God in Africa* (London: S.P.C.K. Press, 1970).
4. Joseph Omosade Awolalu, *Yoruba Beliefs and Sacrificial Rites* (London: Longman, 1979), 275.
5. G. L. Lasebikan, "The Madness of God: An Extermination of Divine Obsessive Compulsive Disorder," 13 Inaugural Lecture (Ajayi Crowther University, 2019).
6. Awolalu, *Yoruba Beliefs and Sacrificial Rites*, 176.
7. Olupona & Sulayman, 3.
8. Idowu, *African Traditional Religion*, 11.
9. Awolalu, *Yoruba Beliefs and Sacrificial Rites*, 1979.
10. Ibid., 117.
11. Ibid., 118.
12. Ibid., 120.
13. Ibid.
14. Ibid., 274–278.
15. Ibid., 276.
16. Ibid., 277–278.
17. Peter Ade Dopamu and Joseph Omosade Awolalu, *West African Traditional Religion* (Ibadan: Onibonje Press, 1979).
18. Peter Ade Dopamu, *Èsù, The Invisible Foe of Man: A Comparative Study of Satan in Christianity Islam and Yorùbá Religion* (Ijebu-Ode, Shebiotimo Publications, 1986), 8–25.
19. Nike Lawal, Matthew N. O. Sadiku, and Ade Dopamu, *Understanding Yorùbá Life and Culture* (Trenton, NJ: Africa World Press 2004).
20. S. O. Oyewole, *Science in the Perspective of African Religion (Afrel), Islam and Christianity*, edited by Ade P. Dopamu, I. O. Umejesi, P. O. Amanze, V. A. Alabi, and S. E. Ododo, 2010; https://www.academia.edu/2516042/SCIENCE_IN_THE_PERSPECTIVE_OF_AFRICAN_RELIGION_AFREL_ISLAM_AND_CHRISTIANITY.

21. Peter Ade Dopamu, "Traditional Medicine with Particular Reference to the Yorùbá of Western Nigeria," in Gloria Thomas-Emeagwali (ed.), *African Systems of Science, Technology and Art: The Nigerian Experience* (London: Karnak House, 2004).
22. W. H. R. Rivers, *Medicine, Magic and Religion* (London: Megan Paul, Trench Trubner and Co. Ltd., 1924), 2.
23. Dopamu, 14.
24. Dopamu, 15.
25. Dopamu, 16.
26. S. S. Farrow, *Faith, Fancies and Fetish, or Yorùbá Paganism* (London: S.P.C.K. Press, 1926), 116–128.
27. J. O. Lucas, *The Religion of the Yorùbás* (Lagos: C.M.S. Bookshop, 1948), 269.
28. M. J. Field, *Religion and Medicine of the Ga People* (London: Oxford University Press, 1937), 11.
29. S. F. Nadal, *Nupe Religion* (London: Routledge and Kegan Paul Ltd, 1954), 6, 7, and 132.
30. J. G. Frazer, *The Golden Bough: A Study in Magic and Religion* (London: Macmillan and Co. Limited, 1950), 11.
31. Frazer, *The Golden Bough*, 12.
32. Dopamu, 14.
33. S. K. Olaleye, "The Limitation of Scientific Method of Analysing Traditional Medicine," *Orita: Ibadan Journal of Religious Studies*, vol. XL, no. 2 (2014): 34 (Ibadan: Department of Religious Studies, University of Ibadan).
34. Stylers Randal, *Making Magic: Religion, Magic and Science in the Modern World* (Oxford: Oxford University Press, 2004), 20.
35. T. M. Sawandili, *Yorùbá Medicine: The Art of Divine Herbology* (Lagos: R.G. Enterprise, 2003), 44.
36. B. Stephen, 5.
37. K. R. Raccette, *When Religion and Medicine Collide* (London: Roland Publishers, 2009), 22.
38. K. Rojcikoya, n.p.
39. S. M. Raji, *Ìjìnlẹ̀ Ofò ÒgẸ̀dẸ̀ at Àásán* (Ibadan: Oníbonòjé Press, 1991), 41.
40. Joshua Odusola, *Ika Méjì: The Poetic Visual Incantation* (Lagos: C.S.S. Bookshop, 2000), 81.
41. S. Manguinhos, *The Magic Universe of Cures: The Role of Magic Practices and Witchcraft in the Universe of 17th Century* (Leicester: MT Press, 2009), 22.
42. Harold G. Koenig, MD, *Medicine and Religion: Twin Healing Traditions* (Pennsylvania: S.M.N. Press, 2012), 42.
43. E. O. Babalola, "The Relevance of Herbal Medicine to the Practice of African Traditional Religion, Islam and Christianity," *EKPOMA Journal of Religious Studies*, vol. 5, no. 1 & 2 (2003).
44. M. A. Bamgboshe, "God and Creation: Christian Perspective," Unpublished Paper presented at the 25th Annual Conference of the Nigerian Association for the Study of Religions (Ago-Iwoye: Olabisi Onabanjo University, 2004), 17.
45. D. O. Ogungbile, 22.
46. R. German, *African Traditional Religion in the Light of the Bible* (Bukuru, Plateau: ACTS Press, 2013), 167.
47. Idowu, *African Traditional Religion*, 15–17.
48. Ibid.

49. Dopamu and Awolalu, *West African Traditional Religion*, 1979.
50. Ibid.
51. Ibid., 21.
52. D. Oguntola-Laguda, *Esu, The Individual and the Society*, 57th Inaugural Lecture (Lagos: Lagos State University, 2017), 9–10.
53. Ibid., 20–21.
54. Dopamu, 14.
55. Dopamu and Awolalu, *West African Traditional Religion*, 1979.
56. Awolalu, 276.
57. Dopamu, 17.
58. Dopamu, 17.
59. Oguntola-Laguda, *Esu, The Individual and the Society*, 6.
60. Dopamu, *op. cit.*, p. 45.
61. Dopamu, 1996.
62. Oguntola-Laguda, *Esu, The Individual and the Society*, 8.
63. Dopamu and Awolalu, *West African Traditional Religion*, 21.
64. Dopamu, *op. cit.*, 17.
65. Ibid., 45.

Index[1]

A

Abacha, Sani, 116
Abimbola, Wande, 243, 383, 384, 386–388, 389n7, 466, 491, 548, 549, 552, 568, 607
Abrahamic Religions, 88
Achebe, 260, 263, 265, 267n20, 267n21, 278, 287n33, 287n36
Adeleke, Adewale, 113, 239n14, 268n36, 411n8, 413
Aderibigbe, Ibigbolade S., 1, 4, 6, 8, 29, 47n1, 47n3, 47n19, 49, 58n2, 59n13, 61, 83n39, 83n41, 88, 98, 107, 119, 131, 141n7, 143, 153n121, 155, 163, 173, 184n15, 185, 197, 207, 219, 231, 238n2, 238n3, 238n7, 241, 257, 271, 289, 303, 317, 329, 347, 357, 365, 383, 391, 400n18, 403, 413, 419, 422, 423, 424n6, 424n12, 424n13, 425n15, 425n20, 425n23, 425n32, 425n36, 425n39, 427, 442, 452, 453n1, 453n5, 453n13, 457–460, 463, 467, 469n3, 469n7, 469n10, 469n11, 469n14, 469n16, 471n38, 474, 487, 494, 497, 515, 528, 529, 534n47, 535, 547, 551, 559, 577, 589, 590, 599, 613, 628

Adewale, Ifabunmi O., 47n14, 113, 324, 325, 328n35, 328n38
Adeyeye, Oni Oba Ogunwusi Enitan, 465
Afghanistan, 376, 381n60
Afolayan, Funso S., 385, 386, 389n5, 530–532, 534n53, 534n56
African Cultural Philosophy (ACP), 293
African Derived Religion, 4
African Diaspora, 1, 3–5, 18, 22, 25, 46, 47, 49, 141n7, 153n21, 241, 244, 245, 247–251, 253n5, 254n17, 285, 314n3, 343n1, 383, 384, 386, 413, 418, 419, 422–424, 424n12, 424n13, 425n15, 425n20, 425n23, 425n40, 426n43, 432, 444, 448, 452, 453, 453n5, 454n28, 460, 469n3, 469n11, 469n16, 470n30, 479, 480, 545n28, 547, 549, 553–555, 557n40, 583, 584
African indigenous religions (AIR), 277, 290, 487, 550, 584
African Philosophy, 13, 59n12, 75, 83n29, 83n54, 83n57, 83n58, 83n63, 84n64, 84n70, 84n80, 84n86, 84n89–91, 106n17, 195n2, 290, 292–295, 297–299, 299n3, 299n4, 299n7, 300n9, 300n22, 300n24, 300n26, 300n33–36, 301n39, 301n42–46, 319, 379n26

[1] Note: Page numbers followed by 'n' refer to notes.

632 INDEX

African Traditional Medicine, 364n12, 391–394, 397, 399, 400n18, 400n21, 513n3, 533n33, 533n35
African Traditional Religion, 1–25, 29–35, 37–40, 43–47, 47n6, 47n13, 47n16, 47n19, 49–59, 61, 88, 95n3, 95n16, 95n21, 98, 104, 105n3, 105n5, 105n8, 106n12, 106n15, 106n16, 106n21–24, 107, 117n2, 119, 129n1, 129n5, 129n6, 129n12, 131, 141n14, 143, 144, 153n5, 153n22, 155, 163, 173–175, 180, 185, 188, 191, 192, 195n12, 195n16, 196n21, 196n24, 196n27, 206n10, 207, 217n23, 217n27, 217n33, 219, 228n17, 228n18, 228n20, 228n23, 228n27, 231, 241, 257, 262, 266n5, 266n8, 271, 277, 288n52, 289, 290, 296, 297, 299, 299n5, 303, 317, 322, 325, 326n10, 329, 331, 347, 350, 353, 357, 361, 365–370, 372–378, 379n16–19, 380n40, 383, 391–394, 396, 399, 399n5, 403–405, 411, 411n1, 411n7, 413–416, 423–428, 430, 431, 435, 437, 437n2, 437n4, 438n19, 438n24, 438n28, 439n36, 439n43, 442–446, 448, 450–452, 453n1, 453n11, 454n43, 455n49, 455n51, 457–460, 462, 463, 468, 469n8, 469n13, 470n29, 474, 480, 482, 483, 483n3, 487–495, 497, 515, 532, 532n1, 533n34, 535, 536, 538, 540, 542, 543, 544n10, 544n22, 545n25, 545n35, 547, 549–551, 555, 555n2, 555n4, 556n14, 556n16, 556n17, 556n25, 556n26, 556n30, 559, 576n2, 576n3 577–578, 580–592, 595, 596n12, 599–605, 607, 609, 609n1, 609n4, 610n16, 613–616, 618, 621–623, 625, 627, 628, 628n2, 628n8, 628n17, 629n43, 629n46, 629n47, 630n49, 630n55, 630n63
African Traditional Religious Movements (ATRM), 448–451
African Union (AU), 397
Afrocentricity, 405
Afterlife, 8, 31, 42, 43, 68, 78, 175, 177, 530
Agada, Obi, 381n61, 468
Aguirre, Begona Venero, 509, 514n29
AIR, *see* African indigenous religions
Ajayi, Jacob F. Adeniyi, 315n12, 344n28, 344n29, 460, 510, 590, 591, 596n3, 596n7, 596n12, 614, 628n5
Akan, 21, 33, 34, 38, 42, 100–102, 145, 175, 347, 348, 351, 354, 355n1, 355n5, 355n14, 355n15, 356n17, 362, 363, 369, 370, 373, 433–436, 439n40, 489, 536, 537, 539–542, 543n9, 544n24, 545n31, 545n33, 550, 560, 584, 607, 610n17
Akan Sankofa, 348
Akindana, Victor, 468
Akintan, Oluwatosin Adeoti, 404, 411n3
Akintunji, Benson, 468
Akoko tree, 35
Akuffo, F. W. K., 348
Akujobi, Remi, 221, 228n9
Alaafin of Oyo, 34
Alagba, 192, 193, 222
Albert, Isaac Olawale, 263, 322, 327n18, 332, 344n13, 344n24, 345n30, 532n8
Alia, Hyacinth, 214
Aliu, Jimoh, 502
All Progressive Congress (APC), 186, 195
Amadiume, Ifi, 315n20, 323, 327n24
Amin, Idi, 116
Amissah, Patrick Kofi, 355n12, 365, 378n3
Ampofo, Oku, 361
Ancestral worship, 20, 22, 36, 37, 43, 51, 78, 112, 114, 134, 147, 149, 150, 157, 167, 169, 178, 182, 209, 214, 224, 233, 234, 236, 243, 339, 341, 342, 358, 502, 503, 518, 519, 524, 526, 536, 537, 540, 542, 544n17, 550, 570, 574
Anderson, Allan, 448, 454n31, 454n34, 468
Andronicus, 65
Angola, 51, 253n7
Anyanwu, K.C., 72, 83n53, 292, 300n10, 300n16
Asante, Molefi Kete, 58n6, 227n1, 304, 314n2, 327n22, 355n12, 405, 411n9, 560, 576n1

Assisted Reproduction Technique (ART), 110, 111, 624
Atheism, 489
Atoba, John, 214
Avruch, Kevin, 336
Awolalu, Joseph Omosade, 2, 24, 25, 38, 47n13, 78, 79, 101, 104, 105n6, 105n8, 106n21, 106n24, 117n2, 129n6, 155, 160n2, 166, 171n7, 171n9, 188, 189, 191, 193, 195n12, 196n16, 243, 344n10, 368, 379n16, 380n40, 403, 411n1, 411n7, 422, 425n37, 427, 437n2, 442, 446, 452, 453n1, 453n11, 455n49, 458, 460, 462, 463, 469n4, 469n8, 469n13, 470n25, 555n2, 590, 599, 601, 607, 609, 613–617, 621, 623, 624, 627, 628, 628n4, 628n6, 628n9, 628n17, 630n49, 630n55, 630n56, 630n63
Ayandele, Emmanuel, 590, 591, 596n3, 596n7, 596n12
Ayer, Alfred Jules, 63, 64

B

Babalola, Ayo, 466
Babalola, E. O., 629n43
Babangida, Ibrahim, 116
Balfour, Arthur James, 535
Balobedu, 227
Bamgboshe, M. A., 621, 629n44
Bangira, Philip Kusasa, 405, 406
Bannerman, Robert, 361
Banta Philosophy, 72
Bantu, 51, 72–74, 83n51, 83n52, 83n55, 83n59, 83n60, 83n62, 134, 141n4, 459, 537
Bascom, William, 247, 544n9, 549
Basden, George T., 404, 411n5
Bastide, Roger, 247, 253n4
Battuta, Ibn, 479, 484n14, 484n15, 489
Bay, Hanson, 220, 228n6, 228n11
Belloc, Hilaire, 261, 262, 267n24
Benin, 145, 148, 231, 376, 377, 381n62, 436, 460, 553, 565, 584, 602
Biden, Joe, 467
Biya, Paul, 116
Bizimana, 42
Black, Peter, 336

Blackwood, Basil Temple, 261, 262, 267n24
Bosman, Willem, 489
Bowen, 564
Brain, Charles Kimberlin, 317, 325n1
Brazil, 11, 18, 49, 236, 243–246, 248–250, 252, 253n7, 371, 384, 389n6, 419, 420, 423, 425n41, 432, 444, 459, 482, 553, 554
Britain, 232, 326n10, 376, 461, 465, 467, 468, 604
Buckley, Anthony, 387, 389n13, 389n16
Buddhism, 8, 30, 173–175, 184n1, 188, 224, 290, 355n3, 368, 579, 583, 584, 594, 604
Bunge, Mario, 67, 82n19, 83n27, 83n28
Burns, James M., 186, 195n1, 195n3
Burundi, 42, 562
Byzantine church, 579

C

Cameron, David, 129n4, 205n1, 376, 381n60
Candomble, 47, 419, 420, 422, 444
Capitalism, 108, 111, 116
Catholicism, 23, 417, 419, 459, 491, 553, 626
Causality, 75
Celtic Druids, 174
China, 164
Christianity, 1–4, 18, 19, 30, 40, 44–47, 49, 57, 70, 96n22, 114, 115, 125, 128, 130n29, 132, 182, 188, 194, 203, 204, 205n8, 207, 208, 211, 215, 219, 224, 236, 238, 243, 259, 272, 277, 279, 286, 290, 319, 321, 326n5, 327n21, 330, 331, 349, 355n3, 357, 368, 374, 376, 377, 386, 392, 395, 399, 399n1, 412n12, 412n13, 428, 430–432, 437, 438n13, 442, 444–447, 451–453, 454n33, 457–464, 466–468, 469n16, 470n18, 470n19, 470n21, 470n22, 470n23, 474, 475, 477–480, 482, 483, 483n4, 483–484n10, 492, 499, 550, 551, 570, 578, 579, 582–584, 587, 591, 594, 596n9, 604, 605, 607, 608, 610n22, 613, 615, 618, 622, 623, 625–628, 628n18, 628n20, 629n43

Chuku, Gloria, 304, 314n3
Chumbow, Beban, 409, 412n22
Colonialism, 13, 108, 209, 220, 225, 259, 263, 265, 269n43, 285, 286, 322, 330, 366, 376, 410, 510, 531, 622
Conflict Transformation Theory, 337
Confucianism, 30, 290, 579, 582
Coppola, Francis Ford, 261
Côte d'Ivoire, 208, 544n16
COVID-19, 165, 464
Cox, Harvey Gallagher, 448, 454n35, 495n3, 495n4, 495n12, 555n4, 556n10
Cuba, 11, 18, 243, 244, 246, 248, 250, 253n11, 371, 384, 416–419, 423, 424n10, 432, 459, 482, 553, 554

D

Dakin, Dakin, 409, 412n22
Danoye-Oguntola, Laguda, 551
Dasylva, Ademola, 501, 502, 513n7, 533n22
David, Ogungile, 551
de Mello, Dofona Zaildes Iracema, 386
de Yemonjá, Mãe Beata, 251, 252
Democratic Governance, 15
Democratic Republic of the Congo (DRC), 537, 539
Diola, 368, 372, 375, 379n21
Doe, Samuel, 116
Dopamu, Peter Adelumo, 2, 24, 25, 38, 47n13, 78, 79, 98, 101, 104, 105n7, 105n8, 106n21, 106n24, 117n2, 123, 124, 129n11, 129n14, 129n19, 129n25, 188, 189, 191, 193, 195n12, 195n16, 196n21, 196n24, 196n27, 344n9, 344n11, 379n17, 422, 425n37, 438n34, 442, 446, 452, 453n1, 453n11, 455n49, 458, 460, 462, 469n8, 469n13, 470n17, 470n25, 495n15, 550, 552, 555n2, 556n13, 556n27, 590, 592, 593, 596n11, 596n16, 600, 601, 606, 607, 613, 614, 618–621, 623–628, 628n17–20, 629n21, 630n49, 630n54, 630n55, 630n57, 630n58, 630n61, 630n63, 630n64
Doyle, Arthur Conan, 261, 262, 267n27
DuBois, W. E. B., 264
Durkheim, Emile, 275, 278, 285, 287n18, 287n34, 288n67, 367, 379n10
Dzer, Matthew, 214

E

Ebola virus, 163
Echekwube, A.O, 78, 295, 296, 298, 300n33–36, 301n39
Egypt, 190, 209, 260, 316n28, 327n22, 475, 476, 492, 535, 593
Eka-Abbasi, 10
Ekeke, 104, 105n1, 106n25, 519, 520, 533n15, 533n20
Ekeopara, 105n1, 106n25, 519, 520, 533n15, 533n20
Ekitiland, 463
Ekpo, Margaret, 307
Elebuibon, Ifayemi, 243, 552
Eliade, Mircea, 264, 268n39, 328n32, 368
Elitism, 116
Ellis, A.B., 243, 253n3, 274, 615, 628n1
Epega, 243
Epistemology, 20, 21, 62, 289, 297, 299, 320, 374, 432, 510, 530, 531, 536, 609
Eschatology, 173, 184n16, 594
Euba, Akin, 235, 238n8
Eurocentric, 21, 51, 68, 366, 403, 405, 490, 499, 535
Eyo Festival, 190, 465, 505

F

Fadele, James, 467, 468
Fadugba, Bayo, 468
Fagunwa, Daniel O., 502, 511
Faleti, Adebayo, 502
Falola, Toyin, 1, 20–23, 29, 49, 61, 88, 98, 107, 119, 131, 143, 155, 163, 171n4, 173, 184n15, 185, 197, 207, 219, 231, 239n10–12, 241,

257, 266n3, 271, 289, 303, 315n11, 315n12, 317, 329, 347, 357, 365, 378n3, 380n49, 383, 391, 403, 413, 422, 425n33, 425n39, 427, 442, 457, 474, 487, 494, 497, 513n7, 513n11, 513n16, 513n20, 513n23, 513n24, 514n31, 515, 533n12, 533n22, 533n23, 533n26, 533n29, 534n38, 534n45, 534n47, 534n53, 547, 559, 577, 589, 599, 613
Fard, Wallace, 477, 478, 481, 484n17
Female Genital Mutilations (FGM), 436
Feminism, 303
Fetishism, 30, 462, 550, 560, 577, 623
Field, M. J., 620, 629n28
Firchow, Peter Edgerly, 261, 262, 267n23, 267n28
Floyd, George, 467, 471n37
France, 260, 602
Frazer, James, 593, 620, 621, 629n30, 629n31
Freud, Sigmund, 145, 153n12, 370

G

Gbadebo, Moses D., 291, 299n7, 299n8
Gbor, John W.T., 293, 300n21
German, R., 621, 629n46
Ghadafi, Muammar, 116
Ghana, 15, 32, 33, 37, 100, 145, 148–151, 152n1, 152n8, 153n26, 153n31, 153n32, 154n34, 154n35, 154n37, 154n42, 154n43, 154n46, 175, 186, 205, 206n10, 206n22, 253n6, 304, 342, 347–351, 353, 355n6, 355n10, 355n12, 355n13, 357–363, 364n12, 433, 435, 439n41, 453, 471n35, 476, 479, 483n3, 489, 529, 533n34, 534n48, 534n50, 536, 539, 584, 606, 607, 610n19, 610n23, 610n24, 613
Global South, 308
Globalization, 18, 115, 126, 127, 143, 152, 202, 215, 313, 319, 396, 399, 407, 410, 474, 482, 483, 547
Golden Stool, 37
Gorongosa, 377, 381n65

Goss, Leonard G., 447, 451, 454n23, 454n47
Gould, Stephen Jay, 260, 267n16
Graham, William Albert, 58n8, 322, 327n18
Greece, 174, 454n30
Guinea, 208, 379n21
Güven, Samet, 259, 265, 267n13, 269n44
Gyeke, Kwame, 369, 373, 379n28
Gyekye, Kwame, 117n3, 274, 277, 287n28, 292, 379n7, 544n24, 545n32

H

Hackett, Rosalind, 411n10, 431–434, 437, 438n24, 438n28, 439n36, 454n16
Hafkin, Jone, 220, 221, 228n6, 228n11
Hall, Everett W., 52, 59n18, 62, 82n15, 106n13, 118n17, 153n16, 602
Hantu, 73–75, 292
Hay, Eloise Knapp, 259, 260, 267n14
Hiebert, Paul, 202, 206n14, 206n20, 206n23
Hinderer, David, 463
Hinduism, 8, 23, 30, 173, 175, 184n4, 188, 290, 355n3, 551, 577–579, 584–586, 604
HIV/AIDS, 200, 215
Hlongwa, Nobuhle Ndimande-, 408, 412n21
Hochschild, Adam, 261
Hollywood, 127, 423
Homosexuality, 13, 313, 314, 325
Horton, Robin, 272, 286n5, 286n10, 431, 438n25
Houphouet-Boigny, Felix, 116
Hume, David, 63, 75, 535, 543n4

I

Ibrahim, Adelodun, 116, 333
Idealism, 65
Idolatry, 30, 98, 103, 244, 443, 461, 462, 489, 623

636   INDEX

Idowu, Bolaji, 2, 23, 24, 32, 37, 47n4, 47n6, 47n8, 47n10, 51, 59n16, 59n17, 68–70, 78–80, 83n32–36, 87, 98, 100, 104, 105n5, 106n12, 106n16, 106n23, 117n2, 120, 129n1, 129n5, 138, 139, 141n14, 141n18, 157, 160n8, 160n9, 170n1, 171n6, 171n13, 184n9, 188, 189, 194, 195n15, 195n19, 233, 243, 258, 266n5, 274–276, 286n2, 286n9, 287n16, 287n19, 287n23, 292, 300n18, 300n19, 368, 369, 379n20, 380n35, 393, 404, 411n7, 421, 422, 424n9, 425n24, 425n28, 425n38, 428, 430, 438n19, 442, 443, 446, 452, 453n1, 453n8, 453n10, 453n11, 454n22, 454n43, 455n49, 455n50, 457, 458, 462, 469n2, 473, 474, 489, 490, 492, 493, 495n10, 551, 552, 556n26, 589–595, 596n1, 596n2, 596n8–10, 596n12, 599, 601, 607, 609, 614–616, 623, 628n2, 628n8, 629n47
Idumwonyia, Itohan Mercy, 376, 381n62
Ifá-Orisa, 11
Igbo land, 214, 215
Ijo Orunmila, 19, 442, 444, 448–453, 453n5, 454n28, 454n30
Ikhidero, Solomon Ijeweimen, 376, 381n62
Illa, 8, 175, 180, 182
Ilogu, Edmund Christopher, 590
India, 174, 611n30
Iroegbu, Panthelon, 64, 67, 82n10–13, 82n23
Islam, 1–4, 18–20, 30, 40, 44–46, 49, 57, 70, 125, 132, 188, 194, 205n8, 208, 211, 215, 219, 238, 243, 272, 277, 286, 326n5, 330, 331, 349, 357, 368, 376, 386, 392, 430–432, 442, 444–446, 452, 453, 457, 474–481, 483, 484n12, 493, 494, 499, 550, 551, 570, 578, 579, 583, 584, 587, 594, 603, 604, 613, 615, 618, 622, 623, 625–627, 628n18, 628n20, 629n43
Isola, Akinwumi, 287n27, 502
Italy, 164, 467, 468

J
Jahn, Janheiz, 73, 74, 83n61, 84n65, 84n66, 141n5, 292, 300n11–14
Jainism, 8, 173, 175, 579, 582
Japan, 164
Jegede, Obafemi, 621
Jesus Christ, 70, 114, 115, 419, 461, 625
Johnson, Samuel, 13, 188, 195n14, 303, 614
Judaism, 23, 30, 40, 219, 243, 368, 492, 551, 577–579, 583, 586, 594

K
Kaakinen, Kaisa, 266, 269n45
Kabila, Joseph, 116
Kagame, Alexis, 74, 75
Kalu, Ogbu, 272, 286n4, 371, 380n33, 380n34, 380n38, 448, 454n33, 460, 470n22, 470n23, 551
Kant, Immanuel, 61, 62, 65, 535, 543n4
Karenga, Maulana, 405
Kaunda, Kenneth, 80, 85n93, 116
Kayode, J.O., 442, 452, 453n1, 455n51, 513n6, 533n24
Kenya, 32, 98, 118n25, 119, 129n3, 130n27, 167, 175, 197, 205n5, 258, 266n9, 562, 589, 594, 614
Kimbangu, Simon, 148
King Leopold, 261, 264, 265
King, Walter, 424n15, 459
Kintu, 73, 74, 292
Kirki, 80
Korzeniowski, Konrad, 266
Kunhiyop, Waje, 281–283, 287n35, 287n48, 288n53
Kuntu, 73, 75, 292
Kuti, Olufunmilayo Ransome, 307
KwaZulu-Natal, 537
Kyeremeh, Ansu, 143, 152n1

L
Lagos State Television (LTV), 502
Lambo (Adeoye), 399
Layiwola, Peju, 231, 238n1
Liberia, 208, 209, 436, 461, 484n10
Lijadu, 243

INDEX

Lucas, Jonathan Olumide, 490, 590, 619, 620, 629n27
Ludwig, Emil, 68, 69, 98, 462, 593, 615
Lugbara, 37, 155, 198, 205n4

M

Magic and Medicine, 6, 37, 119, 129n11, 129n14, 129n19, 129n25, 450
Majeed, Hasskei, 373, 380n47
Mali, 205, 479
Mallios, Peter Lancelot, 264, 266n11, 268n40
Mandela, 116
Manguinhos, S., 621, 629n41
Marx, Karl, 187
Masango, Charles Awe, 498, 513n3, 513n5, 525, 533n33, 533n35
Materialism, 66
Mayemba, Bienvenu, 181, 184n16
Mazama, Ama, 227n1, 372, 380n37, 380n39, 560, 576n1
Mbeki, Thabo, 116
Mbiti, John S., 2, 23, 24, 31, 47n2, 47n5, 47n15, 47n17, 58n1, 59n17, 59n19, 69, 70, 77, 81, 83n37, 83n38, 83n40, 83n42, 85n94–98, 105n4, 117n2, 129n17, 133, 137, 139, 141n1, 141n6, 141n13, 141n17, 153n20, 155, 157, 158, 160n1, 160n6, 160n11, 164, 166–168, 170n2, 171n8, 171n10–12, 206n9, 206n12, 223, 227n2, 228n19, 274, 275, 286n1, 286n7, 287n20, 287n32, 291, 297, 299n6, 301n40, 304, 314n1, 319–321, 324, 326n9–12, 327n17, 328n33, 367, 368, 373, 379n13, 379n22, 380n33, 393, 400n9, 411n7, 428–430, 437n4, 437n10, 438n16, 438n21, 446, 452, 454n42, 455n52, 458, 462, 469n5, 474, 490, 516, 520, 532n2, 532n10, 533n19, 550, 551, 555n1, 578, 588n4, 589, 590, 594–595, 596n17, 597n19, 597n21, 597n23, 599, 601, 607, 609, 615, 628n3
Mead, George Herbert, 414

Mecca, 446, 475, 476, 481, 482
Mende, 33, 37, 209, 213, 370, 537
Menkiti, Ifeanyi, 373
Metaphysics, 62–64, 80, 82, 83, 118n18, 267n11, 287n28
Metz, Thad, 274
Middleton, John, 198, 205n4
Mills, John, 116
Missionaries, 24, 29, 49, 68, 201, 202, 274, 319–321, 337, 347, 367, 377, 430, 458, 460–463, 468, 484n10, 488, 510, 551, 564, 581, 583, 584, 589, 590, 608, 613, 622
Mkhize, Nhlanhla, 408, 412n21
Mlambo, Muzi, 408, 409
Modernism, 146, 410
Modern reproduction technologies (MRT), 284, 285
Mogobe, Ramose B., 297, 301n42, 301n43
Mohammed, Imam Warithu Deen, 481, 484n17
Mohammed, Warithu Deen, 482
Monotheism, 489
More knowledgeable others (MKO), 54, 55
Moremi, 101
Morocco, 475
Mozambique, 377, 381n65, 405
Mubarak, Hosni, 116
Mugabe, Robert, 116
Mugambi, Jesse, 427, 437n1
Muhammad, Muritala, 116, 475, 477, 478, 481, 484n17
Muntu, 72–74, 83n61, 84n65, 84n66, 292, 300n11–14
Myths, 41, 251, 328n32, 415, 501, 502, 519, 596n17

N

Nabofa, Michael Y., 238, 318, 326n7, 590
Nana Buluku, 227
National Agency for Food and Drug Administration and Control (NAFDAC), 395, 398
Nation of Islam, 477, 481
Native American religion, 8

Ndau Festival of the Arts (NdaFA), 17, 404–410
Ndau, Chimanimani, 17, 404–411, 411n11, 412n17
New Religious Movements (NRM), 19, 442, 447–449, 451
New Yam Festival, 386
NGOs, 16, 362, 507
Ngozi, Ezenagu, 409, 410, 412n25
Nigeria, 19, 21, 32, 51, 55, 59n15, 59n20, 61, 71, 78, 88, 95n1, 95n3, 95n6, 95n8, 95n11, 98, 100, 104–109, 113, 121, 128, 129n11, 129n25, 145, 151, 155, 163, 166, 167, 171n5, 175, 185–187, 194, 195n4, 195n8, 195n12, 195n15, 195n19, 205, 206n11, 207–210, 212, 214, 216n1, 216n7, 216n17, 219, 222, 223, 225, 226, 228n16, 231, 235, 236, 238, 239n10–14, 241, 253n6, 258, 262, 271, 278, 280, 281, 284, 287n43, 289, 291, 295, 296, 298, 300n18, 303, 307–309, 312, 314n4, 315n12, 316n30, 326n13, 329–331, 337, 339–342, 344n26, 345n30, 346n57, 346n58, 365, 376, 377, 379n19, 381n59–62, 383, 385, 387–389, 391, 395, 398, 399, 400n7, 400n9, 400n20, 400n24, 400n25, 401n27, 401n28, 411n3–6, 413–415, 418, 422, 424n9, 425n33, 432, 442–451, 453, 454n16, 454n21, 457, 459–461, 463–466, 468, 469n1, 469n3, 469n8, 470n19, 470n32, 47n035, 471n37, 476, 484n10, 487, 491, 495n12, 495n15, 497, 504, 520, 521, 533n24, 533n27, 536, 547, 552, 553, 555n5, 556n13, 556n31, 557n38, 557n40, 557n45, 563, 589–591, 596n1, 596n11, 599, 600, 603, 610n17, 613, 614, 618, 620, 621, 625, 629n21
Nigerian Television Authority (NTA), 502
Nirmal, Arvind P., 404, 411n4
Nkrumah, 348

Nollywood, 127
North Korea, 164
Nyakyusa, 369, 370
Nyamekye, Awuah, 435, 439n40, 439n41
Nyerere, Julius, 186, 195n2
Nzewi, Meki, 233, 238n4, 238n5

O
Obassanjo, Olusegun, 116
Obumo, 10, 101
Odufuye, Wale, 468
Odusola, Joshua, 621, 629n40
Oduwole, Ebun, 325
Ogboni, 44, 208, 209, 213, 216n5, 334, 444, 445, 448
Oguejiofor, J. Obi, 65, 82n14, 293, 300n20
Ogunde, Hubert, 502
Ogungbile, D. O., 621, 629n45
Ogun State Television (OGTV), 502
Ojude Oba Festival, 465
Oke'badan festival, 504
Okonrende, Ade, 468
Okpalo, Christian, 468
Oladele, Orimoogunje, 551
Olaleye, S. K., 621, 629n33
Ọlọgbónméjì, 11, 242
Olorunfumi, Pa, 449, 451
Olufemi, Olaoba, 331
Olupona, Jacob, 58n4, 226, 229n30, 286n4, 286n6, 315n25, 315n26, 316n30, 320, 321, 326n12, 327n17, 380n33, 384, 386, 389n7, 418, 423, 425n17, 425n33, 429, 431–433, 437n5, 437n8, 438n23, 438n24, 438n28, 439n36, 442, 452, 453n2, 453n3, 454n16, 458, 459, 474, 475, 482, 483n1, 483n5, 484n20, 487, 488, 493, 494, 495n3, 495n4, 495n12, 549, 555n4, 556n10, 556n11, 556n29, 556n30, 557n34, 557n36, 557n42, 584, 588n18, 590, 596n2, 628
Omolola, Bayo, 157, 160n7, 379n24
Omoregbe, Joseph, 62, 66, 82n4–6, 82n18, 82n21
Oni, Peter, 190, 194, 292, 300n17, 465

Onibere, G. A., 590, 592
Ontology, 66, 67, 81, 82, 83n27, 84n68, 105n1, 106n25, 533n15, 533n20
Opoku, Kofi Asare, 2, 24, 149, 153n28, 154n42, 490, 536, 538, 544n10, 544n22, 545n25, 599, 600, 606–609, 610n16–26, 611n27–30
Oral Traditions, 40, 513n7, 533n22
Orisha, 459, 465, 476, 477, 496n21, 553–555, 557n38, 557n41
Oseijeman I, Oba, 418
Oshita, Oshita O., 294, 300n26
Oshoffa, Samuel Bileowu, 466
Oshogbo Festival, 190
Osun Osogbo, 342, 464
Osundare, Niyi, 502
Osun-Osogbo, 446, 504, 505
Osun-Osogbo festival, 446, 505
Osun State Broadcasting Corporation (OSBC), 502
Ottoman Empire, 479, 484n16, 579
Ouattara, Alassane, 116
Oyeronke, Olajubu, 226, 229n30, 442, 453n2, 464, 470n33, 551, 555n6

P

P'Bitek, Okot, 535, 543n3
Paganism, 2, 30, 98, 428, 462, 550, 577, 614, 623
Pantheism, 489
Parkin, David, 258, 266n9
Parrinder, Edward Geoffrey, 2, 24, 51, 59n14, 98, 100, 105n2, 105n3, 106n15, 190, 196n23, 211, 217n23, 233, 274, 428, 462, 550, 590, 599–605, 608, 609, 610n7–10, 610n12–14
Parson, William, 285
Pemberton, John, 385, 386, 389n5, 544n11
Pentecostalism, 126, 128, 130n31, 448, 453n5, 453n12, 454n17, 454n20, 454n28, 454n30–32, 454n34, 454n36, 454n41, 454n44, 455n48, 467, 470n35
People's Democratic Party (PDP), 186
Phillips, Charles, 463
Polytheism, 489

Polytheistic, 5, 95, 292, 368, 544n17, 579
Poro, 44, 208, 209
Primary Health Care Training for Indigenous Healers (PRHETIH), 361, 364n12
Pritchard, Edward Evan Evans, 153n24, 319, 320, 326n11, 328n34, 489, 490
Proverbs, 41, 370, 380n31, 414, 415, 502, 503, 513n11, 540, 545n31, 595, 607, 610n21
Provincial Development Coordinator (PDC), 409
Pythagoras, 175

Q

Quadri, 493, 494, 495n15, 555n5
Queen Elizabeth II, 376

R

Raccette, K. R., 621, 629n37
Rahman, Omar bin Abdu, 477
Raji, S. M., 621, 629n39
Randal, Styers, 621, 629n34
Rattray, R. S., 38, 43, 47n20, 274
Redeemed Christian Church of God, North America (RCCGNA), 467, 468, 471n38
Reincarnation, 8, 9, 68, 78, 157–160, 173–180, 182, 183, 298, 497, 501, 518, 585
Rivers, W.H.F., 619
Robinson, David, 258, 263, 266n2, 267n11, 267n29
Rocha, Agenor Miranda, 250, 254n14, 386
Rojcikoya, K., 621, 629n38
Roman Catholic Church, 416, 461
Roper, Hugh Trevor, 260
Ross, Leith, 220, 228n4, 228n13
Russell, Bertrand, 290, 484n12
Rwanda, 376, 377, 380n57, 381n63

S

Sagamu riot, 442, 446
Said, Edward, 264, 265, 268n40, 268n43, 543n2

Salau, Oretayo, 468
Samsara, 78
Samadhi, Fároúnbí Àìná Mosúnmólá Adéwálé, 496n21
Sango, 34, 44, 47, 51, 79, 101, 102, 106n20, 224, 226, 228n28, 244–247, 273, 292, 336, 340, 371, 415–418, 501, 504, 529, 552, 554
Sangomas, 54, 127
Sankara, Thomas, 116
Santeria, 47, 228n29, 416, 417, 419, 420, 425n15, 444, 459, 469n11, 477, 491, 553
Sawandili, T. M., 621, 629n35
Sebald, Winfried Georg, 263–266, 267n11, 267n30, 268n33, 268n41, 269n45
Seko, Mobotu Sese, 116
Seun, Abilawon, 621
Shango, 44, 371, 380n36, 432, 459
Shona, 110, 175, 409
Shorter, Alyward, 126, 129n3, 129n13, 129n23, 177, 184n10, 295, 300n37
Sierra Leone, 33, 37, 100, 209, 461
Sijuwade, Oni Olubuse, 465
Sikhism, 551, 582
Simpson, George, 386, 387, 389n11, 389n15
Singapore, 164, 328n32, 532n7
Sithole, Pindai, 408, 412n20
Slave Trade, 11, 150, 154n37, 424, 458, 461, 468, 469n3, 479, 553
Smith, Edwin W., 68, 148, 258, 262, 266n2, 267n26, 344n16, 346n64, 483n7
Sodipo, J. Olubi, 75–77, 84n71–77, 87, 294, 300n25
Solomon, Ayoub bin, 376, 381n62, 477
South Africa, 54, 59n25, 116, 125, 127, 195n4, 227, 238n4, 238n5, 317, 346n55, 376, 380n54, 380n58, 411n11, 412n20, 434, 437n3, 437n6, 438n17, 438n22, 448, 474, 537, 606
South Korea, 164
Southern Gombe, 280
Spain, 164
Spencer, Herbert, 148
Spivak, Gayatri Chakravorty, 321, 327n16

Stamer, Josef, 20
Stenning, Keith, 260, 267n18
Stephen, B., 621, 629n36
Suega, Stephen, 214
Suicide, 165
Supreme Being, 4–7, 15, 21, 31–34, 37–40, 42–44, 51, 52, 68, 71, 88–95, 98–102, 104, 105, 119, 131, 133–135, 137–140, 146, 151, 155–159, 168, 170, 177, 233, 258, 272, 273, 275, 276, 291, 292, 296, 297, 304, 310–313, 331, 348, 351, 365, 368–373, 375, 377, 378, 416, 422, 430–432, 435, 443, 453, 458, 501, 503, 505, 519, 520, 523, 528, 593, 595, 627
Swem Oath, 341
Swem, U Bumun, 340, 341

T
Tabitha, Olatunji, 409, 410, 412n25
Talbot, 51, 59n15, 233, 620
Taylor, Charles, 116, 268n38, 279, 281, 326n13, 397, 400n22, 411n4
Tempels, 72–75, 83n51, 83n52, 83n55, 83n59, 83n60, 83n62
Ter Haar, Gerrie, 129n7, 206n22, 432, 433, 437, 438n32, 439n47
Thomas, Donald E., 116, 184n2, 258, 266n1, 323, 327n25, 327n26, 462, 629n21
Tiv, 71, 73, 78, 83n29, 90–94, 95n4, 95n6–9, 95n11–13, 95n15, 95n20, 96n22, 96n24, 177, 208, 210, 212–214, 295, 296, 300n21, 331, 339, 340, 394, 396, 400n24, 400n25, 443
Townsend, Henry, 268n38, 418, 424n15, 425n16, 425n18, 462, 463
Traditional African Religions (TAR), 290, 291
Traditional Festivals, 149, 151, 154n46
Traditional Knowledge (TK), 507, 509, 516
Traditional Medicine, 205, 206n26, 360, 391, 393, 395–397, 399, 400n7, 400n8, 400n18, 400n20, 400n21, 401n27, 401n28, 618, 629n21, 629n33

Trinidad, 11, 243, 244, 246, 248, 253n11, 371, 432, 554
Tunisia, 475
Turner, Lorenzo, 145, 146, 153n13, 153n14, 247, 320, 326n15, 483n7, 610n8
Tutuola, Amos, 502, 511
Tylor, Sir Edward, 148, 293, 367, 488

U

Ubuntu, 153n16, 297, 301n42, 366, 375, 380n55
Uche, Samuel Emeka Kanu, 82n14, 591, 596n8
Uduigwomen, A.F., 293, 294, 300n22, 300n24, 300n26
Uganda, 175, 198, 266n8, 433, 594
Unah, Jim, 61, 63, 67, 68, 82n1, 82n7–9, 82n25, 83n30, 83n31
UNESCO, 326n3, 410, 464, 548, 549, 611n29
United Kingdom, 164, 594
United States of America (USA), 19, 46, 50, 175, 323, 384, 388, 389, 419, 432, 434, 458, 459, 465, 467, 468, 469n11, 471n36, 491, 553–555, 557n45, 606
Urbanization, 116, 278, 399, 437
Utov, Christopher, 93, 214
Uzoma, Joel, 468

V

van den Berg, M.E.S., 374, 380n46, 380n51
van Lambalgen, Michiel, 260, 267n18
Verger, Pierre, 247, 250, 315n23
Vilakazi, Herbert, 409, 412n23
Voodoo, 47, 459, 553
Vygotsky, Lev S., 4, 53–58, 59n23, 59n24, 59n28

W

Wambebo, Charles, 395
Wang, M.A, 92, 95n15
Wariboko, Nimi, 285, 288n62, 373, 374, 378n3, 380n49

Weber, Max, 413
Wellington, Wotogbe-Weneka, 551
Welsh, John, 280
Wenger, Susan, 464, 494, 495, 496n22, 622
Westermann, Dierich, 33, 47n9, 327n20, 615
Whitehead, Alfred North, 66, 82n20
Williamson, S.G., 371
Wilson, Godfrey, 228n24, 279, 284, 288n56, 288n59, 369, 379n25
Wiredu, Kwasi, 274, 369, 373, 379n26
Witchcraft, 12, 68, 73, 77, 78, 109, 121, 123, 124, 127, 128, 198, 199, 202, 203, 210, 211, 213–215, 217n37, 274, 290, 298, 313, 331, 339, 341, 416, 429, 436, 489, 619
Wolff, Robert P., 65, 82n15, 82n16
World Bank, 410
World Health Organization (WHO), 360, 364n7, 364n8, 379n6

X

X, Malcolm, 477, 481, 482, 484n13, 484n19
Xhosa, 430

Y

Yaro, Mahmet, 477
Yemoja, 51, 99, 225, 226, 336, 340, 417
Yorùbá, 19, 21, 23, 51, 55, 99–104, 185, 188–191, 193, 194, 222, 223, 225, 226, 235–237, 238n8, 242–252, 252n1, 252n2, 253n11, 254n23, 258, 273, 275, 278, 305, 309–311, 321, 323–325, 331, 333, 336, 339, 340, 368, 371, 372, 383–389, 415, 536–541, 543n9, 544n24, 545n28, 547, 549, 550, 552–554, 555n7, 556n15, 556n29, 557n32, 557n34, 557n36–39, 557n42, 577, 591–593, 604, 616, 618–621, 624–628, 629n21, 629n26, 629n27, 629n35
Yoruba Traditional Religion, 11, 626
Yorùbáland, 189–192, 194, 238, 334, 336, 384, 619, 621

Z

Zambia, 175, 180, 182, 205, 438n25, 537
Zande, 537
Zimbabwe, 110, 121, 175, 228n14, 262, 403, 405, 406, 408, 411n10, 411n11, 411n12, 412n17
Zone of Proximal Development (ZPD), 54, 56
Zoroastrianism, 579
Zulu, 54, 153n16, 375, 430, 537

Printed in the United States
by Baker & Taylor Publisher Services